%

ADVERTISING NOW. ONLINE

ED. JULIUS WIEDEMANN

ADVERTISING NOW.
ONLINE

TASCHEN

HONG KONG KÖLN LONDON LOS ANGELES MADRID PARIS TOKYO

ESSAYS

CHAPTERS

BOB GREENBERG
CHAIRMAN, CEO AND CHIEF CREATIVE OFFICER OF R/GA

After the interactive baby was thrown out with the dot-com bathwater in 2000, it took four years to re-establish the credibility of the interactive channel as a worthwhile marketing investment.

WE ARE STARTING TO SEE A NEW ROLE FOR INTERACTIVE – AS THE LEAD DISCIPLINE FOR MANY CLIENTS.

Why now?

First, because the Web represents the leading edge of technologically enabled consumer control. The era of media-driven mass marketing is rapidly coming to an end, as consumers migrate from "out-bound" channels like scheduled television viewing and print to "inbound" channels like the Internet, video game systems, iPods, convergent mobile phone devices, and PVRs. In the new "on-demand" era, the opportunities to use media to reach consumers are eroding with every change in habit that technology fosters.

MARKETERS ARE EMBRACING INTERACTIVE BECAUSE IT ALIGNS

WITH THE DRAMATIC CHANGES THAT HAVE OCCURRED IN THE LIVES OF THEIR CUSTOMERS.

Second, interactivity enables marketers to escape the confines of traditional brand messaging and build deeper, richer relationships with consumers. Outbound marketing revolves around the crafting of "brand narratives," brief stories—usually 30 seconds long—that seek to differentiate brands from their competitors. Inbound marketing in an on-demand world—as represented by the Web—enables marketers to elevate their dialogue with consumers to achieve what we call "brand transformation." These experiences are not narratives or stories. In fact, they are not really ads. They are new forms of customer interaction, which can transform the relationship between marketer and consumer.

A great example of this is NIKE iD, where consumers can design their own shoes and apparel. NIKE iD began as a Website and has since extended the experience to online banners, digital signage and a New York City retail space. NIKE iD is not an advertisement, but any consumer who uses it changes his perception of NIKE from a brand solely about athletic performance to a brand that also inspires and enables self-expression and personalization.

NO MERE ADVERTISEMENT COULD ACHIEVE SO MUCH. THAT KIND OF CHANGE MUST COME FROM A FIRSTHAND EXPERIENCE.

Après que le bébé interactif a été jeté avec l'eau du bain « .com », il a fallu quatre ans pour rétablir la crédibilité du support interactif comme investissement marketing valable.

NOUS COMMENÇONS À ENTREVOIR UN NOUVEAU RÔLE POUR L'INTERACTIF, CELUI D'UNE DISCIPLINE PHARE POUR DE NOMBREUX ANNONCEURS.

Pourquoi maintenant ?

Premièrement, parce que le Net représente la pointe du progrès technologique en terme de contrôle par le consommateur. L'époque du marketing de masse véhiculé par les médias touche à sa fin, et les consommateurs délaissent les canaux « sortant » comme les programmes télévisés à heure fixe ou la presse écrite pour se tourner vers des canaux « entrant » comme Internet, les jeux vidéos, les iPods, les appareils convergents de téléphonie mobile et les magnétoscopes numériques. Dans cette nouvelle ère « à la demande », les occasions d'atteindre les consommateurs via un média fluctuent selon les changements d'habitudes encouragés par la technologie.

SI LES ANNONCEURS ADOPTENT L'INTERACTIF, C'EST QU'IL S'ALIGNE SUR LES CHANGEMENTS RADICAUX APPARUS DANS LA VIE DE LEURS CONSOMMATEURS.

INTRODUCTION

Deuxièmement, l'interactivité permet aux annonceurs d'échapper au carcan du message de marque et d'établir des relations plus riches et plus profondes avec les consommateurs. Le marketing « sortant » s'articule autour de l'élaboration d'un schéma narratif, une histoire courte (30 secondes en général), qui cherche à différencier une marque de ses concurrents. Le marketing « entrant », dans un monde à la demande comme le Net, permet aux annonceurs d'élever leur dialogue avec les consommateurs pour atteindre ce que nous appelons la « transformation de marque ». Ces expériences ne sont pas des schémas narratifs ou des histoires. En fait, elles ne sont pas vraiment des publicités. Ce sont de nouvelles formes d'interaction, capables de transformer la relation entre la marque et le consommateur.

Un parfait exemple de cette évolution est Nike iD, où les consommateurs peuvent dessiner leur tenue et leur propre paire de chaussures. Nike iD a démarré comme un site Internet, et a depuis élargi l'expérience à des bannières en ligne, un affichage digital dynamique et une boutique de vente à New York.

Nike iD n'est pas une publicité, mais chaque consommateur qui l'utilise change sa perception de Nike, d'une marque uniquement centrée sur les performances sportives à une marque qui encourage la personnalisation et l'expression individuelle.

UNE SIMPLE PUBLICITÉ N'AURAIT PAS PU RÉUSSIR UN TEL EXPLOIT. SEULE L'EXPÉRIENCE INDIVIDUELLE L'A RENDU POSSIBLE.

Nachdem 2000 das interaktive Kind mit dem dot-com-Bad ausgeschüttet worden war, dauerte es vier Jahre, bis die Glaubwürdigkeit des interaktiven Werbekanals als lohnende Marketing-Investition wiederhergestellt war.

WIR SEHEN NUN EINE NEUE ROLLE FÜR INTERAKTIVITÄT: ALS KÖNIGSDISZIPLIN FÜR VIELE KUNDEN.

Warum gerade jetzt?

Erstens, weil das Web die führende Rolle der technologisch möglichen Konsumentenkontrolle repräsentiert. Die Ära des medienorientierten Massenmarketings geht schnell zu Ende, da sich die Konsumenten von „outbound"-Kanälen wie Fernsehen ab- und „inbound"-Kanälen wie dem Internet, Videospielen, iPods, konvergenten Mobilfunkgeräten und PVRs zuwenden. In der neuen „on-demand"-Ära werden die Gelegenheiten, die Konsumenten durch Medien zu erreichen, mit jeder technologischen Änderung untergraben.

IM MARKETING WIRD INTERAKTIVITÄT BEGRÜSST, DA SIE DEN DRAMATISCHEN VERÄNDERUNGEN IM LEBEN DER KUNDEN ENTSPRICHT.

Zweitens ermöglicht die Interaktivität dem Marketing, die traditionellen Grenzen der traditionellen Markenbotschaften zu überschreiten

und tiefere, intensivere Beziehungen zu den Konsumenten aufzubauen. Outbound Marketing dreht sich um das Erzählen von „brand narratives", kurzen Geschichten – normalerweise 30 Sekunden lang –, mit denen sich die Marke von ihrer Konkurrenz absetzen möchte. Inbound Marketing ermöglicht es, in einer „on-demand"-Welt – wie sie im Web repräsentiert wird – den Dialog mit den Konsumenten zu verbessern und damit die so genannte „Markentransformation" zu erreichen. Diese neuen Werbeformen sind keine Geschichten oder Erzählungen. Sie sind nicht einmal wirkliche Werbespots. Sie sind eine neue Form der Interaktion mit den Kunden, die die Beziehung zwischen Marketing und Konsument tiefgreifend verändern kann.

Ein Beispiel hierfür ist NIKE iD, mit der Konsumenten ihre eigenen Schuhe und Kleidung entwerfen können. NIKE iD begann als Webseite und hat die Aktion seitdem mit Online-Bannern, digitalen Werbeflächen und einer New York City-Verkaufsfläche ausgeweitet. NIKE iD ist keine Werbung; aber jeder Konsument, der es benutzt, ändert seine Wahrnehmung von NIKE als Marke für Athleten zu einer Marke, die außerdem zu einem eigenen Ausdruck inspiriert und Individualität ermöglicht.

WERBUNG ALLEIN KÖNNTE DIES NICHT ERREICHEN. DIESE ART VON VERÄNDERTER WAHRNEHMUNG KANN NUR DURCH EINE DIREKTE ERFAHRUNG ENTSTEHEN.

MATT FREEMAN
CEO OF TRIBAL DDB WORLDWIDE

Matt Freeman runs Tribal DDB Worldwide's global network. Under Matt's leadership, Tribal DDB Worldwide has become one of the largest and most award-winning interactive agencies in the world. Tribal DDB consistently ranks as one of the Top-10 companies in the interactive industry as measured by revenue, media clout and creativity. Matt was a founding partner and Chief Creative Officer of DDB Digital in the US, one of the six companies that combined to form Tribal DDB Worldwide. Matt's work has won every major industry award including Cannes Lions, Art Directors Club, New York Festivals, ANDYs, Effies, and "Best of Show" at the One Show Interactive. He has served as a judge for the Cannes International Advertising Festival and has served as interactive chairman of the Clio Awards, the One Show and the International Andy Awards. Matt has also been recognized by publications including Wall Street Journal, New York Times, CNN, CNBC, CBS MarketWatch, Forrester Research, AdAge, Adweek and Creativity. Prior to his life in advertising, Matt worked for MTV, wrote for several magazines and was a prep school English teacher. He has

a B.A. in English and art history from Dartmouth College and attended the School of Visual Arts.

T: What do you thing will be the next 10 most explored digital communication mediums?

MF: Mobile, iTV, Video Games, Blogs, Podcasts, Social Networks, RFID, Digital Home Networks, Nanotech-Imbedded packaging and Robots. Lots and lots of Robots.

T: Online advertising is still a small portion of the whole marketing budget. How do you think it will change?

MF: It will continue its inevitable march toward dominance, but the line between "traditional" and "digital" will also disappear. If you are buying interactive advertising on digital cable, who knows where the line can be drawn. We will continue to see integration accelerate for both media companies and agencies alike.

T: Why should companies be going online more?

MF: Because companies need consumers. And in the majority of cases, consumers are spending largest segments of their media consumption time online.

T: What is different about having digital means to build a brand?

MF: The most fundamental new question brands

need to answer in the digital world is: "how should our brand behave?" The leap from brand communication to brand interaction requires a three-dimensional, behavioral character that is not required of brands in broadcast-only media.

T: One of the biggest advantages of advertising online is the increase in control you have over customer's behaviour. How do you think it is changing advertising agencies?

MF: I actually do not believe that online advertising increases consumer control. In fact, one of the greatest advantages online marketers possess is their innate permission-based approach to consumers. When you fundamentally believe you need to earn consumer attention rather than simply buy it, you have an immediate advantage in an "on-demand" media landscape.

T: A good campaign always starts with a good idea. So how do you think that digital means can empower a campaign?

MF: Digital media allow the consumer to become a part of the campaign. The most powerful new medium we have discovered is not digital, but rather consumers themselves.

THE EXPONENTIAL FORCE OF VIRAL AND SOCIAL NETWORKS OF ALL KINDS WILL INCREASINGLY DETERMINE SUCCESS FOR MARKETING CAMPAIGNS.

LEADING AN ONLINE AGENCY

T: What was the most successful campaign you have ever done? And why?

MF: I am not sure about successful, but the campaign that had the greatest impact on my personal perspective was the IBM chess match between Gary Kasparov and their Deep Blue supercomputer. We covered the match in real time online for fans around the world, interviewed folks in the audience like Milos Forman and George Plimpton.

THE CONNECTIONS WE PROVIDED BETWEEN THE EPIC MAN/ MACHINE BATTLE AND THE REST OF THE WORLD FELT SO VITAL AND EXCITING, I WILL NEVER FORGET IT. IT WAS ALSO A BIT SCARY. THE MACHINE WON.

T: Consumers are filtering more of what they see and becoming "adavoiders". How do you think that digital advertising/marketing can help brands reach customers?

MF: Marketing seems to be increasingly evolving from a media mogul-determined dictatorship into a consumer-determined meritocracy. I think this is only good news for the long-term health of marketing and commerce. Tectonic shifts in power – often painted as doomsday scenarios – often emerge as much-needed progress.

T: How do you think Blogs and Viral are changing communication?

MF: The medium is the messenger. Consumers are the new creative department. Brands need to work with their own consumers to build equity cooperatively.

T: Mobile is being considered the next way to communicate. It is personal and we carry them 24/7. How do you think it will influence advertising in the future?

MF: I am not exactly sure, but I certainly am hoping more people will switch their phones to "vibrate." Silence is golden.

———

Matt Freeman dirige le réseau Tribal DDB Worldwide. Sous sa direction, la société est devenue une des agences interactives les plus développées et les plus primées du monde. Tribal DDB se place régulièrement dans les 10 meilleures compagnies de l'industrie interactive en terme de recettes, d'impact média et de créativité. Matt Freeman a été fondateur puis directeur de création de DDB Digital aux Etats-Unis, une des six compagnies qui ont fusionné pour donner naissance à Tribal DDB Worldwide. Ses travaux ont été récompensés dans les concours professionnels les plus prestigieux, dont les Lions de Cannes, l'Art Directors Club, le New York Festival, les Andys, les Effies, et le OneShow. Il a été juge aux Lions de Cannes, et président des Clio Awards, du One Show, et des Andys. Matt Freeman a été mis à l'honneur par le Wall Street Journal, le New York Times, CNN,

CNBC, CBS MarketWatch, Forrester Research, AdAge, Adweek et Creativity. Avant sa carrière publicitaire, Matt Freeman a travaillé pour MTV, a collaboré à plusieurs magazines et enseigné l'anglais dans une école privée. Il a obtenu une licence d'anglais et d'Histoire de l'Art à Dartmouth et a étudié à l'Ecole des Arts Visuels.

T: Quels seront d'après vous les 10 supports de communication numériques les plus explorés ?

MF: Les téléphones portables, la télévision numérique, les jeux vidéos, les blogs, les Podcast, les communautés virtuelles, les Tag RFID, les réseaux numériques domestiques, les emballages utilisant la nanotechnologie et les robots. Beaucoup, beaucoup de robots.

T: La publicité en ligne ne représente souvent qu'une petite partie du budget marketing global. Cela va-t-il changer ?

MF: Elle continuera inévitablement à progresser vers plus de domination, mais la séparation entre publicité traditionnelle et publicité électronique disparaîtra aussi. Si l'on achète de la publicité électronique qui sera diffusée par le câble, où se trouve la ligne de séparation ? Nous verrons l'intégration s'accélérer, à la fois pour les sociétés de média et pour les agences.

T: Pourquoi les entreprises devraient-elles se tourner vers Internet ?

MF: Parce qu'elles ont besoin de clients. Et dans la majeure partie des cas, les usagers consacrent l'essentiel de leur consommation média à Internet.

T: Qu'apporte la pub en ligne à la construction d'une image de marque ?

MF: La question essentielle à laquelle doivent répondre les annonceurs concernant l'univers numérique est celle-ci : « Comment doit se comporter notre marque ? » Passer de la communication de marque à l'interaction de marque exige une personnalité et un comportement tridimensionnel que n'exige pas la communication exclusivement télévisuelle.

T: Un des plus gros atouts de la publicité en ligne est la marge de contrôle que l'on exerce sur le comportement du consommateur. Cela affecte-t-il le fonctionnement des agences spécialisées ?

MF: Je ne suis pas d'avis que cela permette un contrôle accru du consommateur. Pour moi, l'atout des marketeurs en ligne, c'est qu'ils doivent approcher le consommateur en lui demandant son autorisation. Quand on croit fondamentalement qu'on doit gagner l'attention du consommateur plutôt que de l'acheter, cela vous donne un avantage certain dans un paysage médiatique de plus en plus « à la demande ».

T: Une bonne campagne naît toujours d'une bonne idée. En quoi les moyens numériques peuvent-ils apporter plus d'efficacité ?

MF: Les médias électroniques permettent au consommateur de participer à la campagne. Le média le plus puissant que nous venons de découvrir n'est pas numérique, c'est le consommateur lui-même.

LA FORCE EXPONENTIELLE DES MESSAGES VIRAUX ET DES COMMUNAUTÉS VIRTUELLES DE TOUTES SORTES DÉTERMINERONT DE PLUS EN

PLUS LE SUCCÈS OU L'ÉCHEC D'UNE CAMPAGNE PROMOTIONNELLE.

T: Quelle a été votre campagne la plus réussie ? Et pourquoi ?

MF: J'ignore si elle a eu du succès, mais la campagne qui a eu le plus d'impact sur ma vision personnelle a été la partie d'échec disputée par Gary Kasparov et le superordinateur d'IBM Deep Blue. Nous avons retransmis la rencontre en direct sur Internet pour des fans du monde entier, et interviewé des spectateurs dans le public comme Milos Forman et George Plimpton.

METTRE EN RELATION LE MONDE ENTIER AVEC CETTE LUTTE ÉPIQUE ENTRE L'HOMME ET LA MACHINE A ÉTÉ PALPITANT ET BOULEVERSANT. JE NE L'OUBLIERAI JAMAIS. C'ÉTAIT AUSSI UN PEU EFFRAYANT, CAR C'EST LA MACHINE QUI A GAGNÉ.

T: Les consommateurs « filtrent » ce qu'ils regardent, et deviennent même anti-pubs. Comment le marketing et la publicité en ligne peuvent-ils aider les marques à atteindre leur public ?

Le marketing semble évoluer d'une dictature de magnats des médias vers une méritocratie de consommateurs. Je pense que c'est une bonne nouvelle pour la bonne santé à long terme du marketing et du commerce. Des changements tectoniques de pouvoir, souvent dépeints comme des scénarios de fin du monde, se révèlent souvent des progrès utiles.

T: En quoi les blogs et la communication virale modifient-ils le paysage ?

MF: Le médium est le messager. Les consommateurs forment le nouveau département créatif. Les marques ont besoin de travailler en accord avec les consommateurs afin de bâtir une relation équitable.

T: On considère que les téléphones portables seront le prochain moyen de communiquer. C'est un objet personnel que l'on porte 24 heures sur 24 et 7 jours par semaine. Comment vont-ils influencer la publicité à l'avenir ?

Je ne sais pas trop, mais ce que j'espère, c'est que les gens les mettront plus souvent sur le mode vibreur. Le silence est d'or.

Matt Freeman leitet das globale Netzwerk von Tribal DDB Worldwide. Unter seiner Führung ist Tribal DDB Worldwide eine der größten und am meisten mit Preisen ausgezeichneten interaktiven Agenturen der Welt geworden. Im Moment steht sie bei den 10 Top-Unternehmen in der interaktiven Branche an erster Stelle, gemessen an Einnahmen, Schlagkraft in den Medien und Kreativität. Matt Freeman war Gründungspartner und Kreativleiter von DDB Digital in den USA, eines der sechs Unternehmen, die zusammen Tribal DDB Worldwide formen. Freemans Arbeiten haben alle wichtigen Auszeichnungen der Branche gewonnen, darunter Cannes Lions, Art Directors Club, New York Festivals, ANDYs, Effies und „Best of Show" bei One Show Interactive. Er saß in der Jury des International Advertising Festivals in Cannes und war interaktiver Vorsitzender bei den Clio Awards, der One Show und den International Andy Awards. Außerdem ist er von Publikationen wie Wall Street Journal, New York Times, CNN, CNBC, CBS MarketWatch, Forrester Research, AdAge und Adweek and Creativity gewürdigt worden. Vor seinem Leben in der Werbung arbeitete Freeman bei MTV, schrieb für verschiedene Zeitschriften und war Englischlehrer. Er machte am Dartmouth College seinen B.A. in Englisch und Kunstgeschichte und besuchte die School of Visual Arts.

T: Was werden Ihrer Meinung nach die nächsten 10 meistverwendeten digitalen

Medien sein?

MF: Handys, iTV, Videospiele, Blogs, Podcasts, Netzwerke unter Freunden, RFID, Digitale Heimnetzwerke, Nanotech-integrierte Pakete und Roboter. Eine ganze Menge Roboter.

T: Online-Werbung nimmt im gesamten Marketing-Budget bisher eine kleine Rolle ein. Inwieweit, glauben Sie, wird sich dies ändern?

MF: Es wird seinen unvermeidlichen Weg in Richtung Dominanz gehen, aber die Trennung zwischen „traditionell" und „digital" wird auch verschwinden. Wenn man im Digitalfernsehen interaktive Werbung kaufen kann – wer weiß, wo man die Grenze ziehen kann. Wir werden sehen, dass sich die Integration beschleunigen wird – für Medienunternehmen und Agenturen gleichermaßen.

T: Warum sollten Unternehmen mehr online gehen?

MF: Weil Unternehmen Konsumenten brauchen. Und in den meisten Fällen verbringen die Konsumenten den größten Teil der Zeit ihres Medienkonsums online.

T: Was ändert sich durch den digitalen Aufbau einer Marke?

MF: Die grundlegende neue Frage, die sich Marken in der digitalen Welt stellen müssen, ist folgende: „Wie soll sich unsere Marke präsentieren?" Der Sprung von Markenkommunikation zu Markeninteraktion erfordert einen dreidimensionalen Verhaltenscharakter, den man bei ausschließlich im Fernsehen oder Radio gesendeten Medien nicht braucht.

T: Einer der größten Vorteile von Werbung online ist die wachsende Kontrolle über das Kundenverhalten. Wie wird dies Ihrer Meinung nach die Werbeagenturen verändern?

MF: Ich glaube nicht wirklich, dass online die Konsumentenkontrolle wächst. Tatsächlich besteht der größte Vorteil für das Marketing in seiner Annäherung an den Kunden, die auf Erlaubnis basiert. Wenn man fest daran glaubt, dass man die Aufmerksamkeit des Konsumenten verdienen muss, anstatt sie einfach zu kaufen, hat man einen direkten Vorteil in der „on-demand"-Medienlandschaft.

T: Eine gute Kampagne beginnt immer mit einer guten Idee. Wie kann man eine Kampagne mit digitalen Mitteln verbessern?

MF: Durch digitale Medien wird der Konsument Teil der Kampagne. Das stärkste neue Medium, das wir entdeckt haben, ist nicht digital, sondern das sind die Konsumenten selbst.

DIE EXPONENTIELLE STÄRKE VIRALER UND SOZIALER NETZWERKE ALLER ART WIRD ZUNEHMEND DEN ERFOLG VON MARKETINGKAMPAGNEN BESTIMMEN.

T: Welche Ihrer Kampagnen war die erfolgreichste? Und warum?

MF: Ich bin mir nicht sicher, ob es die erfolgreichste war, aber die Kampagne, die die größte Wirkung auf meine persönliche Perspektive hatte, war das IBM-Schachspiel zwischen Gary Kasparov und ihrem Deep Blue Supercomputer. Wir strahlten das Match live für die Fans aus aller Welt aus und interviewten Leute im Publikum wie Milos Forman und George Plimpton.

DIE VERBINDUNG, DIE WIR ZWISCHEN DEM EPISCHEN KAMPF VON MANN UND MASCHINE UND DEM REST DER WELT HERSTELLTEN, WAR SO AUFREGEND, DASS ICH DAS GEFÜHL NIE VERGESSEN WERDE. ES WAR AUCH EIN WENIG ANGSTEINFLÖSSEND. DIE

MASCHINE GEWANN.

T:Konsumenten filtern immer mehr von dem, was sie sehen, und werden zu „Werbungsvermeidern". Wie kann digitale Werbung/Marketing den Marken helfen, Kunden zu erreichen?

MF: Marketing wandelt sich scheinbar zunehmend von einer von Mogulen gesteuerten Diktatur in eine konsumenten-bestimmte Leistungsgesellschaft. Ich finde, dass sind gute Neuigkeiten für die langfristige Gesundheit von Marketing und Geschäft. Aus tektonischen Machtverschiebungen, die oft als Untergangsszenarien ausgemalt werden, entsteht oft längst notwendiger Fortschritt.

T: Wie werden Blogs und Viral-Marketing die Kommunikation verändern?

MF: Das Medium ist der Botschafter. Konsumenten sind die neue Kreativabteilung. Marken müssen für kooperative Fairness mit ihren eigenen Kunden zusammenarbeiten.

T: Das Handy ist der nächste Weg zur Kommunikation. Es ist persönlich, und wir haben es Tag und Nacht bei uns. Wie wird es die Werbung in Zukunft beeinflussen?

MF: Ich bin nicht ganz sicher, aber ich hoffe wirklich, dass mehr Leute ihren Vibrationsalarm einschalten werden. Schweigen ist Gold.

001

FOOD & BEVERAGE

FEATURED ON THE DVD **CAMPAIGN:** Burger King Subservient Chicken <www.subservientchicken.com>. **PRODUCT:** Burger King TenderCrisp Sandwich. **YEAR:** 2004. **AGENCY:** Crispin Porter + Bogusky <www.cpbgroup.com>. **PRODUCTION TIME:** 1 month. **EXECUTIVE CREATIVE DIRECTOR:** Alex Bogusky. **CREATIVE DIRECTOR:** Andrew Keller. **INTERACTIVE CREATIVE DIRECTOR:** Jeff Benjamin. **ASSOCIATE CREATIVE DIRECTOR:** Rob Reilly. **COPYWRITER:** Bob Cianfrone. **ART DIRECTOR:** Mark Taylor. **ILLUSTRATOR:** Pres Rodriguez. **PROGRAMMER:** Barbarian Group. **MEDIA CIRCULATED:** In-store posters, broadcast TV, magazine inserts, live appearances. **AWARDS:** Cannes Cyber Lions 2004 (Gold, Bronze), London International (Winner: Interactive category, Finalist for Weird, Wonderful Work and Food categories), Viral Awards 2005 (Winner: Most Creative Use of Technology), Andy Awards (Silver), O'Toole (Tier Winner-Big Agency), One Show (Yahoo Big Idea Chair, Interactive Best of Show, Pencils-2 Gold interactive, Finalist in Innovative and Friendster categories), D&AD (Silver pencil, Silver nomination), Webby Awards (Humor nominee, Weird and Wonderful nominee), CA Interactive (Winner), Clio (Grand Clio, Gold in Brand building, Gold), Won the Yahoo Big Idea Chair for the Andy Awards 2005, Marketing Innovation of the year.

 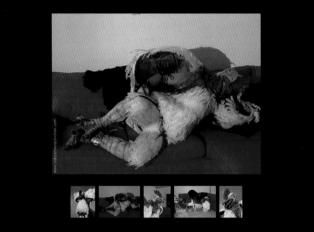

CONCEPT: We launched the Burger King TenderCrisp Sandwich within the "Have it your way" brand message. To show how customers really can have it their way with chicken, we created a large subservient chicken that does almost anything anyone asks. Type commands, and tell the chicken what do. The chicken then does what it is told. The chicken – much like the sandwich - satisfies everyone's personal tastes and preferences, no matter how unique. **RESULTS:** 15 million hits the first 5 days. Word spread completely virally. Once the site and chicken were seeded mainstream we added more branding, commercials and easter egg commands to keep people talking and passing the site around. Now with well over 400 million hits to Subservient Chicken and a significant increase in chicken sales that can be directly linked to the success of the site – this site has showed how successful an advertiser can be when they entertain and let people discover the message and brand.

CONCEPT : Le lancement du burger au poulet TenderCrisp s'intègre dans la campagne « Faites comme vous voulez ». Pour évoquer l'étendue des choix proposés au consommateur de poulet, nous avons conçu un personnage déguisé en poulet qui fait quasiment tout ce qu'on lui demande. Il suffit de taper un ordre dans la boîte de dialogue et le poulet s'exécute. Le poulet, comme le hamburger, satisfait les goûts et les désirs de chacun, aussi uniques soient-ils. **RÉSULTATS :** 15 millions de visites les 5 premiers jours. La nouvelle s'est propagée de façon virale. Une fois que le site et le personnage furent bien implantés dans le public, nous avons ajouté d'autres publicités et d'autres fonctions avec des œufs de Pâques afin que les visiteurs relaient le site et en discutent entre eux. Avec plus de 400 millions de visiteurs et une belle augmentation des ventes de poulet directement attribuable au succès de la pub, le site a démontré qu'un annonceur peut connaître le succès en distrayant les gens et en les laissant découvrir seuls le message et la marque.

KONZEPT: Wir führten Burger Kings TenderCrisp Sandwich innerhalb der „Have it your way"-Markenbotschaft ein. Um zu zeigen, dass Kunden von ihrem Hühnchen alles bekommen, schufen wir ein großes unterwürfiges Huhn, das fast alles tut, was man verlangt: Man tippt Befehle ein, und das Huhn befolgt sie. Es erfüllt – wie das Sandwich – jeden persönlichen Geschmack und Vorzug, egal, wie speziell sie ausfallen. **ERGEBNISSE:** 15 Millionen Treffer in den ersten fünf Tagen. Es verbreitete sich absolut viral. Als die Seite und das Huhn erst einmal gestreut waren, brauchten wir mehr Werbespots und Osterei-Befehle, damit die Leute weiterhin darüber sprachen und die Seite weiter verteilten. Mit nun über 400 Millionen Treffern und einem bedeutenden Anstieg der Hühnchenverkäufe, die direkt vom Erfolg der Seite abgeleitet werden können, hat die Seite gezeigt, wie erfolgreich Werbung sein kann, wenn sie unterhaltsam ist und die Leute Botschaft und Marke entdecken können.

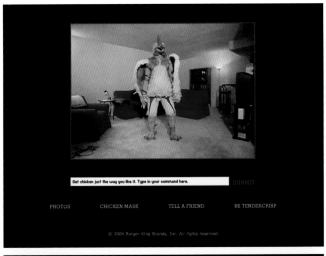

FEATURED ON THE DVD **CAMPAIGN:** Cacique – "Hear the call" <www.escuchalallamada.com>. **PRODUCT:** Cacique Rum. **YEAR:** 2005. **AGENCY:** DoubleYou <www.doubleyou.com>. **PRODUCTION TIME:** 2,5 month. **CREATIVE TEAM:** Daniel Solana, Joakim Borgström, Blanca Piera, Emma Pueyo, Xavi Caparrós, Nacho Guijarro, Lisi Badía, Daniel González, Davis Lisboa (idea based on the offline campaign of Ms. Rushmore). **PROGRAMMER:** Xavi Caparrós, Jose Rubio, Álvaro Sandoval. **TECH ASPECTS:** Macromedia Flash. **MEDIA CIRCULATED:** MSN, Yahoo!, El Mundo, Wanadoo, Ya.com.

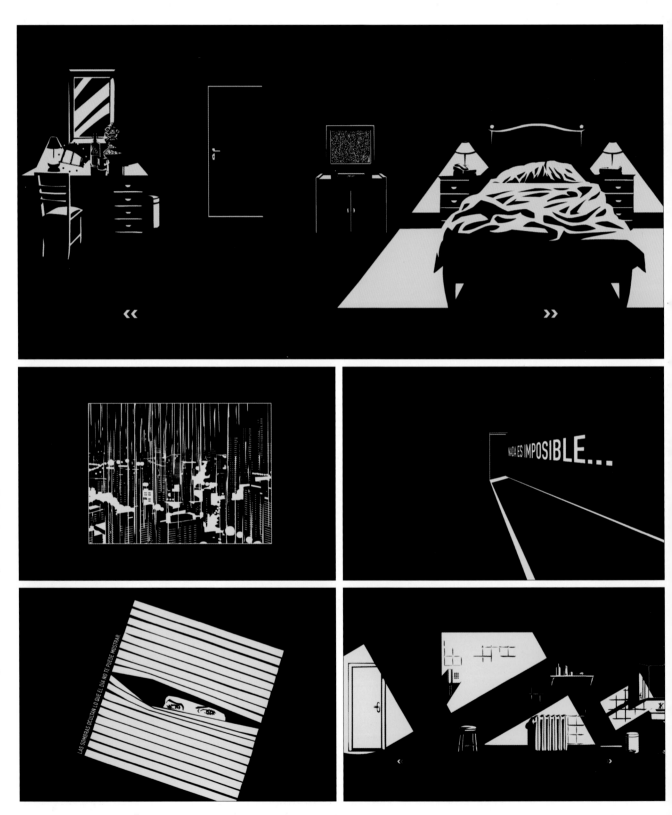

CONCEPT: A website that isn't a website, it's a journey. The journey starts at *escuchalallamada.com*, where the visitor is greeted by a ringing telephone. You answer, and a whispering voice suggests you follow the instructions for a whole new experience. You accept, the voice guides you out from that website, you surf the Internet, visit a blog, cross a jungle which becomes a city, and end up in a motel room which is empty, but for a presence, and an invitation to see something real, but unusual: a show.

CONCEPT : C'est un site qui n'est pas un site, mais un voyage. Le voyage commence sur *escuchalallamada.com*. Sur la page d'accueil, un téléphone sonne. Quand vous décrochez le combiné, une voix vous susurre de suivre les instructions et vous propose de vivre une aventure. Si vous acceptez, la voix vous invite à la suivre, sortir du site, naviguer sur le Net, visiter un blog, traverser une jungle qui se transforme en ville, et finir dans un hôtel où il n'y a personne, seulement une présence et une invitation à voir une chose réelle bien qu'inattendue : un spectacle.

KONZEPT: Eine Webseite, die keine ist – sie ist eine Reise. Sie startet auf *escuchalallamada.com*, wo der Besucher von einem klingelnden Telefon begrüßt wird. Nimmt man es ab, gibt eine flüsternde Stimme Instruktionen für eine völlig neue Erfahrung. Akzeptiert man die Anweisungen, führt die Stimme den Besucher von der Webseite weg, man surft im Netz, besucht einen Blog, durchquert einen Dschungel, der sich in eine Stadt verwandelt, und landet in einem Motelzimmer, das leer ist bis auf eine Einladung, etwas Reales, aber Ungewöhnliches zu sehen: eine Show.

CONCEPT: Interactive advertising explores the "light" concept essence for Coca-Cola in a minimalist, simple and objective way.

CONCEPT : La publicité interactive explore la nature du concept « allégé » de Coca-Cola sur un mode minimaliste, simple et objectif.

KONZEPT: Interaktive Werbung leuchtet das „Light"-Konzept für Coca-Cola auf minimalistische, einfache und neutrale Weise aus.

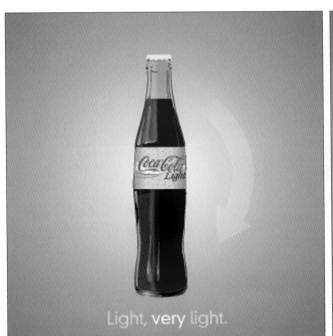

FEATURED ON THE DVD **PRODUCT:** Coca-Cola Blak. **YEAR:** 2005. **AGENCY:** DoubleYou <www.doubleyou.com>. **PRODUCTION TIME:** 3 weeks. **CREATIVE TEAM:** Joakim Borgström, Frédéric Sanz, Blanca Piera, Emma Pueyo, Trini Rodríguez, Natalie Long. **PROGRAMMER:** Jordi Martínez, Joakim Borgström. **TECH ASPECTS:** Macromedia Flash. **MEDIA CIRCULATED:** E-mail.

CONCEPT: E-mail teaser for the international launch of the new Coca-Cola Blak.

KONZEPT: E-Mail-Teaser für den internationalen Launch der neuen Coca-Cola Blak.

CONCEPT : Accroche sous forme d'e-mail pour le lancement international du nouveau Coca-Cola Blak.

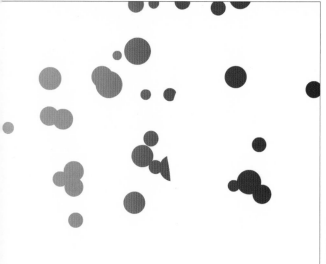

FEATURED ON THE DVD **CAMPAIGN:** World Chill. **PRODUCT:** Coca-Cola Zero. **YEAR:** 2005. **AGENCY:** Crispin Porter + Bogusky <www.cpbgroup.com>. **CREATIVE DESIGN:** Digit <www.digitlondon.com> **PRODUCTION:** Digit <www.digitlondon.com>. **PRODUCTION TIME:** 6 weeks. **ART DIRECTOR:** Andrew Dean. **PRODUCER:** Justin Vir. **DESIGNER:** Henry Brook. **PROGRAMMER:** Jamie Ingram, Adam Frankel, Ray Hilton, Ellen Sundh. **TECH ASPECTS:** Macromedia Flash, sound – voice overs. **AWARDS:** Future Marketing Award 2006 (Best Branded Community Project online).

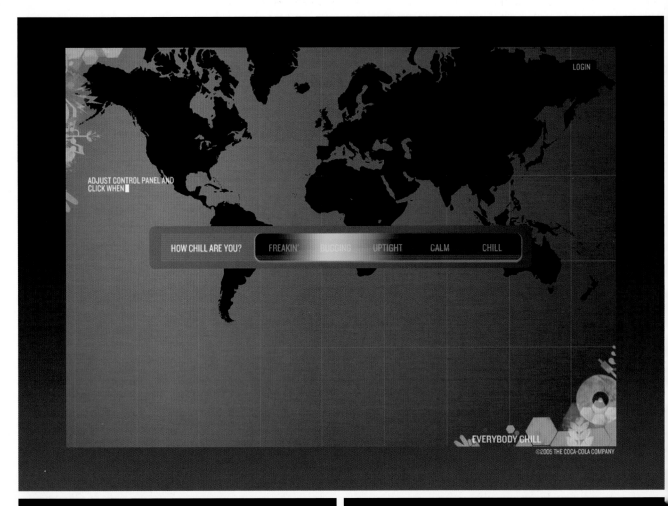

CONCEPT: Coke Zero is the latest diet incarnation of Coca Cola. Produced to taste more like regular Coke than Diet Coke, it has zero calories and is aimed at a male target audience. **BRIEF:** To work with Coke's advertising agency, Crispin Porter + Bogusky, to bring to life their "World Chill" strategy and apply it to a digital destination in five languages. **SOLUTION:** Digit created an integrated website, screensaver and desktop application for a global audience within a very tight timescale (6 weeks). A global, map-based community was built that constantly monitored the level of "chill" around the world. Users were able to zoom in on their location, mark it with a "Chill Pin" and leave a mood reading from "Freakin" to "Chill" and a statement to explain why they felt that way. The site provided up-to-date, global "chill levels" that could also be updated by users via a desktop application, and which fed live data to the screensaver every 5 seconds. This created an ever changing and engaging on-line experience that consumers actively contributed to.

CONCEPT : Coke Zero est le dernier avatar des boissons allégées de Coca-Cola. Conçu pour se rapprocher du goût du Coca classique plutôt que de celui du Coca allégé, il contient « zéro calorie » et s'adresse à un public masculin. **MISSION :** Collaborer avec l'agence de pub de Coca, Crispin Porter + Bogusky, animer leur stratégie «cool attitude mondiale » et décliner une version électronique en cinq langues. **SOLUTION :** Digit a réalisé un site intégré, un écran de veille et une application destinés à une audience planétaire dans un délai très serré (six semaines). Un réseau mondial fut constitué pour mesurer à chaque instant le niveau de « cool attitude » aux quatre coins du monde à l'aide d'une mappemonde. Les internautes pouvaient faire un zoom sur leur région, la marquer d'une épingle et laisser un billet d'humeur allant de « speedé » à « cool » accompagné d'un message justifiant leur état d'esprit. Le site incluait une mise à jour des niveaux de relaxation mondiale qui pouvait également être modifiée par les internautes via une application spéciale, les nouvelles données s'affichant sur l'écran de veille toutes les cinq secondes. Les consommateurs ont participé activement à cette expérience évolutive et captivante.

KONZEPT: Coke Zero ist die neueste Diät-Erfindung von Coca-Cola. Sie soll mehr nach normaler Cola schmecken, als dies bei Cola Light der Fall ist, hat null Kalorien und zielt auf eine männliche Zielgruppe ab. **AUFGABE:** In Zusammenarbeit mit Coca-Colas Werbeagentur Crispin Porter + Bogusky ihre „World Chill"-Strategie ins Leben rufen und sie digital in fünf Sprachen anwenden. **LÖSUNG:** Digit entwickelte eine integrierte Webseite, einen Bildschirmschoner und eine Desktop-Anwendung für ein globales Publikum innerhalb kürzester Zeit (6 Wochen). Eine globale Gemeinschaft wurde aufgebaut, die ständig den „Chill"-Level weltweit überwacht. Die Benutzer konnten auf ihren Standort zoomen, ihn mit einem „Chill Pin" markieren und eine Laune zwischen „Freaking" und „Chill" angeben – mit einer Erklärung, warum sie sich so fühlten. Die Seite lieferte aktuelle, globale „Chill-Level", welche durch die Benutzer mit einer Desktop-Anwendung aktualisiert werden konnten, die alle fünf Sekunden Live-Daten an den Bildschirmschoner lieferte. Dadurch wurde eine sich stets verändernde Online-Darstellung geschaffen, zu der Benutzer aktiv beitrugen.

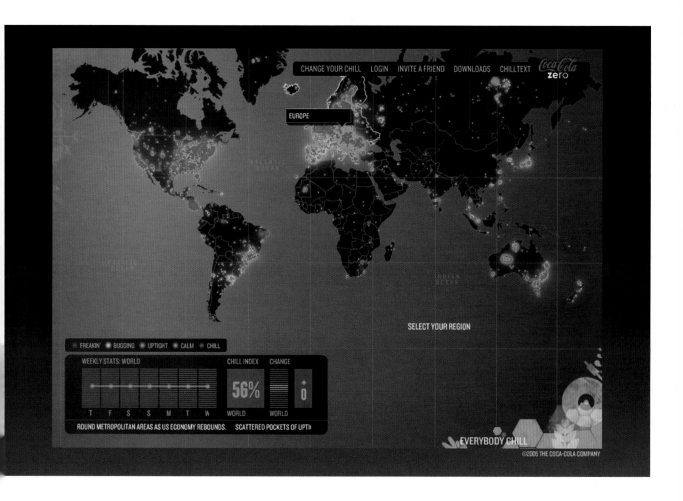

CONCEPT: Interactive advertising with brand experience based at the most practiced sport in Brazil.

CONCEPT : Publicité interactive de présentation de la marque basée sur le sport le plus populaire du Brésil.

KONZEPT: Interaktive Werbung mit Markenpräsentation auf der Grundlage der in Brasilien am meisten praktizierten Sportart.

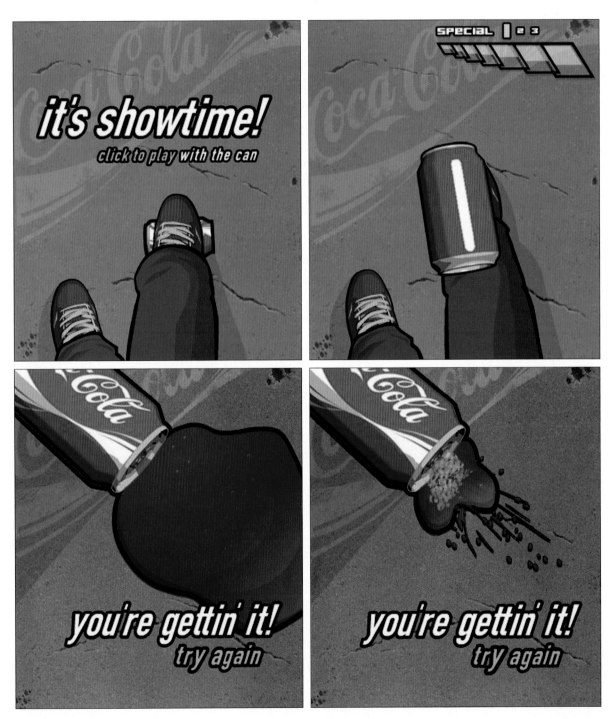

FEATURED ON THE DVD **CAMPAIGN:** Coke website <www.cocacola.com.br>. **CLIENT:** Coca-Cola. **YEAR:** 2005. **AGENCY:** AgênciaClick <www.agenciaclick.com.br>.

CONCEPT: Inspired by the most recognized Coke Symbol, the Brazilian Coke's Website merges all of strategic in a unique interactive experience.

CONCEPT : S'inspirant du célébrissime logo de la marque, le site brésilien englobe toute la stratégie de Coca dans une aventure interactive unique.

KONZEPT: Inspiriert von dem meist erkannten Cola-Symbol vereint die Cola-Webseite Brasiliens alle Strategien in einem einzigartigen interaktiven Ansatz.

CONCEPT: Interactive advertising Tutorial. Instructions for a perfect performance to drink Tequila like Mexicans. Learn and have fun.

KONZEPT: Interaktive Werbung. Anleitung, wie man Tequila wie ein Mexikaner trinkt. Lernen und Spaß haben.

CONCEPT : Site de publicité interactive offrant des instructions pour déguster la tequila comme de parfaits Mexicains. Suivez le guide et amusez-vous.

FEATURED ON THE DVD **CAMPAIGN:** Jungle Duty. **CLIENT:** Chiquita Banana Company. **AGENCY:** LOWE Tesch <www.lowetesch.com>. **ART DIRECTOR:** Patrik Westerdahl. **COPYWRITER:** Cissi Högkvist. **ACCOUNT DIRECTOR:** Måns Tesch. **ACCOUNT MANAGER:** Anna Kjellmark. **MOTION DESIGNER:** Daniel Isaksson, Tobias Löfgren. **FILM PRODUCTION:** Oskar Bård (Hobbyfilm). **3D ANIMATION:** Against all odds. **MUSIC:** Bunker. **ILLUSTRATOR:** Lennart Molin. **CLIENT'S SUPERVISOR:** Max Stenbäck.

CONCEPT: For twelve years Chiquita has been working together with the Rainforest Alliance to reduce strain on the environment because of banana farms – and now we invite you to join. Jungle Duty is an interactive film where the user watch over the rainforest by giving a helping hand to some of the inhabitants and divert some of the inhabitants attention. In return for the rangers contribution Chitquita will adopt rainforest – and the better ranger the more rainforest.

CONCEPT : Chiquita collabore depuis douze ans avec la Rainforest Alliance pour réduire l'impact des bananeraies sur l'environnement, et aide celle-ci à recruter de nouveaux adhérents. *Jungle Duty* est un film interactif où le visiteur protège la forêt tropicale en donnant un coup de main aux habitants et en distrayant l'attention des criminels. En contrepartie de votre contribution, Chiquita « adopte » une forêt tropicale. Plus vous êtes efficace, plus elle sauve de forêts.

KONZEPT: Seit 12 Jahren arbeitet Chiquita mit der Rainforest Alliance zusammen, um die negativen Auswirkungen zu reduzieren, die Bananenfarmen auf die Umwelt haben – und nun laden wir Sie dazu ein, mitzumachen. „Jungle Duty" ist ein interaktiver Film, in dem der Benutzer auf den Regenwald aufpasst, indem er einigen Einwohnern hilft und die Aufmerksamkeit von anderen ablenkt. Als Gegenleistung für den Beitrag des Rangers setzt sich Chiquita für den Regenwald ein – je besser der Ranger, umso mehr Regenwald.

FEATURED ON THE DVD **CAMPAIGN:** Doritos website <www.doritos.com> **PRODUCT:** Doritos. **YEAR:** 2005. **AGENCY:** Tribal DDB Dallas <www.tribalddb.com>. **PRODUCTION TIME:** 3 months. **EXECUTIVE CREATIVE DIRECTOR:** Scott Johnson. **ASSOCIATE CREATIVE DIRECTOR:** Dave Gibson. **ASSOCIATE CREATIVE DIRECTOR:** Michael Carpenter. **ART DIRECTOR:** Tien Pham. **ART DIRECTOR:** Kelly McCullough. **PROGRAMMER:** Andrew Langley, Chris Griffith (Game Developer). **TECH ASPECTS:** Macromedia Flash, full-motion video, games, sound, original music. **MEDIA CIRCULATED:** AOL and Yahoo sponsorships, other banner ads. **AWARDS:** Cannes Lions (Shortlist).

CONCEPT: This site is about living life in the now. To communicate that idea, we created a window which people walk by and touch to release icons onto the home page. Users can capture these and enter the codes on them to unlock a variety of downloads, including games, music, videos, and more. The idea is to provide a constant stream of evanescent content that is designed to surprise and delight.

CONCEPT : Le site encourage la vie dans l'instantanéité. Pour communiquer cette idée, nous avons créé une fenêtre que le visiteur doit franchir pour libérer des icones sur la page d'accueil. On doit les attraper et entrer un code qui déclenche une variété d'éléments à té-

lécharger, dont des jeux, de la musique, des vidéos et autres. L'idée est de proposer un flux constant de contenu évanescent destiné à surprendre et enchanter.

KONZEPT: Bei dieser Seite geht es um das Leben im Hier und Jetzt. Um diese Idee zu kommunizieren, schufen wir ein Fenster, an dem Leute vorbeigehen, es berühren und dadurch Icons auf der Homepage auslösen. Benutzer können diese einfangen und Codes eingeben, um eine Vielzahl von Downloads zu entschlüsseln, darunter Spiele, Musik, Videos und mehr. Die Idee besteht darin, einen konstanten Fluss mit schwindendem Inhalt zu liefern, der überraschen und erfreuen soll.

CONCEPT: When it comes to French wines, people are often turned off the "snob factor." Our challenge was to create a web experience to help demystify French wines and show that even the novice wine drinker can enjoy a wine from France. We did it by creating a site with all the flair and passion of the region. Information on the wines and their regions was woven into every aspect of the site – from love letters to food pairing, and even a faux French glossary. During the promotion, sales of French wines increased by 37% over the same period last year.

CONCEPT : Concernant les vins français, les consommateurs sont souvent rebutés par l'image de snobisme. Notre défi était de créer une expérience internet qui permettrait de démythifier les vins français et montrer que même un néophyte peut les apprécier. Nous avons conçu un site qui rappelle le style et l'esprit du pays. Des informations sur les vins et les terroirs infiltrent chaque aspect du site, agrémentées de lettres d'amour, de recettes culinaires, et même d'un faux glossaire français. Durant la campagne, les ventes de vins français ont connu une hausse de 37% comparé à la même période l'année précédente.

KONZEPT: Wenn es um französische Weine geht, ist man oft vom „Snob-Faktor" abgeschreckt. Unsere Herausforderung bestand darin, eine interaktive Webseite zu entwickeln, die französische Weine entmystifizierte und zeigte, dass auch ein Weintrinker, der kein Kenner ist, französischen Wein genießen kann. Dies taten wir, indem wir eine Seite mit dem Flair und der Leidenschaft des Landes entwarfen. Informationen über die Weine und ihre Regionen waren in alle Aspekte der Seite verwoben – von Liebesbriefen über passendes Essen bis hin zu einem französischen Glossar. Während der Werbeaktion stieg der Verkauf französischer Weine um 37% im Gegensatz zum gleichen Zeitraum im Vorjahr.

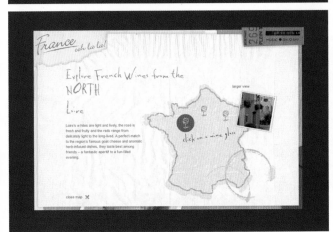

FEATURED ON THE DVD **CAMPAIGN:** NESTEA Ice website <www.nesteaice.com>. **PRODUCT:** NESTEA Ice. **YEAR:** 2005. **AGENCY:** Juxt Interactive <www.juxtinteractive.com>. **PRODUCTION TIME:** 3 months. **CREATIVE DIRECTOR:** Todd Purgason. **ART DIRECTOR:** Jorge Calleja. **FLASH DESIGNER:** Brian Miller, Kenneth Macy. **PROGRAMMER:** Victor Allen, Christian Ayotte. **TECH ASPECTS:** Macromedia Flash, FLV, Quicktime video, MP3 audio. **AWARDS:** London International Advertising Awards (Interactive Media Winner - Beverages category), HOW Interactive Design Awards (Outstanding Winner). **HITS ON THE PAGE:** 40,000 per week.

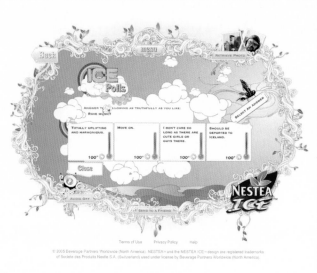

CONCEPT: The NESTEA Ice site was created to help build awareness for a new Ready to Drink tea beverage from Nestea. The product is unique, in that it has a cooling ingredient that actually subtly numbs your mouth when you drink it. We developed the tag line "Absurdly Cold", and this served as the positioning point for the site. We wanted to create a site that had a novel and comical tone with fun and somewhat absurd content. The target audience is college-age males and females, so we created entertaining and viral content so that this demographic would share with friends. Enhancing the interactivity, we built a custom T-shirt application to make the brand more relevant to the youth culture. **RESULTS:** NestealCE.com was hugely successful in generating extensive awareness of the product among college-age males. The site was visited by over 40,000 uniques per week during the three-month campaign, and was lauded by numerous design and beverage industry authorities, including named Best Beverage Site by the London International Advertising Awards. It has been blogged all over the world, and already honored by several design authorities (Macromedia, Favourite Site of the Day, Comm Arts).

CONCEPT : Le site de NESTEA Ice a été conçu pour promouvoir une boisson instantanée à base de thé fabriquée par Nestea. Le produit est unique, dans le sens qu'il contient un ingrédient rafraîchissant qui engourdit légèrement la bouche quand on le boit. Nous avons trouvé le slogan « Ridiculement froid » et elle a servi de positionnement pour le site. Nous voulions adopter un ton comique et présenter un contenu quelque peu absurde. Le public ciblé étant les étudiants des deux sexes, nous avons créé un contenu amusant et viral que cette population pourrait partager entre amis. Pour améliorer l'interactivité, nous avons proposé une application de personnalisation de T-shirts afin que la marque soit plus en phase avec la culture jeune. **RÉSULTATS :** NestealCE.com a connu un énorme succès en terme d'augmentation de notoriété chez les étudiants masculins. Le site a reçu plus de 40 000 visiteurs par semaine pendant les trois mois de la campagne, et a été salué par nombre de professionnels de l'industrie agroalimentaire. Il a reçu le prix du meilleur site de boissons aux LIAA. Il a été repris dans des blogs du monde entier et a été récompensé par plusieurs sociétés de design (Macromedia, Favorite Site of the Day, Comm Arts).

KONZEPT: Die NESTEA Ice-Seite wurde entwickelt, um ein Bewusstsein für das neue Instant-Teegetränk von Nestea aufzubauen. Das Produkt ist insofern einzigartig, als es einen kühlenden Inhaltsstoff enthält, der den Mund beim Trinken leicht betäubt. Wir entwickelten die Überschrift „Absurdly Cold", die als Positionierungspunkt für die Seite dient. Wir wollten eine Seite mit einem neuartigen und witzigen Ton entwickeln, mit spaßigem und leicht absurdem Inhalt. Die Zielgruppe besteht aus Männern und Frauen im Studentenalter; deshalb kreierten wir einen unterhaltsamen und viralen Inhalt, den man mit Freunden teilen kann. Um die Interaktivität zu erhöhen, bauten wir eine Anwendung ein, mit der man eigene T-Shirts gestalten kann, um die Marke für die Jugendkultur relevant zu machen. **ERGEBNISSE:** NestealCE.com war bei der Erzeugung eines breiten Bewusstseins des Produkts bei Männern im Studentenalter extrem erfolgreich. Während der dreimonatigen Kampagne wurde die Seite von über 40 000 Einzelpersonen pro Woche besucht, von vielen Autoritäten aus der Design- und Getränkeindustrie gelobt und unter anderem von den London International Advertising Awards zur Best Beverage Site gewählt. Sie wurde weltweit gebloggt und bereits von einigen Design-Autoritäten gelobt (Macromedia, Favourite Site of the Day, Comm Arts).

Terms of Use   Privacy Policy   Help

© 2005 Beverage Partners Worldwide (North America). NESTEA™ and the NESTEA ICE™ design are registered trademarks
of Societe des Produits Nestle S.A. (Switzerland) used under license by Beverage Partners Worldwide (North America).

FEATURED ON THE DVD **CAMPAIGN:** Peperami Noodles Army <www.goneabitnoodles.co.uk>. **YEAR:** 2005. **AGENCY:** AKQA <www.akqa.com>. **PRODUCTION TIME:** 3 months. **ART DIRECTOR:** James Capp. **COPYWRITER:** Colin Byrne. **GROUP ACCOUNT DIRECTOR:** Richard Hedges. **LEAD CREATIVE:** Miles Unwin. **SENIOR SOFTWARE ENGINEER:** Joel Godfrey, Miriam Healy. **SENIOR WEB DEVELOPER:** Sachin Shah. **CREATIVE DEVELOPER:** Marcus van Malsen, Dan Wood. **MOTION DESIGNER:** Stephen Clements. **DESIGNER:** Ian Byrne. **WEB EDITOR:** Tony Sears. **SENIOR QA MANAGER:** Tony Unwin. **TECH ASPECTS:** Macromedia Flash, video, sound. **AWARDS:** Cannes Cyber Lions (Gold). Gramia Awards (Gold).

OBJECTIVE: Unilever asked us to turn the noodle-slurping men of Britain away from the path of boring noodles and show them how with new Peperami Noodles, "Peperami takes the mundane and makes it more interesting." **STRATEGY:** Our first insight was that young men are much more liable to indulge in the kind of mental craziness that characterizes the Peperami brand when they're in groups. We also knew that by making the creative funny enough, they'd do a lot of the work for us by passing the message on to their mates. **SOLUTION:** And so the Peperami Noodles Army (PNA) was born – an entire army of lads whose sole ambition is to take boring things and liven them up. Via embedded video on a website, lads were invited to explore the training camp, watch and send on recruitment films and join the PNA themselves. They could also download a mobile phone wallpaper and ringtone featuring the distinctive voice of The Animal. Meanwhile, the recruitment films were seeded across over 50 websites, and AKQA stunned Sun readers by making the entire home page of the Sun newspaper online "peel back" to reveal an alternative page where every story was about the PNA. Interactive skyscrapers and banners also featured on sites including Zoo and XFM, where The Animal goaded lads into creating slices for Peperami Noodles by putting him through a chopping machine. Offline activity included a TV campaign, DM and sampling, and PR activity that gave lads the chance to win a PNA survival kit featured in numerous magazines, including "letter of the week" in Zoo). **RESULTS:** Unilever had to step-up production of Peperami Noodles to satisfy demand following the launch of the campaign. The recruitment film "Russian Chess" was viewed over 500,000 times virally. The Sun activity drove 25,000 visitors to the site in a single day. 250,000 lads visited the site in two weeks. The activity was highly commended across a variety of media, described as "like looking at the future of the ad industry" in the press.

OBJECTIFS : Unilever nous a demandé d'encourager les amateurs de nouilles à délaisser leur marque habituelle pour adopter la marque Peperami qui « donne du piment au quotidien ». **STRATÉGIE :** Notre première idée a été que les hommes ont plus tendance à se laisser aller au délire qui caractérise la marque Peperami lorsqu'ils sont en groupe. Nous avions aussi que si nous réussissions à rendre le message assez attrayant, ils feraient le reste du travail à notre place, en passant le message à leurs copains. **SOLUTION :** C'est ainsi que l'Armée des Peperami Noodles vit le jour. Une armée entière de types dont la seule ambition est de transformer les corvées en une partie de plaisir. Via une vidéo incluse dans le site, les internautes sont invités à visiter le camp d'entraînement, visionner des scènes de recrutement, et s'engager finalement dans l'Armée des Peperami Noodles. Ils peuvent aussi télécharger un fond d'écran de portable ainsi qu'une sonnerie avec la voix de l'Animal. Dans le même temps, les annonces de recrutement furent introduites sur 50 autres sites et AKQA étonna les lecteurs du Sun en installant une page d'accueil transparente sur le site du journal, qui une fois soulevée faisait apparaître une deuxième page où tous les articles concernaient l'Armée des Peperami. Des bannières et des gratte-ciels interactifs apparurent sur des sites comme ceux des magazines Zoo et XFM, où l'Animal poussait les gars à fabriquer des nouilles Peperami en le mettant dans une machine à trancher. L'activité hors ligne comprenait un spot télévisé, du marketing direct et une campagne de presse qui offrait la possibilité de gagner un kit de survie de l'Armée. **RÉSULTATS :** Unilever dut augmenter la production de Peperami Noodles pour satisfaire la demande suite au lancement de la campagne. La vidéo de recrutement « Echiquier Russe » a été visionnée plus de 500 000 fois de façon virale. Le Sun a attiré 25 000 visiteurs sur le site en une seule journée. 250 000 personnes on visité le site en deux semaines. L'expérience a été largement commentée dans de nombreux médias, qui l'ont décrite comme « la publicité de du futur ».

ZIEL: Unilever bat uns, die Nudel-schlürfenden Männer Englands weg von langweiligen Nudeln zu lenken und ihnen zu zeigen, wie Peperami-Nudeln „das Banale interessanter machen". **STRATEGIE:** Unsere erste Einsicht bestand darin, dass sich junge Männer viel eher in Gruppen der Verrücktheit hingeben, die die Peperami-Marke auszeichnet. Außerdem wussten wir, dass sie uns einen Großteil der Arbeit abnehmen und die Botschaft in ihrem Freundeskreis verbreiten würden, wenn wir die Werbung lustig genug aufzogen. **LÖSUNG:** So wurde die Peperami Noodles Army (PNA) geboren – eine ganze Armee von Jungs, deren einziger Ehrgeiz darin besteht, langweilige Dinge aufzupeppen. Durch ein in die Webseite eingebettetes Video wurden junge Männer eingeladen, das Trainingslager zu durchforsten, Rekrutierungsfilme anzusehen und zu verschicken und selbst der PNA beizutreten. Außerdem konnten sie einen Handy-Hintergrund und einen Klingelton mit der markanten Stimme von The Animal herunterladen. Währenddessen wurden die Rekrutierungsfilme auf über 50 Webseiten gestreut, und AKQA erstaunte Leser der Sun, indem sich die ganze Homepage der Zeitung online abschälen ließ und eine alternative Seite zum Vorschein brachte, auf der es bei jeder Story um die neue PNA geht. Interaktive Skyscraper und Banner erschienen auch auf anderen Seiten, darunter Zoo und XFM, wo The Animal-Jungs angestachelt werden, Scheiben für Peperami Noodles zu schneiden, indem sie sie in eine Hackmaschine stecken. Offline-Aktivitäten gab es in Form einer Fernsehkampagne, Direct Marketing und Sampling sowie PR-Aktivitäten, die Männern die Chance gaben, ein PNA Survival Kit zu gewinnen (das in zahlreichen Magazinen erschien, unter anderem im „Letter of the Week" in Zoo). **ERGEBNISSE:** Unilever musste die Produktion von Peperami Noodles erhöhen, um der Nachfrage nach dem Launch der Kampagne nachzukommen. Der Rekrutierungsfilm „Russian Chess" wurde über 500 000 Mal viral angeschaut. Die Aktivität von The Sun führte an einem einzigen Tag 25 000 Besucher auf die Seite. 250 000 Männer besuchten die Seite innerhalb von zwei Wochen. Sie wurde von vielen Medien empfohlen und in der Presse als „Zukunft der Online-Werbeindustrie" beschrieben.

CAMPAIGN: Red Bull Air Race.   **PRODUCT:** Red Bull.   **YEAR:** 2005.   **AGENCY:** Less Rain <www.lessrain.co.uk>.   **PRODUCTION TIME:** 3 weeks.   **COST IN HOURS OF WORK:** 120 h.   **CONCEPT/DESIGN:** Carsten Schneider.   **VIDEO EDITING:** Mikkel Due Pedersen.   **CONCEPT:** Vassilios Alexiou.   **PROGRAMMER:** Luis Martinez.   **TECH ASPECTS:** Macromedia Flash, video for 5 different connection speeds, original music score.   **HITS ON THE PAGE:** Over 1 million (in the first two weeks).

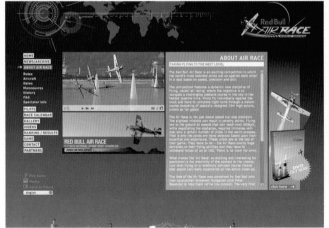

CONCEPT: We were asked to create a viral mailout promoting the 2005 Red Bull Air Race in the UK. We came up with a game that puts you inside the cockpit of one of the world's best aerobatic pilots, Petert Besenyei, and asks you to copy his moves as closely as possible while he takes part in a real Red Bull Air Race. Intelligent bandwidth detection and streaming technology is in place to ensure optimum performance and experience for all connection speeds. **RESULTS:** The key goal of this site was to visualize the physical stress an Air Race Pilot is going through during a race. By creating a simple yet engaging game based on video footage from inside the cockpit, we successfully communicated this to a broader audience. Within just two weeks, the game was played over 230,000 times.

CONCEPT : Créer une campagne promotionnelle par mailing viral pour le Red Bull Air Race 2005 en Grande-Bretagne. Nous avons conçu un jeu de simulation qui vous place dans le cockpit de l'appareil d'un des meilleurs pilotes acrobatiques du monde, Peter Besenyei, et vous invite à reproduire ses figures aussi précisément que possible, tandis qu'il participe à une compétition. Une détection de bande passante intelligente et une technologie de flot continu assure une performance optimale quelque soit le débit de connexion. **RÉSULTATS :**

Le but principal du site était de visualiser la tension physique que subit un pilote d'avion pendant une course. En concevant un jeu simple et captivant basé sur des images vidéo de l'intérieur du cockpit, nous avons transmis le message à un large public. En deux semaines seulement, la partie a été jouée plus de 230 000 fois.

KONZEPT: Wir wurden beauftragt, ein virales Mailout zu entwickeln, um Werbung für das 2005 Red Bull Air Race in Großbritannien zu machen. Wir erfanden ein Spiel, das Benutzer ins Cockpit von einem der weltbesten Kunstflugpiloten, Peter Besenyei, versetzt, wo man seine Bewegungen so ähnlich wie möglich nachmachen kann, während er an einem echten Red Bull Air Race teilnimmt. Intelligente Erkennung der Bandbreite und der Streaming-Technologie sorgen für eine optimale Leistung und Darstellung für alle Verbindungsgeschwindigkeiten. **ERGEBNISSE:** Ziel dieser Seite war die Visualisierung des körperlichen Stresses, dem ein Air-Race-Pilot während eines Rennens ausgesetzt ist. Durch die Entwicklung eines einfachen, aber einnehmenden Spiels, das auf Filmmaterial vom Inneren des Cockpits basiert, kommunizierten wir dies erfolgreich einem breiteren Publikum. Innerhalb von nur zwei Wochen wurde das Spiel über 230 000-mal gespielt.

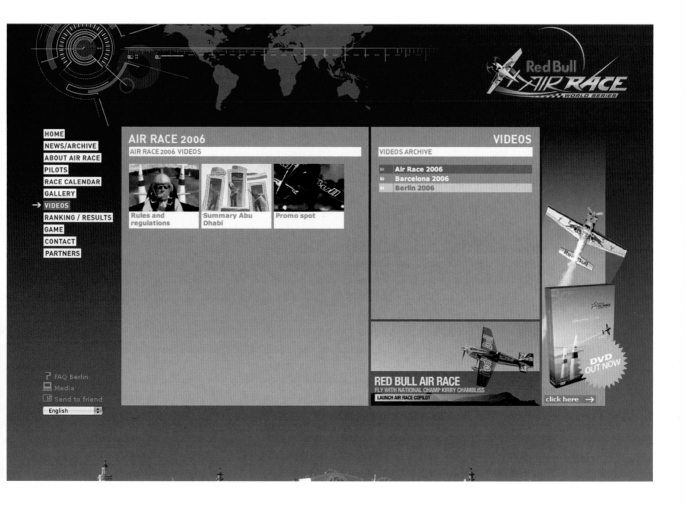

FEATURED ON THE DVD **CAMPAIGN:** Pepsi Pro Contest – Roberto Carlos. **PRODUCT:** Pepsi. **CLIENT:** Pepsi Co. **YEAR:** 2006. **AGENCY:** AlmapBBDO <www.almapbbdo.com.br>. **CREATIVE DIRECTOR:** Marcello Serpa, Sérgio Mugnaini. **ART DIRECTOR:** Sérgio Mugnaini, César Finamori. **COPYWRITER:** Luciana Haguiara, Dulcídio Caldeira. **DESIGNER:** Sérgio Mugnaini. **TECHNICAL DIRECTOR:** Flavio Ramos. **PRODUCER:** Ana Maria Machado. **DIRECTOR:** Tarsem. **ACCOUNT EXECUTIVE:** Ricardo Taunay, Joanna Guinle. **ADVERTISER'S SUPERVISORS:** Gustavo Siemsem; Luciana Fortuna. **FILM PRODUCTION:** Radical Media. **MOTION DESIGNER:** Ricardo de Almeida Martins. **TRACK/VOICE OVER:** Barrera Prod. **PRODUCTION TIME:** 40 days for the hole online campaign. 5 days to shoot the video for the game. 5 months to film Pepsi commercial. **TECH ASPECTS:** Macromedia Flash, 3D Studio Max, sound. **AWARDS:** El Ojo de IberoAmerica 2005 (Gold); MMonline/Msn 2005 (Merit); London Festival 2005 (Shortlist).

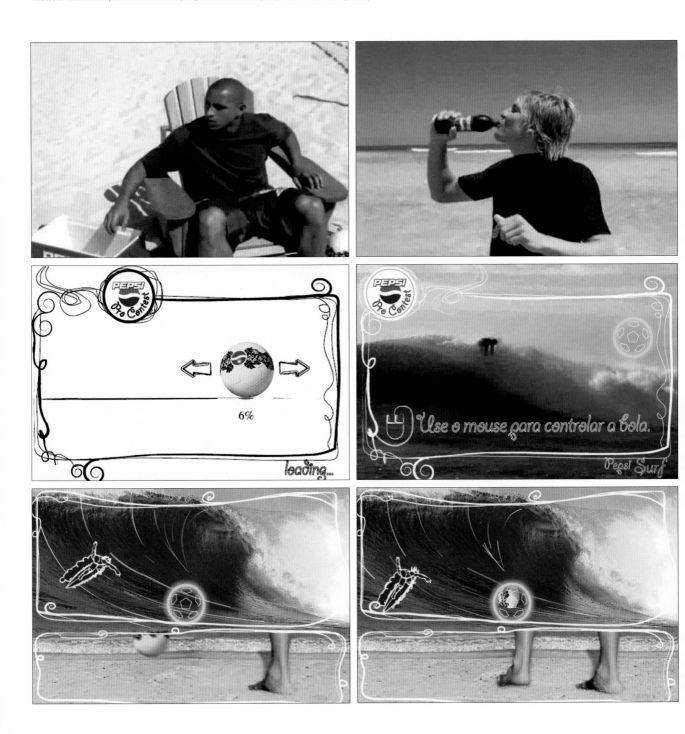

BACKGROUND PROFILE: Pepsi launched a worldwide campaign with the biggest soccer players of the world in uncommon situations. This film had Roberto Carlos as a main actor, with a Pepsi and a surfer without any fear. **CONCEPT:** The challenge was to find an innovative and unusual format that added value to the film on the Internet. **SOLUTION:** A superstition that mixes the film with a game developed for the action: Pepsi Pro-Contest. Before initiating the film, the player Roberto Carlos is seated in front of the sea, almost ready to drink his Pepsi. A surfer passes running and steals the Pepsi can of his hands. Robert Carlos is very upset. The film stops at this point and the users are invited to play. The game is in flash and the player has to kick the ball to knock down the surfer of the wave and to get back the Pepsi. Finished the game, the film continues where Roberto Carlos kicks the ball right in the surfer and the Pepsi can come back through the waves. **RESULTS:** Page-views had been more than 400,000 and 17,112 users had played, remaining about 5,2 minutes in the game.

CONTEXTE : Pepsi a lancé une campagne internationale avec les plus grands joueurs de football du monde placés dans des situations étranges. Dans un film, Roberto Carlos joue le rôle principal, accompagné d'un surfeur qui n'a peur de rien. **CONCEPT :** Trouver un format inhabituel et innovant qui donne de la valeur ajoutée au film sur internet. **SOLUTION :** Un hybride superstitiel de film et de jeu conçu pour le Pepsi Pro-Contest. Au début du film, le joueur Roberto Carlos est assis face à la mer, prêt à boire son Pepsi. Un surfeur passe en courant et lui vole la canette des mains. Roberto Carlos est furieux. Le film s'arrête à ce moment-là et les visiteurs sont invités à jouer. Le jeu est en format Flash et le joueur doit tirer dans le ballon pour faire tomber le surfeur de la vague et récupérer la canette. Le jeu terminé, le film reprend, Roberto Carlos envoie le ballon sur le surfeur et une vague lui rapporte la canette de Pepsi. **RÉSULTATS :** On a enregistré 400 000 visiteurs et 17 112 joueurs ont participé, restant environ 5,2 minutes en ligne.

HINTERGRUND: Pepsi startete eine weltweite Kampagne mit dem größten Fußballstar der Welt in ungewöhnlichen Situationen. Roberto Carlos spielt im Film eine Hauptrolle, zusammen mit einer Pepsi und einem furchtlosen Surfer. **KONZEPT:** Die Herausforderung bestand darin, ein innovatives und ungewöhnliches Format zu finden, das den Film im Internet noch interessanter machte. **LÖSUNG:** Ein Superstitial, das den Film mit einem Spiel kombinierte: Pepsi Pro-Contest. Bevor der Film beginnt, sitzt der Spieler Roberto Carlos am Meer, um seine Pepsi zu trinken. Ein Surfer rennt vorbei und reißt ihm die Dose aus den Händen. Roberto Carlos ist sehr ärgerlich. An diesem Punkt endet der Film, und der Benutzer wird zum Spiel eingeladen. Es ist ein Flash-Spiel, bei dem der Spieler den Ball treten muss, um den Surfer von der Welle zu werfen und die Pepsi wiederzubekommen. Am Ende des Spiels fährt der Film fort: Roberto Carlos kickt den Ball direkt auf den Surfer, und die Pepsi schwimmt durch die Wellen zurück. **ERGEBNISSE:** Die Seite wurde über 400 000-mal angesehen, und 17 112 Personen spielten für jeweils ca. 5,2 Minuten das Spiel.

FEATURED ON THE DVD **CAMPAIGN:** Ted Ferguson <www.tedferguson.com>. **PRODUCT:** Bud Light. **YEAR:** 2006. **AGENCY:** DDB Chicago <www.tribalddb.com>. **PRODUCER:** Domani Studios <www.domanistudios.com>. **PRODUCTION TIME:** 2 weeks. **CREATIVE TEAM:** Domani Studios. **PROGRAMMER:** Domani Studios. **TECH ASPECTS:** Macromedia Flash AS 2.0, Audio, XML. **MEDIA CIRCULATED:** Offline broadcast spots.

CONCEPT: Create a vibrant interactive micro site that supports Bud Light's Ted Ferguson broadcast commercials. The Ted character had a surprising online following on blogs and message boards, but their was no definitive place to access more information about Ted's life, stunts, and live appearances. Tedferguson.com features daily updates, video podcasts, and viral video clips each working together to spread Ted's love. **RESULTS:** This Micro-Site has been a solid extension of the offline spots. Allowing users to download and share video clips, as well as subscribe to a Ted Ferguson podcast has helped ensure that a successful broadcast campaign can be a extended online.

CONCEPT : Créer un site interactif dynamique pour soutenir la campagne télévisée de Ted Ferguson sur la Bud Light. Le personnage de Ted connaît un engouement étonnant sur les blogs et les forums, mais il n'existait pas d'endroit où obtenir des infos sur sa vie, ses pitreries et ses apparences publiques. Tedferguson.com offre des mises à jour quotidiennes, des téléchargements vidéo, des clips viraux, tous destinés à accroître la popularité de Ted.

RÉSULTATS : Le micro-site est devenu une extension importante des spots hors ligne. La réussite d'une campagne télévisée peut être étendue au domaine d'internet, comme l'a démontré le succès des offres de téléchargement et d'échange de clips vidéo, y compris par podcast.

KONZEPT: Eine dynamische, interaktive Microsite erstellen, die die gesendeten Ted-Ferguson-Spots von Bud Lights unterstützt. Ted war in Blogs und Foren zwar sehr präsent, aber es gab keinen bestimmten Ort, wo man mehr Informationen über Teds Leben, Stunts und Live-Auftritte erhalten konnte. Tedferguson.com enthält tägliche Aktualisierungen, Video-Podcasts und virale Videoclips, die miteinander wirken, um Teds Liebe zu verbreiten. **ERGEBNISSE:** Diese Microsite war eine solide Erweiterung der Offline-Spots. Benutzer können Videoclips austauschen und herunterladen sowie sich für einen Ted-Ferguson-Podcast registrieren. Dadurch wurde die erfolgreich gesendete Kampagne online erweitert.

FEATURED ON THE DVD **CAMPAIGN:** So Big. So Bold. So Be Ready. <www.miniswirlz.com>. **PRODUCT:** Kellogg's Mini-Swirlz. **YEAR:** 2006. **AGENCY:** Freedom Interactive Design <www.freedominteractivedesign.com>. **PRODUCTION TIME:** 6 weeks. **COST IN HOURS OF WORK:** 320 h. **CREATIVE TEAM:** Freedom Interactive Design. **PROGRAMMER:** Shea Gonyo, Josh Ott. **TECH ASPECTS:** Macromedia Flash. **MEDIA CIRCULATED:** Banner campaign ran on web properties including Nick.com, 4Kids.com, Disney.

CONCEPT: Leverage assets from Leo Burnett's television campaign for Kellogg's Mini-Swirlz. We created a mini-quiz and a game within this fun microsite.

KONZEPT: Unterstützung von Leo Burnetts Fernsehkampagne für Kelloggs Mini-Swirlz. Wir entwickelten ein Mini-Quiz und ein Spiel innerhalb dieser Spaß-Microsite.

CONCEPT : Exploiter les bénéfices de la campagne télévisée de Leo Burnett pour les Mini-Swirlz de Kellogg's. Nous avons crée un mini-quizz et un jeu dans un micro-site rigolo.

CAMPAIGN: YO! Sushi <www.yosushi.co.uk>. PRODUCT: Samurai Scorchers. YEAR: 2006. AGENCY: Large <www.largedesign.com>. PRODUCTION TIME: 4 weeks. COST IN HOURS OF WORK: 160 h. CREATIVE TEAM: Jim Boulton, Rene Christoffer, Tone Lage. PROGRAMMER: Jesper Lycke, Martin Whiteley. TECH ASPECTS: Macromedia Flash, audio. HITS: 45,000 new registered users.

CONCEPT: Deliver a fun Japanese-led online experience, just like the real thing.

CONCEPT : Offrir une expérience en ligne à la japonaise, comme si on y était.

KONZEPT: Eine lustige, japanisch-orientierte und authentische Online-Erfahrung liefern.

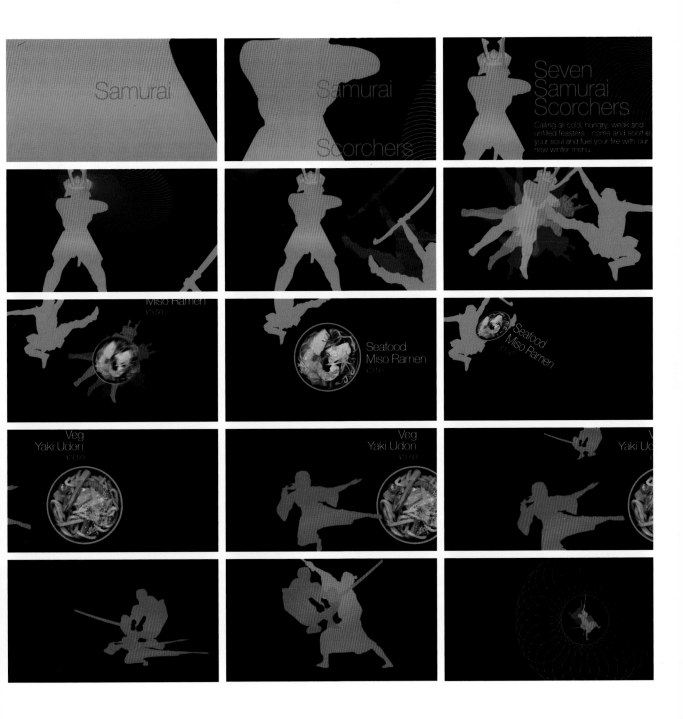

CAMPAIGN: Heineken Green Room Sessions <www.greenroomsessions.se>. **PRODUCT:** Heineken. **YEAR:** 2005. **AGENCY:** Farfar <www.farfar.se>. **PRODUCTION TIME:** 2 months. **CREATIVE TEAM:** Jakob Swedenborg, Jonas Andersson, Per Hansson, Erik Norin, Anders Gustavsson. **PROGRAMMER:** Bo Gustafson.

CONCEPT: The Heineken Green Room Sessions is a series of events where a select audience is treated with free admission to concerts with some of the hottest musical acts all about. The over all advertising concept for The Heineken Green Room Sessions is "rhythm", so we created a site where you gain access to the content simply by making a rhythm.

CONCEPT : Les Green Room Sessions sont une série de manifestations où un public sélectionné est invité gratuitement aux concerts des groupes les plus branchés du moment. Le concept général de la communication des Green Rooms est le rythme, nous avons donc conçu un site sur lequel le contenu est accessible en composant une séquence rythmique.

KONZEPT: Die Heineken Green Room Sessions bestehen aus einer Reihe von Events mit den angesagtesten Bands, die es gerade gibt. Das allgemeine Werbekonzept für die Heineken Green Room Sessions ist „Rhythmus", also wurde eine Seite erstellt, auf die man Zugriff erhielt, indem man einen Rhythmus klopfte.

FEATURED ON THE DVD **CAMPAIGN:** Boy. **CLIENT:** Bauducco Cookies. **PRODUCT:** Mini-Cake "Gulosos" Bauducco. **YEAR:** 2005. **AGENCY:** AlmapBBDO <www.almapbbdo.com.br>. **CREATIVE DIRECTOR:** Sergio Mugnaini. **ART DIRECTOR:** Caetano Carvalho. **COPYWRITER/DIRECTOR:** Luciana Haguiara. **DESIGNER:** Carmelo Di Lorenzo, Ricardo Almeida. **TECHNICAL DIRECTOR:** Flavio Ramos. **PRODUCER:** Ana Maria Machado. **ACCOUNT EXECUTIVE:** Martha Almeida, Joanna Guinle. **ADVERTISER'S SUPERVISOR:** Carlo Andrea. **PRODUCTION TIME:** 30 days. **TECH ASPECTS:** Macromedia Flash, video, sound. **AWARDS:** Cannes Lions 2005 (Shortlist), El Ojo de IberoAmerica 2005 (Bronze), MMonline/MSN 2005 (Merit), London Festival 2005 (Shortlist).

BACKGROUND: Bauducco, a remarkable brand in Brazil for its traditional "panettone", also has a special cookie line for the kids: Gulosos Bauducco. "Gulosos" means greedy. **THE IDEA:** A campaign the shows to the parents and also to the kids how amusing and nutritional can be eating Mini-cakes Gulosos Bauducco. **SOLUTION:** A video superstitial. A little boy is completely bored while eating his breakfast. Without any note, when the user rollover the movie, the cursor turns as a little hand that holds a Bauducco mini-cake. The little boy turns as monster, jumps on the cake and ate it. **VOICE OVER:** "Mini-cake Gulosos Bauducco. The healthy and delicious way to star your miniogre's day."

CONTEXTE : Bauducco, une marque de brioches célèbre au Brésil, produit aussi une ligne de biscuits pour enfants : Gulosos Bauducco. « Gulosos » signifie gourmand. **OBJECTIF :** Montrer aux parents et aux enfants qu'il est amusant et bon pour la santé de manger des mini-biscuits Gulosos Bauducco. **SOLUTION :** Une vidéo en format superstitiel. On voit un enfant qui s'ennuie devant son petit-déjeuner. Sans aucune indication, quand on fait défiler les images, le curseur prend la forme d'une petite main qui tient un biscuit Bauducco. Le petit garçon se transforme alors en monstre qui se jette sur le biscuit et le dévore. **EN VOIX OFF :** « Les biscuits Gulosos Bauducco. La façon saine et délicieuse de démarrer ta journée de petit ogre ».

HINTERGRUND: Bauducco ist in Brasilien eine starke Marke für die traditionelle „Panettone" und stellt außerdem eine spezielle Keksmarke für Kinder her: Gulosos Bauducco. „Gulosos" bedeutet „gierig". **DIE IDEE:** Eine Kampagne, die Eltern und Kindern vor Augen führt, wie viel Spaß es macht, die kleinen Kuchen zu essen, und wie nährstoffreich Gulosos Bauducco sind. **LÖSUNG:** Ein Video-Superstitial. Ein kleiner Junge langweilt sich beim Frühstück. Ohne irgendeinen Hinweis verwandelt sich der Mauszeiger, wenn man ihn über den Film bewegt, in eine kleine Hand, die ein Bauducco hält. Der kleine Junge verwandelt sich in ein Monster, springt auf den Keks und isst ihn. **HINTERGRUNDSTIMME:** „Gulosos Bauducco. Der gesunde und leckere Start in den Tag."

CAMPAIGN: Dado Spitze. **PRODUCT:** Bavaria Premium Beer. **YEAR:** 2006. **AGENCY:** Euro RSCG 4D São Paulo <www.eurorscg4d.com.br>. **CHIEF CREATIVE OFFICER:** Alon Sochaczewski. **CREATIVE DIRECTOR:** Touché. **COPYWRITER:** Fábio Pierro, André Arteze. **ART DIRECTOR:** Touché, Valter Klug. **DESIGNER:** Ricardo Cazzo, Rodrigo Zannin, Danielle Roveri. **PROGRAMMER:** Pedro Son, Fábio Augusto Soares. **TECH ASPECTS:** Macromedia Flash, MSN Messenger.

CONCEPT: Artificial intelligence for a Beer seems a crazy idea, but this is what the campaign proposes. A live chat with a fictitious member of the brewery.

CONCEPT : Utiliser l'intelligence artificielle pour promouvoir de la bière semble une idée un peu folle, mais c'est ce que la campagne propose. Un chat en direct avec un membre imaginaire de la brasserie.

KONZEPT: Künstliche Intelligenz klingt im Zusammenhang mit Bier nach einer verrückten Idee, aber dies ist es, was die Kampagne vorschlägt: ein Live Chat mit einem fiktiven Mitarbeiter der Brauerei.

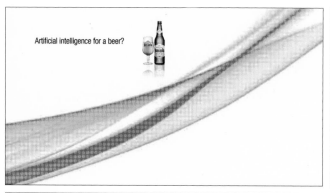

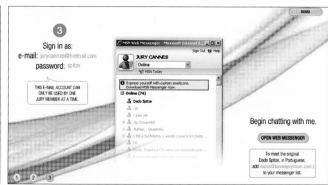

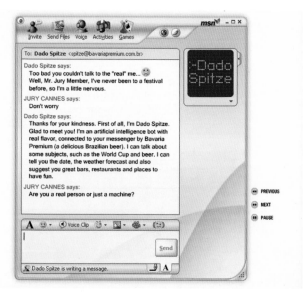

FEATURED ON THE DVD **CAMPAIGN:** Message in a Bottle <www.messageintospace.com>. **PRODUCT:** Zywiec Beer. **YEAR:** 2005. **AGENCY:** Max Weber <www.maxweber.com>. **CREATIVE TEAM:** Marcin Talarek, Krzysztof Dykas, Grzegorz Mogilewski, Andrzej Kryszpiniuk, Bartek Witulski, Mieszko Saktura. **PROGRAMMER:** Marek Brun, Piotr Tracki. **TECH ASPECTS:** Macromedia Flash. **AWARDS:** Eurobest 2005 (Bronze), Epica 2005 (Shortlist).

CONCEPT: The client asked us to come up with something inspiring that will attract new users by use word-of-mouth only. We developed the idea giving people ability to preserve a fragment of their thoughts, emotions and ideas for future generations. Users can write text messages on Zywiec website. Then gathered messages will be converted in to radio waves and broadcast in to space where they will last forever and will be able to be discovered by future generations. Messages were sent on 2/22/2006 from NCSFCT/Evpatoria Telescope located in Crimea, Ukraine.

CONCEPT : Le client nous a chargés de trouver une idée originale pour attirer de nouveaux visiteurs uniquement par le bouche à oreille. Nous avons proposé aux gens de conserver un fragment de leurs pensées, idées ou sentiments pour les générations futures. L'internaute peut écrire des messages sur le site internet de Zywiec. Les messages collectés sont convertis en ondes radio et diffusés dans l'espace où elles demeureront à jamais et pourront être découvertes par les générations futures. Les messages furent envoyés le 22/02/2006 du télescope NCSFCT/Eupatoria situé en Crimée.

KONZEPT: Der Kunde wollte etwas Inspirierendes von uns, das ausschließlich durch Mundpropaganda neue Benutzer anziehen würde. Wir entwickelten die Idee, es den Leuten zu ermöglichen, ein Fragment ihrer Gedanken, Gefühle und Ideen für zukünftige Generationen zu erhalten. Sie können auf der Zywiec-Webseite Textbotschaften schreiben. Die gesammelten Botschaften werden dann in Radiowellen konvertiert und ins All gesendet, wo sie für immer existieren und von zukünftigen Generationen entdeckt werden können. Am 22. Februar 2006 wurden die Botschaften vom NCSFCT/Evpatoria-Teleskop in Crimea, Ukraine, gesendet.

FEATURED ON THE DVD **CAMPAIGN:** Draw Your Own Tube! **PRODUCT:** Kalles Caviar. **CLIENT:** Abba Seafood. **YEAR:** 2006. **AGENCY:** Forsman & Bodenfors <www.fb.se>. **PRODUCTION TIME:** 1 month. **WEB DIRECTOR:** Martin Cedergren. **ART DIRECTOR:** Joakim Blondell. **COPYWRITER:** Martin Ringqvist, Jacob Nelson. **ACCOUNT EXECUTIVE:** Greger Andersson. **ACCOUNT MANAGER:** Jenny Edvardsson. **PRODUCER:** Martin Sandberg. **PROGRAMMER:** B-Reel. **PRODUCER:** B-Reel. **TECH ASPECTS:** Macromedia Flash. **MEDIA CIRCULATED:** Online ads, TVC. **AWARDS:** Favorite Website Award 2006.

CONCEPT: The famous Swedish caviar, Kalles, invites you to design your own tube and win a boxful of your very own real tube creations.

CONCEPT : Kalles, célèbre marque suédoise de pâte de caviar en tube, vous invite à dessiner votre propre tube et gagner une boîte remplie des tubes de votre création.

JOHAN TESCH
CREATIVE DIRECTOR OF LOWE TESCH

Johan Tesch started Tesch & Tesch in 1996, focusing soon on digital advertising. As the business rapidly prospered, he merged with Lowe Advertising group to form Lowe Tesch in 2002. Johan Tesch is personally leading the creative forces of LoweTesch in their search of the advertising of tomorrow. He has won several awards in the last years including Gold in Cannes the last two years. He has served in several international and national advertising juries and chief editor of the webmagazine *Meinhof*.

Twelve years ago a Swedish advertising magazine asked a couple of students to comment on the future of advertising. I happened to be one of them. My theory was that in the future people would be able to choose whether they would like to watch advertising or not. And one day some people would have had enough of the so-called commercialization of their public space.

Take your local community for example. In theory there's nothing stopping you from removing the advertising surrounding you. Since your community actually receives money from renting out space for bill-

boards in the streets, subways etc, the community has the choice to say no to the money and clear their environment of advertising messages. So in some places a majority would vote for an advertising-free community and, if needed, they would raise the taxes to cover the loss of money. It probably wouldn't be that much per head. If the choice was presented to the citizens I thought that many would follow this path. This would then spread to other communities in the country and eventually all over the world.

PEOPLE WOULD REALIZE THAT THEY ACTUALLY HAVE A CHOICE, AND THIS IN TURN WOULD LEAD TO THE DEATH OF ADVERTISING. AT LEAST AS WE KNOW IT TODAY. I WAS PROBABLY JUST LOOKING FOR SOMETHING CLEVER TO SAY, BUT MAYBE THERE WAS SOMETHING TO IT.

It seems like we are beginning to see a new era of consumer choice in advertising.

The hidden consumer

When people find new ways of consuming media where the advertisers can't follow, our industry has a problem. Digital TV, TIVOs, downloading of TV series, renting video online, and the search-for-information use of Internet are examples of new habits in media consumption which puts the advertisers in a tricky situation. They cannot reach people only by buying media anymore. So when people are hiding, how can they get the consumer's attention?

The new creative director

Since the advertising can't find the people anymore, I guess the people will have to find the commercials themselves. And if they have spend some time and effort to find these ads, they'd better be damned good. The campaign that succeeds in attracting people by their own free will is the new advertising. Those that don't will be rejected. This means that we have a power shift in the industry. Suddenly the consumer is in charge.

THE ADVERTISING INDUSTRY HAS TRIED TO COMMUNICATE WITH SOMEONE LYING IN A COUCH HALF ASLEEP FOR A LONG TIME NOW. FINALLY THIS MAN HAS WOKEN UP.

He's now in front of his computer, actually deciding what advertising he wants to see. It is on his terms now. He is calling the shots. He is the new Creative Director. So, how do you please this guy?

How to get your idea approved

The secret to many of the smash hits lately is to succeed in entertaining people with something new and clever, and at the same time say something profound about the core of the product. Only then will people stop what they are doing and lower their guard and be willing to sacrifice a couple of minutes of their time to interact with your brand. But then you must be able to dance. And dare to do so.

Take one of last year's winners in Cannes –The

THE DEATH OF ADVERTISING AS WE KNOW IT

Locktite Superglue. It manages to entertain people in a new and clever way (write stuff on a computer glued to the wall for the whole world to see) as well say a core message about the product (super strong glue). An extra feature was the live element – it could fall down anytime, maybe when you were watching. They managed to reach people who don't give a damn about glue, but guess what they will be buying next time.

THE NEW CREATIVE DIRECTOR WILL OF COURSE APPROVE THE TV COMMERCIALS AS WELL. THE SAME RULES APPLY HERE. IN THE SONY BRAVIA CASE, THEY MANAGED TO ENTERTAIN PEOPLE WITH THIS SIMPLE, BUT WONDERFUL IDEA.

It said something about the product (colour) and had an excellent wow-element in the "Did they really drop all those balls?" reaction.
When it finally aired in Sweden, everybody had already seen it and been blown away by the ad on the Internet. So when you saw it on TV, it felt more like a celebration of the magnificent ad you had already seen on the web.

The end of Riesen

The good news is that it will bring an end to commercials that don't please the new CD. One example is the mighty Riesen Family. Personally I have nothing against the product. I think that I might like it. It's just impossible to buy the product when you think of the happy Riesen family. Although I don't think violent thoughts very often, this gives me a sudden urge to destroy things. They look happy and all, but you still get the feeling that they have their neighbours in the freezer. So, power to the people.

The creative challenge

The bad news is that people are not easy to please. The new creative challenge is to make people interested, to make them give up a few minutes of their time to listen to our message – often when they are working or looking for something on the web, in a totally different mindset.

IT'S OUR JOB TO TAP THEM ON THEIR SHOULDER AND MAKE THEM INTERESTED IN SOMETHING ELSE. MOST OF US WOULD PREFER TO DO THIS IN A SMART AND CLEVER WAY. SOME OF US CHOOSE THE EASY WAY.

The future of Internet advertising could be darkened by drunk teenagers, dancing midgets and chimpanzees on skateboards. Which, of course, could make a great commercial, but not necessarily so. Well, I guess it's up to the audience to sort that out now. Their taste will dictate tomorrow's advertising. When another 12 years has passed we'll probably know the score. Maybe I'll write another article reflecting on some stuff I wrote a long time ago for an advertising publication just trying to be clever. See you then.

Johan Tesch fonde Tesch & Tesch en 1996, et se consacre vite à la publicité sur Internet. Après une croissance rapide, il s'associe au groupe Lowe Advertising et donne naissance à Lowe Tesch en 2002. Johan Tesch dirige les forces créatives de l'agence dans leur quête de la publicité de demain. Il a remporté récemment plusieurs récompenses dont le Lion d'Or à Cannes les deux années passées. Il a été membre de plusieurs jurys nationaux et internationaux et a été rédacteur en chef du magazine en ligne *Meinhof*.

Il y a douze ans, un magazine spécialisé suédois a interrogé quelques étudiants sur l'avenir de la publicité. Il se trouve que j'étais l'un d'eux. J'ai émis alors l'opinion qu'à l'avenir, les gens seraient en mesure de choisir de regarder ou non la publicité. Et qu'un beau jour, ils en auraient assez de la commercialisation de leur espace public.
Prenons par exemple votre municipalité. En théorie, rien ne vous empêche de faire disparaître la publicité environnante. Puisque la municipalité reçoit de l'argent pour louer les espaces publicitaires dans les rues, les stations de métro et autres, elle peut faire le choix de renoncer à l'argent et de débarrasser l'environnement des messages publicitaires. Ainsi une majorité d'administrés pourrait voter en faveur d'un espace public sans publicité, et si besoin est, augmenter les impôts pour compenser la perte des recettes. Sans que cela coûte très cher à chacun pour autant. Si l'on proposait cette option aux citoyens, je pense qu'ils seraient nombreux à l'adopter. L'exemple pourrait alors être suivi par d'autres municipalités du pays, voire par le monde entier.

WHEN PEOPLE FIND NEW WAYS OF CONSUMING MEDIA WHERE THE ADVERTISERS CAN'T FOLLOW, OUR INDUSTRY HAS A PROBLEM.

LES GENS SE RENDRAIENT COMPTE QU'ILS ONT EFFECTIVEMENT LE CHOIX, ET CELA ENTRAÎNERAIT FINALEMENT LA MORT DE LA PUBLICITÉ. DU MOINS SOUS SA FORME ACTUELLE. JE CHERCHAIS SANS DOUTE À ME RENDRE INTÉRESSANT À L'ÉPOQUE DE CETTE DÉCLARATION, MAIS CEPENDANT IL Y AVAIT DE L'IDÉE.

Car il semble que nous soyons à l'aube d'une ère où le consommateur dictera ses choix en matière de publicité.

Le consommateur caché

Quand les annonceurs ne peuvent pas suivre les nouveaux modes d'utilisation des médias par le public, l'industrie a du souci à se faire. La télévision numérique, le boîtier TiVo, le téléchargement de séries télé, la location de vidéo en ligne, et l'utilisation d'Internet à des fins de recherches sont des exemples de nouvelles habitudes de consommation des médias qui mettent les annonceurs dans une situation délicate. Ils ne peuvent plus atteindre leur cible en se contentant d'acheter de l'espace. Comment attirer l'attention du consommateur, lorsque celui-ci est caché ?

Le nouveau directeur de création

Puisque la publicité ne peut plus trouver les gens, j'imagine que ceux-ci devront dénicher eux-mêmes les publicités. Et si cela leur réclame du temps et des efforts, les pubs ont intérêt à être bonnes ! La nouvelle publicité est celle qui réussira à séduire les gens de leur plein gré. La campagne qui échouera sera rejetée. Nous assistons ainsi à un changement de pouvoir au sein de notre industrie. Le consommateur a soudain pris la main.

L'INDUSTRIE PUBLICITAIRE A TENTÉ DE COMMUNIQUER AVEC

UN HOMME ASSOUPI DANS UN CANAPÉ DEPUIS DÉJÀ UN CERTAIN TEMPS. MAIS IL S'EST RÉVEILLÉ.

Il est aujourd'hui devant son ordinateur, et il décide quelle publicité il veut regarder. C'est lui qui dicte ses conditions, qui impose sa règle du jeu. C'est lui le nouveau directeur de création. Alors comment faire pour lui plaire ?

Faire accepter ses idées

Les nombreuses publicités qui ont connu un succès retentissant dernièrement sont celles qui ont réussi à distraire le public de façon intelligente et inédite, tout en transmettant un message profond sur la nature du produit. Ce n'est qu'à cette condition que le consommateur baisse sa garde et accepte de sacrifier quelques minutes de son temps pour interagir avec une marque. Il faut alors savoir saisir la balle au bond. Et oser.
Prenons l'un des lauréats à Cannes l'an passé, la Superglue Locktite. Il réussit à distraire de manière originale (quelqu'un écrit sur un écran collé au mur à la vue de tous), tout en communiquant un message sur le produit (une colle extra-forte). Un élément supplémentaire était l'enregistrement en direct, l'ordinateur pouvait tomber, juste au moment où vous regardiez. Le spot a réussi à séduire les gens qui se fichent de la colle forte, mais ils ne manqueront pas de l'acheter s'ils en ont besoin un jour.

LE NOUVEAU DIRECTEUR DE CRÉATION DOIT ÉGALEMENT APPROUVER LES SPOTS TÉLÉVISÉS. LA MÊME RÈGLE S'APPLIQUE ALORS. DANS LE CAS DE SONY BRAVIA, LE PUBLIC A ÉTÉ SÉDUIT PAR UNE IDÉE SIMPLE MAIS INGÉNIEUSE.

Elle communiquait sur le produit (un téléviseur couleur) tout en provoquant une réaction de surprise. « Ils ont vraiment jeté toutes ces balles ? » Quand le spot a été diffusé en Suède, tout le monde l'avait déjà admiré sur Internet. Le voir à la télévision était comme une consécration de la magnifique vidéo visionnée sur le site.

La fin de Riesen

La bonne nouvelle, c'est que ce changement va entraîner la disparition des publicités qui déplaisent au nouveau directeur de création. Comme la famille Riesen, par exemple. Personnellement, je n'ai rien contre le produit. Je pourrais même l'aimer. Seulement il m'est impossible d'acheter le produit en pensant à la gentille famille Riesen. Bien que je ne sois pas de nature impulsive, cette pub me donne envie de tout casser. Les Riesen ont l'air heureux et tout, mais on a le sentiment qu'ils ont enfermé les voisins dans le congélateur. Le peuple au pouvoir, donc.

Le défi créatif

La mauvaise nouvelle, c'est que le public est difficile à satisfaire. Le nouveau défi créatif consiste à intéresser les gens, les encourager à consacrer quelques minutes de leur temps à écouter votre message, quand ils sont en train de travailler ou de chercher une info sur Internet, dans un tout autre état d'esprit.

NOUS DEVONS LEUR DONNER UNE TAPE SUR L'ÉPAULE ET LES ATTIRER VERS AUTRE CHOSE. LA PLUPART D'ENTRE NOUS PRÉFÉRERAIENT LE FAIRE DE MANIÈRE SUBTILE, MAIS D'AUTRES CHOISISSENT LA FACILITÉ.

L'avenir de la publicité en ligne pourrait être assombri par des ados ivres, des nains qui dansent et des chimpanzés en skateboards. Cela pourrait faire une bonne pub, mais pas forcément. Je pense que c'est au public de faire le tri. Ses goûts dicteront la pub de demain. Dans une douzaine d'années, nous pourrons sans doute faire un bilan. J'écrirai peut-être alors un autre article pour commenter une déclaration que j'ai faite jadis dans un magazine spécialisé, histoire de me rendre intéressant. Rendez-vous dans douze ans !

Johan Tesch gründete 1996 Tesch & Tesch, das sich auf digitale Werbung konzentrierte. Als das Unternehmen schnell florierte, verschmolz es mit der Lowe Advertising Group, um 2002 Lowe Tesch zu formieren. Johan Tesch führt die kreativen Kräfte von Lowe Tesch auf ihrer Suche nach der Werbung von morgen. Er gewann in den letzten Jahren einige Auszeichnungen, darunter zweimal Gold in Cannes. Er war Mitglied in einigen nationalen und internationalen Werbejurys und Herausgeber des Webmagazins *Meinhof*.

Vor zwölf Jahren fragte ein schwedisches Magazin für Werbung ein paar Studenten nach ihrer Meinung zur Zukunft der Werbung. Einer von ihnen war ich. Nach meiner Theorie würden die Menschen der Zukunft wählen können, ob sie Werbung sehen wollen oder nicht. Und eines Tages würden alle genug von der so genannten Kommerzialisierung ihrer Umgebung haben.

Denken Sie zum Beispiel an Ihren eigenen Wohnort: Theoretisch hält Sie nichts davon ab, die Werbung um Sie herum zu entfernen. Da Ihr Ort tatsächlich Geld dafür erhält, dass er Werbeflächen in den Straßen, U-Bahnen etc. vermietet, besteht theoretisch die Möglichkeit, Nein zum Geld zu sagen und die Umwelt von Werbebotschaften zu befreien. An einigen Orten würde eine Mehrheit für eine werbefreie Gemeinde stimmen und, wenn nötig, die Steuern erhöhen, um den Geldverlust auszugleichen. Es wäre pro Kopf wahrscheinlich nicht viel. Ich glaubte, wenn den Bürgern diese Wahl angeboten werden würde, würden viele dieser Richtung folgen. Dies würde sich in andere Gebiete des Landes und schließlich auf der ganzen Welt ausbreiten.

DEN MENSCHEN WÜRDE KLAR WERDEN, DASS SIE TATSÄCHLICH DIE WAHL HABEN – WAS ZUM

TOD DER WERBUNG FÜHREN WÜRDE. ZUMINDEST DER ART VON WERBUNG, WIE WIR SIE HEUTE KENNEN. ICH WOLLTE WAHRSCHEINLICH NUR ETWAS INTELLIGENTES SAGEN, ABER VIELLEICHT LAG WAHRHEIT DARIN.

Es sieht so aus, als beginne heute tatsächlich eine neue Ära: die der freien Entscheidung des Kunden.

Der versteckte Konsument

Wenn die Menschen neue Wege des Medienkonsums einschlagen, denen die Werbeleute nicht folgen können, hat unsere Branche ein Problem. Digitales Fernsehen, TiVo, Downloaden von TV-Serien, online Videos ausleihen und die Informationssuche im Internet sind Beispiele für die neuen Gewohnheiten im Medienkonsum, die Werber in eine verzwickte Situation bringen. Sie können die Menschen nicht mehr allein durch den Kauf von Werbezeiten erreichen. Wenn sich der Kunde also versteckt, wie gewinnt man seine Aufmerksamkeit?

Der neue Kreativdirektor

Da die Werbung die Menschen nicht mehr findet, werden folglich die Menschen die Werbung selber finden müssen. Und wenn sie dafür einige Zeit aufgewendet haben, sollte die Werbung verdammt gut sein. Eine Kampagne, die freiwillig aufgesucht wird – das ist die neue Werbung. Plötzlich hat der Konsument die Kontrolle.

DIE WERBEBRANCHE VERSUCHT SCHON SEIT LÄNGERER ZEIT, MIT JEMANDEM ZU KOMMUNIZIEREN, DER IM HALBSCHLAF AUF DER COUCH DÖST. NUN IST DIESER JEMAND ENDLICH AUFGEWACHT.

Er sitzt vor seinem Computer und entscheidet selbst, welche Werbung er sehen möchte. Er bestimmt die Regeln. Er ist der neue Kreativdirektor. Wie stellen sie diesen Typen zufrieden?

Wie Ihre Idee gut ankommt

Das Geheimnis vieler der jüngsten Werbeerfolge besteht darin, dass man die Menschen erfolgreich mit etwas Neuem und Cleverem unterhält und gleichzeitig etwas Grundlegendes über den Kern des Produktes aussagt. Nur dann werden die Leute innehalten und ein paar Minuten ihrer Zeit opfern, um mit Ihrer Marke zu interagieren. Aber Sie müssen auch tanzen können. Und es wagen, zu tanzen.

Nehmen Sie einen der letzten Gewinner in Cannes – The Locktite Superglue. Man wird auf eine neue und intelligente Weise unterhalten (schreiben Sie auf einen Computer, der an der Wand klebt und von der ganzen Welt gesehen werden kann), und gleichzeitig wird die Kernaussage des Produktes (extrem starker Kleber) vermittelt. Ein zusätzliches Feature war das Live-Element – der Computer konnte jeden Augenblick zu Boden fallen, vielleicht, während Sie zusahen. Es wurden Menschen erreicht, die sich keine Spur für Klebstoff interessieren, aber raten Sie, welchen Kleber sie nächstes Mal kaufen werden.

DER NEUE KREATIVDIREKTOR WIRD NATÜRLICH AUCH DIE TV-SPOTS ANNEHMEN. HIER GELTEN DIESELBEN REGELN. IM FALL VON SONY BRAVIA GELANG ES, DIE LEUTE MIT EINER EINFACHEN, ABER WUNDERVOLLEN IDEE ZU UNTERHALTEN.

Der Spot sagte etwas über das Produkt aus (Farbe) und hatte einen großartigen Wow-Effekt durch die „Ließen sie wirklich alle Bälle fallen?"-Reaktion. Als der Spot schließlich in Schweden gesendet wurde, hatte ihn jeder schon im Internet gesehen und sich begeistern lassen. Als man ihn dann im Fernsehen sah, fühlte es sich eher wie eine Feier des Großartigen an, das man aus dem Netz kannte.

Das Ende von Riesen

Die gute Nachricht ist, dass jene Spots ein Ende haben werden, die dem neuen Konsumenten nicht

WENN DIE MENSCHEN NEUE WEGE DES MEDIENKONSUMS EINSCHLAGEN, DENEN DIE WERBELEUTE NICHT FOLGEN KÖNNEN, HAT UNSERE BRANCHE EIN PROBLEM.

gefallen. Ein Beispiel hierfür ist die große Familie Riesen. Ich persönlich habe nichts gegen das Produkt. Ich glaube, es würde mir schmecken. Aber es ist einfach unmöglich, das Produkt zu kaufen, wenn man an die glückliche Riesen-Familie denkt. Auch wenn ich sonst nicht oft gewalttätige Gedanken hege, löst sie den plötzlichen Impuls in mir aus, etwas zerstören zu wollen. Sie sehen glücklich aus, aber man wird den Gedanken nicht los, dass sie die Leichen ihrer Nachbarn in der Gefriertruhe aufbewahren. Also: Die Macht den Menschen!

Die kreative Herausforderung

Die schlechte Nachricht ist, dass die Leute nicht einfach zufrieden zu stellen sind. Die neue kreative Herausforderung besteht darin, ihr Interesse zu wecken, sie dazu zu bringen, einige Minuten ihrer Zeit zu opfern, um unsere Botschaft zu hören – meist, während sie arbeiten oder im Netz surfen, mit etwas ganz anderem im Hinterkopf.

ES IST UNSERE AUFGABE, IHNEN AUF DIE SCHULTER ZU KLOPFEN UND IHRE AUFMERKSAMKEIT AUF ETWAS ANDERES ZU LENKEN. DIE MEISTEN VON UNS BEVORZUGEN ES, DIES AUF EINE KLUGE UND CLEVERE ART ZU TUN. EINIGE VON UNS WÄHLEN DEN EINFACHEN WEG.

Die Zukunft der Internetwerbung könnte von betrunkenen Teenagern, tanzenden Zwergen und Schimpansen auf Skateboards überschattet werden. Was natürlich einen tollen Spot ergeben könnte; aber nicht unbedingt. Nun, ich denke, es liegt am Publikum, das zu entscheiden. Sein Geschmack wird die Werbung von morgen diktieren. In 12 Jahren werden wir vielleicht wissen, wie es geht. Vielleicht werde ich dann einen weiteren Artikel schreiben, in dem ich über Dinge reflektiere, die ich vor langer Zeit für eine Veröffentlichung geschrieben habe, um clever zu erscheinen. Bis dann.

THE FUTURE OF INTERNET ADVERTISING COULD BE DARKENED BY DRUNK TEENAGERS, DANCING MIDGETS AND CHIMPANZEES ON SKATEBOARDS. WHICH, OF COURSE, COULD MAKE A GREAT COMMERCIAL, BUT NOT NECESSARILY SO.

L'AVENIR DE LA PUBLICITÉ EN LIGNE POURRAIT ÊTRE ASSOMBRI PAR DES ADOS IVRES, DES NAINS QUI DANSENT ET DES CHIMPANZÉS EN SKATEBOARDS. CELA POURRAIT FAIRE UNE BONNE PUB, MAIS PAS FORCÉMENT.

DIE ZUKUNFT DER INTERNETWERBUNG KÖNNTE VON BETRUNKENEN TEENAGERN, TANZENDEN ZWERGEN UND SCHIMPANSEN AUF SKATEBOARDS ÜBERSCHATTET WERDEN. WAS NATÜRLICH EINEN TOLLEN SPOT ERGEBEN KÖNNTE; ABER NICHT UNBEDINGT.

002

MEDIA

FEATURED ON THE DVD **CAMPAIGN:** Commando VIP <www.commando-vip.com>. **CLIENT:** Five. **AGENCY:** 20:20 London <www.2020london.co.uk>. **PRODUCTION TIME:** 1 month. **CREATIVE TEAM:** Peter Riley (Creative Partner), Hugo Bierschenk (Creative), Dean Woodhouse (Creative). **PROGRAMMER:** Simon James. **TECH ASPECTS:** Sound, Adobe After Effects, Macromedia Flash, Wavelab. **MEDIA CIRCULATED:** Email.

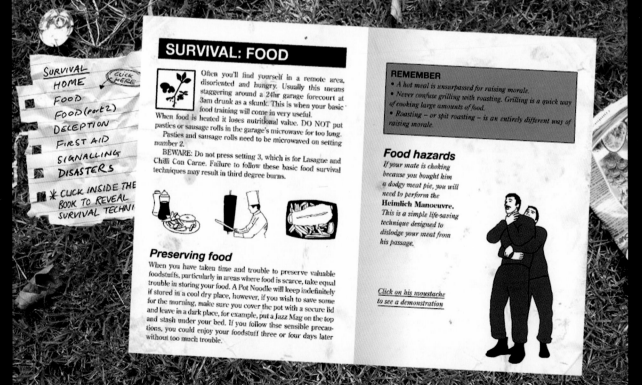

CONCEPT: Launch this hard-man reality TV series to young men. We were asked to investigate the use of mobile communications to create a 'mobile viral' effect. **INSIGHTS:** On first viewing, the show looks as though it is about a bunch of celebrities training as Commandos. However, the true appeal of the show lies in the fact that the celebs THINK they are coming across as macho, capable heroes. The reality is that the editing and voice-over is hilariously setting them up for a spectacular fall. They think they're hard as nails. We see them as bungling VIPs. **SOLUTION:** Be a pro: learn the rules of the urban jungle. A website that looked like an SAS training manual. It was in fact an urban survival guide and featured essential tips on How To Catch A Cheating Girlfriend; How to Blag Your Way Into A Nightclub and How To Give Mouth-To-Mouth To A Young Lady (also known as 'Speed Dating'). Additionally, a series of mobile animations showed survival techniques being demonstrated by our hapless Commando VIPs – all with predictably disastrous results.

CONCEPT : Lancer la série de télé-réalité auprès d'un public jeune et masculin. Une enquête préalable des usages en terme de téléphonie mobile devait contribuer à l'élaboration d'un effet viral. **IDÉE :** À la première vision, l'émission présente un groupe de célébrités qui suit un entraînement commando. Cependant, le véritable intérêt est que les célébrités se prennent pour des héros et des machos, alors que le montage et le commentaire en voix off les placent en position d'échec. Ils se voient comme des durs à cuire, et nous les voyons comme des VIP empotés. **SOLUTION :** Soyez un pro : apprenez les règles de la jungle urbaine. Le site est construit comme un manuel d'instruction du GIGN. Il s'agit en fait d'un guide de survie dans la ville, qui présente des conseils pour démasquer une copine infidèle, entrer gratuitement en boîte de nuit, ou faire du bouche-à-bouche à une demoiselle (autrement appelé *speed dating*). En outre, une série d'animations pour mobiles montrent l'infortuné commando faire la démonstration de quelques techniques de survie, qui s'avèrent toutes désastreuses.

KONZEPT: Launch einer Reality-Fernsehserie für junge Männer. Wir sollten die Verwendung von Handy-Kommunikation untersuchen, um einen „mobilen viralen" Effekt zu erzielen. **EINSICHTEN:** Beim ersten Ansehen wirkt die Show, als handele sie von einer Gruppe Prominenter, die trainieren, um Kommandotruppen zu werden. Die wahre Anziehungskraft der Show entsteht jedoch dadurch, dass die Promis GLAUBEN, dass sie als Machos, als tolle Helden rüberkommen. In Wirklichkeit jedoch werden sie durch Bearbeitung und Hintergrundstimme entlarvt. Sie glauben, sie seien hart wie Stahl; wir sehen sie als vor sich hin stümpernde VIPs. **LÖSUNG:** Sei ein Profi: Lerne die Regeln des urbanen Dschungels. Eine Webseite, die wie eine SAS-Trainingsanleitung aussieht. Tatsächlich war es ein Überlebensführer für die Stadt mit Tipps zu „Wie entlarvt man eine untreue Freundin", „Wie kommt man in einen Nachtclub" und „Wie man in möglichst kurzer Zeit möglichst viele Frauen kennen lernt" (auch als „Speed Dating" bekannt). Zusätzlich zeigte eine Reihe von Handy-Animationen von unseren unglückseligen Kommandotruppen-VIPs demonstrierte Überlebenstechniken – mit vorhersehbar desaströsen Ergebnissen.

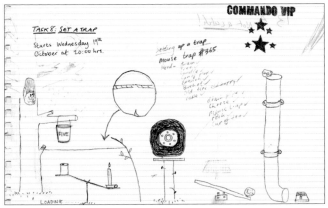

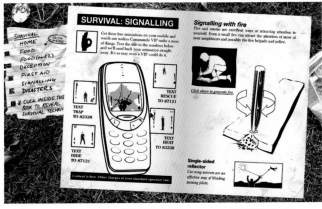

FEATURED ON THE DVD **CAMPAIGN:** Carbon Copy Killer. **CLIENT:** Five – CSI:New York. **AGENCY:** 20:20 London <www.2020london.co.uk>. **PRODUCTION TIME:** 3 months. **CREATIVE TEAM:** Peter Riley (Creative Partner), Hugo Bierschenk (Creative), Dean Woodhouse (Creative). **PROGRAMMER:** Simon James. **TECH ASPECTS:** film, sound, Adobe After Effects, Cepstral, Macromedia Flash, Wavelab, PHP/SQL, 3D Studio, Maya, Shake, Adobe Premiere, Apple Quicktime Pro. **MEDIA CIRCULATED:** Email. **AWARDS:** Direct Marketing Association (UK), Campaign Digital Awards (UK), John Caples International Advertising Awards (New York), Cannes International Advertising Awards.

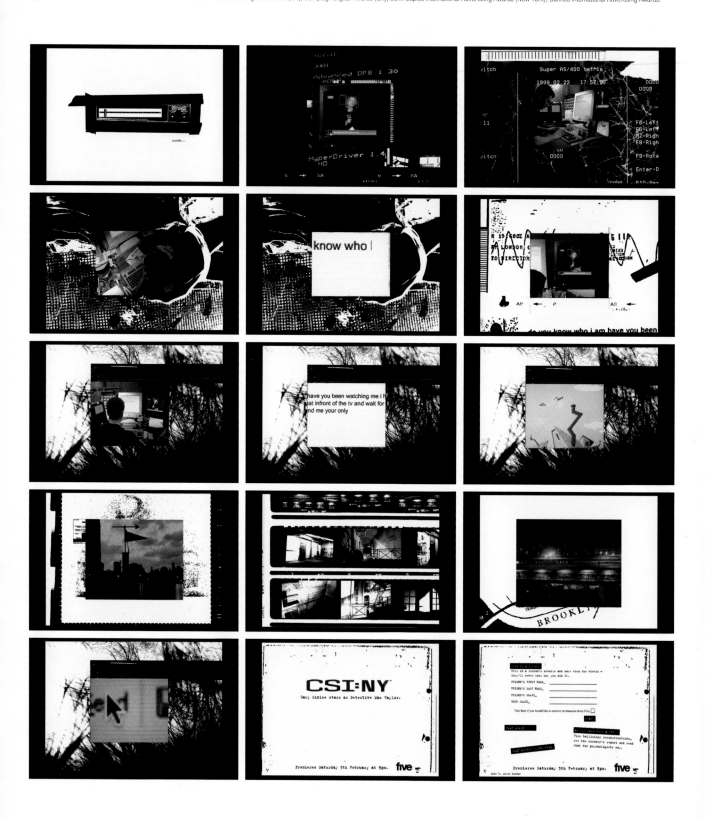

THE BRIEF: We were asked to launch the 3rd Show in the franchise CSI:NY in Britain for channel Five by combining e-mail, Internet film and direct mail as never before. In fact – something you've never seen or heard before... **THE IDEA:** Create a killer campaign showing a made-up serial killer. A viral and direct mail campaign (shot on location in Brooklyn) showed the fictitious "Carbon Copy Killer" confessing his crimes. But the killer has a sick twist: he only murders people with the same name. AND IT'S YOUR NAME! And your name appears in TV and press news bulletins in the film. And the killer speaks your name. HE SPEAKS YOUR NAME! SEND IT TO A FRIEND AND THEIR NAME IS SPOKEN AND SHOWN. Two days later if you've viewed the film then a direct mail pack is despatched to your home with forensic evidence, news reports and an invitation to tune in – ALL PERSONALIZED WITH YOUR NAME. **THE RESULT:** An extra million viewers above forecasts for the opening episode: from 2.2M to 3.2M – a 50% increase. The all-important profile of 16-34 adults also doubled. A MARKETING FIRST that not only shows your name but the computer speaks your name.

BRIEFING : Lancer la campagne du volet new-yorkais de la série CSI en Grande-Bretagne pour la chaîne Five en combinant une campagne d'e-mails, de films Internet et d'envois postaux à une échelle inégalée. En fait, quelque chose qu'on n'avait encore jamais vu ou entendu. **IDÉE :** Créer une campagne présentant un tueur en série imaginaire. Une campagne de mailing viral (tournée à Brooklyn) montrait le fictif Tueur Homonyme en train d'avouer ses crimes. Mais le meurtrier a une sale manie : il ne tue que les gens qui ont le même nom. Et c'est le vôtre ! Votre nom apparaît alors dans les flash infos du film. Et le meurtrier prononce votre nom. Il prononce votre nom ! Si l'on envoie le lien à un ami, son nom aussi sera cité ! Si vous visionnez le film, deux jours après vous recevez par courrier un colis

contenant des preuves légistes, des articles de journaux et une invitation à regarder la série, l'ensemble personnalisé à votre nom. **RÉSULTAT :** Un million de spectateurs de plus que prévus pour le premier épisode, de 2,2 à 3, 2 millions, soit une hausse de 50%. La tranche primordiale des 16-34 ans double également. L'opération a été la première du genre, car elle ne se contentait pas de montrer votre nom, mais le faisait aussi prononcer par l'ordinateur.

DIE AUFGABE: Der Launch der dritten Show der Franchise-Serie CSI:NY in England für Kanal Five durch eine noch nie da gewesene Kombination aus E-Mail, einem Internetfilm und Direktwerbung. Etwas, was man noch nie zuvor gesehen oder gehört hatte ... **DIE IDEE:** Eine Killerkampagne entwickeln, die einen erfundenen Serienmörder zeigt. Eine virale und direkte Mailkampagne (vor Ort in Brooklyn gefilmt) zeigte den fiktiven „Carbon Copy Killer", wie er Verbrechen gestand. Er tötet jedoch eine besondere Methode: Er tötet nur Menschen mit einem bestimmten Namen. UND ES IST DEIN NAME! Im Film erscheint er im Fernsehen und in der Presse. Und der Killer nennt deinen Namen. ER SAGT DEINEN NAMEN! SENDE ES AN FREUNDE, UND IHRE NAMEN WERDEN GENANNT UND GEZEIGT. Zwei Tage, nachdem du den Film gesehen hast, wird ein Paket zu dir nach Hause geschickt, das forensische Beweise, Nachrichten und eine Einladung, die Sendung einzuschalten, enthält – ALLES MIT DEINEM EIGENEN NAMEN PERSONALISIERT. **DAS ERGEBNIS:** Eine Million mehr Zuschauer der ersten Folge als vorausgesagt: von 2,2 Millionen auf 3,2 Millionen – ein Anstieg von 50%. Die wichtige Zielgruppe der 16- bis 34-Jährigen verdoppelte sich ebenfalls. EIN EINMALIGES MARKETING, das deinen Namen nicht nur zeigt, sondern der Computer spricht ihn sogar aus.

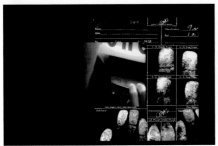

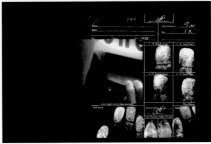

FEATURED ON THE DVD **CAMPAIGN:** The Farm <www.thereturnofthefarm.com>. **CLIENT:** Five. **AGENCY:** 20:20 London <www.2020london.co.uk>. **PRODUCTION TIME:** 1 month. **CREATIVE TEAM:** Peter Riley (Creative Partner), Hugo Bierschenk (Creative), Dean Woodhouse (Creative). **PROGRAMMER:** Simon James. **TECH ASPECTS:** Film, sound, Adobe After Effects, Macromedia Flash, Wavelab, 3D Studio, Maya, Shake, Adobe Premiere, Apple Quicktime Pro. **MEDIA CIRCULATED:** Email.

CONCEPT: The Farm goes where no reality TV series dare tread. Deliberately silly and with a raggle-taggle bunch of washed-up celebs, it's being groomed as a staple of the Five programming calendar. Viewers vote to send the party-poopers packing with the winner donating £100,000 to their fave charidee. **OBJECTIVES:** Make viewers aware that The Farm was returning. And it's bigger than ever. Larger than life, even. **STRATEGY:** Reality TV was perceived as downmarket and band-wagonesque. We held our hands up and admitted that this was meant to be silly and irreverent, and our audience appreciated our honesty. This is a strategy for TV that doesn't take itself seriously – delicious tea-time telly for the masses, where the unexpected is to be expected. The top-secret contestant list included a dizzy blonde; an aging lothario; a young hunk and an eccentric old man. Throw in a ridiculous plotline with a bunch of monster farm animals and you have all the makings of a typical B-Movie. We created "The Return of The Farm" – a trailer of a spoof B-Movie where ham-fisted acting and over-egged dialogue are the order of the day. Delivered over the Internet, we milked every opportunity to reach as wide an audience as possible, including a secret 3D version (the Internet's first 3D movie) that could only be seen if you'd been direct mailed a pair of our special 3D glasses. **RESULTS:** viewing figures peaked at 12% over targets and 8% up on last year. In TV ad revenue terms, 8% is a pot of gold at the end of the rainbow.

CONCEPT : La Ferme va plus loin que n'a osé le faire aucune émission de télé-réalité. Délibérément farfelue et mettant en scène une bande disparate de célébrités sur le retour, l'émission a été conçue comme un élément phare de la programmation de la chaîne Five. Les spectateurs votent pour éliminer les ramasseurs de bouse et le gagnant reçoit 100 000 livres à offrir à une association caritative. **OBJECTIFS :** Informer les téléspectateurs du retour de La Ferme. Plus grande que jamais, et plus vraie que nature. **STRATÉGIE :** La télé-réalité était considérée comme un marché bas de gamme et opportuniste. Nous avons relevé le défi en reconnaissant que l'émission était délibérément idiote et irrévérencieuse, et le public a apprécié notre franchise. C'est une télévision qui ne se prend pas au sérieux, qui propose un divertissement grand public, où l'inattendu est attendu. La liste des participants comprend une blonde évaporée, un don Juan vieillissant, un jeune et beau mec et un vieil homme excentrique. Ajoutez à cela un scénario ridicule et un troupeau d'animaux mons-

trueux, et vous avez tous les ingrédients d'un film de série B. Nous avons conçu « Le retour de La Ferme » comme une parodie de bande-annonce où des acteurs maladroits déclament des dialogues absurdes. Nous avons exploité tous les moyens à notre disposition pour atteindre un public aussi large que possible, dont une version en 3D (le premier film en ligne en 3D) que l'on ne pouvait visionner que si l'on avait reçu au préalable des lunettes spéciales. **RÉSULTATS :** Les chiffres d'audience ont dépassé les prévisions de 12% et ont gagné 8% par rapport à l'an passé. En terme de recettes publicitaires, 8% est déjà une poule au œufs d'or.

KONZEPT: The Farm wagt sich dorthin, wo sich keine andere Reality-Fernsehserie hintraut. Freiwillig albern, mit einer bunten Gruppe von gescheiterten Promis, stellte es einen Höhepunkt im Programmkalender von Five dar. Zuschauer wählen die Spaßbremsen heraus, wobei der Gewinner £100 000 an seine favorisierte Wohltätigkeitsorganisation spendet. **ZIEL DER KAMPAGNE:** Den Zuschauern bewusst machen, dass The Farm zurückkehrt – größer als je zuvor. Sogar in Überlebensgröße. **STRATEGIE:** Reality-TV wurde als anspruchslos und niveaulos wahrgenommen. Wir erhoben unsere Hände und gaben zu, dass es tatsächlich albern und respektlos sein sollte, und das Publikum schätzte unsere Ehrlichkeit. Dies ist eine Strategie für Fernsehen, das sich selbst nicht ernst nimmt – gemütliches Nachmittagsprogramm für die Massen, wo das Unerwartete zu erwarten ist. Die streng geheime Liste der Kandidaten enthielt eine dümmliche Blondine, einen alternden Schürzenjäger, einen jungen Schönling und einen exzentrischen alten Herrn. Geben Sie eine lächerliche Handlung mit einem Haufen Monster-Bauernhoftiere hinzu, und sie haben alles, was zu einem typischen B-Movie gehört. Wir entwickelten „The Return of the Farm" – den Trailer eines verulkenden B-Movies, bei dem ungeschickte Schauspielerei und überzogene Dialoge an der Tagesordnung sind. Wir versuchten, über das Internet mit Hilfe einer geheimen 3D-Version (der erste 3D-Film im Internet), die man nur mit einer zugesandten speziellen 3D-Brille sehen konnte, ein so breites Publikum wie möglich zu erreichen. **ERGEBNISSE:** Die Zuschauerzahlen überstiegen die Erwartungen um 12%, und im letzten Jahr um 8%. In Bezug auf Werbeeinkünfte im Fernsehen sind 8% der Traum aller Etatleiter.

CAMPAIGN: Howard's Studio. **PRODUCT:** Howard Stern Sirius Studio site. **YEAR:** 2005. **AGENCY:** Digit <www.digitlondon.com>. **PRODUCTION TIME:** 1 month. **CREATIVE DIRECTOR:** Mike Bennett. **LEAD DESIGNER:** Andrew Dean. **COPYWRITER:** Joe Brennan. **PRODUCER:** Clemmie Barth von Wehrenalp. **ACCOUNT DIRECTOR:** Rob Tripas. **PROGRAMMER:** Jamie Ingram. **TECH ASPECTS:** Macromedia Flash. **AWARDS:** TBC.

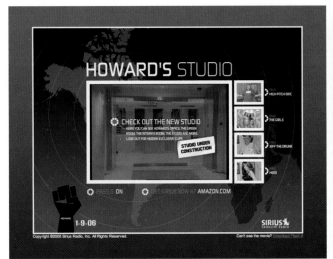

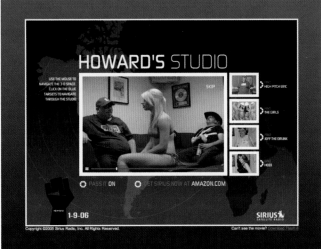

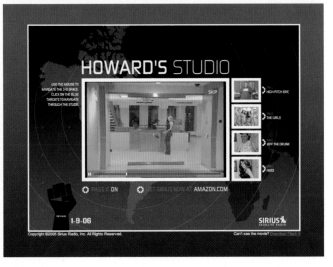

CONCEPT: Howard Stern is America's number one 'Shock Jock'. Attracting millions of listeners every day, he is as well known for his battles with the sensors as his outrageous radio show. Formally syndicated on radio stations throughout the United States, he recently signed an exclusive deal with subscription-based satellite radio service, Sirius. **BRIEF:** to create an edgy, viral, teaser site to inform Howard's existing fans, and potential new listeners about his new home on Sirius satellite radio. As well as ticking all the Howard Stern boxes in terms of content, the site should also drive consumers to Sirius and encourage them to sign up to the service for when his show went live in early 2006. **SOLUTION:** Using an innovative mix of 3D content and streaming video, we created a virtual Sirius Studio that allowed visitors behind-the-scenes access to Stern's preparations for his new show. Fans could explore the building to discover content including videos of the usual suspects Heidi Cortez, Jeff the Drunk, High Pitch Eric and the Scores Girls. We also encouraged users to invite friends to the site by creating a messaging tool that sent out invites apparently from one of Howard's side kicks. On sending an invite, exclusive content on the site was unlocked for the user to view and their message appeared as graffiti on the studio walls.

CONCEPT : Howard Stern est l'animateur radio le plus provocateur des Etats-Unis. Il attire chaque jour des millions d'auditeurs, et il est aussi célèbre pour ses conflits avec la censure que pour l'extravagance de ses émissions. Tout d'abord membre d'un syndicat de distribution pour les radios de tous le pays, il a récemment signé une exclusivité avec un service payant de radio par satellite, Sirius. **BRIEFING :** Créer un site de promo viral et survolté pour informer les fans de Stern et les nouveaux auditeurs potentiels de sa nouvelle apparition sur la radio Sirius. Reprenant les thèmes de prédilection de Stern en terme de contenu, le site encourage les gens à s'abonner à Sirius pour le démarrage de l'émission en direct prévu pour début 2006. **SOLUTION :** Par un mélange inédit de contenu en 3D et de vidéo en flot continu, nous avons reproduit un studio virtuel qui permettait aux visiteurs d'avoir accès aux coulisses de la préparation de la nouvelle émission. Les fans pouvaient aussi visiter les locaux et découvrir des vidéos de ses acolytes, comme Heidi Cortez, Jeff the Drunk, High Pitch Eric et les Score Girls. Nous avons également encouragé les internautes à parrainer leurs amis à l'aide d'un dispositif de messagerie qui envoyait des invitations signées d'un comparse de Stern. En envoyant l'invitation, le contenu du site s'exposait à la vue du visiteur et le message s'affichait sous forme de graffiti sur les murs du studio.

KONZEPT: Howard Stern ist Amerikas „Shock Jock" Nummer Eins. Mit Millionen Hörern täglich ist er sowohl für seine Kämpfe mit den Zensoren als auch für seine skandalöse Radioshow bekannt. Formal einer Interessengemeinschaft von Radiosendern aus den ganzen USA angeschlossen, unterschrieb er kürzlich einen Exklusiv-Vertrag mit dem auf Mitgliedschaft basierenden Satellitenradio-Dienst Sirius. **AUFGABE:** Eine virale Teaser-Seite erstellen, die Howards existierende Fans und potenzielle neue Hörer über seine neue Sendung auf Sirius informiert. Neben der Bereitstellung von umfassendem Inhalt zu Howard Stern soll die Seite außerdem Verbraucher zu Sirius locken und sie dazu ermuntern, Mitglieder zu werden, wenn seine Show Anfang 2006 live startet. **LÖSUNG:** Mit Hilfe eines innovativen Mix von 3D-Inhalt und Streaming-Video erstellten wir ein virtuelles Sirius-Studio, in dem Besucher hinter die Kulissen schauen und Sterns Vorbereitungen für seine neue Show sehen konnten. Fans konnten das Gebäude erforschen und Inhalte wie Videos der üblichen Verdächtigen entdecken: Heidi Cortez, Jeff the Drunk, High Pitch Eric und die Scores Girls. Außerdem ermunterten wir die Besucher, Freunde auf die Seite einzuladen, indem wir ein Messaging-Tool erstellten, das Einladungen von Howards Kumpeln versandte. Beim Versenden einer Einladung wurde exklusiver Seiteninhalt entschlüsselt, und die Botschaft erschien als Graffiti auf den Studiowänden.

FEATURED ON THE DVD **CAMPAIGN:** MDN.tv. **PRODUCT:** MDN. **YEAR:** 2004. **AGENCY:** Tribal DDB Dallas <www.tribalddb.com>. **PRODUCTION TIME:** 3 months. **EXECUTIVE CREATIVE DIRECTOR:** Scott Johnson. **ASSOCIATE CREATIVE DIRECTOR:** Dave Gibson. **ART DIRECTOR:** Tien Pham. **COPYWRITER:** Darrell Loden. **PROGRAMMER:** Chris Isom. **TECH ASPECTS:** Macromedia Flash, stop-motion animation, sound, games. **MEDIA CIRCULATED:** Online media.

CONCEPT: The site is for a television series that ran on Spike TV during the summer of 2004. The concept mirrors the irreverent, bizarre humor of the show that is designed to appeal to the young men who are watching television at 1:00 in the morning.

KONZEPT: Diese Seite gehört zu einer Fernsehserie, die im Sommer 2004 auf Spike TV lief. Das Konzept spiegelt den respektlosen, bizarren Humor der Show, die junge Männer ansprechen soll, die um 1 Uhr morgens fernsehen.

CONCEPT : Le site est celui d'une série télévisée diffusée sur Spike TV pendant l'été 2004. Le concept reflète l'humour bizarre et irrévérencieux du programme destiné à séduire les jeunes qui regardent la télé à une heure du matin.

FEATURED ON THE DVD **CAMPAIGN:** Pre Menstrual Syndrome. **PRODUCT:** MSN Woman/PMS Magazine. **CLIENT:** MSN Brasil. **YEAR:** 2003. **AGENCY:** AgênciaClick <www.agenciaclick.com.br>. **AWARDS:** Cannes Lions 2003 (Bronze).

CONCEPT: Funny and interactive advertising for female online magazine.

CONCEPT : Publicité amusante et interactive pour un magazine féminin en ligne.

KONZEPT: Lustige interaktive Werbung für ein weibliches Online-Magazin.

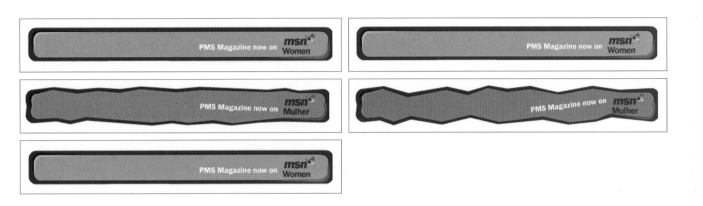

FEATURED ON THE DVD **CAMPAIGN:** Sabrina Setlur SABS <www.sabrinasetlur.de>. **PRODUCT:** 3p – Sabrina Setlur. **YEAR:** 2003. **AGENCY:** Neue Digitale <www.neue-digitale.de>. **PRODUCTION TIME:** September 2003 – October 2003. **CREATIVE TEAM:** Olaf Czeschner, Bejadin Selimi. **TECH ASPECTS:** Macromedia Flash, Adobe Photoshop, Adobe After Effects. **MEDIA CIRCULATED:** Internet. **AWARDS:** Mobius Awards 2005 (Gold), Epica 2004 (Bronze), The One Show Interactive 2004 (Silver), Art Directors Club Deutschland 2004 (Silver).

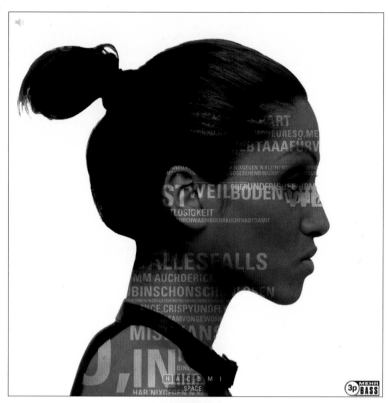

CONCEPT: Promotional, artistically-inspired presentation website for German Hip Hop artist Sabrina Setlur and her new album "SABS", *3p Gesellschaft für Kommunikation mbH*, Rödelheim. Sabrina Setlur's new online presence allows users to take on the artist's perspective, and to actively participate in her philosophy, her personality, and the new album SABS. **THE GOAL:** to transport the ambitious element in Sabrina's music to the Internet with an experimental approach. By breaking up the linear rules of conventional interviews, the section "Close Up" offers fans the possibility to lead their own special interview with Germany's most successful black music singer. The same experimental approach is reflected in the navigation, thereby letting Sabrina's personality unfold itself undisturbed by menu items. Additionally, typographic and sound effects reflect the playfully handling of words and samples typical for Sabrina's music.

CONCEPT : Site de présentation et de promotion artistique de la chanteuse allemande de hip-hop Sabrina Setlur pour la sortie de son troisième album, SABS. Le nouveau site de Sabrina permet aux visiteurs de partager la vision de l'artiste en découvrant sa philosophie, ses goûts et sa musique. **OBJECTIF :** Refléter les ambitions musicales de Sabrina dans une démarche expérimentale. En cassant les règles linéaires de l'interview classique, la rubrique « Portrait » offre aux fans la possibilité de mener leur propre interview avec la chan-

teuse de rap la plus populaire d'Allemagne. Le mode de navigation procède de la même approche, laissant la personnalité de Sabrina se développer seule, sans besoin d'intervenir dans le menu. De plus, des effets audio et typographiques rappellent les combinaisons de mots et de samples caractéristiques du style de l'artiste.

KONZEPT: Künstlerisch-inspirierte Werbeseite zur Präsentation der deutschen Hip-Hop-Sängerin Sabrina Setlur und ihres neuen Albums „SABS", 3p Gesellschaft für Kommunikation mbH, Rödelheim. Sabrina Setlurs neuer Online-Auftritt ermöglicht es den Benutzern, die Perspektive der Künstlerin einzunehmen und aktiv an ihrer Philosophie, ihrer Persönlichkeit und ihrem neuen Album SABS teilzuhaben. **DAS ZIEL:** das ehrgeizige Element von Sabrinas Musik mit einem experimentellen Ansatz ins Internet zu transportieren. Durch die Durchbrechung der Gesetzmäßigkeiten konventioneller Interviews bietet der Bereich „Close up" den Fans die Möglichkeit, ihr eigenes Interview mit Deutschlands erfolgreichster schwarzer Sängerin zu führen. Derselbe experimentelle Ansatz wird durch die Navigation reflektiert, so dass sich Sabrinas Persönlichkeit ungestört von Menüpunkten entfalten kann. Zusätzlich spiegeln Soundeffekte den spielerischen Gebrauch von Worten, der typisch für Sabrinas Musik ist.

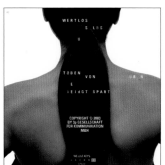

FEATURED ON THE DVD **CAMPAIGN:** Guardian Jobs <www.guardian.co.uk>. **YEAR:** 2004-2005. **AGENCY:** Tribal DDB London. <www.tribalddb.com>. **PRODUCTION TIME:** 5 weeks (x2). **MAINTENANCE:** Two campaigns – May 2004 and Jan 2005. **CREATIVE TEAM:** Ben Clapp, Alex Braxton, Amy Gould. **PROGRAMMER:** James Robb. **TECH ASPECTS:** Macromedia Flash, HTML, pen and paper. **MEDIA CIRCULATED:** Online advertising.

CONCEPT: While you sit bored at your desk, chewing your biro. Guardian Jobs tirelessly goes about finding you the job of your dreams. The campaign is intended to demonstrate the activity and dynamism of The Guardian's intelligent job match service, while avoiding long-winded technical explanations of how it works. A visitor to Guardian Unlimited could literally uncover Guardian Jobs working behind the scenes on the website with the mega-expandable banner, and the repeated use of smaller placements was designed to make best use of repeated presence to maximise the all hands to the pumps effect. **RESULTS:** Guardian jobs is now the fastest growing UK jobs site. Page impressions are 200% up on pre-launch month, and 100% above target for year 1. Users – the prime driver for online only advertising revenues – are 72% up. ABCe regularly audits traffic – January audit was 584k users and 11.8m page impressions. Users – 50% above target for year 1. Jobmatch subscribers – 200% above target for year 1.

CONCEPT : Tandis que vous vous ennuyez au bureau à mâchouiller votre stylo, Guardian Jobs cherche sans relâche à vous dénicher le poste de vos rêves. La campagne doit démontrer le dynamisme et l'activité des petites annonces du journal The Guardian, tout en évitant de longues et fastidieuses explications sur son mode de fonctionnement. Le visiteur du site de Guardian Unlimited peut littéralement observer l'activité de la rubrique grâce à une bannière extensible, et l'utilisation d'encarts plus petits multiplie les signes de présence afin d'optimiser la visibilité. **RÉSULTATS :** Guardian Jobs est le site d'annonces d'emploi qui bénéficie de la plus forte croissance en Grande-Bretagne. Le nombre de pages vues a augmenté de 200% le mois du lancement et de 100% la première année. Le nombre d'utilisateurs, qui détermine les recettes des agences en ligne, a augmenté de 72%. ABCe mesure régulièrement le trafic, et l'audit de janvier a comptabilisé 584 000 visiteurs et 11,8 million de pages vues. Nombre de visiteurs : 50% de plus que l'objectif pour la première année. Nombre d'inscrits : 200% de plus que l'objectif pour la première année.

KONZEPT: Während Sie gelangweilt an Ihrem Schreibtisch sitzen und auf Ihrem Kuli herumkauen, sucht Guardian Jobs unermüdlich nach Ihrem Traumjob. Die Kampagne soll die Aktivität und Dynamik von The Guardians intelligentem Jobservice demonstrieren, und gleichzeitig langatmige technische Erklärungen vermeiden. Ein Besucher von Guardian Unlimited kann mit dem erweiterbaren Banner auf der Webseite buchstäblich Guardian Jobs aufdecken, wie es im Hintergrund arbeitet. Die wiederholte Verwendung von kleineren Platzierungen wurde entworfen, um den Effekt, dass alle Elemente stets in Bewegung sind, maximieren. **ERGEBNISSE:** Guardian Jobs ist heute die am schnellsten wachsende Jobseite in Großbritannien. Die Klicks auf die Seite sind um 200% angestiegen und haben das Ziel des ersten Jahres um 100% überstiegen. Die Zahl der Benutzer – ausschlaggebend für ausschließlich online geschaltete Werbung – stieg um 72%. Regelmäßiger Seitenverkehr – Audit im Januar: 584 000 Benutzer und 11,8 Millionen Klicks auf die Seite. Benutzer – 50% mehr als im ersten Jahr erwartet. Registrierte Benutzer – 200% mehr als im ersten Jahr erwartet.

CAMPAIGN: The Independent. **YEAR:** 2005. **AGENCY:** Large <www.largedesign.com>. **PRODUCTION TIME:** 6 weeks. **COST IN HOURS OF WORK:** 240 h. **CREATIVE DIRECTOR:** Lars Hemming Jorgensen, Jim Boulton, Rene Christoffer. **PROGRAMMER:** Jesper Lycke. **TECH ASPECTS:** Lightwave, Adobe After Effects, Adobe Premiere, audio.

CONCEPT: The world is changing and so is The Independent.

CONCEPT : Le monde change, et le journal aussi.

KONZEPT: Die Welt verändert sich – und so auch The Independent.

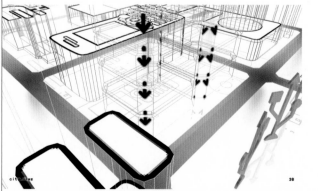

FEATURED ON THE DVD **CAMPAIGN:** TUSH Magazine <www.tushmagazine.com>. **YEAR:** 2005-2006. **AGENCY:** SiteSeeing, Interaktive Medien <www.zeppzepp.com>. **PRODUCTION TIME:** Permanent since March 2005. **MAINTENANCE:** June 2005. **COST IN HOURS OF WORK:** 60 h. **CREATIVE TEAM:** Peter Zepp, Katharina Moelle. **PROGRAMMER:** Jan Loseries. **TECH ASPECTS:** HTML, Macromedia Flash, video, sound, 3D. **MEDIA CIRCULATED:** Print, web.

CONCEPT: TUSH is a beauty magazine published several times per year. Each new edition has its own micro-site, and all the micro-sites are linked for ease of surfing from one to another. The banners and interstitial video serve to direct the visitor's attention to the magazine.

CONCEPT : TUSH est un magazine de beauté qui paraît plusieurs fois dans l'année. A chaque édition correspond un micro-site, et tous les sites sont liés entre eux, permettant ainsi de surfer de numéro en numéro. Les bannières et l'interstitiel vidéodoivent attirer l'attention du visiteur sur le magazine.

KONZEPT: TUSH ist ein Beauty-Magazin und erscheint viermal im Jahr. Für jede Ausgabe wird auch eine neue Microsite entwickelt. Alle Microsites sind miteinander verlinkt – so kann man zwischen den einzelnen Ausgaben wechseln. Die Seiten fungieren als Teaser und sollen Neugierde auf das Magazin wecken.

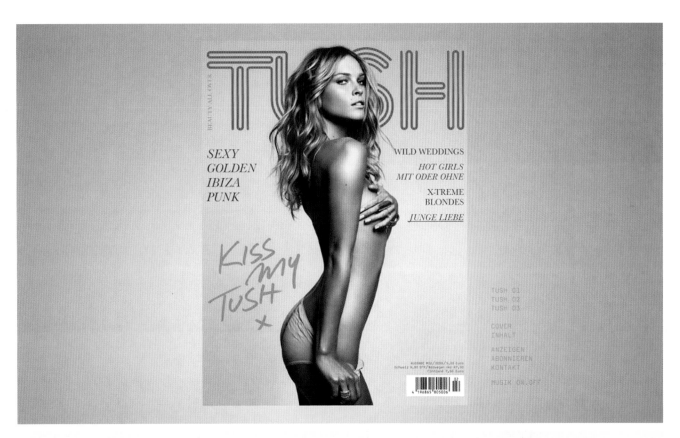

FEATURED ON THE DVD CAMPAIGN: Dinossaur. **CLIENT:** Super Interessante Magazine. **AGENCY:** AlmapBBDO <www.almapbbdo.com.br>. **PRODUCTION TIME:** 5 days. **TECH ASPECTS:** Macromedia Flash, video, sound.
CREATIVE DIRECTOR: Sérgio Mugnaini. **ART DIRECTOR:** Felipe Lima, Cesar Finamori. **COPYWRITER:** Dulcidio Caldeira. **DESIGNER:** Felipe Lima. **TECHNICAL DIRECTOR:** Flavio Ramos. **PRODUCER:** Ana Maria Machado.
ACCOUNT EXECUTIVE: Francisco Meirelles, Joanna Guinle. **AWARDS:** Cannes Festival 2005 (Silver), El Ojo de Ibero America 2005 (Silver), London Festival 2005 (Shortlist), MMonline/Msn 2005 (Bronze).

BACKGROUND: Superinteressante magazine always brings interesting and amazing subjects. **THE IDEA:** The challenge was to show that the magazine is surprising and indispensable in an integrated campaign between on and offline. **SOLUTION:** Expandable banner. While it is closed we see a person seated in a rock. The call is: "If you don't read, you won't know what you're missing. Rollover." The image expands and we can see that the rock is just a bit of the head of an enormous skeleton of dinossaur embedded. Claim: "Superinteressante Magazine. Knowledge is super."

CONTEXTE : Le magazine Super Interessante propose toujours des sujets surprenants et intéressants. **IDÉE :** Montrer que le magazine est étonnant et indispensable par une campagne intégrée en ligne et hors ligne. **SOLUTION :** Une bannière extensible. Quand elle est fermée, on voit une personne assise sur un rocher. Le slogan : « Si vous ne lisez pas, vous ne saurez jamais ce que vous ratez. Déroulez. » L'image s'agrandit et on s'aperçoit que le rocher est une partie de la tête d'un énorme squelette de dinosaure. Accroche : « Le magazine Super Interessante. La connaissance est super. »

HINTERGRUND: Das Magazin Superinteressante enthält immer interessante und faszinierende Themen. **DIE IDEE:** Die Herausforderung bestand darin, in einer Kombination von Offline- und Online-Kampagne zu zeigen, dass das Magazin überraschend und unverzichtbar ist. **LÖSUNG:** Erweiterbares Banner. Ist es geschlossen, sehen wir eine Person, die auf einem Stein sitzt. Der Slogan lautet: „Wenn Sie nicht lesen, wissen Sie nicht, was Sie verpassen. Starten Sie jetzt." Das Bild breitet sich aus, und wir sehen, dass der Stein Teil eines riesigen Dinosaurierskeletts ist. Aussage: „Superinteressante Magazin. Wissen ist super."

CAMPAIGN: Slam Dunk. **CLIENT:** Takehiko Inoue. **YEAR:** 2005. **AGENCY:** Dentsu Inc. <www.dentsu.com>. **CREATIVE DIRECTOR:** Naoto Oiwa, Yasuharu Sasaki. **COPYWRITER:** Yasuharu Sasaki. **ART DIRECTOR:** Yusuke Kitani. **PROGRAMMER:** Hiroki Nakamura. **TECH ASPECTS:** Macromedia Flash. **MEDIA CIRCULATED:** Website. **AWARDS:** One Show Interactive 2005 (Gold), CLIO Awards 2005 (Bronze).

CONCEPT: A campaign commemorating the sale of the 100 million copies of "Slam Dunk", a basketball-themed comic series. The comic's creator used the campaign as a way to personally thank readers. The website allowed users to leave messages from the perspective of audience members looking at the world of the comics "Slam Dunk".

CONCEPT : Une campagne pour fêter la vente de 100 millions de copies de *Slam Dunk*, une série de bande dessinée japonaise ayant pour thème le basket-ball. L'auteur du manga s'est servi de la campagne pour remercier personnellement ses lecteurs. Les visiteurs peuvent laisser des messages et donner leur point de vue sur l'univers de *Slam Dunk*.

KONZEPT: Eine Kampagne, die an den Verkauf von 100 Millionen Exemplaren von „Slam Dunk" erinnert, eine Comicreihe über Basketball. Der Comiczeichner dankte mit dieser Kampagne seinen Lesern. Auf der Webseite konnten die Benutzer Nachrichten aus der Perspektive von Publikumsmitgliedern hinterlassen, die die Welt des Comics „Slam Dunk" betrachteten.

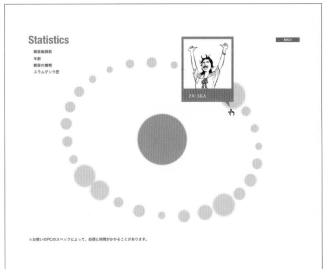

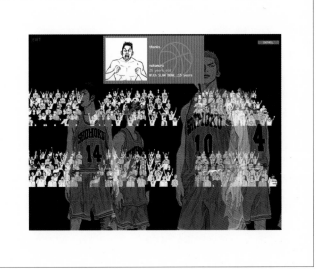

FEATURED ON THE DVD **CAMPAIGN:** Alfie launch. **YEAR:** 2004. **AGENCY:** Big Spaceship <www.bigspaceship.com>. **CREATIVE DIRECTOR:** Daniel Federman. **ART DIRECTOR:** Jens Karlsson. **PRODUCER:** Edward Looram.
ANIMATOR: David Chau, Andrew Payne. **DESIGNER:** Lisa Weatherbee, Ron Thompson. **PROGRAMMER:** Tai U, Christian Stadler. **COPYWRITER:** Karen Dahlstrom. **SOUND DESIGNER:** Daniel Federman. **VIDEO:** Jens Karlsson.
AWARDS: FlashInTheCan Awards (Finalist), SXSW Web Awards (Finalist), WebAwards (Outstanding Website Award), Davey Awards (Silver), Webby Awards (Webby Worthy), STEP Best of Web Design Annual (Sept/Oct 2005).

CONCEPT: A stylish remake of the 1966 film, Alfie explores the life of the charming womanizer Alfie Elkins and his realization that perhaps there is more to life than simply oneself. Influenced by the sparse Mod design of the '60s, the site reflects the film's sexy style, humor, and personality. Features for getting to know Alfie and the women in his world a little better include "Ask Alfie", a horoscopes guide, customizable wallpapers, and a personality test for both blokes and birds. Throughout the site, video clips of Alfie set forth his unconventional and cheeky wisdom.personality test for both blokes and birds. Throughout the site, video clips of Alfie set forth his unconventional and cheeky wisdom.

CONCEPT : Remake stylisé du film de 1966, Alfie décrit la vie du charmant séducteur Alfie Elkins et sa découverte qu'il n'y a pas que soi-même dans la vie. S'inspirant du design minimaliste des années 60, le site reflète le style sexy, l'humour et la personnalité du film. Les rubriques permettant de faire plus ample connaissance avec le héros et ses conquêtes comprennent un horoscope, un test de personnalité pour filles et garçons et des fonds d'écran. A l'intérieur du site, des clips vidéo de Alfie présentent sa philosophie singulière et impertinente.

KONZEPT: Ein schickes Remake des Originalfilms Alfie von 1966 beleuchtet das Leben des charmanten Frauenhelden Alfie Elkins und seine Erkenntnis, dass es im Leben vielleicht mehr gibt als einen selbst. Vom kargen Mod-Design der 60er beeinflusst, reflektiert die Seite den sexy Stil, Humor und Persönlichkeit des Films. Es gibt Features, mit denen man Alfie und seine Frauen besser kennen lernt, wie „Ask Alfie", ein Horoskop-Führer, Hintergrundbilder, die man selber entwerfen kann, und einen Persönlichkeitstest für Jungs und Mädchen. Durch die ganze Seite ziehen sich Videoclips von Alfie, in denen er seine unkonventionellen und frechen Weisheiten von sich gibt.

FEATURED ON THE DVD **CAMPAIGN:** Underworld: Evolution <www.entertheunderworld.com>. **YEAR:** 2005. **AGENCY:** Big Spaceship <www.bigspaceship.com>. **CREATIVE DIRECTOR:** Michael Lebowitz. **ART DIRECTOR:** Jens Karlsson. **PRODUCER:** Karen Monahan, Peter Karlsson. **ANIMATOR:** Tyson Damman, Joel Szymanski, Zander Brimijoin, Bjorn Fagerholm, Jens Karlsson. **DESIGNER:** Joel Szymanski, Tyson Damman, Jens Karlsson, Bjorn Fagerholm. **PROGRAMMER:** Jamie Kosoy. **COPYWRITER:** Karen Dahlstrom. **SOUND DESIGNER:** Chris Wei.

CONCEPT: Kate Beckinsale rises from the nether regions to reprise her role as Selene – death dealer and heroine – in Underworld: Evolution. To capture the spirit of the centuries-old battle between Vampires and Lycans, we built a cutting edge site with medieval flair. In fact, Big Spaceship went above and beyond web shop protocol to broker a deal between Sony Pictures and Macromedia. The fruit of this progressive partnership: Big Spaceship was able to create the first major motion picture campaign and first game of this scope done entirely in the new Flash 8. **RESULT:** A game with over 60,000 registered users in only the first two weeks, using the most robust game engine Big Spaceship has crafted to date.

CONCEPT : Kate Beckinsale revient des enfers pour incarner le rôle de Sélène, héroïne et passeuse de mort dans le jeu *Underworld : Evolution*. Pour rendre l'esprit de la bataille ancestrale entre les Vampires et les Lycans, nous avons réalisé un site sophistiqué dans un style médiéval. En réalité, Big Spaceship a transgressé les usages commerciaux en vigueur en obtenant un accord entre Sony Pictures et Macromedia. Le fruit de ce nouveau partenariat : la première campagne cinéma et jeu en réseau de cette ampleur conçue entièrement dans le nouveau format Flash 8. **RÉSULTAT :** Le jeu a enregistré plus de 60 000 utilisateurs dans les deux premières semaines, et a utilisé le moteur de jeu le plus puissant jamais réalisé par Big Spaceship.

KONZEPT: Kate Beckinsale steigt aus der Unterwelt auf, um ihre Rolle als Selene – Death Dealer und Heldin – in „Underworld: Evolution" wieder aufzunehmen. Um den Geist des jahrhundertealten Kampfes zwischen Vampiren und Werwölfen einzufangen, erstellten wir eine innovative Seite mit mittelalterlichem Flair. Tatsächlich überstieg Big Spaceship seine Möglichkeiten jenseits des Web-Shop-Protokolls, um einen Deal zwischen Sony Pictures und Macromedia zu erreichen. Das Ergebnis dieser fortschrittlichen Partnerschaft: Big Spaceship konnte seine erste große Motion-Picture-Kampagne und das erste Spiel dieser Größenordnung komplett im neuen Flash 8 entwickeln. **ERGEBNIS:** Ein Spiel mit über 60 000 registrierten Benutzern innerhalb der ersten zwei Wochen, mit dem robustesten Spielantrieb, den Big Spaceship bis heute gefertigt hat.

FEATURED ON THE DVD **CAMPAIGN:** Sin City launch. **YEAR:** 2005. **AGENCY:** Big Spaceship <www.bigspaceship.com>. **CREATIVE DIRECTOR:** Michael Lebowitz. **ART DIRECTOR:** D. Garrett Nantz. **TECHNOLOGY LEAD:** Joshua Hirsch. **PRODUCER:** Karen Monahan. **ANIMATOR:** Michael Dillingham. **DESIGNER:** Michael Dillingham, Dexter Cruz. **PROGRAMMER:** Jamie Kosoy. **COPYWRITER:** Drew Horton. **PRODUCTION ARTISTS:** George Murray. **AWARDS:** Creativity 35 Design Annual (In-Book), WebAwards (Outstanding Website Award), Davey Awards (Silver), Favourite Website Awards (Site of the Day).

CONCEPT: From the pages of the Sin City graphic novels, director Robert Rodriguez painstakingly created an almost frame-for-frame homage to the Frank Miller series. In keeping with the film and the novels, the site reflects the gritty, noir sensibility and high-contrast black-and-white imagery that defines the look of Sin City. The Sin City destination site was developed in two phases: the first phase was created to build awareness and credibility within the existing Sin City fan base. Information about Frank Miller and the graphic novels themselves was introduced early in the campaign, with original art and sketches. The translation of the characters from page to screen became the focus of the site, assuring fans that both Miller and Rodriguez were making every effort to remain faithful to the source material. The second phase shifted focus from the avid to casual fan, reaching out to both the gaming and film audiences online and drawing them into the dark world of Sin City. Production information, games and the star-power of the film's cast were used to promote the film to the casual movie-going audience online. Five online games were developed for the site. In four mini-games, the user plays as one of the characters in the film: Hartigan, Marv, Gail and Dwight. In the 'Old Town Rumble', users control all characters in a game of strategy, attack and defense. Additional features include the 'Sin City ID', and 'Custom Desktops' where users can create their own Sin City artwork to save and download.

CONCEPT : D'après la bande dessinée Sin City, le cinéaste Robert Rodriguez a réalisé un hommage à la série de Frank Miller, quasiment image par image. Fidèle à l'esprit du film et de la BD, le site reflète le réalisme, le désenchantement et le noir et blanc contrasté qui font le style de Sin City. Le site a été réalisé en deux phases : la première devait assurer la promotion et la crédibilité du film au sein de la communauté de fans avertis. Des informations sur Frank Miller et ses romans graphiques furent introduites dès le début de la campagne, avec des dessins inédits. L'adaptation à l'écran des personnages du livre devint le cœur du site, assurant aux fans que Frank Miller et Robert Rodriguez faisaient leur possible pour rester fidèle à l'ouvrage d'origine. La deuxième phase s'adressait plutôt au fan occasionnel, visant le public amateur de jeux et de films en ligne, et tentait de les attirer dans l'univers

sombre de Sin City. Des informations sur le tournage et les acteurs, ainsi que des jeux, ont contribué à promouvoir le film auprès des internautes qui vont de temps en temps au cinéma. Cinq jeux en ligne ont été développés pour le site. Dans quatre d'entre eux, l'internaute peut endosser l'identité d'un des personnages du film : Hartigan, Marv, Gail et Dwight. Dans le dernier, *Old Town Rumble*, le joueur contrôle tous les personnages dans un jeu de stratégie, d'attaque et de défense. On trouve en outre des applications pour créer et télécharger ses propres visuels suivant les modèles de Sin City.

KONZEPT: Der Regisseur Robert Rodriguez schuf aus den Seiten der Sin-City-Comics sorgfältig eine beinahe Bild-für-Bild-Hommage an die Frank Miller-Reihe. Um mit Film und Comics mitzuhalten, spiegelt die Seite die düstere Atmosphäre eines Film Noir und die kontrastreiche Schwarz-Weiß-Bilderwelt, die den Look von Sin City ausmachen. Die Sin City-Seite wurde in zwei Phasen entwickelt: Die erste sollte Bewusstsein und Glaubwürdigkeit innerhalb der existierenden Fangemeinde aufbauen. Schon früh wurden Informationen über Frank Miller und die Comics selbst in der Kampagne mit Originalzeichnungen und -skizzen eingeführt. Die Seite konzentrierte sich auf die Übersetzung der Figuren von der Buchseite auf den Bildschirm, um den Fans zu versichern, dass sowohl Miller als auch Rodriguez alle Anstrengungen unternahmen, dem zu Grunde liegenden Material gerecht zu werden. Die zweite Phase verschob den Fokus von dem begeisterten zum zufälligen Fan und versuchte, das Spiel- und Filmpublikum online zu erreichen und sie in die dunkle Welt von Dark City zu ziehen. Produktionsinfos, Spiele und der Starbonus der Filmbesetzung wurden eingesetzt, um bei den zufälligen Kinobesuchern online Werbung für den Film zu machen. Fünf Online-Spiele wurden entwickelt. In vier Minispielen spielt der Benutzer eine der Filmfiguren: Hartigan, Marv, Gail oder Dwight. In „Old Town Rumble" kontrolliert der Spieler alle Figuren in einem Strategiespiel. Als zusätzliche Features gibt es die „Sin City ID" und „Custom Desktops", wo Benutzer ihr eigenes Sin-City-Artwork erstellen, speichern und downloaden können.

FEATURED ON THE DVD **CAMPAIGN:** Trauma launch. **CLIENT:** Warner Brothers. **AGENCY:** 20:20 London <www.2020london.co.uk>. **PRODUCTION TIME:** 1 month. **CREATIVE TEAM:** Peter Riley (Creative Partner), Hugo Bierschenk (Creative), Dean Woodhouse (Creative). **PROGRAMMER:** Dave Luff. **TECH ASPECTS:** Film, sound, Adobe After Effects, Macromedia Flash, Wavelab, PHP/SQL, 3D Studio, Maya, Shake, Adobe Premiere, Apple Quicktime Pro. **MEDIA CIRCULATED:** Email. **AWARDS:** D&AD (UK).

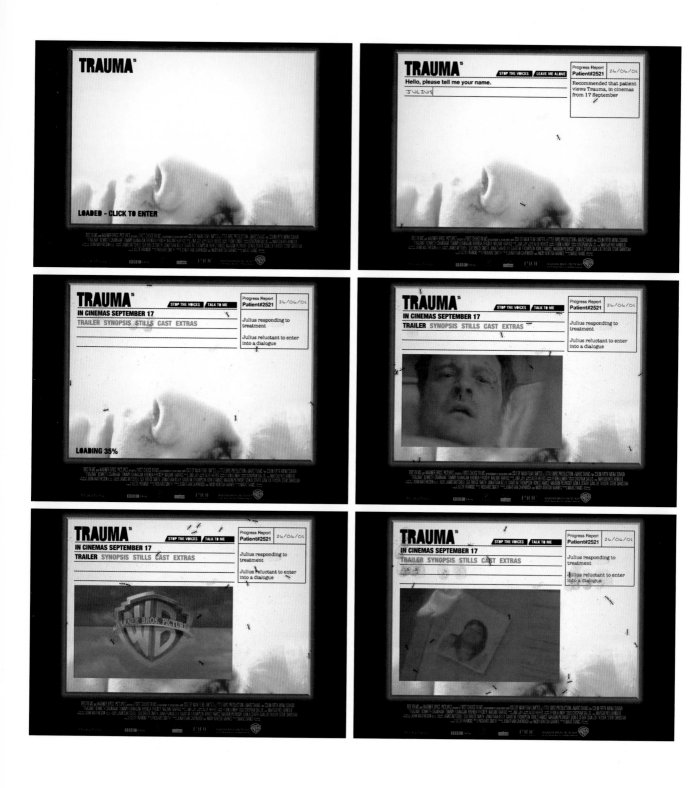

THE BRIEF: To launch the movie 'Trauma' starring Colin Firth (Bridget Jones' Diary), and Mena Suvari (American Beauty). **THE IDEA:** We wanted to reinvent the rules of film marketing. We sent an e-mail link to a list of movie buffs. But the link opened what looked like a typical film website forum and chatroom. And tucked away in some of the chatroom posting was the mention of... YOUR NAME. When you clicked on the video you saw an interview with Colin Firth plus excerpts from the film. But the twist was that we shot special 'on-set' footage and had Colin voice-over how he was disturbed by some unexplained events during the shooting of the film. He talks about a strange event in one scene of a name that kept appearing. We see a corpse on a gurney. Etched into the corpse's arm with a knife is YOUR NAME. SEND IT TO A FRIEND AND THEIR NAME APPEARS. **THE RESULT:** The Trauma launch was so successful that over 50% of people who viewed our film forwarded it to a friend. Above all the movie chatrooms and forums for websites such as Empire and Ain't it Cool News were buzzing with talk of how Colin Firth was talking about a film with YOUR NAME in it. You simply can't buy that kind of word-of-mouth referral.

BRIEFING : Lancer le film Trauma, avec Colin Firth (Le Journal de Bridget Jones) et Mena Suvari (American Beauty). **IDÉE :** Réinventer les règles du marketing en matière de cinéma. Nous avons envoyé un lien url à une liste de passionnés de cinéma. Le lien ouvrait ce qui ressemblait à un forum ou un groupe de discussion sur le cinéma. Seulement votre nom apparaissait dans la liste des messages reçus. En cliquant sur la vidéo, on voyait une interview de Colin Firth et des extraits du film. L'astuce est que nous avions enregistré des scènes sur le plateau de tournage et en voix off, Colin Firth racontait qu'il avait été troublé par de mystérieux événements lors du tournage. Il donne l'exemple d'une scène où un nom

n'arrêtait pas d'apparaître. On voit alors un cadavre sur un brancard. Gravé au couteau sur le bras du mort apparaît votre nom. Si vous faites suivre à un ami, c'est son nom qui apparaîtra. **RÉSULTAT :** Le lancement a eu un tel succès que plus de 50% des gens qui ont visité le site l'ont fait suivre à des amis. En outre, sur les forums spécialisés en cinéma, on ne parlait que de l'histoire de Colin Firth mentionnant votre nom dans un film. C'est le genre de phénomène de bouche à oreille qui ne peut pas s'acheter.

DIE AUFGABE: Launch des Films „Trauma" mit Colin Firth („Schokolade zum Frühstück") und Mena Suvari (American Beauty). **DIE IDEE:** Wir wollten die Regeln des Film-Marketings neu erfinden und sandten einen E-Mail-Link an eine Liste von Filmfans. Was der Link öffnete, sah wie eine typische Filmwebseite mit Forum und Chat aus. Aber in einem der Chatbeiträge versteckt wurde ... DEIN NAME genannt. Klickte man das Video an, sah man ein Interview mit Colin Firth und Auszüge aus dem Film. Das Besondere war, dass wir spezielles Filmmaterial vom Set hatten und Colin im Hintergrund von unerklärlichen Vorfällen während des Drehs berichtet, die ihm Angst eingejagt hatten. Er erzählt von einem merkwürdigen Ereignis in einer Szene, in der immer wieder ein Name auftauchte. Wir sehen eine Leiche auf einer Krankentrage. Mit einem Messer ist DEIN NAME in den Arm der Leiche geritzt. SENDE ES AN FREUNDE, UND IHRE NAMEN ERSCHEINEN. **DAS ERGEBNIS:** Der Launch von „Trauma" war so erfolgreich, dass über 50% der Leute, die unseren Film sahen, ihn an einen Freund weiterleiteten. In allen Filmchats und Foren für Webseiten wie Empire oder Ain't it Cool News wurde darüber gesprochen, wie Colin Firth von einem Film erzählt, in dem DEIN NAME vorkommt. Diese Art von Mundpropaganda kann man einfach nicht kaufen.

FEATURED ON THE DVD **CAMPAIGN:** War of the Worlds launch. **YEAR:** 2005. **AGENCY:** Big Spaceship <www.bigspaceship.com>. **CREATIVE DIRECTOR:** Daniel Federman. **ART DIRECTOR:** James Widegren. **STRATEGY LEAD:** Matthew Lipson. **PRODUCER:** Drew Horton, Edward Looram. **ANIMATOR:** James Widegren, Tai U. **DESIGNER:** James Widegren. **PROGRAMMER:** Tai U, Lee Semel. **COPYWRITER:** Drew Horton. **SOUND DESIGNER:** James Widegren. **PRODUCTION ARTISTS:** Andrew Payne, Christine Yu. **AWARDS:** Creativity 35 Design (Gold), HOW Magazine Interactive Design (Merit), Davey Awards (Silver), WebAwards (Standard of Excellence), Favourite Website Awards (Site of the Day).

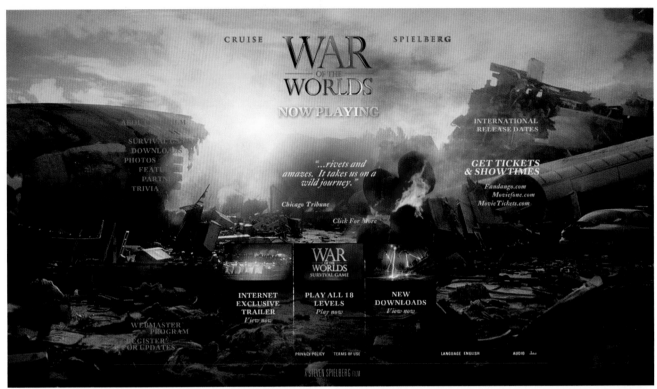

CONCEPT/RESULTS: As the tagline goes, "The last war on Earth won't be started by humans." Steven Spielberg's return to the extra terrestrial sci-fi genre was one of the most anticipated and successful movies of 2005. The online blitz necessary to support the dream team pairing of Cruise and Spielberg meant putting together a campaign that felt truly massive. Over the course of nearly a year, two sites, two full branding campaigns, a webmaster outreach program and a multi-player strategy game were launched to support the film. The site was designed to exhibit the enormity of the movie, using full-screen shots to show the large-scale desolation of Spielberg's vision. Further demonstrating the massive scale, the War of the Worlds Online Survival Game features 18 harrowing maps of gameplay and is one of the most ambitious multi-player Flash games of its kind to date. The webmaster outreach program provided thousands of genre and fan sites with syndicated content, in the form of video, stills, game boards and other promotional content. The proprietary architecture of the webmaster program managed nearly a thousand registered webmasters and their referrals to the War of the Worlds main site.

CONCEPT/RÉSULTAT : Pour citer la dernière réplique du film de Spielberg : "La guerre ultime ne sera pas déclenchée par les humains ». Le retour de Steven Spielberg au genre de science-fiction extraterrestre a été un des succès les plus attendus de l'année 2005. Le seul travail nécessaire pour soutenir le duo de choc Cruise-Spielberg consistait à concevoir une campagne en ligne à très grande échelle. En l'espace d'un an, deux sites, deux campagnes produits, une application pour administrateur de site et un jeu de stratégie en réseau ont été lancés pour promouvoir le film. Le site devait refléter la démesure du film, et utilisait des images plein écran pour rendre l'atmosphère de désolation voulue par le cinéaste. Quant à la portée gigantesque, le jeu en ligne présente 18 niveaux de jeu et c'est le jeu en réseau le plus ambitieux réalisé à ce jour sous format Flash. Le programme pour webmaster a fourni à des milliers de sites de fans des infos autorisées sous forme de vidéos, de photos, de jeux et autres contenus promotionnels. L'application déposée a attiré presque un millier de webmasters sur le site principal de La Guerre des Mondes.

KONZEPT/ERGEBNISSE: Die Überschrift lautet: „Der letzte Krieg der Erde wird nicht von den Menschen begonnen." Steven Spielbergs Rückkehr zum außerirdischen Science-Fiction-Genre war einer der am meisten erwarteten und erfolgreichsten Filme 2005. Der nötige Online-Auftritt, um die Zusammenarbeit des Dreamteams Cruise/Spielberg zu unterstützen, musste eine wirklich massive Kampagne sein. Innerhalb eines knappen Jahres wurden zwei Webseiten, zwei komplette Markenkampagnen, ein Webmaster-Outreach-Programm und ein Strategiespiel für mehrere Spieler ins Leben gerufen, um für den Film zu werben. Die Seite sollte das Ausmaß des Films zur Schau stellen und zeigte mit Vollbildaufnahmen die groß angelegte Trostlosigkeit von Spielbergs Vision. Zusätzlich zeigte das War-of-the-Worlds-Online-Spiel 18 grauenhafte Spielkarten und ist eines der ambitioniertesten Flash-Spiele für mehrere Spieler, das es bisher gab. Das Webmaster-Outreach-Programm sorgte für Tausende von Genre- und Fanseiten mit geschütztem Inhalt in Form von Videos und Bildern aus dem Film, Spielen und anderen Werbeinhalten. Die geschützte Architektur des Webmasterprogramms sorgte für fast 1000 registrierte Webmaster und ihre Empfehlungen der Hauptseite von Krieg der Welten.

FEATURED ON THE DVD **CAMPAIGN:** Wolf Creek launch. **YEAR:** 2005. **AGENCY:** Big Spaceship <www.bigspaceship.com>. **CREATIVE DIRECTOR:** Michael Lebowitz. **ART DIRECTOR:** D. Garrett Nantz. **PRODUCER:** Karen Monahan, Catherine Patterson, Drew Horton. **DESIGNER:** D. Garrett Nantz, Cathy Davenport, Ron Thompson. **PROGRAMMER:** Caleb Johnston. **COPYWRITER:** D. Garrett Nantz, Doug Sepler, Carl Nyman, Drew Horton. **PRODUCTION ARTISTS:** Christine Yu, Bjorn Fagerholm, Staffan Estberg.

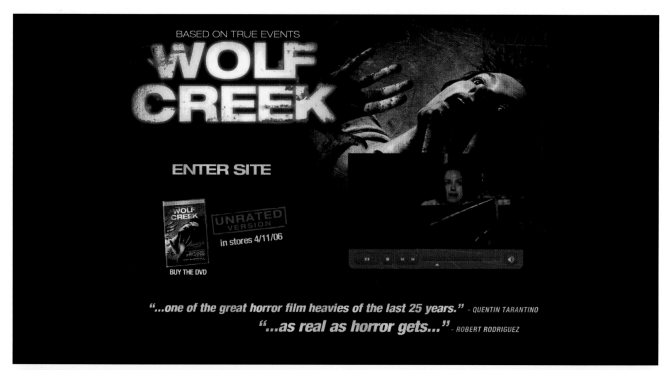

CONCEPT: Based on a true story, Wolf Creek is the tale of three happy-go-lucky college kids who get far more then they bargained for on their hiking trip in the Australian Outback. The site mimics the mounting tension of the film by plunging visitors unexpectedly into creepy panoramic environments in much the same way the film characters find themselves in confusing and progressively scarier situations. Tapping into the conspiracy-theory blog trend, Big Spaceship also created a second site for the film called thekilleroutback.com.au Ostensibly written by an Australian serial-killer fanatic, this blog is full of gory images, research on the missing-persons phenomenon in Australia, and Aussie-slang-laden conjectures as to whether the right person has been caught or whether he is still out there.

CONCEPT : Basé sur une histoire vraie, Wolf Creek raconte les péripéties de trois étudiants insouciants qui ont leur dose d'aventure lors d'une randonnée dans l'arrière-pays australien. Le site imite le suspense du film en plongeant les visiteurs dans des environnements sinistres, tout comme les personnages du film se trouvent dans des situations étranges et de plus en plus effrayantes. Exploitant la tendance de la théorie du complot qu'on trouve sur les blogs, l'agence a aussi réalisé un second site pour le film, nommé thekilleroutback.com.

Ecrit par un fan australien de tueurs en série, le blog est plein d'images sanglantes, d'études sur le phénomène des disparitions de personnes, et d'hypothèses concernant leur cachette et leur capture.

KONZEPT: Wolf Creek basiert auf einer wahren Geschichte von drei unbekümmerten Studenten, die bei ihrem Trekkingurlaub in Australien mehr erleben, als ihnen lieb ist. Die Seite spiegelt die steigende Spannung des Films, indem sie Besucher überraschend in unheimliche Umgebungen versetzt – auf dieselbe Art, in der sich die Filmfiguren in verwirrenden und immer mehr Angst einjagenden Situationen wiederfinden. Im Zuge des Trends von Verschwörungstheorien in Blogs entwickelte Big Spaceship außerdem eine zweite Seite für den Film: thekilleroutback.com.au. Der Blog wurde von einem australischen Serienmörder-Fanatiker geschrieben und ist voll blutiger Bilder und Forschungen über das Missing-Persons-Phänomen in Australien sowie Mutmaßungen in australischem Slang, ob die richtige Person gefasst wurde oder sich der Killer immer noch irgendwo da draußen befindet.

FEATURED ON THE DVD **CAMPAIGN:** Webradio For Everyone! **CLIENT:** Radio Sweden. **YEAR:** 2005. **AGENCY:** Forsman & Bodenfors <www.fb.se>. **PRODUCTION TIME:** 1 month. **WEB DIRECTOR:** Martin Cedergren. **ART DIRECTOR:** Johan Eghammer, Silla Öberg. **COPYWRITER:** Anna Qvennerstedt. **DESIGN/3D:** Lars Jansson, Viktor Larsson, Christofer Beskow. **ACCOUNT EXECUTIVE:** Andreas Engstrand, Hans Andersson. **ACCOUNT MANAGER:** Nicole van Rooij Ekström. **PROGRAMMER:** Thomson. **TECH ASPECTS:** Macromedia Flash. **MEDIA CIRCULATED:** Online ads, radio, poster. **AWARDS:** Eurobest 2005 (Finalist).

CONCEPT: The purpose is to get new listeners, make the audience listen in a new way and inform people that SR now has 15 digital channels on the web. The campaign was up one day on Aftonbladet.se (the largest newspaper in Sweden) and was backed by the Swedish Radio's own site and trailers on SRs FM-broadcast. The number of listeners increased by 400% and over 140,000 downloaded their own desktop radio. The take over ads were live broadcasted and gave each channel its own visual identity. They were also timed and appeared on different times during the day, e.g. the live soccer broadcasting was between 7 pm and 9 pm.

CONCEPT : Attirer de nouveaux auditeurs, changer les habitudes d'écoute du public et l'informer que la radio nationale suédoise possède à présent 15 canaux numériques sur le Net. La campagne a paru par voie de presse dans Aftonbladet, (le plus grand journal de Suède) et a été soutenue par le site officiel de la radio, ainsi que par des annonces sur la bande FM. Le nombre d'auditeurs a augmenté de 400% et plus de 140 000 personnes ont télé-chargé la station. Des annonces supplémentaires ont été diffusées sur les ondes et ont donné à chaque station une identité visuelle propre. Elles ont été diffusées à des heures précises de la journée, par exemple lors de la retransmission en direct de matchs de foot entre 19 et 21 heures.

KONZEPT: Das Ziel bestand darin, neue Hörer zu finden, das Publikum zu einer neuen Art des Hörens zu bewegen und die Leute zu informieren, dass SR nun 15 digitale Kanäle im Web hat. Die Kampagne lief auf Aftonbladet.se (die größte Zeitung Schwedens) und wurde von der Seite des schwedischen Radios und durch auf SR gesendete Trailer unterstützt. Die Höreranzahl stieg um 400%, und über 140 000 Personen luden ihr eigenes Desktop-Radio herunter. Die Spots wurden live gesendet und gaben jedem Kanal seine eigene visuelle Identität. Sie waren außerdem zeitlich festgelegt und erschienen zu verschiedenen Tageszeiten, z.B. wurde das Live-Fußballspiel zwischen 19 und 21 Uhr gesendet.

LARS HEMMING JORGENSEN
CREATIVE DIRECTOR OF LARGE DESIGN

Regular appearances on BBC's 7 O'Clock News, TagesThema on ARD German TV and The Mathew Bannister show on FiveLive has cemented Lars' position as one of the authorities of his industry. With a background in art direction, photography, online strategy and marketing, Lars H. Jorgensen is one of the most interesting characters in the competitive creative arena. His innovative and successful work for dynamic companies such as Agent Provocateur, Bang & Olufsen, YO! Sushi, MTV, AEGON Asset Management and Siemens Mobile attest to his level of dedication and experience.

Lars Jorgensen cames to London via a series of international stopovers and schools, from Iran, London, Jakarta, Luxembourg, Copenhagen, Brussels and finally London again. After studying psychology in Brussels, England's creative environment called, and Lars came to work in design and marketing. Following an MA at the prestigious Hypermedia Research Centre and after meeting his business partner, Jim Boulton, he established Large.

Lars is a Course Director at The Chartered Institute of Marketing and The Chartered Society

of Designers, runs The London eBusiness Club Masterclasses, sits on the board of Scandinavian fashion label Kudo and even performs on the London stand-up circuit – although with slightly different material.

You can have the best website in the world, but if you don't have visitors, you don't have an online side to your business. The online market is by far the most competitive area for companies to enter as cost of entry is low. It's possible for an individual to give the impression of a multinational corporation, which also makes it very exciting. The challenge for big players is then to cement their authority online without being bullish or arrogant.

WE BELIEVE IT IS NO LONGER APPROPRIATE TO DISTINGUISH BETWEEN ONLINE OBJECTIVES AND BUSINESS OBJECTIVES. A WEBSITE IS A BUSINESS TOOL LIKE ANY OTHER AND NEEDS TO MEET BUSINESS OBJECTIVES ACCORDINGLY.

Online brand building therefore not only has to have high impact and constantly re-affirm brand appeal, it also needs to drive the sales process.

Online initiatives that survive and thrive in the challenging environment of the web are those that understand and embrace recognised online behaviour, harnessing these behaviour patterns to the mutual benefit of the brand and the consumer. The aim is not simply to create a great campaign but to develop a strategy that will maximise online exposure

to the brand and fulfil the three fundamental brand objectives:
- to drive frequency (generate traffic)
- to drive conversion (encourage trial & loyalty)
- to drive internal alignment (improve brand clarity & consistency)

Drive frequency

Most companies of any size have a website, most fail because they fail to communicate with the intended audience. It's easy to waste a lot of time, money and energy on a website that looks great but fails to converse with your customers or employees. Developing a great online campaign requires much more than great design and an understanding of technology. It requires a creative and pragmatic approach to thinking about how to exploit technology and maximise its impact. It is vital to leverage technology to realise business benefits.

ONLINE MARKETING INITIATIVES BEGIN BY UNDERSTANDING WHO YOU ARE COMMUNICATING TO AND CONTROLLING THE NARRATIVE FLOW. IT'S VITAL TO UNDERSTAND THAT IF BRAND AWARENESS IS GENERATED THROUGH TV ADVERTISING THEN SUCH THINGS AS 'EASE OF SPELLING' FOR A URL IS ESSENTIAL OR IT HAS TO BE EASY TO FIND ON GOOGLE (WHERE ELSE!).

Other effective efforts when driving traffic is to pro-

ONLINE BRAND BUILDING

duce work, which creates talking points. It's a fact that word-of-mouth is the strongest promotional channel of a new product or service. By creating work which is visually outstanding, intelligent, user-friendly and much more, you are destined to have users talking about it. Not only that, but some of these users will work in media and there's a good chance you'll end up on TV, radio or in the press and then you're suddenly being promoted to an audience of thousands.

Drive conversion

A well-branded service or product is only one half of the transaction equation; the other half is an understanding of the audience. Identifying the characteristics of your customer base will help to determine how to structure content, messages, and design. The object is to develop a detailed and accurate picture of the customer, to ensure the team can adopt a customer, rather than a marketing mindset.
Customer profiles aid marketers throughout the creative process by breaking down the demographic data into information they can easily relate to. The more specific we can be, the more targeted the communication material will be.

BY CREATING A COLLECTION OF PROFILES, WE CAN BEGIN TO "HUMANISE" THE DEMOGRAPHIC DATA AND DEVELOP PERSONALISED STORIES THAT CLEARLY DEFINE THE COMMUNICATION GOALS.

Once these personalities are in place we can then develop the key messages we would like to communicate to each specific audience and use these as concrete reference points for any creative execution.
The average conversion on a website is 1%. Get a lot of traffic but do nothing else and you will increase turnover, but not conversion. However, try to really understand who is responding to your communication and what their needs are and you can see a serious increase in achieving your objectives. The best exercise is to build profiles of your online audience. Knowing things like how often they go online, which sites they visit, their typical online tasks, etc will give you a clear indication of their experience and what they like and dislike.

ANOTHER INTERESTING STATISTIC IS THE FACT THAT 50% OF USERS NEVER GET PAST THE HOMEPAGE. THIS OBVIOUSLY INDICATES THAT HALF OF THE VISITORS DID NOT SEE ANYTHING INTERESTING OR APPEALING ENOUGH TO EVEN CLICK ONCE.

This incredible statistic is surprisingly easy to improve. Users are as diverse as anywhere in the world and therefore it's necessary to segment your audience, ideally to a maximum of 6 segments. The next step is to ensure that you cater for the 6 audiences at the first point of contact. They will then click what appeals to them immediately selecting which segment they fit into themselves and allowing you to give the best messages for this group of people.

Large's viewpoint on creating long-term strategies has changed over the past few years. Before, it was all about controlling the brands and setting up strict guidelines. Although, some brand essence still needs to be maintained it is increasingly much more important to have fresh up-to-date content.

THE BEST WEBSITE IN THE WORLD WILL NOT EVEN BE HALF AS GOOD THE SECOND TIME YOU SEE IT IF IT HASN'T CHANGED. YOU'RE LUCKY IF USERS COME BACK THE THIRD TIME. WHEN ASKING OUR DELEGATES AT THE COURSES WE RUN FOR THE CHARTERED INSTITUTE OF MARKETING, MOST PEOPLE SELECT BBC.CO.UK AS THEIR FAVOURITE SITE. THERE'S ALWAYS SOMETHING NEW WHEN YOU DROP BY.

Successful companies will invest seriously in creating unique content for their online initiatives over the next years and their customer relationships will be stronger and last longer. The world is changing. Are you?

Drive internal alignment

What's the point of having great ideas if you can't agree on them? The critical business issue in building brands is rather astonishingly a lack of internal alignment. We have defined stakeholder input and momentum as 'mission critical' on all of our projects. A significant investment in time is spent on work-

YOU CAN HAVE THE BEST WEBSITE IN THE WORLD, BUT IF YOU DON'T HAVE VISITORS, YOU DON'T HAVE AN ONLINE SIDE TO YOUR BUSINESS.

shops, defining the desired outcomes and establishing a set of criteria by which to evaluate all activities. This ensures rational decisions and evaluation.

Des apparitions régulières aux infos de 19h sur la BBC, à TagesThema sur la chaîne allemande ARD et au Mathew Bannister Show sur la station de radio Five Live ont fait de Lars une autorité reconnue en matière de publicité. Avec une formation initiale en direction artistique, photographie, stratégie en ligne et marketing, Lars H. Jorgensen est l'une des personnalités les plus intéressantes de l'arène créative. Ses travaux novateurs et couronnés de succès pour des sociétés dynamiques comme Agent Provocateur, Bang & Olufsen, YO!Sushi, MTV, Aegon Asset Management et Siemens Mobile attestent de son expérience et de son niveau d'engagement.

Lars Jorgensen est arrivé à Londres après une série d'étapes et d'écoles internationales en Iran, à Londres, à Jakarta, au Luxembourg, à Copenhague et à Bruxelles. Après des études en psychologie à Bruxelles, il a été attiré par le foisonnement créatif de Londres et il est venu travailler dans le design et le marketing. Après une maîtrise au prestigieux Hypermedia Research Centre et après avoir rencontré son partenaire commercial Jim Boulton, il a fondé Large.

Lars H. Jorgensen est directeur d'études au Chartered Institute of Marketing et au Chartered Society of Designers, il dirige les masterclass au London eBusiness Club, siège au conseil d'administration de la société de stylisme scandinave Kudo et se produit aussi sur la scène théâtrale de Londres, dans un registre assez différent.

Vous pouvez avoir le meilleur site du monde, si vous n'avez pas de visiteurs, vous n'augmenterez pas votre activité économique. Le marché Internet est de loin le plus concurrentiel, car le coût d'entrée y est faible. Un simple particulier peut donner l'impression

d'être une entreprise multinationale, et c'est aussi ce qui rend ce média passionnant. Le défi pour les grandes marques est d'affirmer leur position dominante en ligne sans se montrer arrogant ou brutal.

NOUS PENSONS QU'IL N'EST PLUS APPROPRIÉ DE DISTINGUER ENTRE LES OBJECTIFS EN LIGNE ET LES OBJECTIFS D'AFFAIRES. UN SITE INTERNET EST UN OUTIL COMMERCIAL COMME UN AUTRE ET DOIT RÉPONDRE AUX OBJECTIFS STRATÉGIQUES EN CONSÉQUENCE.

La stratégie de marque en ligne doit donc avoir un impact fort et réaffirmer constamment l'attractivité de la marque, tout en générant des transactions commerciales.

Les initiatives en ligne qui survivent et prospèrent dans l'environnement concurrentiel du Net sont celles qui comprennent et reconnaissent les comportements en ligne, et exploitent ces modèles de comportement pour le bénéfice mutuel de la marque et du consommateur. Le but n'est pas seulement de concevoir une bonne campagne, mais de développer une stratégie qui assure une exposition maximale de la marque et remplisse les trois objectifs fondamentaux suivants :

• Encourager la fréquentation (générer du trafic)
• Déclencher la conversion (encourager l'essai et la fidélité)
• Assurer l'alignement interne (améliorer la clarté et la cohérence de la marque)

Encourager la fréquentation

Parmi les entreprises de toutes tailles qui ont un site Internet, la plupart échouent car elles ne réussissent pas à communiquer avec le public désiré. Il est facile de perdre beaucoup de temps, d'argent et d'énergie sur un site qui est esthétique mais qui ne parvient pas à s'adresser aux consommateurs ou aux employés concernés. La réalisation d'une bonne campagne en ligne ne se limite pas à un bon design et une compréhension de la technologie. Elle nécessite

surtout une approche créative et pragmatique afin d'exploiter la technologie et maximiser son impact. Il est essentiel de s'appuyer sur la technologie pour réaliser des bénéfices commerciaux.

SAVOIR À QUI L'ON S'ADRESSE ET CONTRÔLER LE FLUX NARRATIF SONT UN PRÉALABLE AU LANCEMENT D'UN PROJET. IL EST CAPITAL DE COMPRENDRE QUE SI LA NOTORIÉTÉ DE LA MARQUE VIENT D'UNE PUBLICITÉ TÉLÉVISÉE, ALORS SON ADRESSE URL DOIT ÊTRE FACILE À ÉPELER ET ÊTRE RAPIDEMENT REPÉRABLE SUR GOOGLE (OÙ D'AUTRE ?).

Un autre moyen efficace d'attirer la fréquentation est de produire un travail de qualité, ce qui fait parler de vous. Il est avéré que le bouche à oreille est le canal de promotion le plus important pour un nouveau produit ou un nouveau service. En produisant un travail visuellement remarquable, intelligent, chaleureux ou autre, les usagers parleront forcément de vous. Non seulement cela, mais certains de ces usagers travailleront dans les médias et il y a des chances que vous finissiez par être cité dans la presse, sur une chaîne de radio ou de télévision, où vous toucherez tout à coup des milliers de personnes.

Déclencher la conversion

Si la notoriété d'un service ou d'un produit est une variable de l'équation des ventes, l'autre variable est la compréhension du public cible. Identifier les caractéristiques de son groupe de consommateurs aide à structurer le contenu, les messages et le design d'une campagne. Le but est de dresser un portrait détaillé et réaliste du consommateur, afin de s'adapter à celui-ci, plutôt que de lui imposer une vision marketing.

Les profils de consommateurs aident les annonceurs dans le processus créatif en transformant des données démographiques en informations auxquelles ils peuvent se rapporter. Plus on est précis, plus

VOUS POUVEZ AVOIR LE MEILLEUR SITE DU MONDE, SI VOUS N'AVEZ PAS DE VISITEURS, VOUS N'AUGMENTEREZ PAS VOTRE ACTIVITÉ ÉCONOMIQUE.

le matériel de communication sera ciblé.

EN RASSEMBLANT UNE COLLECTION DE PROFILS, ON PEUT COMMENCER À « HUMANISER » LES DONNÉES DÉMOGRAPHIQUES ET DÉVELOPPER DES HISTOIRES PERSONNALISÉES QUI DÉFINISSENT CLAIREMENT LES OBJECTIFS DE COMMUNICATION.

Une fois que ces personnalités sont en place, on peut développer les messages clés que l'on veut transmettre à chaque public spécifique et les utiliser comme des points de références concrets pour toute exécution créative.

La conversion moyenne d'un site Internet est de 1%. Se contenter de bonnes mesures de trafic augmente certes la notoriété, mais pas la conversion. A l'inverse, si l'on essaie de savoir quelle population répond à la communication et quels sont ses besoins, on augmente nettement ses chances d'atteindre ses objectifs. Le meilleur exercice est de dresser le profil de son public en ligne. A quelle fréquence il se connecte, quels sont les sites qu'il visite, quels tâches il accomplit sur le Net etc, donnera une indication précise de son expérience, de ce qu'il aime ou n'aime pas.

UNE AUTRE STATISTIQUE INTÉRESSANTE EST LE FAIT QUE 50% DES USAGERS NE DÉPASSENT JAMAIS LA PAGE D'ACCUEIL. CELA INDIQUE À L'ÉVIDENCE QUE LA MOITIÉ DES VISITEURS N'ONT RIEN VU D'INTÉRESSANT OU DE SUFFISAMMENT ATTRAYANT POUR CLIQUER NE SERAIT-CE QU'UNE FOIS.

Cette incroyable statistique est étonnamment facile à améliorer. Les usagers étant aussi variés que les hommes dans le monde, il est donc nécessaire de segmenter son public, avec un maximum idéal de 6 segments. L'étape suivante est de s'assurer que l'on s'adresse bien aux 6 segments dès le premier point de contact. Les usagers cliqueront alors sur ce qui les attire, sélectionnant immédiatement le segment auquel ils correspondent, ce qui permet de transmettre le meilleur message possible à ce groupe précis.

L'opinion de Large concernant les stratégies à long terme a évolué au cours des dernières années. Auparavant, il s'agissait de gérer les marques et de se poser des directives claires. Bien que la nature de certaines marques ait besoin d'être préservée, il devient de plus en plus important de proposer un contenu actualisé.

LE MEILLEUR SITE DU MONDE SERA DEUX FOIS MOINS BON À VOTRE DEUXIÈME VISITE S'IL N'A PAS ÉVOLUÉ ENTRE-TEMPS. ET VOUS AUREZ DE LA CHANCE SI L'USAGER REVIENT MÊME UNE TROISIÈME FOIS. QUAND NOUS DEMANDONS LEUR AVIS AUX PARTICIPANTS DES COURS QUE NOUS DONNONS AU CHARTERED INSTITUTE OF MARKETING, LA PLUPART CITENT BBC.CO.UK COMME LEUR SITE PRÉFÉRÉ. CAR IL PROPOSE DES NOUVEAUTÉS À CHAQUE VISITE.

Dans les années à venir, les entreprises auront du succès en investissant sérieusement dans le contenu créatif de leur site en ligne, et leur relation avec la clientèle n'en sera que plus durable et plus solide. Le monde évolue. Et vous ?

Assurer l'alignement interne

A quoi sert d'avoir de bonnes idées si elles n'emportent pas l'adhésion ? Le problème critique de la stratégie de marque est, de façon assez surprenante, un manque d'alignement interne. Nous intégrons le dynamisme et la vision des parties prenantes comme élément vital sur tous nos projets. Nous consacrons un temps significatif à la tenue d'ateliers ou nous définissons ensemble les résultats souhaités et établissons un ensemble de critères qui serviront à évaluer toutes les activités. Cela assure des décisions et des évaluations rationnelles.

Regelmäßige Auftritte in den Abendnachrichten der BBC, in den Tagesthemen der ARD und in der Mathew Bannister Show auf FiveLive hat Jorgensens Stellung als eine der Autoritäten der Branche gefestigt. Mit einem Hintergrund in Art Direction, Fotografie, Online-Strategie und Marketing ist Lars H. Jorgensen eine der interessantesten Persönlichkeiten im kreativen Umfeld. Seine innovative und erfolgreiche Arbeit für dynamische Unternehmen wie Agent Provocateur, Bang & Olufsen, YO! Sushi, MTV, AEGON, Asset Management und Siemens Mobile beweisen seinen hohen Grad an Hingabe und Erfahrung.

Lars Jorgensen kam durch eine Reihe internationaler Stationen und Schulen nach London: vom Iran, London, Jakarta, Luxemburg, Kopenhagen, Brüssel und schließlich wieder London. Nach dem Studium der Psychologie in Brüssel folgte er dem Ruf von Englands kreativem Umfeld und arbeitete im Design und Marketing. Nach seinem MA am angesehenen Hypermedia Research Centre und nachdem er seinen Unternehmenspartner, Jim Boulton, kennengelernt hatte, gründete er Large.

Lars Jorgensen ist Kursdirektor am Chartered Institute of Marketing und der Chartered Society of Designers, leitet Meisterklassen im London eBusiness Club, sitzt im Gremium des skandinavischen Modelabels Kudo und tritt sogar im Londoner Stand-up-Theater auf – allerdings mit etwas anderem Material.

Man kann die beste Webseite der Welt haben, aber wenn niemand sie wahrnimmt, ist der Online-Auftritt des Unternehmens fehlgeschlagen. Weil die Kosten niedrig sind, ist der Online-Markt das am härtesten umkämpfte Gebiet für die Selbstdarstellung

MAN KANN DIE BESTE WEBSEITE DER WELT HABEN, ABER WENN NIEMAND SIE WAHRNIMMT, IST DER ONLINE-AUFTRITT DES UNTERNEHMENS FEHLGESCHLAGEN.

von Unternehmen. Ein einziger Mensch kann den Anschein eines multinationalen Konzerns erwecken – was das Ganze auch sehr aufregend macht. Die Herausforderung für große Firmen besteht darin, ihre Autorität online zu demonstrieren, ohne zu selbstsicher oder arrogant zu wirken.

WIR GLAUBEN, DASS ES NICHT LÄNGER ANGEMESSEN IST, ZWISCHEN ONLINEZIELEN UND UNTERNEHMENSZIELEN ZU UNTERSCHEIDEN. EINE WEBSEITE IST EIN UNTERNEHMENSWERKZEUG WIE JEDES ANDERE AUCH UND MUSS DEMENTSPRECHENDE ERFOLGE ERREICHEN.

Markenbildung online muss daher nicht nur eine große Wirkung erzielen und die Marke ständig bestätigen, sondern sie muss auch den Umsatz nach oben treiben.

Online-Initiativen, die in der herausfordernden Umgebung des Netzes überleben und gedeihen, sind solche, die das Online-Verhalten verstehen und zum beidseitigen Nutzen von Marke und Konsument einsetzen. Das Ziel besteht nicht nur darin, eine große Kampagne ins Leben zu rufen, sondern auch, eine Strategie zu entwickeln, die die Publicity einer Marke online maximiert und die folgenden drei grundlegenden Ziele erfüllt:
• Erhöhung der Besucherrate (Verkehr auf der Seite erzeugen)
• Erhöhung der Conversion-Rate (Erprobung & Loyalität anregen)
• interne Einigkeit vorantreiben (Klarheit und Profil der Marke verbessern)

Erhöhung der Besucherrate

Die meisten Firmen, egal, wie groß sie sind, haben eine Webseite. Die meisten scheitern jedoch an der Kommunikation mit ihrer Zielgruppe. Man vergeudet leicht eine Menge Zeit, Geld und Energie auf eine Webseite, die fantastisch aussieht, aber sich nicht mit Kunden oder Mitarbeitern unterhalten kann.

Die Entwicklung einer guten Online-Kampagne erfordert mehr als nur ein großartiges Design und ein Verständnis für die Technologie. Man braucht einen kreativen und pragmatischen Ansatz zum Einsatz der Technologie und der Maximierung ihrer Wirkung. Es ist entscheidend, wie man die Technologie bestmöglich nutzt.

ONLINEMARKETING-INITIATIVEN BEGINNEN DAMIT, ZU VERSTEHEN MIT WEM MAN KOMMUNIZIERT, UND DEN ERZÄHLFLUSS DEMENTSPRECHEND ZU KONTROLLIEREN. WENN DAS BEWUSSTSEIN FÜR EINE MARKE DURCH FERNSEHWERBUNG ERZEUGT WIRD, DANN SIND DINGE WIE EINE EINFACH ZU BUCHSTABIERENDE URL WICHTIG, ODER DASS MAN LEICHT BEI GOOGLE (WO SONST!) GEFUNDEN WIRD.

Eine andere effektive Maßnahme besteht in der Erzeugung von Dingen, über die man spricht. Es ist eine Tatsache, dass Mundpropaganda der stärkste Werbekanal neuer Produkte oder Dienste ist. Wenn man eine Webseite erstellt, die visuell außergewöhnlich, intelligent, benutzerfreundlich und vieles mehr ist, kann man sich sicher sein, dass darüber gesprochen werden wird. Und nicht nur das: Einige der Benutzer arbeiten in den Medien, so dass eine gute Chance besteht, dass man in Fernsehen, Radio oder Presse landet und plötzlich von einem riesigen Publikum promotet wird.

Erhöhung der Conversion-Rate

Gut vermarktete Produkte oder Dienste sind nur die halbe Miete; die andere Hälfte ist das Verstehen des Publikums. Die Identifizierung der Eigenschaften des Kundenstamms verhilft dazu, Inhalt, Botschaften und Design richtig zu strukturieren. Ziel ist es, ein detailliertes und akkurates Bild des Kunden zu entwickeln, um sicherzustellen, dass das Team einen Kunden bedient und keinen Marketer.

Kundenprofile helfen dem Marketing während des kreativen Prozesses, indem sie die demografischen Daten in Informationen übersetzen, auf die sie sich einfach beziehen können. Je spezifischer man sein kann, umso zielgerichteter wird das Kommunikationsmaterial sein.

IST DIESE BASIS ERARBEITET, KANN MAN DIE KERNAUSSAGEN ENTWICKELN, DIE MAN JEDEM SPEZIFISCHEN PUBLIKUM KOMMUNIZIEREN MÖCHTE, UND SIE ALS KONKRETE BEZUGSPUNKTE FÜR JEDWEDE KREATIVE ANWENDUNG VERWENDEN.

Die durchschnittliche Conversion-Rate auf einer Webseite ist 1 %. Herrscht viel Verkehr, aber tut man sonst nichts, wird man den Umsatz erhöhen, aber nicht die Conversion-Rate. Versucht man jedoch, zu verstehen, wer auf die Kommunikation reagiert und welche Bedürfnisse bestehen, erhält man einen starken Anstieg beim Erreichen der Ziele. Die beste Übung besteht darin, Profile des Online-Publikums zu erstellen. Wenn man weiß, wie oft die Benutzer online gehen, welche Seiten sie benutzen, was sie online erledigen etc., erhält man einen klaren Hinweis auf ihre Erfahrungen und das, was sie mögen und nicht mögen.

EINE ANDERE INTERESSANTE STATISTIK IST DIE TATSACHE, DASS 50 % NIE ÜBER DIE STARTSEITE EINE WEBSEITE HINAUS KOMMEN. DIES ZEIGT OFFENSICHTLICH, DASS DIE HÄLFTE DER BESUCHER NICHTS SEHEN, WAS INTERESSANT ODER ANSPRECHEND GENUG WÄRE, UM AUCH NUR EIN EINZIGES MAL WEITERZUKLICKEN.

Diese unglaubliche Statistik lässt sich überraschend einfach verbessern. Benutzer sind so unterschiedlich wie überall auf der Welt; daher ist es notwendig, dass man das Publikum in maximal sechs Segmente unterteilt. Der nächste Schritt besteht darin, sicherzustellen, dass man diesen sechs Gruppen vom ersten Blick an etwas bietet. Sie werden dann sofort das Segment wählen, dass zu ihnen passt und in dem man die besten Botschaften für die jeweilige Gruppe präsentieren kann.

Larges Standpunkt über langfristige Strategien hat sich in den letzten Jahren geändert. Früher ging es um die Kontrolle der Marke und das Festsetzen strenger Regeln. Auch wenn das teilweise noch nötig ist, wird es zunehmend wichtiger, den Inhalt auf dem neuesten Stand zu halten.

festlegt, nach denen alle Aktivitäten bewertet werden. Dies stellt rationale Entscheidungen und Wertungen sicher.

DIE BESTE WEBSEITE DER WELT WIRD NICHT MEHR HALB SO GUT SEIN, WENN SIE SICH BEIM ZWEITEN BESUCH NICHT VERÄNDERT HAT. MAN HAT GLÜCK, WENN JEMAND DIE SEITE EIN DRITTES MAL BESUCHT. WENN WIR DIE BESUCHER UNSERER KURSE, DIE WIR IM CHARTERED INSTITUTE OF MARKETING ABHALTEN, NACH IHRER LIEBLINGSSEITE BEFRAGEN, NENNEN DIE MEISTEN BBC.CO.UK. ES GIBT DORT JEDES MAL ETWAS NEUES ZU SEHEN.

Erfolgreiche Unternehmen werden in den kommenden Jahren viel investieren, um einzigartige Online-Inhalte zu kreieren, und ihre Kundenbeziehungen werden so stärker und halten länger. Die Welt verändert sich. Und Sie?

Interne Einigkeit

Was nützen die besten Ideen, wenn man sich nicht darauf einigen kann? Überraschenderweise liegt der kritische Punkt beim Aufbau von Marken in einem Mangel an interner Übereinkunft. Der Input von Teilhabern ist bei all unseren Projekten eine kritische Angelegenheit. Ein großer Anteil investierter Zeit wird für Workshops verwendet, in dem man die gewünschten Ergebnisse definiert und Kriterien

003

MISCELLANEOUS

CAMPAIGN: Ants: A Pencil Odyssey. **PRODUCT:** One Show 2005 Call for Entries. **CLIENT:** The One Club for Art & Copy. **YEAR:** 2004. **AGENCY:** Dentsu Inc. <www.dentsu.com>. **CREATIVE DIRECTOR:** Hirozumi Takakusaki, Yasuharu Sasaki. **COPYWRITER:** Yasuharu Sasaki. **ART DIRECTOR:** Hirozumi Takakusaki. **DESIGNER:** Yusuke Kitani. **PHOTOGRAPHER:** Kenichiro Tenjinki. **PROGRAMMER:** Hiroki Nakamura, Kampei Baba. **TECH ASPECTS:** Macromedia Flash. **MEDIA CIRCULATED:** Website. **AWARDS:** Cannes Lions 2005 (Silver), tokyo.interactive.ad.awards.jp 2005 (Silver), CLIO Awards 2005 (Silver).

CONCEPT: Ants trying to get to a pencil are used as a metaphor for copywriters and art directors competing for New York's One Show Awards 2005. The website features an interactive game in which a player's ant races to reach One Show's iconic pencil trophy. The journey to the pencil contains many obstacles, some of which may elicit wry smiles from advertising industry insiders.

CONCEPT : Des fourmis essayant d'attraper un crayon sont vues comme le symbole des rédacteurs et directeurs artistiques qui rivalisent pour obtenir une récompense à l'édition 2005 du OneShow de New York. Le site présente un jeu interactif dans lequel une fourmi incarnant le joueur court pour attraper un crayon, trophée iconique de la manifestation. Le trajet qui mène à la victoire est semé d'embûches, dont quelques-unes devraient faire grimacer les professionnels de l'industrie publicitaire.

KONZEPT: Ameisen, die einen Bleistift jagen, werden als Metapher für Texter und Artdirektoren verwendet, die um New Yorks One Show Awards 2005 konkurrieren. Die Webseite enthält ein interaktives Spiel, in dem die Ameise des Spielers in einem Rennen der Bleistifttrophäe der One Show hinterherjagt. Auf dem Weg zum Bleistift gibt es viele Hindernisse – einige werden Insidern der Werbebranche ein Lächeln entlocken ...

CAMPAIGN: AppealNow.com <www.appealNow.com>.   YEAR: 2005.   AGENCY: Nitro London.   PRODUCTION TIME: 2 days.   CREATIVE TEAM: Sandy, Alan Cinnamond.   AWARDS: Cannes Cyber Lions (Gold: Bingo, Kicking).

OBJECTIVES AND RESULTS: To encourage motorists to fight incorrect parking tickets by using the AppealNow.com™ website. The AppealNow.com™ viral ad campaign exceeded my wildest expectations – it was fantastic. As soon as the viral ads were put on our website they got full page coverage in the Evening Standard and were featured on the ITV 6 o'clock and 10 o'clock news. Traffic to the website initially increased by a factor of 3,560% and the website reached a traffic ranking in Alexa of 113,176 out of the several billion websites on the Internet! The AppealNow.com name is now internationally known and according to the latest Google figures there were 174 links to us from websites around the world. On one website which featured one of our viral ads, in a seven day period the viral ad was viewed by no less than 490,000 people! We estimate that at least 4 million people have seen our viral ads. This is an amazing result for a small company like ours and is due to the brilliance of the Great Guns production team and the fantastic actors.

OBJECTIFS ET RÉSULTATS : Encourager les automobilistes à contester les amendes de stationnement abusives grâce au site AppealNow.com™. La campagne virale pour le site a dépassé nos attentes les plus folles, c'était fantastique. Dès la sortie des annonces virales sur le site, on nous a consacré une page entière dans le *Evening Standard* et on nous a cités dans les journaux d'informations de 18h et 22h sur la chaîne ITV 6. La fréquentation du site a d'abord été multipliée par 3,56 % et le site a été classé 113,176 par Alexa, sur plusieurs milliards de sites internet ! Le nom du site AppealNow.com est aujourd'hui mondialement

connu et selon les derniers chiffres de Google, 174 sites répertorient notre lien. Sur l'un des sites hébergeant notre publicité virale, celle-ci a été vue par rien moins que 490 000 personnes en sept jours. Nous estimons qu'au moins 4 millions de personnes ont vu nos annonces. C'est un résultat extraordinaire pour une petite société comme la nôtre, nous la devons au talent des acteurs et à l'équipe de production de Great Guns.

KONZEPT: Ziele und Ergebnisse: Fahrer ermutigen, gegen inkorrekte Strafzettel mit Hilfe der Webseite AppealNow.com™ vorzugehen. Diese virale Anzeigenkampagne übertraf meine wildesten Erwartungen – sie war fantastisch. Sobald die viralen Anzeigen auf unserer Webseite platziert waren, wurden sie ganzseitig im Evening Standard besprochen und in beiden Abendnachrichten auf ITV gesendet. Die Besucherrate auf der Seite stieg um einen Faktor von 3560% an und im Ranking von Alexa stieg sie auf 113 176 – von den Milliarden Seiten im Internet! Der Name AppealNow.com ist nun international bekannt. Nach den neuesten Zahlen von Google führen 174 Links von Webseiten aus aller Welt zu uns. Auf einer Webseite, die eine unserer viralen Anzeigen enthielt, wurde diese innerhalb von sieben Tagen von 490 000 Menschen betrachtet! Wir schätzen, dass mindestens 4 Millionen Menschen unsere viralen Anzeigen gesehen haben. Dies ist ein erstaunliches Ergebnis für ein kleines Unternehmen wie unseres und ist auf die Brillanz des Produktionsteams von Great Guns und die fantastischen Schauspieler zurückzuführen.

FEATURED ON THE DVD **CAMPAIGN:** NZ Army Recruitment <www.army.mil.nz>. **PRODUCT:** Recruitment – Force 9. **YEAR:** 2005. **AGENCY:** Saatchi & Saatchi <www.saatchi.com>. **PRODUCTION TIME:** 6 weeks. **COST IN HOURS OF WORK:** 25 h. **CREATIVE TEAM:** Tom Eslinger, Brian Merrifield. **PROGRAMMER:** David Colqhuhoun. **TECH APSECTS:** Macromedia Flash, sound. **MEDIA CIRCULATED:** A mixture of broad and niche sites were used. The broad reaching media were chosen for their ability to drive reach, awareness of the brand and get the URL in front of people. The niche-targeted media were chosen because they are 'cool' and influential with youth. We allocated 25% of the on-line budget to youth skewed channels eg NZ Girl, Surf, Game Planet, Fantasy Rugby and Modify my Car and 75% to more broad reaching sites such as TradeMe, Hotmail and XtraMSNToday. TV and cinema advertising were also used to drive traffic to the site. **AWARDS:** Axis NZ (Gold), Award AUS (Silver, Bronze), One Show Interactive (3 Finalists), Future Marketing Awards (Finalist).

CONCEPT: Force 9 is an online interactive game that sends players on missions into hostile territory and tests their ability for various Army careers. It was created to educate and attract potential recruits to New Zealand's Army. A series of 4 online banners, derived directly from gameplay, were produced to drive people to the site. **RESULTS:** Over 25,000 click throughs from banner advertising in the first 4 weeks. 79,160 visits and 10,971 registered users in the first three and a half months. A conversion rate of 7.33%, well ahead of the benchmark average of 5% in New Zealand. Hits on the page: 41,152 visits to Force 9 in the first 4 weeks and 5,000 conversions to registration. The Army have been meeting end exceeding in their intake numbers, and anecdotally, the quality of recruits – particularly officers, has improved.

CONCEPT : Force 9 est un jeu interactif en ligne qui envoie les joueurs en mission dans des territoires hostiles et teste leurs aptitudes pour différentes carrières militaires. Il a été conçu pour sensibiliser et attirer des futures recrues dans l'armée néo-zélandaise. Une série de quatre bannières en ligne, dérivées directement du jeu, ont été réalisées pour attirer les gens sur le site. **RÉSULTATS :** Plus de 25 000 clics sur les bannières dans les quatre premières semaines. 79 160 visiteurs et 10 971 visiteurs inscrits dans les trois premiers mois et demi. Un taux de conversion de 7,33%, bien supérieur à la moyenne de référence de 5% en Nouvelle-Zélande. Appels de fichier : 41 152 visites sur Force 9 dans les quatre premières semaines, dont 5 000 nouvelles inscriptions. Les besoins de recrutement de l'armée ont été remplis et même dépassés, et pour l'anecdote, le niveau des officiers recrutés s'est amélioré.

KONZEPT: Force 9 ist ein interaktives Online-Spiel, das Spieler auf Missionen in feindliches Gebiet schickt und ihre Fähigkeit für verschiedene Militärkarrieren testet. Es wurde erstellt, um potenzielle Rekruten für Neuseelands Armee zu informieren und anzuwerben. Eine Reihe von vier Online-Bannern, die direkt vom Spiel abgeleitet waren, wurde produziert, um Leute auf die Seite zu lenken. **ERGEBNISSE:** Über 25 000 Click-Throughs von der Bannerwerbung in den ersten vier Wochen. 79 160 Besuche und 10 971 registrierte Benutzer in den ersten dreieinhalb Monaten. Eine Conversion-Rate von 7,33%, dem Durchschnitt von 5% in Neuseeland weit voraus. Seitenhits: 41 152 Besucher in den ersten vier Wochen und 5000 Konversionen zur Registrierung. Die Anzahl der Neuaufnahmen in die Armee stieg – und es verbesserte sich die Qualität der Rekruten, vor allem der Offiziere.

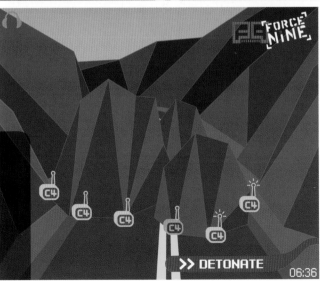

FEATURED ON THE DVD **CAMPAIGN:** AXE Pulse, Germany <www.axe.de>. **YEAR:** 2005. **AGENCY:** AKQA <www.akqa.com>. **PRODUCTION TIME:** 4 months. **CREATIVE TEAM:** James Capp, Laura Grant, Colin Byrne, Miles Unwin, Dan Wood, David Dekker, Steve Clements, Martin Wolfinger, Tony Sears, Tony Unwin. **TECH ASPECTS:** Macromedia Flash, video streams.

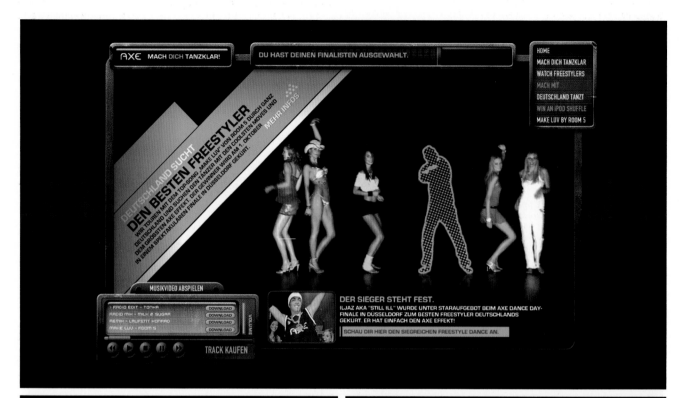

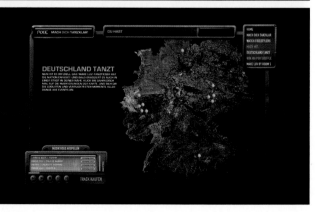

OBJECTIVE: To promote their new Pulse fragrance in Germany, Axe (called Lynx in the UK) launched a nationwide dance competition using videoclips of real guys freestyling to the "Make Luv" track in clubs and city centres. Our challenge was to create a fun, rich and hard-working web presence that would turn a cool idea into a genuine social phenomenon. **STRATEGY:** To impress a tough audience of 15-24 year-old guys, our website used embedded video of specially cast Axe girls, who in turn acted as guides. As an extra incentive, every can of Pulse was issued with a unique code, which guys could enter on the website for a chance to win a limited edition Axe-branded iPod every hour. **SOLUTION:** Axe took cameras, Axe girls and the track across Germany and invited video submissions over the web. Site users cast their votes, and the finalists competed in a televised event in Cologne, in front of an audience of 2,000 people. The site featured over 300 video clips, dynamic league tables and the option to create viral campaigns for favourite dancers. There was also a video dance tutorial from the Axe girls and an interactive map featuring Axe dance events. We also used message boards and club sites to create Dance Mobs (flash mobs to music), attracting groups of up to 500 people to dance in city centres. **RESULT:** The site had video clips of over 300 dancers freestyling to the Axe track. Over 250,000 guys voted. People stayed at the site for an average of over 10 minutes. The Axe Track "Make Luv" got to number 1 in the charts. Through the Dance Mobs, people did the Axe dance in the streets in Germany's five biggest cities over five weeks. Sales of Axe Pulse rose 19%.

OBJECTIF : Pour promouvoir son nouveau parfum Pulse en Allemagne, la marque Axe (qui s'appelle Lynx en Grande-Bretagne) a organisé un concours de danse national accompagné de clips vidéo de jeunes gens improvisant sur le titre « Make Luv » dans les boîtes de nuit et dans les rues. Le défi était de créer une présence en ligne ludique, riche et soutenue qui transformerait une idée sympa en un phénomène de société. **STRATÉGIE :** Pour impressionner un public difficile de garçons de 15-24 ans, le site intégrait une vidéo de jolies danseuses, les filles Axe, qui avaient le rôle d'hôtesses. Comme incitation supplémentaire, chaque vaporisateur de Pulse portait un code numérique unique que l'on tapait sur le site pour gagner toutes les heures un iPod en édition limitée. **SOLUTION :** L'équipe de Axe partit avec des caméras, les danseuses, et la bande audio pour se balader dans tout le pays, tout en encourageant les jeunes à envoyer leurs vidéos sur le site. Les usagers pouvaient voter pour les meilleurs danseurs, et les finalistes s'affrontaient au cours d'un événement télévisé à Cologne, devant un public de 2 000 personnes. Le site présentait plus de 300 clips, un classement dynamique des participants, et la possibilité de créer des annonces vi-

rales pour ses danseurs favoris. Il y avait aussi un tutoriel de danse animé par les danseuses Axe et une carte interactive pour situer les différents compétitions. Nous avons aussi utilisé les forums et les sites de boîtes de nuit pour lancer des Dance Mobs (mobilisation éclair pour danser), attirant des groupes de 500 personnes pour danser dans les centres-ville. **RÉSULTAT :** Le site a réuni des vidéos de plus de 300 danseurs s'exprimant sur le titre de Axe. Plus de 250 000 garçons ont voté. Les visiteurs sont restés en ligne plus de 10 minutes en moyenne. Le titre de Axe, « Make Luv », a été numéro un au hit-parade. Grâce aux Dance Mobs, les jeunes ont dansé dans les rues des cinq plus grandes villes d'Allemagne pendant cinq semaines. Les ventes de Axe ont augmenté de 19%.

ZIEL: Axe veranstaltete zur Promotion seines neuen Deos Pulse einen deutschlandweiten Tanzwettbewerb, bei dem Videoclips verwendet wurden, in denen echte Menschen freestyle zum „Make Luv"-Song in Clubs und Innenstädten tanzten. Unsere Aufgabe war es, eine lustige, starke Webpräsenz zu erstellen, die eine coole Idee in ein soziales Phänomen verwandelte. **STRATEGIE:** Um ein anspruchsvolles Publikum von 15- bis 24-jährigen Männern zu beeindrucken, integrierten wir ein Video mit speziell für Axe gecasteten Mädchen, die als Führerinnen fungierten. Als Extra war jedes Deodorant mit einem einzigartigen Code versehen, den man auf der Webseite eingeben konnte und so die Chance erhielt, jede Stunde einen limitierten iPod mit Axe-Werbung zu gewinnen. **LÖSUNG:** Axe fuhr mit Kameras, Mädchen und dem Song durch Deutschland und lud über das Web zu Video-Einsendungen ein. Seitenbenutzer gaben ihre Stimmen ab, und die Finalisten traten auf einem im Fernsehen ausgestrahlten Event in Köln vor einem Publikum von 2000 Menschen gegeneinander an. Die Seite enthielt über 300 Videoclips, dynamische Liga-Tabellen und die Option, virale Kampagnen für favorisierte Tänzer zu starten. Es gab auch einen Videotanzlehrgang von den Axe-Mädchen und eine interaktive Karte, die auf Tanzevents von Axe hinwies. Außerdem verwendeten wir Message Boards und Clubseiten, um Dance Mobs zu erzeugen (Flash Mobs zu Musik), die Gruppen von bis zu 500 Leuten zum Tanzen in Innenstädte lockten. **ERGEBNIS:** Die Seite erhielt Videoclips von über 300 Tänzern, die freestyle zum Axe-Song tanzten. Über 250 000 Männer wählten. Die Leute blieben durchschnittlich über zehn Minuten auf der Seite. Der Axe-Song „Make Luv" landete auf Platz 1 der Charts. Durch die Dance Mobs tanzten Leute den Axe-Tanz in den Straßen der fünf größten Städte Deutschlands über fünf Wochen lang. Der Verkauf von Axe Pulse stieg um 19%.

FEATURED ON THE DVD **CAMPAIGN:** Clickmore <www.clickmore.com>. **CLIENT:** Unilever. **YEAR:** 2006. **AGENCY:** AKQA <www.akqa.com>. **PRODUCTION TIME:** 4 months. **CREATIVE TEAM:** Colin Byrne, James Capp, Richard Hedges, Michael Austin, Miles Unwin, Sophie Dobson, Sofie Khachik, Ajaz Ahmed, David Wiltshire, William Cookson, Ben Brook, Steven Soloman, Roy James, Emile Swain, Tony Sears, Alia Burley, Emma Witkowski, Abraham Azam, Carlton Shaw. **PROGRAMMER:** Dan Wood, David Dekker, Stephen Clements. **TECH ASPECTS:** Macromedia Flash; Akamai content delivery. **MEDIA CIRCULATED:** TV, outdoor, press, PR, online.

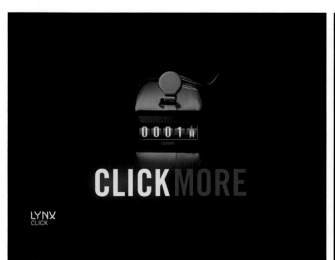
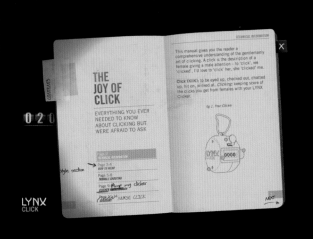

FEATURED ON THE DVD **CAMPAIGN:** Loading. **PRODUCT:** Ariel. **CLIENT:** Procter & Gamble. **YEAR:** 2005. **AGENCY:** Del Campo Nazca Saatchi & Saatchi, Argentina. **ACCOUNT EXECUTIVE:** Andrea Diquez, Carla Paloma Miralles, Verónica Guerra. **CREATIVE DIRECTOR:** Chavo D'Emilio. **COPYWRITER:** Hernán Rebaldería. **ART DIRECTOR:** Daniel Fierro, Pablo Tajer. **DESIGNER:** Mariano Espagnol. **PRODUCTION MANAGER:** Adrián Aspani, Cosme Argerich. **PROGRAMMER:** Mariano Espagnol.

CONCEPT: As Ariel's page loads, dirty garments enter a washing machine on screen. When progress is up to 100%, the garments appear spotless and Ariel's homepage can be entered. **OBJECTIVE:** To transform the loading phase of Ariel's Web Page into a creative peace that relates to washing. A dramatization of the benefits of using Ariel.

CONCEPT : Pendant le chargement de la page d'accueil du site, on voit du linge sale pénétrer dans une machine à laver. Quand la page est entièrement chargée, les vêtements ressortent propres et on peut entrer dans le site. **OBJECTIF :** Transformer le temps de chargement de la page d'accueil en une création relative à la marque. Une illustration des avantages à utiliser Ariel.

KONZEPT: Wenn sich Ariels Seite lädt, wird auf dem Bildschirm schmutzige Wäsche in eine Waschmaschine gesteckt. Sind 100% erreicht, erscheint die Wäsche blitzsauber, und Ariels Homepage kann betrachtet werden. **ZIEL:** Die Ladezeit von Ariels Webseite in ein interaktives Element zu transformieren, das sich auf Waschen bezieht. Eine Dramatisierung der Vorteile von Ariel.

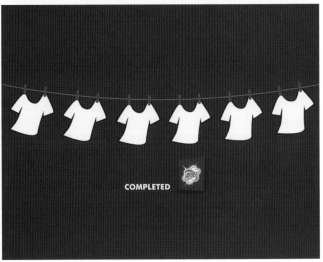

FEATURED ON THE DVD **CAMPAIGN:** Dear Mr B. **PRODUCT:** Systembolaget. **YEAR:** 2005. **AGENCY:** Forsman & Bodenfors <www.fb.se>. **PRODUCTION TIME:** 2 months. **WEB DIRECTOR:** Martin Cedergren. **ACCOUNT EXECUTIVE:** Maria Zachrisson, Hans Andersson. **ACCOUNT MANAGER:** Yara Anttila. **DESIGNER:** Lotta Dolling. **ART DIRECTOR:** Joakim Blondell. **COPYWRITER:** Johan Olivero, Anna Qvennerstedt. **AGENCY PRODUCER:** Charlotte Most, Martin Sandberg. **DIRECTOR:** Tomas Alfredsson. **PROGRAMMER:** B-Reel. **PRODUCER:** B-Reel, Efti. **TECH ASPECTS:** Macromedia Flash. **MEDIA CIRCULATED:** DR, Print, Virals. **AWARDS:** Flash Forward 2006 (Finalist), Favorite Website Award 2005.

CONCEPT: Systembolaget's task – limiting alcohol-related problems in Sweden – is affected by decisions made by the leaders of the European Union in Brussels. So for the 50th anniversary Systembolaget wanted to tell European Commission President José Manuel Barroso how important we think this is and why we have an alcohol monopoly in Sweden. That's why Systembolaget sent him a letter and put an ad in Financial Times. The film is made especially for the net, e.g. different scenes are played random in different versions.

CONCEPT : La mission de Systembolaget, limiter les problèmes dus à l'alcool en Suède, est dépendante des décisions prises par les dirigeants de l'Union Européenne à Bruxelles. Pour son cinquantième anniversaire, Systembolaget voulait expliquer au président de la Commission Européenne José Manuel Barroso l'importance de sa mission et pourquoi la société détient le monopole de la vente d'alcool en Suède. Systembolaget lui a donc écrit

une lettre, et a placé un encart dans le *Financial Times*. Le film a été tourné spécialement pour le Net, différentes versions présentent des scènes qui s'enchaînent suivant un ordre aléatoire.

KONZEPT: Systembolagets Aufgabe – die durch Alkohol entstandenen Probleme in Schweden zu bekämpfen – ist von Entscheidungen der EU in Brüssel betroffen. Daher wollte Systembolaget beim 50. Jubiläum José Manuel Barroso, Präsident der Europäischen Kommission, wissen lassen, für wie wichtig wir dies halten und warum wir in Schweden ein Alkoholmonopol haben. Darum sandte Systembolaget ihm einen Brief und setzte eine Anzeige in die Financial Times. Der Film wurde speziell für das Internet erstellt, z. B. werden verschiedene Szenen in zufälliger Reihenfolge in unterschiedlichen Versionen gezeigt.

FEATURED ON THE DVD **CAMPAIGN:** Fogged Up. **CLIENT:** Buenos Aires Zoo. **YEAR:** 2005. **AGENCY:** Del Campo Nazca Saatchi & Saatchi, Argentina. **ACCOUNT EXECUTIVE:** Pablo Ordoñez, Cecilia Senesi. **CREATIVE DIRECTOR:** Chavo D'Emilio. **COPYWRITER:** Mariano Serkin, Guadalupe Pereira. **ART DIRECTOR:** Javier Lourenco. **DESIGNER/PROGRAMMER:** Denken. **PRODUCTION MANAGER:** Adrián Aspani, Cosme Argerich.

CONCEPT: On the banner, a lion's face can be seen. When rolled over, the lion roars and fogs up the screen with its breath. **SUPER:** Animals very close. Buenos Aires Zoo logo.

CONCEPT : Sur une bannière, apparaît la gueule d'un lion. Quand on la déroule, le lion rugit et son haleine couvre l'écran de buée. **LÉGENDE :** « Les animaux vus de très près ». Puis apparaît le logo du zoo de Buenos Aires.

KONZEPT: Auf dem Banner ist das Gesicht eines Löwen zu sehen. Wenn man mit der Maus darüberfährt, brüllt der Löwe und beschlägt den Bildschirm mit seinem Atem. **DARÜBER:** Tiere ganz nah. Logo Buenos Aires Zoo.

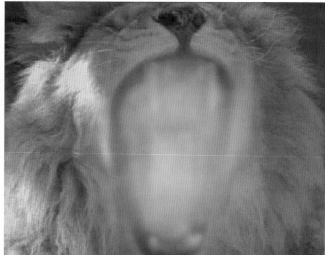

CONCEPT: An E-commerce website doesn't necessarily need to reproduce already established models as market patterns, especially when the focus is on children. The Furry Island website was a promotional initiative for the children's day which became permanent due to its success. All stuffed animals sales were reverted to funds for environmental research in order to preserve endangered species.

CONCEPT : Un site de vente en ligne ne réclame pas forcément que l'on reproduise des modèles déjà existant de schématisation du marché, surtout lorsqu'on vise les enfants. Le site Furry Island est une initiative promotionnelle conçue pour la Journée des Enfants, et qui est devenue pérenne suite à son succès. Les recettes des ventes d'animaux en peluche ont été reversées à des organisations écologiques afin de préserver des espèces en danger.

KONZEPT: Eine E-Commerce-Webseite, die es nicht nötig hat, schon etablierte Modelle als Marktmuster zu reproduzieren, vor allem, wenn der Fokus auf Kinder gerichtet ist. Die Webseite von Furry Island war die Werbeinitiative für den Children's Day, die dank ihres Erfolgs eine ständige Internetpräsenz erhielt. Der gesamte Verkaufserlös der Stofftiere wurde an die Umweltforschung für den Schutz gefährdeter Arten gespendet.

FEATURED ON THE DVD **CAMPAIGN:** FutureReady <www.futureready.org>. **AGENCY:** Tribal DDB Chicago <www.tribalddb.com>. **PRODUCTION TIME:** 2 months (conception to launch). **COST IN HOURS OF WORK:** 2,742 h. **ART DIRECTOR:** Brian Trecka. **COPYWRITER:** Robin Kurzer. **LEAD DESIGN:** Vic Sanchez. **DESIGNER/PROGRAMMER:** Ryan Page. **DESIGNER:** Ryan Wolin. **INFORMATION ARCHITECT:** Cori Stankowicz. **PROGRAMMER:** Scott Boyce. **TECH ASPECTS:** Adobe Illustrator, Adobe Photoshop, Macromedia Flash, Macromedia Dreamweaver, pencil and paper. **MEDIA CIRCULATED:** online banner ads, email blasts, print ads (developed by DDB mainline).

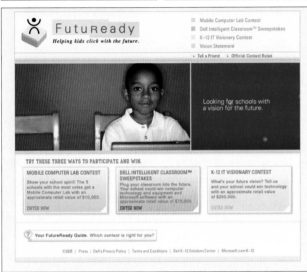

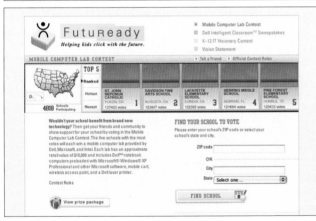

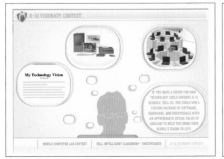
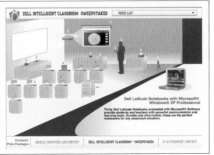

CONCEPT: FutureReady is a collaboration between Dell and Microsoft aimed at helping K-12 schools build 21st Century literate students and increase workforce preparedness. In an effort to create awareness for their vision, Dell and Microsoft launched a promotion providing over $1 million to innovative schools with an eye towards the future of education. Therefore, Tribal DDB created futureready.org, a dynamic, visually engaging site that served as the primary destination for entry into the promotion. More specifically, 3 distinct participation areas of the site included: Mobile Lab Contest: A "popularity contest" of sorts where individuals within the education field could register their school on the site and encourage their peers, students and community to vote online. Schools could track their progress on the site by animated flash trackers that tallied votes in real time and ranked the schools appropriately. Customizable elements and downloads also helped encouraged users to promote their school to victory. The top 5 schools in terms of the most votes won a Mobile Lab. Intelligent Classroom Sweepstakes: A sweepstakes that encouraged individuals in the education field to reach out to their peers and gather their contact info. Schools received one entry per valid contact provided and a random drawing selected 2 winners to receive an Intelligent Classroom for their school. IT Visionary Contest: A contest that encouraged the appropriate individuals within the education field (IT Decision Makers, Tech Savvy Teachers, etc) to share their IT vision for the future. Entries were judged and the top 3 submissions each won $250K to help bring their vision for their school to life. **RESULTS:** In the 2 months the promotion was live over 8,000 schools entered the Mobile Lab contest, over 15,000,000 votes were cast in the Mobile Lab Contest, over 30,000 educators entered the IC Sweepstakes, over 1,500 Essays were submitted to the Technology Vision Contest. Also: Participating schools really used the custom PDFs that we concepted and made available... Search for FutureReady on Google and you'll see examples of how they used them, such as posting the customized PDFs to their own Web sites. Participating schools also came up with inventive, team building exercises like "all night vote-a-thons" and also got the local press to cover their efforts.

CONCEPT : FutureReady est le fruit d'une collaboration entre Dell et Microsoft destiné à aider les écoles K-12 à instruire les élèves du XXIème siècle et former la population active. Afin de sensibiliser le public au projet, Dell et Microsoft ont lancé une opération offrant 1 million de dollars à des écoles novatrices tournées vers l'éducation de l'avenir. Tribal DDB a donc créé futureready.org, un site dynamique au graphisme attrayant qui servait de base pour participer à l'opération. Le site affichait trois domaines de participation distincts. Le « Mobile Lab Contest » : Une espèce de concours de popularité où les professionnels de l'éducation pouvaient inscrire leur école et encourager leurs collègues et leurs étudiants à voter en ligne. Les écoles pouvaient suivre leur progression sur le site grâce à des indicateurs qui comptaient les voix en temps réel et effectuaient le classement approprié. Des éléments personnalisés à télécharger encourageaient les usagers à mener leur école à la victoire. Les cinq premières écoles en terme de nombre de voix gagnaient un laboratoire informatique tout équipé. Le « Intelligent Classroom Sweepstakes » : Une loterie qui encourage les professionnels de l'éducation à communiquer avec leurs pairs et mettre leurs contacts en commun. Les écoles recevaient un bulletin pour chaque contact validé et un tirage au sort sélectionnait deux gagnants qui remportaient un ensemble complet d'ordina-teurs, de logiciels et d'imprimantes pour leur école. Le « IT Visionary Contest » : Un concours qui encourage les professionnels (responsables de programmes, enseignants spécialisés et autres) à partager leur vision des technologies de l'information. Les participants étaient évalués et les trois meilleurs candidats recevaient chacun 250 000 dollars pour réaliser leur projet au sein de leur école. **RÉSULTATS :** Pendant les deux mois de l'opération, plus de 8 000 écoles ont participé au concours du « Mobile Lab ». Plus de 15 000 000 votes ont été enregistrés dans cette section, plus de 30 000 éducateurs ont participé à la loterie « IC », et plus de 1 500 mémoires ont été soumis au concours « IT Visionary ». Les écoles candidates ont fait un large usage des fichiers PDF que nous leur avons fournis. Si vous tapez le nom du site sur Google, vous pourrez avoir un aperçu de la façon dont ils les ont utilisés, en les intégrant par exemple à leurs propres sites internet. Les écoles ont également conçu des exercices de groupe inventifs, comme le « votathon », et ont amené la presse locale à s'intéresser à leurs efforts.

KONZEPT: FutureReady ist eine Kollaboration zwischen Dell und Microsoft, die darauf abzielt, K-12-Schulen zu helfen, gebildete Schüler für das 21. Jahrhundert auszubilden und die Bereitschaft zur Berufstätigkeit zu erhöhen. In dem Bemühen, ein Bewusstsein für ihre Vision zu erzeugen, stellten Dell und Microsoft in einer Werbeaktion über 1 Million US $ für innovative Schulen mit einem Auge auf die Zukunft der Bildung bereit. Daher erstellte Tribal DDB futureready.org, eine dynamische, visuell einnehmende Webseite, die als Startpunkt für die Teilnahme an der Promotion diente. Drei unterschiedliche Teilnahmebereiche der Seite enthielten: Mobile Lab Wettbewerb: eine Art „Beliebtheitswettbewerb", bei dem Personen aus dem Bildungsumfeld ihre Schule auf der Seite registrieren konnten und ihre Freunde, Schüler und die Gemeinde aufforderten, online für die Schule zu stimmen. Schulen konnten den Verlauf auf der Seite mit animierten Flash-Trackern verfolgen, die Stimmen in Echtzeit zählten und die Schulen entsprechend einordneten. Nach eigenem Wunsch gestaltbare Elemente und Downloads ermutigten Benutzer, für ihre Schule zu werben. Die fünf Schulen, die die meisten Stimmen erhielten, gewannen ein Mobile Lab. Intelligentes Klassenzimmer-Lotto: ein Lotto, das Personen im Bildungsbereich anspornte, Kontaktdaten von Freunden zu sammeln. Pro gültigem Kontakt erhielten Schulen einen Eintrag, und eine Zufallsziehung wählte zwei Gewinner aus, die ein Intelligentes Klassenzimmer für ihre Schule erhielten. IT Visionary Wettbewerb: Ein Wettbewerb, der entsprechende Personen aus dem Bildungsumfeld (IT-Fachleute, Lehrer mit Computererfahrung etc.) aufforderte, ihre IT-Vision für die Zukunft darzulegen. Eingereichte Visionen wurden beurteilt, und die drei Besten gewannen jeweils 250 000 $, damit sie ihre Vision für ihre Schule realisieren konnten. **ERGEBNISSE:** Innerhalb der zweimonatigen Werbeaktion nahmen über 8000 Schulen am Mobile Lab-Wettbewerb teil, über 15 000 000 Stimmen wurden gezählt, über 30 000 Lehrer nahmen am Lotto teil, über 1500 Essays wurden eingereicht. Außerdem verwendeten die teilnehmenden Schulen tatsächlich die von uns konzipierten PDFs. Gibt man FutureReady bei Google ein, sieht man Beispiele dafür, wie sie verwendet wurden, z. B. die Einbindung der PDFs in ihre eigenen Webseiten. Teilnehmende Schulen erstellten außerdem erfindungsreiche, teamfördernde Übungen. In lokalen Zeitungen wurde darüber berichtet.

CAMPAIGN: Interactive Salaryman <www.interactive-salaryman.com>. **YEAR:** 2004. **AGENCY:** Dentsu Inc. <www.dentsu.com>. **CREATIVE DIRECTOR:** Naoto Oiwa, Yasuharu Sasaki. **ART DIRECTOR:** Yusuke Kitani. **COPYWRITER:** Yasuharu Sasaki. **PROGRAMMER:** Hiroki Nakamura. **TECH ASPECTS:** Macromedia Flash. **MEDIA CIRCULATED:** Website. **AWARDS:** One Show Interactive 2005 (Gold), CLIO Awards 2005 (Bronze).

CONCEPT: A self promotional website showcasing Dentsu's award-winning creative work in the interactive field. The site also introduces Dentsu's top interactive creators.

KONZEPT: Eine Webseite mit Eigenwerbung, die Dentsus preisgekrönte kreative Arbeit auf dem interaktiven Gebiet darstellt. Sie zeigt außerdem Dentsus beste interaktive Schöpfer.

CONCEPT : Un site d'auto-promotion présentant le travail créatif largement primé de l'agence Dentsu, dans le domaine interactif. Le site présente aussi les meilleurs créatifs de l'agence dans la discipline.

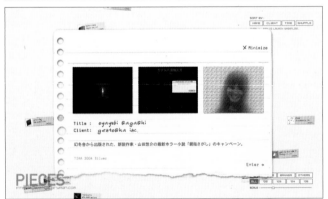

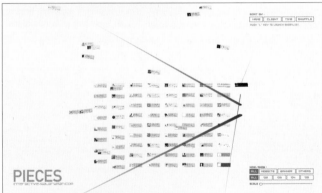

FEATURED ON THE DVD **CAMPAIGN:** Kudo launch <www.kudo.dk>. **YEAR:** 2004. **AGENCY:** Large <www.largedesign.com>. **PRODUCTION TIME:** 3 weeks. **COST IN HOURS OF WORK:** 80 h. **CREATIVE TEAM:** Lars Hemming Jorgensen, Jim Boulton, Rene Christoffer. **PROGRAMMER:** Jesper Lycke, Martin Whitely. **TECH ASPECTS:** Macromedia Flash.

CONCEPT: An uncomplicated Flash experience to provide Kudo with a platform for launching in Europe. **RESULTS:** A very successful European launch with 300% increase in Kudo visitors at the bi-annual Copenhagen International Fashion Fair.

CONCEPT : Une simple expérience en Flash offrant une plateforme pour le lancement de Kudo en Europe. **RÉSULTATS :** Un lancement très réussi en Europe avec une hausse de 300% de visiteurs au rendez-vous semestriel de l'International Fashion Fair de Copenhague.

KONZEPT: Eine unkomplizierte Flash-Seite, die Kudo eine Plattform für ihre Einführung in Europa bietet. **ERGEBNISSE:** Ein sehr erfolgreicher europäischer Launch, mit einem Besucheranstieg von 300% bei Kudo auf der Internationalen Modemesse in Kopenhagen.

CAMPAIGN: IPEX Bra. YEAR: 2005. AGENCY: Firstborn <www.firstbornmultimedia.com>. PRODUCTION TIME: 2,5 months. COST IN HOURS OF WORK: 300 h. PRODUCER: Luba Shekhter, Firstborn. CREATIVE TEAM: Zo Bjorgvinsson, Miles McManus (Victoria's Secret); Vas Sloutchevsky, Joon Yong Park (Firstborn). PROGRAMMER: Joon Yong Park. TECH ASPECTS: Macromedia Flash, audio, video. MEDIA CIRCULATED: Victoria's Secret website.

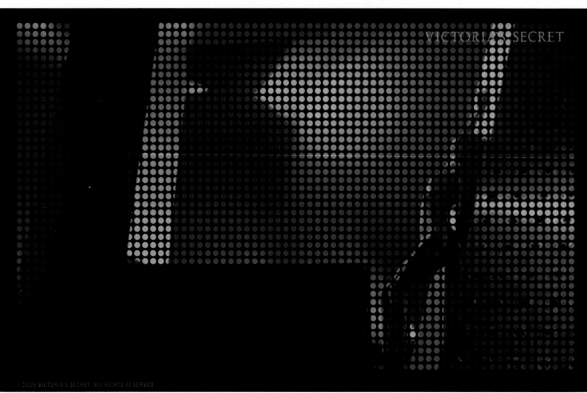

CONCEPT: To support the launch of its revolutionary bra, IPEX, Victoria's Secret approached Firstborn to design and develop an all-Flash interactive mini-site all about the new bra. The look and feel of the site, which lives in a pop-up, reflected the beautiful and sensual campaign imagery and incorporated the scientifically-charged elements of IPEX. Having previously worked on projects such as the Blue London Jeans website and Pink landing page, Firstborn was thrilled at the opportunity to once again join forces with Victoria's Secret's dedicated Internet team. **RESULTS:** The launch of the IPEX bra was a major success for Victoria's Secret, it was accompanied by large billboards, TV spots, and magazine spreads. This interactive campaign educated the consumer and emphasized the importance of technology.

CONCEPT : Pour soutenir le lancement de son soutien-gorge révolutionnaire, IPEX, la marque Victoria's Secret a chargé Firstborn de concevoir et développer un mini-site interactif en format Flash. L'apparence du site, concentré dans une fenêtre *pop-up*, reflète l'imagerie élégante et sensuelle de la campagne, tout en incorporant les caractéristiques « scientifiques » de l'IPEX. Ayant déjà travaillé sur des projets comme le site du Blue London Jeans et celui de Pink, nous avons été ravis d'avoir l'occasion de collaborer à nouveau avec l'équipe passionnée de Victoria's Secret. **RÉSULTATS :** Le lancement du soutien-gorge IPEX a été un énorme succès pour la marque, il s'est accompagné d'une campagne d'affichage, de spots télé, et d'encarts magazine. Cette campagne interactive informait sur le produit en soulignant l'importance de la technologie.

KONZEPT: Um die Einführung ihres revolutionären BHs IPEX zu unterstützen, beauftragte Victoria's Secret Firstborn damit, eine interaktive Flash-Minisite darüber zu entwerfen und zu entwickeln. Der Look der in einem Pop Up befindlichen Seite reflektierte die schöne und sinnliche Bilderwelt der Kampagne und verkörperte die wissenschaftlichen Elemente von IPEX. Firstborn hatte vorher an Projekten wie der Webseite von Blue London Jeans gearbeitet und war begeistert, nochmal die Gelegenheit zu bekommen, mit Victoria's Secrets engagiertem Internet-Team arbeiten zu können. **ERGEBNISSE:** Der Launch des IPEX-BH war für Victoria's Secret ein großer Erfolg. Er wurde von großen Werbeplakaten, Fernsehspots und Magazinwerbung begleitet. Die interaktive Kampagne informierte den Kunden und betonte die Wichtigkeit der Technologie.

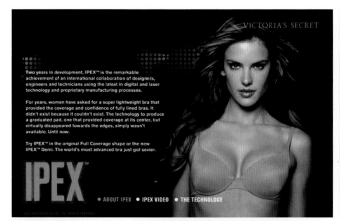

FEATURED ON THE DVD **CAMPAIGN:** Autumn EHT & Nursery. **PRODUCT:** John Lewis Direct. **YEAR:** 2005. **AGENCY:** Agency.com <www.agency.com>. **COST IN HOURS OF WORK:** 857 h. **CREATIVE TEAM:** Adrian Peters, David Wellington. **PROGRAMMER:** Perry Cooper, Paul Collins. **MEDIA CIRCULATED:** Bounty.com; iVillage.com; Junior.com; TimesOnline.com; MSN.co.uk. **SOUND DESIGNER:** James Widegren. **TECH ASPECTS:** Macromedia Flash, video, sound. **AWARDS:** IAB Creative Showcase; Eurobest 2005 (Bronze).

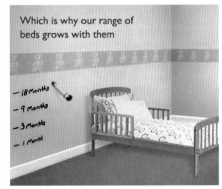

CHALLENGE: To create a new, innovative campaign for JohnLewis.com, targeting time-poor ABC1 men and women with products from: 1. Nursery and 2. Electrical & Home Technology. This was John Lewis Direct's first foray into using rich media. To drive acquisition as well as promote customer retention and loyalty. To inspire new customers to consider JohnLewis.com and attract existing customers to shop online. **SOLUTION:** We created two highly innovative campaigns bringing the product ranges to life for the audiences. We created bespoke video footage: the "Nursery Furniture" execution uniquely uses video and the overlay shows a baby sitting in the centre of your screen. He picks up and plays with a pop-up box which reads: "We know how playful babies can be. That's why our nursery range of furniture is built to last." This plays to John Lewis' reputation of understanding their customers' needs. As the baby shakes the pop-up box the words tumble and fall out of place. Another key element of the online campaign is the invitation to interact with the units via simple, yet powerful concepts which highlight JohnLewis.com's range, quality, and expert knowledge with a human touch. The executions include: marking the age of your child on the wall to visually show what the size bed they need; taking a shot with a digital camera which then prints the image through a range of digital printers. All the executions push the limits of the medium to promote high levels of engagement and interaction with consumers. **RESULTS:** Primary Performance Indicators. 49% average click-through-rate (CTR) achieved for the "Nursery Furniture" overlay. Ad impressions were 18% higher than anticipated for the overall campaign. The campaign achieved 402% higher traffic to the site than planned. Secondary Performance Indicators. Achieved return on investment of 50%.

DÉFI : Imaginer une nouvelle campagne innovante pour John Lewis, visant les hommes et les femmes pressés des classes moyennes et supérieures. La boutique propose des produits de puériculture, et des appareils électroménager et technologiques. C'était la première incursion de John Lewis dans le *rich media*. Le but était d'encourager les ventes ainsi que la fidélité des clients. Nous devions amener les clients potentiels à envisager JohnLewis. com et attirer les clients existants vers la boutique en ligne. **SOLUTION :** Nous avons conçu deux campagnes très innovantes afin de présenter la gamme de produits au public. Une vidéo faite sur mesure, le module « Mobilier enfant » utilise la vidéo de façon unique, et le fond de page montre un bébé assis au centre de l'écran. Il ramasse et joue avec un carré *pop-up* où est inscrit : « Les bébés sont joueurs. C'est pourquoi notre mobilier a été conçu pour durer ». Le message exploite la réputation de la marque quant à sa compréhension des désirs de sa clientèle. Quand le bébé secoue le carré, les mots dégringolent et s'éparpillent. Un autre élément important de la campagne est l'invitation à interagir avec les modules via des concepts simples mais puissants qui soulignent la variété des produits de la marque, leur qualité et leur technicité, avec une touche de chaleur humaine. Parmi les exécutions proposées : une toise virtuelle qui indique la dimension du lit adaptée à votre enfant, et un appareil numérique qui prend une photo et l'imprime différemment selon l'imprimante choisie. Toutes les exécutions repoussent les limites du support et encouragent un haut niveau d'engagement et d'interaction avec le consommateur. **RÉSULTATS :** Indice principal : 49% en moyenne de taux de clics pour le module « Mobilier enfant ». Le nombre de pages vues a été de 18% supérieur aux prévisions pour toute la campagne. La campagne a généré un taux de fréquentation du site supérieur de 402% aux prévisions. Indice secondaire : Retour sur investissement de 50%.

AUFGABE: Eine neue, innovative Kampagne für JohnLewis.com für die Zielgruppe von ABC1-Männern und -Frauen mit Zeitmangel zu entwickeln, mit Produkten aus: 1. Kinderzimmer und 2. Elektronik & Heimtechnologie. Dies war John Lewis' erster Ausflug in die Verwendung von Rich Media. Es sollte sowohl Akquise betrieben als auch die Beibehaltung von Kunden und ihrer Loyalität gefördert werden. Neue Kunden sollten JohnLewis.com in Erwägung ziehen, und existierende Kunden sollten vom Online-Einkauf überzeugt werden. **LÖSUNG:** Wir entwickelten zwei extrem innovative Kampagnen, die die Bandbreite der Produkte für das Publikum zum Leben erweckten. Wir erstellten maßgeschneidertes Videomaterial: Die „Kinderzimmermöbel"-Ausführung verwendet ein Video, und das Overlay zeigt ein Baby, das in der Mitte des Bildschirms sitzt. Es spielt mit einer Pop-Up-Box, auf der steht: „Wir wissen, wie spielfreudig Babys sein können. Deshalb halten unsere Kinderzimmermöbel viel aus." Dies entspricht dem Ruf von John Lewis, die Bedürfnisse der Kunden zu verstehen. Wenn das Baby die Box schüttelt, wackeln und verschieben sich die Worte. Ein weiteres Schlüsselelement der Online-Kampagne ist die Einladung, mit den Einheiten zu spielen – durch simple, aber starke Konzepte, die JohnLewis.coms Auswahl, Qualität und Fachwissen mit menschlicher Note betonen. Die Ausführungen schließen Folgendes ein: Das Alter des Kindes wird auf der Wand markiert, um visuell zu zeigen, wie groß das Bett sein muss; ein Foto kann mit einer Digitalkamera geschossen werden, die das Foto mit mehreren digitalen Druckern druckt. Alle Ausführungen gehen an die Grenzen des Mediums, um einen hohen Level an Einbeziehung und Interaktion der Kunden zu gewährleisten. **ERGEBNISSE:** Primäre Leistungsindikatoren. 49% durchschnittliche Click-Through-Rate (CTR) für den „ Kinderzimmermöbel-Overlay. Die Ad Impressions waren um 18% höher, als es für die gesamte Kampagne erwartet wurde. Sie erzielte einen Verkehr, der um 402% höher war als geplant. Sekundäre Leistungsindikatoren. Erreichter ROI: 50%.

Find an MP3 player to store your music collection

Apple iPod shuffle 512MB

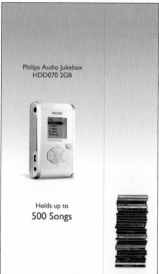

Holds up to
240 Songs

▲
drag

▲
drag

Philips Audio Jukebox HDD070 2GB

Holds up to
500 Songs

Apple Mini Ipod 4GB

Holds up to
1,000 songs

Creative Zen Micro MP3 Player 5GB

Holds up to
1,250 songs

Sony MP3 Walkman NW-HD5 20GB

Holds up to
5,000 songs

Apple iPod Photo 60GB

Holds up to
15,000 songs

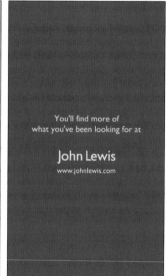

You'll find more of
what you've been looking for at

John Lewis

www.johnlewis.com

Click to take a picture

Epson Stylus Printer, C66

High Resolution Printing

HP Deskjet Printer, 3845

Compact and Quiet

HP All-In-One Printer, PSC1610

A4 Borderless Printing

Click here to find the perfect printer

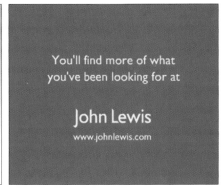

You'll find more of what you've been looking for at

John Lewis

www.johnlewis.com

If you're looking for a laptop

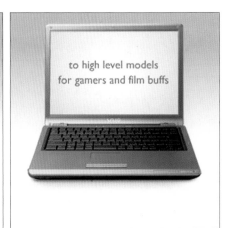

We've got entry level models for email and internet users

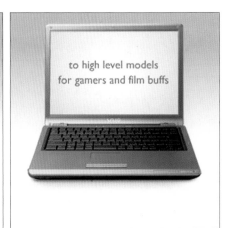

to high level models for gamers and film buffs

You'll find more of what you've been looking for at

John Lewis

www.johnlewis.com

Including a 90 day free helpline for all desktop and laptop computers.

FEATURED ON THE DVD **CAMPAIGN:** Jonathan Meese "Képi blanc – nackt". **PRODUCT:** Schirn Kunsthalle Frankfurt: exhibition Jonathan Meese "Képi blanc – nackt". **YEAR:** 2004. **AGENCY:** Neue Digitale <www.neue-digitale.de>.
PRODUCTION TIME: December 2005 – March 2004. **CREATIVE TEAM:** Olaf Czeschner, Bejadin Selimi. **PROGRAMMER:** Bejadin Selimi. **TECH ASPECTS:** Macromedia Flash, Quicktime Player. **MEDIA CIRCULATED:** Internet.
AWARDS: Mobius Awards 2005 (Silver), ADC Deutschland 2005 (Bronze), Epica 2004 (Bronze), The New York Festival 2004 (Silver), London International Advertising Award (Finalist).

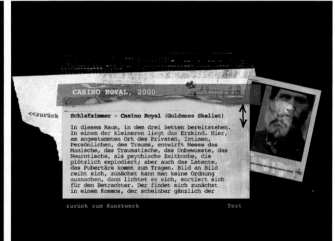

CONCEPT: Meese's pseudo-psychotic universe is a flood of pictures, texts, figures and their attitudes. Whether film, radio, TV program, or history book: nobody featuring in one of these seems to be safe from becoming part of his installations. Creating a concomitantly interactive and informative experience of the Exhibition: Képi blanc, nackt (White Cap, Naked) by internationally renowned artist Jonathan Meese, which could be seen from 16 January to 12 April 2004 in one of Germany's most renowned exhibition institutions. NEUE DIGITALE has created a multimedia cosmos for the artist Jonathan Meese and his exhibition: on the Internet and with terminals that were situated in Schirn Kunsthalle Frankfurt. The user can look at the different rooms of photos and exhibits. The application is programmed completely in Macromedia-Flash. This ensures an atmosphere of dynamic and contagious animation. NEUE DIGITALE has also used the techniques of Quicktime Player to show the different rooms of the exhibition. The user gets the chance to see everything in a quasi-realistic way. **RESULTS:** Just like the German Artist himself, the application should also provoke and polarize the audience. It uses characteristics – like a fibrillation and a swoosh that makes the new media appear imperfect.

CONCEPT : L'univers pseudo-psychotique de Jonathan Meese est un flot d'images, de texte et de personnages en action. Qu'ils soient tirés de films, d'émissions radio et télévisées ou de manuels d'histoire, aucun des personnages n'est à l'abri de figurer dans ses installations. Nous avons conçu une expérience à la fois pédagogique et interactive de l'exposition « Képi blanc, nackt » de l'artiste mondialement réputé Jonathan Meese, qui s'est tenue du 16 janvier au 12 avril dans l'une des galeries d'art les plus renommées d'Allemagne. Neue Digitale a réalisé un univers multimédia pour l'artiste et son exposition, sur internet et sur des bornes installées au Schirn Kunsthalle de Francfort. L'usager peut visiter les différentes salles d'exposition, et admirer photos et autres œuvres. L'application est entièrement programmée en Flash Macromedia, ce qui assure le caractère dynamique de l'ambiance et de l'animation. Neue Digitale a également utilisé le format Quicktime pour montrer les différentes pièces. L'internaute peut ainsi visiter l'exposition de façon quasi-réaliste. **RÉSULTATS :** Tout comme l'artiste allemand lui-même, l'application doit provoquer et polariser le public. L'utilisation supplémentaire d'un effet de fibrillation et de sifflement contribue à faire apparaître le support imparfait.

KONZEPT: Meeses pseudo-psychotisches Universum ist eine Flut von Bildern, Texten, Figuren und deren Verhalten. Ob Film, Radio, Fernsehprogramm oder Geschichtsbuch: Niemand, der in einem dieser Medien vorkommt, ist sicher davor, Teil seiner Installationen zu werden. Ein interaktives und informatives Erlebnis der Ausstellung sollte entwickelt werden: „Képi blanc, nackt" des international bekannten Künstlers Jonathan Meese, die vom 16. Januar bis zum 12. April in einer von Deutschlands bekanntesten Ausstellungshallen zu sehen war. NEUE DIGITALE erstellte für den Künstler und seine Ausstellung einen Multimedia-Kosmos: im Internet und mit Terminals in der Schirn Kunsthalle Frankfurt. Der Betrachter kann sich die verschiedenen Räume mit Fotos und Ausstellungsstücken ansehen. Die gesamte Anwendung wurde mit Macromedia-Flash programmiert, wodurch eine Atmosphäre von dynamischer und ansteckender Animation entsteht. NEUE DIGITALE verwendete außerdem die Technik des Quicktime-Players, um die Ausstellungsräume zu zeigen. Der Benutzer kann alles auf quasi realistische Art sehen. **ERGEBNISSE:** Wie der deutsche Künstler selbst, sollte die Anwendung das Publikum provozieren und polarisieren. Sie verwendet Effekte wie Flimmern und Rauschen, die das neue Medium unperfekt erscheinen lassen.

FEATURED ON THE DVD **CAMPAIGN:** Kid Cupid V-Day Game <http://domanistudios.com/kidcupid>. **YEAR:** 2005. **AGENCY:** Domani Studios <www.domanistudios.com>. **TECH ASPECTS:** Flash AS 2.0, audio, XML. **MEDIA CIRCULATED:** Banner placements. **AWARDS:** Step Magazine's Interactive Annual, How Magazine Interactive Annual.

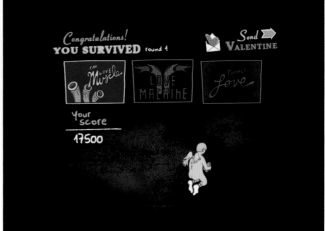

CONCEPT: Create an original interactive Game and e-Card pair that allow users to send Valentine's Day Cards that transform into playable online games. **RESULTS:** This Viral marketing piece was really effective. We received over 100,000 UNIQUE visitors in less than 7 Days. Not bad for a small-ish interactive shop. We created a 3D space in flash that gave the game depth while the illustrations put a smile of users faces.

CONCEPT : Créer une carte postale électronique et un jeu interactif qui permettent aux usagers d'envoyer une carte de Saint-Valentin qui se transforme en jeu en ligne. **RÉSULTATS :** Cette annonce de marketing viral s'est avérée très efficace. Nous avons reçu plus de 100 000 visiteurs uniques en moins de 7 jours. Ce n'est pas mal pour une minus-cule boutique en ligne. Nous avons conçu un espace 3D en Flash qui donnait de la profondeur au jeu tandis que les illustrations apportaient le sourire aux usagers.

KONZEPT: Ein originelles interaktives Spiel und eine E-Card erstellen, mit denen Benutzer Valentinskarten verschicken können, die sich in Online-Spiele verwandeln. **ERGEBNISSE:** Dieses virale Marketing war sehr effektiv. Wir erhielten über 100 000 Besucher in weniger als sieben Tagen – nicht schlecht für einen relativ kleinen interaktiven Shop. Wir entwickelten einen 3D-Raum in Flash, der dem Spiel Tiefe verlieh, während die Illustrationen die Spieler zum Schmunzeln bringen.

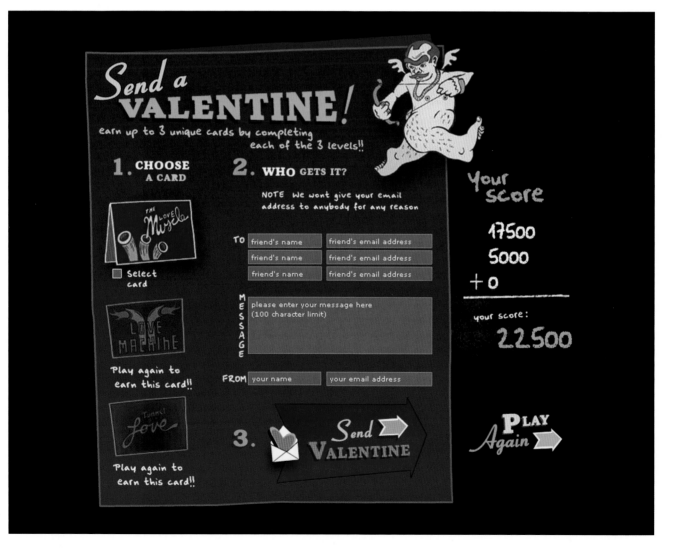

CAMPAIGN: Exo-Force <www.exo-force.co.uk>. PRODUCT: LEGO Exo-Force. YEAR: 2006. AGENCY: Large <www.largedesign.com>. PRODUCTION TIME: 4 weeks. COST IN HOURS OF WORK: 80 h. PRODUCER: Elizabeth Rankich. CREATIVE TEAM: Lars Hemming Jorgensen, Stephen Shaw, Steffen List. PROGRAMMER: Jesper Lycke. TECH ASPECTS: Macromedia Flash, video footage from Exo-Force promo. MEDIA CIRCULATED: Carat.

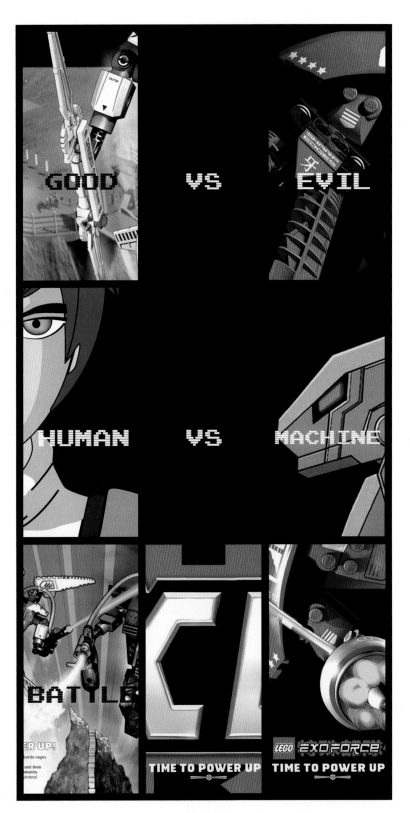

CONCEPT: Vying for control of the planet, an exiled group of humans fight for their existence against malicious renegade robots, intent on destroying the human mountain stronghold. The banner ads appeal to action-hungry young teens who are love LEGO, but need more game experience from their toy purchases

CONCEPT : Rivalisant pour le contrôle du monde, un groupe d'humains exilés luttent pour survivre contre de méchants robots rebelles, désireux de détruire la forteresse des humains. La bannière s'adresse aux enfants amateurs de LEGO qui ont soif d'action, et qui veulent plus d'aventure dans leur achat de jouets.

KONZEPT: Eine ausgeschlossene Gruppe von Menschen kämpft um ihre Existenz und Kontrolle über den Planeten gegen böse abtrünnige Roboter, die die menschliche Hochburg zerstören wollen. Die Bannerwerbung zielt auf Action-hungrige junge Teenager ab, die LEGO lieben, aber noch mehr Anregungen für das Spielen mit Einkäufen brauchen.

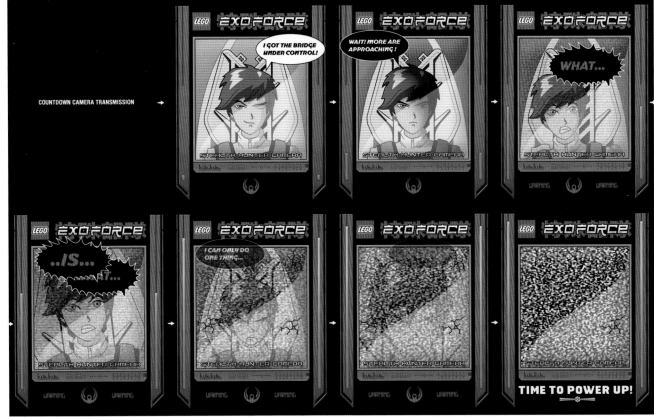

FEATURED ON THE DVD **CAMPAIGN:** MadeinMTL.com <www.madeinmtl.com>. **YEAR:** 2005-2006. **AGENCY:** BlueSponge <www.bluesponge.com>, Locomotion <www.locomotionfilms.com>. **PRODUCTION TIME:** 2 years (versions 1.0 and 2.0). **COST IN HOURS OF WORK:** 5,312 hours (since January 2005) + 10,000 hours (before January 2005). **PRODUCER:** Fady Atallah (BlueSponge), Nicolas Fonseca (Locomotion). **CREATIVE DIRECTOR:** Ralph Dfouni. **DIRECTOR:** Mouna Andraos, Marian Kolev. **PROJECT MANAGER:** Jean Doat, Marc Dfouni. **ARTISTIC DIRECTOR:** Kevin Kit Lo (based on an original design by Valérie Picard). **EDITOR:** Sébastien Tétreault, Marie-Ève Brisson. **CONTENT MANAGER:** Isabelle Charbonneau, Émilie Grenier. **COPYWRITER:** Guillaume Blanchet, Melora Koepke, Alexandra Mcintosh, Esther Pilon, Craig Silverman, John W. Stuart. **SOUND:** DJ Chrystelle. **MUSIC:** Régine Chassagne, Maxime Morin-Champion, Patrick Watson. **PHOTO:** Norma Nixon, Brigitte Henry. **TECHNICAL DIRECTOR:** Octavian Mihai, Oscar Garavito. **PROGRAMMER:** Philippe Dion, Vladimir Bodourov, Alex Serban. **FLASH:** Arnaud Blaszkowski. **TECH ASPECTS:** Video, sound, 15 000 images, Macromedia Flash, database, PHP, AMF middleware. **MEDIA CIRCULATED:** Postcards, print ads, viral content. **AWARDS:** BIMA 2005 London (Gold – Art & Culture), Boomerang 2005 Interactive Communication Award Canada (Winner – Category Art & Culture), Interactive & Alternative Media Awards 2005 New York Festivals (Silver – Travel & Tourism), WebAward USA 2005 (Excellence – Web Site Development), Digital Marketing Awards 2005 Canada (Gold – Website Experience: to elicit an emotional response), CANADA World Summit Award 2005 (Winner - e-culture) The winner of each category will represent Canada at Tunis for the World Summit Award, Cannes Cyber Lions 2005 (Travel, Entertainment & Leisure), Omni Intermedia Award 2005 (Bronze - Documentary, Bronze - Public Service), Vancouver International Digital Festival 2005 (2nd prize - Art), Canadian New Media Awards 2005 (Grand Prize – Excellence Culture, Leisure, arts), Flash Festival en France 2005 (Finalist – Experimental Category), SXSW Interactive Awards 2005 (Grand Prize – Best of Art, Grand Prize – Best of Show), Design Interact 2005 (Website of the week), NetDiver Magazine (Site of the year 2004).

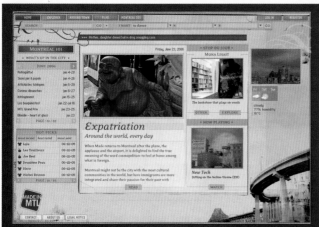

CONCEPT: MadeinMTL is the ultimate tourist guide, a website that gives the user the actual feeling of one of the most live city in the world. MadeinMTL is rich in information, well equipped in terms of navigation tools, and is a true work of art. MadeinMTL.com is powered by Urban Operator, a multi-platform (web, wireless, TV) digital content system for the promotion of cities, regions, events or brands, that creates a singular representation of a city online, with multiple entries to find, locate and explore the places that compose the fabric and moods of Montreal. Urban Operator is a compelling application that reinvents touristic exploration and widens the possibilities of mobile media delivery. MadeinMTL is intended to promote the urban life in Montreal. It gives the tourist who's never set foot in Montréal a unique perspective on the city and helps the born Montrealer to rediscover his hometown.

RESULTS: MadeinMTL.com is a rich media application site that enables the user to explore the city through 15,000 photographs, 400 texts, 50 hours of video, 40 sound bites, as well as 25 short films that truly capture the spirit of Montreal in a virtual experience. MadeinMTL has reached two main targets: Men and Women, between 18 and 35 years, inhabitant in Montreal and in love with their city and accustomed Visitors, tourists occasional, student and professional foreigners who want to be able to count on a friend who knows the city. Moreover, MadeinMTL has built a solid relationship with several partners including the 400 institutions, organizations, companies and various merchants present on the site, and also with other media and touristic partners who seek to join the same audience. MadeinMTL is a single example of treatment and use of the new media technology in the documentation of the life of a City and the sharing of its experiment with a vast audience. When people tell us they would love to visit the city after they've explored MadeinMTL, we feel we have succeeded in our intentions.

CONCEPT : MadeinMTL est le summum du guide touristique, un site qui offre à l'usager une véritable plongée dans une des villes les plus animées du monde. MadeinMTL est riche d'informations, bien équipé en terme d'outils de navigation, et c'est une véritable œuvre d'art. Le site est optimisé par Urban Operator, un système de contenu numérique multi-plateforme (internet, télévision, mobile) pour la promotion de villes, régions, événements ou marques. Il réalise une représentation originale d'une ville en ligne, grâce à de multiples entrées pour situer et explorer les endroits qui composent la nature et l'atmosphère de Montréal. Urban Operator est une application passionnante qui réinvente la visite touristique et élargit les possibilités des supports numériques mobiles. MadeinMTL est destiné à promouvoir la vie culturelle à Montréal. Il offre à celui qui n'y a jamais été un point de vue unique sur la ville, et permet aux habitants de Montréal de redécouvrir leur ville.

RÉSULTATS : MadeinMTL.com est un site d'application en *rich media* qui permet à l'usager de visiter la ville grâce à 15 000 photographies, 400 textes, 50 heures de vidéo, 40 ex-traits sonores et 25 courts métrages qui captent l'esprit de la ville à travers une expérience virtuelle. Le site a atteint deux cibles principales : hommes et femmes, entre 18 et 35 ans, habitants à Montréal et amoureux de leur ville, et visiteurs réguliers, touristes occasionnels, étudiants et travailleurs étrangers qui ont besoin de se reposer sur un ami qui connaît la ville. De plus, MadeinMTL a noué une relation solide avec de nombreux partenaires dont 400 institutions, organisations et entreprises commerciales présents sur le site, ainsi qu'avec d'autres médias et partenaires touristiques qui cherchent à toucher le même public. MadeinMTL illustre parfaitement la capacité des nouvelles technologies numériques à communiquer l'expérience d'une ville et la faire partager à un vaste public. Quand des gens nous disent que notre site leur a donné envie de venir visiter Montréal, nous avons le sentiment d'avoir accompli notre mission.

KONZEPT: MadeinMTL ist der ultimative Touristenführer – eine Webseite, die dem Benutzer das Gefühl gibt, in einer der lebhaftesten Städte der Welt zu leben. MadeinMTL ist reich an Informationen, mit guten Navigationswerkzeugen ausgestattet und ein wahres Kunstwerk. MadeinMTL.com wird von Urban Operator, einem digitalen Multiplattform-Contentsystem (Web, Wireless, TV), für die Werbung für Städte, Regionen, Events oder Marken angetrieben. Es erstellt eine singuläre Repräsentation einer Stadt online, mit zahlreichen Einträgen, um die Orte, die die Stimmung von Montreal ausmachen, zu lokalisieren und zu erforschen. Urban Operator ist eine faszinierende Anwendung, die die touristische Erkundung neu erfindet und die Möglichkeiten mobiler Medien erweitert. MadeinMTL soll für das urbane Leben in Montreal werben. Es bietet dem Touristen, der die Stadt noch nie betreten hat, eine einzigartige Perspektive auf die Stadt und hilft dem in Montreal Geborenen, seine Heimatstadt neu zu entdecken. **ERGEBNISSE:** MadeinMTL.com ist eine Rich-Media-Anwendung, mit der man die Stadt mit 15 000 Fotos, 400 Texten, 50 Videostunden, 40 Soundbites und 25 Kurzfilmen, die den Geist von Montreal in einem virtuellen Erlebnis einfangen, entdecken kann. MadeinMTL hat zwei Hauptzielgruppen erreicht: Männer und Frauen zwischen 18 und 35 Jahren, die in Montreal leben und ihre Stadt lieben, und Besucher, Gelegenheitstouristen, Studenten und berufstätige Fremde, die sich auf einen Freund verlassen wollen, der die Stadt kennt. Außerdem hat MadeinMTL eine solide Beziehung mit mehreren Partnern aufgebaut, darunter 400 Institutionen, Organisationen, Unternehmen und verschiedene Händler, die auf der Seite präsentiert werden, und mit anderen Medien- und Touristenpartnern, die dasselbe Publikum suchen. MadeinMTL ist ein einzigartiges Beispiel für den Umgang mit und Gebrauch von neuer Medientechnologie in der Dokumentation des Lebens einer Stadt und die Beteiligung eines breiten Publikums bei diesem Experiment. Wenn uns jemand sagt, dass er die Stadt gern besuchen möchte, nachdem er MadeinMTL erforscht hat, dann verbuchen wir das als Erfolg.

FEATURED ON THE DVD **CAMPAIGN:** Method Come Clean <www.comeclean.com>. **PRODUCT:** Method Home Products. **YEAR:** 2005. **AGENCY:** Crispin Porter + Bogusky <www.cpbgroup.com>. **PRODUCTION TIME:** 1 month. **EXECUTIVE CREATIVE DIRECTOR:** Alex Bogusky. **INTERACTIVE CREATIVE DIRECTOR:** Jeff Benjamin. **ASSOCIATE CREATIVE DIRECTOR:** Franklin Tipton. **ART DIRECTOR:** Mike Ferrare. **COPYWRITER:** Franklin Tipton, Bob Cianfrone, Paul Johnson, Evan Fry, Dustin Ballard, Jake Mikosh, Larry Corwin, Ronny Northrop, David Gonzalez, Mike Howard, Brian Tierney, Ryan Kutscher, Jackie Hathiramani, Justin Kramm. **PROGRAMMER:** Juan Morales, Jason Soros, Barbarian Group. **AWARDS:** One Show & One Show Interactive 2005 (Finalist), Webby Awards 2005 (Beauty and Cosmetic), CLIO 2005 (Bronze, Shortlist), Young Guns (Bronze), Cannes Cyber Lions 2005 (Grand Prix).

CONCEPT: We launched a viral campaign for Method with the Come Clean website. This viral website lets people start fresh by letting them confess to things they have done – it captures people's confessions and then streams them in a screensaver and on the website. When confessions are entered a woman's voice reacts to the confessions and tells you how what you've done is wrong but that you are forgiven. **RESULTS:** Comeclean.com has received well over 280,000 confessions. It has captured the attention of many as noted by blogs of all different languages. To date the site has reached close to 3 million hits.

CONCEPT : Nous avons lancé une campagne virale pour Method grâce au site Come Clean (Avouez). Ce site viral offre aux usagers de prendre un nouveau départ en avouant des fautes qu'ils ont commises, il enregistre les confessions puis les diffuse sur le site et sur un écran de veille. Quand on entre sa confession, une voix de femme réagit et vous dit que vous avez effectivement mal agi, mais que vous êtes à présent pardonné. **RÉSULTATS :**

Comeclean.com a reçu plus de 280 000 confessions. Il a attiré l'attention de nombreux internautes, comme l'attestent des blogs dans toutes les langues. Jusqu'à ce jour, le site a enregistré près de 3 millions de pages vues.

KONZEPT: Wir eröffneten eine virale Kampagne für Method mit der Come-Clean-Webseite. Mit dieser viralen Seite können Leute neu anfangen, indem sie vergangene Dinge beichten – sie sammelt die Geständnisse und lässt sie in einen Bildschirmschoner und auf die Webseite fließen. Wenn die Geständnisse eingegeben werden, reagiert eine weibliche Stimme darauf und erklärt, dass man falsch gehandelt hat, aber einem vergeben wird. **ERGEBNISSE:** Comeclean.com erhielt über 280 000 Geständnisse. Es erregte große Aufmerksamkeit, was durch zahlreiche Blogs in verschiedenen Sprachen bezeugt wird. Bis heute hat die Seite fast 3 Millionen Treffer erzielt.

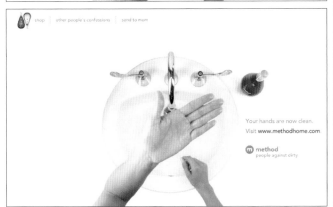

FEATURED ON THE DVD **CAMPAIGN:** MoMA: Contemporary Voices <www.moma.org/contemporaryvoices>. **YEAR:** 2005. **AGENCY:** Big Spaceship <www.bigspaceship.com>. **CREATIVE DIRECTOR:** Michael Lebowitz. **ART DIRECTOR:** James Widegren, Jens Karlsson. **PRODUCER:** Drew Horton. **PROGRAMMER:** Kimba Granlund. **PRODUCTION ARTISTS:** Tyson Damman. **AWARDS:** Davey Awards (Gold), HOW Magazine Interactive Design Annual (Merit), Macromedia (Site of the Day), WebAwards (Standard of Excellence), Moluv's Pick, STEP Best of Web Design Annual (Sept/Oct 2005).

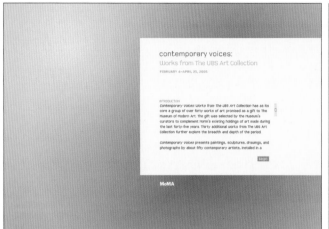

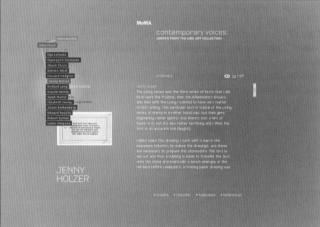

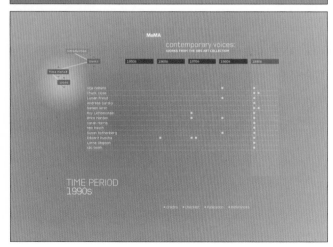

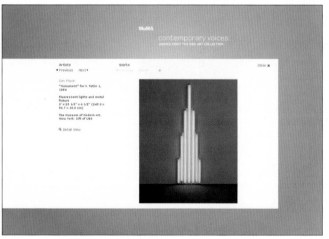

CONCEPT: Culled from the UBS Art Collection, the Contemporary Voices collection showcases the work of thirty-seven major modern and contemporary artists. As a companion to Contemporary Voices, this website highlights the artwork in the exhibition and the words of the artists themselves. Experimenting with unconventional materials, spaces and techniques, each artist asks the audience to appreciate not only the aesthetic image, but the construction and mechanics that went into its creation. As the works themselves represent a wide variety of styles, themes and media, the site uses a contextual navigation to guide visitors through the seventy-plus works in the exhibition. Browsing by artist, visitors can read biographies and excerpts of interviews, hear audio clips and view featured artwork. Visitors may also be able to use a timeline interface to view artists' pieces by creation date or medium to gain a greater context of the periods in which the pieces were created.

CONCEPT : Extraite de la UBS Art Collection, l'exposition « Contemporary Voices » présente les travaux de trente-sept artistes modernes et contemporains majeurs. Pour accompagner cet événement, le site fait un tour d'horizon des œuvres exposées et des réflexions des artistes eux-mêmes. Expérimentant des matériaux, des techniques et des espaces originaux, chaque artiste propose au public de découvrir non seulement l'aspect esthétique de son œuvre, mais aussi la démarche et les mécanismes qui l'ont nourri. Les travaux présentés reflétant une grande diversité de styles, de thèmes et de supports, le site utilise une na-

vigation contextuelle pour guider les visiteurs à travers les quelques soixante-dix œuvres exposées. En naviguant par nom d'artiste, on peut lire des biographies et des extraits d'interviews, écouter des clips audio et regarder les œuvres. On peut également utiliser une interface chronologique pour observer les œuvres des artistes par date de création ou par support, et obtenir ainsi le contexte historique et artistique dans lequel les œuvres ont été réalisées.

KONZEPT: Die Sammlung Contemporary Voices, entliehen von der UBS Art Collection, zeigt die Arbeiten von 37 großen modernen und zeitgenössischen Künstlern. Als Begleiter stellt die Webseite die Kunstwerke der Ausstellung und Zitate der Künstler selbst dar. Jeder Künstler experimentiert mit unkonventionellen Materialien, Räumen und Techniken und bittet das Publikum, nicht nur das ästhetische Bild, sondern auch die Konstruktion und die Mechanik, die in das Schaffen einflossen, zu schätzen. Die Werke selbst repräsentieren ein breites Spektrum von Stilen, Themen und Medien; die Seite verwendet eine kontextabhängige Navigation, um die Besucher durch die über 70 Werke der Ausstellung zu führen. Nach Künstlern sortiert, kann der Besucher Biografien und Auszüge von Interviews lesen, Audioclips hören und Kunstwerke ansehen. Man kann auch ein Zeitleisten-Interface verwenden, um die Kunstwerke nach Datum oder Medium sortiert anzusehen, so dass ein größerer Kontext der Perioden sichtbar wird, in denen die Werke entstanden.

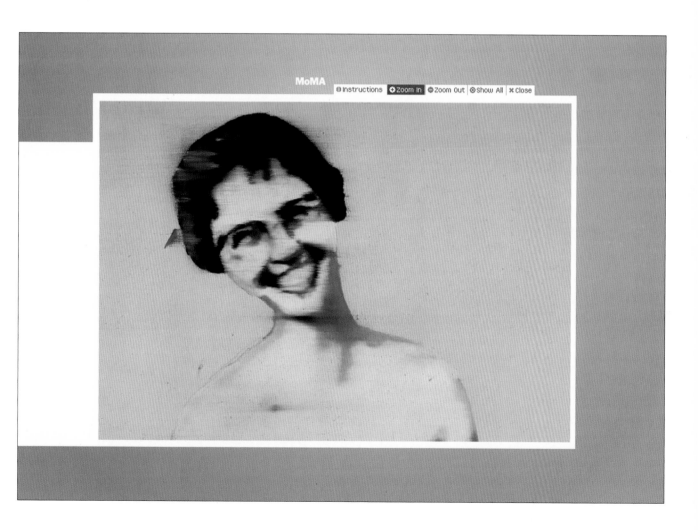

FEATURED ON THE DVD **CAMPAIGN:** National Aids Trust. **AGENCY:** Saatchi & Saatchi <www.saatchi-interactive.com>. **PRODUCTION TIME:** 2 days. **COST IN HOURS OF WORK:** 20 h. **ART DIRECTOR:** Jo Smetham. **COPYWRITER:** Dan Cole. **CREATIVE DIRECTOR:** Charbak Bhattacherjee. **FLASH DESIGNER/PROGRAMMER:** Maya Haiman. **TECH ASPECTS:** Macromedia Flash. **MEDIA CIRCULATED:** Email.

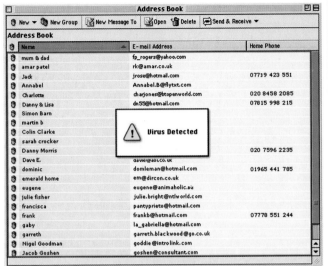

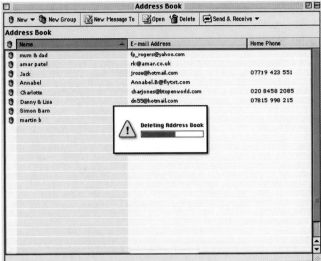

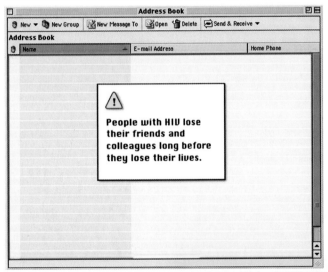

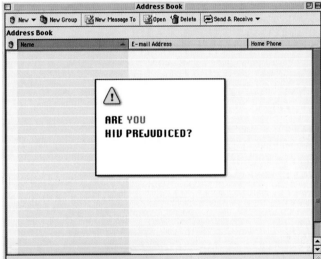

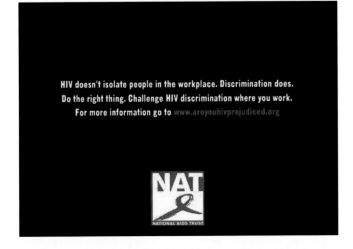

RESULTS: This viral was distributed by the National Aids Trust to raise awareness of new, tighter legislation outlawing discrimination in the workplace. HIV prejudice in particular is at its most visible in the workplace with sufferers reporting feelings of isolation and rejection from their colleagues. The viral, disguised as an important message for employers, directed recipients to a web-link. Upon opening, however, the computer immediately warned that it had picked up a virus. The virus then appeared to delete their address book in front of their eyes. As panic set in, a message appeared – "People with HIV lose their friends and colleagues long before they lose their lives." Reaction was positive, particularly amongst business leaders and large-scale employers. There was also evidence that the e-mail was passed on to a wider audience, as NAT reported a significant upsurge in page viewings on their website during the normally static January period.

RÉSULTAS : Cette annonce virale a été diffusée par National Aids Trust (association de lutte contre le sida) pour informer de la nouvelle législation condamnant la discrimination dans le milieu du travail. Les personnes touchées par le virus HIV sont particulièrement discriminées dans le milieu du travail, et rapportent des sentiments d'isolation et de rejet de la part de leurs collègues. La publicité, qui prend la forme d'un message important pour les employeurs, dirigent l'internaute vers un site. Dès qu'on clique pour entrer, l'ordinateur vous alerte qu'il a été victime d'un virus. Le virus se met alors à détruire le contenu de votre carnet d'adresses sous vos yeux. Un message apparaît alors que la panique vous saisit et signale : « Les victimes du HIV perdent leurs collègues et leurs amis bien avant de perdre la vie ». La réaction a été positive, particulièrement chez les dirigeants d'entreprises et les grands employeurs. Nous avons aussi eu la preuve que le e-mail a été relayé à une grande échelle, car NAT a rapporté une hausse importante du nombre de pages vues sur son site pendant le mois de janvier, période habituellement calme.

ERGEBNISSE: Dieses Viral wurde vom National Aids Trust verteilt, um das Bewusstsein für eine neue, strengere Gesetzgebung bezüglich Diskriminierung am Arbeitsplatz zu wecken. Vorurteile gegenüber HIV im Besonderen sind am Arbeitsplatz am besten sichtbar: Betroffene berichten über Isolation und Zurückweisung durch Kollegen. Das Viral, als wichtige Botschaft für Mitarbeiter getarnt, führte die Empfänger zu einem Weblink. Öffnete man diesen jedoch, warnte der Computer sofort vor einem Virus. Dieses Virus löschte scheinbar das Adressbuch vor den Augen des Benutzers. Panik entstand – und eine Botschaft erschien: Menschen mit HIV verlieren ihre Freunde und Kollegen lange bevor sie ihr Leben verlieren. Die Reaktion war positiv, besonders unter Geschäftsführern und Arbeitgebern großer Firmen. Die E-Mail wurde offenbar an ein breites Publikum verteilt: NAT berichtete von einem signifikanten Anstieg der Treffer auf ihrer Webseite während der normalerweise konstanten Periode im Januar.

CAMPAIGN: terakoya-kururinpa.jp <http://terakoya-kururinpa.jp>. **PRODUCT:** World Terakoya Movement. **CLIENT:** National Federation of UNESCO Associations in JAPAN. **YEAR:** 2005. **AGENCY:** Dentsu Inc. <www.dentsu.com>. **ART DIRECTOR:** Hirozumi Takakusaki. **COPYWRITER:** Fumihiko Sagawa. **CREATIVE DIRECTOR:** Testu Goto. **DESIGNER:** Yusuke Kitani. **PHOTO:** Yusuke Kitani. **PROGRAMMER:** Hiroki Nakamura. **TECH ASPECTS:** Macromedia Flash. **MEDIA CIRCULATED:** Website. **AWARDS:** tokyo.interactive.ad.awards.jp 2005 (Bronze), One Show Interactive 2005 (Finalist), London international awards 2005 (Finalist), 2005 NY ADC (Merit).

CONCEPT: Illiteracy is sadly a fact of life for many people around the world. The World Terakoya Movement, carried out by the National Federation of UNESCO Associations in Japan (NFUAJ) provides opportunities to those people to start their education. The purpose of the website is to introduce this movement with "KURURINPA" characters, designed by Dentsu creators, that become different characters when flipped over. The navigator of the website is a pair of child's hands. The hands on the screen write as you command from typing a keyboard. The letters that appear then are desperately unsuccessful. The website experience provides us with the reality that approximately one billion people around the world are either children unable to go to school or illiterate adults and we have to help provide these people with an education.

CONCEPT : L'analphabétisme est une triste réalité pour de nombreuses personnes dans le monde. Le World Terakoya Movement, sous l'égide de la Fédération Nationale des Associations de l'Unesco au Japon (NFUAJ) offre des possibilités aux personnes illettrées d'avoir accès à l'éducation. Le but du site est de présenter ce mouvement grâce à des personnages Kururinpa, dessinés par les créateurs de Dentsu, qui se transforment quand on les retourne. Le navigateur du site est représenté sous la forme de deux mains d'enfant. Les mains sur l'écran doivent écrire ce que vous tapez sur le clavier. Mais les lettres qui apparaissent sont hélas toutes erronées. L'expérience illustre le fait qu'environ un milliard de personnes dans le monde sont soit des enfants qui n'ont pas accès à l'école soit des adultes illettrés, et que nous devons contribuer à leur offrir une éducation.

KONZEPT: Analphabetismus ist für viele Menschen weltweit eine traurige Tatsache. Die World Terakoya Bewegung der National Federation of UNESCO Associations in Japan (NFUAJ) bietet diesen Menschen Gelegenheit, mit ihrer Bildung zu beginnen. Der Zweck der Webseite besteht in der Einführung dieser Bewegung mit „KURURINPA"-Figuren, die von den Dentsu-Schöpfern gestaltet wurden und sich in andere Figuren verwandeln, wenn sie umgedreht werden. Der Navigator der Webseite besteht aus einem Paar Kinderhände, die schreiben, wenn man etwas mit der Tastatur tippt. Die erscheinenden Buchstaben sind falsch. Dies macht uns die Realität von ca. einer Milliarde Menschen weltweit erfahrbar – entweder Kinder, die nicht zur Schule gehen können, oder erwachsene Analphabeten. Wir müssen helfen, damit diese Menschen eine Bildung erhalten.

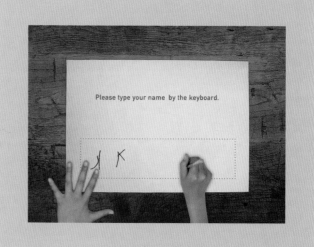

FEATURED ON THE DVD   **CAMPAIGN:** NIVEA BEAUTÉ Baroccoco Look Product Special <www.nivea.de/baroccoco>.   **PRODUCT:** NIVEA BEAUTÉ Baroccoco Product Range.   **YEAR:** 2005.   **AGENCY:** Fork Unstable Media <www.fork.de>.   **CREATIVE TEAM:** Christophe Stoll, Anna Mentzel, Oliver Kauselmann, Klaudia Plettner.   **PROGRAMMER:** Dominik Schmid.   **TECH ASPECTS:** Macromedia Flash.

CONCEPT: The NIVEA BEAUTÉ Baroccoco Look Product Special is part of an integrated brand communication which also includes a print and TV campaign and various online activities. Our aim was to creatively translate the promotion's message to the Internet. **RESULTS:** Next to the web special, which combines contents and images of the print campaign with elaborate illustrations and sound design, we are also in charge of newsletters, banners and co-operations with web portals. Interactive features such as sweepstakes and e-mail shopping lists as well as personalized mailings enhance customer services while the strategic coordination of all online activities has generated synergies for both offline and online promotions.

CONCEPT : Le site de produit Nivea Beauté Baroccoco fait partie d'une communication de marque globale qui inclut des annonces presse et télé, ainsi que diverses actions en ligne. Notre objectif était de retranscrire le message promotionnel sur internet. **RÉSULTATS :** En plus du site internet, qui combine images et rédactionnel des annonces presse dans un design graphique et sonore élaboré, nous nous chargeons aussi des bulletins d'information, des bannières et de la coopération avec les portails internet. Des éléments interactifs, comme une loterie, une liste de courses virtuelles et des courriers personnalisés améliorent la relation client. La coordination stratégique de toutes les activités en ligne a assuré la synergie de la promotion en ligne et hors ligne.

KONZEPT: Das NIVEA BEAUTÉ Baroccoco Look Produkt-Special ist Teil einer integrierten Markenkommunikation, die auch eine Print- und Fernsehkampagne und mehrere Online-Aktivitäten einschließt. Unser Ziel bestand darin, die Werbebotschaft kreativ ins Internet zu übersetzen. **ERGEBNISSE:** Neben dem Web-Special, das Inhalte und Bilder der Printkampagne mit kunstvollen Illustrationen und Sound kombiniert, waren wir für Newsletter, Banner und Kooperationen mit Webportalen verantwortlich. Interaktive Features wie Lotto, E-Mail-Einkaufslisten oder personalisierte Mailings verbessern den Kundenservice, während die strategische Koordination aller Aktivitäten online Synergien für Offline- und Online-Werbung erzeugt hat.

FEATURED ON THE DVD CAMPAIGN: NIVEA BEAUTÉ Online Make-Up Studio <www.nivea.com/mus>. PRODUCT: NIVEA BEAUTÉ Product Range. YEAR: 2005. AGENCY: Fork Unstable Media <www.fork.de>. CREATIVE TEAM: Christophe Stoll. PROGRAMMER: Florian Finke, Jan-Michael Studt. TECH ASPECTS: Macromedia Flash, fully localizable by WYSIWYG CMS-system, automatic adjustment to local assortment specifics, dynamic server-side rendering of product effects on model images.

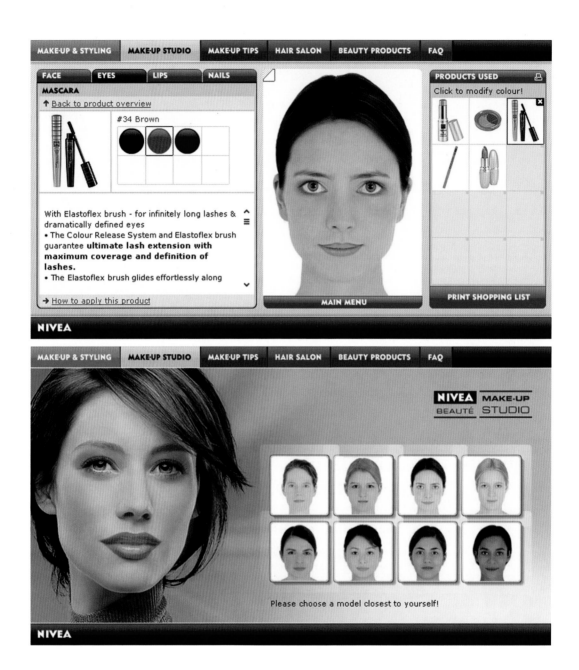

CONCEPT: An easy accessible yet highly comprehensive online make-up tool for women around the world: the most important goal for the production of NIVEA BEAUTE's Online Make-Up Studio. Without any technical restrictions, users should be able to try on all of the various products for face, eyes, lips and nails in all conceivable colour and texture combinations. **RESULTS:** He result is photorealistic and highly effective: users are guided through the complete palette of products and colors until they find their very personal make up. Professional beauty tips and tricks as well as an overview of all NIVEA BEAUTE products top off one of this beauty counselling site. Users can save their look, print it, send it via e-mail or completely change it again. In a recent survey users report that they regularly use this tool to try out NIVEA BEAUTE products before actually buying them. Since its launch the Make-Up Studio plays a vital part in NIVEA BEAUTE's marketing mix. It is part of print ads, newsletters, online co-operations, press releases and TVCs (URL integration).

CONCEPT : Proposer un outil de maquillage en ligne polyvalent et facile d'accès, destiné aux femmes du monde entier, voilà l'objectif du studio de maquillage en ligne de Nivea. Sans aucune limitation technique, l'utilisatrice doit être en mesure d'essayer tous les produits de maquillage pour le visage, les yeux, les lèvres et les ongles, dans toutes les couleurs et les combinaisons de texture possible. **RÉSULTATS :** La création est visuellement réaliste et très efficace : l'usager est guidé à travers la palette complète de produits et de couleurs afin de réaliser son maquillage personnel. Des conseils et des astuces beauté, ainsi qu'un tour d'horizon de la gamme de produits Nivea constituent les atouts de ce site

dédié à la beauté. On peut enregistrer son nouveau look, l'imprimer, l'envoyer par e-mail ou le rectifier entièrement. Un récent sondage a révélé que les femmes utilisent régulièrement cet outil pour tester des nouveautés avant de les acheter. Depuis son lancement, le studio de maquillage virtuel joue un rôle essentiel dans la stratégie commerciale globale de Nivea. Il accompagne les annonces magazine, les bulletins d'informations, la coopération en ligne, les communiqués de presse et le filtrage url (intégration aux annuaires).

KONZEPT: Ein einfach zugängliches und gut verständliches Make-up-Tool online für Frauen aus aller Welt: das wichtigste Ziel für die Herstellung von NIVEA BEAUTÉs Online-Make-up-Studio. Benutzer sollen ohne technische Grenzen alle Produkte für Gesicht, Augen, Lippen und Nägel in allen möglichen Farb- und Strukturkombinationen ausprobieren können. **ERGEBNISSE:** Das Ergebnis ist fotorealistisch und höchst effektiv: Benutzer werden durch die komplette Produkt- und Farbpalette geführt, bis sie ihr persönliches Make-up gefunden haben. Professionelle Schönheitstipps und -tricks sowie ein Überblick über alle Produkte von NIVEA BEAUTÉ runden diese Schönheitsratgeberseite ab. Benutzerinnen können ihren Look speichern, ausdrucken, per E-Mail versenden oder wieder komplett verändern. In einer Umfrage berichteten Benutzerinnen kürzlich, dass sie dieses Tool regelmäßig benutzen, um NIVEA BEAUTÉ-Produkte auszuprobieren, bevor sie sie kaufen. Seit seinem Launch spielt das Make-up-Studio in NIVEA BEAUTÉs Marketing-Mix eine herausragende Rolle. Es ist Teil von Printanzeigen, Newslettern, Online-Kooperationen, Pressemitteilungen und TVCs (URL-Integration).

FEATURED ON THE DVD **CAMPAIGN:** NIVEA BEAUTÉ Stay Real Product Special <www.nivea.com/stayreal>. **PRODUCT:** NIVEA BEAUTÉ Stay Real Liquid Foundation (plus additional products out of the Stay Real line). **YEAR:** 2005.
AGENCY: Fork Unstable Media <www.fork.de>. **CREATIVE TEAM:** Jan Kallwejt, Anna Mentze. **PROGRAMMER:** Florian Finke. **TECH ASPECTS:** Macromedia Flash.

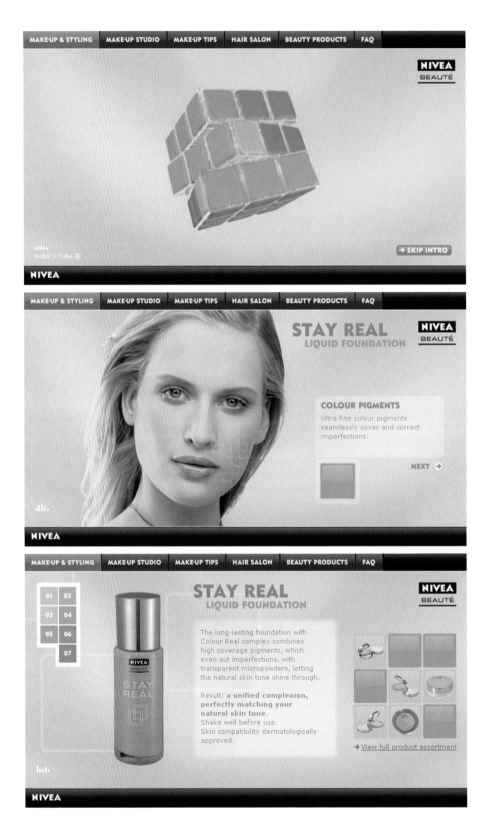

CONCEPT: As vital part of an integrated brand communication which also includes a print and TV campaign, the goal of the web special was to introduce a new liquid foundation for NIVEA BEAUTÉ and its range of monochromatic colours. They communicate the benefit of the product: the ultra fine colour pigments that make a seamless surface. It's just like arranging the little squares of a Rubik's Cube... **RESULTS:** Playful and completely in-line with the classic communication: Fork's very first 80's product special. As all international NIVEA online specials, it is connected to a modular CMS and is ready for local adaptation for up to 48 country versions.

CONCEPT : Comme partie essentielle de la communication globale de marque qui inclut une campagne presse et télévision, l'objectif du site était de présenter un nouveau fond de teint Nivea et sa gamme de tons monochromatiques. Il informe sur les avantages du produit : les pigments de couleurs ultrafins qui unifient le teint. C'est comme d'arranger les petits carrés d'un Rubik's Cube. **RÉSULTATS :** Ludique et en phase avec la communication traditionnelle, c'est le premier site de produit réalisé par Fork. Comme tous les sites internationaux de Nivea, il est connecté à un système de gestion de contenu modulaire et peut être adapté localement à quelques 48 pays.

KONZEPT: Als entscheidender Teil einer integrierten Markenkommunikation, die eine Print- und Fernsehkampagne einschließt, besteht das Ziel des Web-Specials darin, eine neue flüssige Grundierung für NIVEA BEAUTÉ und ihre Auswahl monochromatischer Farben einzuführen. Es kommuniziert die Vorteile des Produkts: die ultrafeinen Farbpigmente, die eine nahtlose Oberfläche gewährleisten – als würde man kleine Vierecke eines Rubik-Würfels anordnen ... **ERGEBNISSE:** Spielerisch und passend zur klassischen Kommunikation: Forks erstes 80er Produkt-Special. Wie alle internationalen Online-Specials von NIVEA ist es mit einem modularen CMS verbunden und für bis zu 48 Länderversionen adaptierbar.

FEATURED ON THE DVD **CAMPAIGN:** NIVEA FOR MEN Configurator <www.nivea.com/configurator>. **PRODUCT:** NIVEA FOR MEN Product Range. **YEAR:** 2005. **AGENCY:** Fork Unstable Media <www.fork.de>. **CREATIVE TEAM:** Christophe Stoll, Dominik Wilhelm, Joachim Fraatz. **PROGRAMMER:** Joachim Fraatz, Benjamin Herholz, Florian Finke. **TECH ASPECTS:** Macromedia Flash, XML, fully localizable by WYSIWYG CMS-system, automatic adjustment to local assortment specifics.

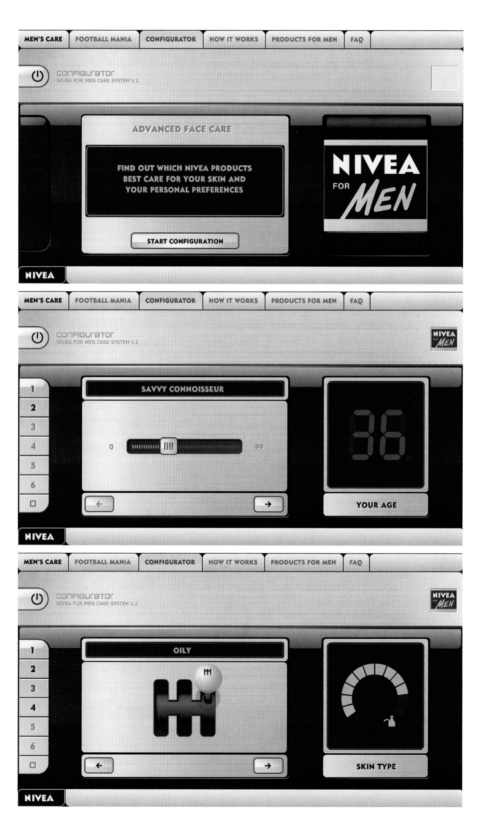

CONCEPT: Playfully introducing men to the topic of face care was our main goal. **RESULTS:** NIVEA FOR MEN's Configurator uses quite a few tech-gadget-like metaphors in order to help men overcome their inhibitions. Based on a modular CMS the Configurator is ready for local adaptation for up to 48 country versions and their local assortments.

CONCEPT : L'objectif était de sensibiliser les hommes à la question des soins pour le visage de façon ludique. **RÉSULTATS :** Le site utilise quelques métaphores de gadgets technologiques afin d'aider les hommes à dépasser leurs inhibitions. Basé sur un système de gestion de contenu modulaire, le configurateur se prête à l'adaptation de 48 versions et déclinaisons différentes.

KONZEPT: Unser Ziel war es, Männer spielerisch in das Thema Gesichtspflege einzuführen. **ERGEBNISSE:** NIVEA FOR MENs Konfigurator verwendet einige Metaphern zu technischen Geräten, um Männern zu helfen, ihre Hemmschwelle zu überwinden. Auf modularer CMS basierend, ist der Konfigurator für bis zu 48 Länderversionen und deren lokale Sortimente adaptierbar.

FEATURED ON THE DVD **CAMPAIGN:** NIVEA FOR MEN Soccer Mania banner flight. **PRODUCT:** NIVEA FOR MEN Product Range. **YEAR:** 2006. **AGENCY:** Fork Unstable Media <www.fork.de>. **CREATIVE TEAM:** Roman Hilmer, Jan Kallwejt, Stefanie Weber, Tilo Göbel. **PROGRAMMER:** Jan Kallwejt, Tilo Göbel. **TECH ASPECTS:** Macromedia Flash.

CONCEPT: Tough task for the beginning of soccer mania year 2006: promote an online soccer game in such a way that it is recognized on first glance amongst the plethora of print and online ads that are being published at the same time. **RESULTS:** Creative texts, neat and playful illustrations, unusual diversity of motifs: by these means we arrest the attention of both men and women at the same time.

CONCEPT : Mission délicate pour début 2006, l'année de la folie du foot : promouvoir un jeu de football reconnaissable au premier regard parmi une multitude d'annonces diffusées simultanément dans la presse et sur le Net. **RÉSULTATS :** Légende créative, illustrations drôles et soignées, grande variété de motifs : par ces moyens nous attirons l'attention des hommes et des femmes à la fois.

KONZEPT: Eine schwierige Aufgabe für den Beginn des Fußballmanie-Jahres 2006: Für ein Online-Fußballspiel so zu werben, dass es auf den ersten Blick in dem Überfluss an Print- und Online-Anzeigen, die zur selben Zeit veröffentlicht werden, erkennbar ist. **ERGEBNISSE:** Kreative Texte, spielerische Illustrationen, ungewöhnliche Vielseitigkeit von Motiven: Damit erregen wir Aufmerksamkeit von Männern und Frauen.

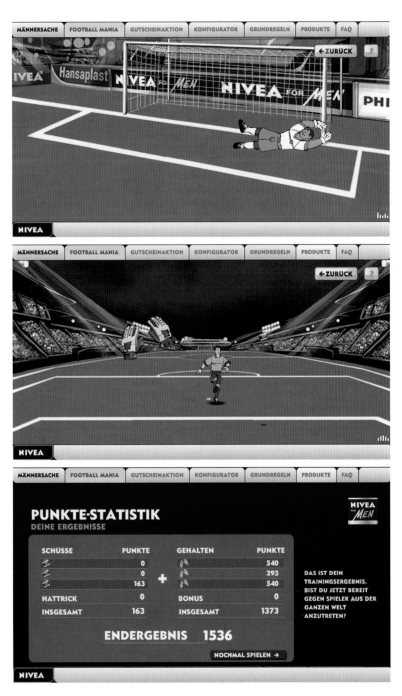

FEATURED ON THE DVD **CAMPAIGN:** NIVEA Hand Range Product Special <www.nivea.de/hand>. **PRODUCT:** NIVEA Hand Product Range. **YEAR:** 2005. **AGENCY:** Fork Unstable Media <www.fork.de>. **CREATIVE TEAM:** Jan Kallwejt, Anna Mentzel, Klaudia Plettner. **PROGRAMMER:** Dominik Schmid. **TECH ASPECTS:** Macromedia Flash.

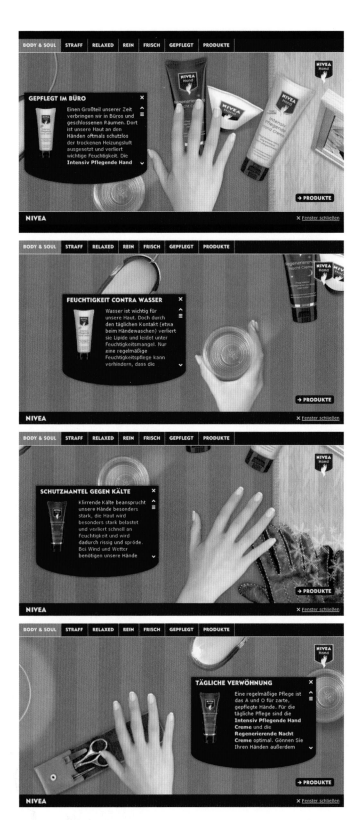

CONCEPT: As vital part of an integrated brand communication which also includes a print and TV campaign and various online activities, our objective for the web special was to introduce the complete care range of NIVEA Hand for the German NIVEA website. Conceptually, we opted for a "hands-on" approach. **RESULTS:** The user navigates and explores the special by moving an actual hand with which he or she can "touch" and find out about products and other hand care- related objects leading to more care tips.

CONCEPT : Dans le cadre d'une communication de marque intégrée qui inclut des annonces presse et télévision ainsi que des opérations en ligne, l'objectif était de présenter la gamme complète des produits de soin pour les mains sur le site allemand de Nivea. De façon conceptuelle, nous avons opté pour une démarche « manuelle ». **RÉSULTATS :** L'usager navigue dans le site en déplaçant l'image d'une main qui touche et manipule les produits de soins spécifiques, tout en révélant d'autres conseils beauté.

KONZEPT: Als entscheidender Teil einer integrierten Markenkommunikation, die eine Print- und Fernsehkampagne einschließt, besteht das Ziel des Web-Specials darin, die komplette Handpflegeserie von NIVEA für die deutsche NIVEA-Webseite einzuführen. Vor diesem Hintergrund entschieden wir uns für einen praktischen Ansatz. **ERGEBNISSE:** Der Besucher navigiert und kundschaftet das Special aus, indem er eine tatsächliche Hand bewegt, mit der man Produktinformationen und andere Objekte, die sich auf Handpflege beziehen, „berühren" kann und so zu weiteren Pflegetipps gelangt.

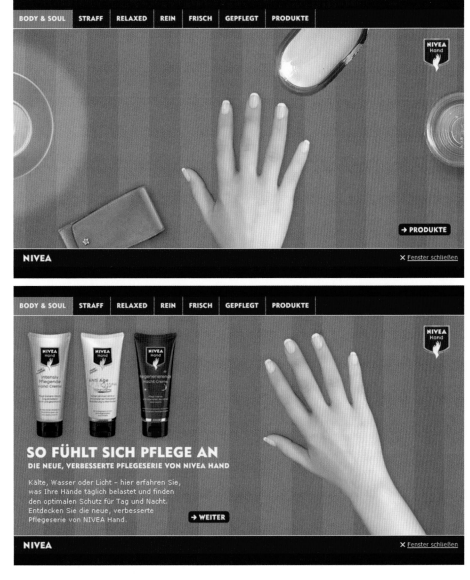

FEATURED ON THE DVD **CAMPAIGN:** NOAH – Pet Sematary Campaign Website <www.petsematary.de>. **YEAR:** 2005. **AGENCY:** Fork Unstable Media <www.fork.de>. **CREATIVE TEAM:** Roman Hilmer, Christophe Stoll, Anna Mentzel, Tilo Göbel, Holger Illing. **PROGRAMMER:** Florian Finke. **TECH ASPECTS:** Macromedia Flash.

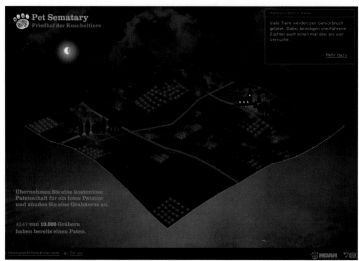

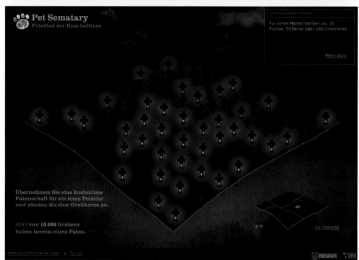

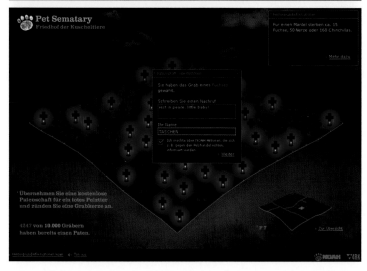

CONCEPT: For a campaign of animal rights activist NOAH – Menschen für Tiere e.V., we created the website "Pet Sematary", a virtual memorial to fur animals. The challenge was in conveying the sad facts in a new and unique way that manages to arouse a public already numbed by the usual gory, visceral details of animal abuse. Our concept of Pet Sematary is based on an immediate and creative approach: users are asked to adopt a grave, light a candle and write an obituary for a fur animal while an overview indicates how many other graves have been adopted already. Thus, all participating animal lovers are linked in a glowing network of lights – an ongoing wake to shake up the fur wielding public. **RESULTS:** Pet Sematary deals with the ugly subject in a modern and aesthetically appealing way without diminishing the inherent horror of the situation. Thus, we created a platform that allows people to get involved and "make a difference", albeit a small one. Furthermore, up-to-date background information fills them in on the basics of fur farming and trade including alarming furry facts and numbers and a list of fur loving fashion labels.

CONCEPT : Pour la campagne du défenseur des droits des animaux Noah, nous avons conçu le site « Pet Sematary », un cimetière virtuel pour les animaux à fourrure. Le défi était de transmettre la triste réalité de façon inédite pour sensibiliser un public déjà abasourdi par les détails sanglants et cruels des sévices infligés aux animaux. Le concept du cimetière virtuel est basé sur une approche créative immédiate : les usagers doivent réserver une tombe, allumer une bougie et écrire une notice nécrologique pour un animal tandis qu'un récapitulatif indique le nombre de tombes déjà réservées. Les amoureux des animaux sont ainsi reliés entre eux par un faisceau de petites lueurs, destiné à éveiller la conscience des amateurs de fourrure. **RÉSULTATS :** Le cimetière virtuel aborde le sujet de façon esthéti-que et attrayante sans pour autant atténuer l'horreur de la situation. Nous avons ainsi réalisé une plateforme qui permet aux gens de s'engager et faire une différence, aussi minime soit-elle. De plus, des informations mises à jour renseignent les usagers quant aux réalités économiques liées à l'industrie de la fourrure, accompagnées de chiffres alarmants, et offre une liste de marques de confection qui n'ont pas recours à l'exploitation des animaux.

KONZEPT: Für eine Kampagne der Tierrechtaktivisten von NOAH – Menschen für Tiere e.V. erstellten wir die Webseite „Pet Sematary", eine virtuelle Gedenkstätte für Pelztiere. Die Herausforderung bestand in der Vermittlung der traurigen Fakten auf neue und einzigartige Weise, die eine Öffentlichkeit anregt, die von den gewöhnlichen abscheulichen Details schon abgestumpft ist. Unser Konzept von Pet Sematary basiert auf einem unmittelbaren und kreativen Ansatz: Benutzer werden gebeten, ein Grab zu adoptieren, eine Kerze anzuzünden und einen Nachruf für ein Pelztier zu schreiben, während eine Übersicht anzeigt, wie viele Gräber bereits adoptiert worden sind. Dadurch werden alle teilnehmenden Tierfreunde durch ein leuchtendes Netzwerk von Lichtern verbunden – ein fortwährender Weckruf, der die Pelz handhabende Öffentlichkeit aufrütteln soll. **ERGEBNISSE:** Pet Sematary beschäftigt sich mit dem hässlichen Thema auf moderne und ästhetische Weise, ohne den Horror der Situation zu beschönigen. Dadurch erzeugten wir eine Plattform, durch die Menschen involviert wurden und einen Beitrag leisten konnten – wenn auch einen kleinen. Außerdem erläutern aktuelle Hintergrundinformationen die Grundzüge von Landwirtschaft und Handel, einschließlich alarmierender Zahlen und Fakten sowie einer Liste von Fashion Labels, die Pelz verarbeiten.

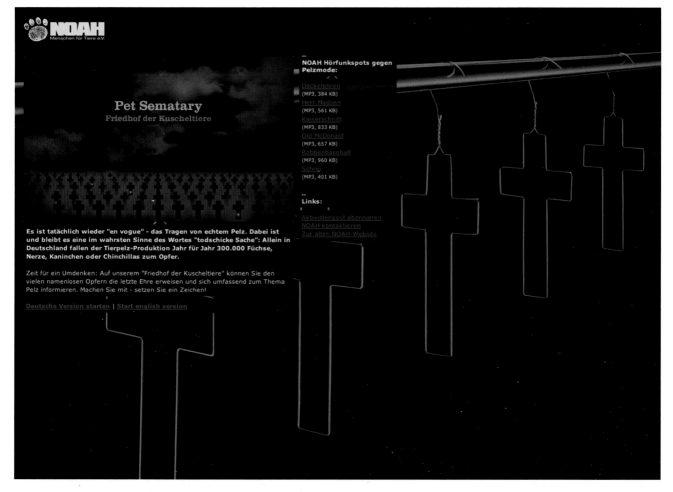

FEATURED ON THE DVD **CAMPAIGN:** Someone To Turn To. **PRODUCT:** NSPCC. **YEAR:** 2004. **AGENCY:** Agency.com London <www.agency.com>. **COST IN HOURS OF WORK:** 406 h. **CREATIVE TEAM:** Olly Robinson, Steve Whiteley. **PROGRAMMER:** Perry Cooper, Tom Gregory. **TECH ASPECTS:** Macromedia Flash, video, sound. **MEDIA CIRCULATED:** TimesOnline.com; iVillage.com; DailyMirror.co.uk; AOL.co.uk. **AWARDS:** Campaign Digital Awards 2005 (Grand Prix); IAB Creative Showcase; Revolution Awards 2005 (Finalist); Imperatives Best Ad Campaign 2005; IAC Best of Show Rich Media 2005; Cannes Cyber Lions 2005 (Finalist); MIXX Awards 2005 (Bronze).

CHALLENGE: The NSPCC asked Agency.com to test online advertising to engage a potential audience of younger donors. The primary objective for this campaign was to generate response, with the intention of conversion to donate, to the NSPCC site, www.nspcc.org.uk. The secondary objective was to generate awareness of the long-standing Full Stop campaign. **STRATEGY & SOLUTION:** Agency.com first identified three key donor segments, their propensity to donate, their donation behavior, and their motivators. From this, three complementary creative routes were created: The 'Emotive' route (executions 'Alone' and 'Seven') targets female-oriented segments (women below 45) that donate in response to emotional triggers. Media focused on female oriented sites such as handbag.com, iVillage and the Mirror; The 'Rational' route (executions 'Court' and 'Languages') targets the male-oriented segment (males 35-45 with children) that want to see what they will get for their money. 'Languages' was specifically tailored to each media property used, including Sky Sports, Mirror and ITV.com; 'Go100' ('Sink', 'Bike' and 'Changing Room') targets all segments with the insight that younger audiences can prefer pro-active fund-raising to passive donation. The campaign concept, 'Every child needs someone to turn to', integrated with the concurrent Brand TV activity. **RESULTS:** The goals set were for response: In the first 4 weeks, we set the goal of a 0.31% response rate, delivering 5,798 clicks through to the NSPCC site. Effectiveness: 648% of the targeted responses were delivered in the first month of the campaign. The average click-through rate was 1.95% – over 6 times the projections. Click-through rates on the emotive execution, 'Seven', peaked at 17%. **EFFICIENCY:** Cost per click (CPC) was £0.41, only 16% of the planned CPC of £2.64. Media Buying costs were also minimized, coming in under budget at £7.96 CPM (see left).

DÉFI: Le NSPCC a chargé Agency.com de tester une campagne en ligne pour sensibiliser une population de jeunes donateurs potentiels. L'objectif principal était de générer une réponse et de la convertir en donation sur le site nspcc.org.uk. L'objectif secondaire était de sensibiliser à la campagne pérenne Full Stop. **STRATÉGIE ET SOLUTION :** Agency.com a d'abord identifié trois segments principaux de donateurs, leur propension à verser des dons, leur comportement face aux dons et leurs motivations. A partir de là, trois axes créatifs ont été élaborés. L'axe « émotif » (exécutions « Seule » et « Sept ») s'adresse au segment féminin (femmes de moins de 45 ans) qui donne en réponse à un déclic émotionnel. Le message a été diffusé sur des sites d'intérêts féminins, comme handbag.com, iVillage et le Mirror. L'axe « rationnel » (exécutions « Tribunal » et « Langues ») s'adresse au segment masculin (pères de famille de 35-45 ans) qui veulent savoir ce qui est fait de leur argent. « Langues » a été conçu sur mesure suivant le support média de destination, Sky Sports, le Mirror ou ITV.com. L'axe « actif » (« Voilà 100 », « Vélo » et « Changer de décor ») s'adresse

à tous les segments avec la notion que le public jeune préfère les collectes de fonds actives plutôt que les donations passives. Le concept de la campagne « Tous les enfants ont besoin de quelqu'un vers qui se tourner », a été intégré dans l'activité publicitaire menée en parallèle sur les chaînes télévisées. **RÉSULTATS :** Nous avions fixé des objectifs de réponse. Dans les 4 premières semaines, nous nous étions fixé un taux de réponse de 0,31%, engendrant 5 798 clics sur le site de NSPCC. Efficacité : 648% de réponses favorables pendant le premier mois de la campagne. Le taux moyen de clics pour l'exécution « Sept » du pôle émotif : 17%. **EFFICACITÉ :** Coût par clic a été de 0,41 livre, c'est-à-dire 16% du coût prévisionnel de 2,64 livres. Le coût d'achat d'espace a été aussi minimisé, atteignant un CPM de 7,96 livres.

HERAUSFORDERUNG: Die NSPCC beauftragte Agency.com damit, Online-Werbung zu testen, um ein potenzielles Publikum jüngerer Spender anzusprechen. Primäres Ziel dieser Kampagne war es, Rückmeldung zu erzeugen, mit der Intention, an die NSPCC-Seite, www.nspcc.org.uk, zu spenden. Sekundäres Ziel war die Erzeugung von Bewusstsein für die anhaltende Full-Stop-Kampagne. **STRATEGIE & LÖSUNG:** Agency.com identifizierte zunächst drei hauptsächliche Spendersegmente, ihre Tendenz zu spenden, ihr Spendeverhalten und ihre Motivation. Davon ausgehend wurden komplementäre kreative Routen erstellt: Die „emotionsgeladene" Route (Ausführungen „Alone" und „Seven") zielt auf weiblich orientierte Segmente ab (Frauen unter 45), die als Reaktion auf emotionale Auslöser spenden; die Medien konzentrieren sich auf weiblich orientierte Seiten wie handbag.com, iVillage und den Mirror. Die „rationale" Route (Ausführungen „Court" und „Languages") zielt auf männlich orientierte Segmente ab (35- bis 45-jährige Väter), die sehen wollen, was sie für ihr Geld bekommen. „Languages" war auf jedes Medium zugeschnitten, das verwendet wurde, darunter Sky Sports, Mirror und ITV.com. „Go100" („Sink", „Bike" und „Changing Room") zielte auf alle Segmente ab, mit der Einsicht, dass jüngeres Publikum aktive Spendenaktionen passivem Spenden vorziehen kann. Das Kampagnenkonzept „Every child needs someone to turn to" passte zur gleichzeitigen Markenaktivität im Fernsehen. **ERGEBNISSE:** Erwartete Reaktionen: In den ersten vier Wochen veranschlagten wir das Ziel auf eine Antwortrate von 0,31%, die 5798 Click-Throughs zur NSPCC-Seite lieferte. Effizienz: Im ersten Monate der Kampagne wurden 648% der Antworten geliefert. Die durchschnittliche CTR war mit 1,95% sechsmal höher als erwartet. Die CTR der emotionsgeladenen Ausführung lag mit 17% an der Spitze. **EFFIZIENZ:** Cost per Click (CPC) lag bei £0,41, nur 16% der geplanten CPC von £2,64. Auch die Unkosten durch Mediakäufe wurden mit £7,96 CPM deutlich minimiert (siehe links).

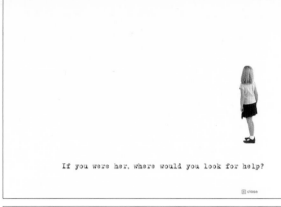

If you were her, where would you look for help?

Abused children can feel isolated and alone.

EVERY WEEK AT LEAST ONE CHILD IS KILLED BY THEIR PARENT OR CARER.

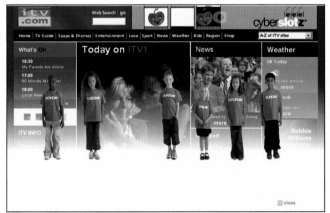

FEATURED ON THE DVD **CAMPAIGN:** Pink Panty Poker. **PRODUCT:** Victoria's Secret Pink. **YEAR:** 2005. **AGENCY:** Crispin Porter + Bogusky <www.cpbgroup.com>. **PRODUCTION TIME:** 2 months. **EXECUTIVE CREATIVE DIRECTOR:** Alex Bogusky. **CREATIVE DIRECTOR:** Scott Linnen. **INTERACTIVE CREATIVE DIRECTOR:** Jeff Benjamin. **ASSOCIATE CREATIVE DIRECTOR:** Tiffany Kosel. **ART DIRECTOR:** Tiffany Kosel. **COPYWRITER:** Scott Linnen. **PROGRAMMER:** Luis Santi (North Kingdom). **TECH ASPECTS:** Macromedia Flash. **AWARDS:** London International 2005 (Finalist), Young Guns 2005 (Gold).

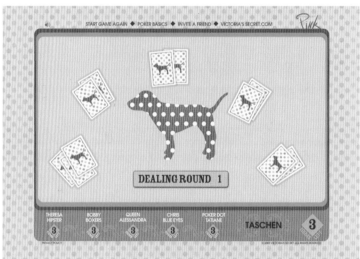

CONCEPT: PINK Panty Poker.com blended online poker, a new collection of Victoria's Secret PINK merchandise and oh yeah, hot supermodels stripping down to their skivvies. The game, aimed at young women but appealing to a large audience of men as well, allows the user to play Five Card Draw Poker against 5 other players (3 women and 2 men). Each time a hand is lost, so is an article of clothing. As each model removes one item, they engage in a playful strip tease, revealing the product in a sexy, fun way. The player with the most clothing remaining at the end of the game is the winner. **RESULTS:** Without any media, the site was promoted virally via e-mails and word of mouth. Within days, the site was the hottest topic on blogs throughout the web. And, after its first two weeks, the site was bringing in almost half a million visitors who were interacting with the site for over 8 minutes at a time.

CONCEPT : Pink Panty Poker.com mêle un jeu de poker en ligne, la nouvelle collection de lingerie Pink de Victoria's Secret, et de magnifiques top models qui font un strip-tease. Le jeu, qui s'adresse aux jeunes femmes mais attire aussi un large public masculin, permet à l'usager de disputer une partie de cartes contre cinq autres joueurs (trois femmes et deux hommes). Chaque fois qu'on perd une manche, le top model enlève un vêtement. A chaque déshabillage, le top model fait un strip-tease, révélant le produit de manière drôle et sexy. Le

joueur qui a gardé le plus de vêtements sur lui est déclaré vainqueur à la fin de la partie. **RÉSULTATS :** Sans aucune publicité, le site a été promu de façon virale via les e-mails et le bouche à oreille. En quelques jours, le site a fait les choux gras de nombreux blogs sur le Net. Après deux semaines de lancement, le site a attiré presque 500 000 visiteurs qui ont interagi plus de 8 minutes en moyenne.

KONZEPT: PINK Panty Poker.com kombinierte Online-Poker, eine neue Kollektion von Victoria's Secret PINK-Artikeln und, oh ja, Supermodels, die sich bis auf ihre Unterwäsche auszogen. Das Spiel zielte auf junge Frauen ab, aber auch auf ein größeres Publikum von Männern. Man kann gegen fünf andere Spieler Strip-Poker spielen (drei Frauen und zwei Männer). Jeder, der verliert, muss ein Kleidungsstück ausziehen. Wenn ein Model etwas auszieht, vollführt sie einen spielerischen Striptease und zeigt das Produkt auf eine lustige, sexy Art und Weise. Der Spieler, der am Ende noch am meisten anhat, hat gewonnen. **ERGEBNISSE:** Ohne irgendwelche Medien wurde die Seite viral durch E-Mails und Mund-zu-Mund-Propaganda verbreitet. Innerhalb von Tagen war sie in Blogs im ganzen Web Gesprächsthema Nummer eins. Nach zwei Wochen zog die Seite fast eine halbe Million Besucher an, die jeweils über acht Minuten verweilten.

CONCEPT: Five is the UK's fifth terrestrial TV channel. Launched in 2000, it has grown steadily with around 30 million viewers tuning in every week to watch the best in film, American drama and sport. Five was the first terrestrial channel to recognise the popularity of poker, and dedicates Wednesday nights to the game. **BRIEF:** To create an on-line experience to support five's poker show and it's sponsorship by gambling site, PartyPoker.Com. As well as promoting the show, the site should act as a resource for poker fans old and new by giving player profiles, rules of the game, hints and tips, and driving users to the download PartyPoker's gaming software and start playing on line. **SOLUTION:** Avoiding the stereotypical style of many poker sites, we put site users at the heart of The Poker Room, a sophisticated atmospheric, smoky poker club. Sitting at a poker table with five other players (The Cowboy, The Chinaman, The Flirt, The Young Gun and The Intimidator), the user navigates the site using their hand of cards. Each card represented a section of the site ranging from game info and hints and tips, to video tutorials from professionals. The final section of the site linked users through to PartyPoker.com and encouraged them to download the sites software.

CONCEPT : Five est la cinquième chaîne hertzienne de Grande-Bretagne. Lancée en l'an 2000, elle a gagné progressivement en audience pour atteindre quelque 30 millions de téléspectateurs par semaine qui regardent une sélection des meilleurs films, séries américaines et émissions sportives. La chaîne a été la première à reconnaître la popularité du poker, et y consacre les soirées du vendredi. **BRIEFING :** Créer une expérience en ligne pour promouvoir l'émission de poker de Five et son sponsor, le site de jeu PartyPoker.com. Le site devait également servir de base de données pour les amateurs de poker de tous âges en présentant des portraits de joueurs, des règles du jeu, des astuces, et encourager les usagers à télécharger le logiciel de jeu de PartyPoker afin de jouer en ligne. **SOLUTION :** S'éloignant du style stéréotypé de nombreux sites de poker, nous invitons l'usager à pénétrer dans la Salle de Poker, un club enfumé à l'ambiance raffinée. S'asseyant à la table avec cinq autres joueurs (le Cowboy, le Chinois, le Dragueur, la Starlette et l'Intimidateur), l'usager navigue dans le site avec ses cartes en main. Chaque carte renvoie à une rubrique du site : règles du jeu, astuces, et tutoriels vidéo de professionnels. La dernière section du site renvoie les usagers sur PartyPoker.com et les invite à télécharger le logiciel de jeu.

KONZEPT: Five ist der fünfte terrestrische Fernsehkanal in Großbritannien. Im Jahr 2000 eingeführt, ist er stets gewachsen, mit heute ca. 30 Millionen Zuschauern, die jede Woche für die besten Filme, amerikanische Serien und Sport einschalten. Five war der erste terrestrische Kanal, der die Popularität von Poker erkannte, und widmet Mittwochabende diesem Spiel. **AUFGABE:** Ein Online-Erlebnis zu kreieren, das die Poker Show und ihren Sponsor, die Seite PartyPoker.com, unterstützt. Neben Werbung für die Show sollte die Seite als Quelle für junge und alte Pokerfans dienen und Spieler mit Profilen, Spielregeln, Tipps und Tricks versorgen sowie sie zum Download von PartyPokers Spielsoftware und dem Spielen online anregen. **LÖSUNG:** Den stereotypen Stil vieler anderer Pokerseiten vermeidend, stellten wir dem Benutzer in die Mitte von „The Poker Room", einen modernen, verrauchten Pokerclub. Er sitzt mit den anderen fünf Spielern (The Cowboy, The Chinaman, The Flirt, The Young Gun und The Intimidator) am Tisch und navigiert die Seite mit Hilfe ihrer Spielkarten. Jede Karte stellt einen Bereich der Seite dar – von Spielinfo über Tipps und Tricks bis zu Videoanleitungen von Profis. Der letzte Bereich der Seite führte Benutzer zu PartyPoker.com und ermunterte sie zum Download von Software.

FEATURED ON THE DVD **CAMPAIGN:** Retouch. **PRODUCT:** Girl Power. **CLIENT:** Girl Power/Sara Bambder. **YEAR:** 2005. **AGENCY:** Forsman & Bodenfors <www.fb.se>. **PRODUCTION TIME:** 2 weeks. **WEB DIRECTOR:** Martin Cedergren. **ART DIRECTOR:** Sill Öberg. **COPYWRITER:** Jacob Nelson. **ACCOUNT MANAGER:** Anna Chantre. **ACCOUNT EXECUTIVE:** Fredrik Widén. **DESIGNER:** Lars Jansson, Viktor Larsson. **PROGRAMMER:** Itiden. **TECH ASPECTS:** Macromedia Flash. **MEDIA CIRCULATED:** Online ads, campaign site, community. **AWARDS:** Cannes Lions 2005 (Finalist), Epica 2005 (Gold).

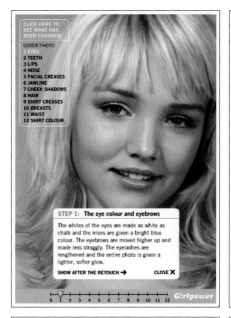

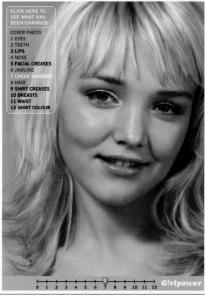

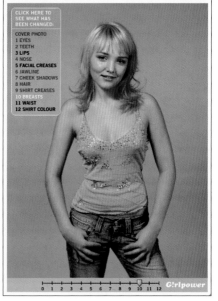

CONCEPT: The media world is becoming increasingly fixated on appearances. And the number of tricks used to achieve the increasingly exaggerated ideals is growing. Many models have plastic surgery and even more are retouched so they appear to have bigger breasts, smaller stomachs or fuller lips. We wanted to show how easy it is to change someone's appearance in this campaign.

CONCEPT : Le monde médiatique se focalise de plus en plus sur les apparences. Et le nombre d'astuces utilisées pour forger une image idéale est en constante augmentation. Nombre de top models ont recours à la chirurgie esthétique et beaucoup d'entre elles sont retouchées numériquement afin d'exhiber des poitrines opulentes, des ventres plats ou des bouches pulpeuses. Nous voulions montrer dans cette campagne avec quelle facilité on peut changer l'apparence des gens.

KONZEPT: Die Medienwelt fixiert sich zunehmend auf Äußerlichkeiten. Die Anzahl von Tricks, diese übertriebenen Ideale zu erreichen, wächst. Viele Models unterziehen sich Schönheitsoperationen, und noch mehr werden retuschiert, so dass sie größere Brüste, flachere Bäuche oder vollere Lippen haben. Mit dieser Kampagne wollten wir aufzeigen, wie leicht es ist, Äußerlichkeiten zu verändern.

FEATURED ON THE DVD **CAMPAIGN:** Santamaria Wirtschaftswundertour Campaign Website <www.santamariatour.de>. **PRODUCT:** Santamaria Wirtschaftswundertour. **YEAR:** 2005. **AGENCY:** Fork Unstable Media <www.fork.de>. **CREATIVE TEAM:** Roman Hilmer, Arndt Dwenger, Tilo Göbel, David Hoffmann, Klaudia Plettner. **PROGRAMMER:** David Hoffmann. **TECH ASPECTS:** Macromedia Flash.

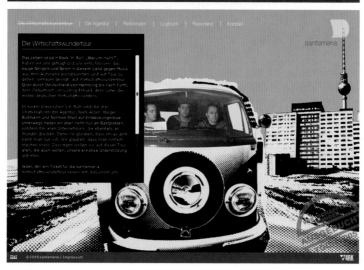

CONCEPT: Our task was to create a promotional website for Santamaria, an agency specialized in creative concepts for advertising campaigns. The Wirtschaftswundertour, an unusual self-promotion which included driving a bus through Germany and spontaneously assisting potential clients, required a public interface for the "traveling advertisers". So we developed a website which offers an authentic glimpse of the mission including real-time updates and pictures. **RESULTS:** Inspired by Swiss travel brochures from the 1920's and 30's we combined the styles of copy art, photomontage and cut-out with the use of strong colors and a simple navigation. The layout centers on the bouncing bus (including a view of the crew behind the windshield) bringing hope and new ideas to the desert of the German "Jammertal". True to the "Wirtschaftswunder" claim the website manages to combine a tongue-in-cheek hint to German post-war optimism with a DIY design aesthetic ranging from the 1920's to the 1980's — a timeless cry for creativity in times of stagnation and depression.

CONCEPT : Notre mission était de créer un site promotionnel pour Santamaria, une agence spécialisée dans les concepts créatifs pour la publicité. Le Wirstschaftswundertour, une auto-promotion originale qui consistait à voyager en bus en Allemagne et aider spontanément des clients, nécessitait une interface publique pour les « publicitaires voyageurs ». Nous avons développé un site qui offre un aperçu authentique de la mission, enrichi de photos et de mises à jour en temps réel. **RÉSULTATS :** S'inspirant des brochures de voyage suisse des années 20 et 30, nous avons combiné les styles du copy-art, du photomontage et du collage dans des couleurs vives et une navigation simple. La maquette met l'accent sur le bus (et l'équipe qui est au volant), symbolisant l'espoir et l'imagination dans le désert du « Jammertal » allemand. Fidèle au slogan, le site mêle une allusion comique à l'optimisme allemand de l'après-guerre aux valeurs esthétiques en vigueur de 1920 à 1980, encourageant la créativité dans une période de stagnation et de dépression.

KONZEPT: Wir sollten eine Werbeseite für Santamaria erstellen, eine Agentur, die auf kreative Konzepte für Werbekampagnen spezialisiert ist. Die Wirtschaftswundertour, eine ungewöhnliche Eigenwerbung, die eine Busfahrt durch Deutschland einschließt, bei der potenzielle Klienten spontan assistieren, erforderte ein öffentliches Interface für die „reisenden Werber". Also entwickelten wir eine Webseite, die einen authentischen Einblick in die Mission gibt, darunter Live-Aktualisierungen und Bilder. **ERGEBNISSE:** Inspiriert von Reisebroschüren aus der Schweiz der 20er und 30er Jahre kombinierten wir die Stile von Copy Art, Fotomontage und Cut Out mit starken Farben und einer simplen Navigation. Das Layout zentriert einen hüpfenden Bus (einschließlich eines Blicks auf die Crew hinter der Windschutzscheibe), der Hoffnung und neue Ideen in die Wüste des deutschen Jammertals bringt. Passend zur „Wirtschaftswunder"-Aussage kombiniert die Webseite einen ironischen Hinweis auf den deutschen Nachkriegsoptimismus mit einer Heimwerker-Designästhetik, die sich zwischen den 20er und 80er Jahren bewegt — ein zeitloser Schrei nach Kreativität in Zeiten von Stagnation und Depression.

FEATURED ON THE DVD **CAMPAIGN:** Reality Advertising. **PRODUCT:** Super Bonder. **YEAR:** 2005. **AGENCY:** Tribal DDB São Paulo <www.dm9ddb.com.br>. **PRODUCTION TIME:** 3 weeks. **ART DIRECTOR:** Cris Santoro, Pedro Gravena, Maurício Mazzariol, Alexandre D'albergaria. **COPYWRITER:** Keke Toledo. **DESIGNER:** Theo Siqueira. **PROGRAMMER:** Mauricio Massaia. **TECH ASPECTS:** Macromedia Flash. **MEDIA CIRCULATED:** Internet. **AWARDS:** Cannes Lions 2005 (Grand Prix).

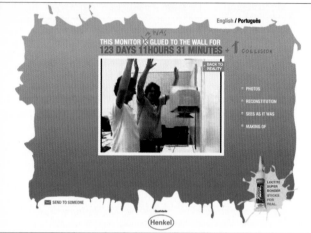

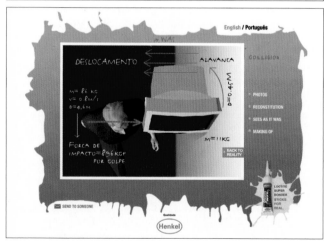

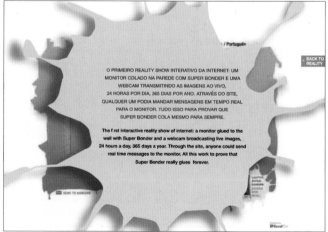

RESULTS: Numbers are rocketing. On Friday, June 24th, 1,113 sites were mentioning the reality piece. Today's statistics, are nearly 2,500 reference sites. Since the piece has been running on the Internet, every two days, the number of access has almost doubled. Today's coverage is more than 79 countries.

RÉSULTATS : Les chiffres explosent. Le vendredi 24 juin, 1 113 sites mentionnaient l'expérience publicitaire en cours. Les statistiques indiquent aujourd'hui 2 500 sites de référence. Depuis que la publicité est diffusée sur internet, tous les deux jours, le chiffre de la fréquentation a quasiment doublé. La diffusion couvre aujourd'hui plus de 79 pays.

ERGEBNISSE: Die Zahlen schießen in die Höhe. Freitag, den 24. Juni, erwähnten 1113 Seiten dieses Reality-Stück. Die heutige Statistik besagt fast 2500 Referenzseiten. Seit es im Internet läuft, verdoppelte sich die Anzahl der Zugänge alle zwei Tage. Das derzeitige Sendegebiet erstreckt sich auf über 79 Länder.

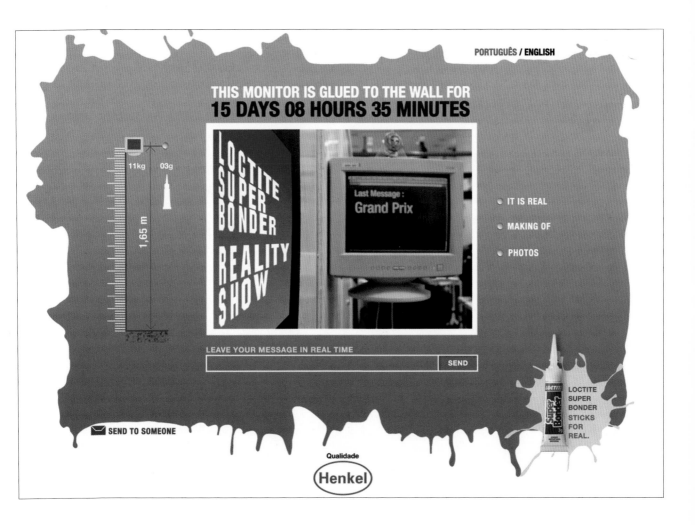

FEATURED ON THE DVD **CAMPAIGN:** Target Design for All <www.target.com/designforall>. **YEAR:** 2004. **AGENCY:** R/GA <www.rga.com>. **BROADBAND:** David Shuff, Laura Pence, Stephen Barnwell. **COPYWRITER:** Jamie McPhee, Mary-Catherine Jones, Melissa Bannon, Nana Brew-Hammond, Nicole Possin, Paul Malmont. **DESIGNER:** Allen Yee, Andrew Clark, Andrew Thompson, Brennan Boblett, Ernest Rowe, Henry Brown, Jeremiah Simpson, Johanna Langford, Josh Mackey, Kazz Ishihara, Kris Kiger, Lara Horner, Lian Chang, Martin Jung, Matt Lawrence, Michael Colella, Natalie Lam, Nick Law, Pablo Gomez, Rich Mains, Sarah Golding, Tracy Levy, William Wong, Winnie Tseng. **INTERACTION DESIGN:** Aya Karpinska, Cindy Jeffers, Diego Bauducco, Elaine Castillo-Keller, Perry Chan, Ted Metcalfe. **PRODUCTION:** Christopher Dugan, John Antinori, Mae Flordeliza. **PROGRAMMER:** Chris Hinkle, Hamid Younessi, Ted Warner, Tom Freudenheim. **STRATEGY AND ANALYTICS:** Briggs Davidson, Erica Millado, Ken O'Donnell, Nicole Victor. **QUALITY ASSURANCE:** Diane Lichtman, Edwin Quan, Jennifer Liang, Michael Shagalov, Patrick Fitzgerald.

CAMPAIGN: Target Clear Rx. **AGENCY:** R/GA <www.rga.com>. **ACCOUNT MANAGEMENT:** Nicole Victor. **COPYWRITER:** Mary Catherine Jones, Paul Malmont. **DESIGNER:** Andy Clark, Johanna Langford, Lian Chang, Ernest Rowe, Allen Yee. **INTERACTION DESIGN:** Ted Metcalfe, Perry Chan. **PRODUCTION:** John Antinori, Elyse Epstein. **PROGRAMMER:** Tom Freudenheim, Chris Hinkle, Sunny Nan. **QUALITY ASSURANCE:** Patrick Fitzgerald.

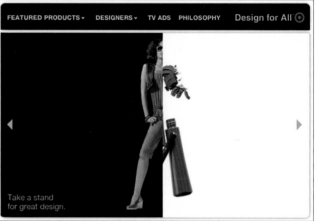

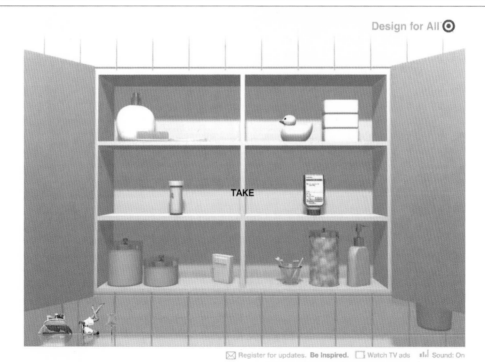

CAMPAIGN: Traumschiff Surprise. **PRODUCT:** Chicken Premiere Surprise, Käsesahne (Food). Key ring, fun watch (Non-food). **YEAR:** 2004. **AGENCY:** Tribal DDB München/Mindmatics <www.tribalddb.de>. **CREATIVE TEAM:** Mick Schneider, Fabian Zarse. **PROGRAMMER:** Michael Mölter; Chrisitan Heydt. **TECH ASPECTS:** Macromedia Flash, sound, film, mobile applications (ring-tones, logos, voice-mail greetings, "fun keys"). **MEDIA CIRCULATED:** over 10 million trayliner (in-store).

CONCEPT: Based on a German cult comedy movie with the same title a McDonald's "Traumschiff Surprise" campaign was staged in the restaurants using an innovative mobile concept. The ingenious story line and the cult status of the film were interpreted as innovative fun experiences with instant entertainment for everyone. The customer could choose between mobile voicemail greetings and ring tones, logos and "fun keys" – an innovation in mobile phone entertainment. The campaign was extended on the McDonald's website with detailed informations about food-offers and mobile fun and exclusive soundfiles. **RESULTS:** Even before the official film premiere, the campaign generated high demand from younger target groups along with increased talk value, in-store experience and massive viral marketing impact.

CONCEPT : S'inspirant d'une comédie allemande culte, nous avons lancé une campagne du même nom pour McDonald's, en utilisant un concept novateur adapté aux téléphones mobiles. Le scénario ingénieux du film et son statut de culte chez les jeunes ont été déclinés dans des expériences amusantes et immédiatement distrayantes pour tous. Le consommateur pouvait choisir entre une messagerie audio, des sonneries d'appel, des logos et des touches fantaisie, une innovation dans le domaine de la communication sur mobile. La campagne a été étendue sur le site de McDonald's, avec des infos sur les offres de menus et les accessoires audio pour mobiles. **RÉSULTATS :** Avant même la sortie officielle du film, la campagne a généré beaucoup de demandes chez les jeunes, un phénomène de bouche à oreille, une hausse de fréquentation des restaurants et un impact massif de marketing viral.

KONZEPT: Basierend auf einem lustigen deutschen Kultfilm mit demselben Titel startete McDonald's in seinen Restaurants eine „Traumschiff Surprise"-Kampagne mit einem innovativen Handy-Konzept. Die geniale Handlung und der Kultstatus des Films wurden als innovative Spaßerfahrung und Unterhaltung für Jedermann interpretiert. Der Kunde konnte zwischen Voicemail-Grüßen und Klingeltönen, Logos und „Fun Keys" wählen – eine Innovation im Handy-Entertainment. Die Kampagne wurde auf die McDonald's-Webseite ausgeweitet, mit detaillierten Informationen über Menü-Angebote und exklusiven Handysounddateien. **ERGEBNISSE:** Schon vor der offiziellen Filmpremiere erhielt die Kampagne großen Zulauf von jüngeren Zielgruppen und viel Mundpropaganda und massive viraler Marketingwirkung.

FEATURED ON THE DVD **CAMPAIGN:** VARTA Experience Online Brand Promotion <www.varta-experience.de>. **PRODUCT:** VARTA Consumer Batteries. **YEAR:** 2005. **AGENCY:** Fork Unstable Media <www.fork.de>. **CREATIVE TEAM:** Hans Schaale, Tons May, Timo Wilks. **PROGRAMMER:** Benjamin Herholz (Flash), Dani Füller (CMS). **TECH ASPECTS:** Macromedia Flash.

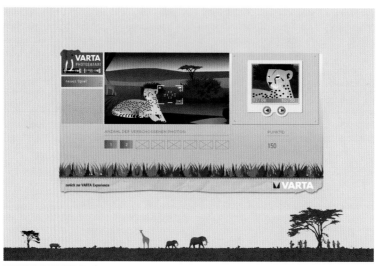

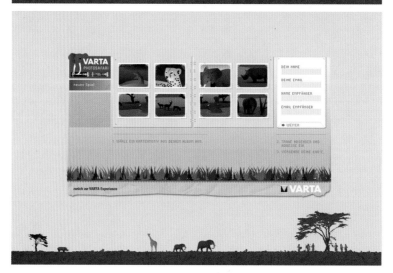

CONCEPT: For VARTA we developed the VARTA Experience, an adventure special combining product promotion with an organized trip into the wilderness. Our aim was to create a microsite that not only provides all the necessary information on the trip but also recruits potential adventurers. **RESULTS:** Interactive contents such as games and mobile applications remind users on and offline of what's going on. Ranging from African-style downloadables to the beautifully illustrated flash-based Safari Game the visual impact of the design also allows users at home to take part in the adventure and makes for an emotional web experience. Most of the contents can be edited by a modular CMS thus providing an efficient and consistent way to update and localize them if required.

CONCEPT : Nous avons développé l'expérience Varta, une aventure qui combine la promotion de produit et un voyage organisé dans la jungle. Le but était de créer un micro-site qui offrirait toutes les infos nécessaires à l'organisation du voyage, tout en recrutant des aventuriers potentiels. **RÉSULTATS :** Le contenu interactif, comme les jeux et les applications pour mobiles tiennent les usagers informés, en ligne et hors ligne. Les éléments à télécharger de style africain, le superbe jeu de safari en Flash et l'impact du design graphique permettent à l'usager de participer à l'aventure depuis chez lui, et contribuent à une expérience émotionnelle. La plupart des contenus peuvent être édités par un système de gestion modulaire, qui permet des mises à jour régulières et des versions locales si besoin est.

KONZEPT: Für VARTA entwickelten wir ein interaktives Abenteuer-Special, das Produktwerbung mit einem organisierten Trip in die Wildnis kombiniert. Wir wollten eine Microsite entwickeln, die nicht nur die notwendigen Informationen enthält, sondern auch potenzielle Abenteurer rekrutiert. **ERGEBNISSE:** Interaktive Inhalte wie Spiele und Handy-Anwendungen halten Benutzer online und offline auf dem Laufenden. Von Downloads im afrikanischen Stil zum kunstvoll illustrierten Safarispiel in Flash – die visuelle Wirkung des Designs ermöglicht es dem Benutzer daheim, durch ein emotionales Weberlebnis am Abenteuer teilzunehmen. Die meisten Inhalte können mit einem modularen CMS editiert werden, so dass man sie bei Bedarf effektiv und konsistent aktualisieren und lokalisieren kann.

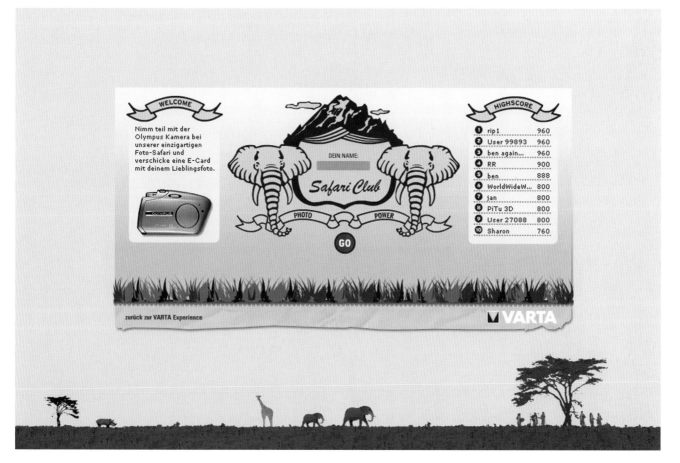

CAMPAIGN: GAP Watch Me Change <www.watchmechange.com>. **PRODUCT:** The Gap. **YEAR:** 2005. **AGENCY:** Crispin Porter + Bogusky <www.cpbgroup.com>. **PRODUCTION TIME:** 2 months. **EXECUTIVE CREATIVE DIRECTOR:** Alex Bogusky. **CREATIVE DIRECTOR:** Andrew Keller, Rob Reilly. **INTERACTIVE CREATIVE DIRECTOR:** Jeff Benjamin. **ART DIRECTOR:** Nick Munoz. **COPYWRITER:** Mike Howard. **DESIGNER:** Rahul Panchal. **PROGRAMMER:** Fuel Industries. **TECH ASPECTS:** Shockwave 3D. **AWARDS:** Future Marketing Awards 2006 (Internet Innovation).

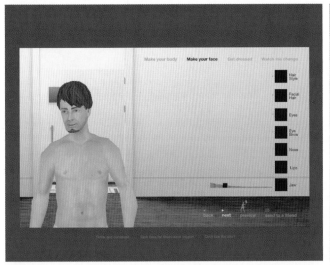

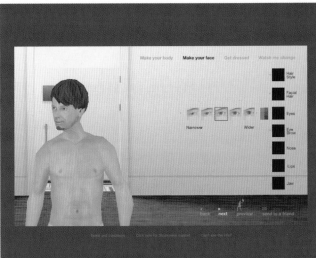

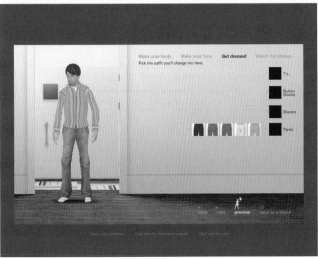

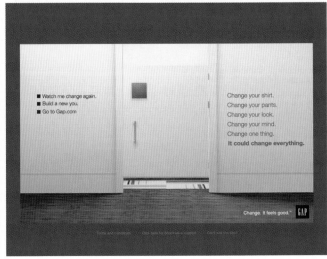

CONCEPT: We launched GAP's watchmechange.com as part of an integrated plan to communicate the transformation of Gap stores in key markets to a completely new look and feel. Each medium in the plan played a different role – some more rational than others. Watchmechange.com was created to link to the aspirational idea of "change": the notion that a small change (such as a new pair of chinos) is just the beginning of what can be many big and beneficial changes. We developed a fully interactive website where we guide users through a detailed step-by-step construction of an online model of themselves. At the end of the model-building process, the character performs a strip-tease dance into the dressing room where they will change into a GAP outfit. **RESULTS:** The success of WMC has been achieved completely virally, with no initial seeding at the launch in July. To date, there have been over 4.5 million total visits and over 1 million unique visitors.

CONCEPT : Nous avons lancé le site de Gap watchmechange.com comme partie intégrante d'une campagne visant à communiquer la transformation des boutiques Gap sur des marchés clés, et leur nouvelle apparence. Chaque support du plan média jouait un rôle différent, certains plus rationnels que d'autres. Watchmechange.com a été élaboré pour illustrer l'aspiration au changement, l'idée qu'un petit changement (comme un nouveau pantalon de coton) peut être la source de changements bénéfiques plus importants. Nous avons développé un site interactif où nous guidons l'usager pas à pas dans la construction

détaillée d'un modèle virtuel de lui-même. A la fin du processus de transformation, le personnage fait un strip-tease dans la cabine d'essayage, avant d'adopter une tenue Gap. **RÉSULTATS :** Le succès du site s'est fait de façon totalement virale, sans aucune annonce préalable au lancement, au mois de juillet. A ce jour, plus de 4,5 millions de visites ont été comptabilisées, ainsi que 1 million de visiteurs uniques.

KONZEPT: Wir führten GAPs watchmechange.com als Teil eines integrierten Plans ein, die Transformation von GAP-Geschäften in einen komplett neuen Look in Schlüsselländern zu kommunizieren. Jedes Medium innerhalb des Plans spielte eine unterschiedliche Rolle – manche rationaler als andere. Watchmechange.com wurde erstellt, um auf die inspirierende Idee von Veränderung zu verweisen: Eine kleine Veränderung (wie ein neues Paar Chinos) ist nur der Anfange von etwas, das viele nützliche Veränderungen nach sich ziehen kann. Wir entwickelten eine komplett interaktive Webseite, auf der wir Benutzer durch eine Schritt-für-Schritt-Konstruktion eines Online-Modells von ihnen selbst führen. Am Ende dieses Prozesses vollführt die Figur im Umkleideraum einen Striptease-Tanz und wechselt in ein GAP-Outfit. **ERGEBNISSE:** Der Erfolg von WMC wurde ausschließlich viral erreicht, ohne vorheriges Streuen beim Launch im Juli. Bis heute gab es über 4,5 Millionen Besuche auf der Seite und über 1 Million einzelne Besucher.

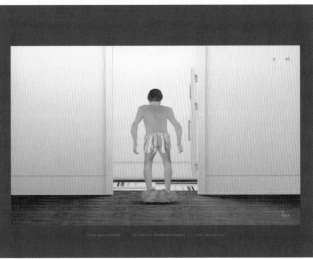

FEATURED ON THE DVD CAMPAIGN: Shine. PRODUCT: Nugget Leather Cleaner. YEAR: 2006. AGENCY: Euro RSCG 4D São Paulo <www.eurorscg4d.com.br>. CHIEF CREATIVE OFFICER: Alon Sochaczewski. CREATIVE DIRECTOR: Touché. COPYWRITER: Fábio Pierro, Nelson Rubens Botega Jr. ART DIRECTOR: Guilherme Médici. DESIGNER: Airton Groba. PROGRAMMER: Edivaldo Braz. TECH ASPECTS: Macromedia Flash. AWARDS: Cannes Cyber Lions 2006 (Shortlist).

CONCEPT: Nugget from Reckitt Benckiser is a traditional paste that gives an intense shine, and protects all types of leather.

CONCEPT : Nugget, de Reckitt Benckiser, est une pâte de cirage traditionnelle qui donne un brillant intense et protège tous les types de cuir.

KONZEPT: Nugget von Reckitt Benckiser ist eine traditionelle Schuhcreme, die intensiven Glanz erzeugt und alle Arten von Leder schützt.

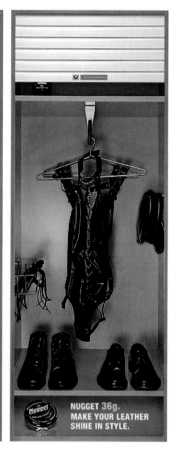

FEATURED ON THE DVD **CAMPAIGN:** It's Me. **PRODUCT:** Nugget Shoe Wax. **YEAR:** 2006. **AGENCY:** Euro RSCG 4D São Paulo <www.eurorscg4d.com.br>. **CHIEF CREATIVE OFFICER:** Alon Sochaczewski. **CREATIVE DIRECTOR:** Touché. **COPYWRITER:** Fábio Pierro. **ART DIRECTOR:** Touché. **PROGRAMMER:** Edivaldo Braz. **TECH ASPECTS:** Macromedia Flash, webcam. **AWARDS:** Cannes Cyber Lions 2006 (Shortlist).

CONCEPT: Liquid Nugget from Reckitt Benckiser is a wax that provides intense shine and protection to shoes.

CONCEPT : Liquid Nugget, de Reckitt Benckiser, est un cirage qui protège les chaussures et les fait briller.

KONZEPT: Liquid Nugget von Reckitt Benckiser ist ein Wachs, der für intensiven Glanz und Pflege von Schuhen sorgt.

FEATURED ON THE DVD **CAMPAIGN:** Oops! **PRODUCT:** Poliflor. **YEAR:** 2006. **AGENCY:** Euro RSCG 4D São Paulo <www.eurorscg4d.com.br>. **CHIEF CREATIVE OFFICER:** Alon Sochaczewski. **CREATIVE DIRECTOR:** Touché. **COPYWRITER:** Fábio Pierro, Nelson Rubens Botega Jr. **ART DIRECTOR:** Touché. **DESIGNER:** Airton Groba. **TECH ASPECTS:** Macromedia Flash. **AWARDS:** Cannes Cyber Lions 2006 (Gold).

CONCEPT: Poliflor is an effective furniture polisher that protects the surfaces where it is applied, leaving them shiny, smooth and preventing the adherence of dirt.

CONCEPT : Poliflor est un vernis pour meubles très efficace. Il protège les zones d'application, les rend brillantes et lisses, et repousse la poussière.

KONZEPT: Poliflor ist eine effektive Möbelpolitur, die Oberflächen schützt. Nach Gebrauch sind sie glatt und glänzend und weisen Dreck ab.

FEATURED ON THE DVD **CAMPAIGN:** Monalisa. **PRODUCT:** Rodasol. **YEAR:** 2005. **AGENCY:** Euro RSCG 4D São Paulo <www.eurorscg4d.com.br>. **CHIEF CREATIVE OFFICER:** Alon Sochaczewski. **CREATIVE DIRECTOR:** Touché. **COPYWRITER:** Fábio Pierro. **ART DIRECTOR:** Valter Klug. **TECH ASPECTS:** Macromedia Flash. **AWARDS:** Colunistas Brasil 2005 Awards (Gold); Colunistas São Paulo 2005 Awards(Gold); MMOnline/Msn 2005 Awards (Bronze); About de Comunicação Integrada e Dirigida 2005 (Silver); Cannes Cyber Lions 2005 (Bronze); NY Festivals 2005 (Merit); ADC Awards 2006 (Merit); CLIO 2006 Awards (Shorlist); One Show 2006 (Finalist); CCSP 2006 Awards (Bronze); FIAP 2006 Awards(Silver).

CONCEPT: Rodasol is a multi-purpose insecticide that exterminates flies, long-legged creatures and mosquitoes, even if they are out of sight.

KONZEPT: Rodasol ist ein Multizweck-Insektizid, das gegen Fliegen, langbeinige Kreaturen und Moskitos eingesetzt werden kann – sogar, wenn diese außer Sichtweite sind.

CONCEPT : Rodasol est un insecticide universel qui extermine les mouches, les insectes à longues pattes et les moustiques, même lorsqu'on ne les voit pas.

FEATURED ON THE DVD **CAMPAIGN:** One for All. **PRODUCT:** Rodasol. **YEAR:** 2005. **AGENCY:** Euro RSCG 4D São Paulo <www.eurorscg4d.com.br>. **CHIEF CREATIVE OFFICER:** Alon Sochaczewski. **CREATIVE DIRECTOR:** Touché. **COPYWRITER:** Fábio Pierro. **ART DIRECTOR:** Fábio Matiazzi, Touché. **TECH ASPECTS:** Macromedia Flash. **AWARDS:** Cannes Cyber Lions 2005 (Silver, Shortlist); About de Comunicação Integrada e Dirigida 2005 (Gold).

CONCEPT: Rodasol is an advanced insecticide formula that performs outstandingly in exterminating flying insects.

CONCEPT : La formule avancée de l'insecticide Rodasol élimine particulièrement bien les insectes volants.

KONZEPT: Rodasol ist ein hoch entwickeltes Insektizid, das einzigartig bei der Bekämpfung fliegender Insekten wirkt.

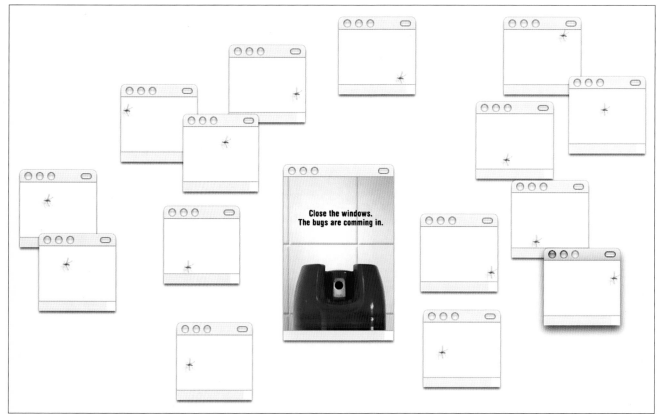

CONCEPT: Interactive advertising that materializes a blind experience.

CONCEPT : Publicité interactive qui illustre les problèmes de cécité.

KONZEPT: Interaktive Werbung, die ein Erlebnis materialisiert.

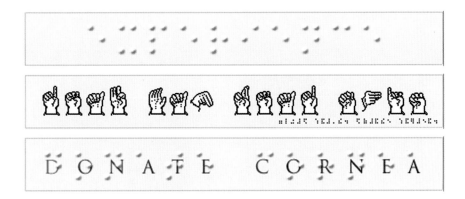

CAMPAIGN: Levis anti-fit. PRODUCT: Levis 501's. YEAR: 2005. AGENCY: Farfar <www.farfar.se>. PRODUCTION TIME: 1 month. CREATIVE TEAM: Jennie Arvenäs, Pellen. PROGRAMMER: Bo Gustafson.

CONCEPT: The new Levis 501's are anti fit and so are the people featured on this site. We've found five young individuals who do their own thing and have a strong focus on expressing themselves without worrying what regular people thinks. Here, we let them tell their own story. The site lets visitors explore things for themselves and offers the opportunity to claim the spot as the sixth and final "anti-fit".

CONCEPT : Les nouveaux Levis 501 sont "anti-fit" (mal ajustés), comme le sont les personnes qui figurent sur le site. Nous avons choisi cinq jeunes gens qui font ce qui leur plaît, et qui sont attachés à leur expression personnelle sans se soucier de l'opinion publique. On leur donne la parole pour raconter leur propre histoire. Le site permet aux visiteurs d'explorer par eux-mêmes et offre la possibilité de qualifier le spot de sixième et ultime "anti-fit".

KONZEPT: Die neuen Levis 501 sind „anti-fit" – genau wie die Menschen, die auf dieser Seite vorgestellt werden. Es sind fünf junge individuelle Personen, die ihr eigenes Ding durchziehen und sich selber ausdrücken, ohne sich darüber Gedanken zu machen, was andere über sie denken. Hier erzählen sie ihre Geschichte. Besucher können die Seite eigenständig erforschen.

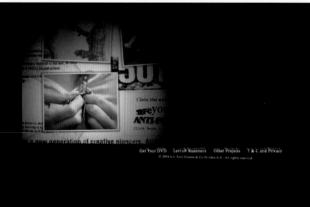

FEATURED ON THE DVD **CAMPAIGN:** "Run". **PRODUCT:** Cia. Athletica. **YEAR:** 2005. **AGENCY:** Tribal DDB São Paulo <www.dm9ddb.com.br>. **PRODUCTION TIME:** 2 weeks. **ART DIRECTOR/COPYWRITER/PROGRAMMER:** Mauricio Mazzariol. **TECH ASPECTS:** Macromedia Flash, sound. **MEDIA CIRCULATED:** Internet. **AWARDS:** Cannes Cyber Lions 2005 (Gold).

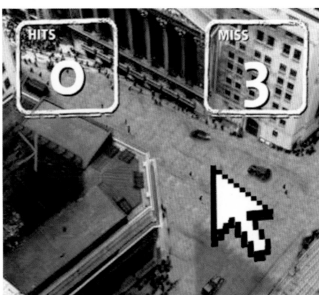

CAMPAIGN: Driver's Eye. PRODUCT: Driver Safety. CLIENT: Japan Advertising Council. YEAR: 2004. AGENCY: Dentsu Inc. <www.dentsu.com>. PRODUCER: Hajime Kawamura, Kuniyuki Manji (Excite Japan Co., Ltd.). PRODUCTION TIME: 1 month. CREATIVE DIRECTOR: Shoichi Tamura. ART DIRECTOR: Momoko Kobayashi, Hiroki Nakamura. DESIGNER: Momoko Kobayashi. COPYWRITER: Shoichi Tamura. PRODUCER: Masataka Hosogane. TECH ASPECTS: Macromedia Flash. MEDIA CIRCULATED: Banner. AWARDS: Cannes Lions 2005 (Silver), tokyo.interactive.ad.awards.jp 2005 (Gold), London International Awards 2005 (Winner).

CONCEPT: A banner ad warning people not to use their mobile phones while driving. Users are invited to drive the car in the banner at the top of the screen. Soon after, a mobile phone starts to ring in the banner on the right hand side. As soon as the driver picks up the phone, the entire screen cracks into pieces.

CONCEPT : Une bannière alerte le public sur les dangers du téléphone mobile au volant. Les usagers sont invités à conduire la voiture sur la bannière en haut de l'écran. Un téléphone se met alors à sonner sur la droite de la bannière. Dès que le conducteur décroche, l'écran entier tombe en morceaux.

KONZEPT: Eine Banneranzeige warnt, während des Autofahrens nicht das Handy zu benutzen. Benutzer werden eingeladen, das Auto im Banner oben auf dem Bildschirm zu fahren. Kurz danach beginnt rechts im Banner ein Handy zu klingeln. Sobald man es abhebt, zerfällt der gesamte Bildschirm in Stücke.

CONCEPT: The website recreates a contemporary art gallery and adds an interactive element that explores the visitor's experience.

CONCEPT : Le site en ligne recrée une galerie d'art contemporain et ajoute un élément interactif qui enrichit l'expérience du visiteur.

KONZEPT: Die Webseite stellt eine moderne Kunstgalerie dar und fügt ein interaktives Element hinzu, welches das Besuchererlebnis untersucht.

FEATURED ON THE DVD CAMPAIGN: Stockholm the Musical <www.stockholmthemusical.com>. YEAR: 2006. AGENCY: Farfar <www.farfar.se>. PRODUCTION TIME: 1 month. CREATIVE TEAM: Tom Erikssen, Johan Öhrn, Nicke Bergstrom, Marten Forslund, Per Hansson. PROGRAMMER: Bo Gustafsson.

CONCEPT: Stockholm wants to sing for you! You can also make a customized version for a friend. The purpose of the campaign is to promote Stockholm to people living in London.

KONZEPT: Stockholm will für Sie singen! Sie können auch eine eigene Version für Freunde erstellen. Ziel der Kampagne ist es, in London für Stockholm zu werben.

CONCEPT : Stockholm vous a concocté une comédie musicale ! On peut aussi fabriquer une version personnalisée pour un ami. Le but de la campagne est de faire la promotion de Stockholm pour des gens vivant à Londres.

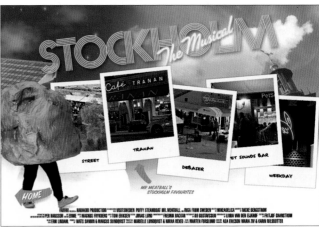

FEATURED ON THE DVD **CAMPAIGN:** Swim 10 Year Anniversary. **PRODUCT:** Swim Collection from Victoria's Secret. **YEAR:** 2005. **AGENCY:** Firstborn <www.firstbornmultimedia.com>. **PRODUCTION TIME:** 2,5 months. **COST IN HOURS OF WORK:** 300 h. **PRODUCER:** Luba Shekhter, Firstborn. **CREATIVE TEAM:** Victoria's Secret: Zo Bjorgvinsson, Miles McManus. Firstborn: Vas Sloutchevsky. **PROGRAMMER:** Dan LaCivita. **TECH ASPECTS:** Macromedia Flash, audio, video. **MEDIA CIRCULATED:** Victoria's Secret website.

CONCEPT: 2005 marked the 10th anniversary of Victoria's Secret's Swim Collection. To commemorate a decade of success, style and sexy, Victoria's Secret hosted an event and published an exclusive book, SEXY, featuring the works of three photographers who captured the collection's essence. Following the event, Firstborn developed a commemorative mini-site which features exclusive footage from behind the scenes of the swim shoot, photographs from the party as well as editorial content for the press and public. **RESULTS:** the online campaign did a great job of supporting the event, and letting people know that Victoria's Secret Swim Collection was only getting better. VIPs were presented with a special book commemorating the decade of beautiful swimwear and the models who sported them.

CONCEPT : L'année 2005 a marqué le dixième anniversaire de la collection de maillots de bain de Victoria's Secret. Pour commémorer une décennie de succès, de style et de beauté, la marque a organisé une rétrospective et publié un livre exclusif, Sexy, qui réunit le travail de trois photographes ayant su capter l'esprit de la collection. A la suite de l'opération, Firstborn a développé un mini-site commémoratif qui présente des images inédites des coulisses des séances photo, des images de la réception privée et un contenu éditorial des-

tiné à la presse et au public. **RÉSULTATS :** La campagne en ligne a bien soutenu l'événement, tout en informant sur l'exceptionnelle qualité des maillots de bain de la marque. Les VIP se sont vu offrir un livre commémorant les dix ans de la collection et célébrant les mannequins qui l'ont portée.

KONZEPT: 2005 markierte das 10-jährige Jubiläum von Victoria's Secrets Schwimmkollektion. Um ein Jahrzehnt des Erfolgs und Stils zu feiern, veranstaltete Victoria's Secret ein Event und veröffentlichte ein exklusives Buch, das die Arbeit von drei Fotografen enthält, die die Essenz der Kollektion einfingen. Nach dem Event entwickelte Firstborn eine Minisite, die exklusives Material hinter den Kulissen des Shots beinhaltet, Fotos der Party und Texte für Presse und Öffentlichkeit. **ERGEBNISSE:** Die Online-Kampagne war in der Unterstützung des Events sehr erfolgreich und ließ die Leute wissen, dass Victoria's Secrets Schwimmkollektion immer besser wird. In einem speziellen Buch wurden VIPs präsentiert, um an das Jahrzehnt schöner Schwimm-Mode und die Models, die sie vorführten, zu erinnern.

FEATURED ON THE DVD **CAMPAIGN:** "Lupi". **CLIENT:** Proanima. **YEAR:** 2005. **AGENCY:** AgênciaClick <www.agenciaclick.com.br>. **AWARDS:** Golden Bell – Festival Internacional de Língua Portuguesa em Portugal.

CONCEPT: Simple communication with a rather emotional and strong concept.

CONCEPT : Communication simple suivant un concept fort et émotionnel.

KONZEPT: Simple Kommunikation mit einem emotionalen und starken Konzept.

CAMPAIGN: IFAW. PRODUCT: Seal Campaign 2005. YEAR: 2005. AGENCY: Fork Unstable Media <www.fork.de>. CREATIVE TEAM: Silke Krieg. PROGRAMMER: Silke Krieg. TECH ASPECTS: Macromedia Flash.

CONCEPT: Help the International Fund for Animal Welfare (IFAW) create awareness for the millions of seals being slaughtered for commercial reasons. **RESULTS:** No frightening images but rather beautiful illustrations; According to IFAW this made it easier to place these ads free of charge in Germany's most visited online portals (RTL, AOL, Web.de to name but a few). We did not charge IFAW for our work either.

CONCEPT : Aider l'IFAW, organisation de défense des animaux, à sensibiliser le public aux millions de phoques massacrés pour des raisons commerciales. **RÉSULTATS :** Pas d'images terrifiantes, mais plutôt de belles illustrations. D'après l'IFAW, cela a permis de faire héberger gratuitement les bannières par les plus grands portails allemands (RTL, AOL, Web.de entre autres). Nous n'avons pas facturé IFAW pour ce travail.

KONZEPT: Dem International Fund for Animal Welfare (IFAW) helfen, ein Bewusstsein für die Millionen von Robben zu erzeugen, die für kommerzielle Zwecke geschlachtet werden. **ERGEBNISSE:** Keine unheimlichen Bilder, sondern schöne Illustrationen: Laut IFAW erleichtert dies die kostenlose Platzierung der Anzeigen auf Deutschlands meistbesuchten Online-Portalen (RTL, AOL, Web.de, um nur einige zu nennen). Auch wir verlangten für unsere Arbeit von IFAW kein Honorar.

Daniel Solana has worked as a creative in such agencies as Interalas Bates, Solución BDDP, Young & Rubicam Barcelona and Contrapunto Madrid. In 1997 he founded DoubleYou, an interactive advertising agency, in which he has been responsible for interactive communication projects for clients such as Audi, Evax, San Miguel, Nike, Seat, Turismo de España, Yahoo!, and others. DoubleYou leads the awards tables among Spain's interactive agencies and is also one of Europe's most widely acclaimed agencies. In 2003, it was named Agency of the Year in the San Sebastián Advertising Festival. In 2004, DoubleYou won more prizes than any other Spanish agency at the festival, including the "Gran Premio" in the interactive categories, and that same year it also won the Cyberlions Grand Prix, at the Cannes Festival. Solana has spoken at a range of national and international congresses on Internet advertising, and was also president of the first interactive advertising jury of the San Sebastián festival, and a member of the jury for such international festivals as Cannes, the Clio Awards in Chicago, One Show Interactive, New York Festival and the London International Advertising Awards.

A changing scene

Advertising is changing, much more deeply than it seems, and the Internet and the new media are undoubtedly the silent motor driving these changes. A simple glance at the complex present-day Internet advertising scenario and its development is sufficient to see that we are dealing with a fundamentally different form of communication to advertising as than previously understood. It is also developing and transforming at a much faster pace, so fast indeed that we are unable to assimilate the changes. Not so many years earlier, there were essentially only two formats on the Internet: banners –simple GIF technology, and websites –content storage platforms.

TODAY, THERE ARE SO MANY FORMATS THAT THEY DEFY CLASSIFICATION: RICH MEDIA BANNERS, ONLINE SPOTS, ANIMATED AND ELECTRONIC POSTERS, DIGITAL BROCHURES, COMMUNITY-GENERATING PLATFORMS, VIRTUAL PRESS CONFERENCES AND EVENTS, GUERRILLA MARKETING, VIRAL OR SUBVIRAL MARKETING, DIGITAL PRODUCT PLACEMENT AND AMBIENT MARKETING.

What kind of medium is it that allows us to use so many different and varied formats?
It is as if creativity, the need to come up with new ideas, had leapt out from its normal secluded place of hiding –the 20 or 30 seconds given over to advertising spots or the din A4 page of a standard magazine– in its fervour to reach the daily life of its target audience. Eventually "rich media" might end up meaning "do whatever occurs to you".

Undoubtedly, its tremendous versatility and flexibility are two of the main characteristics of advertising in today's new context. In my opinion, however, the most important aspect of the new advertising is not its disconcerting versatility and flexibility; rather what is truly significant is that the interactive advertising items, while undoubtedly advertising –expressly intended to be persuasive, emotional, involving... are essentially computer applications, that is, programs, software. Beyond the fact that they may be small in scale, landscape or full-screen format, independently of whether the message is graphic or audiovisual, whether its aim is to sell an image, position a brand, or to effect a promotional call to action, advertising items are defined and generated by means of programming codes, that is, they are completely different in nature. They are not static, unalterable ads, to be consumed. This is organic matter, that can evolve and develop in response to the consumer's interaction. They behave.

At present, this behaviour is elementary. By moving the cursor over the surface of the ad, something happens: a sudden change of colour, the appearance of a new text, or some means of eliciting user interaction. Something very simple, almost silly, yet deep-down what is important is that a rich media advertising item is genetically a member of the same species as, for example, Deep Blue, a software program sufficiently sophisticated to take on

International Advertising Awards.

CHANGES, CHANGES, CHANGES

chess grand masters. The only point differentiating one item from another is complexity —the DNA is the same: both are computer programs. Until now, interactive advertising reacted as a primitive living organism reacts, i.e., via elementary stimuli, yet in the long-term it is logical to think that it will become more sophisticated, and that this advertising will be equipped to take more complex decisions, to learn, or think and, depending on what they think, to act. We must ask ourselves how are advertisers to employ all this extraordinary power once we learn to handle it for creative ends.

A changing public

The media and setting for brand communication are changing, because the Internet is transforming them. The advertising message is also changing, because advertisements are not only seen or heard, but can also react to public response and may even change of their own accord and take their own decisions. And the user, i.e., the consumer is also changing. The target is no longer a target, a sitting duck exposed to the piercing darts of a daring advertising pitch. Now, it's a moving target, a zapping, illusive, Internet-surfing target that deactivates pop-ups by means of blocking mechanisms and who, sooner or later, will have software enabling him or her to eliminate advertising from his television screens.

TODAY'S PUBLIC, AND MORE IMPORTANTLY, TOMORROW'S PUBLIC, IS AN INFORMED ONE; PERFECTLY AWARE OF WHAT ADVERTISING IS AND HOW IT

OPERATES, IT SEES IT AS ITS RIGHT TO MAKE DEMANDS ON BRANDS AND MAY EVEN LAUNCH AN ANTI-BRAND INTERNET CAMPAIGN IF IT FEELS IT HAS BEEN THE VICTIM OF MANIPULATION OR TRICKERY.

Over and beyond the successive waves of Internet phenomena, including, in their time, flash mobs, P2Ps, and more recently, blogs, today's trend is towards an interconnected society, with multiple information dissemination points, and individuals capable of generating spontaneous communication phenomena which may reach universal dimensions. And these will compete with the traditional media, or may even run campaigns which prove more far-reaching than those of the major brands.

A changing language

Never before in my professional life have I been so assailed by doubts about the foundations of this discipline. For example, brevity. Traditionally, advertising was an exercise in synthesis, concise in project definition — the brief! and concise in its message —USP! We have so little time, let's just say one thing. This approach always struck me as being entirely reasonable.
Nevertheless, from the perspective of interactive advertising, time and space are treated differently. A programmed advertising item can take up as much time and space as we like. It's no longer a question of the 20 seconds allocated for a spot, or the limited format of a bottom page advertising strip. A

rich media banner may be a simple, fleeting, unidirectional message, yet it can also, if we wish, be expanded by "mouse over" and become a much deeper matter indeed! A site? a microsite? it may last for an instant, or 20 minutes, or for four hours; it may contain the information of a din A4 page or of 1000 such pages. Who says that advertisers have to keep it brief in this new context? Of course, we can't expect the consumer to be so interested in the brand that he or she will be willing to waste time on a never-ending advertisement, yet is it really an advertisement that's required in order to attain our communication objectives in this new setting?

IF YOU ARE TRYING TO CONSTRUCT A SOLID RELATIONSHIP BETWEEN THE BRAND AND THE CONSUMER, AND HOPING TO GET THAT RELATIONSHIP OFF TO A FLYING START, ARE WE GOING TO LIMIT OURSELVES TO A SINGLE CATCH-PHRASE TO CAPTURE THE CONSUMER'S ATTENTION?

And then what's to happen if the public reacts to our offer? Do we repeat the same line?
In this new scenario, advertising must take on a different guise. And rather than just penning a once-off slogan encapsulating the benefits of a given product or searching for, creating or locating the perfect jingle to identify the brand, agencies must undertake a multiplicity of tasks. Building virtual scenarios for interaction with the brand, experiencing contact with and tactile recognition of the product; designing set-

UNDOUBTEDLY, ITS TREMENDOUS VERSATILITY AND FLEXIBILITY ARE TWO OF THE MAIN CHARACTERISTICS OF ADVERTISING IN TODAY'S NEW CONTEXT.

tings for meetings with the public; acting as hosts in the homes of the brand's corporate buildings; writing scripts or stories that begin when someone watches a spot but which may continue for hours, days or weeks on sites or by means of major cross-media experiences; building platforms for recreational learning about product benefits; creating intensive emotional experiences in a unique event based around the intangible value of a brand; reaching agreements with supports in order to provide "no holds barred" demonstrations or rational proof of product advantages; establishing and nurturing dialogue between companies and their present or potential clients; popularising a new brand by means of a complex campaign comprising viral spots or virtual ambient marketing.

We are on the threshold of extraordinarily exciting new times for the world of advertising. Or who knows, perhaps we have already started to live in them. Changes!

Daniel Solana a travaillé comme créatif chez Interalas Bates, Solución BDDP, Young & Rubicam Barcelona et Contrapunto Madrid. En 1997, il fonde Double You, une agence de publicité interactive qui va gérer les projets de clients comme Audi, Evax, San Miguel, Nike, Seat, Turismo de España, Yahoo ! et autres. Double You est l'agence la plus primée d'Espagne, et c'est l'une des plus réputée d'Europe. En 2003, elle a été élue Agence de l'Année au festival de publicité de Saint-Sébastien. En 2004, Double You a remporté à ce même festival plus de récompenses que n'importe quelle autre agence espagnole, dont le premier prix dans la section publicité interactive, et la même année elle a aussi remporté le Cyber Lion de Cannes. Solana a participé à de nombreux congrès nationaux et internationaux sur la publicité en ligne, a été président du jury du festival de Saint-Sébastien, et membre du jury aux Lions de Cannes, aux Clio Awards de Chicago, au OneShow de New York et aux LIAA.

Changement de décor

La publicité change, plus profondément qu'il n'y paraît, et Internet et les nouveaux médias sont incontestablement les moteurs silencieux de ces changements. Il suffit de regarder la complexité du scénario actuel de la publicité en ligne et son évolution pour comprendre que nous avons affaire à une forme de communication fondamentalement différente de ce que nous connaissions jusqu'ici. Elle se développe et se transforme aussi beaucoup plus vite, si vite que nous avons du mal à assimiler les changements. Il n'y a pas si longtemps, il n'existait que deux formats principaux sur Internet : les bandeaux (simple technologie GIF) et les sites (plateforme de stockage de contenu).

AUJOURD'HUI, IL Y A TELLEMENT DE FORMATS DIFFÉRENTS QU'ILS DÉFIENT TOUTE CLASSIFICATION : LES BANNIÈRES EN RICH MEDIA, LES SPOTS EN LIGNE, LES AFFICHES ANIMÉES ET ÉLECTRONIQUES, LES BROCHURES NUMÉRIQUES, LES PLATEFORMES COMMUNAUTAIRES, LES CONFÉRENCES DE PRESSE ET LES ÉVÉNEMENTS VIRTUELS, LE GUÉRILLA MARKETING, LE MARKETING VIRAL OU SUBVIRAL, LE PLACEMENT ÉLECTRONIQUE DE PRODUIT ET LE MARKETING SENSORIEL.

Quel est donc ce média qui nous permet d'utiliser des formats aussi variés ?

C'est comme si la créativité, le besoin de trouver de nouvelles idées, était sorti de son repaire habituel, les 20 ou 30 secondes consacrées aux spots télé, ou la récurrente page A4 des magazines, pour tenter d'atteindre son public cible dans sa vie quotidienne. Finalement, rich media pourrait signifier : « fais ce qui te passe par la tête ».

Sa souplesse et sa fantastique polyvalence sont incontestablement deux des principales caractéristiques de la publicité dans le nouveau contexte actuel. Mais d'après moi, cependant, l'aspect essentiel de cette nouvelle publicité n'est ni sa flexibilité ni sa polyvalence. Ce qui est vraiment significatif, c'est que les modules interactifs, qui restent de la publicité, avec le but avoué de persuader, d'émouvoir ou de mobiliser, sont surtout des applications informatiques, des programmes et des logiciels. Quelle que soit la taille (réduite, panoramique ou plein écran), que le message soit graphique ou sonore, qu'il tende à vendre une image, positionner une marque, ou inciter à l'achat, les créations publicitaires sont définies et générées par des codes de programmation, c'est-à-dire qu'elles sont différentes par nature. Ce ne sont pas des pubs statiques, inaltérables, faites pour être consommées. C'est un matériau organique, qui peut évoluer et se développer en réponse à l'interaction du consommateur. Elles ont un comportement propre.

Pour l'heure, ce comportement est élémentaire. En promenant le curseur sur la surface d'une pub, il se passe quelque chose : un changement de couleur, l'affichage d'un nouveau texte, ou une invitation à l'interaction. Une chose très simple, presque idiote, et pourtant au fond ce qui est important, c'est qu'une pub en rich media est génétiquement de la même espèce que disons, Deep Blue, un programme assez sophistiqué pour défier les plus grands joueurs d'échecs. La complexité est la seule chose qui différencie deux créations. C'est un peu comme l'ADN, les deux sont des programmation informatiques. Jusqu'ici, la publicité interactive a réagi à la façon d'un organisme vivant primitif, en réponse à des stimuli élémentaires, mais à long terme il est logique de penser qu'elle deviendra plus sophistiquée, qu'elle sera conçue pour prendre des décisions plus subtiles, pour apprendre, raisonner, et agir en conséquence. Il faut se demander comment les publicitaires emploieront ce pouvoir extraordinaire, une fois qu'ils l'auront maîtrisé à des fins de création.

Changement de public

Le décor et le support de la communication évoluent, parce qu'Internet les transforme. Le message publicitaire change aussi, car les pubs ne sont

SA SOUPLESSE ET SA FANTASTIQUE POLYVALENCE SONT INCONTESTABLEMENT DEUX DES PRINCIPALES CARACTÉRISTIQUES DE LA PUBLICITÉ DANS LE NOUVEAU CONTEXTE ACTUEL.

pas seulement vues ou entendues, mais elles peuvent aussi réagir en fonction de la réponse du public, voire changer de leur propre chef et prendre leurs propres décisions. Et l'utilisateur, autrement dit le consommateur, change aussi. La cible n'est plus une cible, un pantin immobile exposé aux flèches d'un message publicitaire. C'est une cible mouvante, une cible insaisissable, qui zappe, surfe sur Internet, désactive les fenêtres pop-up par des mécanismes de blocage, et qui un jour ou l'autre, possédera un logiciel lui permettant d'éliminer la publicité de son écran télévisé.

LE PUBLIC D'AUJOURD'HUI, ET PLUS ENCORE LE PUBLIC DE DEMAIN, EST UN PUBLIC INFORMÉ, PARFAITEMENT AU COURANT DE CE QU'EST LA PUBLICITÉ ET SON FONCTIONNEMENT, ET CONSIDÈRE QU'IL A LE DROIT D'EXIGER DES CHOSES DES MARQUES, ET PEUT MÊME LANCER UNE CAMPAGNE ANTI-MARQUE S'IL ESTIME AVOIR ÉTÉ VICTIME D'UNE MANIPULATION OU D'UNE SUPERCHERIE.

Au-delà des vagues successives de phénomènes Internet, incluant en leur temps, la mobilisation éclair (flash mob), le P2P, et plus récemment, les blogs, la tendance actuelle va vers une société interconnectée, avec de multiples points d'information disséminés, et des individus capables de générer des phénomènes de communication spontanés qui peuvent atteindre une portée mondiale. Rivalisant avec les médias traditionnels, ces nouvelles campagnes auront peut-être même plus de portée que celles des grandes marques.

Changement de langage

De toute ma carrière, je n'avais jamais autant douté des fondamentaux de notre discipline. La brièveté, par exemple. Jusqu'ici, la publicité était un exercice de synthèse, de concision dans la définition du pro-

jet : le briefing ! Et de concision dans le message : l'avantage unique ! Le temps est compté, contentons-nous de dire une seule chose. Cette approche m'a toujours semblé extrêmement raisonnable.
Néanmoins, dans la publicité interactive, le temps et l'espace sont traités différemment. Une publicité en ligne peut prendre autant de temps et d'espace qu'on le désire. Il n'est plus question de respecter les 20 secondes accordées au spot, ou le format limité d'un bandeau pub en bas de page. Une bannière en rich média peut transmettre un message simple, flottant et unidirectionnel, mais elle peut aussi, si on le désire, s'étendre avec la souris à un message beaucoup plus profond. Un site, un micro-site ? Cela peut durer un instant, ou 20 minutes, ou quatre heures. Elle peut contenir l'information d'une page A4, ou de mille pages A4. Qui a dit que les publicitaires devaient être concis, dans ces conditions ? On ne peut évidemment pas attendre du consommateur qu'il soit assez passionné par la marque pour perdre son temps sur une publicité sans fin, mais espère-t-on vraiment que la publicité remplisse notre objectif de communication dans ce nouveau contexte ?

SI NOUS VOULONS CONSTRUIRE UNE RELATION STABLE ENTRE LA MARQUE ET LE CONSOMMATEUR, ET LUI FAIRE PRENDRE UN BON DÉPART, ALLONS-NOUS NOUS CONTENTER D'UN SLOGAN POUR CAPTIVER L'ATTENTION DU CONSOMMATEUR ?

Et si le public réagit à notre offre, allons-nous répéter la même phrase ?
Dans ce nouveau scénario, la publicité doit prendre une nouvelle apparence. Et au lieu de rédiger un slogan unique renfermant les avantages d'un produit ou d'un service donné, de réaliser le jingle idéal qui identifie une marque, les agences devront assumer une variété de taches. Imaginer des scénarios virtuels d'interaction avec la marque, des expériences de contact et de reconnaissance tactile avec le produit, des points de rendez-vous avec le public, des animations au sein des entreprises de la marque, des scripts ou des histoires qui commencent quand

on regarde un spot mais qui peuvent aussi continuer pendant des heures, des jours ou des semaines sur des sites ou autres supports hybrides, des plateformes ludiques expliquant les atouts d'un produit, des expériences émotionnelles lors d'événement basé sur la valeur intangible d'une marque, des accords entre différents supports pour offrir sans limite la démonstration ou la preuve rationnelle des atouts d'un produit, des points de dialogue entre les entreprises et leurs clients présents ou futurs, et la promotion d'une marque par une campagne intégrée de spots viraux et de marketing sensoriel.
Nous sommes à l'aube d'une époque passionnante pour l'univers de la publicité. Mais qui sait, cette époque a peut-être déjà commencé. Place aux changements !

Daniel Solana arbeitete als Kreativer in Agenturen wie Interalas Bates, Solución BDDP, Young & Rubicam Barcelona und Contrapunto Madrid. 1997 gründete er DoubleYou, eine interaktive Werbeagentur, wo er für interaktive Kommunikationsprojekte für Kunden wie Audi, Evax, San Miguel, Nike, Seat, Turismo de España, Yahoo! und andere verantwortlich war. DoubleYou hat mehr Auszeichnungen als irgendeine andere Interaktivagentur Spaniens erhalten und ist außerdem eine von Europas angesehensten Agenturen. 2003 erhielt sie den Titel Agency of the Year beim San Sebastián Advertising Festival. 2004 gewann DoubleYou die meisten Preise beim Festival, einschließlich des „Gran Premio" in der interaktiven Kategorie, und im selben Jahr gewannen sie außerdem den Cyberlions Grand Prix beim Cannes Festival. Solana hielt bei zahlreichen nationalen und internationalen Kongressen Vorträge über Internetwerbung und war Präsident der ersten Jury für interaktive Werbung beim San Sebastián Festival sowie Jurymitglied bei internationalen Festivals wie Cannes, den Clio Awards in Chicago, One Show Interactive, New York Festival und den London International Advertising Awards.

ZWEIFELLOS SIND DIE ENORME VIELSEITIGKEIT UND FLEXIBILITÄT ZWEI DER GRUNDLEGENDEN EIGENSCHAFTEN DER WERBUNG IN IHREM NEUEN KONTEXT.

Eine andere Umgebung

Die Werbung ändert sich viel tief greifender als es scheint; und das Internet und die Neuen Medien sind ohne Zweifel der stille Motor, der diese Veränderungen antreibt.

Ein Blick auf die komplexe aktuelle Internetwerbung und ihre Entwicklung reicht aus, um zu bemerken, dass wir es mit einer völlig anderen Form der Kommunikation in der Werbung zu tun haben als vorher. Außerdem entwickelt und transformiert sie sich so schnell, dass wir die Veränderungen nicht alle aufnehmen können. Vor nicht allzu vielen Jahren gab es im Wesentlichen nur zwei Formate im Internet: Banner – simple GIF-Technologie – und Webseiten – Plattformen für Inhalt.

HEUTE GIBT ES SO VIELE FORMATE, DASS SIE DER KLASSIFIZIERUNG TROTZEN: RICH-MEDIA-BANNER, ONLINE-SPOTS, ANIMIERTE UND ELEKTRONISCHE PLAKATE, DIGITALE BROSCHÜREN, PLATTFORMEN, DIE EINE GEMEINSCHAFT GENERIEREN, VIRTUELLE PRESSEKONFERENZEN UND EVENTS, GUERILLA-MARKETING, VIRALES ODER SUBVIRALES MARKETING, DIGITALE PRODUKTPLATZIERUNG UND AMBIENT-MARKETING.

Welches andere Medium erlaubt uns die Verwendung so vieler verschiedener Formate?

Es ist, als wenn Kreativität, das Bedürfnis nach neuen Ideen, aus ihrem Versteck gesprungen wäre – den 20 oder 30 Sekunden von Werbespots oder der DIN-A4-Seite eines Standardmagazins –, in ihrem Verlangen, den Alltag ihrer Zielgruppe zu erreichen. Irgendwann könnte „Rich Media" bedeuten: „Tu, was du willst!"

Zweifellos sind die enorme Vielseitigkeit und Flexibilität zwei der grundlegenden Eigenschaften der Werbung in ihrem neuen Kontext. Meiner Meinung

nach ist der wichtigste Aspekt der neuen Werbung jedoch nicht ihre beunruhigende Vielseitigkeit und Flexibilität; eher ist die Tatsache von Bedeutung, dass die Gegenstände der interaktiven Werbung – obwohl sie zweifellos Werbung sind und überzeugend, emotional und involvierend sein sollen – im Wesentlichen Computeranwendungen sind, d.h. Programme und Software. Abgesehen davon, dass sie klein sein oder den ganzen Bildschirm ausfüllen können, unabhängig davon, ob die Botschaft grafisch oder audiovisuell ist, ob sie ein Image verkaufen, eine Marke positionieren oder ein Aufruf zum Handeln sein will: Die Werbegegenstände werden durch Programmiercode definiert und generiert, d.h. sie unterscheiden sich in ihrer Natur. Sie sind keine statischen, unveränderbaren Anzeigen zum Konsumieren. Sie bestehen aus organischem Material, das sich in Erwiderung auf die Interaktion mit dem Verbraucher entwickeln kann. Sie legen ein bestimmtes Verhalten zutage.

Zurzeit ist dieses Verhalten elementar. Indem man den Zeiger über die Oberfläche der Anzeige bewegt, passiert etwas: eine plötzliche Farbänderung, das Erscheinen von neuem Text oder etwas, dass den Nutzer für Interaktion gewinnt. Etwas Simples, fast Albernes; aber wirklich wichtig ist, dass die Gegenstände der Rich-Media-Werbung genetisch Mitglieder derselben Art sind – zum Beispiel Deep Blue, ein Softwareprogramm, das weit genug entwickelt ist, um es mit Schachmeistern aufnehmen zu können. Das einzige, was einen Gegenstand vom anderen unterscheidet, ist die Komplexität. Die DNA ist dieselbe: Es sind Computerprogramme. Bis jetzt reagierte interaktive Werbung wie ein primitiver lebender Organismus, d.h. durch einfache Stimulation. Langfristig ist es jedoch logisch anzunehmen, dass sie sich weiterentwickeln wird und mit komplexeren Entscheidungen wird umgehen können, lernen, denken oder – je nachdem, was sie denkt – handeln können wird. Wir müssen uns fragen, wie Werber diese außergewöhnliche Macht einsetzen sollen, wenn wir lernen, sie für kreative Zwecke zu nutzen.

Eine andere Öffentlichkeit

Die Medien für Markenkommunikation ändern

sich, weil das Internet sie transformiert. Die Werbebotschaften ändern sich auch, weil Werbung nicht nur gesehen oder gehört wird, sondern auch auf öffentliche Reaktionen reagieren oder sich sogar eigenständig ändern und eigene Entscheidungen treffen kann. Und der Benutzer, d.h. der Verbraucher, ändert sich ebenfalls.

Das Ziel ist nicht länger ein Ziel, eine Ente, die den Pfeilen ausgesetzt ist, die die Werbung mutig auf sie abschießt. Das Ziel ist nun beweglich: ein umschaltendes, trügerisches, im Internet surfendes Ziel, das Pop Ups durch das Blockieren von Mechanismen deaktiviert und früher oder später Software haben wird, mit der man Werbung vom Fernsehbildschirm verbannen kann.

DIE HEUTIGE UND, VIEL WICHTIGER, DIE ZUKÜNFTIGE ÖFFENTLICHKEIT IST INFORMIERT. SIE WEISS, WAS WERBUNG IST UND WIE SIE FUNKTIONIERT UND BETRACHTET ES ALS IHR RECHT, FORDERUNGEN AN MARKEN ZU STELLEN ODER SOGAR EINE ANTI-MARKEN-INTERNETKAMPAGNE INS LEBEN ZU RUFEN, WENN SIE SICH ALS OPFER VON MANIPULATION ODER BETRÜGEREIEN SIEHT.

Bei der Welle der Internetphänomene einschließlich Flash Mobs oder P2Ps und, in jüngerer Zeit, Blogs, geht der Trend hin zu einer vernetzten Gesellschaft mit multiplen Verbreitungspunkten von Informationen und Einzelpersonen, die spontane Kommunikationsphänomene erzeugen, die universale Dimensionen bekommen können. Und diese werden mit den traditionellen Medien konkurrieren oder sogar eine Kampagne ins Leben rufen, die viel weit reichender ist als die einer großen Marke.

Eine andere Sprache

Niemals zuvor in meinem Berufsleben wurde ich derart von Zweifeln an den Grundfesten dieser

Disziplin bestürmt. Zum Beispiel die Kürze. Werbung war traditionell eine Synthese und präzise in der Projektdefinition – die Kürze! Und präzise in der Botschaft – USP! Wir haben so wenig Zeit, also sagen wir nur eine Sache. Dieser Ansatz kam mir immer absolut vernünftig vor.

Gleichwohl werden Raum und Zeit aus der Perspektive der interaktiven Werbung anders gehandhabt. Eine programmierte Werbeeinheit kann so viel Zeit und Raum einnehmen, wie wir wollen. Es ist keine Frage von 20 Sekunden mehr, die einem Spot zugewiesen wurden, oder des begrenzten Formats eines Werbebandes unten auf der Seite. Ein Rich-Media-Banner kann eine einfache, flüchtige, einseitige Botschaft sein; aber es kann auch, wenn man es so möchte, durch Darüberfahren mit der Maus erweitert und zu einer tieferen Angelegenheit werden. Eine Seite? Eine Microsite? Die Beschäftigung mit ihr kann einen Moment, 20 Minuten oder vier Stunden dauern; die Seite kann die Information einer DIN-A4-Seite enthalten oder 1000 solcher Seiten umfassen. Wer sagt, dass sich Werber in diesem neuen Kontext kurz fassen müssen? Wir können natürlich vom Verbraucher nicht erwarten, dass er sich so für die Marke interessiert, dass er sich Zeit für eine unendliche Werbung nimmt; aber braucht man wirklich eine Werbeanzeige, um Kommunikationsziele in dieser neuen Umgebung zu erreichen?

WERDEN WIR UNS BEI DEM VERSUCH, EINE SOLIDE BEZIEHUNG ZWISCHEN MARKE UND KUNDE VON BEGINN AN AUFZUBAUEN, DAHINGEHEND BESCHRÄNKEN, DIE AUFMERKSAMKEIT DES KUNDEN MIT NUR EINEM SCHLAGWORT ZU GEWINNEN?

Und was passiert, wenn die Öffentlichkeit auf unser Angebot reagiert? Wiederholen wir dasselbe Schlagwort?

In diesem neuen Szenario muss die Werbung eine andere Gestalt bekommen. Bevor man einen einmaligen Slogan niederschreibt, der die Vorteile eines bestimmten Produkts einfängt, oder den perfekten Jingle zur Identifizierung der Marke sucht oder kreiert, müssen Agenturen eine Vielzahl von Aufgaben durchführen: virtuelle Szenarien für die Interaktion mit der Marke aufbauen, wobei sie Kontakt mit und fühlbare Wiedererkennung des Produktes erfahren; Szenerien für Treffen mit der Öffentlichkeit entwerfen; sich mit den jeweiligen Kunden beraten; Skripts oder Storys schreiben, die beginnen, wenn jemand einen Werbespot sieht, die aber stunden-, tage- oder wochenlang auf Seiten oder durch Cross-Media-Anwendungen andauern können; Plattformen errichten, wo man spielerisch die Vorteile des Produktes erfahren kann; mit einem einzigartigen Event, das auf dem unfassbaren Wert des Produktes basiert, intensive emotionale Erfahrungen schaffen; Einigung mit Geldgebern erzielen, um „Es sind alle Mittel erlaubt"-Demonstrationen oder vernünftige Beweise für die Vorteile des Produktes zu liefern; einen Dialog zwischen Unternehmen und ihren derzeitigen oder potenziellen Klienten aufbauen und pflegen; eine neue Marke durch eine komplexe Kampagne beliebt machen, die virale Spots oder virtuelles Ambient-Marketing beinhaltet.

Wir stehen an der Schwelle zu außergewöhnlich aufregenden neuen Zeiten in der Welt der Werbung. Oder, wer weiß, vielleicht haben wir schon begonnen, darin zu leben. Alles ist anders!

004

SERVICE
& RETAILERS

CAMPAIGN: 3M Everywhere. **PRODUCT:** 3M. **YEAR:** 2005. **AGENCY:** AKQA <www.akqa.com>. **CREATIVE TEAM:** Kerry Finlay, Miles Unwin, Kevin Russell. **PROGRAMMER:** David Dekker. **TECH ASPECTS:** Macromedia Flash, film, music, interactivity on hotspots. **MEDIA CIRCULATED:** Two online advertising campaigns ran to drive traffic to the site to reach the niche target audiences (e.g. banners and skyscrapers on The New Scientist, The Engineer, Manufacturing Talk and HSM Search). An outbound email and DM campaign also drove traffic to the site. **AWARDS:** Shortlisted for 'Campaign: Best B2B Campaign' and 'Revolution: Best B2B Service'.

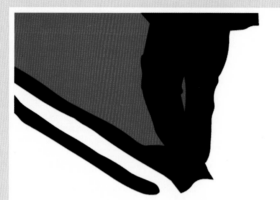

WIN AN iMac G5

3M innovation is all around you. You're never far from something we've created or helped to build - but you may not always realise it. See if you can spot 15 of our innovations in our short movie for a chance to win a prize in our monthly draw:

- Spot **10 or more** for a chance to win one of three portable DVD players
- Spot **all 15** for a chance to win an iMac G5

SEE THE ▶
PRIZES

PLAY NOW ▶

This competition is only open to business customers, you'll be asked to complete a short qualifying questionnaire as part of your entry. Please read our competition rules

3M *Innovation*

INNOVATIVE SOLUTIONS
whoever you are, whatever your business

GAME STARTS IN 15 SECONDS
HERE'S HOW TO PLAY

- When the film starts, use your mouse to guide the red target and find the 15 3M hotspots.
- When the target flashes green, click to reveal the hidden innovation.
- Find 10 or more to enter the monthly prize draw – find all 15 to enter the grand prize draw.
- Play again to improve your score - the hotspots already found will be remembered.

3M *Innovation*

🔊 | SHOW ME WHERE THEY ARE | START AGAIN | SKIP **3M** *Innovation*

OBJECTIVE: Most people know that 3M make stuff. If pressed they might even name Post-it® notes and Scotch® tape. But ask them to name some of the other approximately 49,998 things that 3M produces and they would struggle to name more than two or 3. It's this lack of familiarity with the breadth of solutions that 3M asked us to address for a small, influential and loyal audience of health care, health and safety, production, engineering and purchasing professionals. **SOLUTION:** We produced an industry first: a 60-second interactive movie, featuring a businessman's journey from his home to the Eurostar Terminal at Waterloo, and asking visitors to identify 15 hidden hot-spots that demonstrated how 3M technology was involved in the story. Visitors who spotted more than 10 were entered in a prize draw. They could also delve further into the site for more in-depth content if they wished. The site was promoted through banner activity targeted at niche B2B websites. In addition, promotional e-mails were sent to specified e-mail addresses acquired from Mardev and Findlay data lists. **RESULTS:** The brand familiarity, brand favourability and purchase intent scores increased by 21% on average among the 3M Everywhere competition entrants (compared to a survey concluded before exposure to the 3M Everywhere game). The site attracted 4,469 unique visitors. Average dwell time of over eight minutes. 1,590 competition entries (this is a conversion rate of 35% from site visitors to competition entries). On average over 84% of visitors played the game and 60% of them played more than once. Hits on the page: There were 17,258 game start impressions.

OBJECTIF : La plupart des gens savent que 3M fabrique des choses. Si l'on insiste, ils pourront même citer les Post-it ou le Scotch. Mais si on leur demande de citer un des quelques 49 998 autres produits que fabrique 3M, ils auront du mal à en nommer plus de deux ou trois. La société nous a chargé de traiter le manque de familiarité des consommateurs avec sa gamme de produits, en nous adressant à un public de professionnels fidèles et influents dans les domaines de la santé, de la sécurité, de la production, de l'ingénierie et des services achats. **SOLUTION :** Une première dans la discipline : un film interactif de 60 secondes, où l'on suit le trajet d'un homme d'affaires qui sort de chez lui pour se rendre au terminal de l'Eurostar à la gare de Waterloo. L'internaute doit identifier sur ce trajet 15 produits issus de la technologie 3M. Ceux qui réussissent à en retrouver plus de dix participent à une tombola. On peut aussi explorer le site plus avant si l'on souhaite plus d'informations

sur les produits. Le site fut annoncé sous forme de bannières sur le réseau interentreprise. Des e-mails furent aussi envoyés à un fichier d'adresses acquis chez Mardev et Findlay. **RÉSULTATS :** La notoriété, l'image favorable et les intentions d'achat ont augmenté de 21% en moyenne parmi les utilisateurs du jeu, comparé à une étude similaire avant l'utilisation du jeu. Le site a attiré 4,469 utilisateurs uniques, avec une durée moyenne de session de plus de huit minutes. On a comptabilisé 1,590 consultations de formulaires (taux de conversion de 35% par rapport au nombre de visiteurs). Plus de 84% des visiteurs ont joué au jeu et 60% d'entre eux ont joué plus d'une fois. 17,258 ouvertures d'application du jeu ont été recensées.

ZIEL: Die meisten Leute wissen, dass 3M etwas herstellen. Bei weiterem Nachfragen fielen ihnen vielleicht sogar Post-it®-Blöcke und Scotch®-Klebeband ein. Aber wenn sie weitere der ungefähr 49 998 Produkte von 3M nennen wollten, könnten sie wahrscheinlich kaum mehr als zwei oder drei finden. Es ist dieser geringe Bekanntheitsgrad, an dem wir arbeiten sollten, um ein kleines, einflussreiches und treues Publikum im Bereich Gesundheitswesen, Produktion, Ingenieurwesen und Einkauf anzusprechen. **LÖSUNG:** Wir produzierten zunächst einen einminütigen Film für unsere Webseite, in dem ein Geschäftsmann auf seinem Weg von zu Hause zum Eurostar Terminal in Waterloo begleitet wird. Wir baten Besucher der Seite, 15 versteckte Hotspots zu identifizieren, die demonstrierten, wie 3M-Technologie in die Story involviert war. Besucher, die mehr als 10 entdeckten, nahmen an einer Verlosung teil. Sie konnten auf Wunsch auch tiefer in die Seite eintauchen. Für die Seite wurde mit Bannern auf Nischen-B2B-Webseiten geworben. Zusätzlich wurden Werbemails an bestimmte E-Mail-Adressen verschickt, die wir aus Datenlisten von Mardev and Findlay akquiriert hatten. **ERGEBNISSE:** Die Vertrautheit mit der Marke, die Vorliebe für die Marke und die Einkaufsabsicht stiegen innerhalb des 3M-Everywhere-Wettbewerbs im Durchschnitt um 21% (im Vergleich zu einer Umfrage vor dem 3M-Everywhere-Spiel). Die Seite zog 4 469 Besucher an, die im Durchschnitt über acht Minuten verweilten. 1 590 Personen nahmen am Wettbewerb teil (das ist eine Conversion-Rate von 35% der Seitenbesucher zu Wettbewerbteilnahmen). Im Durchschnitt spielten 84% der Besucher das Spiel; 60% davon mehr als einmal. Hits auf der Seite: 17 258 Mal wurde der Startbutton des Spiels angeklickt.

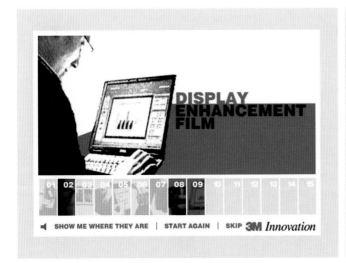

CAMPAIGN: American Express Dream Lists. **PRODUCT:** American Express Cards International. **YEAR:** 2004-2005. **AGENCY:** OgilvyOne North America <www.ogilvy.com>. **CREATIVE TEAM:** Jan Leth, Sung Chang, Mat Zucker, Peter DiBartolo, Jeff Kopay, Glori Kilmnick. **PROGRAMMER:** Scott Gordon. **DIRECTOR OF ENGINEERING:** Scott Stark. **SENIOR PROJECT ENGINEER:** Jonathan Schnapp. **MULTIMEDIA DEVELOPER:** Pierre Legagneur. **PROJECT ENGINEER:** Misha Ali. **APPLICATION DEVELOPER:** Yefim Krasnyanskiy. **SENIOR QUALITY ASSURANCE TESTER:** Julia Jia. **TECH ASPECTS:** Macromedia Flash, sound, XML, TreeMapping. **MEDIA CIRCULATED:** Online advertising, a variety interactive executions of advertisements – all rich media.

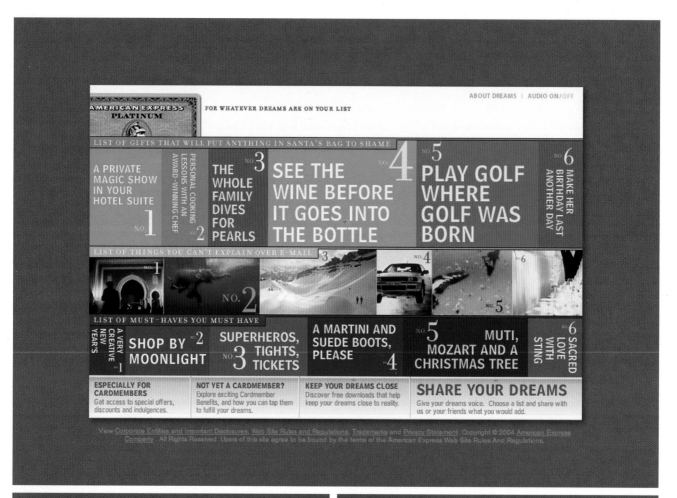

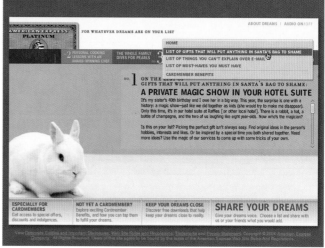

CONCEPT: OgilvyOne developed five country market sites that enable visitors to deepen their relationship with American Express and activate their membership by leveraging access to experiences (as part of an integrated, 360 campaign). The site experience for "Lists" is an interactive window into what's uniquely possible with the American Express Card. By expanding on the offline "Lists" as well as offering never-seen-before, compelling, interesting information served in the form of "lists", American Express' international targets find: Ideas for what you can do with your membership; Insight into what others are doing; Inspiration to act on it for yourself (acquisition/usage). The sites enable prospects to engage with the brand and experience the benefits of membership, while Cardmembers are advantaged by the valuable benefits at their disposal. **RESULTS:** Media and creative beat projected CTR (click-through rate) by more than 25%, exceeding industry performance standard. Lists campaign destination site surpassed engagement goals. Average time spent on site by visitors more than double what was projected. 70% of all visitors viewed multiple product benefit pages exceeding estimates. Significant positive impact in brand metrics were achieved with communications integrating the web showing the highest impact. 4+ Frequency Increases: (Communications integrated with the Web has highest impact). Aided Ad Awareness 26%. Message Association 96%. Winner of Gold New York Addy Award (2004) for excellence in Rich Media Interactive. Phase 2 of the evolution of the Lists campaign strategy was rolled out in August with additional product launches planned for September through the remainder of 2005.

CONCEPT : OgilvyOne a développé cinq sites nationaux qui permettent aux visiteurs d'approfondir leur relation avec American Express et activer leur adhésion en offrant une expérience de marque, dans le cadre d'une campagne intégrée. La rubrique « listes » est une fenêtre interactive qui présente les avantages exclusifs de la carte de membre American Express. Venant en complément des offres hors ligne, le site propose à ses clients internationaux des infos originales sur la façon d'utiliser sa carte, des exemples d'autres utilisateurs, et des invitations à personnaliser son usage (acquisition et usage). Le site permet aux futurs clients d'interagir avec la marque et de faire un tour d'horizon des avantages de l'adhésion, tandis que les adhérents disposent d'avantages tangibles. **RÉSULTATS :** On a mesuré 25% de hausse sur le taux de clics, ce qui dépasse la norme des performances

dans le domaine. La fréquentation du site a dépassé les objectifs. La durée moyenne d'une session est deux fois supérieure aux prévisions. 70% des visiteurs ont dépassé les estimations concernant le nombre de pages vues. Les mesures d'impact ont indiqué que les meilleures performances revenaient aux différents supports électroniques. La notoriété a augmenté de 26%, la mémorisation du message de 96%. Le site a remporté la Médaille d'Or aux New York Addy Awards en 2004 pour l'excellence de sa création *rich media*. La deuxième phase de la stratégie a été développée au mois d'août, et comprend de nouveaux lancements de produit échelonnés sur l'année 2005.

KONZEPT: OgilvyOne entwickelten Seiten für den Markt in fünf Ländern, auf denen Besucher ihre Beziehung zu American Express vertiefen und ihre Mitgliedschaft aktivieren können (Teil einer integrierten 360°-Kampagne). Unter „Listen" findet man ein interaktives Fenster, in dem die einzigartigen Möglichkeiten, die die American Express Card bietet, dargestellt werden. Durch die Ausweitung auf die Offline-„Listen" und neue, spannende und interessante Informationen finden internationale Zielgruppen außerdem Ideen, wie man eine Mitgliedschaft nutzen kann, Einblicke in das, was andere tun, Inspiration für eigene Aktivitäten (Akquisition/Verwendung). Die Seite ermöglicht Interessenten, sich mit der Marke auseinander zu setzen und die Vorteile einer Mitgliedschaft zu erfahren, während Mitglieder sich von den Vorteilen ihrer Mitgliedschaft überzeugen können. **ERGEBNISSE:** Die erwartete CTR (Click-Through-Rate) lag um 25% höher als erwartet und übertraf damit den Leistungsstandard der Branche. Die durchschnittliche Verweildauer auf der Seite war doppelt so hoch wie erwartet. 70% der Besucher betrachteten die verschiedenen Seiten mit den Produktvorteilen und übertrafen damit die Schätzungen. Bedeutende positive Wirkung wurde in der Metrik erreicht, wobei web-integrierende Kommunikationsmittel die beste Wirkung erzielten. Steigerung der Häufigkeit (mit dem Web verknüpfte Kommunikation hat die größte Wirkung). Bekanntheitsgrad 26%. Erfolgreiche Vermittlung der Botschaft 96%. Gewinner von Gold beim New York Addy Award (2004) für hervorragende Leistungen bei interaktiven Rich-Media-Lösungen. Phase 2 der Evolution der Listen-Kampagnenstrategie wurde im August 2005 eingeläutet, mit zusätzlichen geplanten Produkteinführungen für September und den Rest des Jahres hindurch.

FEATURED ON THE DVD   **CAMPAIGN:** The Agent Provocateur Sale <www.agentprovocateur.com>.   **YEAR:** 2005.   **AGENCY:** Large <www.largedesign.com>.   **PRODUCTION TIME:** 3 weeks.   **COST IN HOURS OF WORK:** 80 h.
CREATIVE TEAM: Lars Hemming Jorgensen, Jim Boulton, Rene Christoffer, Rory McHarg.   **PROGRAMMER:** Jesper Lycke, Martin Whitely.   **TECH ASPECTS:** Macromedia Flash, PHP.   **AWARDS:** D&AD Annual.

CONCEPT: A simple, but sexy campaign offering readers fantastic lingerie at a discount while stocks last. **RESULTS:** The sale was cut short by a week due to lack of goods – they'd had sold out early.

CONCEPT : Une campagne simple et sexy offrant aux visiteurs de la lingerie à prix soldé dans la limite des stocks. **RÉSULTATS :** La vente a été arrêtée une semaine plus tôt que prévu due à une pénurie de produits, tout est parti très vite.

KONZEPT: Eine einfache, aber sexy Kampagne, die den Lesern schöne Unterwäsche zu reduzierten Preisen bei gleich bleibendem Angebot bietet. **ERGEBNISSE:** Der Ausverkauf wurde um eine Woche verkürzt, weil die Ware so schnell vergriffen war.

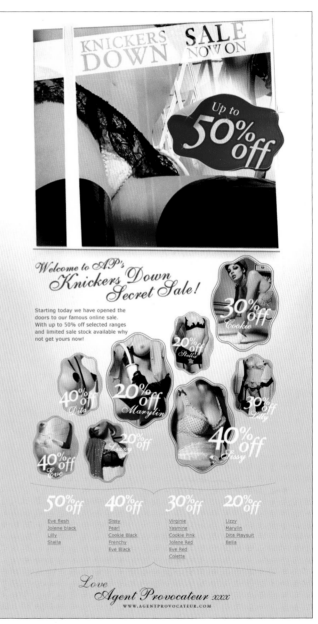

FEATURED ON THE DVD **CAMPAIGN:** Atrapalo.com <www.atrapalo.com>. **PRODUCT:** Screensaver. **YEAR:** 2005. **AGENCY:** DoubleYou <www.doubleyou.com>. **PRODUCTION TIME:** 2 weeks. **CREATIVE TEAM:** Daniel Solana, Emma Pueyo, Blanca Piera, Xavi Caparrós. **PROGRAMMER:** Xavi Caparrós. **TECH ASPECTS:** Macromedia Flash.

CONCEPT: True to the concept defining the brand (run to catch all opportunities), Atrápalo gave its users an experimental screen-saver for Christmas, in which 40 runners mark the hours of the clock.

CONCEPT: Fidèle au slogan qui définit la marque : « Saisir toutes les opportunités », Atrapalo offre aux internautes un écran de veille expérimental en guise de cadeau de Noël, sur lequel 40 coureurs figurent les heures d'une horloge.

KONZEPT: Gemäß dem Markenkonzept (Rennen, um alle Gelegenheiten zu ergreifen) schenkte Atrápalo seinen Benutzern einen experimentellen Bildschirmschoner zu Weihnachten, auf dem 40 Läufer die Stunden auf der Uhr markieren.

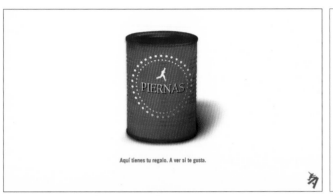

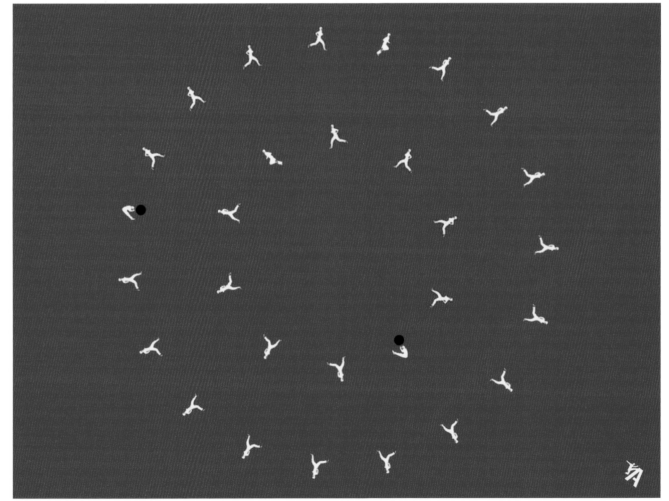

CONCEPT: Entertaining promotional action for the Children for the biggest private bank of Latin America.

KONZEPT: Unterhaltsame Werbeaktion für die Tochterfirma der größten privaten Bank Lateinamerikas.

CONCEPT : Promouvoir de façon distrayante l'action caritative de la plus grande banque privée d'Amérique latine en faveur de l'enfance.

FEATURED ON THE DVD **CAMPAIGN:** Borders Giftmixer 3000. **PRODUCT:** Borders Bookstore. **YEAR:** 2004. **AGENCY:** Crispin Porter + Bogusky <www.cpbgroup.com>. **PRODUCTION TIME:** 2 months. **EXECUTIVE CREATIVE DIRECTOR:** Alex Bogusky. **CREATIVE DIRECTOR:** Tim Roper. **INTERACTIVE CREATIVE DIRECTOR:** Jeff Benjamin. **ART DIRECTOR:** Joon Young Park, Michael Ferrare. **COPYWRITER:** Tim Roper, Lydia Langford, Ryan Kutscher, Justin Kramm. **PROGRAMMER:** Firstborn Multimedia. **MEDIA CIRCULATED:** Magazine Inserts, Broadcast TV. **AWARDS:** One Show & One Show Interactive 2005 (Finalist), CLIO 2005 (Bronze), CA Interactive 2005 (Winner), London International 2005 (Finalist).

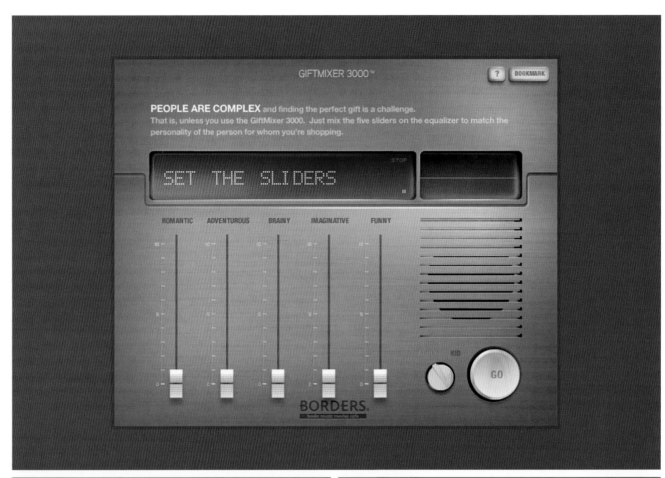

CONCEPT: The Giftmixer 3000 helps people find the perfect gift for their family and friends in a fun and unexpected way.

KONZEPT: Der Geschenkmixer 3000 ermöglicht es, das perfekte Geschenk für Familie und Freunde auf ungewöhnliche Weise zu finden.

CONCEPT : Le Giftmixer 3000 aide les usagers à dénicher le cadeau idéal pour leurs amis ou leur famille, sous une forme distrayante et inattendue.

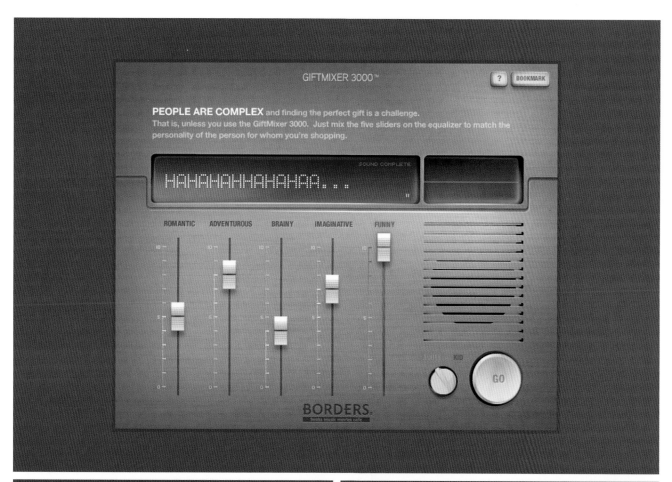

FEATURED ON THE DVD CAMPAIGN: BP Ultimate. TITLE: Baby. AGENCY: 20:20 London <www.2020london.co.uk>. PRODUCTION TIME: 3 months. CREATIVE TEAM: Peter Riley (Creative Partner), Hugo Bierschenk (Creative), Dean Woodhouse (Creative). PROGRAMMER: Dave Luff. TECH ASPECTS: Film, sound, Adobe After Effects, Macromedia Flash, Wavelab, PHP/SQL, 3D Studio, Maya, Shake, Adobe Premiere, Apple Quicktime Pro. MEDIA CIRCULATED: Email.

OBJECTIVES: BP Ultimate is the premium fuel range of BP. BP Ultimate really is the performance fuel of the future. **CONCEPT:** Create interest and debate. Make some noise so consumers can find out how their car can perform like never before. **STRATEGY:** Fuel is boring and no product in the category has a clear brand personality. We considered the product benefits so unambiguous and easy to understand that they needed an honest and simple delivery. This thought, allied to BP's long-term environmental heritage, led to the idea of the Ultimate Baby. Albie (as we christened him) really is the ultimate brand spokesperson. He's advanced and intelligent like the product; feisty and straight-talking like the brand. **SOLUTION:** An e-mail link was sent to the Nectar database that clicked through to an Internet film showing Albie playing at home. When his mum's not looking his baby scribbles turn into pie charts and fuel-performance graphs. As he explains the benefits of using Ultimate, he crawls over to the family's computer where he types you an e-mail. Right on cue, as the film finishes, there's the real e-mail in your inbox, triggered automatically by reaching the end of the film. This e-mail further explains the benefits of using Ultimate and points you in the direction of the website. A Digital DM invitation to see for yourself the advanced thinking behind BP Ultimate fuels. **RESULTS:** Evaluation results, summary of improvements to business performance 1.25 million views and 270,000 forwards. Positive words from Jeremy Clarkson and Quentin Willson in the motoring press and contribution to BP Ultimate reaching year 5 targets in just 2 years!

OBJECTIFS : BP Ultimate est la marque de supercarburant de BP, le carburant à hautes performance de l'avenir. **CONCEPT :** Eveiller l'intérêt et encourager la discussion. Faire du bruit afin que les automobilistes découvrent les nouvelles possibilités de leur voiture. **STRATÉGIE :** Le carburant est un produit ennuyeux et aucun produit de cette catégorie ne possède de personnalité tranchée. Les avantages du produit étaient si évidents et simples à comprendre qu'ils avaient besoin d'une communication franche. Cette notion, alliée à l'héritage environnemental de BP nous a conduit à l'Ultimate Baby. Le petit Albie (comme nous l'avons baptisé) est le porte-parole de la marque. Il est brillant et intelligent comme le produit, fougueux et spontané comme elle. **SOLUTION :** Un e-mail envoyé sur la base de données Nectar renvoie l'usager sur une vidéo en ligne montrant Albie en train de jouer chez lui. Quand sa mère ne le regarde pas, Albie gribouille des graphiques de performances. Il nous explique les atouts du carburant, puis marche à quatre pattes vers l'ordinateur familial pour vous envoyer un e-mail. Dès que le film est fini, l'e-mail arrive dans votre boîte de réception, déclenché automatiquement. Le message vous décrit en détail les avantages du produit et vous dirige vers le site de la marque, où vous êtes invités à partager la philosophie de la société pétrolière. **RÉSULTATS :** 1,25 million de pages vues et 270 000 recommandations. Les journalistes J. Clarkson et Q. Willson en ont fait l'éloge dans la presse automobile, et les objectifs de BP sur cinq ans ont été atteints en seulement deux ans.

AUFTRAG UND ZIELSETZUNG: BP Ultimate ist das Premiumkraftstoff-Angebot von BP. BP Ultimate ist der Leistungskraftstoff der Zukunft. Diese Botschaft galt es zu vermitteln. **KONZEPT:** Interesse und Debatten wecken. Aufmerksamkeit erregen, damit Konsumenten herausfinden können, wie ihr Auto laufen kann wie nie zuvor. **STRATEGIE:** Kraftstoff ist langweilig und kein Produkt, das eine klare Markenpersönlichkeit hat. Wir hielten die Vorteile des Produktes für so klar und einfach zu verstehen, dass sie ehrlich und simpel vermittelt werden sollten. Dieser Gedanke führte zusammen mit dem langfristigen Umwelterbe von BP zur Idee des Ultimate Baby. Albie (so tauften wir ihn) ist der ultimative Ansprechpartner für die Marke. Er ist so fortschrittlich und intelligent wie das Produkt; energiegeladen und geradeheraus wie die Marke. **LÖSUNG:** Ein E-Mail-Link wurde an die Nectar-Datenbank gesendet, die einen Internetfilm startete, der Albie zu Hause beim Spielen zeigte. Als seine Mutter nicht hinsieht, werden aus den Kritzeleien des Babys Tabellen und Grafiken zur Kraftstoffleistung. Während er die Vorteile von Ultimate erklärt, krabbelt er zum Familiencomputer und schreibt von dort eine E-Mail an Sie. Exakt in dem Moment, in dem der Film zu Ende ist, finden Sie tatsächlich eine E-Mail in Ihrem Posteingang, die automatisch durch den Schluss des Films ausgelöst wurde. Sie enthält weitere Erläuterungen der Vorteile von Ultimate sowie den Verweis zur Webseite – eine digitale Direct-Marketing-Einladung, die Ihnen das fortschrittliche Denken hinter BP Ultimate-Kraftstoffen vor Augen führt. **ERGEBNISSE:** Auswertungsergebnisse und Zusammenfas-sung der Verbesserungen der Unternehmensleistung: 1,25 Millionen Ansichten und 270 000 weiterführende Klicks. Positive Reaktionen von Jeremy Clarkson und Quentin Willson in der Motorpresse, und Beitrag zum Erreichen der 5-Jahres-Ziele von BP Ultimate in nur 2 Jahren!

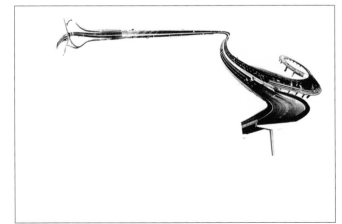

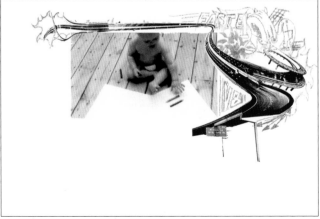

FEATURED ON THE DVD **CAMPAIGN:** Dream Kitchens for Everyone. **CLIENT:** IKEA Sweden. **YEAR:** 2005-2006. **AGENCY:** Forsman & Bodenfors <www.fb.se>. **PRODUCTION TIME:** 3 months. **CREATIVE TEAM:** Mathias Appelblad, Andreas Malm, Anders Eklind, Karin Frisell, Fredrik Jansson, Anders Hegerfors, Mikko Timonen, Nina Andersson, Jerry Wass. **PROGRAMMER:** Kokokaka. **PRODUCER:** Kokokaka, Sammarco, Stop, Syndicate. **TECH ASPECTS:** Macromedia Flash. **MEDIA CIRCULATED:** Online ads, magazine, press, TVC, viral. **AWARDS:** Flash Forward 2006 (Winner), Eurobest 2005 (Silver).

CONCEPT: It began with a simple brief: Make kitchen inspiration and show that IKEA's kitchens are functional, have great design, great quality and low price.

KONZEPT: Es begann mit einem einfachen Auftrag: Präsentieren Sie auf inspirierende Weise die Funktionalität, das großartige Design, die hohe Qualität und den günstigen Preis von IKEA-Küchen.

CONCEPT : Susciter l'enthousiasme autour des cuisines et montrer que celles qu'on trouve chez IKEA sont fonctionnelles, esthétiques, bon marché et résistantes.

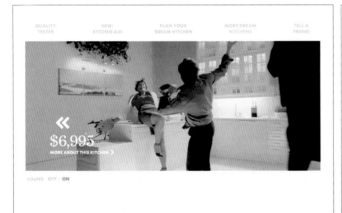

DREAM KITCHENS FOR EVERYONE.

ORGANIZE YOUR KITCHEN   QUALITY TESTER   NEW! KITCHEN AID   PLAN YOUR DREAM KITCHEN   TELL A FRIEND   MORE DREAM KITCHENS

$3,499
MORE ABOUT THIS KITCHEN ▶

SOUND OFF / **ON**

ORGANIZE YOUR KITCHEN   QUALITY TESTER   NEW! KITCHEN AID   PLAN YOUR DREAM KITCHEN   TELL A FRIEND   MORE DREAM KITCHENS

$3,695
MORE ABOUT THIS KITCHEN ▶

SOUND OFF / **ON**

ORGANIZE YOUR KITCHEN QUALITY TESTER NEW! KITCHEN AID PLAN YOUR DREAM KITCHEN TELL A FRIEND MORE DREAM KITCHENS

RIGHT NOW! BUY A KITCHEN FOR $1,295 AND GET $129 TO SPEND AT IKEA.

$2,999

FAKTUM kitchen with **TIDAHOLM** cabinets and **VARIABEL** countertops.

MORE PICTURES

Prices do not include appliances, custom-built sinks, faucets, lighting, or cabinet hardware.

BACK

© Inter IKEA Systems B.V. 2006

IKEA
DREAM KITCHEN FOR EVERYONE.

ORGANIZE YOUR KITCHEN QUALITY TESTER NEW! KITCHEN AID PLAN YOUR DREAM KITCHEN TELL A FRIEND MORE DREAM KITCHENS

RIGHT NOW! BUY A KITCHEN FOR $1,295 AND GET $129 TO SPEND AT IKEA.

$2,399

FAKTUM kitchen with **NEXUS** cabinets and **VARIABEL** countertops.

MORE PICTURES

Prices do not include appliances, custom-built sinks, faucets, lighting, or cabinet hardware.

BACK

© Inter IKEA Systems B.V. 2006

IKEA
DREAM KITCHEN FOR EVERYONE.

CONCEPT: Diamond Schmitt Architects was looking for a way to raise its international profile. The firm has a well-established reputation in Canada, but is little known in Europe and the US. The current trend for large institutional projects is to make a big splash by hiring architects like Frank Gehry or Rem Koolhaas, both of whom are far more focused on dramatic form and less on buildings that are user-focused and context-sensitive. DS wants to compete with these 'superstars' more effectively.

CONCEPT : Le cabinet d'architectes Diamond Schmitt désire améliorer sa notoriété au niveau international. Il jouit en effet d'une réputation établie au Canada, mais il est peu connu en Europe et aux Etats-Unis. Les grandes institutions ont tendance à faire sensation en engageant des sommités comme Frank Gehry ou Rem Koolhaas, qui sont tous deux plus intéressés par l'esthétique que par le côté fonctionnel et contextuel des constructions. La société DS cherche à rivaliser efficacement avec ces superstars.

KONZEPT: Diamond Schmitt Architects suchten nach einer Möglichkeit, ihr internationales Profil zu schärfen. Das Unternehmen genießt einen guten Ruf in Kanada, ist aber in Europa und den USA kaum bekannt. Der momentane Trend bei großen Prestige-Projekten besteht darin, Aufsehen zu erregen, indem man Architekten wie Frank Gehry oder Rem Koolhaas engagiert – beide konzentrieren sich eher auf die dramatische Form als auf Gebäude, die auf Menschen und Kontexte ausgerichtet sind. DS will mit diesen „Superstars" effektiver konkurrieren.

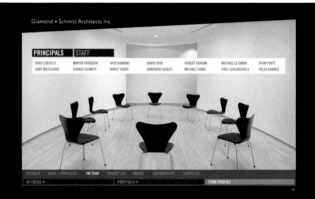

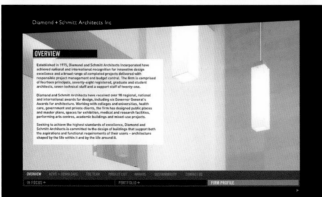

FEATURED ON THE DVD **CAMPAIGN:** Colour Chemistry. **PRODUCT:** Dulux. **YEAR:** 2004-2005. **AGENCY:** Agency.com London <www.agency.com>. **COST IN HOURS OF WORK:** 345 h. **CREATIVE TEAM:** Adrian Peters, David Wellington. **PROGRAMMER:** Wil Bevan, Rob Mills, Karl Reynolds, Dan Harman. **TECH ASPECTS:** Macromedia Flash. **MEDIA CIRCULATED:** All banner executions were specifically conceptualised for the sites they were to appear on – dating, fashion and celebrity related sites, such as: Channel4 Homes, Glamour.com, Handbag.com, UK Style, ivillage and Lycos. For example the rock star execution appeared on sites including <Ticketmaster.co.uk>. **AWARDS:** IAB Creative Showcase; Creative Review Annual 2005; One Show Interactive 2005; Horizon Interactive Awards 2005; D&AD Awards 2005; IAC Best Consumer Goods Rich Media; Cannes Cyber Lions 2005 (Bronze); MIXX Awards 2005 (Gold); Campaign Digital Awards 2005; IMA Awards 2005 Consumer Goods & Best Use of Rich Media; Eurobest 2005 Awards (Finalist).

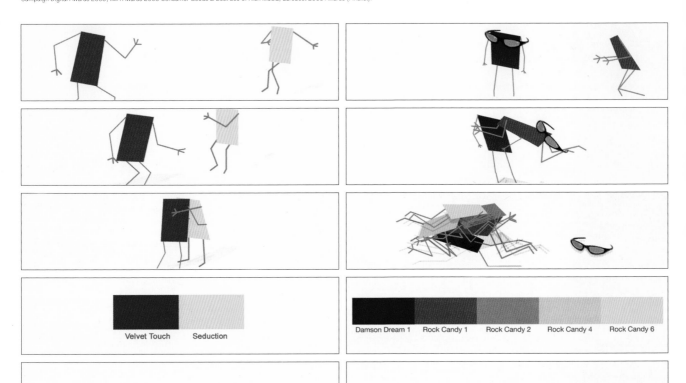

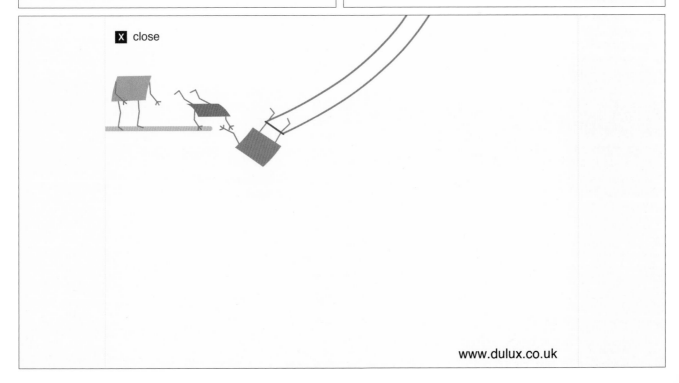

CHALLENGE: Dulux repositioned as 'colour experts' in the marketplace with a newly rede-signed website which provided an interactive experience to position Dulux as a personal 'colour expert', helping customers realize their creative projects. The campaign intended to raise brand awareness online of the new brand positioning and aimed to drive traffic to the new and revamped Dulux site-specifically to the online 'Mousepainter' application. **SOLUTION:** The ATL and online advertising brief was materially the same; Dulux reposi-tioned as colour experts in the marketplace via Colour Chemistry; a helpful way of making colour combining easy. The role of the advertising was to encourage people to embark on their creative journey with Dulux. The online advertising campaign integrated with the above the line concept of "some colours are just made for each other," harnessed specifically for the online medium with a unique creative style. In the ads, colour swatches are character-ized, or 'humanized'. Different colour swatches are seen interacting in different scenarios i. e. two swatches coming together in an embrace, or one swatch climbing from banner to banner in order to get to the other swatch, reinforcing the notion that "some colours are just made for each other." Each creative execution was specifically tailored around the media format or placement for that particular unit. The Roadblock and Overlay executions both specifically 'play' with the format as part of the ad, with the swatches climbing between pop-ups or across the screen from banner to skyscraper, and so on. The online art direction was unique in producing the human element to the swatches. Every movement was origi-nally filmed with a camcorder as live footage of people. This was traced, frame by frame, into Flash in order to create human like movements. **RESULTS:** Click through rates of up to 3.8%. Overall traffic to Dulux.co.uk up 60% during the campaign. Cost Per Click £1.56. Booked impressions versus actual impressions was 113%. 30% of all traffic to the site from the online advertising resulted in a key action. After the success of the new website and corresponding campaign, Agency.com was appointed in 2004 as the Interactive Agency of record for Dulux UK, covering creative development, online advertising and inter-active consultancy for the next three years.

DÉFI : Repositionner Dulux sur le marché de la peinture comme un spécialiste de la couleur grâce à un remodelage de son site. Celui-ci offre une expérience interactive qui aide les consommateurs à mener à bien leurs envies créatives. La campagne en ligne vise à aug-menter la notoriété de la marque et encourager l'utilisation de l'application « Mousepainter ». **SOLUTION :** Le briefing pour la pub en ligne et hors ligne se propose de positionner Dulux comme un expert de la couleur via Colour Chemistry, une application facilitant la combinai-son des couleurs. La pub doit encourager le public à embarquer pour un voyage créatif. Le slogan de la campagne en ligne : « Certaines couleurs sont faites l'une pour l'autre » était décliné dans un style créatif unique. Les échantillons de couleurs sont caractérisés, comme personnifiés. Ils interagissent selon plusieurs scénarios, ils s'approchent pour s'enlacer, grimpent sur les bannières pour se rejoindre, tout est fait pour renforcer la notion d'entente et d'harmonie entre couleurs. Chaque module créatif a été réalisé sur mesure selon le canal de destination. Les applications Roadblock et Overlay permettent de jouer sur les différen-ces de formats comme partie intégrante de la pub, avec des couleurs qui grimpent entre les fenêtres *pop-up*, qui traversent l'écran d'une bannière à une autre, etc. La direction artisti-que a supervisé les éléments « humains » des couleurs. Les mouvements ont d'abord été exécutés par des hommes et enregistré avec une caméra. Puis image par image ils ont été décalqués et convertis en format Flash afin d'imiter au plus près les mouvements humains. **RÉSULTATS :** Le taux de clics a connu une hausse de 3,8%. Le trafic global du site Dulux. co.uk a augmenté de 60% pendant la campagne. Coût par clic : 1,56 livre. Le nombre de pages vues a dépassé de 113% les prévisions. 30% du trafic sur le site a généré une ac-tion. Suite au succès du nouveau site et de la campagne en ligne, Agency.com a été nom-mée agence interactive exclusive pour Dulux UK, et sera chargée des activités de conseil et de développement pendant les trois prochaines années.

AUFGABE: Dulux positionierten sich als „Farbexperten" neu auf dem Markt, mit einer neu gestalteten, interaktiven Webseite, um Dulux als persönlichen „Farbexperten" zu präsentie-ren, der Kunden hilft, ihre kreativen Projekte zu realisieren. Die Kampagne wollte den Bekanntheitsgrad der Marke online erhöhen und zielte darauf ab, die Besucher der neu auf-gemachten Dulux-Seite zu leiten, besonders zur „Mousepainter"-Anwendung. **LÖSUNG:** Der Auftrag für ATL und die Online-Werbung war praktisch derselbe: Dulux als Farbexperten auf dem Markt mit seinem interaktiven Tool „Colour Chemistry" neu zu positionieren; ein praktischer Weg, Farbkombinationen einfach zu gestalten. Die Rolle der Werbung bestand darin, Leute dazu zu animieren, ihre kreative Reise mit Dulux anzutreten. Die Online-Werbekampagne integrierte oben Erwähntes mit dem Konzept „Manche Farben sind ein-fach füreinander gemacht", das besonders für das Online-Medium mit einem einzigartigen kreativen Stil umgesetzt wurde. In den Anzeigen werden Farbmuster charakterisiert oder „vermenschlicht". Man sieht verschiedene Muster in unterschiedlichen Szenarien, d.h. zwei Muster kommen in einer Umarmung zusammen, oder ein Muster klettert von Banner zu Banner, um zum anderen zu gelangen, um damit die Idee zu unterstreichen, dass „manche Farben einfach füreinander gemacht sind". Jede kreative Ausführung war speziell auf das Medienformat oder die Platzierung der jeweiligen Einheit zugeschnitten. Die Roadblock-und Overlay-Ausführungen „spielen" jeweils mit dem Format als Teil der Anzeige, wobei die Muster zwischen Pop Up-Fenstern oder über den Bildschirm von Banner zu Skyscraper klettern usw. Das Webdesign war einzigartig in der Form, wie es die Muster mit dem menschlichen Element versah. Jede Bewegung kam ursprünglich von wirklichen Menschen, die mit dem Camcorder aufgenommen worden waren. Dies wurde, Frame für Frame, in Flash umgewandelt, um menschliche Bewegungen zu erzeugen. **ERGEBNISSE:** Click-Through-Raten von bis zu 3,8%. Allgemeine Besucherrate auf dulux.co.uk stieg während der Kampagne um 60%. Kosten pro Klick: £1,56. 30% der Besucher, die durch Online-Werbung zu der Seite gelenkt wurden, verweilten länger, um z. B. die interaktiven Tools auszuprobieren. Nach dem Erfolg der neuen Webseite und der korrespondierenden Kampagne wurde Agency.Com 2004 als Interaktive Agentur von Dulux UK mit der kreativen Entwicklung, Online-Werbung und interaktiven Beratung für die nächsten drei Jahre beauftragt.

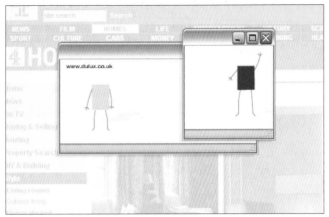
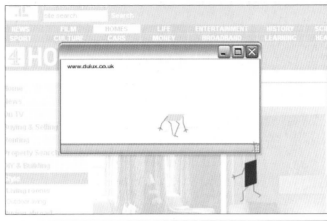
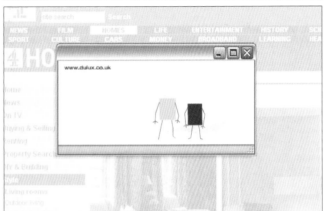
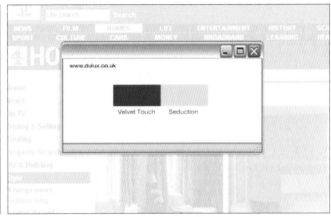

4 | TV Listings | E4
Text Only | T4
Site A-Z | FilmFour

site search | Search

www.DULUX.co.uk

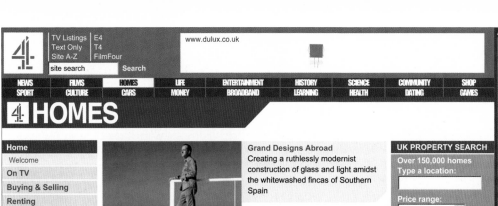

NEWS | FILMS | HOMES | LIFE | ENTERTAINMENT | HISTORY | SCIENCE | COMMUNITY | SHOP
SPORT | CULTURE | CARS | MONEY | BROADBAND | LEARNING | HEALTH | DATING | GAMES

4 HOMES

Home

Welcome

On TV

Buying & Selling

Renting

Property Search

DIY & Building

Style

Buying abroad

Chat, vote & win

Forum

Property from property

Money

SEARCH

GO

All 4 Homes:

Grand Designs Abroad
Creating a ruthlessly modernist construction of glass and light amidst the whitewashed fincas of Southern Spain

On TV

Location Location Location Phil and Kirstie help people find their dream homes without breaking the bank

Housetrapped In The Sun Dream turned to nightmare? Tell us about it.

New

Win A Weekend In Paris When you vote for the Best Private Develop - ment of the year

Tantalising Tiles Some of the most exciting new tile designs for your home

Don't Miss

The Mind of Estate Agents A psychological profile of the people selling your home

House Price Index How much has the value of your house changed in the last year?

UK PROPERTY SEARCH

Over 150,000 homes
Type a location:

Price range:

Min Price

Max Price

Min bedrooms:

Min Beds

☐ New homes only GO

www.dulux.co.uk

4HOMES MAIL

GO

Enter your email to sign up to the 4Home newsletter

ASK THE EXPERT

Got a question for our DIY expert Tony Lush? Pop your question into our DIY forum and our DIY expert Tony Lush will pick one a week to answer.

www.dulux.co.uk

FEATURED ON THE DVD **CAMPAIGN:** JC – The Store. **CLIENT:** JC – Jeans & Clothes. **YEAR:** 2004. **AGENCY:** Forsman & Bodenfors <www.fb.se>. **PRODUCTION TIME:** 1 month. **CREATIVE TEAM:** Mathias Appelblad, Andreas Malm, Fredrik Jansson, Jerry Wass. **PROGRAMMER:** Kokokaka, Stink. **PRODUCER:** Kokokaka. **TECH ASPECTS:** Macromedia Flash. **MEDIA CIRCULATED:** Online ads, TVC. **AWARDS:** Cannes Lions 2005 (Silver), CLIO 2005 (Finalist), Eurobest 2005 (Finalist), The Golden Egg Award 2005 (Finalist), London International Advertising Awards (Finalist), New York Festivals 2005 (2 Gold, 1 Silver), One Show 2005 (Silver), Flash Forward 2006 (Winner).

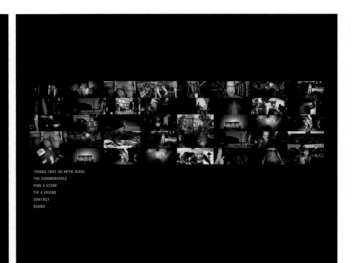

CONCEPT: Jeans & Clothes deliver an interactive store to reflect the emotional experience of a pair of jeans.

CONCEPT : Jeans & Clothes propose une boutique en ligne qui reflète l'expérience émotionnelle de l'achat d'une paire de jeans.

KONZEPT: Jeans & Clothes bieten einen interaktiven Shop, um die emotionale Erfahrung beim Kauf einer Jeans zu reflektieren.

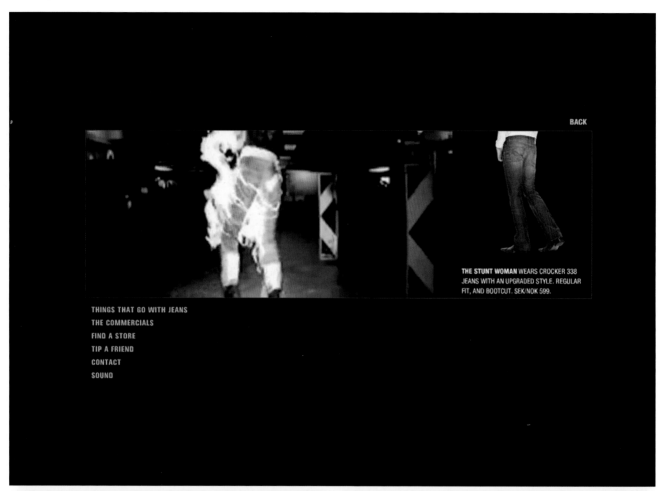

FEATURED ON THE DVD CAMPAIGN: PDK <www.pdk.pl>. **CLIENT:** Powszechny Dom Kredytowy (PDK). **COUNTRY:** Poland. **YEAR:** 2004-2005. **AGENCY:** Max Weber <www.maxweber.com>. **PRODUCTION TIME:** 1 year.
CREATIVE TEAM: Grzegorz Mogilewski, Krzysztof Dykas, Mateusz Subieta, Małgorzata Wo Niakowska, Marcin Talarek. **PROGRAMMER:** Lukasz Dyszy. **TECH ASPECTS:** Macromedia Flash. **AWARDS:** Cannes Cyber Lions 2004
(Gold), Silver Drum, New York Festivals (Bronze World Medal), Favourite Website Awards (Site of the Month), Ultrashock Bombshock.

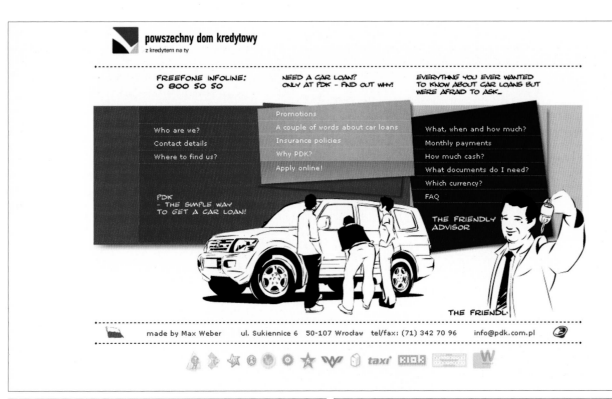

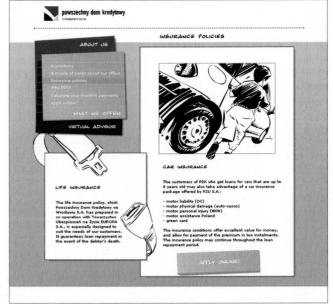

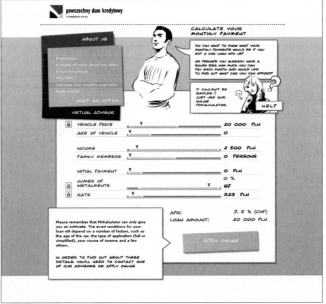

CONCEPT: The aim of the campaign was to support PDK in entering a market of car-credits operators. Max Weber was responsible for creation of CI for PDK as well as for all possible Internet activities. Main assumption was to leave financial nomenclature in order to make communication clear and easy. We dismissed all empty and unemotional pictures and replaced them with characteristic animations. We bet on PDK's distinguishable design and innovative tools which enable users to make decision about credits. **RESULTS:** In may 2004, after six-months-works, we published service www.pdk.pl, which gathered 20,000 entries in first 48 hours – everything without preceding promotions of any kind. Afterwards, new websites, supportive to PDK's main, were created – PDKlub (trustworthy program) and PDKpartner (a platform for cooperation with used cars dealers) published every three months. There was no assistance of traditional Internet campaigns while launching the brand. Nevertheless, the first year of PDK's functioning brought 200,000,000 zł of turnover and its creative line made and still makes it highly distinguishable from other financial organizations.

CONCEPT : Soutenir l'entrée de PDK sur le marché des sociétés de crédits automobiles. Max Weber a supervisé la campagne en ligne de PDK, ainsi que tous les autres modules internet. Il fallait délaisser la nomenclature financière afin de réaliser une communication simple et claire. Nous avons fait disparaître les images froides et techniques et les avons remplacées par des animations. Nous avons parié sur le design caractéristique de PDK et ses outils novateurs qui permettent aux clients de choisir leurs crédits. **RÉSULTATS :** En mai 2004, après six mois de travail, nous avons réalisé pdk.pl, qui a attiré 20 000 entrées dans les premières 48 heures, sans aucune annonce préalable. Ultérieurement, d'autres si-

tes ont vu le jour en complément du premier, PDKlub (programme de fidélité) et PDKpartner (plateforme de coopération destinée aux vendeurs de voitures d'occasion). Le lancement de la marque n'a bénéficié d'aucune autre forme de publicité en ligne. Néanmoins, la première année de fonctionnement de PDK a rapporté 200 000 zlotys de transactions et son positionnement créatif l'a distingué d'autres sociétés financières.

KONZEPT: Das Ziel der Kampagne war die Unterstützung von PDK beim Eintritt in den Markt von Anbietern zur Autokauffinanzierung. Max Weber war sowohl für die Entwicklung einer CI für PDK verantwortlich als auch für die umfangreichsten Internetaktivitäten. Die Voraussetzung war, die finanzielle Nomenklatur auszulassen, um die Kommunikation klar und einfach zu machen. Wir ersetzten alle starren und nicht-emotionalen Bilder durch charakteristische Animationen. Wir setzten auf das unverwechselbare Design von PDK und innovative Tools, die es den Benutzern ermöglichen, eine Entscheidung über Kredite zu treffen. **ERGEBNISSE:** Im Mai 2004, nach sechsmonatiger Arbeit, starteten wir die Seite www.pdk.pl, die innerhalb der ersten 48 Stunden 20 000 Besucher hatte – ohne irgendwelche vorangegangenen Werbemaßnahmen. Danach wurden Webseiten entwickelt, die PDKs Hauptseite unterstützten: PDKlub (vertrauenswürdiges Programm) und PDKpartner (eine Plattform für die Kooperation mit Gebrauchtwagenhändlern), die alle drei Monate aktualisiert wurden. Es gab beim Launch der Marke keine zusätzlichen gebräuchlichen Internet-Kampagnen. Dennoch erzielte PDK im ersten Jahr einen Umsatz von 200 000 000 Zloty, und seine kreative Linie macht PDK immer noch klar unterscheidbar von anderen Finanzierungsanbietern.

FEATURED ON THE DVD **CAMPAIGN:** PG Tips – Wallace and Gromit <www.pgmoment.com>. **PRODUCT:** PG Tips. **YEAR:** 2005. **AGENCY:** AKQA <www.aqka.com>. **COUNTRY:** USA. **EXECUTIVE CREATIVE DIRECTOR:** James Hilton, Nick Turner. **ART DIRECTOR:** Jim Bucktin, Tiina Bjork. **COPYWRITER:** Phil Wilce, Miles Unwin. **SENIOR COPYWRITER:** Michael-Jason Hobbs. **MOTION GRAPHICS:** Stephen Clements. **CREATIVE DEVELOPER:** Greg Mullen, Rick Williams. **SENIOR QA MANAGER:** Tony Unwin. **WEB EDITOR:** Tony Sears. **SENIOR SOFTWARE ENGINEER:** Miriam Healy. **CREATIVE DEVELOPMENT DIRECTOR:** Andy Hood. **SOFTWARE ENGINEER:** Jez Brewster. **WEB DEVELOPER:** Mario Theodorou. **SENIOR DESIGNER:** Chris Williams. **JUNIOR DESIGNER** Chris Walker. **DESIGNER:** Win Kwok, Shahpour Abbasvand. **SENIOR CREATIVE:** John Mintoft. **GROUP ACCOUNT DIRECTOR:** Richard Hedges. **ACCOUNT DIRECTOR:** David Bentley. **SENIOR ACCOUNT MANAGER:** Jacqui Smith. **TECH ASPECTS:** ERN was designed to fit with the Wallace & Grommit style and era without being an exact match –he therefore takes the form of an old Fridge that has been converted into a machine for making tea. 3D Studio Max was used to model and animate ERN and the environment in which he lives; it was also used to create many of the interactive elements like the menu board and the tea rigs. ERN was then rendered into a series of movies that fit together in various combinations to create a seamless, interactive, experience. Flash was then used to create the interaction and to add the finishing touches to the 3D animation. **AWARDS:** Revolution Awards 2006 (Shortlist).

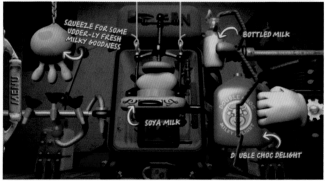

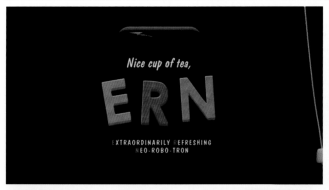

OBJECTIVE: PG Tips asked our team to support its sponsorship of the first full-length Wallace & Gromit movie launch with a campaign site at pgmoment.com. The characters and the brand were a great fit; as British as you can get, they practically never stop drinking tea. We wanted to build some original content around this relationship that would help recruit some new PG Tips drinkers, and remind people that PG Tips is fun and different. It was squarely aimed at Mums and kids, but had to be appealing to everyone. **STRATEGY:** We asked ourselves, what would supreme inventor Wallace come up with if he had to turn his hand to tea making? The answer was ERN (Extremely Refreshing Neo-Rotational-Brew-a-liser), a mechanical fridge that managed to make the simple act of making a cuppa into something supremely complicated. ERN provided both the site's content and interface - the aim was to inspire consumers to enter their own "cuppa-contraption" designs for the chance to win £10,000. **SOLUTION:** To achieve the effect we wanted, we had to create and animate our own computer-generated ERN (and his environment) from scratch. We studied Oscar-winner Nick Park's animation and sent our Creatives to meet the Aardman team. The result was a contraption worthy of Wallace himself. Users were able to interact with the machine to create their own version of the perfect cuppa and enter a prize draw. They were also able to design and print their own Aardman style character; the CGI environment provided the interface to watch a sneak preview of the movie and exclusive Aardman animation clips too. **RESULTS:** By promoting ERN on pack and through advertising, home page visits increased by over 600%. Stats indicate that around 60% of visitors spent at least 15 minutes interacting with the site.

OBJECTIF : PG Tips a sponsorisé le premier long métrage de Wallace et Gromit, et nous a chargés de le faire savoir grâce au site pgmoment.com. Les personnages du film et la marque correspondaient en tous points. Typiquement anglais, ils n'arrêtent quasiment jamais de boire du thé. Il nous fallait trouver un contenu original rendant compte de cette connivence, et attirer de nouveaux buveurs de thé en leur rappelant que TG Tips est unique et amusant. Le message était clairement destiné aux mamans et leurs enfants, mais il devait pouvoir séduire tout le monde. **STRATÉGIE :** Nous nous sommes demandé : « Quelle machine fabriquerait Wallace le super inventeur s'il devait faire du thé ? » La réponse fut ERN (Néo-Infuseur Extrêmement Rafraîchissant), un frigo mécanique qui réussissait à faire d'un un acte aussi simple que préparer du thé une merveille de complication technique. ERN a inspiré le contenu et l'interface du site. Il s'agissait d'encourager les internautes à réaliser leur propre machine à thé et concourir pour remporter 10 000 livres. **SOLUTION :**

Pour réaliser l'effet recherché, il a fallu créer et animer notre propre machine ERN et son environnement. Nous avons étudié l'animation de Nick Park et envoyé nos créatifs rencontrer l'équipe des studios Aardman. Le résultat est un bidule digne de Wallace lui-même. Les usagers ont pu interagir avec la machine pour créer leur propre version de la tasse de thé idéale et participer à un tirage au sort. Ils ont pu aussi dessiner et imprimer leur propre personnage selon le style du studio, et l'interface permettait de visionner la bande-annonce du film ainsi que d'autres vidéos des studios Aardman. **RÉSULTATS :** Grâce au lancement de ERN, le nombre de visiteurs sur le site a augmenté de 600%. Les statistiques indiquent qu'environ 60% des visiteurs ont passé au moins un quart d'heure à interagir avec le site.

AUFGABE: PG Tips baten unser Team um Unterstützung, um den Launch des ersten Wallace & Gromit-Films in Spielfilmlänge mit einer Kampagnenwebseite unterpgmoment.com zu sponsern. Die Charaktere und die Marke passten gut zusammen: Wie es britischer kaum geht, trinken Wallace und Gromit fast ununterbrochen Tee. Um diese Beziehung herum wollten wir originellen Inhalt erstellen, der neue Teetrinker anwarb und die Leute daran erinnern sollte, dass PG Tips Spaß machen und anders sind. Die Kampagne zielte auf Mütter und Kinder ab, sollte aber jedem gefallen. **STRATEGIE:** Wir fragten uns: Was würde der Erfinder Wallace für eine Idee haben, wenn es darum ging, Tee zu kochen? Die Antwort lautete ERN (Extremely Refreshing Neo-Rotational-Brew-a-liser = Extrem erfrischender Neo-Rotations-Aufbrüher), ein mechanischer Kühlschrank, der den einfachen Akt des Teekochens in etwas extrem Kompliziertes verwandelt. ERN bot sowohl den Inhalt als auch die Oberfläche der Seite – Ziel war es, Konsumenten dazu zu inspirieren, ihren eigenen „Tee-Apparat" zu entwerfen und hierbei die Chance zu haben, £ 10 000 zu gewinnen. **LÖSUNG:** Um den gewünschten Effekt zu erzielen, mussten wir unseren eigenen computererzeugten ERN (und seine Umgebung) von Grund auf generieren. Wir untersuchten die Animationen des Oscar-Gewinners Nick Park, und unser Kreativteam traf das Team von Aardman. Das Ergebnis war ein Apparat, der Wallace alle Ehre machte. Benutzer konnten mit der Maschine interagieren, um ihre eigene Version der perfekten Tasse Tee zu entwerfen und am Gewinnspiel teilzunehmen. Außerdem konnten sie ihren eigenen Charakter im Stil von Aardman entwerfen und drucken; mit der CGI-Umgebung konnte man eine Sneak Preview des Films oder exklusive Aardman-Animationen anschauen. **ERGEBNISSE:** Durch die Promotion von ERN und durch Werbung erhöhte sich die Besucherquote der Seite um 600%. Laut Statistik verweilten ca. 60% der Besucher mindestens 15 Minuten aktiv auf der Seite.

FEATURED ON THE DVD **CAMPAIGN:** Reflex Kolo – Sanitec Kolo <www.saniteckolo.com/reflex>. **PRODUCT:** Reflex Kolo coat. **YEAR:** 2005. **AGENCY:** Max Weber <www.maxweber.com>. **CREATIVE TEAM:** Krzysztof Dykas, Grzegorz Mogilewski, Marcin Talarek, Bartek Witulski, Mieszko Saktura. **PROGRAMMER:** Marek Brun, Piotr Tracki. **TECH ASPECTS:** Macromedia Flash. **AWARDS:** Golden Drum 2005 (Silver).

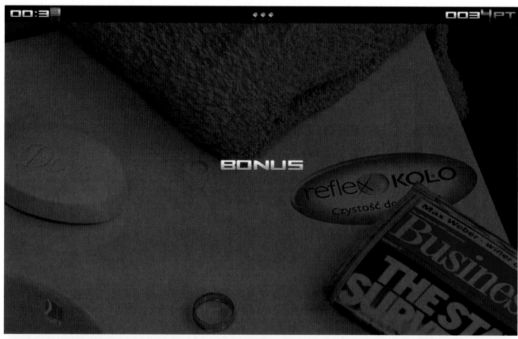

CONCEPT: Reflex Kolo is a modern coat which protects bath ceramic and glass surfaces from depositing of dust, dirt and contaminants. 'Reflex Kolo' is a viral advergame giving players an opportunity to steer a water drop laying on a sink covered by Reflex Kolo surface. The core idea was to build an interactive droplet acting and looking like a real one in real Reflex Kolo environment.

CONCEPT : Reflex Kolo est un revêtement qui protège les carrelages et les surfaces vitrées des traces d'eau, des dépôts de poussière et de bactéries. Le jeu en ligne permet aux utilisateurs de faire couler des gouttes d'eau sur un évier traité avec Reflex Kolo. Le jeu interactif permet de recréer de façon virtuelle un environnement réaliste.

KONZEPT: Reflex Kolo ist eine moderne Abdeckung, die Keramik im Bad und Glasoberflächen vor Staub und Verunreinigungen schützt. „Reflex Kolo" ist ein virales Werbespiel, bei dem Spieler einen Wassertropfen auf einer Spüle, die mit einer Reflex-Kolo-Oberfläche überzogen ist, steuern können. Die Idee bestand darin, ein interaktives Tröpfchen zu erzeugen, das in einer realen Reflex-Kolo-Umgebung wie ein echtes aussieht und reagiert.

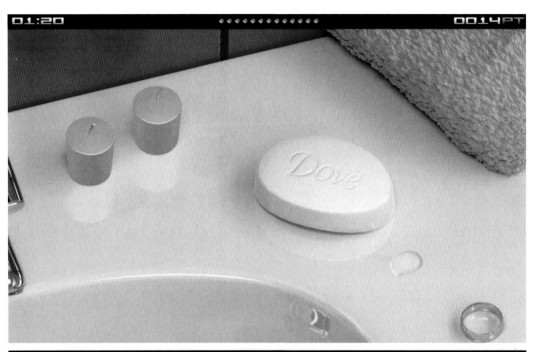

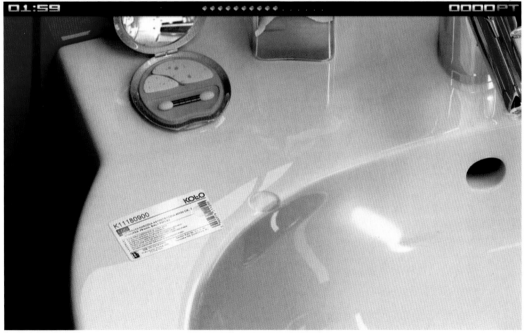

FEATURED ON THE DVD **CAMPAIGN:** Royal Caribbean's "Freedom of the Seas" <www.freedomoftheseas.com>. **AGENCY:** Arnold Worldwide <www.arnoldworldwide.com>. **CHIEF CREATIVE OFFICER:** Ron Lawner. **EXECUTIVE CREATIVE DIRECTOR:** Jay Williams, Tony Quin. **CREATIVE DIRECTOR:** Stephen Potter, Adam Boozer. **ART DIRECTOR/DESIGNER:** David Chung. **COPYWRITER:** Nicole Berard. **PRODUCER:** Heather Wischmann. **INFORMATION ARCHITECT:** Melissa Goldstein. **ACCOUNT SERVICE:** Kate Walters. **TECH ASPECTS:** Animation, audio, compositing, Macromedia Flash, video. **PRODUCTION:** IQ Interactive.

CONCEPT: FreedomoftheSeas.com was created to introduce the launch of the new Freedom family of ships and to educate consumers about Freedom of the Seas' many exciting and innovative features. Through frequent microsite updates, consumers are kept up-to-date on the ship's progress under construction as well as on the latest features and amenities onboard the ship as Royal Caribbean slowly reveals them to the public in the year leading up to the ship's launch. By utilizing 3D architectural renderings supplemented with full motion video, seamlessly composited into the scenes, we have been able to create an unprecedented, fully immersive experience that literally puts viewers on the ship. **RESULTS:** With users spending an average of over 8 minutes per visit, and almost 20% clicking to view more information about Freedom cruises, the site has proven extremely effective at both building awareness and driving sales.

CONCEPT: FreedomoftheSeas.com a été créé pour le lancement de la nouvelle flotte de paquebots Freedom afin d'informer le public sur les nouvelles caractéristiques des bateaux. Grâce à des mises à jour régulières des micro-sites, les consommateurs peuvent suivre les avancées de la construction des bateaux, découvrir les nouveaux services à bord pendant l'année qui précède leur mise en service. L'interprétation en 3D et les inserts vidéo contri-buent à une expérience d'immersion totale qui place littéralement le consommateur sur le pont du paquebot. **RÉSULTATS :** Les visiteurs ont passé en moyenne 8 minutes sur le site, et 20% d'entre eux ont cliqué pour obtenir des informations complémentaires sur les croisières. Le site a brillamment réussi à promouvoir la notoriété de la marque et générer des transactions.

KONZEPT: FreedomoftheSeas.com wurde für den Launch der neuen Schiff-Familie Freedom entwickelt, und um Konsumenten über die aufregenden und innovativen Features von Freedom of the Seas zu informieren. Durch permanente Aktualisierung der Seite werden Besucher stets auf den neuesten Stand bezüglich des Schiffbaus und der Einrichtungen und des Komforts an Bord gebracht, den Royal Caribbean der Öffentlichkeit im Jahr vor dem Launch langsam enthüllt. Durch die Verwendung von 3D-Video-Übertragungen, die übergangslos in Szenen zusammengesetzt sind, haben wir eine noch nie da gewesene, unmittelbare Erfahrung erzeugt, die den Betrachter auf das Schiff versetzt. **ERGEBNISSE:** Benutzer verweilen im Durchschnitt über 8 Minuten auf der Seite, und fast 20% klicken weiter, um mehr Informationen über Freedom-Kreuzfahrten zu erhalten. Dies zeigt, dass die Seite extrem effektiv war, um Interesse zu wecken und Verkäufe zu erhöhen.

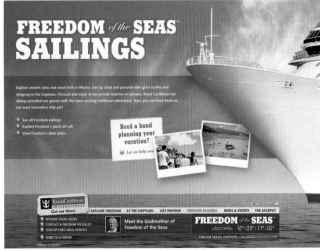

FEATURED ON THE DVD **CAMPAIGN:** Starwood Meetings. **CLIENT:** Starwood Hotels and Resorts. **YEAR:** 2005. **AGENCY:** Domani Studios <www.domanistudios.com>. **PRODUCTION TIME:** 2 weeks. **CREATIVE TEAM:** Domani Studios. **PROGRAMMING:** Domani Studios. **TECH ASPECTS:** Macromedia Flash AS 2.0, XML. **MEDIA CIRCULATED:** banner advertisements.

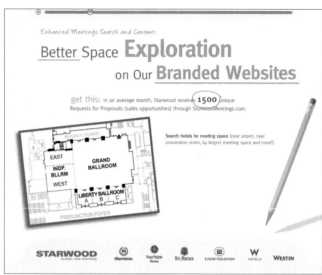

CONCEPT: Create a narrative presentation that walks users through Starwood Hotels and Resorts meeting capabilities for its business travelers. **RESULTS:** Short text about the results achieved: This Micro-Site has been very successful in promoting Starwood Meetings. The site is highly informative without feeling too consuming or cumbersome. Users responded that they liked the presentation approach and were left with enough information to feel really good about setting up a meeting or corporate event.

CONCEPT : Réaliser un dispositif narratif qui invite les usagers à visiter les Hôtels et centres de conférence Starwood, et découvrir leur gamme de services. **RÉSULTATS :** Le micro-site s'est révélé un excellent outil de promotion de la marque. Le contenu du site est instructif sans être pesant et compliqué pour autant. Les usagers ont apprécié l'approche de la présentation et se sont sentis suffisamment informés pour l'organisation pratique de leurs conférences ou de leurs réunions.

KONZEPT: Es galt, eine narrative Präsentation zu erstellen, bei der Benutzer durch Starwood Hotels und Anlagen spazieren können und ihnen die Möglichkeiten für Geschäftsreisende begegnen. **ERGEBNISSE:** Diese Microsite war bei der Werbung für Starwood Meetings sehr erfolgreich. Sie ist sehr informativ, ohne zu aufwändig oder umständlich zu wirken. Benutzer mögen den Präsentationsansatz und erhalten genug Informationen, um mit einem guten Gefühl ein Meeting oder eine Firmenveranstaltung planen zu können.

FEATURED ON THE DVD **CAMPAIGN:** The Bad Luck Test. **CLIENT:** IF Insurance. **YEAR:** 2005. **AGENCY:** Forsman & Bodenfors <www.fb.se>. **PRODUCTION TIME:** 3 months. **WEB DIRECTOR:** Jonas Sjövall, Martin Cedergren. **ART DIRECTOR:** Lotta Ågerup. **COPYWRITER:** Oskar Askelöf. **ACCOUNT MANAGER:** Sara Linde, Jenny Karlsson. **ACCOUNT EXECUTIVE:** Meta Ågren, Anders Härneman. **PROGRAMMER:** B-REEL. **PRODUCER:** B-REEL. **TECH ASPECTS:** Macromedia Flash. **MEDIA CIRCULATED:** Online ads, TVC, radio. **AWARDS:** Epica 2005 (Bronze), Eurobest 2005 (Silver), Favorite Website Award 2005, Flash Forward 2006 (Winner), London International Advertising Awards 2005 (Winner).

CONCEPT: Bad luck is something that everybody gets their share of – and something that If, the insurance company, has been dealing with for about 150 years. The Bad Luck test is not a scientific test but rather a way to get your awareness in terms of safety to decrease the risk of you having bad luck. The test will take approximate 10 minutes and underway we will give you tips and hints on how to improve your safety awareness status.

CONCEPT : La malchance est une chose que nous connaissons tous, et qui est pris en charge depuis 150 ans par la compagnie d'assurances If. Le test de malchance que nous avons conçu n'a rien de scientifique mais vise à éveiller la vigilance afin de diminuer les risques d'accident. Il prend environ 10 minutes à remplir et prodigue des astuces et des conseils pour améliorer sa vigilance au quotidien.

KONZEPT: Jeder hat mal Pech – und die Versicherung beschäftigt sich seit über 150 Jahren damit. Der Bad-Luck-Test ist nicht wissenschaftlich, sondern erhöht das Bewusstsein für Sicherheit, um das Risiko im Falle eines Unglücks zu verringern. Der Test dauert ca. 10 Minuten. Währenddessen erhält man Tipps und Hinweise, wie man sein Bewusstsein für Sicherheit verbessern kann.

FEATURED ON THE DVD **CAMPAIGN:** Burning Home. **PRODUCT:** Answer Seguro On-Line <answeronline.com.ar>. **YEAR:** 2005. **AGENCY:** Del Campo Nazca Saatchi & Saatchi, Argentina. **CREATIVE DIRECTOR:** Chavo D'Emilio. **COPYWRITER:** Hernán Rebaldería. **ART DIRECTOR/DESIGNER:** Daniel Fierro, Pablo Tajer. **PROGRAMMER:** Damián Lubenfeld. **PRODUCTION MANAGER:** Adrián Aspani, Cosme Argerich. **ACCOUNT EXECUTIVE:** Pablo Ordoñez, Esteban Tarling. **AWARDS:** Gramado Festival – Galo du Prata (Silver), Diente 2005 (Gold), New York Festivals – Interactive & Alternative Media Awards – Simple Banner (Silver), YoungGuns Festival – Cyberactive Online Advertising (Silver).

CONCEPT: The banner recreates the toolbar of an Internet browser, over the user's real toolbar. The "home" button catches fire. At that point the message "Insure your house" appears, and later the Answer Seguro Online logo. If clicked, the banner links the user to the Home Insurance information page. **OBJECTIVE:** To communicate the existence of Answer Seguro Online's Home Insurance Plan.

CONCEPT : Une bannière imitant une barre d'outils vient se superposer à la véritable barre sur l'écran de l'usager. Le bouton accueil « Home » s'enflamme. Le message « Assurez votre résidence » s'affiche alors, suivi du logo de Answer Seguro Online. Si l'on clique sur la bannière, elle vous envoie sur la page d'accueil de la compagnie d'assurances. **OBJECTIF :** Communiquer l'existence de la police d'assurance de Answer Seguro.

KONZEPT: Das Banner hat die Form der Werkzeugleiste eines Internetbrowsers über der tatsächlichen Werkzeugleiste des Benutzers. Der „Home"-Knopf fängt Feuer, woraufhin der Text „Versichern Sie Ihr Heim" erscheint und später das Logo von Answer Segure Online. Klickt man darauf, führt das Banner den Benutzer zur Informationsseite über Hausversicherungen. **ZIEL:** Die Existenz von Answer Seguros Online-Hausversicherungsplan zu kommunizieren.

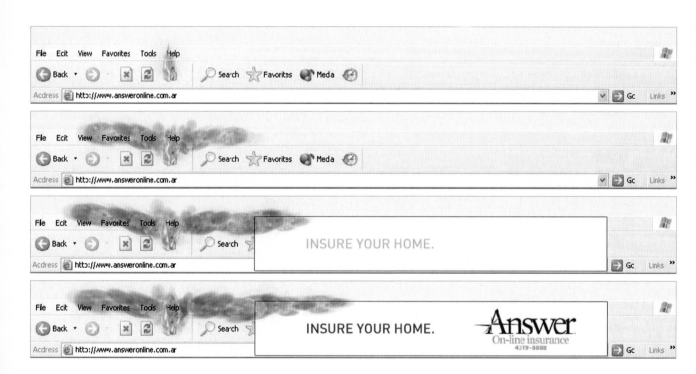

FEATURED ON THE DVD **TITLE:** Man. **PRODUCT:** Answer Seguro On-Line <www.answeronline.com.ar>. **YEAR:** 2005. **AGENCY:** Del Campo Nazca Saatchi & Saatchi, Argentina. **ACCOUNT EXECUTIVE:** Pablo Ordoñez, Esteban Tarling, Vicky Patron Costas. **CREATIVE DIRECTOR:** Chavo D'Emilio. **COPYWRITER:** Mariano Serkin, Guadalupe Pereira. **ART DIRECTOR:** Javier Lourenco. **DESIGNER/WEB DEVELOPER/PROGRAMMER:** Denken **PRODUCTION MANAGER:** Adrián Aspani, Cosme Argerich, **AWARDS:** Gramado Festival – Galo du Prata (Silver), Diente 2005 (Gold), New York Festivals – Interactive & Alternative Media Awards – Beyond the Banner (Silver), YoungGuns Festivals – Cyberactive Online Advertising (Finalist).

CONCEPT: On the banner we see a man that looks suspicious. He is whistling and trying to look distracted. When the banner is rolled over, the young man runs towards the cursor, grabs it and runs off screen with it. Super: "When you least expect it, you can be robbed." The Answer Seguro Online logo appears.

CONCEPT : Sur une bannière, apparaît un individu à l'air louche. Il siffle en se donnant un air dégagé. Quand on déroule la bannière, le jeune homme se précipite sur le curseur, s'en empare et fuit hors champ. Slogan : « Quand on s'y attend le moins, on peut se faire dévaliser ». S'affiche alors le logo de l'assureur Answer Seguro Online.

KONZEPT: Auf dem Banner ist ein verdächtig aussehender Mann dargestellt. Er pfeift vor sich hin und versucht, unauffällig zu wirken. Wenn sich das Banner umdreht, rennt der Mann auf den Cursor zu, ergreift ihn und verschwindet vom Bildschirm. Text: „Wenn Sie es am wenigsten erwarten, können Sie bestohlen werden." Das Logo von Answer Seguro Online erscheint.

When you least expect it, you can get robbed.

FEATURED ON THE DVD   **CAMPAIGN:** Time is Money <www.wheredidthetimego.com>.   **PRODUCT:** BT Broadband.   **CLIENT:** British Telecom.   **YEAR:** 2004.   **AGENCY:** Agency.com London <www.agency.com>.   **COST IN HOURS OF WORK:** 542 h.   **CREATIVE TEAM:** Paul Banham, Karl Reynolds.   **PROGRAMMER:** Karl Reynolds, Wil Bevan.   **TECH ASPECTS:** Macromedia Flash, animation, sound.   **MEDIA CIRCULATED:** Viral.   **AWARDS:** IAB Creative Showcase August 2004, Viral Awards 2005 (Best Art Direction/Design), Revolution Creative Award 2005, IAC Awards 2005 (Best of Show Microsite).

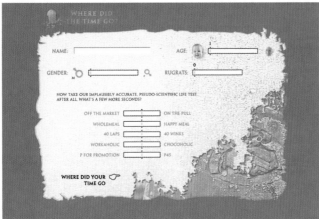 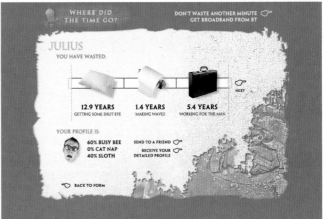

BUSINESS PROBLEM: As the broadband marketplace becomes increasingly competitive and the marketing landscape more and more cluttered, BT were looking for a way to cut through the noise and answer the question "Why Broadband from BT?" **CAMPAIGN OBJECTIVES:** Raise awareness and generate consideration for BT Broadband Basic. **TARGET AUDIENCE:** 21-28 professionals with dial-up connections at home. **SOLUTION:** A playful viral application that allows the user to, through answering some basic questions around their lifestyle, map out the story of their life so far. What have they been up to? What kind of person are they? And, above all, where has all the time gone? Having engaged and entertained the target and made them think about their lives a little, we paid off the interaction with a subtle brand message urging them not to waste another minute waiting for slow downloads by signing up to BT Broadband. The application was seeded through text links on news and lifestyle sites as well as integrated placements on The Sun Online's viral chart, Lycos' Cheeky E-mails Chart and Yahoo's 'office attachment' sections. All of these channels were highly relevant to Broadband's viral application. Viral e-mails were also sent out internally. **OBJECTIVE:** Deliver a post-experience pop-under that capitalizes on impulse clicks in a non-intrusive manner. **RESULTS:** Phenomenal viral success on a small media-seeding budget. Over 690,000 unique sessions were registered on the "Where did the time go" micro site with 40,000 repeat visitors. Average session length was over 4 minutes. The "send to a friend" application was used over 15,000 times. Application was forwarded on by e-mail an average of 1.7 times. Despite this being predominantly a branding campaign, it delivered over 500 Broadband sales at a CPA of under £40 (not much higher than corresponding response-driven campaign elements)

CONTEXTE : Sur un marché de fournisseurs d'accès haut débit de plus en plus compétitif, dans un paysage de plus en plus encombré, BT cherche à se frayer une voie et se pose la question : « Pourquoi choisir le haut débit de BT ? ». **OBJECTIFS :** Promouvoir la marque et susciter les intentions d'achat en faveur de BT. **PUBLIC CIBLE :** La tranche des actifs de 21 à 28 ans qui possèdent une connexion internet chez eux. **SOLUTION :** Une application ludique et virale qui permet à l'usager de faire un bilan de sa vie, grâce à des questions simples sur son style de vie. Qu'a-t-il fait récemment ? Comment se décrit-il ? Et surtout, qu'a-t-il fait de son temps ? Après avoir amusé les internautes et les avoir fait réfléchir un peu à leur vie, un message leur conseille de ne plus perdre leur temps avec une connexion bas débit et de s'abonner plutôt au haut débit. L'application apparaissait grâce à un lien hypertexte placé dans des sites de vie quotidienne, ainsi que sur le site du journal The Sun. Lycos le référençait sous la section e-mails amusants, et Yahoo dans celle des services bureautiques. Tous ces canaux étaient adaptés à l'application virale. Des e-mails ont aussi

été envoyés de façon interne. Le but était d'offrir une expérience interactive qui s'appuie sur des clics d'impulsion sur un mode non intrusif. **RÉSULTATS :** Un succès viral phénoménal pour un petit budget plurimédia. Plus de 690 000 visiteurs ont été enregistrés sur le micro-site, 40 000 visiteurs sont venus plus d'une fois. La durée moyenne d'une session était supérieure à 4 minutes. L'application de recommandation a été utilisée 15 000 fois. Elle a été transférée par e-mail 1,7 million de fois en moyenne. Bien que la campagne ait concerné avant tout la notoriété, elle a rapporté plus 500 nouveaux contrats pour un coût par acquisition inférieur à 40 livres (quasiment autant que la campagne promotionnelle d'abonnements).

PROBLEM DES UNTERNEHMENS: Der Breitband-Markt wird zunehmend hart umkämpft und die Marketing-Landschaft immer unübersichtlicher. BT suchte nach einem Weg, sich darin bemerkbar zu machen und die Frage zu beantworten: „Warum ein BT-Breitband?" **ZIELE DER KAMPAGNE:** Erhöhung des Bekanntheitsgrades und Heranführen neuer Kunden an BT Broadband Basic. **ZIELPUBLIKUM:** 21- bis 28-jährige Berufstätige mit Internetanschluss zu Hause. **LÖSUNG:** Eine spielerische, virale Anwendung, die es den Benutzern ermöglicht, sich durch das Beantworten einiger grundlegender Fragen bezüglich ihres Lifestyles mit ihrem bisherigen Leben auseinander zu setzen. Was haben sie bisher gemacht? Was für eine Art Person sind sie? Und vor allem, wo ist die Zeit geblieben? Indem man die Zielgruppe unterhalten und sie dazu gebracht hat, ein wenig über ihr Leben nach-zudenken, zahlt sich die Interaktion mit einer subtilen Markenbotschaft aus, die sie anregt, keine weitere Minute mit dem Warten auf langsame Downloads zu vergeuden, indem sie sich bei BT Broadband anmelden. Die Anwendung war sowohl durch Textlinks auf Nachrichten- und Lifestyleseiten als auch durch integrierte Platzierungen auf der viralen Skala von The Sun Online, Lycos' Cheeky E-Mails Skala und Yahoos „Büro-Anhang"-Bereichen gestreut. All diese Kanäle waren für die virale Anwendung von Broadband extrem relevant. Außerdem wurden intern virale E-Mails versendet. **ZIEL:** Ein Pop Under zu liefern, das auf eine unaufdringliche Weise impulsive Klicks aktiviert. **ERGEBNISSE:** Phänomenaler viraler Erfolg mit einem kleinen Medienbudget. Auf der „Where did the time go"-Microsite wurden über 690 000 einzelne Sessions registriert, mit 40 wiederkehrenden Besuchern. Die durchschnittliche Länge der Sessions betrug über vier Minuten. Von der „send to a friend"-Anwendung wurde über 15 000 Mal Gebrauch gemacht. Die Anwendung wurde per E-Mail durchschnittlich 1,7 Millionen Mal weitergeleitet. Obwohl dies hauptsächlich eine Markenkampagne war, initiierte sie über 500 Broadband-Verkäufe bei einem CPA von unter £40 (nicht viel höher als entsprechende reaktionsgesteuerte Kampagnen).

FEATURED ON THE DVD **CAMPAIGN:** Pocketbooks. **PRODUCT:** Speedy Broadband. **CLIENT:** Telefônica. **YEAR:** 2004. **AGENCY:** Dm9DDB, São Paulo, Brazil. **PRODUCTION TIME:** 90 days. **CREATIVE DIRECTOR:** Sergio Valente, Pedro Cappeletti, Fernanda Romano. **ART DIRECTOR:** Sérgio Mugnaini. **COPYWRITER:** Fabio Victoria. **LEAD DESIGNER:** Sérgio Mugnaini. **DESIGNER ASSISTANT:** Raul Arantes. **FLASH DEVELOPER:** Raul Arantes. **ILLUSTRATOR:** Jairo Rodrigues Braga, Flávio Zoia, Daniel Martins. **FILM PRODUCER:** Jodaf. **SOUND PRODUCER:** Ludwig-Van! **ACCOUNT MANAGER:** Fernanda Romano. **TECH ASPECTS:** Macromedia Flash, video, sound. **AWARDS:** Cannes Lions 2004 (Bronze), New York Festivals 2004 (Gold), Mmonline/Msn 2004 (Silver), Clube de Criação de São Paulo 2004 (Bronze), Festival In Msn/Meio & Mensagem 2004 (Silver), One Show Interactive 2005 (Merit), London Festival 2005 (Shortlist).

CONCEPT: "Realtime." **SOLUTION:** We create a 30" spot TV with interaction during this film. Than, we produce this book in 3D, during this process, we started to develop all the animations and films and then, we join everything. Than, we produce this book in 3D and invited some artists to join in our project.

CONCEPT : Le temps réel. **SOLUTION :** Nous avons réalisé un spot télé de 30 secondes permettant l'interaction. Puis nous avons produit un livre en 3D. Nous avons développé les films et l'animation et nous avons combiné l'ensemble. Nous avons invité des artistes à se joindre au projet.

KONZEPT: „Zeitnah." **LÖSUNG:** Wir kreierten einen 30-Sekunden-Spot mit Interaktion. Dann produzierten wir dieses Buch in 3D und entwickelten währenddessen alle Animationen und Filme. Schließlich verbanden wir alles miteinander und luden Künstler ein, an unserem Projekt teilzunehmen.

FEATURED ON THE DVD **CAMPAIGN:** Roaming Brazil–Japan. **PRODUCT:** TIM International Roaming. **YEAR:** 2005. **AGENCY:** Euro RSCG 4D São Paulo <www.eurorscg4d.com.br>. **CHIEF CREATIVE OFFICER:** Alon Sochaczewski. **CREATIVE DIRECTOR:** Touché. **COPYWRITER:** Fábio Pierro. **ART DIRECTOR:** Rodrigo Buim, Touché. **PROGRAMMER:** Edivaldo Braz. **TECH ASPECTS:** Macromedia Flash. **AWARDS:** Cannes Cyber Lions 2005 (Bronze); About de Comunicação Integrada e Dirigida 2005 Awards (Silver); CCSP 2006 (Shortlist); FIAP 2006 (Shortlist).

CONCEPT: TIM is the mobile phone carrier that has introduced GSM technology in Brazil. Among other services, TIM offers automatic roaming in over 200 countries.

CONCEPT : TIM est l'opérateur de téléphonie mobile qui a lancé la technologie GSM au Brésil. Entre autres services, TIM propose l'itinérance automatique dans plus de 200 pays.

KONZEPT: TIM ist die Handyfirma, die die GSM-Technologie in Brasilien eingeführt hat. Neben anderen Services bietet TIM automatisches Roaming in über 200 Ländern an.

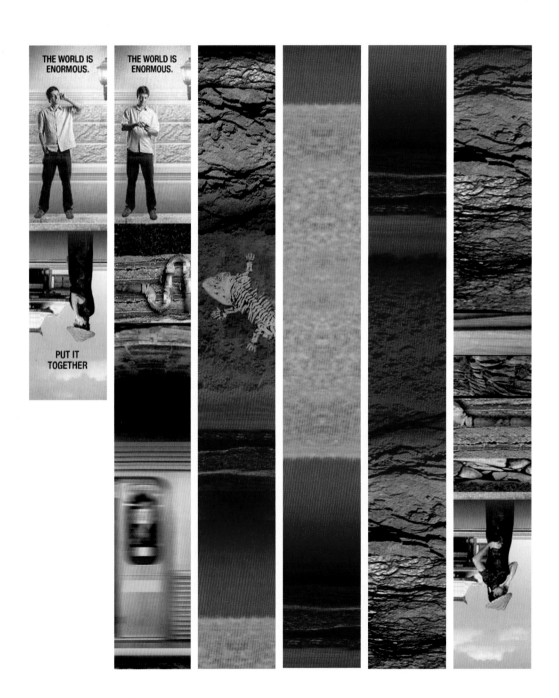

CAMPAIGN: Leonardo LED. **PRODUCT:** LED. **YEAR:** 2004. **AGENCY:** Large <www.largedesign.com>. **PRODUCTION TIME:** 6 weeks. **COST IN HOURS OF WORK:** 200 h. **CREATIVE TEAM:** Lars Hemming Jorgensen, Jim Boulton, Rene Christoffer. **PROGRAMMER:** Jesper Lycke. **TECH ASPECTS:** Macromedia Flash, audio. **AWARDS:** Macromedia (Site of the Day).

CONCEPT: A highly emotional audio visual experience to create market awareness of Leonardo's new LED product range. The products are actually programmable and allows owners to decide on their colours, animation and speed.

CONCEPT : Expérience audiovisuelle très émotionnelle qui vise à mieux faire connaître la nouvelle gamme de produits d'éclairage LED de Leonardo. Les produits sont eux-mêmes programmables et permettent à l'usager de choisir la couleur, l'animation et la vitesse.

KONZEPT: Eine emotionale audio-visuelle Erfahrung auf höchster Ebene, um auf Leonardos neue LED-Produktlinie aufmerksam zu machen. Die Produkte sind programmierbar: Benutzer können eigene Farben, Animationen und Geschwindigkeiten wählen.

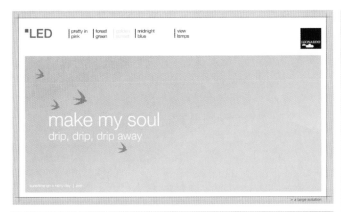

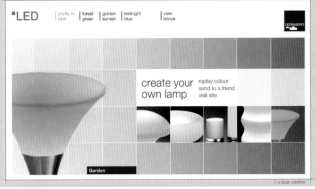

FEATURED ON THE DVD **CAMPAIGN:** "Hats" – Brokeback Moutain DVD. **PRODUCT:** 2001 Video New Releases. **YEAR:** 2006. **AGENCY:** Euro RSCG 4D São Paulo <www.eurorscg4d.com.br>. **CHIEF CREATIVE OFFICER:** Alon Sochaczewski. **CREATIVE DIRECTOR:** Touché. **COPYWRITER:** Fábio Pierro, André Arteze. **ART DIRECTOR:** Giuliano Bissacot, Ricardo Cazzo. **PROGRAMMER:** Marcelo Olandim. **TECH ASPECTS:** Macromedia Flash. **AWARDS:** Cannes Cyber Lions 2006 (Shortlist).

CONCEPT: The video store 2001 which has a collection ranging from classic and cult movies to the latest releases, is presenting the DVD Brokeback Mountain, winner of 3 Oscars.

CONCEPT : Le magasin vidéo 2001, dont la collection va des films classiques et cultes aux dernières nouveautés, présente le DVD du film Brokeback Mountain, qui a reçu 3 Oscars.

KONZEPT: Der Videoladen 2001 besitzt ein breites Sortiment, von Klassikern über Kultfilme bis zu den neuesten Veröffentlichungen, und präsentiert die DVD Brokeback Mountain, Gewinner von 3 Oscars.

FEATURED ON THE DVD **CAMPAIGN:** Lenscrafters <www2.lenscrafters.com>. **PRODUCT:** Featherwates Complete Lenses made with Scotchgard. **YEAR:** 2005. **AGENCY:** Large <www.largedesign.com>. **PRODUCTION TIME:** 4 weeks. **COST IN HOURS OF WORK:** 360 h. **CREATIVE TEAM:** Lars Hemming Jorgensen, Jim Boulton, Stephen Shaw, John Taylor. **PROGRAMMER:** Jesper Lycke. **TECH ASPECTS:** Macromedia Flash, film, audio.

CONCEPT: Rich media narrative campaign outlining features and benefits of the brand new lenses exclusive to Lenscrafters.

CONCEPT : Campagne en *rich media* soulignant les caractéristiques et les atouts des nouveaux verres de lunettes fabriqués en exclusivité par Lenscrafters.

KONZEPT: Eine narrative Rich-Media-Kampagne skizziert die Eigenschaften und Vorteile der neuen, exklusiven Kontaktlinsen von Lenscrafters.

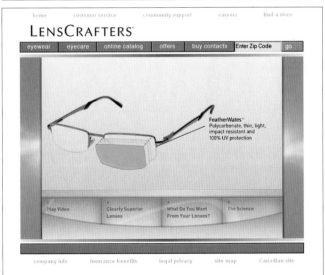

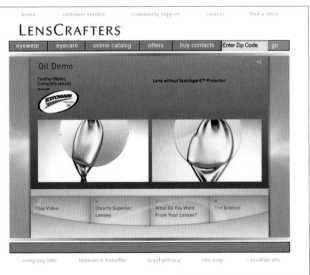

CAMPAIGN: Convinient Life. **PRODUCT:** Pharmaceutical Products. **CLIENT:** Sankyo Co., Ltd. **YEAR:** 2004. **AGENCY:** Dentsu <www.dentsu.com>. **CREATIVE DIRECTOR :** Takeshi Mizukawa. **ART DIRECTOR :** Kaori Mochizuki. **TECHNICAL DIRECTOR :** Hiroki Nakamura. **TECH ASPECTS:** Macromedia Flash. **AWARDS:** Cannes Lions 2004 (Silver).

CONCEPT: A banner ad portraying a hardworking life consisting solely of sitting at the computer and sleeping. The humorous ad warns against such an unhealthy lifestyle.

KONZEPT: Ein Banner stellt eine Person vor, die nur abwechselnd vor dem Computer sitzt und schläft. Die humorvolle Anzeige warnt vor einer derart ungesunden Lebensweise.

CONCEPT : Une bannière décrit une vie de labeur passée à s'asseoir devant un ordinateur avant d'aller se coucher. Le ton humoristique alerte sur les dangers pour la santé d'un mode de vie aussi statique.

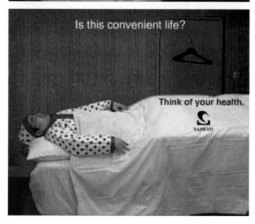

FEATURED ON THE DVD **CAMPAIGN:** Pocket Lover. **PRODUCT:** Mobile Advertising C&A. **CLIENT:** C&A. **YEAR:** 2004-2005. **AGENCY:** AgênciaClick <www.agenciaclick.com.br>. **COUNTRY:** Brazil.

CONCEPT: First initiative in Brazil for mobile advertising integrating brand and cellular phone.

CONCEPT: Première initiative brésilienne de promotion de marque sur le réseau de téléphonie mobile.

KONZEPT: Die erste Werbekampagne in Brasilien für Handys, die Marke und Handy integriert.

FEATURED ON THE DVD CAMPAIGN: "We'll meet at the fridge." <www.stickyjam.de>. PRODUCT: Sticky Jam. YEAR: 2005. AGENCY: SiteSeeing, Interaktive Medien <www.zeppzepp.com>. PRODUCTION TIME: 2 months. COST IN HOURS OF WORK: 90 h. CREATIVE TEAM: Peter Zepp, Katharina Moelle. PROGRAMMER: Jan Loseries. TECH ASPECTS: Macromedia Flash, video, HTML. HITS ON THE PAGE: 60,800 individual users (March 2005 – February 2006).

CONCEPT: Sticky Jam, producer of exceptional art and advertising magnets, asked SiteSeeing to design a modern and engaging company presentation. They developed a funny implementation of the sticky jam claim "Meet you at the fridge." With digital video technology, a hand puts magnets and corporate information on the website. **RESULTS:** The extraordinary implementation of the site lead to many links that refer to the website. With the support of the banner ad on a design portal, sales of magnets increased significantly. By now, sticky jam has established itself as a producer of exceptional magnets on the European market.

CONCEPT : Sticky Jam, fabricant de magnets artistiques et publicitaires a chargé Site Seeing de concevoir un site moderne et engageant afin de promouvoir son activité. L'agence a développé une implémentation distrayante accompagnée du slogan « Rendez-vous devant le frigo ». Grâce à une technologie de vidéo numérique, on voit une main poser des magnets qui apportent des renseignements sur la société. **RÉSULTATS :** La remarquable réalisation a fait l'objet de commentaires sur de nombreux sites, qui ont repris et propagé le lien. Grâce à une bannière installée sur un portail de design, les ventes de magnets ont augmenté de façon significative. Aujourd'hui, Sticky Jam s'est positionné en Europe comme un des fabricants leader de magnets.

KONZEPT: Sticky Jam, Hersteller außergewöhnlicher Kunst- und Werbemagneten, hat SiteSeeing damit beauftragt, eine moderne und ansprechende Unternehmenspräsentation zu gestalten. Entstanden ist eine einfallsreiche und lustige Umsetzung des sticky-jam-Spruchs Wir treffen uns am Kühlschrank. Mit digitaler Videotechnik pappt eine Hand die Magneten und Firmeninfos auf die Website. **ERGEBNISSE:** Dank der ungewöhnlichen Umsetzung der Seite gelang es Sticky Jam, sehr viele Links auf die Website verweisen zu lassen. Durch die Bannerwerbung auf einem Designportal wurde der Verkauf von Magneten auf der Website merklich erhöht. Mittlerweile hat sich Sticky Jam als Hersteller von außergewöhnlichen Magneten auf dem europäischen Markt etabliert.

FEATURED ON THE DVD **CAMPAIGN:** TAM Testimonial. **PRODUCT:** TAM Express Courier. **YEAR:** 2004. **AGENCY:** Dm9DDB, São Paulo, Brazil <www.dm9ddb.com.br>. **PRODUCTION TIME:** 30 days. **CREATIVE DIRECTOR:** Sergio Valente, Pedro Cappeletti, Fernanda Romano. **ART DIRECTOR:** Sérgio Mugnaini. **COPYWRITER:** Fabio Victoria. **FLASH DEVELOPER:** Raul Arantes, Fabricio Zuardi. **FILM PRODUCER:** On Film. **SOUND PRODUCER:** Lua Web. **TECH ASPECTS:** Macromedia Flash, video, sound. **AWARDS:** Cannes Lions 2004 (Silver), Mmonline/Msn 2004 (Bronze), One Show Interactive 2005 (Merit), London Festival 2005 (Shortlist).

THE IDEA: "You have two kind of delivery companies. Fast and slow." TAM Express is a company that deliveries whatever you want. The Best Quality of TAM is: they are extremely fast and organized. **SOLUTION:** we made an interactive 30" spot film that the user can interact with.

IDÉE : « Il existe deux sortes de services de livraison, les lents et les rapides ». TAM Express est une société qui vous livre tout ce que vous désirez. Leur meilleur atout : leur rapidité et leur sens de l'organisation. **SOLUTION :** Un film de 30 secondes qui engage l'interaction du visiteur.

DIE IDEE: „Es gibt zwei Arten von Lieferfirmen. Schnelle und langsame." TAM Express ist ein Unternehmen, das liefert, was immer Sie möchten. Die beste Eigenschaft von TAM ist: Sie sind extrem schnell und gut organisiert. **LÖSUNG:** Wir erstellten einen interaktiven 30-Sekunden-Spot, mit dem der Benutzer interagieren kann.

MIKE JOHN OTTO
CREATIVE DIRECTOR AT INTERONE WORLDWIDE

Creative Director at INTERONE Worldwide, an agency of the worldwide BBDO Network. He studied Visual Communication with a focus on Digital Design at the University of Applied Science Münster. During his studies he worked as a freelancer for advertising agencies and design offices, among others for BBDO Interactive in Düsseldorf. His final paper was a digital work about the subcultures in England, which received several awards and was published many times. After he graduated, he worked as a freelancer in London before he became Senior Designer at the agency Razorfish. After two years he started working as an Art Director at Elephant Seven. 2002 he became Senior Art Director at INTERONE in Hamburg. There he started with working for the BMW brand; since May 2005 he has been the responsible Creative Director for the MINI brand, among others. At the same time he works on his own projects at his studio stereoplastic.com and is the founder of the label Coft1.com.

From everywhere, you can hear classic advertising complaining. The high art of the 30 sec-

ond commercial – the so-called lead discipline – is supposed to be through. Ads are becoming either more expensive or less good. According to market research studies, they hardly ever reach their potential target group. People like to watch them for entertainment, but the decision to buy something happens to be on the Internet. This is admittedly not true for all products, but the development is interesting and forward-looking. Widespread advertising increasingly becomes an image for the brand, but does not sell the product.

THE SHINY WORLD OF ADVERTISING AS WE KNOW IT CHANGES RAPIDLY. WHILE ONLINE CAMPAIGNS USED TO BE SMILED AT, AND WEBSITES SOMETIMES LOOKED JUST LIKE A CATALOGUE ONLINE, THE MEDIUM IS NOW MORE SELF-CONFIDENT AND SUCCESSFUL THAN EVER.

And while at professional online campaigns nowadays their own shooting, costly 3D use and films has become a standard for premium brands, the development already goes a step further: mobile measures already support global campaigns with outdoor advertising, posters with mms numbers which the user can use to load information straight on his mobile, or with hard facts about the product you can load from the online special. The potential customer can choose how much information he wants and how to consume it. The mobile phone has not only here become an allround device: In Japan, for example, you can already pay your underground ticket via chip.

BUT THE INTERNET DOES NOT STAND STILL EITHER. A FEW YEARS AGO, THE LAUNCH OF THE FLASH TECHNOLOGY REVOLUTIONIZED THE MEDIUM; NOW IT IS FAST BROADBAND WITH ITS UNLIMITED POSSIBILITIES OF EVEN WATCHING MOVIES WITHOUT HAVING TO WAIT FOR LONG.

PlayStation is already connected to the net, which suggests advertising is built into the games. The new secret weapon is called "in-game advertising". Placed cleverly in the game, it reaches the kids even if they do not watch television.

In the game, you pass a poster that shows the latest sports car. If you click on the poster, you get to the online special where you can configure your vehicle. Or you can take a test drive around the next corner in the game. Pie in the sky? Not really. The real and the virtual world is connecting with each other more and more in order to become one. The latest example are the developments in Asia where people buy the latest Adidas sneakers not only for themselves, but also for their virtual self on the net, in chats or games. What else does a brand need other than being such a cult that buyers not only consider the three stripes important in the shoe shop, but also spend money on the three pixel lines for their virtual self? It will become increasingly important to be familiar with the latest technology. Tools like "google earth" are used as an advertising platform. Adidas has already translated this into action: One of the current football games uses this technology to provide support for the questions in

ADVERTISING IS DEAD. LONG LIVE ADVERTISING!

the game. Although this is not applicable to the masses yet, the road is clear and will become broadly accepted.

The agencies and their clients will have to re-think things, too. Their task is not getting any easier because they have to trust and keep up with each other. The outside world is not black and white any-more. Specialists are more important than ever! Even more important is staff with a wide and inte-grative way of thinking.

THERE USED TO BE INFORMATION ARCHITECTS AT THE ONLINE AGENCIES AND COPYWRITERS AT THE ADVERTISING AGENCIES. NOW YOU NEED A CREATIVE THINKER WHO RECONCILES BOTH AND THINKS MULTIMEDIA. ONLINE ART DIRECTORS HAVE TO DEVELOP STORIES, AND OFFLINE ART DIRECTORS HAVE TO LEARN TO USE THE INTERNET FOR MORE THAN CHECKING THEIR EMAILS. DARE! IT'S FUN!

The immediate, professional and target-set-ting approach is gaining acceptance. For instance, a customer used to go to a car dealer to get some advice. Then he would take home a pile of bro-chures, leaving with as many questions as he had had before his visit. Nowadays he browses the net, has a 3D look at the car, contacts his local dealer and fixes an appointment. The retailer welcomes the customer in a lounge, has all the necessary data at hand and explains the security features on a 40"

TFT screen in a relaxing atmosphere – features the customer does not see and hopes he does not to have to buy, but is convinced by the consultant that he actually needs them. This is a project that has recently been realized for BMW. 3D becomes more and more important.

MUSIC VIDEOS, TV COMMERCIALS AND ONLINE SPECIALS HAVE BEEN – EVEN BEFORE "MATRIX" – INFLUENCED BY GAMES. WHETHER IT IS AN EFFECT OR A STORY – ONE THING IS FOR SURE: IF WITHIN THE HUGE MASS OF ADVERTISING MESSAGES JUST ONE THING IS REMEMBERED, A LOT HAS BEEN ACHIEVED.

Is advertising dead? Not at all – it is more in-teresting than ever! The traditional thinking of online and offline is being taken over by clever direct ad-vertising. Interactive television will forge links. What will measure a successful brand in the future are the channels it serves and how it approaches a spe-cial target group. Instead of commercials getting on peoples nerves by interrupting their favourite movie on television, there will be more advertising "on de-mand" wrapped in films, shows or games. This way, the user themselves decide when they want to get information on a product. And if they choose to do that, it is certain that they are interested in purchas-ing the product. On the following pages, this book will present the latest and most innovative adver-tising that has recently been developed. And this is only the beginning!

We are living in the most exciting times ever. Advertising is not dead, just different. Or, like an IKEA commercial said: "Discover the possibilities!"

Directeur artistique chez Interone Worldwide, une agence du réseau BBDO. Il a étudié la communication visuelle à l'Université des Sciences Appliquées de Münster, avec une spécialisation en design numérique. Pendant ses études, il a travaillé en free-lance pour des agences de pub et de design, entre autres BBDO Interactive à Düsseldorf. Son mémoi-re de fin d'études, une création numérique sur les sous-cultures britanniques, a reçu plusieurs prix et a été largement publié. Une fois diplô-mé, il a travaillé comme free-lance à Londres avant d'être nommé responsable du design à l'agence Razorfish. Deux ans plus tard, il dé-bute comme directeur artistique chez Elephant Seven. Il est nommé en 2002 directeur artis-tique chez Interone à Hambourg. Il commence alors à travailler pour la marque BMW. Depuis 2005, il est directeur de création pour la Mini, entre autres. Il mène en parallèle des projets personnels dans son studio Stereoplastic et a fondé le label Coft1.

De tous côtés, on entend les complaintes de la publicité traditionnelle. Le grand art du spot de 30 secondes, la discipline supposée reine, passe pour obsolète. Les publicités sont soit trop chè-res, soit moins bonnes. Et selon les analyses mar-keting, elles atteignent rarement leur public cible.

IS ADVERTISING DEAD? NOT AT ALL – IT IS MORE INTERESTING THAN EVER!

Les gens aiment les regarder pour se distraire, mais la décision d'achat d'un produit est déterminée par Internet. Cela n'est pas vrai pour tous les produits bien sûr, mais ce développement est intéressant et révélateur pour l'avenir. La publicité à grande échelle est vecteur d'image pour la marque, mais ne fait pas vendre le produit.

L'UNIVERS SCINTILLANT DE LA PUBLICITÉ TEL QU'ON LE CONNAÎT ÉVOLUE RAPIDEMENT. ON A UN TEMPS MÉPRISÉ LES CAMPAGNES EN LIGNE, ET CONSIDÉRÉ LES SITES COMME DE SIMPLES CATALOGUES ÉLECTRONIQUES, MAIS LE MÉDIUM EST AUJOURD'HUI PLUS CONFIANT ET PLUS PROSPÈRE QUE JAMAIS.

Alors que certaines campagnes en ligne bénéficient de leur propre tournage, que l'utilisation onéreuse de films et d'images 3D est devenue la norme pour les grandes marques, l'évolution a déjà fait un pas de plus : les placements sur mobiles soutiennent les campagnes hors ligne, les affiches promotionnelles donnent des numéros MMS que l'on peut composer pour télécharger des informations directement sur son téléphone, quand on ne le fait pas à partir du site officiel. Le client potentiel peut choisir quelle quantité d'information il veut recevoir, et sous quelle forme. Le mobile est devenu un outil polyvalent. Au Japon par exemple, on peut déjà payer son ticket de métro grâce à la puce de son téléphone.

MAIS INTERNET N'EST PAS EN RESTE. IL Y A QUELQUES ANNÉES, LE LANCEMENT DE LA TECHNOLOGIE FLASH A RÉVOLUTIONNÉ LE SUPPORT. AUJOURD'HUI, C'EST LE HAUT DÉBIT ET SES POSSIBILITÉS ILLIMITÉES, DONT CELLE DE REGARDER UN FILM SANS ATTENDRE BIEN LONGTEMPS QU'IL SOIT TÉLÉCHARGÉ.

La PlayStation est déjà connectée au Net, ce qui permet des annonces publicitaires au sein des jeux. La nouvelle arme fatale est l'intégration de publicité au sein des jeux vidéo. Placé habilement dans le jeu, elle atteint les enfants même s'ils ne regardent pas la télé.

Ainsi dans un jeu de rally, on croise une affiche du dernier modèle de voiture de sport. Si on clique sur l'affiche, elle vous renvoie sur le site de la marque, où l'on peut configurer son propre véhicule. On peut également s'inscrire pour l'essayer un peu plus loin dans la partie. Promesses en l'air ? Pas exactement. Le monde réel et virtuel s'interconnectent de plus en plus pour ne faire qu'un. L'exemple le plus récent se trouve en Asie, où les gens ont acheté des basket Adidas pour eux-mêmes, puis pour leur personnage virtuel sur le Net, dans les jeux ou les groupes de discussion. Que demander de plus pour une marque ? Le culte est tel que les acheteurs ne cherchent pas les trois bandes dans le seul magasin, mais dépensent aussi de l'argent pour équiper leur personnage virtuel de trois bandes de pixels ! Il sera de plus en plus important d'être familiarisé avec les dernières technologies. Des outils comme Google Earth servent de plateforme publicitaire. Adidas est déjà passé à l'action. Un des jeux de football actuel utilise cette technique d'intégration pour faire progresser le joueur au sein d'un questionnaire. Bien que cela ne soit pas encore applicable au grand public, la voie est ouverte et sera largement acceptée.

Les agences et les annonceurs devront aussi re-réfléchir. Leur tache n'est pas simplifiée, car ils devront se faire confiance et évoluer les uns en même temps que les autres. Le monde n'est plus en noir et blanc. Les spécialistes sont plus importants que jamais. Et ce qui compte par-dessus tout, c'est d'avoir une équipe possédant un esprit ouvert et une vision globale du monde.

ON TROUVAIT AUTREFOIS DES ARCHITECTES DE L'INFORMATION DANS LES AGENCES EN LIGNE, ET DES RÉDACTEURS DANS LES AGENCES DE PUB. AUJOURD'HUI ON A BESOIN D'UN CRÉATEUR INVENTIF QUI CONCILIE LES DEUX ET PENSE MULTIMÉDIA. LES DIRECTEURS ARTISTIQUES MULTIMÉDIA DOIVENT APPRENDRE À INVENTER DES HISTOIRES, ET LEURS HOMOLOGUES HORS LIGNE DOIVENT APPRENDRE À SE SERVIR D'INTERNET POUR AUTRE CHOSE QUE RELEVER LEURS E-MAILS. ESSAYEZ DONC, C'EST RIGOLO !

L'approche directe, professionnelle et ciblée est de plus en plus acceptée. Par exemple, un client allait chez un concessionnaire pour avoir des conseils. Il rentrait chez lui avec un tas de brochures sous le bras, et autant de questions qu'avant sa visite. Aujourd'hui il surfe sur le Net, regarde la voiture qui l'intéresse en 3D, puis il contacte son revendeur local pour un rendez-vous. Le vendeur accueille son client dans un salon, a toutes les données en main et explique les derniers équipements de sécurité sur un écran de 40 pouces dans une ambiance décontractée. De nouvelles options que le client ne regarde pas vraiment car il espère ne jamais devoir s'en servir, mais le vendeur le convainc de leur utilité. Ce projet a été récemment réalisé pour BMW. La 3D devient de plus en plus importante.

LES VIDÉO CLIPS, LES PUBS TÉLÉ ET LES SITES INTERNET ONT ÉTÉ, BIEN AVANT MATRIX, INFLUENCÉS PAR LES JEUX. QUE CELA SOIT UNE TENDANCE OU UNE RÉALITÉ, UNE CHOSE EST SÛRE : SI DANS LA MASSE ÉNORME DE MESSAGES PUBLICITAIRES ON NE RETIENT QU'UNE SEULE INFO, ALORS LE BUT EST ATTEINT.

La publicité est morte ? Pas du tout, elle est plus passionnante que jamais ! La séparation classique entre publicité en ligne et hors ligne est comblée par la publicité directe. La télévision interactive forgera de nouveaux liens. Le succès d'une marque se mesurera à l'avenir au canal qu'elle utilise et à sa façon d'approcher son groupe cible. A la place des pubs qui agacent les téléspectateurs en interrompant leur film, nous trouverons plus de pubs « à la demande » intégrées dans des films, des émissions ou des jeux. Ainsi le consommateur choisira le moment où il désire être informé sur un produit. Et s'il choisit de le faire, c'est qu'il est intéressé pour l'achat du produit. Dans les pages suivantes, vous pourrez découvrir les publicités les plus intéressantes et les plus novatrices récemment réalisées. Et ce n'est qu'un début !

Nous vivons une époque palpitante. La publicité n'est pas morte, elle est simplement différente. Ou pour citer une pub d'IKEA : « Explorez les possibles ! »

Arbeitet als Creative Director bei der INTERONE Worldwide, Agentur des weltweiten BBDO Netzwerkes. Er studierte Visuelle Kommunikation mit dem Schwerpunkt Digitales Design an der Fachhochschule in Münster. Während seines Studiums hat er früh als freier Mitarbeiter für Werbeagenturen und Design-Büros gearbeitet, unter anderem als langjähriger freier Mitarbeiter für die BBDO Interactive in Düsseldorf. Seine Abschlussarbeit, eine digitale Arbeit über die Subkulturen Englands, erhielt mehrere Awards und wurde mehrmals publiziert. Nach dem Studium arbeitete er zunächst frei in London, bis er dann als Senior Designer bei der Agentur Razorfish begann. Nach zwei Jahren bei Razorfish startete er als Art Director bei Elephant Seven, bis er Anfang 2002 als Senior Art Director zu der INTERONE in Hamburg ging. Dort arbeitete er zunächst für die Marke BMW und betreut seit Mai 2005 als Creative Director unter anderem die Marke MINI. Nebenbei arbeitet er an eigenen Projekten mit seinem Studio stereoplastic.com und ist Gründer des Labels Coft1.com.

Überall hört man die klassische Werbung sich beklagen! Die hohe Kunst des 30-Sekunden-Spots – die so genannte „Königsdisziplin" – soll

am Ende sein. Die Werbespots werden entweder immer teurer oder immer stumpfer. Sie erreichen laut Marktforschungsstudien kaum die potenzielle Zielgruppe. Man schaut sie sich gerne an und lässt sich unterhalten, aber die Kaufentscheidung erfolgt im Internet. Das mag zwar zugegebenermaßen nicht auf alle Produkte zutreffen, aber die Entwicklung ist interessant und zukunftsweisend. Breit gestreute Werbung bleibt immer mehr ein reiner Imageträger für die Marke, aber verkauft das Produkt nicht.

DIE SCHÖNE WERBEWELT, WIE WIR SIE KENNEN, VERÄNDERT SICH RASANT. WÄHREND FRÜHER ONLINE-KAMPAGNEN BELÄCHELT WURDEN UND INTERNET-SEITEN TEILWEISE AUSSAHEN, ALS OB MAN EINEN KATALOG ONLINE GESTELLT HÄTTE, IST DAS MEDIUM HEUTE SO SELBSTBEWUSST UND ERFOLGREICH WIE NIE ZUVOR.

Und während professionelle Online-Kampagnen mit einem eigenen Shooting, aufwändigem 3D-Einsatz und einem Filmdreh für viele Premium-Marken längst zum Standard geworden sind, geht die Entwicklung bereits einen Schritt weiter: Mobile Maßnahmen unterstützen jetzt schon globale Kampagnen, sei es im Verbund mit Outdoor-Werbung, beispielsweise mit Plakaten, die eine MMS-Nummer tragen, mit welcher der Handy-Besitzer sich Infos direkt und mobil auf sein Handy laden kann, oder als mobile Weiterführung mit den „Hard Facts" eines Produktes – geladen aus dem Online-Special. Der potenzielle Kunde kann selbst wählen, wie viele Informationen er braucht und auf welche Art er diese konsumieren möchte. Das Handy ist nicht nur bei uns zum Allround-Gerät geworden. In Japan zum Beispiel wird mittlerweile per Chip schon das U-Bahn-Ticket bezahlt.

DOCH AUCH DAS INTERNET STEHT NICHT STILL. WÄHREND VOR EINIGEN JAHREN DIE EINFÜHRUNG DER FLASH-

TECHNOLOGIE DAS MEDIUM REVOLUTIONIERT HAT, IST ES NUN DIE IMMER SCHNELLER WERDENDE BANDBREITE DES NETZES MIT DEN UNBEGRENZTEN MÖGLICHKEITEN, NUN AUCH GANZE FILME ONLINE ZU STELLEN, OHNE LANGE WARTEN ZU MÜSSEN.

Die Playstation ist längst mit dem Internet verbunden, und was liegt näher, als in den Games auch Werbung zu betreiben. „In-Game Advertising" lautet die neue Geheimwaffe. Werbung, geschickt platziert in einem Spiel, erreicht die Kids, auch wenn sie keine Lust haben fernzusehen.

Man läuft im Spiel an einem Plakat vorbei, auf dem der neueste Sportwagen zu sehen ist. Klickt man auf das Plakat, gelangt man zum Online-Special und kann sein Fahrzeug konfigurieren. Oder man kann an der nächsten Ecke im Game selbst eine kleine Testfahrt machen. Zukunftsmusik? Keineswegs. Überhaupt scheinen sich die reale und die virtuelle Welt immer mehr zu verbinden und eins zu werden. Jüngstes Beispiel ist die Entwicklung in Asien, wo viele selbst für ihre virtuellen Ichs im Netz, in Chats oder Games die neuesten Adidas-Sneaker kaufen. Was kann sich eine Marke mehr wünschen, als so sehr Kult zu sein, dass die Käufer nicht nur im Schuhgeschäft Wert auf die drei Streifen legen, sondern selbst für die drei Pixellinien auf den Schuhen ihres virtuellen Ichs Geld ausgeben. Dabei wird es immer wichtiger werden, sich in den neuesten Techniken auszukennen. Tools wie „Google Earth" werden bereits als Plattform für Werbung genutzt. Adidas hat dies schon umgesetzt. Eins der derzeitigen Fußball-Games nutzt die Technik als Unterstützung für die Fragen im Spiel. Zwar ist das noch nicht massentauglich, aber der Weg ist klar und wird Schule machen.

Dies erfordert aber auch ein Umdenken bei den Agenturen und ihren Kunden. Die Aufgabe wird dadurch nicht leichter, denn beide müssen miteinander Schritt halten und einander vertrauen. Die Welt dort draußen ist nicht so schwarz-weiß wie lange geglaubt. Spezialisten sind wichtiger denn je! Noch

DIE WERBUNG IST TOT? WOHL KAUM – SIE IST INTERESSANTER DENN JE GEWORDEN!

wichtiger sind Mitarbeiter, die möglichst breit und integrativ denken können!

FRÜHER GAB ES INFORMATIONS-ARCHITEKTEN BEI DEN ONLINE-AGENTUREN UND TEXTER BEI DEN WERBEAGENTUREN. NUN WIRD IMMER MEHR NACH DEM KREATIVEN KONZEPTER GESUCHT, DER BEIDES VEREINT UND MULTIMEDIAL DENKEN KANN. ONLINE-ART-DIREKTOREN MÜSSEN STORYS ENTWICKELN KÖNNEN UND OFFLINE-ART-DIREKTOREN MÜSSEN LERNEN, DAS INTERNET FÜR MEHR ZU NUTZEN ALS NUR DAZU, IHRE E-MAILS ABZURUFEN. BEIDE SEITEN MÜSSEN SICH WEITER EINANDER ANNÄHERN. TRAUT EUCH! ES MACHT SPASS!

Die direkte, professionelle und zielgenaue Ansprache setzt sich durch. Früher ging man zum Beispiel zum Autohändler und ließ sich beraten. Danach trug man einen Stapel Broschüren nach Hause und hatte genauso viele Fragen wie vor dem Besuch. Heute erkundigt man sich online, schaut sich das Fahrzeug in 3D an, kontaktiert seinen nächstgelegenen Händler und macht einen Termin aus. Der Händler empfängt den Kunden in einer Lounge, hat schon seine Daten und erklärt dem Kunden auf einem 40-Zoll-TFT-Bildschirm in entspannter Atmosphäre die Sicherheitsfeatures, die der Kunde nicht sieht, die er niemals einzusetzen hofft, von deren Wichtigkeit er aber durch den Berater überzeugt wird. Ein Projekt, das vor kurzem für BMW realisiert wurde. Das Thema 3D wird immer wichtiger.

EINFLÜSSE AUS GAMES FLIESSEN NICHT ERST SEIT „MATRIX" IN MUSIKVIDEOS, FERNSEHSPOTS UND ONLINE-SPECIALS EIN. OB ES EIN EFFEKT IST ODER EINE STORY – SICHER IST: WENN

ÜBERHAUPT IN DER MASSE DER WERBEBOTSCHAFTEN ETWAS HÄNGEN BLEIBT, DANN IST SCHON VIEL ERREICHT.

Die Werbung ist tot? Wohl kaum – sie ist interessanter denn je geworden! Das traditionelle Denken von Online und Offline ist passé und wird durch clevere direkte und gezielte Werbung abgelöst. Interaktives Fernsehen wird diese Brücke schlagen und die Grenze verschwinden lassen. In der Zukunft wird eine erfolgreiche Marke daran gemessen werden, welche Kanäle sie bedient und wie sie die immer speziellere Zielgruppe anspricht. Statt von der Werbung genervt zu sein, die den Lieblingsfilm im Fernsehen unterbricht, wird es immer mehr Werbung „on demand" geben, verpackt in Filmen, in Shows oder in Spielen. Auf diese Weise entscheidet der User selbst, wann er etwas über das Produkt erfahren möchte. Dabei kann man sich dann aber auch sicher sein, dass er wirklich ein Kaufinteresse hat. Auf den folgenden Seiten wird dieses Buch das Aktuellste und Innovativste zeigen, das bisher entwickelt wurde. Und das ist nur der Anfang!

Die Zeit ist spannender denn je. Die Werbung ist noch lange nicht tot, nur anders. Oder wie schon ein IKEA-Spot sagte: „Entdecke die Möglichkeiten."

THE AGENCIES AND THEIR CLIENTS WILL HAVE TO RE-THINK THINGS, TOO. THEIR TASK DOES NOT BECOMEIS NOT GETTING ANY EASIER BECAUSE THEY HAVE TO TRUST AND KEEP UP WITH EACH OTHER.

LES AGENCES ET LES ANNONCEURS DEVRONT AUSSI RE-RÉFLÉCHIR. LEUR TACHE N'EST PAS SIMPLIFIÉE, CAR ILS DEVRONT SE FAIRE CONFIANCE ET ÉVOLUER LES UNS EN MÊME TEMPS QUE LES AUTRES.

DIES ERFORDERT ABER AUCH EIN UMDENKEN BEI DEN AGENTUREN UND IHREN KUNDEN. DIE AUFGABE WIRD DADURCH NICHT LEICHTER, DENN BEIDE MÜSSEN MITEINANDER SCHRITT HALTEN UND EINANDER VERTRAUEN.

005

SPORTS & APPAREL

FEATURED ON THE DVD   **CAMPAIGN:** Adidas Originals.   **YEAR:** 2005.   **AGENCY:** Neue Digitale <www.neue-digitale.de>.   **PRODUCTION TIME:** October 2004 – March 2005.   **PRODUCER:** Neue Sentimental Film, Frankfurt
CREATIVE TEAM: Olaf Czeschner, Bejadin Selimi.   **PROGRAMMER:** Jens Steffen.   **TECH ASPECTS:** Macromedia Flash, Adobe After Effects, Adobe Photoshop.   **MEDIA CIRCULATED:** Internet.   **AWARDS:** Eurobest Award (Gold);
Cannes Cyber Lions 2005 (Silver); New York Festivals 2005 (Print, Outdoor, Design: Silver); New York Festivals Interactive (Apparel: Bronze); New York Festivals Interactive (Best use of rich media: Bronze).

CONCEPT: Dancing models present the spring/summer collection 2005 from Adidas Originals on the Internet – in broadband full-screen video which runs at an even higher resolution than on television. The broadband web-special was developed to impress the trendy, highly-demanding target group as a part of an integrated marketing concept. On the Internet, the user can choose how he wants to view the collection. The first choice is Movie Mode, where dancing models present the Adidas Originals collection uninterrupted. In the Interactive Mode, the user can pick and choose which scenes he wants to see and view details of individual products. The lowband version, Product Mode, was created so that even those without a broadband connection can comfortably view the details of the individual styles. **RESULTS:** The interactive video sequences set new benchmarks in the online world, especially in regard to high quality level/low load time ratio and the video also runs on monitors in select stores where adidas products are sold. The project was implemented for a global audience – in 14 languages across 26 countries. The innovative product presentation of adidas originals should raise brand awareness for Adidas among the Internet affine target group. The website should support Adidas "must-have-street-wear" – and sell more products.

CONCEPT : Des mannequins en mouvement présentent en ligne la collection printemps-été 2005 de la ligne Originals de Adidas, dans une vidéo large bande et plein écran qui offre une résolution supérieure à celle de la télévision. La technologie appliquée devait impressionner un public branché et exigeant dans le cadre d'une campagne intégrée. L'utilisateur peut choisir comment il veut regarder la collection. La première option s'appelle « Mode Film », et les mannequins présentent la collection de façon ininterrompue. Dans le « Mode Interactif », on peut choisir la scène que l'on désire voir et regarder un produit en détail. La version basse résolution, « Mode Produit », a été conçue afin que ceux qui n'ont pas de connexion haut débit puissent aussi profiter en détail des modèles présentés. **RÉSULTATS :** Les séquences vidéo interactives ont fait référence dans l'univers en ligne, surtout en ce qui concerne le rapport temps de chargement-niveau de qualité supérieure. La vidéo est également diffusée sur des écrans dans les points de vente Adidas. Le projet a été implémenté pour un public mondial, en 14 langues et dans 26 pays. La présentation novatrice du produit devrait augmenter la notoriété de la marque auprès du groupe cible, et positionner la ligne Originals comme un accessoire indispensable de la mode urbaine.

KONZEPT: Im Internet wird die Frühlings- und Sommerkollektion 2005 von Adidas Originals von tanzenden Models präsentiert – in einer Vollbilddarstellung in besserer Qualität als im Fernsehen. Das Web-Special wurde als Teil eines integrierten Marketing-Konzepts entwickelt, um die moderne und anspruchsvolle Zielgruppe zu beeindrucken. Im Internet kann sich der Benutzer aussuchen, wie er die Kollektion ansehen will: Die erste Möglichkeit ist der Film-Modus, in dem tanzende Models die Kollektion Adidas Originals ohne Unterbrechung vorführen. Im interaktiven Modus kann man einzelne Szenen auswählen und verschiedene Produkte im Detail betrachten. Der Produkt-Modus, die Modem-Version, wurde entwickelt, damit man auch über eine Modem-Verbindung bequem die verschiedenen Stile betrachten kann. **ERGEBNISSE:** Die interaktiven Videosequenzen setzten im Online-Bereich neue Maßstäbe, vor allem bezüglich der hohen Qualität bei geringer Ladezeit. Das Video läuft außerdem in verschiedenen Geschäften, in denen Adidas-Produkte verkauft werden. Das Projekt war für ein globales Publikum entwickelt worden – in 14 Sprachen in 26 Ländern. Die innovative Produktpräsentation von Adidas Originals sollte den Bekanntheitsgrad der Marke innerhalb der Internet-affinen Zielgruppe vergrößern. Die Webseite sollte Adidas' „must-have-street-wear" unterstützen – und mehr Produkte verkaufen.

FEATURED ON THE DVD **CAMPAIGN:** Adidas Sport Style Y-3 Cubes. **PRODUCT:** Adidas Sport Style Y-3. **YEAR:** 2005-2006. **AGENCY:** Neue Digitale <www.neue-digitale.de>. **PRODUCTION TIME:** March 2005 – August 2005. **CREATIVE TEAM:** Olaf Czeschner, Jörg Waldschütz, Peter Kirsch. **PROGRAMMER:** Jens Steffen. **TECH ASPECTS:** Macromedia Flash, Adobe Photoshop, 3D Max. **MEDIA CIRCULATED:** Internet. **AWARDS:** Eurobest Award (Grand Prix); New York Festivals (Interactive Grand Award); New York Festivals Interactive (Gold); Epica Awards (Bronze).

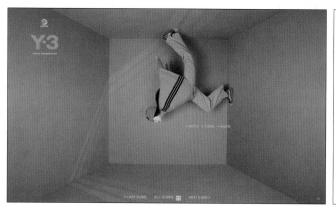

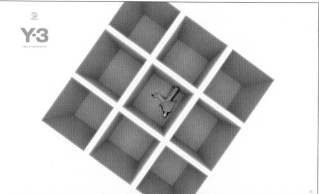

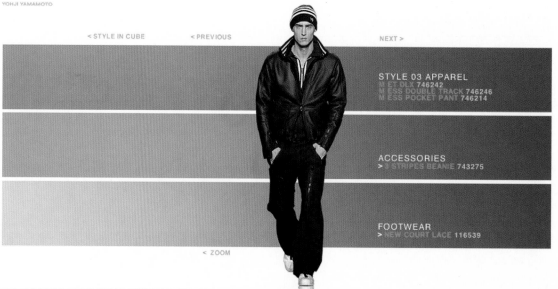

CONCEPT: Y-3 is a high end fashion brand which was developed from a cooperation between Adidas and the japanese designer Yohij Yamamoto. NEUE DIGITALE is already in its third year of looking after the luxury label and has continued to develop the brand since its inception in 2003. The user sees a model in a cube. One click and the model detaches themself from the wall, rotates on an axis and springs into a new acrobatic pose. One further click and the entire room rotates 90 degrees, and with it the model wearing the Y-3 autumn/winter collection 2004/2005, therefore displaying the styles from lots of different views. As well as the styles demonstrated in the cubes, the entire Y-3 collection is displayed in the product area with 53 further outfits, 151 accessories and 62 styles of shoes. **RESULTS:** the Y-3 autumn/winter collection 2005/06 is presented in a new multimedia space dimension, which breaks away from the norm and so has an effect that is bizarre and out of the ordinary. The Y-3 collection is introduced to the lifestyle-oriented consumer exclusively via the Internet – no further medium is used to accompany the broadbrand representation.

CONCEPT : Y-3 est une marque branchée haut de gamme née de la collaboration de Adidas et du styliste japonais Yohji Yamamoto. Neue Digitale gère la marque de luxe depuis déjà trois ans et continue de la développer depuis sa création en 2003. Le visiteur du site voit un mannequin dans un cube. Quand on clique, le mannequin se détache de la paroi, tourne sur lui-même et adopte une nouvelle pose acrobatique. Au clic suivant, le cube fait une rotation de 90 degrés, ainsi que le mannequin qui porte la collection automne-hiver 2004/2005, ce qui expose les articles sous différents angles. Les modèles présentés dans le cube, comme toute la collection Y-3, sont repris dans la rubrique produit, accompagnés de 53 tenues, 151 accessoires et 62 modèles de chaussures. **RÉSULTATS :** La collection automne-hiver 2004/2005 est présentée dans une dimension spatiale hors norme, et produit un effet étrange et frappant. La ligne Y-3 s'adresse aux amateurs de mode uniquement par Internet, aucun autre média n'accompagne la campagne en ligne.

KONZEPT: Y-3 ist eine hochwertige Modemarke, die aus der Zusammenarbeit von Adidas mit dem japanischen Designer Yohij Yamamoto entstanden ist. NEUE DIGITALE betreut das Luxus-Label nun schon seit drei Jahren und entwickelt die Marke seit ihrer Entstehung im Jahre 2003. Der Benutzer sieht ein Model in einem Würfel. Ein Klick, und das Model löst sich von der Wand, dreht sich und springt in eine neue akrobatische Pose. Ein weiterer Klick, und der gesamte Raum rotiert um 90 Grad, und mit ihm das Model, das die Y-3 Herbst- und Winterkollektion trägt, die so aus vielen verschiedenen Blickwinkeln betrachtet werden kann. Neben den Stilen, die in den Würfeln gezeigt werden, wird die gesamte Y-3-Kollektion im Produktbereich mit 53 weiteren Outfits, 151 Accessoires und 62 Paar Schuhen vorgeführt. **ERGEBNISSE:** Dei Herbst- und Winterkollektion 2005/2006 von Y-3 wird in einer neuen Multimedia-Raumdimension präsentiert, die von der Norm abweicht und einen bizarren und außergewöhnlichen Effekt hat. Die Y-3-Kollektion wird dem Lifestyle-orientierten Kunden über das Internet nahe gebracht – diese Repräsentation wird von keinem weiteren Medium begleitet.

FEATURED ON THE DVD **CAMPAIGN:** Adidas Sport Style Y-3 Prêt-à-Porter-Fashionshow. **PRODUCT:** Adidas Sport Style Y-3. **YEAR:** 2004-2005. **AGENCY:** Neue Digitale <www.neue-digitale.de>. **PRODUCTION TIME:** October 2003 – July 2004. **CREATIVE TEAM:** Olaf Czeschner, Bejadin Selimi, Michael Barnutz, Marc Freund. **PROGRAMMER:** Jens Steffen. **TECH ASPECTS:** Macromedia Flash, Adobe After Effects, Adobe Photoshop. **MEDIA CIRCULATED:** Internet. **AWARDS:** Cannes Cyber Lions 2005 (Silver); Eurobest Award (Gold); CRESTA 2005 (Winner); New York Festivals 2005 (Print, Outdoor, Design: Gold); The New York Festival 2004 (Gold); Red Dot: Digital Media (Best of Show); The One Show Interactive 2005 (Gold); D&AD 2005 (Silver); ADC Deutschland 2005 (Silver); Epica 2004 (Silver); London International Advertising Award (Finalist); Econ Jahrbuch der Werbung (Site of the Year 2005).

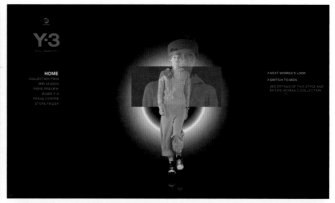
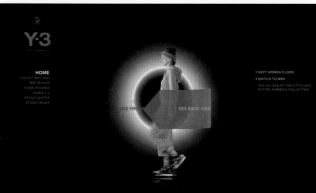
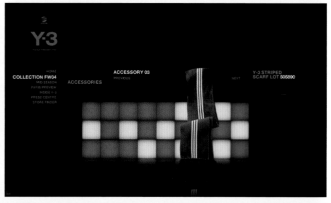
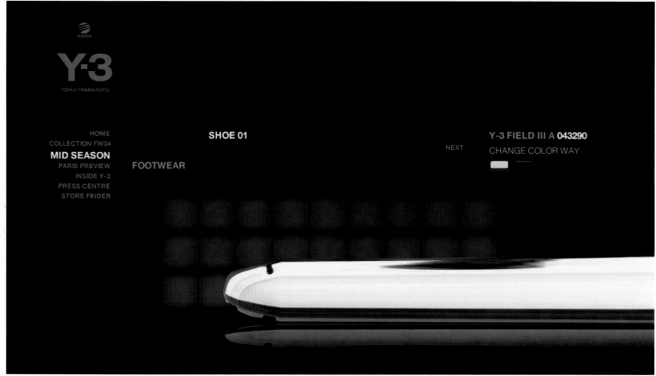

CONCEPT: The collection from the Y-3 fashion label, a collaboration between Adidas and the Japanese designer Yohij Yamamoto, was presented in a dynamic and futuristic way in a Prêt-à-Porter fashion show on the Internet. Models strut down a virtual catwalk, which can be viewed from various angles. This enables the viewer to see how the clothes fall on a real body. NEUE DIGITALE also conceived, carried out post-production work, and implemented a complex video loop taken in a studio against blue and green screens. All styles are completely dynamic and are editable via a specially created Flash-application. **RESULTS:** The implementation of the Adidas Y-3 Prêt-à-Porter fashion show is the first time "fashion in motion" has been presented on the Internet. In no other medium can fashion be so realistically and interactively presented as via the Internet. For Y-3 the Internet is the predominant marketing channel.

CONCEPT : La collection de la ligne Y-3, née de la collaboration entre Adidas et le styliste japonais Yohji Yamamoto, est présentée de façon dynamique et futuriste dans un défilé de prêt-à-porter en ligne. Les mannequins défilent sur un podium virtuel, qui peut être observé de différents point de vue. Cela permet à l'internaute de voir l'effet des vêtements sur une personne en chair et en os. Neue Digitale a aussi conçu et réalisé le travail de post-production, et a intégré une séquence vidéo enregistrée en studio sur des fonds bleu et vert. Tous les modèles sont totalement dynamiques et peuvent être montés grâce à une application spéciale en format Flash. **RÉSULTATS :** Le défilé virtuel de la ligne Y-3 est la première réalisation de « mode en mouvement » jamais présentée en ligne. La présentation interactive et réaliste du défilé n'aurait pu être réalisée dans aucun autre média qu'internet. Pour Y-3, internet est le support marketing prédominant.

KONZEPT: Die Kollektion des Y-3-Modelabels, eine Kooperation zwischen Adidas und dem japanischen Designer Yohij Yamamoto, wurde auf dynamische und futuristische Weise in einer Prêt-à-Porter-Modenschau im Internet präsentiert. Models laufen einen virtuellen Catwalk entlang, der aus verschiedenen Blickwinkeln betrachtet werden kann. Dadurch sieht man, wie die Kleider an einem realen Körper aussehen. NEUE DIGITALE drehte außerdem einen komplexen Video-Loop vor einem Hintergrund von blauen und grünen Bildschirmen. Alle Stile sind absolut dynamisch und können mit einer speziell entwickelten Flash-Anwendung editiert werden. **ERGEBNISSE:** Mit der Adidas Y-3 Prêt-à-Porter-Modenschau wird zum ersten Mal „Mode in Bewegung" im Internet präsentiert. In keinem anderen Medium kann Mode so realistisch und interaktiv dargestellt werden. Für Y-3 stellt das Internet den wichtigsten Marketing-Kanal dar.

CAMPAIGN: Adidas KG3 <www.adidas.com.hk/kg3hk>. **YEAR:** 2006. **AGENCY:** Rice5 <www.rice5.com>. **PRODUCTION TIME:** 1 month. **CREATIVE TEAM:** Tom Shum. **PROGRAMMER:** Mike Lee. **TECH ASPECTS:** Macromedia Flash (FLV), Macromedia Firework, Adobe Photoshop, Adobe After Effects.

CONCEPT: Step inside KG. An exploration on new device. By using webcam as an input tool, users can upload or capture their image and merge theirselves into the TVC. After creating their clip, they can wait for people voting and after a certain time, the highest voters will have a pair of KG3 sneakers as prize.

CONCEPT : Entrer dans l'univers de KG, une nouvelle aventure technologique. Grâce à leur *webcam*, les utilisateurs peuvent enregistrer et retransmettre leur image et se fondre dans l'insert. Après avoir créé leur propre clip vidéo, ils peuvent le soumettre au vote des autres internautes, et celui qui remporte le plus de suffrages gagne une paire de baskets KG3.

KONZEPT: Treten Sie ein in KG. Erforschen Sie es auf neuartige Weise. Mit einer Webcam als Input-Tool kann der Benutzer sein Bild hochladen und wird selbst Teil des TVC. Hat er seinen eigenen Clip erstellt, wird dieser von anderen Nutzern bewertet. Wer die meisten Punkte bekommt, gewinnt ein Paar KG3 Sneakers.

CAMPAIGN: Adidas +10 Recruitment (HK) <www.plus10recruit.com>. **PRODUCT:** Adidas +10. **YEAR:** 2006. **AGENCY:** Rice5 <www.rice5.com>. **PRODUCTION TIME:** 1 month. **CREATIVE TEAM:** Anderw Lee. **PROGRAMMER:** Daniel Yuen. **TECH ASPECTS:** Macromedia Flash (FLV), Macromedia Firework.

CONCEPT: To extend the global +10 concept, a localized +10 recruitment platform is built for drawing teens to participate in this football event. Using local celebrities instead of famous football players is another challenge for drawing football fans attention. **RESULTS:** Still under recruiting. More than 2000 entries within 1 week.

CONCEPT : Etendre le concept global « +10 », et construire une plateforme de recrutement afin d'encourager les adolescents à participer à un tournoi de football dont les équipes sont composées de professionnels et d'amateurs. Utiliser des joueurs régionaux plutôt que des stars internationales est une autre astuce pour attirer les fans. **RÉSULTATS :** Le recrutement continue. Il y a eu plus de 2000 entrées en une semaine.

KONZEPT: Um das globale „+10"-Konzept zu erweitern, wurde eine „+10"-Bewerber-Plattform entwickelt, auf der Teenager durch Malen am Fußball-Event teilnehmen können. Die Verwendung von lokalen Prominenten statt berühmten Fußballspielern ist eine Herausforderung für die malenden Fußballfans. **ERGEBNISSE:** Der Wettbewerb läuft noch; innerhalb der ersten Woche gab es über 2000 Einsendungen.

CAMPAIGN: San Silvestre Vallecana 2003 Race. **YEAR:** 2003. **AGENCY:** DoubleYou <www.doubleyou.com>. **PRODUCTION TIME:** 1 month. **CREATIVE TEAM:** Eduard Pou, Joakim Borgström, Oriol Villar, Anna Coll, Quim Tarrida, Elisabeth Badía. **PROGRAMMER:** Joakim Borgström, Mauricio Mazzariol, Ale Bica, Antonio Buenosvinos, Álvaro Sandoval, Josep Maria Soler, Jose Rubio. **TECH ASPECTS:** Macromedia Flash, Javascript. **MEDIA CIRCULATED:** online ads. **AWARDS:** Cannes Cyber Lions 2004 (Integrated Interactive Campaigns – Grand Prix; Travel, Entertainment and Leisure – Gold); One Show Interactive 2004 (Banners Campaign – Gold; Brand Gaming Website – Silver); El Sol Festival San Sebastián (Interactive – Grand Prix); Club de Creativos (Corporate Website – Silver); FIAP 2004 (Web Film – Gold; Website – Bronze; Web Advertising – Bronze); LAUS Design Awards (Interactive Promotional – Winner; Interactive Campaign – Winner); CLIO Awards 2004 (Consumer/Targeted Site – Bronze).

CONCEPT: "The bear of the famous Madrid's statue has escaped. If you see it, run." The website is an adaptation of this urban legend. The San Silvestre Vallecana offline campaign conceived by the agency Villar&Rosas, is here used as a leitmotiv for the website of the race, experiencing the story from the runner point of view. An inner voice guides the user during the persecution and shows him that, in his mind, the menace of the bear becomes an extra motivation to run. Instead of running away, the runner chases after the bear.

CONCEPT : L'ours de la célèbre statue de Madrid s'est échappé. Si vous le croisez, courez ! Le site est une adaptation de cette légende urbaine. La campagne hors ligne élaborée par l'agence Villar&Rosas est utilisée comme leitmotiv sur le site, et adopte le point de vue du coureur de marathon. Une voix guide l'utilisateur alors qu'il est poursuivi et lui montre que dans sa tête, la menace de l'ours devient une motivation supplémentaire pour courir. Au lieu de fuir devant le danger, c'est le coureur qui poursuit l'ours.

KONZEPT: „Der Bär der berühmten Statue aus Madrid ist entlaufen. Wenn du ihn siehst, renn, so schnell du kannst." Die Webseite ist eine Adaption dieser urbanen Legende. Die Offline-Kampagne für San Silvestre Vallecana, entwickelt von der Agentur Villar&Rosas, wird hier als Leitmotiv für die Webseite des Rennens verwendet, auf der man die Geschichte aus der Sicht des Läufers erfährt. Eine Hintergrundstimme führt den Benutzer während der Verfolgung und zeigt ihm, dass die Bedrohung durch den Bären eine zusätzliche Motivation für den Lauf darstellt. Statt wegzulaufen, verfolgt der Läufer schließlich den Bären.

FEATURED ON THE DVD **CAMPAIGN:** NIKE Gridiron Website. **AGENCY:** R/GA <www.rga.com>. **COPYWRITER:** Josh Bletterman, Thomas Pettus, Michael Spiegel, Craig Grant. **DESIGN:** Nick Law, David Hyung, Troy Kooper, Gui Borchert, Jeremiah Simpson, Lian Chang. **INTERACTION DESIGN:** Matt Walsh. **PRODUCTION:** Winston Binch, Harshal Sisodia, Matt Howell, Chris Emond, Julia Belozersky. **PROGRAMMING:** Sean Lyons, Nick Coronges, Kumi Tominaga, Sarah Grant, Sunny Nan, Lee Walling, Felix Turner, Noel Billig. **QUALITY ASSURANCE:** August Yang, Michele Roman. **VIDEO EDITING:** Can Misirlioglu, Tim Speece.

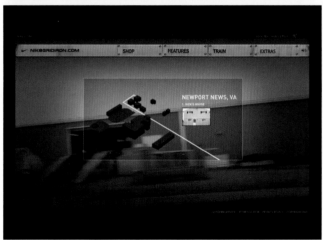

FEATURED ON THE DVD **CAMPAIGN:** NIKE Basketball – Lebron James. **AGENCY:** R/GA <www.rga.com>. **INTERACTION DESIGN:** Yu-Ming Wu. **DESIGN:** ShuZheng Li, Joseph Cartman. **PROGRAMMER:** Charles Duncan, Joseph Cartman. **PRODUCTION:** Harshal Sisodia. **QUALITY ASSURANCE:** Todd Kovner, Michele Roman. **OTHER:** Collaboration with Stardust for After Effects and Design.

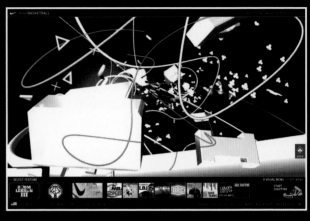

FEATURED ON THE DVD **CAMPAIGN:** Nike Sprint Sister. **YEAR:** 2005. **AGENCY:** DoubleYou <www.doubleyou.com>. **PRODUCTION TIME:** 2 weeks. **CREATIVE TEAM:** Edu Pou, Joakim Borgström, Esther Pino, Blanca Piera, Natalie Long, Nacho Guijarro. **PROGRAMMER:** Joakim Borgström, Nacho Guijarro. **TECH ASPECTS:** Macromedia Flash, Eyeblaster. **MEDIA CIRCULATED:** <http://www.elle.wanadoo.es>.

CONCEPT: We managed to have all the images and texts of Elle's home page in black and white so colour could only be found in the campaign, integrated by a banner, a square, a skyscraper and an eyeblaster that worked together.

CONCEPT : Toutes les pages d'accueil de Elle ont été intégrées en noir et blanc sur le site, la couleur n'apparaissait que dans l'annonce, sous forme de bannière, d'un carré, d'un gratte-ciel et d'une création *rich media* combinés.

KONZEPT: Alle Bilder und Texte auf der Webseite von Elle sind schwarz-weiß, so dass nur die Kampagne farbig ist, die aus einem Banner, einem Quadrat, einem Skyscraper und einem Eyeblaster besteht, die zusammen wirkten.

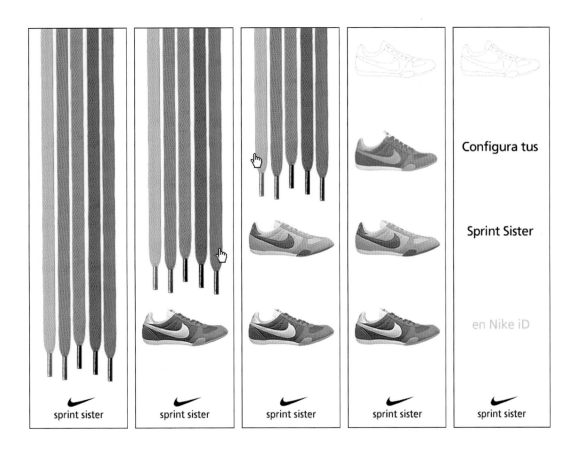

FEATURED ON THE DVD **CAMPAIGN:** NIKE Basketball Family Website. **AGENCY:** R/GA <www.rga.com>. **INTERACTION DESIGN:** Yu-Ming Wu. **DESIGN:** ShuZheng Li, Joseph Cartman. **PROGRAMMER:** Charles Duncan, Joseph Cartman. **PRODUCTION:** Harshal Sisodia. **QUALITY ASSURANCE:** Todd Kovner, Michele Roman. **OTHER:** Collaboration with Stardust for After Effects and Design.

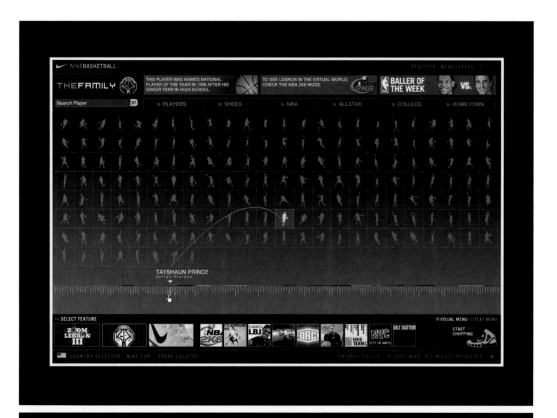

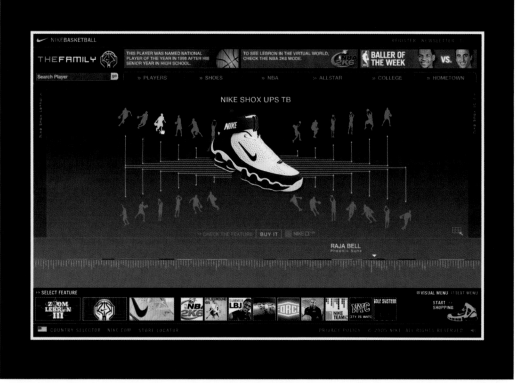

FEATURED ON THE DVD **CAMPAIGN:** NIKE iD Metropop Website. **AGENCY:** R/GA <www.rga.com>. **COPYWRITER:** Thomas Pettus. **DESIGN:** Jerome Austria, Gui Borchert, Elena Sakevich, Phil Lubliner. **INTERACTION DESIGN:** Carlos Gomez de Llarena. **PRODUCTION:** Jennifer Allen, Suzanne Cort. **MEDIA CIRCULATED:** Noel Billig, Christine Reindl. **QUALITY ASSURANCE:** August Yang.

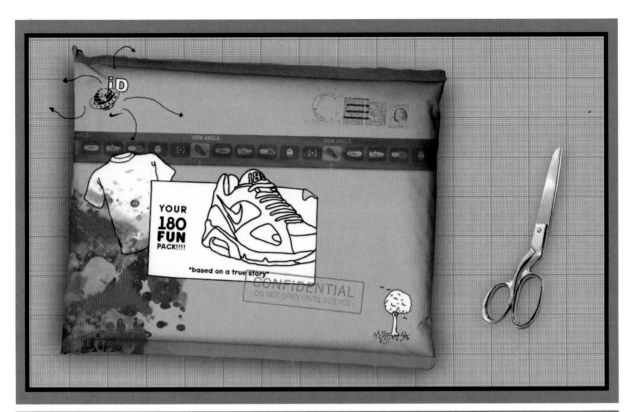

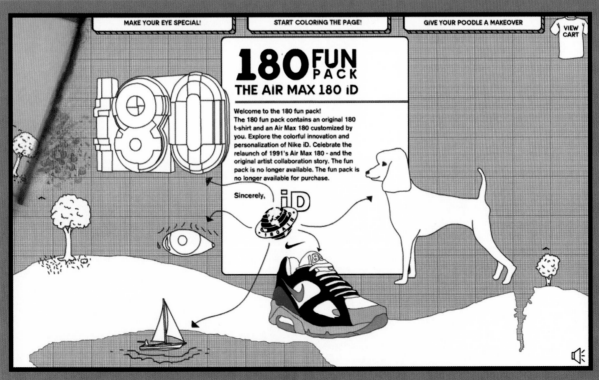

CAMPAIGN: NIKE iD Online Advertising. AGENCY: R/GA <www.rga.com>. ANALYTICS: Briggs Davidson, Erica Millado. COPYWRITER: Mike Spiegel, Scott Tufts. DESIGN: Brian Votow, Troy Kooper. PRODUCTION: Andy Bhatt, Jessica Yin, Matt Howell.

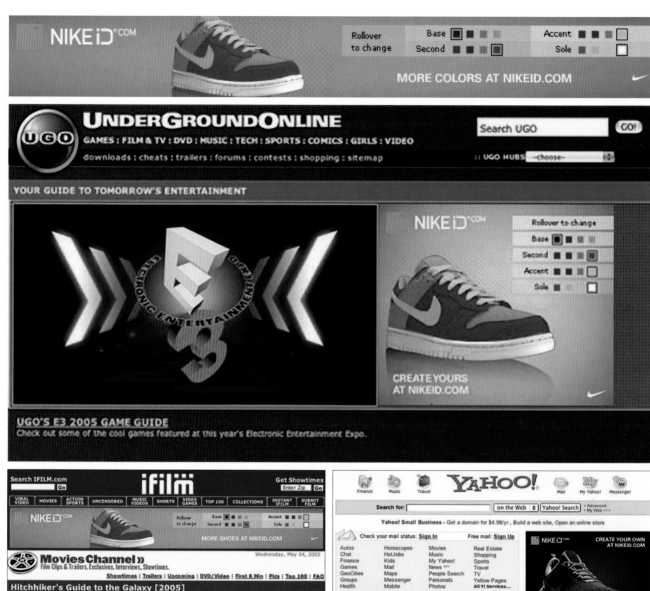

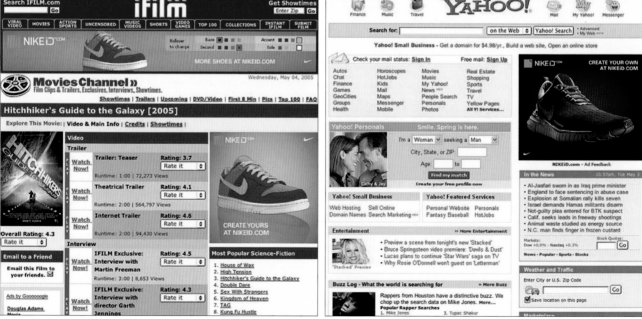

FEATURED ON THE DVD   **CAMPAIGN:** Nike San Silvestre Vallecana 2005.   **YEAR:** 2005.   **AGENCY:** DoubleYou <www.doubleyou.com>.   **PRODUCTION TIME:** 3 months.   **CREATIVE TEAM:** Edu Pou, Oriol Villar, Fernando Codina, Miguel Medina, Marius Zorrilla, Xavi Caparrós, Nacho Guijarro.   **PROGRAMMER:** Xavi Caparrós, Nacho Guijarro, Miguel Medina, Álvaro Sandoval, Nacho Lorente.   **TECH ASPECTS:** Macromedia Flash, Javascript, Java. **MEDIA CIRCULATED:** Marca, AS.

CONCEPT: A timeline-designed navigation website that moves forward to the undefined date Madrid will have its Olympic Games and, in spite of the typical countdown, uses a "count up" to symbolize that with every second that passes this aim is a second closer.

CONCEPT : Le site est conçu comme un tableau chronologique qui avance vers la date indéfinie qui verra Madrid accueillir les Jeux Olympiques, et au lieu d'utiliser un compte à re-bours, il additionne les secondes pour symboliser que chaque moment qui passe rapproche de l'objectif.

KONZEPT: Eine Navigationsseite mit einer Zeitleiste, die sich bis zu dem ungewissen Tag erstreckt, an dem die Olympischen Spiele in Madrid stattfinden werden. Ein „Count up", ein Zähler, soll zeigen, dass dieses Ziel mit jeder Sekunde, die vergeht, näher rückt.

CAMPAIGN: NIKE Gridiron Online Advertising.   AGENCY: R/GA <www.rga.com>.   COPYWRITER: Michael Spiegel.   DESIGN: Troy Kooper, Brian Votaw.   PRODUCTION: Andy Bhatt, Jessica Yin.

ICKY SHUFFLE

DAY 1 WATCH DRILL   DAY 2   DAY 3

TRAIN LIKE TOM BRADY.

NIKEGRIDIRON.COM

TRAIN LIKE TOM BRADY.
THE PROGRAM

NIKEGRIDIRON.COM

DAY 1   DAY 2   DAY 3

CAMPAIGN: nikeplay.com - the game <www.nikeplay.com>. **YEAR:** 2003. **AGENCY:** DoubleYou <www.doubleyou.com>. **PRODUCTION TIME:** 4,5 months. **CREATIVE TEAM:** Joakim Borgström, Esther Pino, Daniel Solana, Blanca Piera, Elisabeth Badía, Jordi Martínez. **PROGRAMMER:** Jordi Martínez, Álvaro Sandoval, Joakim Borgström, Mauricio Mazzariol. **TECH ASPECTS:** Macromedia Flash, Java, Javascript. **AWARDS:** Cannes Cyber Lions 2004 (Viral Marketing – Gold); FIAP 2004 (Web Game – Bronze); El Sol Festival San Sebastián 2004 (Fashion and Home – Gold); LAUS Design Awards 2004 (Interactive Promotional – Finalist); Club de creativos 2004 (Corporate Website – Silver).

CONCEPT: Interactive version of the Nike TAG campaign, representing the classic game of tagging and being tagged. The online experience is based on a conceptual city made of typographic names of streets from cities all over the world. The user, represented as a pointer, must chase and "click" on any of the several other pointers that run and hide in the city. Once this is achieved, run away to avoid being "tagged".

CONCEPT : Version interactive de la campagne Nike TAG, sous la forme d'un jeu de tagué-tagueur. L'expérience en ligne est basée sur une ville virtuelle où l'on retrouve les noms de rues de villes du monde entier. L'utilisateur, représenté par un curseur, doit poursuivre et cliquer sur les autres curseurs qui se dissimulent dans la ville. Une fois que c'est fait, il faut fuir pour éviter d'être tagué.

KONZEPT: Interaktive Version der Kampagne für Nike TAG, die das klassische Spiel vom gegenseitigen Abschlagen repräsentiert. Die Webseite basiert auf dem Konzept einer Stadt, die aus typografischen Straßennamen von Städten aus aller Welt besteht. Der Benutzer muss mit dem Mauszeiger andere Zeiger verfolgen und anklicken, die sich in der Stadt verstecken und vor ihm weglaufen. Hat man dies erreicht, muss man wegrennen, um nicht selbst abgeschlagen zu werden.

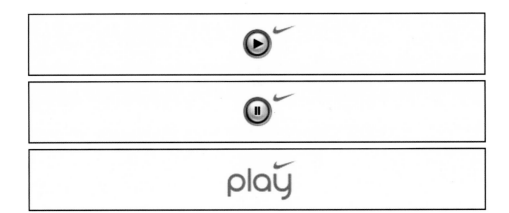

FEATURED ON THE DVD **CAMPAIGN:** NIKE iD <http://NIKEiD.com>. **AGENCY:** R/GA <www.rga.com>. **ANALYTICS:** Erica Millado, Briggs Davidson. **COPYWRITER:** Josh Bletterman, Scott Tufts. **DESIGN:** Marlon Hernandez, Ian Brewer, David Hyung, Michelle Zassenhaus, Lara Horner, Andrew Thompson, John James, Takafumi Yamaguchi, Brian Votaw, Troy Kooper, Allen Yee. **INTERACTION DESIGN:** Richard Ting, Matt Walsh. **PRODUCTION:** Winston Binch, Harshal Sisodia, Matt Howell. **PROGRAMMING/QUALITY ASSURANCE:** Scott Prindle, Sean Lyons, Chuck Genco, Stan Wiechers, Martin Legowiecki, August Yang, Todd Kovner, Michele Roman, Noel Billig, Stuart Buchbinder.

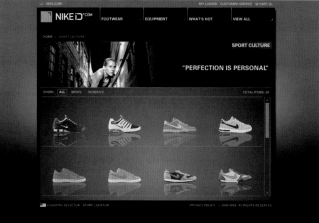

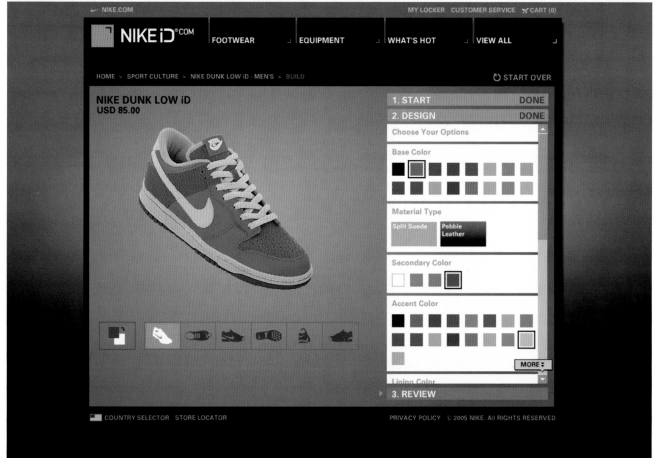

CAMPAIGN: NIKEiD Reuters Sign. AGENCY: R/GA <www.rga.com>. ANALYTICS: Briggs Davidson. COPYWRITER: Mike Spiegel, Josh Bletterman, Scott Tufts. PRODUCTION: Andy Bhatt, Matt Howell. DESIGN: Brian Votaw, Laura Pence, Troy Kooper, Matthew Garton, David Alcorn, Johanna Rustia. INTERACTION DESIGN: Aya Karpinska, Richard Ting. PROGRAMMING/QUALITY ASSURANCE: Ephraim Cohen, John Mayo-Smith, Sean Lyons, Scott Prindle, Chuck Genco, Michael Shagalov, Todd Kovner. THE REUTERS SIGN PRODUCTION TEAM: Dave Jenssen (Creative & Technical VP), Dondi Fusco (Creative & Technical Director), Taiwai Yun and Michael Demaio (Interactive Designer), Kyle Kane (Director/Video Production), Tia Kim (Designer).

FEATURED ON THE DVD **CAMPAIGN:** NITRO Snowboards 2003/04. **PRODUCT:** NITRO Snowboards. **YEAR:** 2003. **AGENCY:** Neue Digitale <www.neue-digitale.de>. **PRODUCTION TIME:** July 2003 – October 2003. **CREATIVE TEAM:** Olaf Czeschner, Rolf Borcherding, Elke Nied, Stefan Schuster. **PROGRAMMER:** Marius Bulla, Jens Steffen, Crizz Gelbach. **TECH ASPECTS:** Macromedia Flash, PHP. **MEDIA CIRCULATED:** Internet. **AWARDS:** Cannes Lions 2004 (Shortlist).

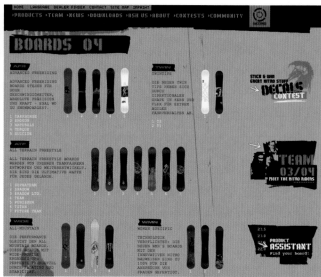

CONCEPT: Website relaunch for snowboard manufacturer Nitro Snowboards, Hofholding. Strengthen Nitro's image through new, interactive features, and create viral e-mails as an integrated part of the website. Nitro's online presentation is designed in an aggressive, yet innovative style using the whole spectrum of the Internet's interactive possibilities: stencils are available for download so the user can design his own snowboards and boots. The practical "Assistant" enables every user to individually configurate his or her Nitro equipment. The extreme viral e-mail section 'D-Mails' features short shocking Flash movies. These are sent from one snowboard fanatic to another and so on and so on – just like a virus. This viral marketing measure brings Nitro products closer to the target group by speaking its language. With its various interactive features and an authentic appearance, Nitro creates an online snowboarding theme park. It is filled with emotions that strengthen the user's identification with the brand.

CONCEPT : Site de lancement pour Hofholding, fabricant des snowboards Nitro. Il s'agit de renforcer l'image de Nitro grâce à de nouveaux éléments interactifs et générer des e-mails viraux. La présentation du produit adopte un style novateur et agressif en utilisant toute la gamme des possibilités interactives. L'internaute peut télécharger des pinceaux pour dessiner ses bottes et son snowboard. Un « assistant » aide l'utilisateur à configurer son équipe-

ment. La rubrique d'e-mail viraux présente des vidéos choc en format Flash. Elles sont transmise d'un fan de snowboard à un autre puis un autre, tout comme un virus. Cette démarche de marketing viral rapproche Nitro de son public cible en parlant le même langage que lui. Grâce à plusieurs éléments interactifs et un style personnel, Nitro crée un parc à thème dédié au snowboard. Son contenu émotionnel renforce l'identification du consommateur avec la marque.

KONZEPT: Relaunch der Webseite für den Snowboard-Hersteller Nitro Snowboards, Hofholding. Nitros Image sollte durch neue, interaktive Features gestärkt und virale E-Mails in die Webseite integriert werden. Die Online-Präsentation ist in einem aggressiven, aber innovativen Stil gestaltet, bei dem das gesamte Spektrum der interaktiven Möglichkeiten im Internet ausgeschöpft wurde: Man kann Schablonen downloaden und damit sein eigenes Snowboard entwerfen. Der praktische Assistent hilft bei der Konfiguration der individuellen Nitro-Ausstattung. Der in hohem Maße virale E-Mail-Bereich enthält kurze, schockierende Flash-Filme. Diese werden von einem Snowboard-Fanatiker zum anderen gesendet – wie ein Virus. Dieses virale Marketing bringt die Nitro-Produkte der Zielgruppe näher, indem es seine Sprache spricht.

JAN LETH
CO-CHIEF CREATIVE OFFICER OF OGILVY NEW YORK

Jan Leth joined OgilvyInteractive (an integrated offering of OgilvyOne) in December of 1996, where he oversees all creative development for a growing list of blue-chip clients including IBM, Ameritrade, Unilever, DHL, American Express, and Kodak. OgilvyInteractive has won numerous awards including the Grand Prix at Cannes, the Grand Clio, the Grand Prix at the LIAA, Caples, Adtech, OneShow and Effies. In 2005, to reflect the growing importance of digital media in all communications channels in the Ogilvy group, Jan was promoted to be Co-Chief Creative Officer of Ogilvy New York.

Jan has chaired the OneShow, the Clios, as well as serving as a judge for the Cannes Lions, the Andy Awards, Adtech, Caples and the Echoes. He is also a member of the Board of Directors of the OneClub.

A good campaign starts with a good idea, no matter if it is online or offline. So how differentiated are creative professions that work with interactive?

Interactive creatives, good ones at least, are really only differentiated from their offline counterparts in two areas.

One is in the sets of tools they use, and the knowledge base of what is doable or could be invented in the digital world. Just as a traditional creative who must be aware of the directors, film production capabilities, etc.

The second, and bigger difference I think, is in their interest in creating opportunities for dialogue rather than a broadcast model. Like a good live performance they thrive on audience participation.

They both however have to be students of culture, past, popular and future, for it is this that makes a great idea, the technology of each media allows for the tangible expression only. Rarely is technology, whether special effects, or new digital capabilities the germ of a lasting concept that will stand the test of time.

In the end results, I suppose offline is more akin to seeing a film, and online a little more like a greatly improved performance, every experience is unique.

What has interactivity brought to the dynamics of advertising?

Again, the sensibility has changed the end result from a monologue to a dialogue. There is a clear sense of a value exchange. Give me something of value, whether it's entertainment, information or utility, and I'll pay attention, relate to, and consider your brand.

We live in an era of "the death of something"...mass media, 30 second spot, etc. Do you think that's true?

Well, I don't believe the 30 sec. spot is dead. For the right brands, and objectives, it's still hard to beat the reach and emotional capabilities of a great TV spot. But I do think the era of that particular format driving everything else is over. And I think mass media is a bit of a question mark. When you have so many options as a consumer, and it's an on demand world, we need to create much more targeted communications plans. Plans that account for the real behavior of consumers, and not ones based on what a media company has bought in bulk.

How different are interactive agencies from traditional advertising agencies?

For the most part I'd say interactive agencies are much more production focused, whereas a good traditional agency is more idea focused.

STAND ALONE INTERACTIVE AGENCIES HAVE CERTAINLY GOTTEN A LEG UP BY THEIR RELENTLESS FOCUS ON DIGITAL TECHNOLOGY, ALLOWING THEM TO INNOVATE IN MANY BRILLIANT WAYS. AT THE SAME TIME THIS HAS SEVERELY LIMITED THEM. THEY DON'T TEND TO BRING A WELL ROUNDED VIEW OF THE WORLD AND THE CONSUMER TO THE TABLE. AND WHILE I'VE JUST SAID TRADITIONAL AGENCIES MAY BE MORE ABOUT IDEAS, THE MAJORITY ARE LIVING IN COMPLETE DENIAL,

IDEAS ARE THE CORE BUSINESS

DISREGARDING THE NEWER DIGITAL PLATFORMS AS A PLACE FOR LAUNCHING THAT BIG IDEA.

Fortunately I feel like I work in a place that has embraced digital, where it has as big a seat at the table as anything else. Where the most important things are innovative insights and ideas that move our clients businesses forward regardless of platforms.

What are the 5 most used digital communications tools today?

Internet, email, mobile, text, IM.

Consumers are becoming prosumers, and at the same time adavoiders, etc. How can interactive help to build brands?

Interactive can help build brands by being where consumers are, (namely online a lot,) in meaningful, relevant ways. If your brand stands for innovation let's say, then demonstrate that innovation, don't just tell me about it. This where interactive can really leapfrog traditional media, by tangible demonstration, or enabling the consumer to experience your brand.

In interactive agencies, results can be tracked with more precision, so the pressure is bigger. How can that pressure help to create more creative campaigns?

First of all you have to make sure there is an agreed upon set of metrics for which you are tracking.

Most online advertising has been treated like DM, judged on click rates. But interactive media is probably the only medium that is equally valid for Brand awareness building, consideration, and the Direct Marketing lead generation. If you are measuring the wrong thing, bad things happen.

But you can use tracking to do better creative work. The problem is, too few people actually test properly. But better creative work ALWAYS performs better! And if you make tests you can prove it.

What are the countries producing the best interactive works?

Brazil, USA, UK, Japan, Sweden.

Are ads on the Internet more appealing than on paper or on TV? Or must they be combined with search-results and other traced parameters to be more effective?

Most ads, online or off are unappealing. Advertising as an industry has gotten away with this because we weren't yet in a consumer controlled world. But we are now, and uninspired marketing, lacking insight and differentiation will begin to fail miserably. Creativity has never been more critical.

YOU CAN CERTAINLY IMPROVE THE EFFECTIVENESS OF ONLINE ADS WITH BEHAVIORAL DATA. AND IT DOES GET QUITE INTERESTING WHEN YOU CAN CUSTOMIZE YOUR CREATIVE CONTEXTUALLY. IT SIMPLY

BECOMES A COST ISSUE AS TO WHETHER THE IMPROVEMENT IS WORTH THE COST.

Banners can be quite annoying and sites even have "intrusion rates" to define how "annoying" they can allow themselves to be. Google lead the way for not using banners. How do you deal with "ad avoidance"?

Relevance, and creativity. I'm sounding a bit repetitive here, but give the consumer something of value. Then you may even leverage another great thing about digital which is the peer-to-peer networking dynamic, where consumers receive the message not from an advertisement but from their trusted friends.

Do you think that the next generation (that today are small kids) are going to behave differently from the 25s + today? What differences might there be?

There will no doubt be some surprises we haven't thought of, or can even predict. But they'll certainly be an even more "always on, always connected" generation that controls what and when they see it. It's a generation that cannot comprehend life before Playstation, and is perfectly at ease in that virtual environment, which will impact other media dramatically. And this will be a global trend as technology uptakes even out worldwide.

Most of the online space for 2006 is already sold out, but still, online accounts for a small

I THINK IT'S ONLY JUST BEGUN TO EXPLODE. WE'VE ONLY BEGUN TO SEE THE CREATIVE POTENTIAL OF THE MEDIUM.

sum in the advertising budget. What would you tell companies to pay attention to?

Don't prejudge the impact your campaign can have by the media budget, and don't segregate your media buying from your strategy and creative work. I think one of the greatest tragedies in the advertising industry was the segregation of media from the creative process. This happened when mass media was still just that, mass. And media companies could increase efficiencies and profit by aggregating and buying in bulk. Well, I don't think bulk buying works in the new fragmented world.

WE HAVE RECENTLY REINTEGRATED OUR DIGITAL MEDIA INTO THE AGENCY, TO WORK AS ONE WITH CREATIVES IN DEVELOPING CAMPAIGNS IDEAS. WE CAN INNOVATE MUCH MORE NIMBLY AND DEVELOP CREATIVE WORK THAT WAS IMPOSSIBLE WHEN THE PROCESSES WERE SEPARATE.

Following on from the previous questions, what problems will Interactive agencies face when online space is almost sold out? Are agencies now going to focus on mobile, PDAs, etc?

A lot of these interactive-only agencies are already developing campaigns that extend across mobile, blogs, IM and assorted other digital venues. In essence though they will increasingly be in the content business, as they will have to generate creative, appealing content that will not only catch people's attention as "advertising" but will attract users to come to them or be referred to them by their peers. But real people in the real world still do things that are not on their computer. And the challenge for stand alone interactive shops will be in integrating their concepts across multiple consumer touchpoints. When you do that you have the killer app.

What is your perspective for interactive

advertising in the next 5 years.

I think it's only just begun to explode. We've only begun to see the creative potential of the medium. And I believe we'll see tremendous growth, with the only thing holding us down being the lack of enough talent, in an industry that has so little history as yet.

Jan Leth rejoint OgilvyInteractive (un service intégré de OgilvyOne) en décembre 1996, où il supervise la création pour le compte d'une longue liste de solides clients comme IBM, Ameritrade, Unilever, DHL, American Express et Kodak. OgilvyInteractive a reçu de nombreuses récompenses dont le premier prix aux Lions de Cannes, aux Clio Awards, aux LIAA, aux Caples, à l'Adtech, au OneShow et aux Effie Awards. En 2005, suite à l'importance croissante du secteur Internet dans les réseaux de communication du groupe Ogilvy, Jan a été promu co-directeur de création de Ogilvy New York.

Jan a siégé au OneShow, aux Clio Awards, et a été membre du jury aux Lions de Cannes, aux Andy Awards, à l'Adtech, aux Caples et aux Echoe Awards. Il siège aussi au conseil de direction du OneClub.

Une bonne campagne naît d'une bonne idée, que ce soit en ligne ou hors ligne. Qu'est-ce qui caractérise les créatifs qui travaillent dans l'interactif ?

Les créatifs qui travaillent dans l'interactif, les bons du moins, se distinguent de leurs homologues hors ligne par deux aspects. Le premier concerne les outils qu'ils utilisent, et la connaissance de base de ce qui est réalisable ou peut être inventé dans l'univers numérique. Tout comme un créatif traditionnel doit prendre en compte les réalisateurs, les capacités de production audiovisuelle et autres. Le deuxième aspect, qui est je crois le plus important, est leur désir de favoriser des occasions de dialogue, plutôt qu'un modèle de simple diffusion. Comme dans le spectacle vivant, ils se nourrissent

de la participation du public. Ils doivent néanmoins posséder des notions de culture populaire, passée et présente, car c'est la base d'un bon concept, et la technologie propre à chaque média n'est qu'une passerelle d'expression. Il est rare que la technologie, qu'il s'agisse d'effets spéciaux ou de nouvelles fonctionnalités numériques soit à l'origine d'un concept capable de résister à l'épreuve du temps. Au final, je suppose que la communication hors ligne est comparable au fait de regarder un film, tandis que la publicité en ligne procède d'une représentation améliorée, où chaque expérience est unique.

Qu'a apporté l'interactivité à la dynamique de la publicité ?

Là encore, la sensibilité a modifié le résultat final en passant d'un monologue à un dialogue. Il y a une notion évidente d'échange de valeur. Donnez-moi de la distraction, des informations ou des services, et je prêterai attention à votre marque et son produit.

Nous vivons une époque de fin de règne... celui des mass media, du spot de 30 secondes... Qu'en pensez-vous ?

Ma foi, je ne pense pas que le spot de 30 secondes soit mort. Pour certaines marques, certains objectifs, il est encore difficile de surpasser la portée et l'impact émotionnel d'un bon spot télé. Mais je crois en revanche que la prépondérance de ce format est terminée. Quant aux mass media, c'est un peu l'incertitude. Quant le consommateur a une multiplicité de choix, que c'est un univers à la demande, c'est à nous de concevoir des plans de communication plus ciblés. Des plans qui tiennent compte du comportement réel du consommateur, et non du budget média de l'annonceur.

Qu'est-ce qui distingue les agences interactives des agences traditionnelles ?

Pour l'essentiel, je dirais que les agences interactives sont plus axées sur la production, tandis qu'une bonne agence traditionnelle se focalise sur le concept.

JE PENSE QU'ELLE EST JUSTE EN TRAIN D'EXPLOSER. NOUS DÉCOUVRONS ENCORE LE POTENTIEL CRÉATIF DE CE MÉDIUM.

LES AGENCES EXCLUSIVEMENT INTERACTIVES SE SONT APPUYÉES SANS RELÂCHE SUR LES AVANCÉES DE LA TECHNOLOGIE NUMÉRIQUE, CE QUI LEUR A PERMIS D'INNOVER SOUS DE NOMBREUX ASPECTS. EN MÊME TEMPS, CELA LES A SÉVÈREMENT LIMITÉES. ELLES ONT TENDANCE À NÉGLIGER LA VISION GLOBALE DU MONDE ET DU CONSOMMATEUR. BIEN QUE J'AI DÉCLARÉ QUE LES AGENCES TRADITIONNELLES SOIENT PLUS AXÉES SUR LES IDÉES, LA MAJORITÉ VIT DANS UN DÉNI TOTAL, ET DÉDAIGNENT LES NOUVELLES PLATEFORMES NUMÉRIQUES POUR LANCER LEURS GRANDES IDÉES.

J'ai la chance de travailler dans une structure qui a intégré le numérique, et cette technologie jouit chez nous d'une place équitable. L'essentiel est d'innover dans les idées et les concepts afin de développer l'activité de nos clients, et cela quelle que soit la plateforme choisie.

Quels sont les cinq outils de communication électronique les plus utilisés aujourd'hui ?

Internet, les e-mails, les téléphones portables, les textos et les MMS.

Les consommateurs sont devenus de plus en plus avertis, et certains rejettent la publicité. En quoi la publicité interactive peut-elle contribuer à la promotion d'une marque ?

La publicité interactive peut promouvoir les marques en étant présente là où se trouvent les consommateurs (à savoir surtout sur le Net), de façon éloquente et pertinente. Si par exemple votre marque symbolise l'innovation, alors faites-en la démonstration, ne vous contentez pas d'en parler. C'est là que la publicité interactive peut vraiment surpasser les mé-

dias traditionnels, dans la démonstration tangible, en permettant au consommateur de faire l'expérience de la marque.

Dans les agences interactives, les résultats peuvent être évalués avec plus de précision, ce qui augmente la pression. Cette pression entraîne-t-elle plus de créativité ?

Il faut tout d'abord s'accorder sur les paramètres qu'on cherche à mesurer. La plupart des publicités en ligne sont traitées comme du marketing direct, en jugeant le nombre de clics. Mais la e-publicité est sans doute la seule à être valable tant au niveau de la visibilité, de la notoriété, que du résultat des ventes. Si l'on mesure les mauvaises variables, c'est un désastre.

LES ANALYSES PEUVENT EFFECTIVEMENT AMÉLIORER LA CRÉATIVITÉ. L'ENNUI, C'EST QUE TRÈS PEU DE GENS S'EN SERVENT CORRECTEMENT. UNE BONNE CRÉATION ENTRAÎNE TOUJOURS DE MEILLEURS PERFORMANCES. IL SUFFIT DE SAVOIR LES MESURER POUR LE PROUVER.

Quels sont les pays qui produisent les meilleurs travaux interactifs ?

Le Brésil, les Etats-Unis, la Grande-Bretagne, le Japon et la Suède.

La publicité sur Internet est-elle plus attrayante que dans la presse ou à la télévision ? Ou bien doit-on croiser les études de résultats et d'autres paramètres afin d'être plus efficace ?

La plupart des publicités, en ligne ou hors ligne, manquent d'attrait. L'industrie publicitaire s'en est bien sortie jusqu'ici car nous n'étions pas dans un monde contrôlé par le consommateur. Mais c'est le cas aujourd'hui, et le marketing qui man-

que d'inspiration et de différenciation sera bientôt voué à l'échec. La créativité n'a jamais été aussi primordiale.

On peut certainement améliorer l'impact de la e-publicité grâce à des études socioéconomiques du public ciblé. Et personnaliser la création de façon contextuelle est une chose passionnante. Reste à décider si le bénéfice recherché mérite un tel investissement.

Les bandeaux publicitaires peuvent être très agaçants et certains sites mesurent même le niveau d'intrusion acceptable afin de définir un plafond à ne pas dépasser. Google a d'ailleurs été le premier à renoncer aux bandeaux. Comment gérez-vous le réflexe anti-pub ?

Par la créativité et la pertinence. J'ai l'air de me répéter, mais il faut offrir de la qualité au consommateur. On peut aussi compter sur un autre aspect positif du format en ligne, qui est le réseau P2P, grâce auquel les internautes reçoivent des messages de leurs amis, plutôt que de l'annonceur.

Pensez-vous que la prochaine génération (les enfants d'aujourd'hui) se comportera différemment des jeunes de plus de 25 ans ? Et de quelle façon ?

Nous aurons forcément des surprises, des choses que nous n'aurons pas prévues. Mais la prochaine génération sera certainement encore plus souvent connectée, elle contrôlera ce qu'elle veut voir, et à quel moment. C'est une génération qui n'envisage pas la vie avant l'arrivée de la PlayStation, et qui est parfaitement à l'aise dans l'environnement virtuel, ce qui aura un énorme impact sur d'autres médias. Et cette tendance se généralisera quand le monde entier aura accès aux nouvelles technologies.

L'essentiel de l'espace publicitaire en ligne est déjà vendu pour l'année 2006, et néanmoins, le budget Internet n'est qu'une infime partie du budget publicitaire global. Quels conseils donneriez-vous aux sociétés ?

ICH GLAUBE, JETZT GEHT ES ERST SO RICHTIG LOS. WIR HABEN GERADE ERST DAS KREATIVE POTENZIAL DES MEDIUMS ERKANNT.

Ne préjugez pas de l'impact de votre campagne par rapport au coût du média, et ne distinguez pas votre achat d'espace de votre stratégie et de vos objectifs.

Je pense qu'un des plus grands drames que connaît l'industrie publicitaire est la ségrégation du média et du processus créatif. Cela remonte à l'époque où les mass media étaient justement cela : massives. Les annonceurs achetaient de l'espace en masse afin d'augmenter le profit et l'efficacité. Je ne pense pas que cette stratégie soit valable dans l'univers actuel plus fragmenté.

NOUS AVONS RÉCEMMENT INTÉGRÉ LE SECTEUR INTERNET AU SEIN DE L'AGENCE, AFIN DE TRAVAILLER EN CONCERTATION AVEC LES CRÉATIFS AU DÉVELOPPEMENT DES IDÉES DE CAMPAGNE. NOUS POUVONS AINSI INNOVER DE FAÇON PLUS SOUPLE, CE QUI ÉTAIT IMPOSSIBLE QUAND LES PROCESSUS ÉTAIENT SÉPARÉS.

En rapport aux questions précédentes, quels problèmes vont rencontrer les agences interactives quand l'espace en ligne sera pratiquement tout vendu ? Les agences se tourneront-elles vers les mobiles, les PDA et autres ?

Beaucoup d'agences exclusivement interactives conçoivent déjà des campagnes adaptées aux portables, aux blogs, aux messageries et autres canaux numériques. Cependant, par nature, elles vont s'axer de plus en plus sur le contenu du message, car elles devront générer des concepts attrayants et novateurs pour attirer l'attention non seulement en tant que publicité, mais inciter les consommateurs à aller vers eux, et à relayer l'information à leur entourage.

Mais les vrais gens dans la vraie vie font encore des choses en dehors de leur ordinateur. Et le défi pour les sociétés dédiées au commerce en ligne sera de décliner leurs concepts à travers des canaux de diffusion multiples. Les chances de réussite sont à ce prix.

Quelles sont vos prévisions pour la publicité interactive dans les cinq prochaines années ?

Je pense qu'elle est juste en train d'exploser. Nous découvrons encore le potentiel créatif de ce médium. Nous allons assister à une croissance extraordinaire, la seule chose qui nous freinera sera la pénurie de talents, car cette industrie a peu de passé derrière elle.

Jan Leth begann im Dezember 1996, bei OgilvyInteractive (eine Tochterfirma von OgilvyOne) zu arbeiten, wo er die gesamte kreative Entwicklung für einen wachsenden Stamm von erstklassigen Kunden leitet, darunter IBM, Ameritrade, Unilever, DHL, American Express und Kodak. OgilvyInteractive gewann zahlreiche Auszeichnungen, unter anderem den Grand Prix von Cannes, den Grand Clio, den Grand Prix von LIAA, Caples, Adtech, OneShow und Effies. 2005 wuchs die Bedeutung der digitalen Medien in allen Kommunikationskanälen der Ogilvy-Gruppe, und Jan Leth wurde zum Co-Kreativdirektor von Ogilvy New York befördert. Er saß der OneShow und Clios bei und war Mitglied der Jury für die Cannes Lions, die Andy Awards, Adtech, Caples und den Echos. Außerdem ist er Vorstandsmitglied des OneClubs.

Eine gute Kampagne beginnt mit einer guten Idee, egal, ob online oder offline. Was aber zeichnet kreative Berufe aus, in denen man interaktiv arbeitet?

Kreative, die im interaktiven Bereich tätig sind, zumindest die guten, unterscheiden sich von ihren Kollegen aus dem Offline-Bereich in zwei Dingen.

ZUM EINEN IN DEN WERKZEUGEN, DIE SIE VERWENDEN, UND

DEM GRUNDWISSEN DARÜBER, WAS IN DER DIGITALEN WELT MÖGLICH IST ODER ERFUNDEN WERDEN KÖNNTE. WIE EIN „TRADITIONELLER" KREATIVER AUCH MUSS MAN SICH DER REGISSEURE, DER MÖGLICHKEITEN DER FILMPRODUKTION ETC. BEWUSST SEIN. ZUM ANDEREN, UND DAS IST DER GRÖSSERE UNTERSCHIED, IN IHRER ABSICHT, GELEGENHEITEN ZUM DIALOG ZU SCHAFFEN STATT EINES SENDEMODELLS. WIE BEI EINER GUTEN LIVE-AUFFÜHRUNG HÄNGT IHR ERFOLG VON DER MITWIRKUNG DES PUBLIKUMS AB.

Beide müssen allerdings die vergangene, gegenwärtige und zukünftige Kultur studieren, denn erst dadurch entsteht eine gute Idee; die Technologie des jeweiligen Mediums bestimmt nur den greifbaren Ausdruck. Technologie – ob durch Spezialeffekte oder neue digitale Möglichkeiten – ist selten der Kern eines langlebigen Konzeptes, das den Test der Zeit besteht.

Letztlich ähnelt offline eher dem Anschauen eines Films, während online einer großartigen, verbesserten Aufführung gleichkommt – alle Erfahrungen sind einzigartig.

Wie hat Interaktivität die Dynamik der Werbung verändert?

Das Endergebnis wurde von einem Monolog in einen Dialog verwandelt. Es herrscht ein deutliches Gefühl der Werteverschiebung. Geben Sie mir etwas Wertvolles – sei es Unterhaltung, Information oder etwas Nützliches –, und ich werde Ihrer Marke Aufmerksamkeit schenken, einen Bezug zu ihr herstellen und sie in Erwägung ziehen.

Wir leben in einer Ära des „Ende von etwas" ... von Massenmedien, dem 30-Sekunden-Spot etc. Glauben Sie, das stimmt?

Nun, ich glaube nicht, dass der 30-Sekunden-Spot tot ist. Für die richtigen Marken und Ziele ist es immer noch schwierig, die Reichweite und emotionalen Kapazitäten eines guten Fernsehspots zu übertreffen. Aber ich glaube, die Ära eines speziellen Formates, das alles andere bestimmt, ist vorbei. Ich denke, Massenmedien sind eine Art Fragezeichen. Sie haben als Verbraucher so viele Möglichkeiten in einer „On-Demand"-Welt, dass unsere Kommunikationspläne viel zielgerichteter sein müssen. Sie müssen dem wirklichen Kundenverhalten gerecht werden und dürfen nicht darauf basieren, was ein Medienunternehmen groß eingekauft hat.

Wie unterscheiden sich interaktive Agenturen von traditionellen Werbeagenturen?

Vor allem konzentrieren sich interaktive Agenturen viel mehr auf die Produktion, die traditionellen eher auf die Idee.
Eigenständige Interaktivagenturen haben sicherlich einen Vorteil dadurch, dass sie sich ausschließlich auf die digitale Technologie konzentrieren, die ihnen viele brillante Möglichkeiten zu Innovationen bietet. Gleichzeitig schränkt sie sie enorm ein. Meist bringen sie keine runde Sicht auf die Welt und die Kunden zustande.
Obwohl ich gerade sagte, dass sich traditionelle Agenturen mehr mit einer Idee befassen, lehnt die Mehrheit von ihnen die neueren digitalen Plattformen als Ort der Einführung dieser großen Idee ab.
Glücklicherweise arbeite ich an einem Ort, der die digitale Welt begrüßt, die an unserem Tisch einen gleichwertigen, wichtigen Platz hat. Wo die wichtigsten Dinge innovative Einsichten und Ideen sind, die die Unternehmen unserer Kunden weiterbringen – egal, auf welcher Plattform.

Was sind heutzutage die 5 meistverwendeten Kommunikationsmittel?

Internet, E-Mail, Handys, SMS, Interaktives Marketing.

Aus Verbrauchern werden „Prosumer" und gleichzeitig Werbevermeider etc. Wie kann

Interaktivität zur Markenbildung beitragen?

Indem sie da ist, wo die Verbraucher sind (hauptsächlich online), und zwar auf bedeutsame, relevante Weise. Steht Ihre Marke beispielsweise für Innovation, dann demonstrieren Sie diese Innovation, erzählen Sie mir nicht einfach nur davon. Hier kann Interaktivität die traditionellen Medien wirklich überholen: durch greifbare Demonstration, oder indem der Konsument die Marke erleben kann.

In interaktiven Agenturen können Ergebnisse präziser verfolgt werden, wodurch sich der Druck erhöht. Wie kann dieser Druck die Kreativität von Kampagnen steigern?

Zuerst müssen Sie sicherstellen, dass man sich auf eine Messweise geeinigt hat, mit der man das Tracking betreibt. Der Großteil der Online-Werbung wurde wie Direct Marketing gehandhabt: Man zählte die Klicks. Aber Interaktivität ist wahrscheinlich das einzige Medium, das gleichermaßen gültig ist für die Bildung des Markenbewusstseins, Kaufentscheidung und Direktvertrieb. Messen Sie das Falsche, passieren schlimme Dinge. Aber Sie können das Tracking für bessere Kreativität verwenden. Das Problem ist, dass nur wenige Leute richtig testen können. Aber bessere Kreativität funktioniert auch IMMER besser! Und wenn Sie testen, können Sie dies beweisen.

Welche Länder produzieren die besten interaktiven Arbeiten?

Brasilien, USA, Großbritannien, Japan und Schweden.

Sind Anzeigen im Internet ansprechender als auf Papier oder im Fernsehen? Oder müssen sie mit Umfrageergebnissen und anderen Parametern kombiniert werden, um effektiver zu sein?

Die meisten Anzeigen, ob online oder offline, sind nicht ansprechend. Werbung ist eine Branche, die bisher damit durchkam, weil wir nicht in einer vom Verbraucher kontrollierten Welt lebten. Aber wir tun

es jetzt, und fantasieloses Marketing, mangelnde Einsicht und Differenzierung werden kläglich versagen. Kreativität wurde nie kritischer betrachtet.

SIE KÖNNEN DIE EFFEKTIVITÄT VON ONLINE-ANZEIGEN DURCH VERHALTENSDATEN SICHERLICH VERBESSERN. UND ES WIRD INTERESSANT, WENN SIE IHRE KREATIVITÄT DEN KONTEXTEN ANPASSEN. ES WIRD EINFACH EINE FRAGE DER KOSTEN SEIN, OB DIE VERBESSERUNG ES WERT IST, UMGESETZT ZU WERDEN.

Banner können nerven, und einige Seiten haben sogar „Störraten", um zu definieren, wie weit sie es sich erlauben können, zu nerven. Google benutzte als erstes keine Banner mehr. Wie kann man mit „Werbevermeidung" umgehen?

Durch Relevanz und Kreativität. Ich wiederhole mich, aber bieten Sie dem Verbraucher etwas Wertvolles. Dann können Sie eine weitere gute Eigenschaft der digitalen Medien nutzen: die Netzwerk-Dynamik, innerhalb derer die Konsumenten eine Botschaft nicht durch Werbung, sondern von ihren Freunden erhalten, denen sie vertrauen.

Glauben Sie, dass sich die nächste Generation (die heute Kleinkinder sind) anders als die heute 25+-Jährigen verhalten wird? Worin könnten die Unterschiede bestehen?

Es wird zweifellos einige Überraschungen geben, an die wir nicht gedacht haben oder die wir nicht einmal vorhersagen können. Aber es wird mit Sicherheit eine „Immer da, immer verbunden"-Generation sein, die bestimmt, was sie wann sieht. Eine Generation, die das Leben vor Erfindung der Playstation nicht nachvollziehen kann und sich mit Leichtigkeit in der virtuellen Umgebung bewegt, deren Wirkung auf andere Medien enorm sein wird. Und dies wird der globale Trend sein, wenn sich die technologischen

Fortschritte weltweit angleichen.

Der Großteil der Online-Marktfläche ist für 2006 schon verkauft, aber innerhalb des Werbebudgets hat Online-Werbung nur einen geringen Stellenwert. Was raten Sie Unternehmen, worauf sie achten sollen?

Verurteilen Sie nicht im Voraus die Auswirkung, die Ihre Kampagne auf das Medienbudget haben kann, und isolieren Sie Ihren Medienkauf nicht von Ihrer Strategie und Kreativität.

Ich glaube, eine der größten Tragödien in der Werbebranche war die Isolation der Medien vom kreativen Prozess. Dies geschah, als Massenmedien nur eins waren: Masse. Medienunternehmen konnten Effizienz und Profit erhöhen, indem sie kumulieren und in Massen einkauften. Nun, ich glaube nicht, dass dies in der neuen fragmentarischen Welt funktioniert.

WIR HABEN UNSERE DIGITALEN MEDIEN KÜRZLICH IN DIE AGENTUR INTEGRIERT, UM BEI DER ENTWICKLUNG VON IDEEN FÜR KAMPAGNEN ALS EINHEIT ZU ARBEITEN. WIR KÖNNEN VIEL SCHNELLER NEUERUNGEN VORNEHMEN UND KREATIV ENTWICKELN, ALS ES VOR DER TRENNUNG DER PROZESSE MÖGLICH WAR.

Um auf die vorherige Frage zurückzukommen: Welche Probleme kommen auf Interaktivagenturen zu, wenn die Online-Marktfläche fast ausverkauft ist? Konzentrieren sie sich nun auf Handys, PDAs etc.?

Die meisten dieser Agenturen entwickeln schon Kampagnen, die sich auf Handys, Blogs, Interaktives Marketing und andere gemischte digitale Anwendungen erstrecken. Im Wesentlichen werden sie sich jedoch mehr und mehr den Inhalten zuwenden, da sie kreative, ansprechende Inhalte erzeu-

gen müssen, die nicht nur als „Werbung" Interesse wecken, sondern auch bewirken, dass die Benutzer davon angezogen oder sie von Freunden darauf aufmerksam gemacht werden. Aber reale Menschen in der realen Welt tun immer noch Dinge, die in keinem Zusammenhang mit ihrem Computer stehen. Und die Herausforderung für eigenständige interaktive Shops wird darin bestehen, ihre Konzepte in multiple Verbraucher-Bezugspunkte zu integrieren. Wenn sie das tun, werden sie den gewünschten Erfolg haben.

Was ist Ihre Vorhersage für interaktive Werbung in den nächsten 5 Jahren?

Ich glaube, jetzt geht es erst so richtig los. Wir haben gerade erst das kreative Potenzial des Mediums erkannt. Wir werden vermutlich ein riesiges Wachstum sehen – das einzige, was uns am Boden hält, ist der Mangel an kreativen Talenten in einer Branche, die eine so kurze Geschichte hat.

I DON'T BELIEVE THE 30 SEC. SPOT IS DEAD. FOR THE RIGHT BRANDS, AND OBJECTIVES, IT'S STILL HARD TO BEAT THE REACH AND EMOTIONAL CAPABILITIES OF A GREAT TV SPOT.

MA FOI, JE NE PENSE PAS QUE LE SPOT DE 30 SECONDES SOIT MORT. POUR CERTAINES MARQUES, CERTAINS OBJECTIFS, IL EST ENCORE DIFFICILE DE SURPASSER LA PORTÉE ET L'IMPACT ÉMOTIONNEL D'UN BON SPOT TÉLÉ.

NUN, ICH GLAUBE NICHT, DASS DER 30-SEKUNDEN-SPOT TOT IST. FÜR DIE RICHTIGEN MARKEN UND ZIELE IST ES IMMER NOCH SCHWIERIG, DIE REICHWEITE UND EMOTIONALEN KAPAZITÄTEN EINES GUTEN FERNSEHSPOTS ZU ÜBERTREFFEN.

006

TECHNOLOGY & GAMES

FEATURED ON THE DVD **CAMPAIGN:** Olympus Viral Movies Microsite. **PRODUCT:** Olympus Digital Cameras. **YEAR:** 2005. **AGENCY:** Neue Digitale <www.neue-digitale.de>. **PRODUCTION TIME:** April 2005 – June 2005.
CREATIVE TEAM: Olaf Czeschner, Rolf Borcherding, André Bourguignon. **PROGRAMMER:** Heiko Schweikhardt. **TECH ASPECTS:** All movie characters animated in Macromedia Flash with embedded sound and flash movies.
MEDIA CIRCULATED: Internet. **AWARDS:** Epica Awards (Silver).

CONCEPT: Interpretation of the digital photography campaign "What you choose to remember" within its own microsite and the integration of the viral web films created for it. The newly developed campaign focuses on the quirks of digital photography: three spots which will start online and be spread virally show digital artefacts – such as cropped tourists, a blurry boy or a distorted dog – which act as strangely likeable characters in these films. In keeping with the campaign message, the consumer is asked how they would like to deal with these digital artefacts: "Would you keep a distorted dog or would you delete it?" On the start page a collage of pictures document memories and stories to accompany the photos appear on mouseover. By clicking on any of the main characters which are integrated into this collage the user gets transported to a page where the character lives. This is a kind of intermediate world where the character tries to avoid being deleted by the user. Here the user can interact with the characters, learn about them and watch their web film. At the end of each film the user can playfully try to delete the character. The character runs away from the mouse pointer and tries to hide. After successfully deleting the picture, the user has the chance to send the film to a friend as an E-Card, or to download it in order to send it by e-mail to a larger group of people. **RESULTS:** The campaign idea should be centred on the characters from the films, and extended through interaction with these characters. The Olympus brand should be emotionally loaded and positioned online. The idiosyncratic viral films work especially well on the web. The disturbingly amusing effect of the films is effectively communicated and expanded via the microsite. Interpretation of the digital photography campaign "What you choose to remember" within its own microsite and the integration of the viral web films created for it.

CONCEPT: Déclinaison de la campagne « Choisissez vos souvenirs » pour la marque Olympus au sein de son micro-site, intégrant des films interactifs conçus pour l'occasion. La nouvelle campagne se focalise sur les bizarreries de la photographie numérique, grâce à trois spots en ligne destinés à une communication virale. Ils présentent des artefacts numériques, des gens à qui il manque la tête, un enfant flou, un chien déformé, qui deviennent des personnages étrangement sympathiques. Dans l'esprit de la campagne, le message demande au consommateur ce qu'il ferait de ces artefacts : « Vous gardez la photo du chien déformé ou vous l'effacez ? » Sur la page d'accueil, un collage de photos évocatrices de souvenirs s'anime quand on fait glisser la souris sur les images. En cliquant sur l'un des sujets du collage, l'internaute est envoyé sur une autre page où le personnage s'anime. C'est une espèce d'univers intermédiaire où le personnage va essayer d'éviter d'être effacé.

Le visiteur peut interagir avec lui, apprendre à le connaître et visionner son film. A la fin de chaque film, l'internaute essaie d'effacer le personnage. Celui-ci tente d'échapper au curseur et essaie de se cacher. Une fois qu'on a réussi à effacer l'image, on peut envoyer le film à un ami sous forme de carte électronique, ou bien le télécharger pour faire un envoi groupé. **RÉSULTATS :** La campagne est centrée autour des personnages des films, et encourage l'interaction avec le visiteur. La marque Olympus se positionne en ligne en misant sur l'impact émotionnel. Les petits films singuliers fonctionnent extrêmement bien sur Internet. L'effet amusant et dérangeant est bien communiqué et s'étend au micro-site. Le slogan « Choisissez vos souvenirs » a été parfaitement illustré dans les films viraux réalisés spécialement pour le micro-site.

KONZEPT: Interpretation der digitalen Fotokampagne „What you choose to remember" innerhalb einer eigenen Microsite, und die Integration des viralen Webfilms, der dafür erstellt wurde. Die neu entwickelte Kampagne konzentriert sich auf die Eigenarten digitaler Fotografie: Drei Spots, die sich online und viral verbreiten, zeigen digitale Artefakte wie abgeschnittene Touristen, einen unscharfen Jungen oder einen verzerrten Hund, die wie merkwürdig sympathische Figuren in diesen Filmen agieren. Gemäß der Kampagnenbotschaft wird der Kunde gefragt, wie er mit solchen digitalen Artefakten umgehen würde: „Würden Sie einen verzerrten Hund behalten oder löschen?" Auf der Startseite dokumentiert eine Collage Erinnerungen und Geschichten, die erscheinen, wenn man mit der Maus über die Fotos fährt. Klickt man auf eine der Hauptfiguren, gelangt der Benutzer auf eine Seite, wo die Figur lebt. Dies ist eine Art unmittelbare Welt, wo die Figur versucht, zu vermeiden, dass der Benutzer sie löscht. Der Benutzer kann hier mit den Figuren interagieren, etwas über sie erfahren und ihren Webfilm sehen. Am Ende eines jeden Films kann man spielerisch versuchen, die Figur zu löschen. Sie rennt vor dem Mauszeiger davon und versucht, sich zu verstecken. Hat der Benutzer das Bild erfolgreich gelöscht, kann er den Film einem Freund als E-Card senden oder ihn downloaden, um ihn per E-Mail an eine Gruppe von Leuten zu senden. **ERGEBNISSE:** Die Idee der Kampagne sollte sich um die Filmfiguren zentrieren und durch Interaktion mit ihnen erweitert werden. Die Marke Olympus sollte emotional besetzt und online positioniert werden. Die eigenwilligen Filme funktionieren im Web besonders gut. Die verstörend amüsierende Wirkung des Films wird durch die Microsite effektiv kommuniziert und ausgeweitet: die Interpretation der digitalen Fotokampagne „What you choose to remember" innerhalb einer eigenen Microsite und die Integration viraler Webfilme, die dafür entwickelt wurden.

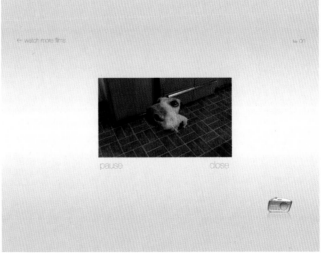

CAMPAIGN: Bang & Olufsen. **YEAR:** 2002. **AGENCY:** Large <www.largedesign.com>. **PRODUCTION TIME:** 40 weeks. **COST IN HOURS OF WORK:** 1,600 hours **CREATIVE TEAM:** Lars Hemming Jorgensen, Jim Boulton.
PROGRAMMER: Jesper Lycke. **TECH ASPECTS:** Macromedia Flash, audio. **MEDIA CIRCULATED:** The world most beautiful – Financial Times.

CONCEPT: Bang & Olufsen are magical, but this is very difficult to communicate unless you experience them in real life. The online campaigns gave users a greater insight into the products and drove them directly into the B&O stores. **RESULTS:** The campaign drove 700 a month into B&O stores, 8% spent £2,800 on average. This resulted in an increase in annual turnover by almost £2 million.

CONCEPT : Les produits Bang & Olufsen sont magiques, mais c'est difficile à illustrer, il vaut mieux en faire l'expérience soi-même. La campagne en ligne a offert aux usagers un meilleur aperçu des produits et les a attirés dans les boutiques de la marque. **RÉSULTATS :**

La campagne a amené 700 personnes par mois dans les boutiques B&O, 8% d'entre elles ont dépensé en moyenne 2 888 livres. Le volume annuel des transactions a augmenté de presque 2 millions de livres.

KONZEPT: Bang & Olufsen sind magisch, aber schwierig zu kommunizieren, so lange man sie nicht im realen Leben erfährt. Die Online-Kampagnen gaben Benutzern eine größere Einsicht in die Produkte und lenkten sie direkt zu den B&O-Geschäften. **ERGEBNISSE:** Die Kampagne führte 700 Personen pro Monat in B&O-Geschäfte, 8% gaben durchschnittlich £2 800 aus. Dies führte zu einem Anstieg des Jahresumsatzes von fast £2 Millionen.

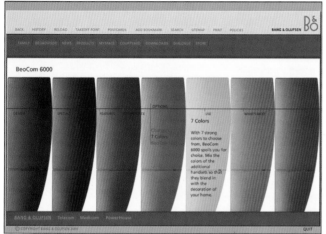

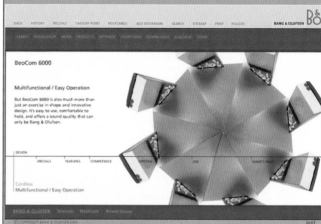

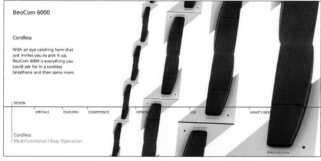

CAMPAIGN: PinkyKoya (Tamagocchi Girl). **PRODUCT:** PinkyKoya. **YEAR:** 2005. **AGENCY:** Rice5 <www.rice5.com>. **PRODUCTION TIME:** 3 months. **CREATIVE TEAM:** Snowman Tsang. **PROGRAMMER:** Mike Lee.
TECH ASPECTS: Macromedia Flash, Macromedia Flash Video (FLV), Macromedia Firework, Adobe Photoshop, Adobe After Effects.

CONCEPT: It's a video base online game. Your task is, simply please the girl inside the pinky small house, answering questions, playing mini games with her and finally, she will give you a grade on how close the relation among you and her. To make it more realistic, we build a blog in Yahoo HK in order to draw people attention, and play the game. **RESULTS:** More than 180,000 people visited the blog.

CONCEPT: Jeu vidéo en ligne. La mission est simple, il suffit de faire plaisir à la fille à l'intérieur de la petite maison rose, en répondant à ses questions, en jouant avec elle, et finalement, elle vous donne une note qui reflète l'intimité de votre relation. Pour ajouter au réalisme, nous avons créé un blog sur Yahoo HK afin d'attirer l'attention du public, et l'inviter à jouer. **RÉSULTATS :** Plus de 180 000 internautes ont visité le blog.

KONZEPT: Ein Online-Spiel, das auf Video basiert. Man muss das Mädchen in dem kleinen rosa Haus zufrieden stellen, ihm Fragen stellen, mit ihm spielen, bis es schließlich bewertet, wie eng die Beziehung ist. Um es realistischer zu gestalten, errichteten wir einen Blog in Yahoo HK, um die Aufmerksamkeit der Leute zu wecken, damit sie das Spiel spielten. **ERGEBNIS:** Über 180 000 Personen besuchten den Blog.

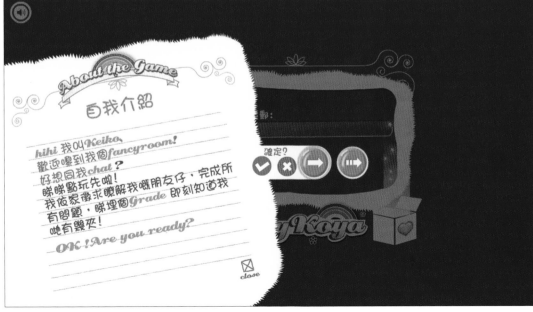

FEATURED ON THE DVD **CAMPAIGN:** IBM Help Desk. **PRODUCT:** IBM Help Desk. **YEAR:** 2005. **AGENCY:** OgilvyOne <www.ogilvyone.com>. **PRODUCTION TIME:** 6 Weeks. **CREATIVE TEAM:** Greg Kaplan, Simon Foster, Al Green, Amy Hodgins, Tom Newsom. **ACCOUNT TEAM:** Scot Beck, Andrew Fair, Mila Babrikova, Nedim Aruz. **PROGRAMMER:** Todd Yard, Tim Murray, Filips Baumanis. **TECH ASPECTS:** streaming video, sound, Macromedia Flash, navigation tools. **MEDIA CIRCULATED:** Flash, Gif and Video banner and custom sponsorships (NY Times) supported through a US campaign as well as simultaneous campaigns from around the world.

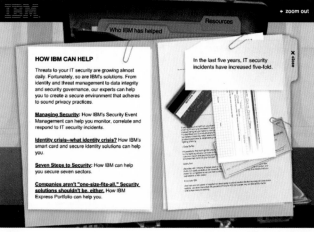

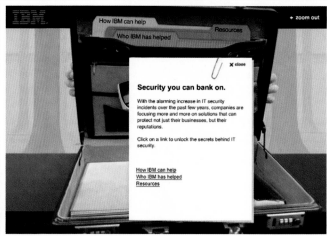

CONCEPT: The World's "Help Desk" is a metaphor for IBM and its ability to help tackle tough problems in business, society, and the world at large. It answers bigger, more complex questions involving social concerns, government, environment, energy, banking, education. The sitelet tells a deeper story about IBM's role in everyday life, today and in the future. It encourages the user to explore the expansive space of the Help Desk and learn that the Help Desk is available to all, with solutions for everyone. IBM is the world's help desk. The help desk is open. **RESULTS:** To date, 50+% of unique-visitor traffic to the On Demand site is attributed to the Help Desk campaign. This is an impressive 31% increase in Advertising-driven traffic to the site over 2004. Our repeat visit rate is 15.2%, an impressive 57% increase over the 2004 average. Average minutes/visit rose to 13.7, an amazing 100+% increase over the 2004 average. 10% of visitors click to featured *ibm.com* sites, moving through a broader and more holistic IBM experience. Regular Customer Value Monitor (CVM) surveys online showed that the Help Desk campaign has had a positive effect on numerous scores: 22% increase over 2004 in our Consideration: IBM as consultant and technology expert. 19% increase over 2004 in our Consideration: Interest in doing business with IBM. 16% increase over 2004 in our Customer Satisfaction: Usefulness of Content 11% increase over 2004 in our Consideration: IBM as innovative company. **BANNERS:** The Help Desk TV, video and flash banners broke the online clutter and provided better than average CTR. The overall banner creative CTR was .21%. Compared to the running average of .09% this CTR is almost 2.3x higher. The streaming video units had the highest CTR at 1.40%. Compared to past video creative the CTR for Help desk video banners was 3.5x higher. The strong brand lift, visitor volume and survey results were underscored by two awards for interactive campaign success in 2005 (New York Festivals & EFFIE). This Help Desk campaign was so successful both online and offline that we are in the process of revising and re-launching a 360 campaign called "Help Desk 2" set to go live on August 29th.

CONCEPT : Help Desk, le service clientèle de la compagnie IBM, symbolise la capacité de celle-ci à résoudre la problématique des entreprises, de la société et du monde en général. Il répond à des questions complexes de société, de politique, d'environnement, d'énergie, de finance et d'éducation. Le site révèle l'importance du rôle que peut jouer IBM dans la vie quotidienne, aujourd'hui comme demain. L'usager est invité à explorer l'espace extensible du Help Desk et découvrir que le service d'assistance est ouvert, accessible à tous, et qu'il a une solution adaptée pour chacun. IBM est le service d'assistance de la planète. **RÉSULTATS :** A ce jour, la hausse de 50% du nombre de visiteurs uniques sur le site est attribuée à la campagne du Help Desk. Sur l'année 2004, le site a connu une hausse de trafic global de 31%. Le taux de visites répétées est de 15,2%, c'est-à-dire 57% de mieux que la moyenne en 2004. La durée moyenne d'une session est passée à 13,7 minutes, 100% de plus que la moyenne de 2004. 10% des visiteurs sont allés sur d'autres sites IBM, pour une expérience holistique et approfondie de la marque. Les mesures d'impact ont montré que la campagne Help Desk a eu un effet positif dans de nombreux domaines.

Concernant l'image d'IBM comme expert en conseil et en technologie : hausse de 22% de réponses positives par rapport à 2004. Concernant l'intérêt porté à IBM : hausse de 19% de réponses favorables par rapport à 2004. Hausse de 16% comparé à 2004 du taux de satisfaction client concernant le contenu du site. Concernant l'image d'IBM comme société innovante : hausse de 11% de réponses positives comparé à 2004. **BANNIÈRES :** Le module Help Desk, la vidéo et les bannières en Flash ont brisé l'encombrement du site et ont généré un taux de clics supérieur à la moyenne. Le taux de clics sur les bannières a été de 0,21%, soit 2,3 fois plus que le taux moyen de 0,09%. Les modules vidéos ont généré le plus fort taux de clics, à savoir 1,40%. Comparé à d'anciens modules vidéos, le taux de clics pour le Help Desk était 3,5 fois plus élevé. Les bons résultats des mesures d'audience, l'augmentation du trafic et de la notoriété, ont été confortés par deux récompenses en 2005, au New York Festival et aux Effies. La campagne a remporté un tel succès en ligne comme hors ligne que nous travaillons actuellement sur une nouvelle campagne intégrée, Help Desk 2, qui sera inaugurée le 29 août.

KONZEPT: Das „Help Desk" der Welt ist eine Metapher für IBM und seine Fähigkeit, bei Problemen im Unternehmen, der Gesellschaft und der Welt als Ganze zu helfen. Es beantwortet größere, komplexere Fragen bezüglich sozialer Probleme, Regierung, Umwelt, Energie, Banking, Erziehung. Die Site erzählt die Geschichte von IBMs Rolle im Alltag – jetzt und in Zukunft und ermuntert den Benutzer, das riesige Help Desk zu erforschen und zu erfahren, dass es jedem zugänglich ist, mit Lösungen für alle. IBM ist ein Help Desk für die ganze Welt. Es ist offen. **ERGEBNISSE:** Bis jetzt wird über 50% der Besucherrate auf der On-Demand-Seite der Help-Desk-Kampagne zugeschrieben. Das ist ein beeindruckender Anstieg von 38% gegenüber 2004. Die Rate der wiederholten Besuche liegt bei 15,2%, ein Anstieg von 57% gegenüber dem Durchschnitt von 2004. 10% der Besucher klicken auf andere ibm.com-Seiten und erleben so eine breiteres, ganzheitliches IBM-Bild. Die Umfrage des Regular Customer Value Monitor (CVM) zeigte, dass die Help-Desk-Kampagne einen positiven Effekt auf zahlreichen Ebenen hatte: 22% Anstieg gegenüber 2004 bei der Anerkennung von IBM als Berater und Technologie-Experte. 19% Anstieg gegenüber 2004 beim Interesse, mit IBM Geschäfte zu machen. 16% Anstieg gegenüber 2004 in unserer Kundenzufriedenheit: Nützlichkeit des Inhalts stieg gegenüber 2004 um 11% bei der Wahrnehmung von IBM als innovativem Unternehmen. **BANNER:** Das Help-Desk-Fernsehen, Video- und Flashbanner sorgten für eine überdurchschnittliche CTR. Die gesamte CTR lag bei 21%; verglichen mit dem derzeitigen Durchschnitt von 09% ist diese CTR fast 2,3-mal höher. Die höchste CTR bei Streaming-Video-Einheiten lag bei 1,40%. Die CTR für Help-Desk-Videobanner lagen verglichen mit vergangenen Videobannern 3,5-mal höher. Die starke Marke, das Besuchervolumen und die Umfrageergebnisse wurden von zwei Auszeichnungen für erfolgreiche interaktive Kampagnen 2005 noch übertroffen (New York Festival & EFFIE). Diese Kampagne war offline und online so erfolgreich, dass wir eine überarbeitete 360°-Kampagne wieder einführten, „Help Desk 2", die am 29. August 2006 startet.

CAMPAIGN: Monsters. PRODUCT: Intel Centrino. YEAR: 2005. AGENCY: Euro RSCG 4D São Paulo <www.eurorscg4d.com.br>. CHIEF CREATIVE OFFICER: Alon Sochaczewski. CREATIVE DIRECTOR: Touché. COPYWRITER: Fábio Pierro, Ana Dolabela. ART DIRECTOR: Rubens Miranda, Rodrigo Buim, Fábio Matiazzi. DESIGNER: Gustavo Vilanova. PROGRAMMER: Michael Figueiredo. TECH ASPECTS: Macromedia Flash. AWARDS: CCSP 2005 (Gold); Gramado Festival 2005 (Silver); Colunistas Brasil 2005 (Silver); CLIO 2005 (Shortlist); One Show 2005 (Merit); Cannes Cyber Lions 2005 (Silver, Shortlist); MMOnline/Msn 2005 Awards (Silver); London International Advertising Awards 2005 (Gold); About de Comunicação Integrada e Dirigida 2005 Awards (Bronze).

CONCEPT: Intel Centrino Technology for wireless nets eliminates a series of limitations found in nets that use connection cables and wires.

KONZEPT: Intel Centrino Technology für kabellose Netze überschreitet eine Reihe von Grenzen, die Netzen mit Kabeln gesetzt sind.

CONCEPT : La technologie Intel Centrino pour les réseaux sans fil élimine tout un ensemble de limitations dont souffrent les réseaux qui utilisent des connexions filaires.

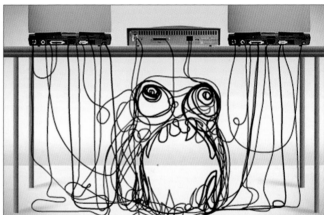

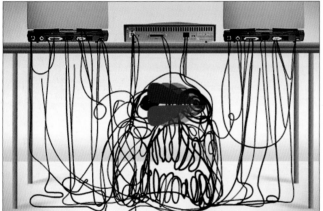

CAMPAIGN: Digital Land. **PRODUCT:** Intel Centrino. **YEAR:** 2005. **AGENCY:** Euro RSCG 4D São Paulo <www.eurorscg4d.com.br>. **CHIEF CREATIVE OFFICER:** Alon Sochaczewski. **CREATIVE DIRECTOR:** Touché.
COPYWRITER: Clóvis La Pastina, Fábio Pierro. **ART DIRECTOR:** Fábio Matiazzi, Diorgenes Wenderly. **PROGRAMMER:** Edivaldo Braz, Marcelo Olandim. **TECH ASPECTS:** Macromedia Flash.

CONCEPT: A fun and game-like website to display and sell the advantages of having a Intel Centrino processor on your computer.

CONCEPT : Un site Internet ludique qui présente les avantages des ordinateurs équipés d'un processeur Intel Centrino.

KONZEPT: Eine lustige Seite mit Spiel, um die Vorzüge eines Intel Centrion Prozessors auf dem eigenen Computer darzustellen.

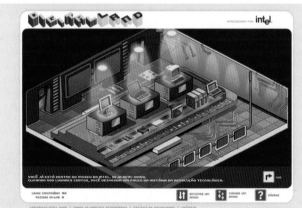

FEATURED ON THE DVD **CAMPAIGN:** Boost Mobile And 1 Streetball <www.boostmobilestreetball.com>. **PRODUCT:** Boost Mobile. **YEAR:** 2005. **AGENCY:** Juxt Interactive <www.juxtinteractive.com>. **PRODUCTION TIME:** 2 months. **CREATIVE DIRECTOR:** Todd Purgason. **ART DIRECTOR:** Jorge Calleja, Adrian Luna. **FLASH DESIGNER:** Brian Miller. **PROGRAMMER:** Khanh Nguyen. **TECH ASPECTS:** Macromedia Flash, video content.

CONCEPT: An exciting micro site launched to promote Boost Mobile's participation in the And 1 Mix Tape Tour, a national showcase of elite street basketball players competing across the nation. Users can learn about individual players on the roster and follow which players have been picked in each market. The site allows users to experience the action without trekking out to their local playgrounds, bringing the latest slamming and jamming right to the user's computer. A blog keeps fans in the know on the latest news, while team info and statistics keep the rotisserie geeks thoroughly satisfied. **RESULTS:** The Boost Mobile Streetball web site promotes Boost's involvement in the And 1 street basketball tour. The site serves as a powerful promotional vehicle, highlighting upcoming games, providing clips from past contests, and giving users a front row seat to the heart-stopping playground action. Site traffic has been solid and steady since site launch, and look for a refresh to the look and feel in Spring 2006.

CONCEPT : Le micro-site rapporte la participation de Boost Mobile au « And 1 Mix Tape Tour », un tournoi national de prestige réunissant les meilleurs joueurs de basket de rue. Le site fournit des infos sur chaque joueur inscrit et présente les sélections de chaque équipe. L'internaute peut suivre les matchs sans avoir besoin de se déplacer sur le terrain de son quartier, et peut admirer les *smashs* et les paniers depuis son ordinateur. Un blog informe les amateurs des dernières nouvelles et le classement des équipes selon leurs performances satisfait la curiosité des fans. **RÉSULTATS :** Le site rend parfaitement compte de l'engagement de Boost Mobile dans cet événement sportif. C'est un vecteur promotionel efficace, annonçant les prohaines rencontres, offrant des clips des anciens matchs, et plaçant l'usager au premier rang de l'action. Le site a connu un trafic important et régulier depuis son lancement, et sera réactualisé au printemps 2006.

KONZEPT: Eine spannende Microsite, die für die Teilnahme von Boost Mobile in der And 1 Mix Tape Tour wirbt, ein nationales Vorzeigeobjekt für die Elite der Straßenbasketballer, die im ganzen Land gegeneinander antreten. Benutzer können sich im Mitgliederverzeichnis über einzelne Spieler informieren und verfolgen, welche Spieler wo ausgewählt wurden. Sie können die Aktionen erleben, ohne zum Spielfeld zu gehen – die Körbe gelangen auf direktem Wege zum Computer des Benutzers. Ein Blog versorgt die Fans mit den neuesten Nachrichten, während Infos zum Team und Statistiken die Grillfreaks zufrieden stellen. **ERGEBNISSE:** Die Seite dient als starke Werbemaßnahme, informiert über künftige Spiele, zeigt Clips vergangener Spiele und bietet Benutzern einen Platz in der ersten Reihe bei atemberaubenden Spielen. Die Besucherrate auf der Seite war seit ihrem Launch beständig und solide und wurde im Frühling 2006 aktualisiert.

FEATURED ON THE DVD **CAMPAIGN:** Tattoo. **CLIENT:** INDT. **YEAR:** 2004. **AGENCY:** AgênciaClick <www.agenciaclick.com.br>. **AWARDS:** Cannes Lions 2004 (Gold).

CONCEPT: Interactive advertising materializes the loyalty and passion for mobiles concept in a fun and irreverent way.

CONCEPT : Une publicité interactive matérialise la fidélité et la passion du public pour les téléphones mobiles sur un mode ludique et impertinent.

KONZEPT: Interaktive Werbung verkörpert die Loyalität und Leidenschaft für das Konzept der Handys auf lustige und respektlose Weise.

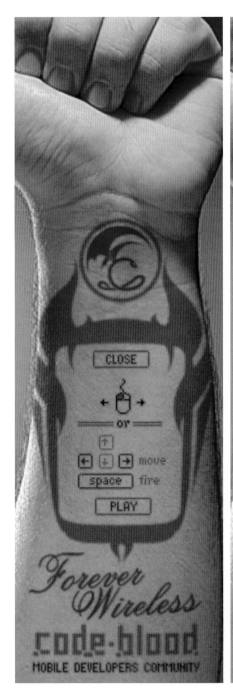

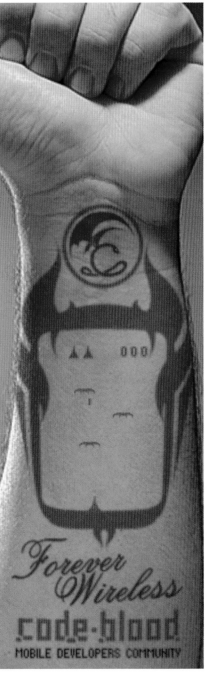

CAMPAIGN: Motoglyph <www.hellomoto.com/motoglyph>. CLIENT: Motorola. · YEAR: 2004-2005. AGENCY: Digit <www.digitlondon.com>. PRODUCTION TIME: 2 months. ART DIRECTOR: Henry Brook. DESIGNER: Stuart Jackson. INTERACTIVE DESIGN: Lars Jessen. PROGRAMMER: Lars Jessen, Jamie Ingram. AUDIO PROGRAMMER: Matthew Paradis. AWARDS: Cannes Cyber Lions.

CONCEPT: Motorola is one of the world's biggest mobile phone handset manufacturers. As well as being at the forefront of handset design, the company also has strong links with the music world and are the first and only manufacturer to put iTunes on a handset. **BRIEF:** To create an interactive experience for the Winter Music Conference in Miami which reinforced Motorola's commitment to music and youth culture. **SOLUTION:** By fusing cutting edge technology and simple tools we created a digital graffiti wall on which users could 'spray' their own unique signature or drawing. We designed and built the unit, which consisted of a digital spray can, an ultrasonic sensor and a back projected screen which combined to make an immersive and entertaining brand experience. Whilst creating a 'signature', Motoglyph also simultaneously generated a soundscape. Both the soundtrack and the image could be sent to the users mobiles to be used as wallpaper and ring tone. **RESULTS:** The Motoglyph won a Lion at Cannes, has created an enormous amount of positive press coverage globally for Motorola, and was commissioned to be part of a major contemporary design exhibition at the Pompidou Centre in Paris. Motorola has purchased the Motoglyph IP from Digit, and enhanced versions of the experience have been created for Motorola in territories including Mexico, Japan, France, Australia and Argentina.

CONCEPT : Motorola est l'un des plus grands fabricants mondiaux de téléphones mobiles. La société, à la pointe du design de combinés, entretient également des liens étroits avec le monde de la musique et elle est la seule à proposer iTunes sur ses appareils. **BRIEFING :** Mettre au point une expérience interactive à l'occasion de la Winter Music Conference de Miami, qui réaffirme l'engagement de Motorola à la musique et à la culture des jeunes. **SOLUTION :** En combinant une technologie dernier cri et un outil élémentaire, nous avons réalisé un mur de *graffitis* numérique sur lequel les usagers pouvaient peindre leur tag ou leur graph personnel. Nous avons conçu et réalisé le module, qui consistait en une bombe de peinture numérique, un capteur ultrasonore et un écran rétro-éclairé qui contribuaient à une expérience d'immersion ludique. L'écriture virtuelle d'une signature s'accompagnait simultanément d'effets sonores. L'image et la musique pouvaient être téléchargés sur le mobile des usagers et servir de fond d'écran et de sonnerie d'appel. **RÉSULTATS :** Le Motoglyph a remporté un Lion à Cannes, suscité nombre de critiques favorables dans la presse et a été sélectionné pour participer à une exposition sur le design contemporain au Centre Pompidou à Paris. Motorola a acheté le protocole Motoglyph à l'agence Digit, et des versions améliorées ont été réalisées pour d'autres pays comme le Mexique, le Japon, la France, l'Australie et l'Argentine.

KONZEPT: Motorola ist einer der größten Handyhersteller der Welt. Vom Vorsprung im Handset-Design abgesehen, hat die Firma außerdem eine gute Verbindung zur Musikwelt und ist der erste und einzige Hersteller, der iTunes in ein Handset integriert hat. **AUFGABE:** Ein interaktives Erlebnis für die Winter Music Conference in Miami zu schaffen, das Motorolas Verpflichtung gegenüber Musik und Jugendkultur unterstreicht. **LÖSUNG:** Durch die Kombination von innovativer Technologie und einfachen Werkzeugen entwickelten wir eine digitale Graffitimauer, auf die Benutzer ihre eigene Unterschrift oder ein Bild „sprayen" konnten. Wir entwarfen und bauten die Einheit, die aus einer digitalen Sprühflasche, einem Überschallsensor und einem Bildschirm bestand, was insgesamt für ein eindringliches und unterhaltsames Markenerlebnis sorgte. Motoglyph kreierte zusammen mit der „Unterschrift" auch einen Sound. Soundtrack und Bild konnten auf die Handys der Benutzer geschickt und als Hintergrundbild und Klingelton verwendet werden. **ERGEBNISSE:** Der Motoglyph gewann einen Löwen in Cannes, erzeugte eine positive weltweite Berichterstattung für Motorola und wurde Teil einer großen zeitgenössischen Designausstellung im Centre Pompidou in Paris. Motorola erwarb den Motoglyph von Digit, und verbesserte Versionen der Anwendung wurden für Motorola unter anderem in Mexiko, Japan, Frankreich, Australien und Argentinien entwickelt.

FEATURED ON THE DVD **CAMPAIGN:** Motorola Ultrashort Film Festival. **PRODUCT:** Motorola c650. **CLIENT:** Motorola. **YEAR:** 2004. **AGENCY:** Ogilvy Interactive Mexico <www.ogilvy.com.mx>. **PRODUCTION TIME:** 2 weeks. **CREATIVE TEAM:** Rafael Jiménez, Geraldina Jiménez, Oscar Mendoza, Luis Falconi. **PROGRAMMER:** Carmen Garcés, Oscar Mendoza. **TECH ASPECTS:** Macromedia Flash interface, the videos where filmed and produced exclusively for the campaign. **MEDIA CIRCULATED:** Banner at <www.hellomoto.com.mx>.

CONCEPT: Motorola's c650 phone is capable of playing a 10 second video. This inspired the launch campaign where we created the first Mexican ultrashort film festival, where people could put together their own video by choosing five different 2" video sequences out of 50 available. After naming their shortfilm (very important to completely understand the short) they would submitted and then competed to win prizes. **RESULTS:** Excellent results with more than 1,000 ultrashort films to watch. The users were enthusiastic for the three week festival, we gathered a professional filmmakers jury for the evaluation of the shortfilms.

CONCEPT : Le combiné Motorola c650 est le seul mobile capable de diffuser une vidéo de 10 secondes. Cela nous a donné l'idée de lancer une campagne en organisant le premier festival mexicain de films « ultracourts ». Les participants pouvaient créer leur propre vidéo en choisissant deux séquences de 2 secondes chacune parmi 50 séquences proposées. Après avoir donné un titre à leur film (essentiel à la compréhension), les participants concouraient pour gagner des prix. **RÉSULTATS :** Plus de 1 000 films ont été reçus. Les usagers ont été enthousiastes durant les trois semaines du festival, et un jury de réalisateurs professionnels s'est chargé d'évaluer les films.

KONZEPT: Motorolas c650-Handy kann ein 10-Sekunden-Video abspielen. Die Launch-Kampagne ließ sich davon inspirieren, als sie das erste mexikanische Ultrakurzfilm-Festival initiierte, wo man sein eigenes Video zusammenstellen konnte, indem man aus 50 verfügbaren 2-Sekunden-Videosequenzen fünf auswählte. Nachdem man seinem Kurzfilm einen Titel gegeben hatte (wichtig, um ihn richtig zu verstehen), wurde er eingereicht, um einen Preis zu gewinnen. **ERGEBNISSE:** Exzellente Ergebnisse mit mehr als 1 000 Ultrakurzfilmen. Die Benutzer waren während des dreiwöchigen Festivals enthusiastisch, und wir konnten professionelle Filmemacher als Jury für die Bewertung der Filme gewinnen.

CAMPAIGN: Motorola 3G "HERE". **PRODUCT:** Motorola 3G phones. **YEAR:** 2005. **AGENCY:** OgilvyOne Paris <www.ogilvy.fr>. **PRODUCTION TIME:** 3 months. **CREATIVE DIRECTOR:** Chris Jones. **ART DIRECTOR:** Sebastien Serandrei. **INFOGRAPHIST:** Guillaume Mary. **PROGRAMMER:** Mathieu Zylberait, Frederic Lim. **TECH ASPECTS:** Macromedia Flash, streaming video, dynamically generated PDFs, Eyeblaster. **MEDIA CIRCULATED:** Major video and music content sites throughout Europe.

CONCEPT: With Motorola 3G phones you can do whatever you want, wherever you are. Supporting a major offline campaign we developed a series of page takeover banners on music and movie sites. The phones sucked all the content from the page demonstrating how videos can now be accessed anywhere. A minisite brought the campaign to life, capturing the imagination of the visitor in a viral competition that invited participants to show how they'd use a 3G phone in an imaginative way. A dynamic tool allowed visitors to create their own Motorola 3G ad. The best idea won a Motorola 3G phone. **RESULTS:** The suction banner generated a huge click through rate of between 1.77 and 3.20 %! The microsite is phase two of the campaign and goes live shortly.

CONCEPT : Avec les mobiles Motorola 3G, on peut faire ce qu'on veut, où on veut. Pour accompagner une grande campagne hors ligne, nous avons intégré des bannières sur des sites consacrés à la musique ou au cinéma. Le téléphone sur la bannière aspirait tout le contenu de la page, démontrant ainsi que les vidéos peuvent être téléchargées de n'importe te où. Un mini-site développait le concept, en proposant un concours où les internautes de-

vaient faire preuve d'imagination dans l'utilisation de leur 3G. Un outil dynamique permettait de réaliser sa propre pub Motorola, et la meilleure proposition remportait un téléphone mobile. **RÉSULTATS :** La bannière a généré un énorme taux de clics, entre 1,77 et 3,2%. Un micro-site constituera la seconde phase de la campagne et sera actif sous peu.

KONZEPT: Mit Motorola 3G-Handys kann man tun, was man will, wo immer man ist. Als Unterstützung einer großen Offline-Kampagne entwickelten wir eine Reihe von Bannern auf Musik- und Kinoseiten. Die Handys saugten den gesamten Inhalt einer Seite auf, um zu demonstrieren, wie man nun von überall Zugang zu Videos hat. Eine Minisite erweckte die Kampagne zum Leben, indem sie einen viralen Wettbewerb ausschrieb, der Teilnehmer dazu einlud, zu zeigen, wie sie ein 3G-Handy auf fantasievolle Weise nutzten. Sie konnten mit einem dynamischen Tool ihre eigene Motorola 3G-Werbung erstellen. Die beste Idee gewann ein Motorola 3G-Handy. **ERGEBNISSE:** Das Saugbanner generierte eine riesige CTR zwischen 1,77 und 3,20%! Die Microsite ist die zweite Phase der Kampagne und erscheint bald.

CAMPAIGN: Mobile Kids "Mokitown" <www.mokitown.de>. **PRODUCT:** Mokitown. **YEAR:** 2002. **AGENCY:** Neue Digitale <www.neue-digitale.de>. **PRODUCTION TIME:** December 2000 – June 2001, ongoing. **CREATIVE TEAM:** Olaf Czeschner, Rolf Borcherding, Angela Fusco. **PROGRAMMER:** Marius Bulla. **TECH ASPECTS:** Macromedia Shockwave, chat, macro games, quiz, child-friendly environment (Bad-Word-Filter). **MEDIA CIRCULATED:** Internet. **AWARDS:** Cannes Cyber Lions 2002 (Bronze), Jahrbuch der Werbung 2002, Epica Awards 2001 (Finalist), Annual Multimedia Yearbook 2002, The New York Festivals 2001 (Silver).

CONCEPT: Online presence for MobileKids, a safety initiative by DaimlerChrysler AG, Stuttgart. International campaign in German and English promoting child awareness of daily dangers in traffic. Children, aged 8–12, can playfully learn how to act correctly. Road traffic education, an unloved chore for children? Not if you look at it from a child's perspective, if you speak the children's language. For this project, NEUE DIGITALE created a whole new world: Mokitown, town of the Mobile Kids. Kids are invited to explore the city, meet other children, chat with them, and experience thrilling adventures. Quizzy, the flying robot, asks challenging questions about road safety, geography, or general knowledge. Mokitown — that is truly seeing the world through children's eyes. **RESULTS:** Design and implementation of a global traffic safety playground for every child in every corner of the world. The community works! Thousands of Mobile Kids from all over the world visit Mokitown and chat with each other on a regular basis. Monthly growth rates range from 20 to 30 per cent. The number of children that use the MobileKids community is constantly increasing — although we did little to advertise the community. Children spend more than 22 minutes in a "session" on average. In 2005, children used the online-platform Mokitown intensively, dealing with the topic of road safety and playfully learning new content. Mokitown is a favourite of children. This is documented by the direct accesses to this site (90.32%). Nearly all children come knowingly and voluntarily to Mokitown. That points to its popularity and a positive word-to-mouth propaganda. A large number of registered users are also Newsletter subscribers (110,000 users worldwide). This indicates a long-term interest in the site and its content.

CONCEPT : Promouvoir MobileKids, une opération de prévention routière initiée par DaimlerChrysler, de Stuttgart. La campagne en anglais et en allemand visait à sensibiliser les enfants aux dangers de la circulation. Les enfants de 8 à 12 ans peuvent apprendre les bons comportements de façon ludique. L'éducation à la sécurité routière, une corvée pour les enfants ? Pas si on l'envisage du point de vue de l'enfant, en parlant son langage. Pour ce projet, Neue Digitale a élaboré tout un univers : Mokitown, la ville des enfants « mobiles ». Les enfants sont invités à explorer la ville, rencontrer d'autres enfants, discuter avec eux, et vivre des aventures palpitantes. Quizzy, le robot volant, pose des questions sur la sécurité, la géographie ou la culture générale. Mokitown reflète la vision enfantine de la ville. **RÉSULTATS :** Design et implémentation d'une aire de jeux de sécurité routière pour les enfants des quatre coins du monde. Et la communauté fonctionne ! Des milliers d'enfants du monde entier visitent Mokitown et discutent entre eux de façon régulière. Le taux de croissance mensuel va de 20 à 30%. Le nombre d'enfants qui utilisent la communauté Mokitown est en hausse constante, bien que nous ayons fait peu de publicité sur la communauté. Les enfants ont passé en moyenne 22 minutes sur le site. En 2005, les enfants ont fait un usage intensif de la plateforme, s'intéressant à la sécurité et s'instruisant tout en jouant. Mokitown est devenu un des sites favoris des enfants. Cela est confirmé par le taux d'accès directs au site, de 90,32%. La plupart d'entre eux viennent sur le site volontairement et en toute connaissance de cause. Cela souligne sa popularité et le bon fonctionnement du bouche à oreille. Un grande nombre d'internautes se sont abonnés au bulletin d'information (110 000 inscrits dans le monde). Cela prouve un intérêt pérenne pour le site et son contenu.

KONZEPT: Online-Präsenz für MobileKids, eine Sicherheitsinitiative der DaimlerChrysler AG, Stuttgart. Internationale Kampagne auf Deutsch und Englisch, die für mehr Aufmerksamkeit der Kinder für die täglichen Gefahren im Straßenverkehr wirbt. Kinder zwischen acht und zwölf können spielerisch lernen, wie man sich richtig verhält. Verkehrserziehung, eine verhasste Anstrengung für Kinder? Nicht, wenn man es aus der Perspektive der Kinder betrachtet und ihre Sprache spricht. NEUE DIGITALE schufen für dieses Projekt eine ganz neue Welt: Mokitown, Stadt der Mobile Kids. Kinder werden eingeladen, die Stadt zu erforschen, andere Kinder zu treffen, mit ihnen zu reden und spannende Abenteuer zu erleben. Quizzy, der fliegende Roboter, stellt Fragen über Straßensicherheit, Geografie oder Allgemeinwissen. Mokitown – hier sieht man die Welt mit Kinderaugen. **ERGEBNISSE:** Design und Implementierung eines globalen Verkehrssicherheits-Spielplatzes für alle Kinder aus allen Ecken der Welt. Die Gemeinde funktioniert! Tausende von Mobile Kids aus aller Welt besuchen Mokitown und unterhalten sich regelmäßig. Die monatlichen Wachstumsraten betragen 20 bis 30%. Die Anzahl der Kinder, die die Mobile-Kids-Gemeinde benutzen, wächst ständig – obwohl wir wenig taten, um dafür zu werben. Kinder verweilen durchschnittlich 22 Minuten auf der Seite. 2005 nutzten Kinder die Online-Plattform Mokitown intensiv, beschäftigten sich mit Straßensicherheit und lernten spielerisch neue Dinge. Dies ist durch die direkten Zugänge auf die Seite dokumentiert (90,32%). Fast alle Kinder kommen wissentlich und freiwillig zu Mokitown. Dies weist auf die Popularität und eine positive Mund-zu-Mund-Propaganda hin. Eine große Zahl der registrierten Benutzer haben außerdem den Newsletter abonniert (110 000 Benutzer weltweit). Dies weist auf ein langfristiges Interesse an der Seite und ihren Inhalten hin.

FEATURED ON THE DVD **CAMPAIGN:** Tre NEC E616 Xtreme.   **CLIENT:** Tre.   **YEAR:** 2004.   **AGENCY:** LOWE Tesch <www.lowetesch.com>.   **CREATIVE DIRECTOR:** Johan Tesch.   **ART DIRECTOR:** Johan Öhrn.   **COPYWRITER:** Tom Eriksen.   **ACCOUNT DIRECTOR:** Mattias Falkendahl.   **AGENCY PRODUCER:** Caroline Déas-Ehrnvall.   **MOTION DESIGNER:** Niklas Fransson.   **PHOTOGRAPHER:** John Gripenholm.   **CLIENT'S SUPERVISOR:** Karin Bill, Jessica Persson.

SYNOPSIS: 3 – the telecom company – is riding a strong tail wind. Their handsets sell like never before. So when they decide to re-release their topselling handset, now in a black coloured limited edition, all hell brakes loose. 3 asked LOWE Tesch to get out on the field and document the havoc.

CONTEXTE : « 3 », l'opérateur de télécom, a le vent en poupe. Ses appareils se vendent comme des petits pains. La remise sur le marché des modèles les plus vendus, dans une édition limitée de couleur noire, a déclenché un véritable raz-de-marée. La société a demandé à LOWE Tesch d'enquêter sur le terrain afin d'expliquer le phénomène.

SYNOPSIS: 3 – das Telecom-Unternehmen – erhält starken Rückenwind. Ihre Handsets verkaufen sich wie nie zuvor. Als sie sich entschieden, ihr bestes Handset in einer limitierten schwarzen Ausgabe herauszugeben, brachen alle Dämme. Sie beauftragten LOWE Tesch damit, das Chaos zu dokumentieren.

CAMPAIGN: Blindfolded Boxing <www.blindfoldedboxing.com>. **PRODUCT:** Nokia N-Gage. **YEAR:** 2005. **AGENCY:** Farfar <www.farfar.se>. **PRODUCTION TIME:** 1 month. **CREATIVE TEAM:** Nicke Bergström, Henrik Berglöf, Jon Dranger, Per Hansson, Anders Gustavsson, Erik Norin. **PROGRAMMER:** Bo Gustafsson. **AWARDS:** Cannes Lions (Bronze), LIIA (Gold), D&AD (Silver), Eurobest (Bronze).

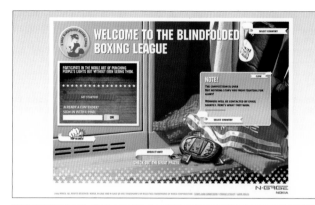

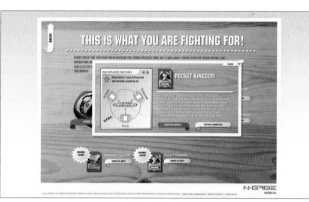

CONCEPT: A clever competition was needed to promote the new N-Gage QD and the latest games releases for Nokia's hand held gaming device. The Answer was a highly original game where the object was to punch the opponent's lights out without being able to see a thing.

KONZEPT: Für das neue N-Gage QD und die neuesten Spiele brauchte man eine clevere Werbung. Sie bestand aus einem originellen Spiel, in dem in dem man seinen Gegner K.o. schlagen musste, ohne ihn zu sehen.

CONCEPT : Il fallait rivaliser d'inventivité pour promouvoir le nouveau N-Gage QD et les derniers jeux sortis sur la console de poche de Nokia. La réponse a été un jeu original où le but était de *puncher* son adversaire dans l'obscurité totale.

CAMPAIGN: Pjotro <www.pjotro.com>. **PRODUCT:** Nokia N91. **YEAR:** 2006. **AGENCY:** Farfar <www.farfar.se>. **PRODUCTION TIME:** 3 months. **CREATIVE TEAM:** Nicke Bergström, Daniel Wall, Per Hansson, Anders Gustavsson, Björn Johansson, Henrik Berglöf, Anna Frick, Marielle Lundquist. **PROGRAMMER:** Bo Gustafsson.

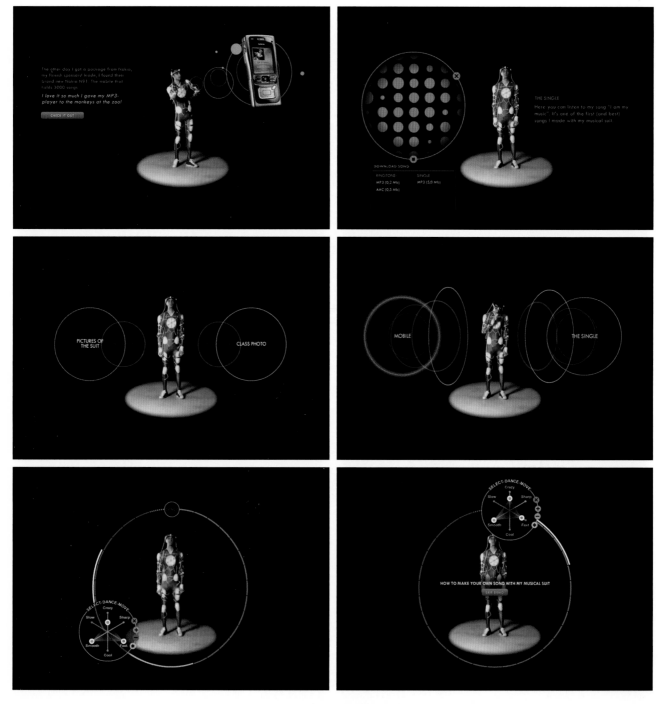

CONCEPT: In order to create some buzz before the release of the Nokia N-91 music phone we created a somewhat odd character by the name of Pjotro. He loves music so much that he became music. A viral clip of his brake through performance on TV led to a site where you could explore his background and test his greatest innovation: The Musical Suit. A totally viral campaign with no media back up.

CONCEPT : Afin de générer un buzz avant le lancement du téléphone et baladeur portable Nokia N-91, nous avons imaginé un personnage un peu étrange du nom de Pjotro. Il aime tellement la musique qu'il finit par l'incarner. Un clip viral d'une performance télévisuelle fictive conduit à un site où l'on peut découvrir la genèse du personnage et tester sa plus grande innovation : la combinaison musicale. La campagne était uniquement virale, sans aucun soutien des autres médias.

KONZEPT: Um vor dem Verkaufsstart des Musikhandys Nokia N-91 für etwas Gesprächsstoff zu sorgen, schufen wir eine etwas merkwürdige Figur namens Pjotro. Er liebte Musik so sehr, dass er selbst zur Musik wurde. Ein viraler Clip seines ersten Erfolgsauftritts im Fernsehen führte zu einer Seite, auf der man seinen Hintergrund erforschen und seine größte Innovation testen konnte: Die Musical Suite. Eine ausschließlich virale Kampagne ohne Unterstützung durch andere Medien.

CAMPAIGN: Bad Quality <www.badqualitysuperglue.com>. **PRODUCT:** Nokia N90. **YEAR:** 2006. **AGENCY:** Farfar <www.farfar.se>. **PRODUCTION TIME:** 1 month. **CREATIVE TEAM:** Jon Dranger, Henrik Berglöf, Nicke Bergström, Rickard Lundberg.

CONCEPT: The really good thing about having a mobile phone with great video capabilities is that you always have it with you if you something worth capturing. We have made a series of films illustrating this and showing off the great picture quality at the same time. The films where spread virally over the Internet.

CONCEPT : L'avantage de posséder un téléphone portable avec de grandes capacités vidéo est qu'on l'a toujours avec soi au cas où l'on verrait quelque chose digne d'être photographié. Nous avons illustré cette idée à travers une série de films qui démontrent également la grande qualité des images obtenues. Les films ont été transmis par Internet de façon virale.

KONZEPT: Das Beste an einem Handy mit Videofunktion ist, dass man es bei jeder Gelegenheit bei sich tragen kann. Wir drehten eine Reihe von Filmen, die dies illustrierten und gleichzeitig die hohe Bildqualität bezeugten. Die Filme wurden viral über das Internet verbreitet.

CAMPAIGN: Snakes. **PRODUCT:** Nokia N-Gage. **YEAR:** 2005. **AGENCY:** Farfar <www.farfar.se>. **PRODUCTION TIME:** 4 months. **CREATIVE TEAM:** Nicke Bergström, Henrik Berglöf, Jon Dranger, Per Hansson, Anders Gustavsson. **PROGRAMMER:** Bo Gustafsson. **AWARDS:** Cannes Lions (Bronze), LIIA (Gold), D&AD (Silver), Eurobest (Bronze).

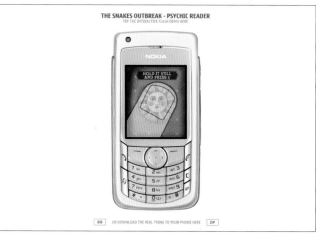

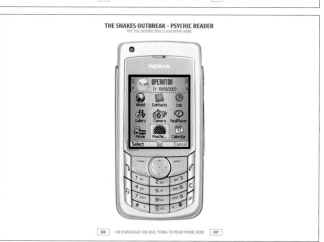

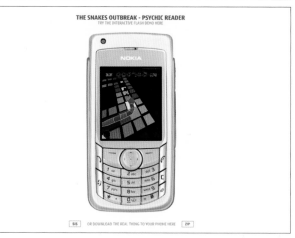

CONCEPT: Snakes is the sequel to Snake, the classic mobile game from Nokia that has lived to be the most played game ever. Although Snakes is a rather impressive game, with smooth 3D graphics and Bluetooth multiplayer capabilities, Nokia is giving it away for free. Owners of Nokia's gaming phone Nokia N-Gage are free to simply download the game and spread it virally to other members of the N-Gage community.

CONCEPT : Snakes est la suite de Snake, le jeu classique pour mobile qui est devenu le jeu le plus joué de tous. Bien que Snakes soit assez sophistiqué, avec des images en 3D et des possibilités Bluetooth de jeu en réseau, Nokia le fournit gratuitement. Les possesseurs de l'appareil Nokia N-Gage peuvent le télécharger gratuitement et l'envoyer de façon virale à d'autres membres de la communauté N-Gage.

KONZEPT: Snakes ist die Fortsetzung von Snakes, dem klassischen Handyspiel von Nokia, das bis heute das meist gespielte Spiel überhaupt ist. Obwohl Snakes mit seinen 3D-Grafiken und Bluetooth-Multiplayer-Funktion ein beeindruckendes Spiel ist, ist es umsonst. Besitzer eines Nokia N-Gage Handys können das Spiel kostenlos downloaden und viral an weitere Mitglieder der N-Gage-Community senden.

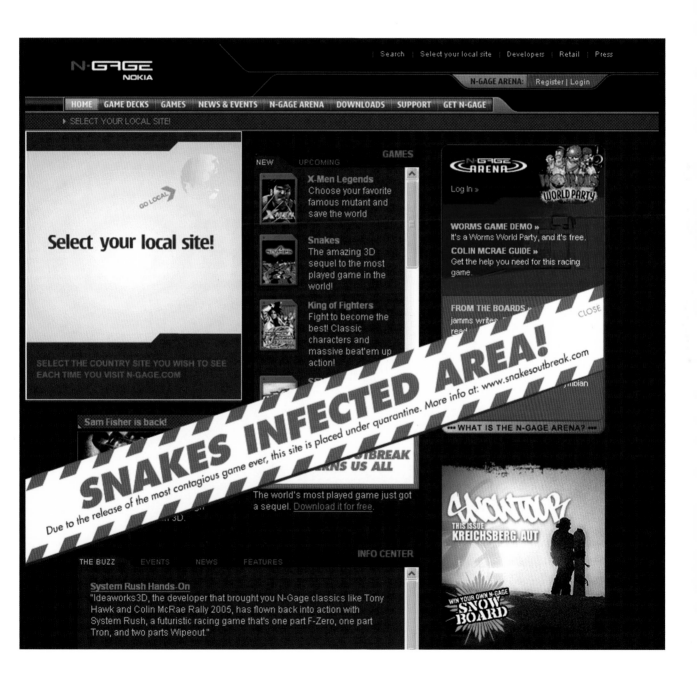

CAMPAIGN: Snakes. **PRODUCT:** Nokia N-Gage. **YEAR:** 2005. **AGENCY:** Euro RSCG 4D São Paulo <www.eurorscg4d.com.br>. **CHIEF CREATIVE OFFICER:** Alon Sochaczewski. **CREATIVE DIRECTOR:** Touché. **COPYWRITER:** Fábio Pierro. **ART DIRECTOR:** Valter Klug, Diorgenes Wenderly. **PROGRAMMER:** Michael Figueiredo. **TECH ASPECTS:** Macromedia Flash. **AWARDS:** About de Comunicação Integrada e Dirigida 2005 (Grand Prix); New York Festivals 2005 (Merit); CCSP 2006 (Shortlist).

CONCEPT: With Snakes, designed for N-Gage 3D game deck cellular, nobody is going to look for serpents anywhere else.

CONCEPT : Avec Snakes, conçu pour la plateforme de jeu mobile N-Gage 3D, personne n'aura l'idée d'aller chercher des serpents ailleurs.

KONZEPT: Mit Snakes, für N-Gage 3D Game Deck Handys entworfen, wird niemand mehr woanders nach Snakes suchen.

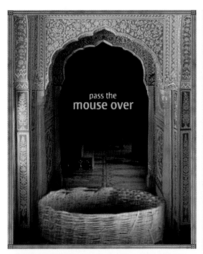
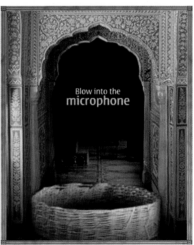

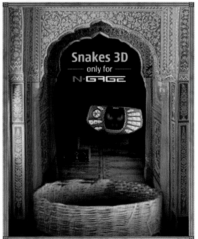

CAMPAIGN: Nokia Trends 2005 Hot Site. PRODUCT: Nokia Trends Festival. YEAR: 2005. AGENCY: Euro RSCG 4D São Paulo <www.eurorscg4d.com.br>. CHIEF CREATIVE OFFICER: Alon Sochaczewski. CREATIVE DIRECTOR: Touché. COPYWRITER: Fábio Pierro, Nelson Rubens Botega Jr. ART DIRECTOR: Rogerio Cassoli, Rodrigo Buim, Valter Klug. DESIGNER: Lucia Silveira, Eduardo Marques. TECH ASPECTS: Macromedia Flash. AWARDS: Gramado Festival 2005 (Bronze); Abanet 2005 Awards (Gold); CCSP 2004 (Merit).

CONCEPT: Nokia Trends website was created to complement the event's communication towards its public. However, the site reached a huge success and became the main tool to spread the news and further information about the event. The special feature of the website was the two-windowed browser, one representing Rio de Janeiro and the other representing São Paulo, which shows perfectly the synchrony between both towns, that hosted the event at the same time.

CONCEPT : Le site Internet Nokia Trends (tendances Nokia) a été conçu comme un complément de la campagne de communication de l'événement au public. Mais l'énorme succès du site en a fait l'outil de communication principal pour diffuser les informations relati-

ves à l'événement. Le point fort du site était la navigation sur deux fenêtres, l'une représentant Rio de Janeiro et l'autre São Paulo, ce qui montrait très bien la correspondance entre les deux villes, qui ont hébergé l'événement en même temps.

KONZEPT: Die Webseite für Nokia Trends sollte das Event durch Kommunikation mit der Öffentlichkeit begleiten. Sie war ein riesengroßer Erfolg und wurde sogar zum stärksten Tool, um Neuigkeiten und Informationen über das Event zu verbreiten. Die Besonderheit lag in dem doppelten Browserfenster: Eines zeigte Rio de Janeiro, das andere São Paulo, um die Synchronie der beiden Städte zu präsentieren, in denen das Event zu gleichen Zeit stattfand.

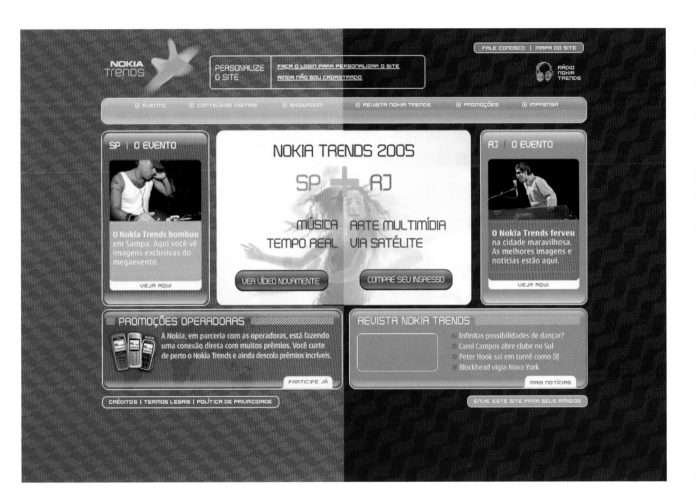

CAMPAIGN: Siemens A52. YEAR: 2004. AGENCY: Large <www.largedesign.com>. PRODUCTION TIME: 2 weeks. COST IN HOURS OF WORK: 160 h. CREATIVE TEAM: Lars Hemming Jorgensen, Jim Boulton, Rene Christoffer.
PROGRAMMER: Jesper Lycke. TECH ASPECTS: Macromedia Flash, audio.

CONCEPT: The A52 was a simple phone, but the campaign was loud, fun and had real impact. It was high pace and set to a catchy soundtrack. **RESULTS:** the phone got a lot of press coverage in Eastern Europe where the campaign ran.

CONCEPT : Le A52 est un téléphone classique, mais la campagne était drôle et retentissante. Le rythme soutenu et la musique accrocheuse lui ont assuré un fort impact. **RÉSULTATS :** La publicité a bénéficié d'une large couverture de la presse en Europe de l'Est où elle était diffusée.

KONZEPT: Das A52 war ein einfaches Telefon, aber die Kampagne war laut, lustig und hatte eine große Wirkung. Sie war temporeich und hatte einen einprägsamen Soundtrack. **ERGEBNISSE:** Das Telefon erhielt eine breite Berichterstattung in der Presse in Osteuropa, wo die Kampagne lief.

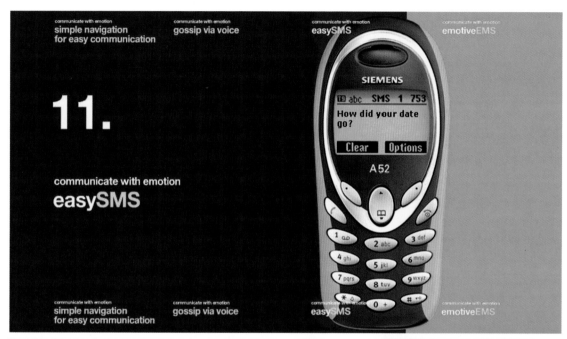

CAMPAIGN: Gear Up – Brasil Telecom. CLIENT: Brasil Telecom. AGENCY: AgênciaClick <www.agenciaclick.com.br>.

CONCEPT: Campaign for a broadband access convokes the best players of on-line gaming to be part of a revolutionary movement.

KONZEPT: Kampagne für Breitband-Zugang, die die besten Spieler von Online-Spielen einberuft, um Teil einer revolutionären Bewegung zu sein.

CONCEPT : La campagne promotionnelle pour l'internet haut débit invite les meilleurs joueurs de jeux en réseau à participer à un mouvement révolutionnaire.

CAMPAIGN: TOSHIBA Presents FM Festival '04. **CLIENT:** TOSHIBA Corporation/TOKYO FM Broadcasting Co., Ltd. **YEAR:** 2004-2005. **AGENCY:** Dentsu Inc. <www.dentsu.com>. **CREATIVE DIRECTOR:** Aco Suzuki. **ART DIRECTOR:** Yugo Nakamura. **FLASH DESIGNER:** Yugo Nakamura, Hisayuki Takagi. **PRODUCER:** Koichiro Tanaka, Masakatsu Kasai. **TECHNICAL DIRECTOR:** Yugo Nakamura. **PROGRAMMER:** Keita Kitamura. **TECH ASPECTS:** Macromedia Flash, sound, film. **MEDIA CIRCULATED:** Internet. **AWARDS:** Cannes Lions 2005 (Gold), tokyo.interactive.ad.awards.jp 2005 (Gold), One Show Interactive 2005 (Silver), CLIO Awards 2005 (Silver).

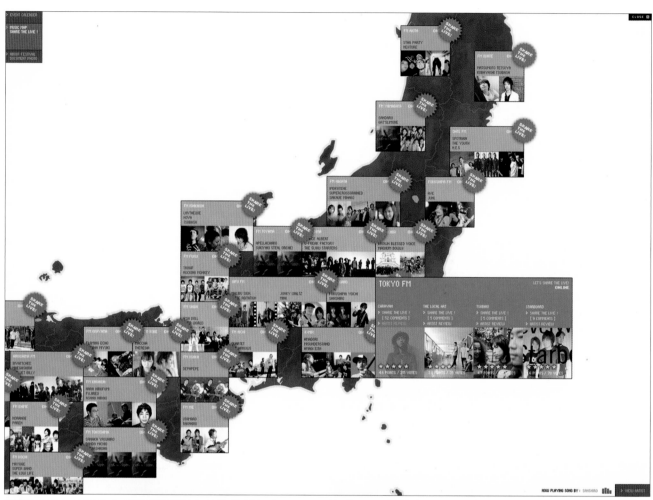

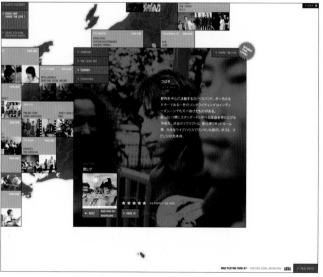

CONCEPT: A campaign site for a nationwide live music and radio event organized by the 38 stations in the JAPAN FM NETWORK, featuring the latest news on indies artists taking part in the event, as well as exclusive live video streaming of the concerts. Real-time audience participation was possible through comments posted as the concerts were in progress.

CONCEPT : Site de campagne concernant l'organisation et la retransmission de concerts par les 38 stations de radio japonaises Japan FM Network. Il présente les dernières infos sur les artistes indépendants qui participent au festival, ainsi que des retransmissions vidéo en direct des concerts. La participation du public en temps réel était illustrée par l'affichage de messages pendant le déroulement des concerts.

KONZEPT: Eine Kampagnenseite für ein landesweites Livemusik- und Radioevent, das von den 38 Stationen des JAPAN FM NETWORK organisiert wurde, und die Neuigkeiten über Indie-Künstler enthielt, die beim Event auftraten, sowie exklusives Live-Video-Streaming der Konzerte. Publikumsteilnahme live war durch Kommentare möglich, die man während der Konzerte senden konnte.

FEATURED ON THE DVD **CAMPAIGN:** Modem AD. **PRODUCT:** ADSL Broadband. **CLIENT:** TELE2. **YEAR:** 2005. **AGENCY:** Forsman & Bodenfors <www.fb.se>. **PRODUCTION TIME:** 2 weeks. **WEB DIRECTOR:** Martin Cedergren. **ACCOUNT EXECUTIVE:** Greger Andersson. **ACCOUNT MANAGER:** Jerk Zander. **DESIGN:** Jonas Sjövall. **ART DIRECTOR:** Kim Cramer. **COPY:** Martin Ringqvist, Lars Jönsson. **AGENCY PRODUCER:** Mathias Appelblad. **PROGRAMMER:** Itiden. **TECH ASPECTS:** Macromedia Flash. **MEDIA CIRCULATED:** Online ads.

CONCEPT: This ad is only visible for those who use a dial up modem (a script detects which connection speed the user have). If you surf with a slow modem the ad will show how fast the page could have been loaded with Tele2 ADSL broadband instead. The ad was put on more heavily loaded sites like MSN.

KONZEPT: Diese Anzeige ist nur für diejenigen sichtbar, die eine Modemverbindung nutzen (ein Script erkennt, welche Verbindungsgeschwindigkeit die Benutzer haben). Surft man mit einem langsamen Modem, zeigt die Anzeige, wie schnell die Seite mit einem Tele2 ADSL Breitband hätte geladen werden können. Die Anzeige wurde auf viel besuchten Seiten wie MSN geschaltet.

CONCEPT : Cette publicité n'est visible que pour ceux qui utilisent un modem à numérotation automatique (un script détecte le débit de connexion de l'usager). Si vous surfez avec un modem lent, la pub vous montre à quelle vitesse la page aurait été chargée avec le haut débit de Tele2. La publicité a également paru sur des moteurs de recherche comme MSN.

CONCEPT: MSN Web Pioneers – The MSN Creative Awards were established to recognize the outstanding advertising featured on MSN.com. This year, MSN wanted to celebrate the people who pushed the limits of technology – the true pioneers of online advertising. The "call for entries" campaign included print ads, banner ads, four online videos, and a Boy Scout style "web pioneer survival guide" which showed, among other things, how to start a fire using web standard fonts.

CONCEPT : Le Web Pioneers, concours de création de MSN, a été organisé pour souligner les publicités novatrices qui figurent sur MSN.com. Cette année, MSN voulait rendre hommage aux créatifs qui repoussent les limites de la technologie, les vrais pionniers de la dis-

cipline. La liste des participants présentait des annonces écrites, des bannières, quatre vidéos numériques et un guide de survie du pionner du Net, dans un style très boy scout, qui expliquait entre autre comment allumer un feu avec des fontes électroniques.

KONZEPT: MSN Web Pioneers – The MSN Creative Awards entstanden, um auf die außergewöhnliche Werbung auf MSN.com hinzuweisen. MSN wollte dieses Jahr die Menschen feiern, die an die Grenzen der Technologie gingen – die wahren Pioniere der Online-Werbung. Die Kampagne schloss gedruckte Anzeigen, Banner, vier Online-Videos und eine „Webpionier-Überlebensanleitung" ein, die unter anderem zeigte, wie man mit Standard-Fonts ein Feuer entfachen kann.

FEATURED ON THE DVD CAMPAIGN: This Is Huge. **PRODUCT:** YAHOO! Music Unlimited. **YEAR:** 2005. **AGENCY:** OgilvyOne Worldwide, San Francisco <www.ogilvy.com>. **PRODUCTION TIME:** 3 months. **CREATIVE DIRECTOR:** Arthur Ceria, Aaron Griffiths, Andy Berndt (Soho Sq.), Jeff Curry (Soho Sq.). **ART DIRECTOR:** Jason Koxvold, Ryan Cochrane, Ryan Gerber, Kara Verhoorn, Josh Rosen (Soho Sq.). **COPYWRITER:** Guy Reingold, Jon Clifton, Larry Johnson, Peter Crosby, Bill Roden, Mark Svartz (Soho Sq.). **GRAPHIC DESIGN/DIGITAL ART:** Christina Markel, Rana Cline, Anusard Korlarpkitkul. **DEVELOPER (INTERACTIVE):** Devin Gillespie, Greg Rotter, Matt Hoover, Scott Johnson, Andy Slopsema, Jamie Lloyd. **PRODUCER:** Dave King, Raul Aristud, Katherine Ground. **ACCOUNT MANAGEMENT:** Tom Conner, Mark Yesayian, Jessica Soriano. **PROOF-READING/QA:** Gina Poggi. **MEDIA CIRCULATED:** Interactive, OOH, collateral.

CONCEPT: We were looking for something iconic, some way of injecting Yahoo!'s fun, ir-reverent brand into the booming digital music arena. We needed to go big. So, of course, we went small. Really, really small. Leveraging the artwork created by Craig Robinson, we decided to personify Yahoo! Music Unlimited's subscription music service through tiny, 8-bit pixel rock stars – every bit as unpredictable and addictive as their real world counter-parts. **RESULTS:** Prior to the launch of the advertising, new account trials were averaging around 830 per day. Immediately following the campaign, those trial numbers tripled to an average of approximately 2,400 per day and the awareness for Yahoo! Music Unlimited's subscription service skyrocketed as the pixel rockstars began appearing everywhere and almost every major U.S. press agency picked up the story.

CONCEPT : Nous recherchions une image iconique capable de véhiculer le côté ludique et insolent de Yahoo au sein de l'arène musicale numérique en pleine expansion. Il fallait voir grand. Alors bien sûr, on a vu petit. Très, très petit. En nous appuyant sur le design graphi-que de Craig Robinson, nous avons personnifié le service d'abonnement musical Music Unlimited grâce à de minuscules rock stars de 8 bits, chaque bit étant aussi imprévisible que son modèle dans la réalité. **RÉSULTATS :** Avant le lancement de la publicité, les nou-veaux abonnements étaient d'environ 830 par jour. Immédiatement après le lancement, ce chiffre a triplé pour atteindre 2 400 abonnements par jour. La notoriété du service musical de Yahoo! a connu son apogée quand les rock stars pixélisées se sont mises à apparaître partout, relayées par la quasi-totalité des agences de presse américaines.

KONZEPT: Wir suchten nach einem Weg, die lustige, respektlose Marke Yahoo! in die digi-tale Musikarena einzuführen. Es war eine große Sache. Also entschieden wir uns natürlich für etwas Kleines. Sehr, sehr klein. Um das Artwork von Craig Robinson in Schwung zu bringen, entschieden wir uns, das Abonnement von Yahoo! Music Unlimited mit winzigen, 8-Bit-Pixel-Rockstars zu personalisieren – alles so unvorhersehbar und süchtig machend wie ihre realen Pendants. **ERGEBNISSE:** Vor dem Launch der Werbung lagen die Neuanmeldungen bei 830 pro Tag. Unmittelbar nach der Kampagne verdreifachte sich die-se Zahl auf einen Durchschnitt von ca. 2400 pro Tag, und das Bewusstsein für den Aboservice von Yahoo! Music Unlimited Aboservice schoss in die Höhe, als die Pixelrockstars überall erschienen und fast jede große Presseagentur der USA die Story aufgriff.

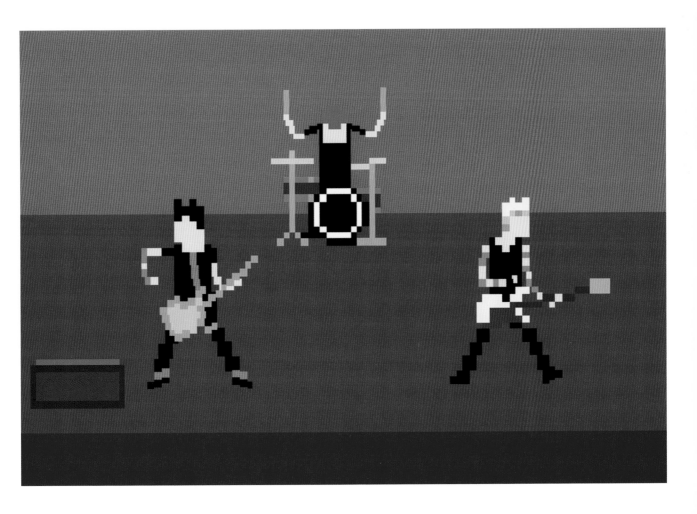

FEATURED ON THE DVD **CAMPAIGN:** 1st Worldwide Search Championship. **YEAR:** 2005. **AGENCY:** DoubleYou <www.doubleyou.com>. **PRODUCTION TIME:** 1 week. **CREATIVE TEAM:** Esther Pino, Daniel Solana, Enric A. Cano, Lisi Badía, Joakim Borgström, Xavi Caparrós. **PROGRAMMER:** Joakim Borgström, Xavi Caparrós. **TECH ASPECTS:** Macromedia Flash, JavaScript. **MEDIA CIRCULATED:** Yahoo!, El Mundo, TPI, Adlink.

CONCEPT: The Masked Searcher faces his efficient competitors to demonstrate his superiority at the moment of searching for something in the net. Who will be the winner in this peculiar combat? The user can select the competing search-engine in the banner, write a search concept and will receive the search results of both competitors real-time on his screen.

CONCEPT : Le Chercheur Masqué affronte ses concurrents afin de démontrer sa supériorité au moment de faire des recherches sur le Net. Qui sera le vainqueur de ce drôle de combat ? L'usager peut sélectionner le moteur de recherche de son choix dans la bannière, entrer une demande et il recevra les résultats des recherches des deux concurrents en temps réel sur son écran.

KONZEPT: Der Masked Searcher tritt seinen Konkurrenten entgegen, um seine momentane Überlegenheit bei der Suche im Internet zu demonstrieren. Wer wird diesen merkwürdigen Kampf gewinnen? Der Benutzer kann eine Suchmaschine im Banner anklicken, ein Suchkonzept schreiben und erhält die Suchergebnisse beider Konkurrenten gleichzeitig auf seinem Bildschirm.

FEATURED ON THE DVD **CAMPAIGN:** Two is one too many. **PRODUCT:** Cisco IP Communication Solutions. **YEAR:** 2004. **AGENCY:** Ogilvy Interactive Worldwide GmbH, Frankfurt, Germany <www.ogilvy-interactive.de>. **PRODUCTION TIME:** 4 weeks. **CREATIVE TEAM:** Ulf Schmidt, Stefanie Lehr, Michael Kutschinski. **PROGRAMMER:** Stefanie Lehr. **MEDIA CIRCULATED:** Macromedia Flash.

CONCEPT: Cisco IP-Communication enterprises can integrate the current telephone network completely into the existing data network. Doing this means companies have only one network instead of two – and will save money for maintenance, administration and replacements. The online banner campaign brought to life the complexity of the unnecessarily doubled infrastructure – and showed the advantage of a converged solution. The users learned that two (networks, goals in football, balls in a game, banner) is one too many. **RESULTS:** The online campaign generated more than 1,000 potential new business customers for Cisco IP Communication, and some of them even requested specific proposals. Considering the fact that this was a business-to-business campaign for a complex solution, the results were outstanding – and that is exactly what Cisco said about the campaign.

CONCEPT : La société Cisco IP-Communication peut intégrer en totalité le réseau téléphonique dans le réseau de données existant. Ainsi les entreprises n'ont plus qu'un seul réseau au lieu de deux, ce qui permet d'économiser sur la maintenance, l'administration et les remplacements. La campagne a voulu démontrer la complexité et l'inutilité d'une double infrastructure, et les avantages d'une solution convergente. L'usager découvre que deux (deux réseaux, deux goals au foot, deux ballons dans un jeu, deux bannières) est souvent un de trop. **RÉSULTATS :** La campagne en ligne a généré plus de 1 000 nouveaux clients potentiels, et certains d'entre eux ont même soumis des demandes de services personnalisés. S'agissant d'une campagne sur le réseau interentreprises, les résultats sont remarquables, et c'est aussi l'avis de l'annonceur.

KONZEPT: Cisco IP-Communication können das derzeitige Telefonnetzwerk komplett in das existierende Datennetzwerk integrieren. Das heißt, Unternehmen haben dadurch ein Netzwerk statt zwei – und sparen Geld für Wartung, Administration und Ersatz. Die Onlinebanner-Kampagne verdeutlichte die Komplexität der unnötigen zweifachen Infrastruktur und zeigte den Vorteil einer konvergierten Lösung. Die Benutzer erfuhren, dass zwei (Netzwerke, Tore beim Fußball, Bälle in einem Spiel, Banner) eins zu viel sind. **ERGEBNISSE:** Die Online-Kampagne warb mehr als 1 000 potenzielle neue Geschäftskunden für Cisco IP Communication. Einige davon baten um spezifische Angebote. Bedenkt man, dass es eine B2B-Kampagne für eine komplexe Lösung war, waren die Ergebnisse herausragend – und genau das sagte Cisco über die Kampagne.

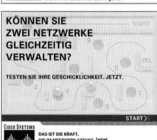

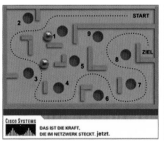
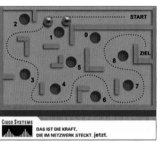

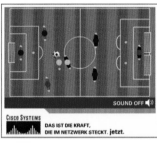

FEATURED ON THE DVD **CAMPAIGN:** Smashing Windows™ – Fifa Street <www.fifastreetmovie.com/uk>. **PRODUCT:** Fifa Street. **CLIENT:** Electronic Arts. **YEAR:** 2004. **AGENCY:** 20:20 London <www.2020london.co.uk>. **PRODUCTION TIME:** 1 month. **CREATIVE TEAM:** Peter Riley (Creative Partner), Hugo Bierschenk (Creative), Dean Woodhouse (Creative). **PROGRAMMER:** Dave Luff, Simon James. **TECH ASPECTS:** film, sound, Adobe After Effects, Macromedia Flash, Wavelab, Flame, 3D Studio Max, Maya, Shake, Adobe Premiere, Apple Quicktime Pro. **MEDIA CIRCULATED:** Email. **AWARDS:** Direct Marketing Association (UK), Campaign Digital Awards (UK), Cannes International Advertising Awards.

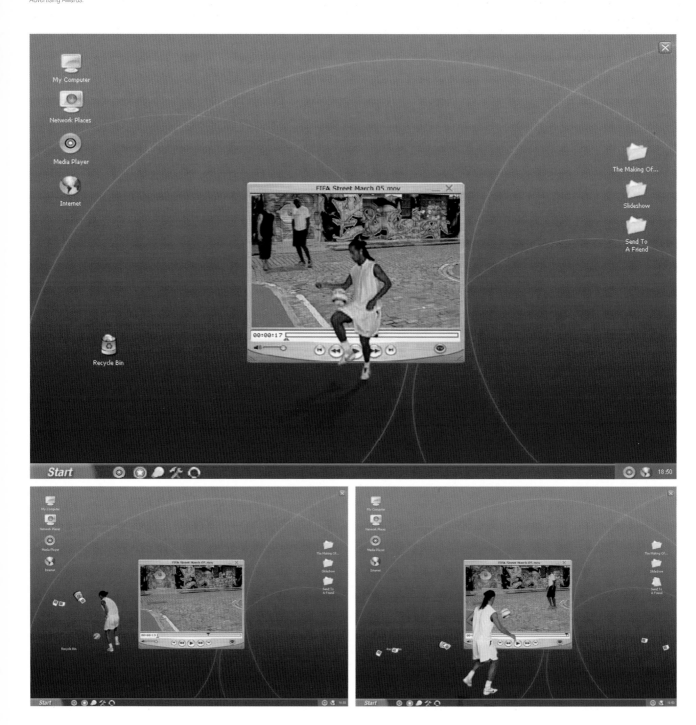

CONCEPT AND COALS: Create a new media communication plan to launch the new FIFA Street football game from Electronic Arts across Europe. The game licenses Ronaldinho, the current World Player of the Year. **INNOVATIVE MEDIA STRATEGY:** imagine if Ronaldinho came to life and interacted with your computer and your mobile phone. **ENGAGING CREATIVITY:** An e-mail link to a viral film shows what seems to be a regular Quicktime movie where Ronaldinho is shown performing ball skills in a film clip. Suddenly, Ronaldinho jumps out of the Quicktime window and dribbles the ball around icons on your desktop – knocking over your computer's trash and desktop folders and ending by kicking the ball against the close button. Additionally games fans can watch the making of the film, view a slideshow and forward to a friend. On your mobile phone, you can watch Ronaldinho head the ball off the side of the phone and knock over your battery icons. **ENCOMPASSING THE AUDIENCE:** the unique Internet and mobile phone film combined the world's biggest games company with the world's best footballer to create a film that fits in with the whole approach of getting closer to street football. **EFFECTIVENESS:** the FIFA Street launch was so successful that the e-mail open rate was over 50%, with over 100,000 unique users in the first 2 weeks, with over 50% of viewers forwarding it to a friend.

OBJECTIFS : Elaborer un plan média pour le lancement européen du jeu de football FIFA Street distribué par Electronic Arts. Le jeu met Ronaldinho en vedette, le détenteur actuel du titre de Meilleur Joueur de l'Année. **STRATÉGIE :** Imaginez que Ronaldinho interagit avec votre ordinateur et votre téléphone mobile. **CRÉATIVITÉ :** Un e-mail renvoie à un film viral ressemblant à un module Quicktime classique, qui présente le joueur en train de faire des passes. Soudain, Ronaldinho sort de la fenêtre Quicktime et se met à dribbler autour des icônes de votre bureau, fait valser la poubelle et les dossiers, et envoie le ballon sur le bouton d'arrêt. Les fans de jeux peuvent également visionner le tournage du film, une gale-

rie de photos et faire suivre le lien à un ami. Sur votre mobile, Ronaldinho frappe le ballon de la tête et renverse l'icône de niveau de charge de la batterie. **ATTIRER LE PUBLIC :** Le film Internet et la création pour mobile ont associé la plus grande société mondiale de jeu et le meilleur joueur du monde dans une démarche visant à se rapprocher du football de rue. **EFFICACITÉ :** Le lancement du jeu a remporté un tel succès que plus de 50% des e-mails ont été ouverts, le site a attiré plus de 100 000 visiteurs uniques dans les deux premières semaines et plus de 50% d'entre eux l'ont fait suivre à un ami.

KONZEPT UND ZIELE: Einen Kommunikationsplan mit neuen Medien für den Launch des neuen FIFA Straßenfußballspiels von Electronic Arts in Europa erstellen. Das Spiel sicherte sich Rechte von Ronaldinho, dem derzeitigen World Player of the Year. **INNOVATIVE MEDIENSTRATEGIE:** Man stelle sich vor, Ronaldinho erwache zum Leben und interagiere mit dem eigenen Computer und Handy. **KREATIVITÄT ANREGEN:** Ein E-Mail-Link zu einem viralen Quicktime-Film, in dem man Ronaldinho spielen sieht. Plötzlich springt er aus dem Quicktime-Fenster und dribbelt den Ball um die Icons auf dem Desktop, stößt Papierkorb und Ordner um und schießt den Ball schließlich auf den Knopf „Schließen". Zusätzlich können Fans die Entstehung des Films und eine Slideshow sehen und sie an Freunde versenden. Auf dem Handy kann man Ronaldinho beobachten, wie er mit dem Ball die Batterie-Icons umstößt. **DAS PUBLIKUM UMFASSEN:** Der einzigartige Internet- und Handyfilm kombinierte das größte Spieleunternehmen der Welt mit dem weltbesten Fußballer und passte damit zu dem Anliegen, dem Straßenfußball näher zu kommen. **EFFIZIENZ:** Der Launch war so erfolgreich, dass die Rate der geöffneten E-Mails bei über 50% lag, mit über 100 000 einzelnen Benutzern in den ersten zwei Wochen. Über 50% der Nutzer leiteten das Spiel an einen Freund weiter.

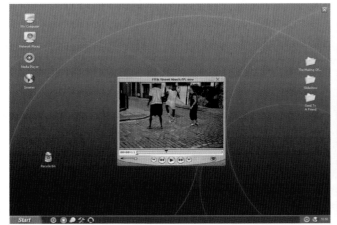

CAMPAIGN: Xbox Forza.   YEAR: 2005.   AGENCY: AKQA <www.akqa.com>.   CREATIVE TEAM: Kevin Russell, James Hilton.   PROGRAMMER: Tristan Celder, Sachin Shah.   TECH ASPECTS: Macromedia Flash, Akamai.

OBJECTIVE: Play Forza Motorsport on Xbox and you enter the obsessive, creative, high-octane world of modified racing, or 'modding'. It was our job to capture the energy and excitement of this emerging scene to entice car-crazy Xbox owners to try the game. **STRATEGY:** The only way truly to understand the passion and dedication of modders is to see them for yourself. Video was the obvious solution, but we wanted something entirely new that would capture the immediacy and pace of the racing scene, as well as showcase the game. **SOLUTION:** We delivered a world first: a large-screen television-style 'broadcast' over the web – FMC.tv. The channel featured a series of documentaries about the world of modding inter-cut with VJ links and advertisements for Forza Motorsport and Xbox Live®. Uniquely, the video stream was independent of user interaction – so every time Xbox owners visited the site they would see something different. The multilingual, pan-European site was supported by extensive online marketing handled by our team, in addition to press, TV and cinema developed by McCann Erickson. Xbox promoted the site via seeding forums and gaming community sites.

OBJECTIF : Jouez à Forza Motorsport sur Xbox et pénétrez dans l'univers débridé, créatif et obsessionnel de la modification de console. Nous devions retranscrire l'énergie et l'excitation de cette nouvelle tendance en invitant les propriétaires de Xbox amateurs de courses autos à essayer le nouveau jeu. **STRATÉGIE :** La seule façon d'appréhender la passion et l'implication des « modders » (adeptes des modifications et du piratage), est encore de les voir à l'oeuvre. La vidéo était une solution évidente, mais nous voulions une chose totalement nouvelle qui capterait le rythme et l'instantanéité d'une course auto, tout en présentant le jeu. **SOLUTION :** En première mondiale, un canal de télévision sur le Net : FMC.tv. Le support présentait une série de documentaires sur l'univers des « modders », entrecou-

pés de liens VJ et de pubs pour la Xbox et le jeu Forza Motorsport. La vidéo était singulièrement indépendante de l'interaction de l'usager, ainsi les propriétaires de Xbox pouvaient-ils visionner une vidéo différente à chacune de leur visite sur le site. Le site européen et multilingue a été soutenu par une grande opération marketing en ligne gérée par notre équipe, qui venait s'ajouter à une campagne de presse, et à des annonces à la télévision et au cinéma gérées par McCann Erickson. La Xbox a promu le site en l'annonçant sur des forums et des communautés de joueurs.

ZIEL: Spiel Forza Motorsport auf Xbox und tritt in die obsessive, kreative, hyper-dynamische Welt des „modified racing", oder „Modding", ein. Unsere Aufgabe bestand darin, die Energie und Aufregung dieser Szene einzufangen, um autoverrückte Xbox-Eigentümer anzulocken, das Spiel auszuprobieren. **STRATEGIE:** Der einzige Weg, die Leidenschaft und Hingabe von Moddern zu verstehen, ist, sie mit eigenen Augen zu sehen. Video war die offensichtliche Lösung, aber wir wollten etwas absolut Neues, das die Unmittelbarkeit und Geschwindigkeit der Rennszene spiegelte und gleichzeitig das Spiel darstellte. **LÖSUNG:** Wir boten etwas komplett Neues: einen großformatigen, fernsehähnlichen Sender über das Web – FMC.tv. Der Kanal beinhaltete einige Dokumentationen über die Welt des Modding, unterbrochen von VJ-Links und Werbung für Forza Motorsport und Xbox Live®. Der Video-Stream war unabhängig von Benutzerinteraktion, wodurch Xbox-Eigentümer jedes Mal, wenn sie die Seite besuchten, etwas anderes sahen. Die multilinguale, paneuropäische Seite wurde durch breites Online-Marketing unseres Teams unterstützt, zusätzlich zu Presse-, Fernseh- und Kinowerbung von McCann Erickson. Xbox warb durch Foren und Spielergemeinden für die Seite.

FEATURED ON THE DVD **CAMPAIGN:** Xbox Origen. **YEAR:** 2005. **AGENCY:** AKQA <www.akqa.com>. **CREATIVE TEAM:** James Hilton, Kevin Russell, Phil Wilce. **PROGRAMMER:** Dan Wood, Sachin Shah. **TECH ASPECTS:** Macromedia Flash, film, sound.

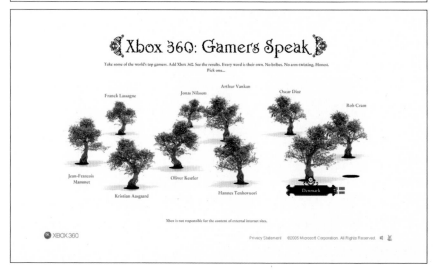

OBJECTIVE: Imagine the most cynical person in the world. Then multiply the cynicism by a factor of ten. You now have something approaching the attitude with which gamers approach marketing messages from console manufacturers. Battle-scarred by past disappointments at the hands of Xbox's competitors, they are inured to hyperbole. It was our job to get these people excited about the launch of Xbox 360. **STRATEGY:** Given the target audience, we knew we could forget about high-blown claims and marketing speak. We'd be justifiably ripped apart in the forums. No. We needed something existential. Something very, very cool – and we needed to let the gamers think they were the only ones who could figure the whole thing out. **SOLUTION:** What on earth do two talking white rabbits and a big tree have to do with Xbox 360? This was the question occupying gamers in the weeks after the launch of the site, hosted by furry friends Didier and Boss. Precisely the effect we were looking for. Following the site's completely un-promoted or seeded launch, additional content was drip-fed until the online chatter reached fever-pitch. Only once gamers had worked themselves up into an explosive frenzy of anticipation was it revealed that Origen is, in fact, a gamers' paradise and gamers were offered eight opportunities to attend. **RESULTS:** 1.5 million visits to the site – an average of 27,713 a day – without any promotion whatsoever.

OBJECTIF : Prenez la personne la plus cynique du monde, puis multipliez son cynisme par dix. Vous obtenez alors un comportement approchant celui des joueurs face aux messages marketing produits par les fabricants de console. Déçus par les opérations de ce type menés par les concurrents de la Xbox, les joueurs sont insensibles à l'hyperbole. Notre mission était pourtant de les intéresser au lancement de la Xbox 360. **STRATÉGIE :** Vu le groupe cible, nous savions que nous devions éviter les slogans racoleurs et le jargon marketing. Nous risquions de nous faire incendier à juste droit sur les forums. Non, il nous fallait quelque chose d'existentiel. Un truc cool, hyper cool, et il fallait laisser penser aux joueurs qu'ils étaient les seuls à pouvoir comprendre l'histoire. **SOLUTION :** Quel est donc le rapport entre deux lapins blancs, un gros arbre et la Xbox 360 ? La question a occupé les joueurs pendant les semaines qui ont suivi le lancement du site, présenté par les deux compères à fourrure Didier et Boss. Exactement l'effet que nous avions recherché. Sans faire aucune espèce de promotion du site, nous avons distillé des infos au compte-gouttes jusqu'à ce les forums bruissent d'hypothèses. Et une fois que les joueurs se sont mis dans un état d'excitation suffisante, nous avons révélé que Origen était en fait un paradis pour joueurs, et ceux-ci se sont vu offrir huit occasions d'assister au lancement. **RÉSULTATS :** 1,5 million de visiteurs sur le site, avec une moyenne de 27 713 personnes par jour, sans aucune forme de promotion.

ZIEL: Stellen Sie sich die zynischste Person der Welt vor. Multiplizieren Sie den Zynismus mit zehn. Dann erhalten Sie annähernd die Einstellung, mit der Spieler den Marketingbotschaften von Konsolenherstellern gegenüberstehen. Mit Kampfverletzungen durch vergangene Enttäuschungen durch Xbox-Konkurrenten versehen, an Übertreibungen gewöhnt – diese Leute mussten wir für den Launch von Xbox 360° begeistern. **STRATEGIE:** Bei der gegebenen Zielgruppe konnten wir hochtrabende Aussagen und Marketingsprache vergessen. Wir würden in den Foren zerrissen werden. Nein. Wir brauchten etwas Existentielles. Etwas extrem Cooles. Und wir mussten die Spieler in dem Glauben lassen, dass sie die Einzigen waren, die das Ganze verstehen könnten. **LÖSUNG:** Was in aller Welt haben zwei sprechende weiße Kaninchen und ein großer Baum mit Xbox 360° zu tun? Das war die Frage, die Spieler in den Wochen nach dem Launch der Seite beschäftigte (Host: Didier und Boss). Genau der Effekt, auf den wir abzielten. Nachdem für den Launch der Seite überhaupt nicht geworben worden war, wurde nach und nach Inhalt hinzugefügt, bis das Online-Geplapper seinen Höhepunkt erreichte. Erst, als sich die Spieler in eine Ekstase der Erwartung hineingesteigert hatten, kam ans Tageslicht, dass Origen ein Paradies für Spieler ist. Ihnen wurden acht Gelegenheiten geboten, teilzunehmen. **ERGEBNISSE:** 1,5 Millionen Seitenbesucher – ein Durchschnitt von 27 713 pro Tag – ohne irgendeine Form von Werbung.

The seed grew into this wonderful tree...

XBOX 360

FEATURED ON THE DVD **CAMPAIGN:** 24: The Game <www.underground-bunker.com>. **PRODUCT:** 24: The Game (Sony PlayStation). **CLIENT:** PlayStation. **YEAR:** 2006. **AGENCY:** 20:20 London <www.2020london.co.uk>. **PRODUCTION TIME:** 5 weeks. **CREATIVE TEAM:** Peter Riley (Creative Partner); Hugo Bierschenk (Creative); Dean Woodhouse (Creative). **PROGRAMMER:** Simon James. **TECH ASPECTS:** Macromedia Flash, Adobe After Effects, Final Cut Pro. **MEDIA CIRCULATED:** Email. **AWARDS:** Cannes Advertising Festival 2006 (Product Launch Strategy – Gold; Consumer Product Campaign – Gold; Media Integration – Silver; Use of Internet – Bronze).

THE BRIEF: The '24' TV series, starring Kiefer Sutherland is the biggest show in Fox's history. Adrenaline, intrigue, and plot twists make it compelling viewing. We needed to launch the computer game spin-off, '24: The Game' by staying true to the Show's values. However, the game goes one step further, allowing YOU to take on the role of a Counter Terrorist Agent. **OBJECTIVES:** Generate interest and excitement around the new game beyond screengrabs and reviews. Create a truly integrated and interactive campaign, one that engages the user across various media (email, SMS, personalized Internet films and direct mail) and gives a real taste of the 24: The Game action and storyline. **STRATEGY BEHIND THE WORK:** Let's treat the marketing campaign as a 'mission' just like the game. Let's reward consumers for their efforts and involvement. And let's create the ultimate interactive experience using new and old media. **RESULTS:** This wasn't just a communication to create awareness or to get a game out to fans but to reward and remind them that Sony and PS2 know about the excitement and interaction of action. An initial e-mail was sent to hard-core gamers on the PS2 database, with 12,169 views of the first film, representing a click through rate of 38.9% (a good result according to the DMA is 15%). 82.9% of those went on to view the second personalized film having received the SMS at the end of the first film in real time. They then went on to receive the DM pack. **WORD OF MOUTH:** When film 1 and 2 were forwarded to a friend, the recipient saw a special combined movie 3. In total this movie was viewed 443,290 times which suggest that each e-mail was opened and viewed and was forwarded 36 times. Overall this equates to delivering a rich brand experience costing a mere 26 pounds per person and delivering an ROI not possible using traditional communications.

EN RÉSUMÉ : La série télévisée « 24 Heures Chrono », avec Kiefer Sutherland, est le programme qui a eu le plus grand succès de l'histoire de la Fox. Adrénaline, intrigue et coups de théâtre sont les ingrédients de la fascination qu'elle a provoquée. Nous voulions lancer le jeu sur console, « 24 Heures Chrono : Le Jeu » en restant fidèles aux valeurs de la série. Mais le jeu va un peu plus loin, car VOUS pouvez jouer le rôle d'un agent de la lutte anti-terrorisme. **OBJECTIFS :** Générer l'intérêt du public et créer un événement autour du nouveau jeu en allant au-delà des captures d'écran et des critiques dans les magazines. Créer une campagne véritablement intégrée et interactive, atteignant l'utilisateur à travers plusieurs supports (e-mail, SMS, films Internet personnalisés et courrier), et qui donne un réel avant-goût de l'action et de l'histoire de 24 Heures Chrono : Le Jeu. **LA STRATÉGIE DERRIÈRE LE TRAVAIL :** Nous avons traité la campagne marketing comme une « mission », exactement comme dans le jeu. Il fallait remercier les consommateurs pour leurs efforts et leur participation, et leur donner la meilleure expérience interactive du marché, en utilisant les supports les plus modernes ainsi que des supports plus traditionnels. **RÉSULTAT :** Il ne s'agissait pas d'une simple campagne de communication pour informer

le public ou pour faire arriver le jeu jusqu'aux fans de la série. Il s'agissait de récompenser le public, et de rappeler que Sony et PS2 s'y connaissent en action et en interaction. On a d'abord envoyé un e-mail aux joueurs invétérés de la base de données de PS2, et le premier film a été visionné 12 169 fois, ce qui représente un taux de clics de 38.9 % (selon DMA, 15 % est un bon résultat). 82,9 % de ces personnes ont continué et ont vu le deuxième film personnalisé après avoir reçu le SMS à la fin du premier film, en temps réel. Puis ils ont continué et ont reçu le pack DM. **BOUCHE À OREILLE :** Lorsqu'un utilisateur faisait suivre les films 1 et 2 à un ami, il recevait un troisième film combiné spécial. Au total, ce film a été vu 443 290 fois, ce qui laisse supposer que chaque e-mail a été ouvert, lu et retransmis 36 fois. Dans l'ensemble, cela équivaut à communiquer de manière très intense et personnalisée autour de la marque pour seulement un quart de dollar par personne. C'est un retour sur investissement qui aurait été impossible avec les outils de communication traditionnels.

AUFGABE: Die TV-Serie „24" mit Kiefer Sutherland ist der größte Erfolg in der Geschichte des Fernsehsenders Fox. Adrenalin, Intrigen und die unerwarteten Wendungen in der Handlung sorgen für ein spannendes Fernseherlebnis. Für das Computerspiel zur Serie, „24: The Game", musste die Qualität der Serie fortgeführt werden. Das Spiel geht jedoch noch einen Schritt weiter, indem es dem Spieler in die Rolle eines terroristischen Agenten versetzt. **ZIELE:** Die Aufmerksamkeit für das Spiel jenseits von Screengrabs und Kritiken wecken. Eine integrierte und interaktive Kampagne, die Benutzer aller Medien (E-Mail, SMS, personalisierte Internetfilme und Post) anspricht und einen Eindruck von Action und Handlungsverlauf des Spiels gibt. **STRATEGIE:** Die Kampagne sollte, wie das Spiel, als „Mission" verstanden werden. Konsumenten sollten für ihre Anstrengungen belohnt werden. Mit Hilfe von neuen und alten Medien wollte man ein ultimatives interaktives Erlebnis schaffen. **ERGEBNISSE:** Hier handelte es sich nicht um bloße Kommunikation, um Aufmerksamkeit zu erregen oder Fans ein Spiel zu präsentieren, sondern die Fans sollten belohnt werden – und man wollte ihnen bewusst machen, dass sich Sony und PS2 bei der Interaktion von Action auskennen. Zunächst wurde eine E-Mail an die Hardcore-Spieler auf der PS2-Datenbank versendet: 12 169 Zuschauer sahen den ersten Film, was einer Clickthrough-Rate von 38,9 % entspricht (laut DMA sind schon 15 % ein gutes Ergebnis). 82,9 % sahen auch den zweiten personalisierten Film, nachdem sie direkt nach dem Ende des ersten Films eine SMS erhalten hatten. Danach bestellten sie das DM-Paket. **MUNDPROPAGANDA:** Leitete man Film 1 und 2 an einen Freund weiter, sah der Empfänger einen speziell kombinierten Film 3. Insgesamt wurde dieser Film 443 290 Mal gesehen – d.h. jede E-Mail wurde 36 Mal geöffnet, angesehen und weitergeleitet. Das bedeutet, dass ein einzigartiges Markenerlebnis für nur ca. 50 Cent pro Person geliefert wurde – und damit ein ROI, der über traditionelle Kommunikationswege nicht möglich gewesen wäre.

FEATURED ON THE DVD **CAMPAIGN:** "fun, anyone?" **PRODUCT:** PlayStation 2. **YEAR:** 2004. **AGENCY:** Ogilvy Interactive Worldwide GmbH, Frankfurt, Germany <www.ogilvy-interactive.de>. **PRODUCTION TIME:** 4 weeks.
CREATIVE TEAM: Andrea Goebel, Thorsten Voigt. **PROGRAMMER:** Thorsten Voigt. **TECH ASPECTS:** Macromedia Flash.

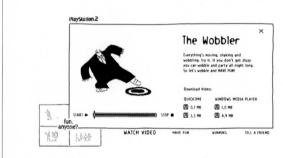

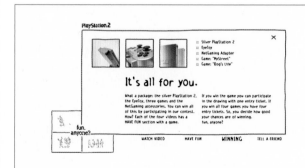

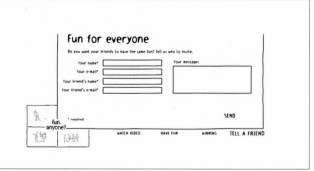

CONCEPT: New characters conquer the Internet: Robogirl, Wobbler, Winner and Laughing Mouth. They make the new PlayStation claim "fun, anyone?" come alive. Each banner ad invites the user to interact with the characters in a way that corresponds to the specific website. On the microsite, the user can not only watch and download the films, he can also interact with each character in four little games to experience them in a new way. Those games are simply fun and with a little bit of luck you can win a PlayStation 2 package.
RESULTS: The average click rate was over 7% which is more than 5 times higher than an average image campaign. The click rates for the microsite were also impressively high. For example, in the first month more than 90,000 users visited the microsite even though only 50,000 monthly visits were expected. Each visitor spent more than 4 minutes on the site. Finally, the "fun, anyone?" campaign has won 10 awards and nominations: Gold at the New York Festivals, the Cresta Awards and the German Multimedia Award and silver at the One Show and nominations at the Clio Awards, ADC New York, ADC Germany, D&AD Awards and Cannes Cyber Lions.

CONCEPT : De nouveaux personnages envahissent Internet : Robogirl, Wobbler et Laughing Mouth. Ils incarnent le slogan de PlayStation : « Qui veut rigoler ? » Chaque bannière invite l'usager à interagir avec les personnages suivant le style du site. Sur le micro-site, l'usager peut visionner et télécharger les films, et participer à quatre petits jeux pour découvrir les personnages sous un nouvel angle. Ces jeux sont distrayants et avec un peu de chance, on peut gagner une PlayStation 2. **RÉSULTATS :** Le taux moyen de clics a dépassé 7%, ce qui est cinq fois supérieur à une campagne d'image ordinaire. Le taux de clics pour le micro-site

a été aussi très élevé. Par exemple, durant le premier mois, plus de 90 000 usagers ont visité le micro-site, alors qu'on attendait seulement 50 000 visiteurs. La durée moyenne d'une session a été de 4 minutes. Finalement, la campagne «Qui veut rigoler ? » a remporté 10 récompenses et nominations. La Médaille d'Or au New York Festival, aux Cresta Awards et aux German Multimedia Awards, la Médaille d'Argent au OneShow, et des nominations aux Clio Awards, ADC New York, ADC Germany, D&A Awards et aux Cyber Lions de Cannes.

KONZEPT: Neue Figuren erobern das Internet: Robogirl, Wobbler, Winner und Laughing Mouth. Sie erwecken den neuen PlayStation-Spruch „fun, anyone?" zum Leben. Jede Bannerwerbung lädt den Benutzer ein, mit den Figuren auf eine Weise zu interagieren, die mit der spezifischen Webseite korrespondiert. Auf der Microsite kann der Benutzer nicht nur Filme sehen und downloaden, sondern er kann auch mit jedem Charakter in vier kleinen Spielen interagieren, um sie auf neue Weise zu erleben. Diese Spiele machen einfach Spaß, und mit ein bisschen Glück kann man eine PlayStation 2 gewinnen. **ERGEBNISSE:** Die durchschnittliche CTR lag bei über 7% und damit fünfmal höher als bei einer normalen Image-Kampagne. Die CTR für die Microsite war ebenfalls beeindruckend hoch. Beispielsweise besuchten im ersten Monat über 90 000 Besucher die Microsite, obwohl man nur 50 000 monatliche Besuche erwartet hatte. Jeder verweilte über vier Minuten auf der Seite. Außerdem gewann die „fun, anyone?"-Kampagne zehn Auszeichnungen und Nominierungen: Gold bei den New York Festivals, den Cresta Awards und dem German Multimedia Award; Silber bei der One Show; Nominierungen bei den Clio Awards, ADC New York, ADC Germany, D&AD Awards und Cannes Cyber Lions.

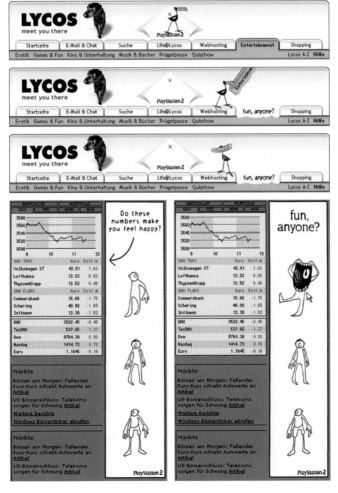

FEATURED ON THE DVD **CAMPAIGN:** Metroid Prime 2 Echoes <http://metroid.com/main.htm>. **PRODUCT:** Metroid Prime 2 Echoes Microsite. **YEAR:** 2005. **AGENCY:** 2Advanced Studios <www.2advanced.com>. **COLABORATION:** Nintendo of America. **PRODUCTION TIME:** 3 weeks. **CREATIVE TEAM:** Eric Jordan, Shane Mielke. **TECH ASPECTS:** Macromedia Flash, video, sound. **AWARDS:** Marcom Creative Awards (Platinum), WebAward (Outstanding), Web Marketing Association's Internet Advertising Awards (Best Entertainment Microsite/Landing Page), Summit Creative Awards (Silver), Orange County Ad Awards (Silver), Horizon Interactive Awards (Silver), TINY Awards (Site of the Day), FWA (Site of the Day).

CONCEPT: Nintendo of America approached 2Advanced Studios to help promote the launch of Metroid Prime 2 Echoes, the latest installment from the wildly successful Metroid game series. The Metroid game series dates back to the original game's release in 1986, therefore the campaign needed to cater to dedicated, long-time Metroid fans. Over 40 domains were registered and launched prior to the game's release to generate a buzz within the large Metroid fanbase. Channel 51 <channel51.org>, Orbis Labs <orbislabs.com>, and the Luminoth Temple Website <luminothtemple.com> were among the domains designed to be part of an underground marketing campaign to virally market the Metroid brand through hints at its plot line. **RESULTS:** The entire campaign was extremely successful in generating a buzz within the long-standing Metroid community. Visitors flooded the online forums to discuss the newly launched websites. Channel 51 received 100,000 visitors within the first 18 days alone. The password-protected section of Orbis Labs received over 25,000 login attempts.

CONCEPT: L'américain Nintendo a chargé les studios 2Advanced de promouvoir le lancement de Metroid Prime 2 Echoes, le dernier volet de la série à succès Metroid. La série des Metroid ayant démarré avec le premier jeu sorti en 1986, la campagne s'adressait donc à des fans de longue date. Quelques 40 noms de domaine furent enregistrés et déposés avant le lancement officiel du jeu afin de générer un buzz au sein de la communauté de fidèles. Parmi les sites destinés à soutenir une campagne de marketing virale, Channel51.org, Orbislabs.com et luminothtemple.com ont distillé des informations sur le scénario du jeu. **RÉSULTATS :** La campagne a réussi à générer un buzz parmi la communauté des amateurs de Metroid. Les visiteurs ont submergé les forums en ligne pour commenter les nouveaux sites. Channel 51 a reçu 100 000 visiteurs en 18 jours. La rubrique de Orbis Labs, dont l'entrée nécessitait un mot de passe, a enregistré plus de 25 000 tentatives de connexion.

KONZEPT: Nintendo in Amerika beauftragte 2Advanced Studios damit, für den Launch der Metroid Prime 2 Echoes zu werben, die neueste Folge der erfolgreichen Metroid-Spielserie. Diese geht zurück auf die Veröffentlichung des Originalspiels 1986; daher musste die Kampagne hingebungsvolle Metroid-Fans ansprechen, die schon seit langem spielen. Über 40 Domains wurden vor der Veröffentlichung des Spiels registriert und eingeführt, um Aufregung innerhalb der großen Metroid-Fangemeinde zu entfachen. Channel 51 <channel51.org>, Orbis Labs <orbislabs.com> und die Luminoth Temple Webseite <luminothtemple.com> waren einige der Domänen, die Teil einer Underground-Marketingkampagne werden sollten, um die Metroid-Marke viral durch Hinweise auf seine Handlung zu vermarkten. **ERGEBNISSE:** Die gesamte Kampagne war äußerst erfolgreich, indem sie Aufregung innerhalb der alteingesessenen Metroid-Gemeinde erzeugte. Die Online-Foren wurden von Besuchern überflutet, die die neuen Webseiten diskutierten. Channel 51 erhielt 500 000 Besucher allein innerhalb der ersten 18 Tage. Im passwortgeschützten Bereich von Orbis Labs gab es über 25 000 Log-ins.

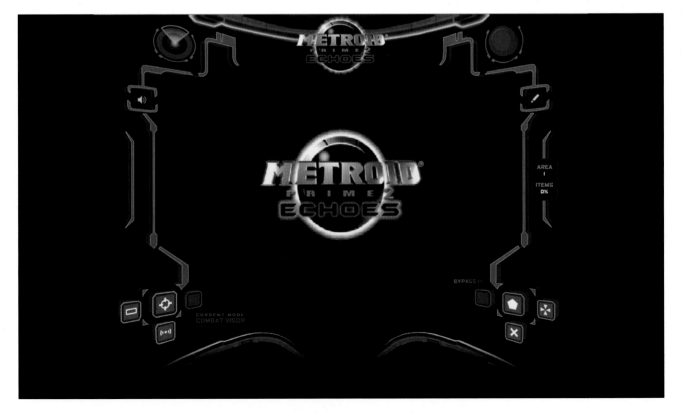

CAMPAIGN: Monopoly Live <www.monopolylive.com>. PRODUCT: Monopoly Here and Now – Special Edition. YEAR: 2005. AGENCY: Tribal DDB London <www.tribalddb.com>. PRODUCTION TIME: 8 weeks. CREATIVE TEAM: Ben Clapp, Chris Jenkins, Jamie Copeland, Alex Braxton, Amy Gould. PROGRAMMER: Chris Walker, Paul James, Matt Oxley, Colin Humphreys. TECH ASPECTS: A dedicated (n+1) platform based on the Redhat Enterprise operating system, Apache 2, TUX and mySQL RDBMS was built to handle all data, process the game updates and deliver all game related content via web, email and SMS in a high traffic environment. The game was played through a Macromedia Flash user interface which communicated in real time to the main game engine using Asynchronous JavaScript and XML (AJAX). The main game engine, responsible for processing all data and updating each user account every fifteen minutes - whilst avoiding cascade overrun - was written in a combination of PHP, Perl (for multithreading) and Shell script (for automatic execution of base level processes). In all, 14 separate servers on two networks were responsible for executing their respective parts of the game process every fifteen minutes, for the 4 weeks. MEDIA CIRCULATED: TV, radio, online, PR, word of mouth.

CONCEPT: When is a taxi not a taxi? When it's a skateboard… To celebrate the launch of Monopoly Here & Now – a fully updated version of the boardgame, we created the biggest game of Monopoly ever played. This was a real-life interactive version played over the streets of London with Taxis as the playing pieces. 18 cabs were fitted with GPS, liveried in Monopoly colours and painted as one of the new movers: Skateboard, Jumbo, Rollerblade, Bus, F1 car, Mobile phone. For 28 days, wherever the cabs went in London was relayed to our website where hundreds of thousands of players competed to be the UK's biggest property tycoon. A dedicated (n+1) platform based on the Redhat Enterprise operating system, Apache 2, TUX and mySQL RDBMS was built to handle all data, process the game updates and deliver all game related content via web, e-mail and SMS in a high traffic environment. The game was played through a Macromedia Flash user interface which communicated in real time to the main game engine using Asynchronous JavaScript and XML (AJAX). The main game engine, responsible for processing all data and updating each user account every fifteen minutes – whilst avoiding cascade overrun – was written in a combination of PHP, Perl (for multithreading) and Shell script (for automatic execution of base level processes). In all, 14 separate servers on two networks were responsible for executing their respective parts of the game process every fifteen minutes, for the 4 weeks. **RESULTS:** The Monopoly 'Here and Now' Limited Edition board game is already one of the best selling games of 2005. This is even more of an achievement if you consider these figures when board game sales are traditionally in a period of hibernation. The PR coverage alone generated well over £2 million of value for Hasbro – nearly five times the cost of the entire campaign. Whilst generating a buzz was a primary objective, there were other significant returns on investment. Monopoly Live has also bolstered the Hasbro CRM database by almost 100,000 opted in users, keen to hear about new developments from Hasbro. The game itself is now a valuable asset for Hasbro, and there are plans to possibly develop the idea further. **NUMBERS:** during the 28 days the site was live, we had over 1 million visitors to the site and 189,699 people played Monopoly Live. Each player played three games on average, and on each visit remained on the site for over five minutes.

CONCEPT : Quand un taxi n'est-il pas un taxi ? Quand c'est un skateboard ! Pour fêter le lancement du Monopoly Here & Now, une version actualisée du célèbre jeu de plateau, nous avons réalisé la plus grande partie de Monopoly jamais jouée. C'est une version interactive et grandeur nature jouée dans les rues de Londres avec des taxis comme pièces. 18 taxis équipés de GPS, habillés aux couleurs du Monopoly et peints comme les nouvelles pièces du jeu : skateboard, Jumbo, rollers, bus, Formule 1, et téléphone mobile. Pendant 28 jours, l'endroit où se rendaient les taxis était relayé au site Internet où des centaines de milliers de joueurs s'affrontaient pour devenir le plus gros propriétaire foncier de Grande-Bretagne. Une plateforme dédiée (N+1) basée sur le système d'exploitation de Redhat Enterprise, Apache 2, et utilisant les applications Tux et mySQL RDBMS a été créée pour gérer toutes les données, traiter les mises à jour et délivrer le contenu relatif au jeu via Internet, les e-mails et les SMS dans un environnement de fort trafic. Le jeu a été joué via une interface utilisateur en Macromedia qui communiquait en temps réel avec le principal moteur de jeu en utilisant les langages Asynchronous JavaScript et XML (AJAX). Le principal moteur de jeu, responsable du traitement des données et des mises à jour usager toutes les quinze minutes, tout en évitant les erreurs de cadence, utilisait une combinaison de programmes PHP, Perl (pour le traitement multiprocessus) et Shell script (pour

l'exécution automatique des tâches du niveau de base) . En tout, 14 serveurs distincts sur deux réseaux étaient chargés d'exécuter leur part des processus du jeu toutes les quinze minutes, et cela pendant 4 semaines. **RÉSULTATS :** La série limitée Here & Now du jeu de plateau fait déjà partie des meilleures ventes du segment en 2005. C'est d'autant plus remarquable que les ventes de jeu de plateau sont actuellement dans une phase d'hibernation. La promotion a généré plus de 2 millions de livres de valeur pour Hasbro, presque cinq fois le coût de la campagne. Alors que le buzz était le premier objectif recherché, il y a eu d'autres formes de retour sur investissement. Monopoly Live a aussi soutenu la gestion des relations avec la clientèle, et près de 100 000 usagers se sont inscrit au bulletin d'information de Hasbro. Le jeu lui-même est aujourd'hui un atout pour la marque et la société envisage de développer l'idée. **CHIFFRES :** Pendant les 28 jours d'activité du site, nous avons reçu plus de 1 million de visiteurs et 189 699 personnes ont joué au Mononopoly Live. Chaque joueur a joué en moyenne trois parties, avec un temps de session supérieure à 5 minutes à chaque visite.

KONZEPT: Wann ist ein Taxi kein Taxi? Wenn es ein Skateboard ist ... Um den Launch von Monopoly Here & Now zu feiern, eine komplett aktualisierte Version des Brettspiels, schufen wir das größte Monopolyspiel, das je gespielt wurde: eine zeitnahe, interaktive Version, die in den Straßen von London mit Taxen als Spielsteinen gespielt wurde. 18 Taxen wurden mit GPS ausgestattet, in Monopoly-Farben eingekleidet und als einer der neuen Spielsteine angemalt: Skateboard, Jumbo, Rollschuh, Bus, F1-Auto, Handy. 28 Tage lang wurden die Orte, zu denen die Taxen fuhren, auf unsere Webseite übertragen, wo Tausende von Spielern darum konkurrierten, Großbritanniens größter Immobilienmagnat zu werden. Eine engagierte (n+1)-Plattform, die auf dem Redhat-Enterprise-System Apache 2, TUX und mySQL RDBMS basierte, wurde gebaut und kontrollierte alle Daten, aktualisierte das Spiel und lieferte allen auf das Spiel bezogenen Inhalt über Internet, E-Mail und SMS, bei einem großen Besucheraufkommen. Das Spiel wurde mit einem Macromedia Flash Interface gespielt, dass durch Asynchronous JavaScript und XML (AJAX) live mit der Hauptspielmaschine kommunizierte. Die Hauptspielmaschine war für die Verarbeitung aller Daten verantwortlich und aktualisierte jedes Benutzerkonto alle 15 Minuten, während sie gleichzeitig einen Überlauf verhinderte. Sie war aus einer Kombination von PHP, Perl (für Multithreading) und Shell Script (für die automatische Ausführung von Basislevel-Prozessen) programmiert. Insgesamt waren 14 separate Server in zwei Netzwerken dafür verantwortlich, ihre jeweiligen Aufgaben vier Wochen lang alle 15 Minuten auszuführen. **ERGEBNISSE:** Das Brettspiel Monopoly „Here & Now" in begrenzter Auflage ist schon eines der meistverkauften Spiele 2005. Das ist eine noch größere Leistung, wenn man berücksichtigt, dass der Brettspielverkauf sich allgemein in einer Phase des Winterschlafs befindet. Die PR allein erzeugte über £2 Millionen Umsatz für Hasbro – fast fünfmal mehr als die Kosten der gesamten Kampagne. Während es das erste Ziel war, Aufregung zu erzeugen, gab es andere bedeutsame ROIs: Monopoly Live hat die Datenbank von Hasbro CRM um fast 100 000 ausgewählte Benutzer erhöht, die sich über die neuen Entwicklungen von Hasbro informieren möchten. Das Spiel selbst leistet nun einen wertvollen Beitrag zu Hasbro, und es ist geplant, die Idee weiterzuentwickeln. **ZAHLEN:** Innerhalb der ersten 28 Tage besuchten über 1 Million Besucher die Seite, und 189 699 Personen spielten Monopoly Live. Jeder spielte durchschnittlich drei Spiele und verweilte über fünf Minuten auf der Seite.

FEATURED ON THE DVD **CAMPAIGN:** Prince of Persia. **YEAR:** 2004. **AGENCY:** Soleil Noir <www.soleilnoir.net>. **PRODUCTION TIME:** 2 days. **TECH ASPECTS:** Macromedia Flash, video. **MEDIA CIRCULATED:** Game portal.

CONCEPT: Online Campaign for Prince of Persia from Ubisoft. Shows the character in action.

KONZEPT: Online-Kampagne für Prince of Persia von Ubisoft, die den Charakter in Aktion zeigt.

CONCEPT : Campagne en ligne pour le jeu Prince of Persia développé par Ubisoft. Montre le personnage en action.

CONCEPT: Online Campaign for XIII game from Ubisoft. Shows the character in action with cell-shading design.

KONZEPT: Online-Kampagne für das Spiel XIII von Ubisoft, das die Charaktere in Aktion zeigt, mit Cell-Shading-Design.

CONCEPT : Campagne en ligne pour la promotion du jeu XIII par Ubisoft. Montre le personnage en action dans un graphisme en cell-shading (effet de reproduction BD).

CONCEPT: online Campaign for Myst Revelation from Ubisoft. Show graphics and environment of game.

CONCEPT : Campagne en ligne de Myst Revelation produit par Ubisoft. Elle présente le design graphique et l'environnement du jeu.

KONZEPT: Online-Kampagne für Myst Revelation von Ubisoft, die Grafiken und die Umgebung des Spiels zeigt.

FEATURED ON THE DVD **CAMPAIGN:** Beyond Good & Evil. **YEAR:** 2004. **AGENCY:** Soleil Noir <www.soleilnoir.net>. **PRODUCTION TIME:** 2 days. **TECH ASPECTS:** Macromedia Flash, video. **MEDIA CIRCULATED:** Game portal.

CONCEPT: Online Campaign for Beyond Good & Evil game from Ubisoft. Show character in action.

CONCEPT : Campagne en ligne pour le jeu Beyond Good and Evil développé par Ubisoft, et montrant un personnage en action.

KONZEPT: Online-Kampagne für das Spiel Good & Evil von Ubisoft, die die Figur in Aktion zeigt.

PJ PEREIRA
EXECUTIVE CREATIVE DIRECTOR OF AKQA

PJ Pereira, 32, is one of the most influential Creatives in the interactive industry worldwide and the Executive Creative Director of AKQA, San Francisco, where he leads the creative work for brands such as Nike, Xbox, Palm, MSN, Target and Visa. He was also one of the founders of AgenciaClick, the most successful Interactive agency in Brazil, and the first Interactive Media Director at DM9DDB, still a strong creative powerhouse at any international competition. He and his teams have won more than 35 awards on the most prestigious international festivals and had already been the President of the Jury on London International Awards (2001) and Cannes Cyber Lions Awards (2005).

Let me tell you a secret: every good creative is a selfish bastard. I say, and immediately admit: there is no way you can be a good professional of creativity without being completely committed to your own grandiosity.

My friend Mauro, for example, is a great creative. One of the best ones I've ever met. You can't go out with him without seeing the guy stop by a scene, an image, a little something that sparked a big idea. Last week, for example, we had dinner with our wives. In a single night, he saw: 1) a TV spot "happening" with the couple discussing at a table beside us, 2) a viral film "arising" from the crazy homeless speaking to an imaginary friend, 3) an interactive game "coming" from the poor waitress bouncing between the tables and 4) a good photo shoot location on the parking lot. Does he never stop?

No, he doesn't. This is how my friend and all the good creatives I know do it – they keep their curiosity and imagination turned on all the time. They see every moment as a creative opportunity, and almost everything they live immediately becomes a great idea – something they would be very proud of doing, showing and bragging about.

And notice that no client, no product, or brief has been mentioned so far!

Not because they don't care, though. Actually, my friend and his kind usually go to work after a prolific night, holiday or weekend full of ideas, just to realize they just don't make sense for any of the projects they are working on. But it's ok, they didn't have those for any client anyway – they had them for themselves, the egotistical people they are. Then, the same way they had the ideas, they forget about them. Or, better, they put them on hold. Because some day, maybe years later, those ideas will suddenly apply for the task on their hands. And at this moment, one client will be completely blown away: "the man had this idea in such a short time? What a genius he is!"

The difference between the masterpiece and just elementary work, more often than you think, is the origin of it. Ideas that just come from a marketer's formal brief, usually are as good as the strategy behind it. And that, most of the time, means a more or less literal interpretation of what marketers often call "best practices" (I'd rather call it "jargon-glamorized repetition").

REALLY INNOVATIVE IDEAS DON'T COME FROM BRIEFS, NEITHER FROM IMPROVING WHAT HAS BEEN DONE BEFORE. THEY COME FROM INSPIRATION, AND INSIGHT, FROM IMPROBABLE COMBINATIONS, SOME RANDOMNESS, AND A GOOD MARKETING SENSE TO IDENTIFY WHEN TO USE THEM – THEN THEY SOLVE A PROBLEM FOR THE BRAND YOU ARE WORKING ON. BREAKTHROUGHS COME FROM SQUEEZING IDEAS WE LIKE INTO PROJECTS WE ARE WORKING ON.

I'm really sorry if this incinerates all your romantic images of how creatives work. As a matter of fact, if it wasn't for these self-seeking people, every similar assignment would get the same ideas – and pay attention now, because this is the key to the secret I'm trying to tell. Selfish brilliant creatives do it because when they add their own experiences to their work, besides putting their own signature on it, they're also making it unique – and that's when ego-trips and brand missions converge.

Family, school, entertainment, newspaper, things you see when you go out for dinner or even some brand archeology exercised by trained self-

LOST IN CONFESSIONS TODAY

ish eyes… The sources are infinite, now, and we can finally sincerely expect that, at that same moment, there will be nobody coming up with the same original idea in another part of the world (the worst nightmare a selfish creative can have).

On the interactive advertising field, however, no other kind of reference is as powerful as technology. And that again is a reason why I picked my friend Mauro among other virtuoso creatives I have worked with: the man is a gadget freak!

BECAUSE OF HIS LOVE FOR TECHNOLOGY, HE IS ALWAYS AHEAD OF THE REST OF HUMANITY IN TERMS OF INTERACTIVE REPERTORY AND THE WAY MACHINES AND PEOPLE INTERACT. AND WHEN YOU CAN COMBINE REAL HUMAN INSIGHTS WITH A FRESH BORN TECHNOLOGY, GREATNESS IS ALMOST AN EASY JOB.

From the transformational experience that is Nike iD to the goofiness of a man-in-a-chicken-costume obeying whatever you type in on Burger King's Subservient Chicken website; from the surprise of a video game bounty hunter calling your mobile phone on Xbox's Perfect Dark Zero to the emotional power of reading a claim for cornea donations in a Braille-written banner ad for Sao Paulo Eye Bank; almost all the big stories in the interactive advertising world come from a seamless combination of technological and human insights. And I can give you an educated guess that all those ideas had been there

for a while before those creatives pitched them for their clients.

If you don't believe me, though, I'm sorry. You won't be able to validate my theory. Cause if you try confirming that at least a good part of any creative's original idea had been hibernating on their authors' mind before they officially had it, they will deny.

Because when it comes to protecting our own improvisational creativity myths, we, selfish bastard creatives, always lie.

PJ Pereira, 32 ans, est un des créatifs les plus influents de l'industrie interactive mondiale, et le directeur de création chez AKQA, à San Francisco, qui a travaillé pour des marques comme Nike, Xbox, Palm, MSN, Target et Visa. Il est également un des membres fondateurs de Agência Click, la plus grande agence interactive du Brésil, et le premier directeur des médias interactifs chez DM9DDB, qui arrive toujours en bonne place dans les concours internationaux. Lui et ses équipes ont remporté plus de 35 récompenses dans de prestigieux festivals, et Pereira a été président du jury au London International Awards en 2001 et aux Cyber Lions de Cannes en 2005.

Je vais vous dire un secret : tout bon créatif est un sale égoïste. Mais je dois aussi le reconnaître : on ne peut pas être un bon professionnel de la création sans être totalement convaincu de son génie.

Mon ami Mauro, par exemple, est un grand créatif. Un des meilleurs que j'aie jamais rencontré.

On ne peut pas se promener avec lui sans qu'il s'arrête devant une scène, une image, quelque détail qui lui inspire un grande idée. La semaine dernière, nous sommes sortis dîner avec nos épouses respectives. En une seule soirée, il a imaginé : 1) un spot télé avec le couple qui dînait à la table voisine, 2) un message viral avec un clochard qui parlait à un copain imaginaire, 3) un jeu interactif avec la serveuse qui courait de table en table, 4) une super séance de photos sur le parking du restaurant. Il ne s'arrête donc jamais ?

Non, effectivement. Chez mon ami comme chez tous les bons créatifs que je connais, la curiosité et l'imagination restent en éveil à toute heure du jour et de la nuit. Chaque instant est une occasion de création, et quasiment tout ce qu'ils vivent se change en idée de concept, une chose qu'ils seraient fiers de faire, et dont ils seraient ravis de se vanter.

Et remarquez que je n'ai pas encore parlé de client, de produit ou de briefing !

Non pas qu'ils s'en fichent, rassurez-vous. Mais de fait, mon ami et ses homologues arrivent souvent au bureau la tête pleine d'idées après une soirée, un week-end ou des congés féconds, pour s'apercevoir que ces idées ne sont nullement adaptées aux projets qui les occupent ce jour-là. Mais qu'importe, ils n'ont pas eu ces idées pour un client, ils les ont eues pour eux-mêmes, sales égoïstes qu'ils sont.

Puis, aussi vite qu'ils ont eu ces idées, ils les oublient. Ou mieux, ils les mettent de côté. Car un jour, des années plus tard peut-être, ces idées pourront servir au travail qu'on leur demande. Et à ce jour-là, le client sera complètement bluffé : « Il a eu cette idée en si peu de temps ? Ce type est un génie ! »

Ce qui différencie un chef-d'œuvre d'un travail ordinaire est plus souvent qu'on ne le croit une question d'origine. Les idées proposées par le service marketing d'un client sont généralement aussi bonnes que la stratégie qui les motive. La plupart du temps, il s'agit plus ou moins d'une interprétation littérale de ce qu'ils nomment les « meilleures pratiques ». (Et que j'appellerais plutôt : « la répétition enrobée de glamour »).

LES IDÉES VRAIMENT NOVATRICES VIENNENT RAREMENT DES BRIEFINGS, NI DE LA SIMPLE AMÉLIORATION DE CE QUI A DÉJÀ ÉTÉ FAIT. ELLES NAISSENT DE L'INSPIRATION, D'UNE VISION PERSONNELLE. ELLES NAISSENT D'ASSOCIATIONS IMPROBABLES, D'UNE PART DE HASARD, ET D'UN SENS AIGU DU MARKETING QUI IDENTIFIE LE MOMENT OPPORTUN, CELUI OÙ CES IDÉES VONT RÉSOUDRE UN PROBLÈME POUR LA MARQUE QUI VOUS OCCUPE. LES AVANCÉES SE FONT EN ADAPTANT LES IDÉES QU'ON AIME AUX PROJETS SUR LESQUELS ON TRAVAILLE.

Si cela détruit votre vision romantique de la façon dont travaillent les créatifs, j'en suis sincèrement navré. Mais à la vérité, si ces égoïstes n'étaient pas là, toutes les missions similaires recevraient des réponses similaires, et écoutez bien, car je vais vous révéler un secret. Les brillants créatifs réussissent car en intégrant leurs propres expériences à leur travail, non contents d'apposer leur signature, ils les rendent aussi unique, faisant ainsi converger leur ego et l'intérêt d'une marque.

La famille, l'école, les spectacles, les journaux, les choses qu'on observe dans la rue, l'analyse des marques faites par un œil expert... Les sources sont infinies, à portée de main, et on peut sincèrement espérer qu'au même moment, dans un autre coin du monde, personne d'autre n'aura la même idée originale (le pire cauchemar d'un créatif égoïste).

Dans le domaine de la publicité interactive toutefois, la référence la plus convaincante est la technologie. Et c'est une raison supplémentaire qui m'a fait choisir mon ami Mauro parmi d'autre virtuoses de la création avec qui j'ai collaboré : c'est un fou de gadgets !

SON AMOUR DE LA TECHNOLOGIE LE PLACE TOUJOURS EN TÊTE DU PELOTON EN TERME DE RÉPERTOIRE INTERACTIF, ET DE COMMUNICATION ENTRE L'HOMME ET LA MACHINE. ET LORSQU'ON COMBINE UNE AUTHENTIQUE VISION PERSONNELLE AVEC UNE TECHNOLOGIE DERNIER CRI, LE SUCCÈS EST PRESQUE GARANTI.

Qu'il s'agisse de l'expérience de transformation de Nike iD, de la maladresse d'un homme déguisé en poulet qui obéit à vos ordres sur le site de Burger King, du vidéogramme d'un chasseur de prime qui vous appelle sur votre mobile pour Dark Zero de la Xbox, de la bannière en braille encourageant le don de cornée pour la Banque de l'Oeil de São Paulo, quasiment tous les grands succès du monde de la pub interactive sont dus à une combinaison idéale de vision humaine et technologique. Et je peux faire le pari averti que toutes ces idées existaient bien avant que les créatifs ne les vendent à leurs clients.

Si vous ne me croyez pas, je le regrette. Vous ne pourrez pas valider ma théorie. Car si vous demandez aux auteurs de ces idées si celles-ci hibernaient dans leur cerveau avant de voir officiellement le jour, ils nieront en bloc.

Car lorsqu'il s'agit de protéger le légendaire caractère d'improvisation de notre créativité, nous les sales égoïstes, sommes toujours prêts à mentir.

PJ Pereira, 32, ist einer der einflussreichsten Kreativen in der interaktiven Branche weltweit und leitender Kreativdirektor von AKQU, San Francisco, wo er die kreative Arbeit für Marken wie Nike, Xbox, Palm, MSN, Target und Visa leitet. Er war auch einer der Gründer von AgenciaClick, der erfolgreichsten Interaktivagentur Brasiliens, und der erste Interaktivmedien-Leiter bei DM9DDB, ein immer noch starkes kreatives Kraftwerk bei jedem internationalen Wettbewerb. Er und seine Teams haben mehr als 35 Auszeichnungen bei den angesehensten internationalen Festivals gewonnen, und er war Präsident der Jury bei den London International Awards (2001) und den Cannes Cyber Lions Awards (2005).

Lassen Sie mich Ihnen ein Geheimnis verraten: Jeder gute Kreative ist ein egoistischer Mistkerl. Ich gebe es sofort zu: Man kann nicht professionell kreativ sein, ohne absolut seiner eigenen Grandiosität verpflichtet zu sein.

Mein Freund Mauro zum Beispiel ist ein großartiger Kreativer. Einer der besten, die ich je traf. Sie können nicht mit ihm ausgehen, ohne dass er bei einer Szene, einem Bild, irgendeiner Kleinigkeit stehen bleibt, aus der eine große Idee entspringt. Letzte Woche beispielsweise aßen wir mit unseren Frauen im Restaurant. In einer einzigen Nacht sah er: 1) ein Fernsehspot „passierte" am Nebentisch, wo ein Paar diskutierte, 2) ein viraler Film „entsprang" einem verrückten Obdachlosen, der mit einem imaginären Freund sprach, 3) ein interaktives Spiel „entstand" durch eine arme Kellnerin, die zwischen den Tischen hin und her sprang, 4) eine gute Foto-Location auf dem Parkplatz. Macht er nie eine Pause?

Nein, tut er nicht. Er nicht, und auch nicht alle anderen guten Kreativen, die ich kenne – ihre Neugierde und Fantasie sind die ganze Zeit eingeschaltet. Sie betrachten jeden Moment als kreative Gelegenheit, und fast alles, was sie erleben, wird sofort zu einer großen Idee – etwas, auf das sie sehr stolz sind und das sie allen zeigen möchten.

Beachten Sie, dass bisher noch kein Kunde, kein Produkt oder Auftrag erwähnt wurde!

Aber nicht, weil es ihnen egal ist. Tatsächlich gehen mein Freund und die anderen normalerweise nach einer produktiven Nacht, einem Urlaub oder Wochenende voller Ideen zur Arbeit, nur um zu merken, dass sie für keines der Projekte, an denen sie arbeiten, Sinn machen. Aber das ist OK, sie hatten die Idee ohnehin nicht für einen Kunden, sondern für sich selbst – Egoisten, die sie sind. Auf dieselbe Art, auf die sie die Ideen hatten, vergessen sie sie wieder. Oder, besser, sie werden auf Eis gelegt. Denn eines Tages, vielleicht Jahre später, werden diese Ideen genau zu einem Auftrag passen. Und in diesem Moment wird ein Kunde begeistert sein: „Der Mann hatte diese Idee in so einer kurzen Zeit? Was für ein Genie!"

Der Unterschied zwischen einem Meisterwerk und einer einfachen Arbeit liegt, öfter als man denkt, im Ursprung. Ideen, die vom förmlichen Auftrag eines Marketers kommen, sind normalerweise so gut wie die Strategie dahinter. Und das bedeutet meistens eine mehr oder weniger wörtliche Interpretation dessen, was Marketer „optimales Verfahren" nennen (ich würde eher „glamourisierte Wiederholung" dazu sagen).

WIRKLICH INNOVATIVE IDEEN KOMMEN WEDER DURCH AUFTRÄGE NOCH DURCH VERBESSERUNGEN VON SCHON DAGEWESENEM. SIE ENTSTEHEN DURCH INSPIRATION, EINSICHT. DURCH UNWAHRSCHEINLICHE KOMBINATIONEN, ETWAS ZUFÄLLIGKEIT UND EINEM GUTEN MARKETINGSINN DAFÜR, WANN SIE ZU VERWENDEN SIND – WENN SIE DAS PROBLEM DER MARKE LÖSEN, AN DER MAN ARBEITET. DURCHBRÜCHE ENTSTEHEN DURCH DIE INTEGRATION VON IDEEN IN PROJEKTE, AN DENEN WIR ARBEITEN.

Es tut mir Leid, wenn Sie jetzt Ihre romantischen Vorstellungen über die Arbeitsweise von Kreativen einäschern müssen. Tatsache ist: Ohne diese eigennützigen Menschen gäbe es bei jeder Aufgabe dieselben Ideen – und passen Sie jetzt genau auf, denn nun kommt der Schlüssel zu dem Geheimnis, das ich verraten will. Egoistische, brillante Kreative wollen ihre Arbeit einzigartig machen, indem sie neben

ihrer Unterschrift ihre eigenen Erfahrungen in die Arbeit einfließen lassen – und dabei zerfließen die Grenzen zwischen Egotrips und Markenaktionen.

Familie, Schule, Unterhaltung, Zeitungen, Dinge, die man sieht, wenn man ausgeht, oder sogar Kampagnen aus längst vergangenen Zeiten mit geschulten egoistischen Augen betrachtet … Die Quellen sind unerschöpflich, und wir können schließlich ganz realistisch erwarten, dass in demselben Moment niemand anders auf der Welt dieselbe originelle Idee hat (der schlimmste Alptraum eines jeden Kreativen).

Auf dem Gebiet der interaktiven Werbung jedoch ist keine andere Art der Referenz so mächtig wie die Technologie. Und dies ist wiederum der Grund, warum ich meinen Freund Mauro aus dem Kreis der Virtuosen ausgewählt habe, mit denen ich bereits arbeitete: Der Mann ist ein Gerätefreak!

DURCH SEINE LIEBE ZUR TECHNOLOGIE IST ER DEM REST DER MENSCHHEIT STETS VORAUS, WAS DAS INTERAKTIVE REPERTOIRE UND DIE ART BETRIFFT, WIE MASCHINEN UND MENSCHEN INTERAGIEREN. UND WENN SIE REALE MENSCHLICHE EINSICHTEN MIT EINER NEUGEBORENEN TECHNOLOGIE KOMBINIEREN, IST GROSSARTIGKEIT FAST EINE EINFACHE ARBEIT.

Von der Transformationserfahrung, die Nike iD darstellt, über die Albernheit eines „Mann-auf-einem-Huhn-Kostüms", der auf alles gehorcht, was man auf Burger Kings unterwürfiges Hühnchen tippt; von der Überraschung eines Kopfgeldjägers aus einem Videospiel, der Sie auf Ihrem Handy auf Xbox' Perfect Dark Zero anruft, bis hin zur emotionalen Schlagkraft einer Werbung für Hornhautspenden auf einem Banner, das in Blindenschrift für die Eye Bank in Sao Paulo geschrieben ist; fast alle großen Storys aus der interaktiven Werbewelt entstehen durch eine nahtlose Kombination von technischen und menschlichen Einsichten. Und ich kann Ihnen

den wohl begründeten Hinweis geben, dass alle diese Ideen schon eine Weile existierten, bevor diese Kreativen sie für ihre Kunden umsetzten.

Es tut mir Leid, wenn Sie mir nicht glauben. Sie werden meine Theorie nicht für gültig erklären können. Denn wenn sie versuchen, zu beweisen, dass mindestens ein großer Teil einer jeden kreativen, originellen Idee schon lange im Geist des Erfinders überwintert hat, wird er es leugnen.

Denn wenn es darum geht, die eigenen improvisierten Kreativitätsmythen zu schützen, lügen wir egoistischen Mistkerle immer.

RICARDO FIGUEIRA
CREATIVE DIRECTOR OF AGÊNCIACLICK

Ricardo Figueira has accumulated many international awards including Cannes Lions, London International Awards Advertising, The OneShow NY, and others.

Participated as jury of the One Show NY, Art Directors, Clio Awards and other international advertising awards. He has already developed more than 300 interactive projects and led creative strategies for clients such as The Coca-Cola Company, MSN, Johnnie-Walker (Diageo), WWF, Fiat, Nike, Sky, BrasilTelecom, Credicard, Bradesco (the largest private bank in South America) and others. Ricardo Figueira is the creative director for AgênciaClick in São Paulo, Brazil, in charge of developing creative strategies through brand experiences and interactive advertising. He was born in the Brazilian capital Brasilia, studied graphic design, and opened his own design company, merging later with AgenciaClick.

Today, there is a new kind of artist, the Internet artist. A brand new kind of creative professional who is supposed to know much more than just techniques in order to express concepts. More than

technological information, he has to know about people in order to deliver interactivity. If, in the past, art was meant to be gazed upon, today the challenge is creating art to be shared, an interactive experience to communicate meaning, make services easy or simply get the expectator emotionally involved.

UNLIKE TRADITIONAL ART EXPRESSED ON PAPER, ON CANVAS OR IN SCULPTURES, DIGITAL ART IS HIGHLY "COMMODITIZED" BY ITS OWN MEDIUM WHICH MAKES THE ARTIST BE IN CONSTANT NEED OF CREATING SOMETHING NEW OR SIMPLY PROVIDING THE EXPECTATOR WITH ORIGINAL AND REMARKABLE EXPERIENCES.

Being so, I must confess that writing about works for the Internet which will be a record of a time or an era is rather complex once there is always the risk of becoming outdated in time, however writing about any future prerogative could be even worse.

Therefore, if there is something that can be claimed, it is that the Internet has created no style, has brought no movement or has consolidated no set of techniques whatsoever that could make up an art movement, on the contrary the Internet made it all possible in real-time and ended up bringing a new attitude, setting up a new great artistic competence criteria, the "innovation".

Ricardo Figueira a remporté de nombreuses récompenses internationales, notamment aux Lions de Cannes, au London International Awards Advertising et au NY OneShow. Il a été juré au OneShow, à l'ADC Awards, aux Clio Awards et autres concours internationaux. Il est à l'origine de plus de 300 projets interactifs et de la stratégie créative de clients comme Coca-Cola, MSN, Johnnie Walker, WWF, Fiat, Nike, Sky, Brasil Telecom, Credicard, Bradesco (première banque privée d'Afrique du Sud) et autres. Ricardo Figueira est directeur de création chez Agência Click à São Paulo, et gère la stratégie créative des marques par de la publicité interactive. Il est né dans la capitale Brasília, a étudié le design graphique et a fondé sa propre agence de design, pour fusionner ensuite avec Agência Click.

Il existe de nos jours une nouvelle espèce d'artiste, l'artiste Internet. Un tout nouveau genre de professionnel de la création qui est censé maîtriser bien plus que de simples technologies afin d'exprimer des concepts. En plus des compétences techniques, il doit avoir une compréhension des êtres humains pour générer de l'interactivité. Si dans le passé, l'art était destiné à être admiré, le défi actuel est de créer un art qui puisse se partager, une expérience interactive qui communique du sens, facilite les services ou suscite simplement l'émotion du spectateur.

CONTRAIREMENT AUX FORMES TRADITIONNELLES DE LA PEINTURE OU DE LA SCULPTURE,

THE NEW ARTIST

L'ART ÉLECTRONIQUE EST HAUTEMENT « MARCHANDISÉ » PAR SON PROPRE SUPPORT, CE QUI OBLIGE L'ARTISTE À RECHERCHER SANS CESSE LA NOUVEAUTÉ, OU À OFFRIR AU SPECTATEUR DES EXPÉRIENCES INÉDITES ET ORIGINALES.

De ce fait, j'avoue qu'écrire sur la publicité en ligne, qui sera le témoin d'une époque ou d'un temps donné, est plutôt délicat, car on risque de devenir obsolète à terme, et s'aventurer dans des prévisions sur son développement serait encore plus périlleux.

Par conséquent, la seule déclaration que l'on puisse faire est qu'Internet n'a engendré aucun style, n'a inspiré aucun mouvement, n'a consolidé aucun ensemble de techniques qui pourraient contribuer à un mouvement artistique quelconque. Au contraire, Internet a rendu tout cela possible en temps réel et a fini par engendrer une nouvelle attitude, en établissant un nouveau critère de compétence artistique : la capacité d'innovation.

Ricardo Figueira hat im Laufe seines Lebens zahlreiche internationale Auszeichnungen erhalten, darunter Cannes Lions, London International Awards Advertising, The OneShow NY und viele andere. Er war Mitglied der Jury von One Show NY, Art Directors, Clio Awards und anderen internationalen Werbeauszeichnungen. Bisher hat er über 300 interaktive Projekte entwickelt und kreative Strategien für Kunden wie The Coca-Cola Company, MSN, Johnnie-Walker (Diageo), WWF, Fiat, Nike, Sky, BrasilTelecom, Credicard, Bradesco (die größte private Bank in Südamerika) und andere geleitet. Ricardo Figueira ist Kreativdirektor bei AgênciaClick in São Paulo, Brasilien, wo er kreative Strategien für Marken und interaktive Werbung entwickelt. Er wurde in der brasilianischen Hauptstadt Brasilia geboren, studierte Grafikdesign und gründete eine eigene Designfirma, die sich später mit AgenciaClick zusammenschloss.

Es gibt heutzutage eine neue Art von Künstler: den Internetkünstler. Ein brandneuer kreativer Beruf, bei dem man sich mit viel mehr als nur der Technik auskennen muss, um Konzepte umzustellen. Um Interaktivität zu liefern, muss sich der Internetkünstler eher mit Menschen als mit technischen Informationen auskennen. In der Vergangenheit lag das Augenmerk auf der Kunst; heute besteht die Herausforderung darin, Kunst zu kreieren, die für jeden zugänglich ist; eine interaktive Erfahrung, die Bedeutung kommuniziert, Dienste vereinfacht oder den Betrachter emotional involviert.

IM GEGENSATZ ZU KUNST AUF PAPIER, LEINWAND ODER IN SKULPTUREN WIRD DIE DIGITALE KUNST STARK DURCH IHR EIGENES MEDIUM BESTIMMT, DAS DEN KÜNSTLER DAZU ZWINGT, STÄNDIG ETWAS NEUES ZU KREIEREN BZW. DEM BETRACHTER ORIGINELLE UND BEMERKENSWERTE

ERFAHRUNGEN ZU LIEFERN.

So, wie die Dinge liegen, muss ich zugeben, dass es eine komplexe Aufgabe ist, über Arbeiten im Internet zu schreiben, als ein Bericht über eine Zeit oder eine Ära, da immer das Risiko besteht, von der Zeit überholt zu werden. Allerdings könnte das Schreiben über die Zukunft noch schwieriger sein...

Wenn es jedoch etwas gibt, das sicher ist, so dies: Das Internet hat keinen Stil entwickelt, keine Bewegung erzeugt oder irgendwelche Techniken konsolidiert, die eine Kunstbewegung hervorgebracht hätten – im Gegenteil: Das Internet machte alles live möglich und schuf eine neue Einstellung, indem es ein neues großes Kompetenzkriterium ins Leben rief: Innovation.

007

TRANSPORT

FEATURED ON THE DVD **CAMPAIGN:** Alfa Romeo 147 – No Tourist Guide. **PRODUCT:** Alfa Romeo 147. **YEAR:** 2004. **AGENCY:** OgilvyInteractive, Italy <www.ogilvy.it>. **PRODUCTION TIME:** 3 months. **COPYWRITER:** Francesca Celi. **GRAPHIC DESIGNER:** Paola Birolo. **SHOOTING/EDITING VIDEO/REPORTING:** Francesco Scarpelli (Tokyo), Erika Rossi (Seattle), Edgar Zippel (Berlin). **CREATIVE DIRECTOR:** Roberta Rossi. **FLASH DEVELOPER:** Paolo Drovetti, Luca Battaglia. **TECH ASPECTS:** Macromedia Flash, video streaming, sound. **MEDIA CIRCULATED:** Website, banner, DEM.

CONCEPT: The site deserts the product site stereotype. It is a website that shuns the commonplace and values those details that often pass unnoticed. The site's design was inspired by the will to bring the travelling spirit alive online, using strong impact images. *No tourist Guide* takes the user to Tokyo, Berlin and Seattle. Every user can virtually visit these beautiful cities, deciding to get lost in their neighbourhoods or take advantage of the "City Tour" navigator. Product information is distributed internally in the neighbourhood areas in a non-invasive way. To capture information about the customers and increase the number of profiled customers, OgilvyInteractive created an online contest. The final prize was a trip to Tokyo, Berlin or Seattle. **RESULTS:** Two months after launch, the site collected more than 2,000 new profiled users and almost 150 requests for new Alfa 147 Test Drive requests.

CONCEPT : Délaissant les stéréotypes de la communication de produit, le site s'écarte des clichés et mise sur des détails qui passent d'ordinaire inaperçus. Le design du site est motivé par la volonté de restituer en ligne l'esprit du voyage, grâce à des images fortes. *No tourist Guide* emmène l'internaute à Tokyo, Berlin et Seattle. On peut visiter ces villes de façon virtuelle, décider de se perdre dans les quartiers ou suivre une visite organisée. Les informations sur le produit sont distillés dans chaque partie de la ville, de façon peu intrusive.

Pour obtenir des informations sur les clients et établir leur profil, l'agence a conçu un concours en ligne. La récompense est un voyage à Tokyo, Berlin ou Seattle. **RÉSULTATS :** Deux mois après le lancement, le site a enregistré 2000 inscriptions d'usagers et environ 150 demandes d'essai sur route de la nouvelle Alfa 147.

KONZEPT: Die Seite verlässt das Produktseiten-Stereotyp. Sie vermeidet Allgemeinplätze und schätzt Details, die man oft nicht bemerkt. Das Design war von dem Wunsch inspiriert, eine Reise mit wirkungsvollen Bildern online zum Leben zu erwecken. *No tourist Guide* bringt den Benutzer tatsächlich nach Tokio, Berlin und Seattle. Jeder kann diese Städte virtuell entdecken, sich in den Stadtteilen verirren oder den "City Tour"-Navigator anwenden. Produktinformationen sind auf unaufdringliche Weise innerhalb der Stadtteile verteilt. Um Informationen über die Kunden zu erlangen und die Anzahl von Kundenprofilen zu erhöhen, veranstaltete OgilvyInteractive einen Online-Wettbewerb. Der Hauptpreis war eine Reise nach Tokio, Berlin oder Seattle. **ERGEBNISSE:** Zwei Monate nach dem Launch hatte die Seite mehr als 2000 neue Benutzerprofile gesammelt und fast 150 Anfragen für eine Testfahrt mit dem neuen Alfa 147.

FEATURED ON THE DVD **CAMPAIGN:** Alfa Romeo Portal <www.alfaromeo.it>. **PRODUCT:** Alfa Romeo. **YEAR:** 2003. **AGENCY:** OgilvyInteractive, Italy <www.ogilvy.it>. **PRODUCTION TIME:** 8 months. **COPYWRITER:** Matteo del Porto. **DESIGNER:** Barbara Pascoli. **CREATIVE DIRECTOR:** Roberta Rossi. **WEB DEVELOPER:** Espin SpA. **TECH ASPECTS:** Macromedia Flash, video streaming. **MEDIA CIRCULATED:** Website, banner, newsletter, DEM.

CONCEPT: At the beginning of 2003, Alfa Romeo asked OgilvyInteractive to completely review its online presence, to be consistent with the new worldwide campaign "beauty is not enough." Ogilvy Interactive identified the website as the main driver for the creation of the brand and product experience. The Alfa Romeo portal represents the evolution of the online presence of Alfa Romeo. OgilvyInteractive identified four main guidelines in developing the Alfa Romeo portal: 1) Give products features a central role to substantiate the brand values. 2) Have a customer centric approach. 3) Use the website as CRM platform to drive demand generation and enhance loyalty. 4) Usability. **RESULTS:** After only one month, the new site increased the number of visits about +500% and it jumped to the second place in the Italian Internet automotive "hit parade", before Audi, Volvo, Ford, Opel... and not too much behind Fiat.

CONCEPT : Au début de l'année 2003, Alfa Romeo a chargé OgilvyInteractive de restructurer entièrement sa présence en ligne, afin d'être en phase avec la nouvelle campagne mondiale « La beauté ne suffit pas ». L'agence a conçu le site comme vecteur principal de l'expérience de marque. Le portail représente l'évolution de la présence en ligne de Alfa Romeo. Son élaboration a suivi quatre grandes lignes directrices. 1) Mettre en avant les qualités des produits pour justifier la valeur de marque. 2) Personnaliser l'approche du client. 3) Faire du site une plateforme de gestion de la relation client pour générer la demande et encourager la fidélité. 4) Ergonomie. **RÉSULTATS :** Au bout d'un mois, le nombre de visiteurs a augmenté de 500% et le site s'est placé au deuxième rang dans le classement des sites automobiles italiens, devant Audi, Volvo, Ford, Opel, et non loin derrière Fiat.

KONZEPT: Anfang 2003 bat Alfa Romeo OgilvyInteractive, seine Online-Präsenz komplett zu überarbeiten, um sie der neuen weltweiten Kampagne „Beauty is not enough" anzugleichen. OgilvyInteractive identifizierte die Webseite als Hauptmotor für die Kreation der Marke und die Produkterfahrung. Das Portal repräsentiert die Evolution der Online-Präsenz von Alfa Romeo. OgilvyInteractive stellte für die Entwicklung des Alfa-Romeo-Portals vier Hauptleitsätze auf: 1. den Produkteigenschaften eine zentrale Rolle zur Bekräftigung der Markenwerte geben. 2. ein kundenzentrierter Ansatz. 3. die Webseite als CRM-Plattform nutzen, um die neue Kunden anzuwerben und sich die Loyalität vorhandener Kunden zu sichern. 4. Nützlichkeit. **ERGEBNISSE:** Nach nur einem Monat erhöhte sich die Anzahl der Besucher um über 500%, und die Seite erreichte den 2. Platz im italienischen Internetauto-Ranking, vor Audi, Volvo, Opel ... und nicht allzu weit hinter Fiat.

FEATURED ON THE DVD **CAMPAIGN:** Attitudes <www.attitudes.org>. **YEAR:** 2005. **AGENCY:** DoubleYou <www.doubleyou.com>. **PRODUCTION TIME:** 3 weeks. **CREATIVE TEAM:** Edu Pou, Anna Coll, Emma Pueyo, David Romero. **PROGRAMMER:** Joakim Borgström, Dani Fernández, Antonio Buenosvinos, Josep María Soler. **TECH ASPECTS:** Macromedia Flash. **AWARDS:** El Sol Festival 2005 (Gold).

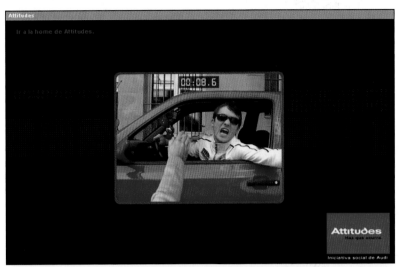

CONCEPT: Attitudes rejects aggressive driving habits by means of a provocative interactive video in which the user is subjected to a verbal attack for a full minute. The end depends on how the user reacts. Apart from the simple and surprising interaction, the main feature of this piece lies in the tone of the monologue spoken by the main actor.

CONCEPT : Attitudes rejette les comportements agressifs au volant au travers d'une vidéo interactive dans laquelle un conducteur est agressé verbalement pendant une bonne minute. La fin va dépendre de la réaction de l'usager. Au-delà de l'interaction simple et surprenante, l'élément essentiel de cette création réside dans le ton du monologue de l'acteur principal.

KONZEPT: Attitudes lehnt aggressives Fahrverhalten ab und verdeutlicht dies mit einem interaktiven Video, in dem der Benutzer eine volle Minute lang einer Verbalattacke ausgesetzt wird. Das Ende hängt davon ab, wie der Benutzer reagiert. Neben der simplen und überraschenden Interaktion liegt ein Hauptmerkmal im Tonfall des Monologes, der von einem Schauspieler gesprochen wird.

FEATURED ON THE DVD **CAMPAIGN:** The Perfect Match. **PRODUCT:** Audi A3 Sportback. **CLIENT:** Audi Cars. **YEAR:** 2004. **AGENCY:** 20:20 London <www.2020london.co.uk>. **PRODUCTION TIME:** 2 months.
CREATIVE TEAM: Peter Riley (Creative Partner), Hugo Bierschenk (Creative), Dean Woodhouse (Creative). **PROGRAMMER:** Dave Luff. **TECH ASPECTS:** film, sound, Adobe After Effects, Macromedia Flash, Wavelab, PHP/SQL, 3D Studio Max, Maya, Shake, Adobe Premiere, Apple Quicktime Pro. **MEDIA CIRCULATED:** Email. **AWARDS:** Direct Marketing Association (UK), Campaign Digital Awards (UK), John Caples International Advertising Awards (New York), Cannes International Advertising Awards.

THE BRIEF: Create an online film to launch the new Audi A3 Sportback across UK and Europe to collect data for test drives. Communicate the brand essence of "Vorsprung Durch Technik" to a hi-tech Internet audience. **THE IDEA:** An email link to a viral film shows scientists conducting tests to determine the 'DNA' of the car and human DNA, and are seen inputting YOUR NAME into various clinical tests. The scientists realise that your DNA and the DNA of the new Audi A3 is identical – revealing that you really are 'The Perfect Match' for the new car. The final shot of the film shows DNA slides from both the car and human tests coming together. YOUR NAME APPEARS OUT OF THE DNA SEQUENCE STRIP. You are 'The Perfect Match' for the new Audi A3 Sportback. When you send the movie to a friend THEIR NAME appears in the movie. More surprising, a couple of days later a mailpack from Audi arrives on your doorstep with your 'test' results, and the actual DNA slide personalised with YOUR NAME. **RESULTS:** The Audi launch was so successful that the email open rate was over 50%, over 65,000 views of the film were recorded and over 50% of viewers forwarded it to a friend. This unique integration of Internet film and direct mail was adopted by Audi Head Office as Global Best Marketing Practice with interest in roll-out from territories as diverse as USA, South Africa and Australia.

BRIEFING : Réaliser un film en ligne pour le lancement de la nouvelle Audi A3 Sportback en Grande-Bretagne et en Europe pour récolter des demandes d'essais sur route. Il fallait communiquer la nature de haute technicité de la marque à un public d'internautes sensible à ce critère. **IDÉE :** Un lien hypertexte vous renvoie à un film montrant des scientifiques au travail. Ils sont en train de procéder à des analyses pour comparer l'ADN de l'homme à celui de la voiture. Ils entrent votre nom dans un fichier et s'aperçoivent que votre ADN et celui de la nouvelle Audi A3 sont identiques, ce qui fait de vous « l'homme idéal ». La dernière scène montre la superposition des deux empreintes génétiques, et votre nom s'affiche sur l'écran. Vous êtes bien l'homme idéal pour la A3. Si vous envoyez le lien à un ami, c'est son nom qui apparaîtra dans le film. Quelques jours après, vous recevez par la poste le résultat de vos tests, accompagné d'une diapositive de votre empreinte génétique. **RÉSULTATS :** Le lancement a connu un tel succès que le taux d'ouverture des e-mails a dépassé 50%. Le film a été visionné 65 000 fois et plus de 50% des internautes l'ont fait suivre à un ami. Cette approche combinée de film et de campagne e-mail a été saluée par la direction de Audi comme Meilleure Pratique Globale de Marketing. L'intérêt pour la marque s'est propagé jusqu'aux Etats-Unis, en Afrique du Sud et en Australie.

DIE AUFGABE: Einen Online-Film für den Launch des neuen Audi A3 Sportback in Großbritannien und Europa entwickeln, um Daten für Testfahrten zu sammeln. Die Markenessenz „Vorsprung durch Technik" einem Hi-Tech Internetpublikum kommunizieren. **DIE IDEE:** Ein E-Mail-Link zu einem viralen Film zeigt Wissenschaftler, die Tests durchführen, um die „DNA" des Autos und die menschliche DNA zu determinieren, und man sieht, wie sie DEINEN NAMEN in verschiedene klinische Tests eingeben. Sie bemerken, dass deine DNA und die DNA des neuen Audi A3 identisch sind – du passt perfekt zum neuen Auto. Die letzte Einstellung des Films zeigt, wie die menschliche DNA und die DNA des Autos zusammenkommen. DEIN NAME ERSCHEINT IN DER DNA-SEQUENZ. Du bist das perfekte Gegenstück für den neuen Audi A3 Sportback. Sendet man den Film an einen Freund, erscheint SEIN NAME im Film. **ERGEBNISSE:** Zwei Tage später kommt per Post sogar ein Paket von Audi mit den Testergebnissen: Der Audi-Launch war so erfolgreich, dass über 50% die E-Mail öffneten, der Film 65 000-mal gesehen wurde und über 50% der Zuschauer ihn einem Freund weiterleiteten. Diese einzigartige Kombination von Internetfilm und Post wurde von Audis Hauptsitz als Global Best Marketing Practice übernommen, mit Interesse daran, es in so verschiedenen Märkten wie den USA, Südafrika und Australien anzuwenden.

FEATURED ON THE DVD **PRODUCT:** Audi A3 Sportback. **YEAR:** 2005. **AGENCY:** DoubleYou <www.doubleyou.com>. **PRODUCTION TIME:** 2 weeks. **CREATIVE TEAM:** Frédéric Sanz, Joakim Borgström, Xavi Caparrós, Nacho Guijarro. **PROGRAMMER:** Xavi Caparrós, Nacho Guijarro, Joakim Borgström. **TECH ASPECTS:** Macromedia Flash, Eyeblaster. **MEDIA CIRCULATED:** Temps de Neu (Televisió de Catalunya), Coches.net, Guia Campsa, ABC.

CONCEPT: The starting point for this piece was the Audi A3 Sportback campaign featuring what were supposed to be the memories of the typical purchaser of this model. To transfer this concept to the web, we opted for a number of interactive items in which a set of Polaroids allowed the users to view these memories before discovering the Audi A3 Sportback. This campaign received the Eyeblaster prize in New York in November 2005, for best international interactive campaign.

CONCEPT : Il s'agissait de décliner la campagne pour la Audi A3 Sportback présentant les souvenirs imaginaires d'un acheteur typique. Pour retranscrire en ligne ce concept, nous avons opté pour plusieurs modules interactifs dans lesquels l'usager regardait une série de Polaroïds avant de découvrir l'Audi A3. La publicité a été désignée Meilleure Campagne Interactive Internationale par Eyeblaster à New York en 2005.

KONZEPT: Der Ausgangspunkt war die Audi A3 Sportback-Kampagne, die die vermeintlichen Erinnerungen eines typischen Käufers dieses Modells darstellte. Um dieses Konzept auf das Web zu übertragen, entschieden wir uns für einige interaktive Elemente, bei denen die Benutzer diese Erinnerungen in einer Reihe von Polaroids betrachten konnten, bevor sie den Audi A3 Sportback entdeckten. Die Kampagne erhielt in New York im November den Eyeblaster-Preis für die beste internationale interaktive Kampagne.

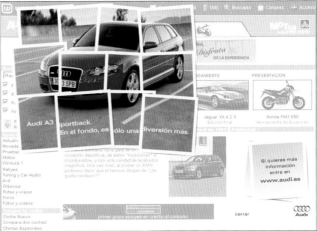

FEATURED ON THE DVD **CAMPAIGN:** 25 years of Quattro. **PRODUCT:** Audi. **YEAR:** 2005. **AGENCY:** DoubleYou <www.doubleyou.com>. **PRODUCTION TIME:** 2 weeks. **CREATIVE TEAM:** Frédéric Sanz, Lisi Badía, Nacho Guijarro, Joakim Borgström, Xavi Caparrós. **PROGRAMMER:** Joakim Borgström, Xavi Caparrós, Nacho Guijarro. **TECH ASPECTS:** Macromedia Flash, Eyeblaster. **MEDIA CIRCULATED:** Autoscout24, viaMichelin, El Mundo, Inetwork, Expansión, Autopistaonline, Terra, Wanadoo, Autocity, Supermotor.

CONCEPT: To mark the 25th Anniversary of its four-wheel drive technology, Audi set out to surprise internauts with an interactive campaign in which users found themselves literally stuck to a banner or a killerpage. On struggling to free themselves the piece becomes a three-page leaflet with video sequences conveying a brief history of the quattro.

CONCEPT : Pour marquer le 25ème anniversaire de sa technologie 4x4, Audi a décidé de surprendre les internautes avec une campagne interactive dans laquelle l'utilisateur se retrouve littéralement collé à une bannière. Tandis qu'il essaye de se libérer, la bannière se change en une brochure de trois pages intégrant des séquences vidéo qui retracent l'historique de la Quattro.

KONZEPT: Um das 25. Jubiläum seiner Vierradtechnik zu feiern, überrascht Audi Internet-User mit einer interaktiven Kampagne, bei der der Benutzer wortwörtlich an einem Banner oder einer Killerpage festklebt. Bei dem Bemühen, sich zu befreien, wird eine dreiseitige Broschüre mit Videosequenzen daraus, die eine kurze Geschichte des Quattro beschreibt.

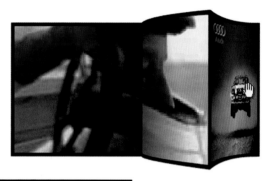

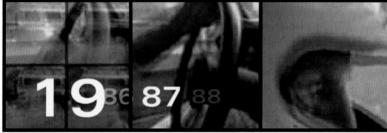

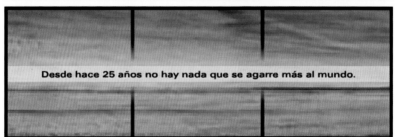

Desde hace 25 años no hay nada que se agarre más al mundo.

FEATURED ON THE DVD   **CAMPAIGN:** "It won't leave you indifferent."   **PRODUCT:** Audi A4.   **YEAR:** 2005.   **AGENCY:** DoubleYou <www.doubleyou.com>.   **PRODUCTION TIME:** 1 week.   **CREATIVE TEAM:** Joakim Borgström, Frédéric Sanz, Blanca Piera, Lisi Badia, Nacho Guijarro, Xavi Caparrós.   **PROGRAMMER:** Xavi Caparrós, Joakim Borgström.   **TECH ASPECTS:** Macromedia Flash.   **MEDIA CIRCULATED:** ABC, Autoscout24, Coches.net, El Mundo, Expansión, KM77, La Vanguardia, Movendus, Repsol YPF, Terra, Via Michelin, Ya.com.

CONCEPT: When transferring the concept of the new Audi A4 campaign "It won't leave you indifferent" to the Internet, we opted for a simple but attention-capturing item which stimulated the internaut to interact with it. It really did become a "demonstration" that the Audi A4 left no one indifferent!

CONCEPT : Pour retranscrire le concept de la nouvelle campagne Audi A4 « Elle ne vous laissera pas indifférent », nous avons conçu un projet simple mais captivant qui invitait l'internaute à participer. Il a fait la démonstration que l'Audi A4 ne laisse personne indifférent.

KONZEPT: Bei der Übertragung des Konzepts der neuen Audi A4-Kampagne „Es wird Sie nicht gleichgültig lassen" entschieden wir uns für etwas Simples, aber Aufmerksamkeit Erregendes, mit dem der Internet-User interagieren konnte. Es wurde wirklich zu einer Demonstration, dass der Audi A4 niemanden gleichgültig ließ!

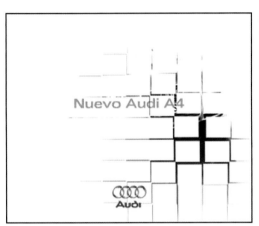
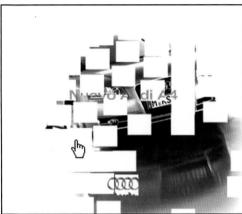

FEATURED ON THE DVD **CAMPAIGN:** Audi Elements <www.audi-elements.com>. **PRODUCT:** Audi A4. **YEAR:** 2004. **AGENCY:** 20:20 London <www.2020london.co.uk>. **PRODUCTION TIME:** 3 months. **CREATIVE TEAM:** Peter Riley (Creative Partner), Hugo Bierschenk (Creative), Dean Woodhouse (Creative). **PROGRAMMER:** Simon James. **TECH ASPECTS:** Film, sound, Adobe After Effects, Macromedia Flash, Wavelab, PHP/SQL, 3D Studio Max, Maya, Shake, Adobe Premiere, Apple Quicktime Pro. **MEDIA CIRCULATED:** Email.

STATEMENT OF BRIEF AND OBJECTIVES: Audi cars are known for being technologically advanced. This is summed up by the Teutonic simplicity of "Vorsprung durch Technik" (VdT). If the cars are ahead of the pack, shouldn't the marketing be also? Digital Direct Marketing was to be used to raise awareness of the restyled Audi A4 compact executive saloon and encourage test drives. **STRATEGY:** We targeted the Audi database of previous purchasers and prospects. These guys – yes, they are mainly men – are secure in both their finances and career and adore gadgets and technology. The kind of bloke who wires his iPod into his car's stereo because he can. Research identified a core truth – these men have an untapped online address book of like-minded friends. If we excite them then they'll tell their friends, and the way to do that is to put them at the centre of the message, not the product. This gave us a powerful connection. **SOLUTION:** An emotive and personalised short online film, shot in black and white, shows the epic struggle between individualism and mass conformity. Set against a backdrop of industrial espionage, a ficticious Japanese corporation denies the existence of "Vorsprung durch Technik", the secret ingredient in every Audi. The heroine singles you out for some under-wraps information and types an email to you. Right on cue, as the film finishes, there's the real email in your inbox, triggered automatically by reaching the end of the film. This email explains the story, shows pictures of the car and points you to the website. A Digital DM invitation to see for yourself the advanced thinking behind Audi and the new A4. **RESULTS:** Evaluation results, summary of improvements to business performance 1.2 million prospects receiving a personalised film from a friend who knew they would be interested. The ultimate in targeted direct communication. This Digital Direct Marketing has been adopted as Global Best Practice by Audi's Head Office in Germany.

OBJECTIFS : Les voitures Audi sont réputées pour leur haute technicité. Cette notion est résumée par la simplicité teutonique *Vorsprung Durch Technik* (Vdt) « Le progrès via la technologie ». Si les voitures sont en tête du peloton, alors le marketing doit l'être aussi. Le marketing électronique direct devait communiquer sur la nouvelle berline de luxe A4 et inviter les consommateurs à venir l'essayer. **STRATÉGIE :** Nous avons ciblé la base de données de propriétaires d'une Audi et de clients potentiels. Ces hommes, car ce sont essentiellement des hommes, ont généralement des revenus et un métier stables, et sont friands de gadgets technologiques. Le genre d'homme qui branche son iPod dans la stéréo de sa voiture. Les sondages ont révélé une vérité essentielle : ces hommes possèdent un carnet d'adresses e-mail d'amis qui leur ressemblent, et qui ne demande qu'à être exploité. Si on les accroche, ils passeront eux-mêmes le message à leurs amis. Il s'agit donc de placer au centre du message non pas le produit, mais l'individu, et d'établir avec lui une relation forte. **SOLUTION :** Un petit film émotif et personnalisé, tourné en noir et blanc, et mettant en scè-

ne le combat épique entre individualisme et conformité sociale. Sur fond d'espionnage industriel, une société japonaise imaginaire réfute l'existence du VdT, le mystérieux gène de toutes les Audi. L'héroïne vous désigne pour tirer l'affaire au clair et vous envoie un e-mail. L'e-mail arrive dans votre boîte à la fin du film, déclenché automatiquement par les dernières images. Le message vous explique votre mission, vous fournit des photos de la voiture et vous dirige sur le site. L'opération de marketing direct vous invite à découvrir la philosophie de Audi et de son dernier modèle de voiture. **RÉSULTATS :** Amélioration quantifiée des performances de la marque. 1,2 million de clients potentiels ont reçu le film par recommandation d'un ami. Cette démarche de marketing électronique direct a reçu le titre de Meilleure Pratique Globale par la direction de Audi en Allemagne.

AUFGABE UND ZIELE: Audis sind dafür bekannt, technologisch fortschrittlich zu sein. Dies wird in dem simplen Slogan „Vorsprung durch Technik" (VdT) zusammengefasst. Wenn die Autos schon ganz vorne sind, sollte es das Marketing nicht auch sein? Digitales Direct Marketing sollte das Bewusstsein für den neu gestylten Audi A4 wecken und zu Testfahrten ermuntern. **STRATEGIE:** Wir zielten auf die Audi-Datenbank früherer und potenzieller Käufer ab. Diese Jungs – ja, es sind hauptsächlich Männer – sind finanziell und beruflich abgesichert und bewundern Geräte und Technik. Die Art von Mann, der seinen iPod im Auto anschließt – weil er es kann. Untersuchungen belegen die folgende Tatsache: Diese Männer besitzen ein dickes Online-Adressbuch, voll mit gleich gesinnten Freunden. Sprechen wir sie an, werden sie ihren Freunden davon berichten; und die richtige Art, dies zu tun, ist, sie in das Zentrum der Botschaft zu rücken – nicht das Produkt. Dies verhalf uns zu einer starken Kundenbeziehung. **LÖSUNG:** Ein emotionsgeladener und personalisierter kurzer Schwarz-Weiß-Online-Film zeigt den epischen Kampf zwischen Individualität und Massenkonformität. Vor dem Hintergrund von Industriespionage gedreht, leugnet eine fiktive japanische Firma die Existenz von „Vorsprung durch Technik", dem geheimen Inhaltsstoff in jedem Audi. Der Held wählt Sie für einige vertrauliche Informationen aus und schreibt Ihnen eine E-Mail. Zum selben Zeitpunkt, an dem der Film aufhört, landet eine E-Mail, die automatisch vom Ende des Films ausgelöst wurde, in Ihrem Posteingang. Diese E-Mail erklärt die Story, zeigt Bilder des Autos und verweist Sie auf die Webseite. Eine digitale Direct-Marketing-Einladung, mit der Sie das fortschrittliche Denken, das hinter Audi und dem neuen A4 steckt, mit eigenen Augen sehen sollen. **ERGEBNISSE:** Bewertungsergebnisse und Zusammenfassung von Verbesserungen der Unternehmensleistung: 1,2 Millionen Kunden erhielten den personalisierten Film von einem Freund, der wusste, dass sie Interesse daran haben würden. Die ultimative gezielte Direktkommunikation. Dieses digitale Direct Marketing wurde von Audis Hauptsitz in Deutschland als Global Best Practice übernommen.

FEATURED ON THE DVD   **CAMPAIGN:** Have you clicked yet?   **PRODUCT:** British Airways e-services.   **YEAR:** 2005.   **AGENCY:** Agency.com London <www.agency.com>.   **COST IN HOURS OF WORK:** 1,112 h.   **CREATIVE TEAM:** Julie Barnes, Sarah Bagner.   **PROGRAMMER:** Alan Lead, Karl Reynolds, Paul Collins.   **TECH ASPECTS:** Video, Macromedia Flash, sound, mobile phone technology.   **MEDIA CIRCULATED:** DigitalHome.com; NewScientist.com; TimesOnline.com; FT.com; Economist.com.   **AWARDS:** Campaign Digital Awards 2005 (Finalist); LIA Awards 2005 (Finalist); Revolution 2006 Best Integrated Marketing (Finalist).

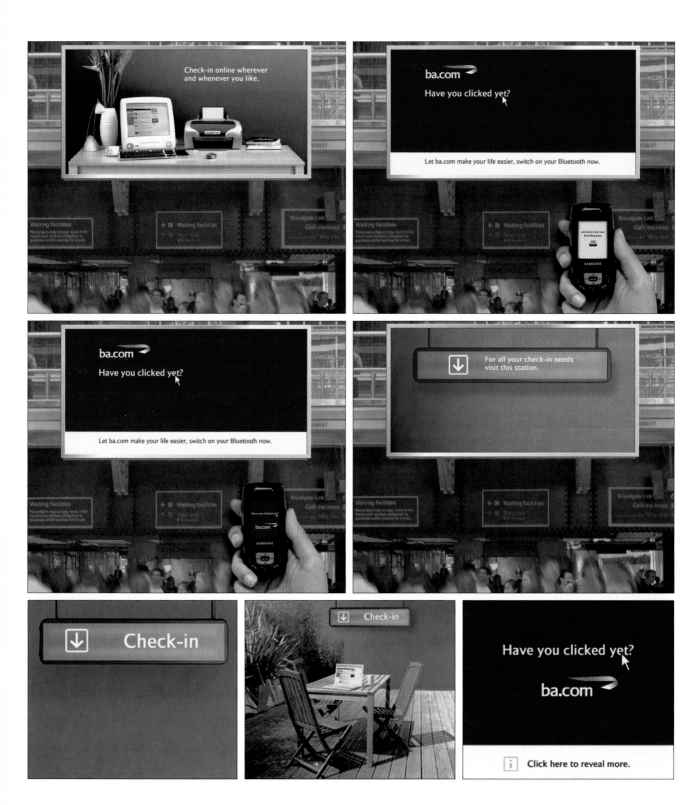

CHALLENGE: British Airways has launched a host of 'e-services', available at *ba.com*, which are set to make travel easier – from printing your own boarding pass, online check-in and self-service check-in, to choosing your own seat and changing your booking. **SOLUTION:** We created a series of innovative, high-impact executions that pushed the boundaries in terms of creative and media placements, creating a truly integrated cross-platform digital campaign. The media plan met the demographics of the target audience – closely matching lifestyle with e-service messaging. The campaign integrated with the ATL proposition "Have you clicked yet?" harnessing digital media's unique qualities to bring the campaign to life. Messages focused on the two main innovations: online check-in and the facility to print your own boarding pass. We used sophisticated animation and photography, coupled with copy that focused on British Airways' intelligent wit, and suggested the benefits in a subtle and emotive way. In this way, we linked the consumers' lifestyle to the core services available. The campaign was delivered through innovative media: ATM screens; Transvision screens including Bluecasting; digital escalator panels at Tottenham Court Road; Oxigen screensaver (corporate screensaver package) and online advertising. **RESULTS:** Media firsts included the use of video overlays in conjunction with margin ads as part of the online campaign generating CTR over 40%; Becoming one of the first advertisers in the UK to run a campaign on digital escalator panels; First airline or travel brand to trial bluecasting in conjunction with large format plasma screens; First 4 weeks showed rich media as strongest creative online, generating click-through rates in excess of 40%.

DÉFI : British Airways a lancé une série de services en ligne, disponibles sur *ba.com*, destinés à faciliter le voyage. On peut imprimer sa carte d'embarquement, procéder à l'enregistrement en ligne, changer son numéro de siège et même sa réservation. **SOLUTION :** Une série d'exécutions novatrices et efficaces qui repoussent les limites en terme de placement média, au centre d'une campagne électronique intégrée. Le plan média a suivi les données démographiques du groupe cible, en adaptant le message au style de vie des usagers. Le slogan « Avez-vous cliqué ? » exploite les capacités particulières du support électronique. Le message insiste sur les deux innovations principales : l'enregistrement en ligne et l'impression de la carte d'embarquement. Une photographie et une animation élaborées accompagnent un texte imprégné d'humour et suggèrent les avantages de manière subtile et émotionnelle. Nous avons ainsi recherché la connivence entre le style de vie des consommateurs et les services proposés. La campagne a été diffusée via des canaux originaux :

écrans ATM, écrans TransVision intégrant le BlueCasting, panneaux d'escalators digitaux dans le métro, écrans de veille animés et publicité en ligne. **RÉSULTATS :** La combinaison inédite de diffusion vidéo et d'encarts pubs au sein de la campagne en ligne a généré une hausse du nombre de clics de plus de 40%. Nous sommes parmi les premiers en Grande-Bretagne à avoir affiché sur les panneaux d'escalators. L'annonceur est un des premiers transporteurs aériens à avoir essayé le BlueCasting associé à des écrans plasma grand format. Les quatre premières semaines ont démontré la supériorité créative du rich media et ont généré une formidable hausse de trafic.

AUFGABE: British Airways führte „E-Dienste" auf *ba.com* ein, die das Reisen leichter machen sollten – vom Drucken der eigenen Bordkarte über Check-In online und Selbstbedienungs-Check-In bis zur eigenen Sitzplatzwahl und Buchungsänderungen. **LÖSUNG:** Wir entwickelten eine Reihe innovativer, wirkungsvoller und in kreativer Hinsicht grenzüberschreitende Ausführungen, indem wir eine integrierte, plattformübergreifende digitale Kampagne starteten. Der Media-Plan orientierte sich an der Zusammensetzung des Zielpublikums, indem die E-Dienste-Botschaften dem Lifestyle entsprachen. Die Kampagne schloss den ATL-Slogan ein „Haben Sie schon geklickt?" und nutzte die einzigartigen Eigenschaften der digitalen Medien, durch die sie ins Leben gerufen wurde. Die Botschaften konzentrierten sich auf die zwei wichtigsten Innovationen: Check-In online und die Möglichkeit, die eigene Bordkarte auszudrucken. Wir verwendeten hochentwickelte Animation und Fotografie in Kombination mit einem Text, der den hohen Standard von British Airways spiegelte und die Vorteile auf subtile und gleichzeitig emotional ansprechende Weise darlegte. Dadurch verbanden wir den Lifestyle der Konsumenten mit dem verfügbaren Service. Die Kampagne wurde durch innovative Medien vermittelt: ATM-Bildschirme, Transvision-Bildschirme einschließlich Bluecasting, digitale Rolltreppenkonsolen an der U-Bahnstation Tottenham Court Road, Oxigen-Bildschirmschoner (Firmenbildschirmschoner-Paket) Werbung online. **ERGEBNISSE:** Die Kampagne integrierte erstmals die Verwendung von Video-Pop Ups in Verbindung mit marginaler Werbung als Teil einer Online-Kampagne und erzeugte damit eine CTR von über 40%; BA wurde einer der ersten Werber in Großbritannien, der eine Kampagne auf digitalen Rolltreppenkonsolen laufen ließ; die erste Flug- bzw. Reisemarke, die Bluecasting in Verbindung mit großformatigen Plasmabildschirmen verwendete; die ersten vier Wochen bewiesen die Stärke von Rich Media, was an Click-Through-Rates von über 40% abzulesen war.

CAMPAIGN: Sleeper Service. PRODUCT: British Airways Club World. YEAR: 2004. AGENCY: Agency.com London <www.agency.com>. COST IN HOURS OF WORK: 654.25 h. CREATIVE TEAM: Olly Robinson, Steve Whiteley.
PROGRAMMER: Perry Cooper, Paul Collins. TECH ASPECTS: Macromedia Flash, sound. MEDIA CIRCULATED: TimesOnline.com; FT.com; NYTimes.com. AWARDS: CIM Travel Advertising 2004 (Silver); IAB Creative Showcase.

CHALLENGE: Passenger surveys revealed that British Airways Club World Travellers, who regularly flew overnight to London Heathrow, wanted to sleep more during their journeys. In spring 2004, British Airways launched an enhanced Club World Sleeper Service. BA wanted to generate awareness and interest in the new developments to the service. **SOLUTION:** The online campaign integrated with ATL campaign and the online media plan mirrored offline positioning, through sites such as *ft.com*, *economist.com*, *times.com* and *classicfm.com*. Pop-ups, superstitial units, banners and larger formats such as MPU (messaging plus units) were used. Successful negotiation of Eyeblaster acceptance allowed us to drive more interactivity. **RESULTS:** Six weeks after the initial launch it had generated an ROI of £24 for every £1 spent online. Interaction rates exceeded expectations, demonstrating the campaign's effectiveness. Within the first week, there were 2.2 million impressions across all creative units. Average interaction rates for the expandable banner and the superstitial were 1.4% and 1.17% respectively.

DÉFI : Un sondage mené auprès des voyageurs du Club World de British Airways qui atterrissent de nuit à l'aéroport d'Heathrow révèle leur désir de dormir plus pendant leurs trajets. Au printemps 2004, British Airways lance donc un service couchettes pour la classe affaires. Le transporteur veut communiquer sur sa nouvelle offre de service et susciter l'intérêt. **SOLUTION :** La campagne en ligne et le plan plurimédia reflètent le positionnement de la marque hors ligne, en apparaissant sur des sites comme *ft.com*, *economist.com*, *times.com* et *classicfm.com*. Des modules superstitiels, des fenêtres pop-up, des bannières et des grands bandeaux sont réalisés. L'autorisation d'employer le format vidéo Eyeblaster nous a permis d'augmenter l'interactivité du site. **RÉSULTATS :** Six semaines après le lancement initial, le site a généré un retour sur investissement de 24 livres pour 1 livre dépensée en ligne. Les taux d'interaction ont dépassé les prévisions, démontrant l'efficacité de la campagne. Dans la première semaine, on a compté 2,2 millions de pages vues quels que soient les modules. Le taux moyen d'interaction pour la bannière extensible et le superstitiel ont été respectivement de 1,4% et 1,17%.

AUFGABE: Passagierumfragen ergaben, dass Reisende mit British Airways Club World, die regelmäßig über Nacht nach London Heathrow flogen, während der Reise mehr schlafen wollten. Im Frühjahr 2004 führte British Airways einen verbesserten Club World Schlafservice ein. BA wollte Interesse für die neuen Entwicklungen des Service wecken. **LÖSUNG:** Die Online-Kampagne spiegelte, zusammen mit der ATL-Kampagne und dem Online-Media-Plan, die Offline-Positionierung durch Seiten wie *ft.com*, *economist.com*, *times.com* und *classifm.com* wider. Es wurden Pop-Up-Fenster, Superstitial-Einheiten, Banner und größere Formate wie MPU (Message Plus Units) verwendet. Durch erfolgreichen Einsatz von Eyeblaster konnten wir die Interaktivität erhöhen. **ERGEBNISSE:** Sechs Wochen nach dem Launch erzeugte es einen ROI von £24 für jedes online ausgegebene £1. Die Interaktionsraten überstiegen die Erwartungen und bewiesen die Effektivität der Kampagne. Innerhalb der ersten Woche wurden auf allen Ebenen der Kampagne 2.2 Millionen Klicks gezählt. Die durchschnittliche Interaktionsrate für ausdehnbare Banner und das Superstitial lag bei jeweils 1.4% und 1.17%.

FEATURED ON THE DVD CAMPAIGN: BMW 1 Series. PRODUCT: BMW 1 Series PDA. YEAR: 2004. AGENCY: Interone Worldwide, Hamburg <www.interone.de>. PRODUCTION TIME: 1,5 month. COST IN HOURS OF WORK: 1,000 h. SENIOR ART DIRECTOR: Mike John Otto. CONTENT DEVELOPMENT: Tim Büsing. SCREEN DESIGN: Jochen Röhling. COPY TEXT: John Dubois. TECHNICAL PROJECT MANAGER: Eckhard Schneider. PRODUCER: RTT Realtime Technology, M.able. TECH ASPECTS: Film, Macromedia Flash, 3D Configurator.

CONCEPT: Within its communication medium, the mobile BMW 1 Series PDA Site is a unique application regarding its design, ergonomics, content and functionality. The design is pragmatic yet fits the brand perfectly and is compatible and optimised for approximately the whole PDA and Palm end devices. The BMW 1 Series PDA site is easy to use thanks to an extremely comprehensive navigation system. Compared to other PDA sites, the application offers a balanced mix of text and images, contains a lot of animations and 3D Clips on each page, displays high-quality images and can be downloaded quickly making it extremely user-friendly. A major plus is the full 3D Visualizer and the 360° 3D Model of the BMW 1 Series. **RESULT:** Strong communication impulse for the brand in quantity and quality. The Module was rolled out into 5 markets.

CONCEPT : Au sein de son réseau de communication, le site PDA de BMW 1 Series est une application unique quant au design, à l'ergonomie, au rédactionnel et aux fonctionnalités. Le design est pragmatique tout en reflétant parfaitement la marque, il est optimisé pour être compatible avec la quasi-totalité des appareils PDA. Le site est simple d'utilisation grâce à un système de navigation polyvalent. Comparé à d'autres sites PDA, l'application offre un mélange équilibré de texte et d'images de qualité supérieure, d'animations et d'inserts en 3D, et sa grande facilité de téléchargement le rend très pratique pour l'usager. La visualisation en 3D et sur 360 degrés des différents modèles de voitures comptent parmi ses plus grands atouts. **RÉSULTAT :** Gros impact commercial, en qualité comme en quantité. Le module a été décliné sur cinq autres marchés.

KONZEPT: Innerhalb ihres Kommunikationsmediums ist die mobile BMW 1-PDA-Seite eine einzigartige Anwendung, was Design, Ergonomie, Inhalt und Funktionalität betrifft. Das Design ist pragmatisch, aber passt perfekt zur Marke und ist für beinahe alle PDA- und Palm-end-Geräte kompatibel und optimiert. Die BMW 1-PDA-Seite ist dank eines leicht verständlichen Navigationssystems einfach zu verwenden. Verglichen mit anderen PDA-Seiten bietet die Anwendung eine ausgeglichene Mischung von Text und Bildern, enthält viele Animationen und 3D-Clips auf jeder Seite, zeigt qualitativ hochwertige Bilder und kann schnell heruntergeladen werden, was sie extrem benutzerfreundlich macht. Ein großer Pluspunkt ist der 3D-Visualizer und das 360°-3D-Modell der BMW 1-Serie. **ERGEBNIS:** Starke Kommunikationsimpulse für die Marke in Quantität und Qualität. Das Modul wurde in 5 Länder ausgeliefert.

PRODUCT: BMW ICS NewMedia. YEAR: 2004. AGENCY: Interone Worldwide <www.interone.de>. PRODUCTION TIME: 4 months. COST IN HOURS OF WORK: 4,000 hours. PRODUCER: RTT – Realtime Technology, Deli Pictures Postproduction. CREATIVE DIRECTOR: Arne Habeman. SENIOR ART DIRECTOR: Mike John Otto. CONTENT DEVELOPMENT: Jan Köpke. SCREEN DESIGN: Jochen Röhling. COPY TEXT: John Dubois. PRODUCER: Jochen Watrall, Ursula Haferstroh. FLASH: Patrick De Jong. FLASH/BACKEND: Wolfgang Müller. TECHNICAL PROJECT MANAGER: Thomas Feldhaus. TECH ASPECTS: The PoS Product Presentation incorporates and combines a wide range of varying media formats. Highlights include interactive 3D models of all BMW vehicles and 3D films illustrating vehicles' technical features. The BMW ICS NewMedia Tool is a all in Macromedia Flash realized Software. It contains rich 3D use, 360° 3D turns of each BMW Model and 3D aswell as Realfilm use to show the safety, design and driving aspects of the whole BMW Range. The Tool is XML feeded and allows to be used in various languages which each BMW Dealer Worldwide can select while using the BMW ICS NewMedia. AWARDS: New York Festivals 2005 (Gold), IF Design Award 2005 (Gold), IAA AWARDS 2004 (Silver), Annual Multimedia 2004.

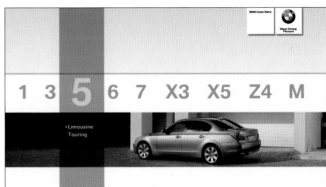

CONCEPT: The BMW ICS NM Presentation displayed on a 40" TFT monitor is the central component of the BMW Consulting Lounge, a "store in store" solution for individualised vehicle advising and sales sessions. Comprehensive and interactive, the ICS NM Presentation supports BMW dealers in providing a personalised customer consultation. In this role, it becomes an essential component of the sales process and reinforces the customer's experience of the brand and the product at the dealership. Contents of the presentation are consequently targeted to the client's interests in the context of vehicle sales – the format of the content "interactive mixed media" and the presentation's operating and navigation concept meet the high demands of a BMW customer advisor. The ICS NM Presentation is designed for use with a high-powered PC and a 40" TFT monitor, with a Bluetooth keyboard, mouse and media pad serving as input devices. **RESULTS:** The Product Presentation supports the customer advisor in conducting an customer-oriented, individualised sales discussion. BMW high technology, innovations and design are displayed in an interactive and animated manner using a number of different media. The specifications outlined in the following make the BMW PoS Product Presentation currently one of a kind on the market : programmed completely in Flash MX, compatible with Content Management Systems, and featuring a display size of 1280 x 768 on a 40" TFT monitor.

CONCEPT : La présentation BMW ICS NM exposée sur un moniteur TFT de 40 pouces est l'élément essentiel de l'Espace Conseil BMW, une « boutique dans la boutique » dédiée au conseil individualisé et aux sessions de vente. Polyvalente et interactive, la présentation ICS fournit au concessionnaire un outil de consultation personnalisée. Il devient un élément essentiel des opérations de vente et accentue l'expérience de marque du consommateur chez le vendeur. Le contenu répond aux intérêts du client en conditions d'achat, tandis que le format interactif et plurimédia satisfait les exigences du conseiller BMW en termes de fonctionnalités et de navigation. La présentation est conçue pour un puissant PC et un

moniteur de 40 pouces, accompagné d'un clavier Bluetooth, d'une souris optique et d'un pavé numérique pour la publication des données. **RÉSULTATS :** La présentation du produit permet au conseiller de vente d'engager une discussion centrée sur le consommateur et ses besoins. La technologie BMW, les innovations et le design sont présentées de façon vivante et interactive via différents canaux. Les caractéristiques de la présentation la rendent unique en son genre sur le marché : tout est programmé en Flash MX, est compatible avec les systèmes de gestion de contenu, et offre une résolution de 1280 x 768 sur un écran de 40 pouces.

KONZEPT: Die Präsentation von BMW ICS NM auf einem 40"-TFT-Monitor ist die zentrale Komponente der BMW-Beratungslounge, eine „Store in Store"-Lösung für persönliche Beratungs- und Verkaufsgespräche. Verständlich und interaktiv unterstützt die ICS-NM-Präsentation BMW-Händler dabei, eine persönliche Kundenberatung anzubieten. In dieser Rolle wird sie zu einer essentiellen Komponente des Verkaufsprozesses und stärkt die Bindung des Kunden an Marke und Produkt. Die Präsentationsinhalte zielen auf die Interessen des Klienten im Kontext des Autoverkaufs ab – das inhaltliche Format „Interactive Mixed Media" und das Navigationskonzept entsprechen den Anforderungen eines BMW-Kundenberaters. Die ICS-NM-Präsentation kann mit einem leistungsfähigen PC und einem 40"-TFT-Monitor verwendet werden, mit einer Bluetooth-Tastatur, Mouse und Mediapad als Input-Geräte. **ERGEBNISSE:** Die Produktpräsentation unterstützt den Kundenberater beim Führen eines kundenorientierten, persönlichen Verkaufsgesprächs. Technologie, Innovationen und Design werden auf interaktive und animierte Art mit verschiedenen Medien gezeigt. Die folgenden Spezifikationen machen die Produktpräsentation von BMW auf dem derzeitigen Markt einzigartig: komplett in Flash MX programmiert, mit Content-Management-Systemen kompatibel, mit einer Displaygröße von 1280 x 768 auf einem 40"-TFT-Monitor.

CAMPAIGN: Who killed the idea? **PRODUCT:** BMW 5 Series. **YEAR:** 2003. **AGENCY:** Interone Worldwide <www.interone.de>. **PRODUCTION TIME:** 2 months. **COST IN HOURS OF WORK:** 2,000 hours. **CREATIVE DIRECTOR:** Mike John Otto. . **ART DIRECTOR:** Mike John Otto. **CONTENT DEVELOPMENT:** Jan Köpke. **SCREEN DESIGN:** Jochen Röhling. **COPY TEXT:** John Dubois. **PRODUCER:** Claudia Frindte. **FLASH:** David Löhr. **FLASH/BACKEND:** Eric Funk. **TECHNICAL PROJECT MANAGER:** Thomas Feldhaus. **AWARDS:** Cannes Cyber Lions (Finalist), Epica Award, Favourite Website Award, IAA Awards (Bronze), IF Design Award, Cresta Award, Worldmedia Festival (Silver).

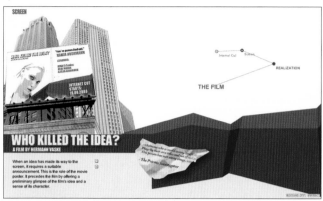

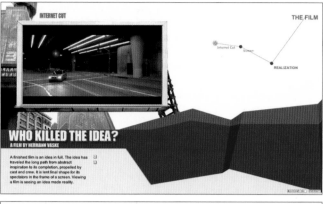

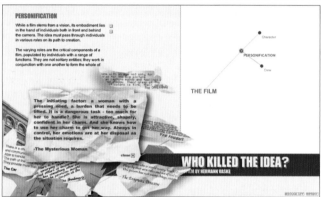

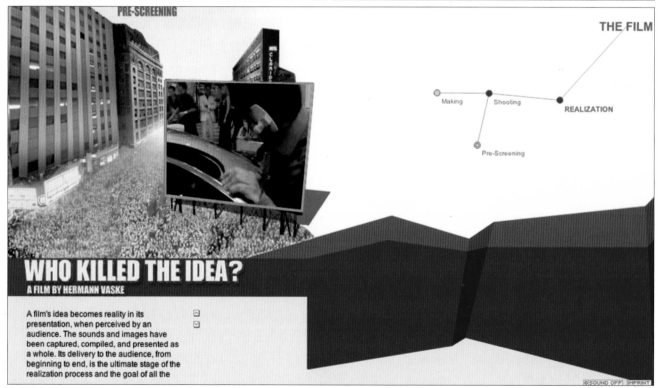

CONCEPT: The website was developed to accompany the production of Hermann Vaske's film "Who killed the idea?", which debuted during the 2003 Cannes Film Festival. Along with Debi Mazar and Nadja Auermann, the new BMW 5 Series also plays a major role in this classic detective story fused with a documentary-style investigation. The investigation focuses on the creation of new ideas and their fate. How does an idea take form and then become realized in a film? The answers to these questions form the backbone of the site's navigation in the branches of the mindmap and allow users to embark on their own investigative journey through the Web site's content. Image and text as well as videos, audio and animation all offer the user a true multimedia experience.

CONCEPT : Le site a été réalisé afin d'accompagner la production du film de Hermann Vaske *Who killed the idea?*, sorti au Festival de Cannes en 2003. Avec Debi Mazar et Nadja Auermann, la nouvelle série BMW 5 joue aussi un rôle de premier plan dans cette histoire policière classique, où l'enquête est menée dans un style documentaire. Au cœur de l'histoire : la naissance des idées, et leur destinée. Comment une idée prend-elle forme dans la réalisation d'un film ? La réponse constitue l'ossature de la navigation dans le site et ses différentes rubriques et permet à l'usager de se lancer dans sa propre enquête. Les images, le texte, les vidéos, l'animation et l'habillage sonore, tout concourt à offrir une véritable expérience multimédia.

KONZEPT: Die Webseite wurde entwickelt, um die Produktion von Hermann Vaskes Film „Who killed the idea?" zu begleiten, der beim Cannes Film Festival 2003 Premiere hatte. Neben Debi Mazar und Nadja Auermann spielt auch die neue BMW5-Serie eine herausragende Rolle in dieser klassischen Detektivstory, die mit einer Ermittlung in dokumentarischem Stil verschmilzt. Diese konzentriert sich auf die Entstehung von neuen Ideen und deren Schicksal. Wie nimmt eine Idee Form an, wie wird sie in einem Film umgesetzt? Die Antworten auf diese Fragen bilden die Basis der Seitennavigation und ermöglichen es dem Benutzer, sich auf seine eigene Forschungsreise durch den Inhalt der Seite zu begeben. Text und Bild sowie Videos, Audio und Animation bieten dem Benutzer ein multimediales Erlebnis.

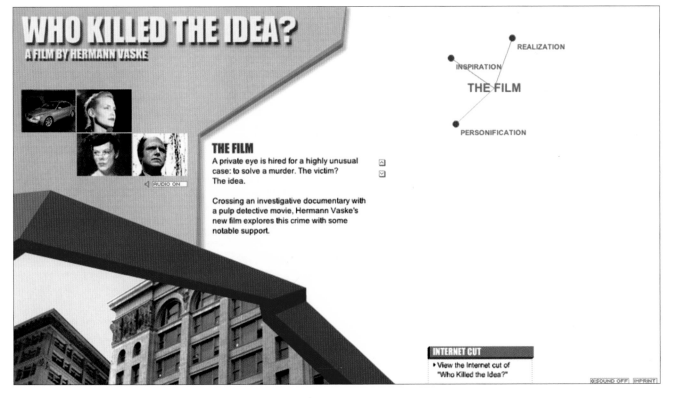

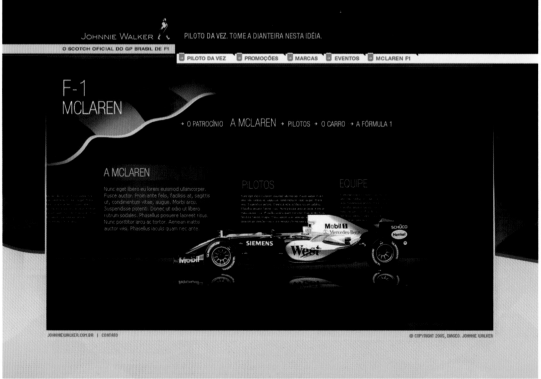

CONCEPT: Stilo Connect's website provides a complete experience with the product through an interactive story. It was the first website to interact with the user on the phone while surfing on the web.

CONCEPT : Le site de Stilo Connect offre une expérience complète du produit à travers une histoire interactive. Le premier site à interagir au téléphone avec l'internaute alors que celui-ci est connecté simultanément à Internet.

KONZEPT: Die Stilo Connect-Webseite bietet eine komplette Produktpräsentation durch eine interaktive Story. Es war die erste Seite, die mit dem Benutzer am Telefon interagierte, während er im Web surfte.

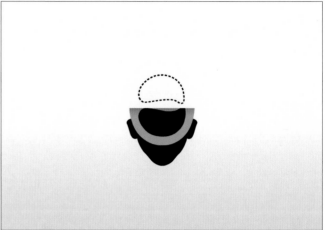

CONCEPT: Idea. This name inspired the hot site concept. As a principal attribute "idea", the name of the car, suggests interactive tools like a fun animation editor. The first on line clay editor.

CONCEPT : Idea. Le nom a déterminé le concept du site. Comme principal attribut, le nom de la voiture nous a inspiré des outils interactifs, comme un réalisateur de films d'animation. C'est le premier réalisateur de pâte à modeler électronique.

KONZEPT: Idea. Dieser Name inspirierte das Seitenkonzept. Die Haupteigenschaft „Idea", der Name des Autos, legte interaktive Tools wie einen Animationseditor nahe. Der erste Editor seiner Art online.

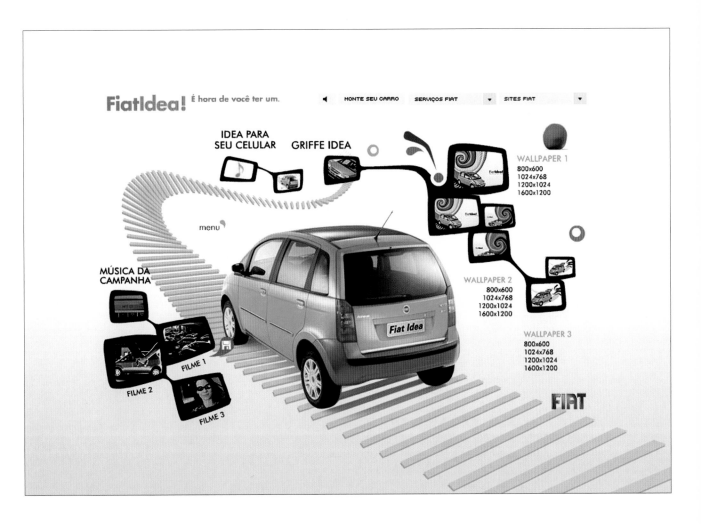

CAMPAIGN: Germanwings Screensaver. **PRODUCT:** Germanwings Realtime Screensaver. **YEAR:** 2004-2005. **AGENCY:** Neue Digitale <www.neue-digitale.de>. **PRODUCTION TIME:** June 2004 – December 2004. **CREATIVE TEAM:** Olaf Czeschner, Bejadin Selimi, Melanie Lenz, André Bourguignon. **PROGRAMMER:** Heiko Schweikhardt. **TECH ASPECTS:** Macromedia Flash, Screentime. **MEDIA CIRCULATED:** Internet. **AWARDS:** Cresta 2005 (Winner), ADC New York (Silver), The One Show Interactive 2005 (Silver), ADC Deutschland 2005 (Silver), Eurobest Award (Silver), New York Festivals Interactive (Bronze).

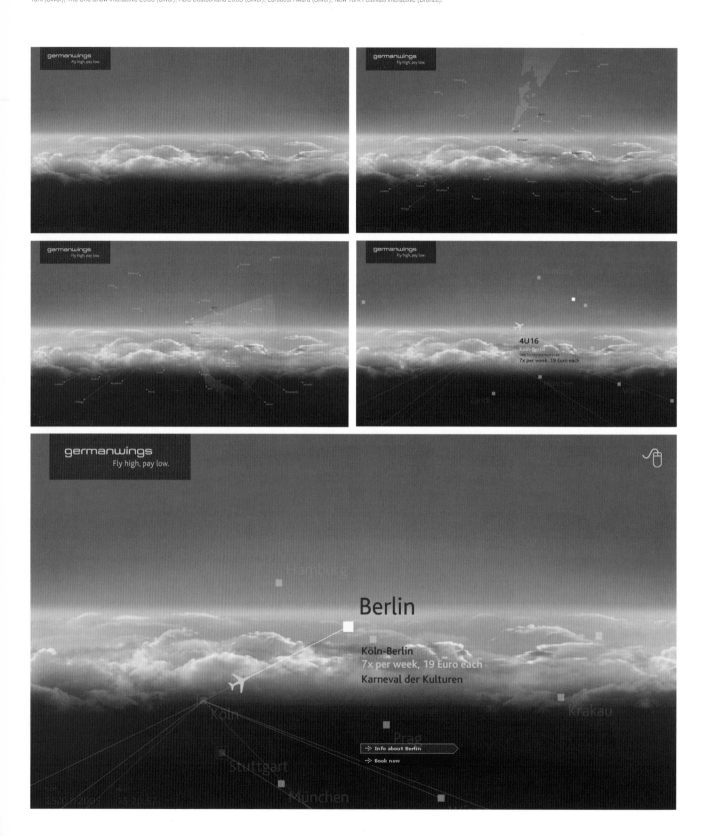

CONCEPT: The Germanwings planes make users want to travel and awaken specific desires. The screensaver's high-level design – combined with the specially featured offers – communicates the Germanwings brand slogan "Fly high, pay low" insistently yet discreetly. The design features a map of Europe, showing the live movement of planes in the Germanwings fleet. The user can see – in real-time – which planes are in the air, which are taking off, and which are landing. The current time is shown and day and night functions are on display. The screensaver changes its appearance according to the time of day. **OVERALL IMPRESSION/TECHNICAL IMPLEMENTATION:** When the user connects to the Internet, the screensaver searches for updates, and new data is automatically loaded. Presentation of flight plans, flight and destination specials and promotions. The user is guided towards booking a flight. Each time the screensaver loads, a different destination is zoomed in upon at random. Destinations can be prioritized by Germanwings. **RESULTS:** The Germanwings real-time screensaver is an innovative hard-sell tool that binds the user to the brand while animating the user to book current specials and promotions. The screensaver supports further Germanwings marketing. Additionally, marketing specials (including those from partners) can be promoted through this platform.

CONCEPT : Les avions Germanwings donnent envie de voyager et éveillent des désirs spécifiques. L'écran de veille au design de haut niveau, accompagné d'offres promotionnelles, communique le slogan de la marque : « Payez peu, voyagez loin », de façon discrète bien qu'insistante. L'interface montre une carte de l'Europe, où l'on peut suivre l'activité des avions de la compagnie Germanwings. L'internaute peut observer en temps réel quels avions sont en vol, quels avions décollent ou atterrissent. Une horloge est affichée, et l'on peut activer des fonctions nuit/jour. L'écran de veille change d'apparence selon les heures de la journée. **IMPRESSION GÉNÉRALE :** Quand l'internaute se connecte, l'écran va rechercher des mises à jour et les données sont chargées automatiquement. On y présente les plans de vol, les vols et les destinations en promotion. L'usager est guidé vers le service de réservation. A chaque mise à jour, une destination est mise en valeur au hasard. Certaines destinations peuvent être choisies en priorité par la compagnie. **RÉSULTATS :** L'écran de veille est un outil agressif novateur qui relie l'usager à la marque tout en l'encourageant à réserver un vol promotionnel. Il affiche aussi d'autres annonces pour Germanwings. En outre, des annonces spéciales, dont celles de partenaires commerciaux, sont aussi hébergées sur cette plateforme.

KONZEPT: Die Flugzeuge von Germanwings wecken bei den Benutzern den Wunsch, fliegen zu wollen. Das Design des Bildschirmschoners befindet sich auf einem hohen Level und kommuniziert – kombiniert mit Sonderangeboten – den Germanwings-Slogan „Fly high, pay low" ständig, aber unaufdringlich. Das Design besteht aus einer Europakarte, die die Bewegungen der Flugzeuge der Germanwings-Flotte live zeigt. Der Benutzer kann in Echtzeit sehen, welche Flugzeuge sich in der Luft befinden und welche gerade starten oder landen. Es werden die Zeit sowie Tag- und Nachtfunktionen angezeigt. Der Bildschirmschoner passt seine Erscheinung der Tageszeit an. **ALLGEMEINER EINDRUCK/ TECHNISCHE IMPLEMENTIERUNG:** Wenn der Benutzer eine Verbindung zum Internet herstellt, sucht der Bildschirmschoner nach Updates, und neue Daten werden automatisch geladen. Flugpläne, Spezialflüge und -ziele sowie Werbeaktionen werden präsentiert. Der Benutzer wird zur Buchung eines Fluges geführt. Jedes Mal, wenn sich der Bildschirmschoner lädt, wird ein anderes, zufälliges Ziel vergrößert. Bestimmten Zielen kann von Germanwings Priorität eingeräumt werden. **ERGEBNISSE:** Der Echtzeit-Bildschirmschoner von Germanwings ist ein innovatives, direktes Tool, das den Benutzer an die Marke bindet und ihn gleichzeitig dazu animiert, die aktuellen Spezialangebote und Promotions zu buchen. Damit unterstützt der Bildschirmschoner das Markenkonzept von Germanwings. Auch für zusätzliche Marketing-Specials (auch von Partnern) kann auf dieser Plattform geworben werden.

CAMPAIGN: Honda Icon Museum <http://www.honda.co.jp/IconMuseum/>. **PRODUCT:** Honda Automobiles. **CLIENT:** Honda Motor Co., Ltd. **YEAR:** 2005. **AGENCY:** Dentsu Inc. <www.dentsu.com>. **PRODUCER:** Morihiro Harano, Toshifumi Oiso. **CREATIVE DIRECTOR:** Yasuharu Sasaki. **ART DIRECTOR:** eBoy <www.eboy.com>, Hirozumi Takakusaki. **COPYWRITER:** Yasuharu Sasaki. **PROGRAMMER:** Hiroki Nakamura, Hiroshi Koike. **TECH ASPECTS:** Macromedia Flash. **MEDIA CIRCULATED:** Website, banner. **AWARDS:** tokyo.interactive.ad.awards.jp 2005 (Gold), Cannes Lions 2005 (Shortlist).

CONCEPT: In this campaign, personal computer desktop icons became an advertising medium. Each of Honda's car models was converted into several pixelized icon versions and given away free over the Internet. The icons became viral-marketing tools, as they leapt from desktop to desktop around offices and between friends.

CONCEPT : Dans cette campagne, les icônes électroniques sont devenues un vecteur de publicité. Chaque modèle de voiture Honda a été converti en plusieurs versions d'icônes pixelisées, offertes gratuitement sur le Net. Les icônes sont devenues des outils de marketing viral, et se sont propagées de bureau à bureau dans les entreprises et entre amis.

KONZEPT: In dieser Kampagne werden persönliche Desktop-Icons zum Werbemedium. Jedes Hondamodell wurde in mehrere gepixelte Icon-Versionen umgewandelt und über das Internet kostenlos weitergegeben. Sie wurden zu viralen Marketingtools, indem sie in Büros und unter Freunden von Desktop zu Desktop sprangen.

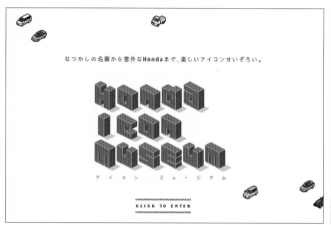

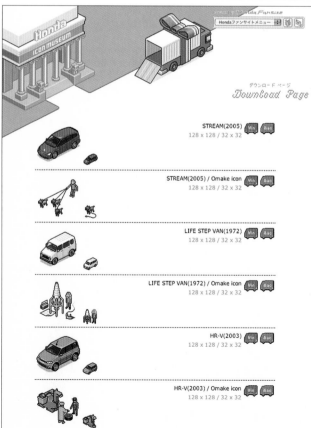

CAMPAIGN: 2006 Lexus GS. PRODUCT: 2006 Lexus GS. YEAR: 2005. AGENCY: Team One <www.teamoneadv.com>. PRODUCTION TIME: 1 month. COST IN HOURS OF WORK: 160 h. CREATIVE TEAM: Jorge Calleja.
PROGRAMMER: Fredrik Stutterheim, Andreas Wannerstedt. TECH ASPECTS: Macromedia Flash, Adobe Photoshop. MEDIA CIRCULATED: 12 units.

CONCEPT: A suite of online advertising that combines beautiful product photography and a straightforward message within the pre-existing Lexus style guide to entice viewers' click-through. **RESULTS:** Exopolis' delivery of this clean and sophisticated campaign helped to demonstrate the studio's versatility and supplied the brand the powerful spotlight they were looking for.

CONCEPT : Une série de publicités en ligne combinent de magnifiques photographies du produit et un message simple et direct dans le style de Lexus pour inciter les visiteurs à cliquer. **RÉSULTATS :** Cette campagne sobre et raffinée a contribué à démontrer la polyvalence du studio Exopolis et a offert à l'annonceur la mise en lumière qu'il désirait.

KONZEPT: Luxuriöse Online-Werbung, die schöne Produktfotografie mit einer klaren Botschaft innerhalb des schon existierenden Lexus-Stilführers kombiniert, um die Besucher zum Click-Through anzuregen. **ERGEBNISSE:** Exopolis klare und fortschrittliche Kampagne demonstrierte die Vielseitigkeit des Studios und rückte die Marke ins Rampenlicht.

FEATURED ON THE DVD **CAMPAIGN:** Zero to Obsession. **PRODUCT:** Lotus Elise. **CLIENT:** Lotus. **YEAR:** 2004. **AGENCY:** 20:20 London <www.2020london.co.uk>. **PRODUCTION TIME:** 3 months. **CREATIVE TEAM:** Peter Riley (Creative Partner), Hugo Bierschenk (Creative), Dean Woodhouse (Creative). **TECH ASPECTS:** Film, sound, Adobe After Effects, Macromedia Flash, Wavelab, PHP/SQL, 3D Studio Max, Maya, Shake, Adobe Premiere, Apple Quicktime Pro. **MEDIA CIRCULATED:** Email. **AWARDS:** Campaign Digital Awards (UK), Precision Marketing Awards (UK), John Caples International Advertising Awards (New York), Cannes International Advertising Awards.

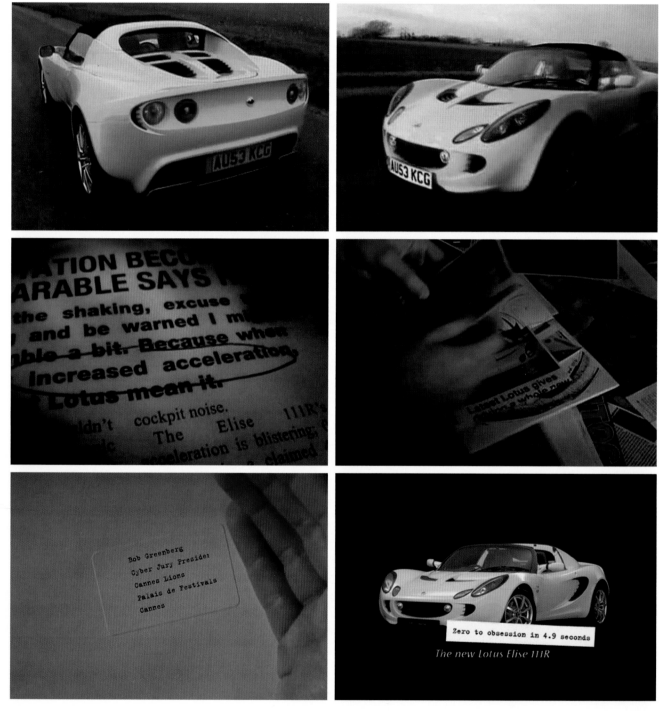

OBJECTIVES: Generate awareness of the new, improved Elise in key countries in Europe. Maximise budgets with PR-worthy creative and promote the Lotus belief of 'Change the Rules'. Test drives will be the indicator of success. Our job was to introduce prospects to the new Elise 111R, so awareness was our job. The elise is a car you could fall in love with at first sight. There's a real obsession surrounding Lotus, from those who make it to those who buy it. It's the kind of car that people point and stare at. **THE IDEA:** Obsession. The maverick British director Ken Russell directed a viral movie for this maverick car brand. The movie is personalised with your name, and encourages you to forward the link to friends as their name appears in the movie when forwarded. The movie shows a scrapbook of Lotus images and articles being collated by a strange figure, then he addresses an envelope to you! 48 hours later the scrapbook lands on your doormat. A car brochure like no other. **RESULTS:** Amazing stand-out in a cluttered viral space and 38.8% response rate. And a new way of integrating online and direct mail.

OBJECTIFS: Communiquer sur le nouveau modèle Elise dans les pays européens. Rentabiliser les budgets avec des créations de qualité et promouvoir la philosophie de Lotus, « changer les règles ». Les demandes d'essais sur route seront les indicateurs du succès. La mission était donc de promouvoir la nouvelle Elise 111R auprès de futurs acheteurs. Le modèle Elise est le genre de voiture dont on peut tout de suite tomber amoureux. La Lotus fait l'objet d'un véritable culte, de la part de ceux qui la fabriquent comme de ceux qui l'achètent. C'est le genre de voiture qui attire tous les regards. **IDÉE :** L'obsession. Le réalisateur Ken Russell a dirigé un film viral pour cette voiture non-conformiste. Le film est personnalisé à votre nom, et vous encourage à envoyer le lien à un ami, dont le nom appa-

raîtra à son tour. Le film montre un étrange personnage en train de compulser un album souvenir, fait de photographies de la Lotus et d'articles divers. On le voit écrire votre nom sur une enveloppe, et 48 heures plus tard, vous recevez l'album photo par la poste. Une brochure qui ne ressemble à aucune autre. **RÉSULTATS :** Enorme impact dans un espace viral surchargé, et un taux de réponse de 38%. Une première dans la combinaison d'envoi postal et de courrier électronique.

ZIELE: Die neue, verbesserte Elise in den europäischen Schlüsselländern ins Bewusstsein rufen. Das Budget mit kreativer PR maximieren und mit dem Lotus-Slogan „Change the Rules" werben. Testfahrten werden der Erfolgsindikator sein. Unsere Aufgabe bestand darin, potenzielle Kunden für die neue Elise 111R zu finden, so dass die Erregung von Aufmerksamkeit unser Job war. Elise ist ein Auto, in das man sich auf den ersten Blick verlieben kann. Bei Herstellern und Käufern herrscht eine regelrechte Obsession, wenn es um Lotus geht. Es ist die Art von Auto, auf das man zeigt und das man anstarrt. **DIE IDEE:** Obsession. Der britische Regisseur und Einzelgänger Ken Russell führte bei einem viralen Film für diese Automarke, die auch ein Einzelgänger ist, Regie. Der Film ist mit Ihrem Namen personalisiert und ermutigt Sie, den Link an Ihre Freunde weiterzuleiten – dann erscheint deren jeweiliger Name im Film. Der Film zeigt ein Sammelalbum mit Lotus-Bildern und Artikeln, die von einer merkwürdigen Person gesammelt werden, die einen Briefumschlag an Sie schickt! 48 Stunden später landet das Buch auf Ihrer Fußmatte. Eine Autobroschüre wie keine andere. **ERGEBNISSE:** Herausragend innerhalb eines überfüllten viralen Raumes und eine Antwortrate von 38,8%. Eine neue Art, Online- und Direktmail zu kombinieren.

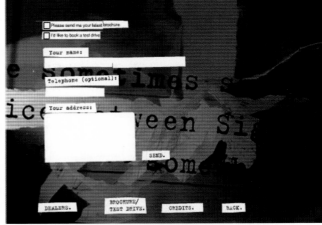

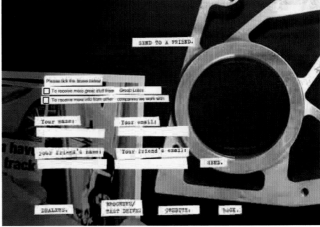

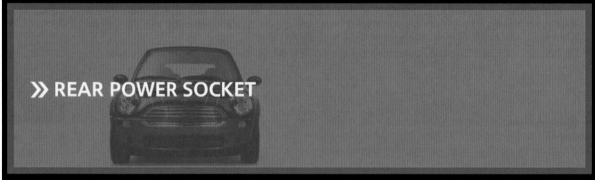

CONCEPT: MINI Canada wanted to show off the features and technology that give MINI total control over icy winter conditions. Ouch! We decided the most interesting way to show "control" was through a character many people identify with that concept – a Dominatrix. After extensive research on the subject, we developed a site that uses voice-over, music, and full motion video of a PVC clad Dominatrix who whips, paddles, flogs, buffs, spanks, and teases a MINI Cooper. User's are invited to "whip around the site" to see a series of short animations demonstrating the practical benefits of each winter feature.

CONCEPT : La filiale canadienne désirait vanter la technologie qui permet à la Mini de garder le contrôle dans des conditions hivernales. Nous avons décidé que la manière la plus intéressante de symboliser le contrôle était de présenter un personnage que les gens pouvaient facilement identifier : Dominatrix. Après avoir mené des recherches sur le sujet, nous avons élaboré un site intégrant une vidéo du personnage, accompagnée de voix off et de musique. Dominatrix, toute vêtue de vinyl, fesse, fouette, caresse, excite et fustige une Mini Cooper. Les internautes sont invités à « cravacher » à l'intérieur du site afin de découvrir une série d'animations présentant les avantages pratiques des nouvelles options.

KONZEPT: MINI Canada wollte die Features und Technik darstellen, die dem MINI totale Kontrolle über eisiges, winterliches Wetter gibt. Aua! Wir entschieden, dass die interessanteste Möglichkeit, „Kontrolle" darzustellen, eine Figur war, mit der man dieses Konzept identifiziert – eine Dominatrix. Nach ausgiebiger Recherche entwickelten wir eine Seite mit Hintergrundstimme, Musik und dem Video einer in Lack gekleideten Dominatrix, die einen MINI Cooper auspeitscht, verhaut, poliert und versohlt. Benutzer werden eingeladen, sich eine Reihe von kurzen Animationen mit den praktischen Vorteilen der Winter-Features anzusehen.

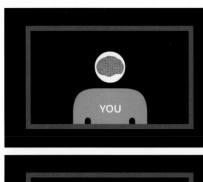

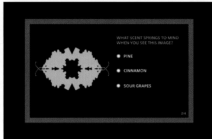

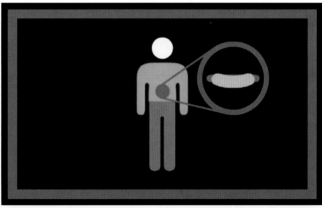

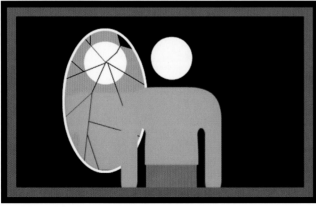

CONCEPT: MINI Canada had compiled a substantial email list of interested consumers from auto shows and other venues. MINI wanted to use a series of four emails to gather important information and whittle this database down into a highly qualified list of leads to pass on to their retailers. The big challenge was to do all this without boring people to tears. We had to get info we needed while still finding a way to reinforce the fun, mischievous MINI brand. We did it by combining music, narration and quirky animation to guide users through the entire experience. We ended up with a cohesive campaign that was both entertaining and informative. And by maintaining a uniform visual style and the same narrator, we developed a strong relationship with users, which translated into very few "opt-outs" throughout the program.

CONCEPT : Mini possède un volumineux listing d'adresses e-mail d'acheteurs potentiels rencontrés sur des salons automobiles ou autres événements. L'entreprise voulait utiliser ces contacts pour collecter des renseignements sur les consommateurs et réduire ensuite cette base de données à un listing détaillé qui serait transmis à ses concessionnaires. La difficulté était d'éviter d'ennuyer le consommateur. Il fallait recueillir les informations que nous voulions tout en maintenant l'esprit ludique et impertinent de la marque. Nous avons combiné musique, narration et animation originale pour accompagner l'internaute dans cette expérience. La campagne s'avéra cohérente, instructive et distrayante à la fois. L'harmonie et la continuité dans le choix du design graphique et sonore a tissé une relation forte avec l'usager, et nous avons essuyé très peu de refus de la part des internautes.

KONZEPT: MINI Canada besaß eine umfangreiche E-Mail-Liste interessierter Kunden von Autoshows und anderen Veranstaltungen. Sie wollten eine Serie von vier E-Mails verwenden, um wichtige Informationen zu sammeln und diese Datenbank auf eine hochqualifizierte Liste reduzieren, die sie an ihre Händler weitergeben wollten. Die große Herausforderung bestand darin, dies alles zu tun, ohne die Leute zu Tode zu langweilen. Wir brauchten Informationen und mussten gleichzeitig die lustige, spitzbübische Marke MINI stärken. Dies taten wir durch die Kombination von Musik, Erzählung und verschrobener Animation, die den Benutzer durch das ganze Erlebnis führte. Es entstand eine zusammenhängende Kampagne, die sowohl unterhaltsam als auch informativ war. Durch einen einheitlichen visuellen Stil und denselben Sprecher entwickelten wir eine enge Beziehung zu den Benutzern, die sich in der geringen Anzahl von Abbrüchen des Programms spiegelte.

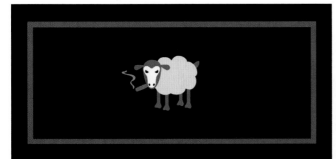

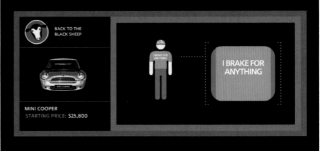

CONCEPT: During the winter months, MINI Canada wanted to shift the focus of their advertising to highlight MINI's outstanding safety features. The challenge was delivering this type of messaging while maintaining MINI's fun and aggressive personality. This banner focuses on MINI's pro-active safety features, such as its exceptional steering technology. This "over the content" banner challenges the user to "click the MINI" as it darts across their screen. The MINI is programmed to constantly move out of the way as the cursor comes near. The message is clear – MINI is great at avoiding impacts

CONCEPT : Pour la saison hivernale, la filiale canadienne de Mini désirait modifier le cœur de son message afin de souligner les remarquables équipements de sécurité de la Mini. Il fallait délivrer ce message tout en conservant l'image tonique et sympathique de la marque. Le bandeau souligne les performances des options de sécurité, en particulier la qualité ex-ceptionnelle de la direction. L'internaute est invité à cliquer sur la Mini tandis qu'elle traverse l'écran à toute vitesse. La voiture est programmée pour s'écarter à chaque fois que le curseur approche. Le message est clair : la Mini sait éviter les chocs.

KONZEPT: Während der Wintermonate wollte MINI Canada seine Werbung auf die herausragenden Sicherheitsstandards von MINI lenken. Die Herausforderung lag darin, diese Art Botschaft gleichzeitig mit MINIs lustiger und energiegeladener Persönlichkeit zu vermitteln. Dieses Banner konzentriert sich auf MINIs aktive Sicherheitsfeatures, wie die außergewöhnliche Lenktechnik. Als „Over the Content"-Banner fordert es den Benutzer auf, den MINI anzuklicken, während dieser sich über den Bildschirm bewegt. Er ist so programmiert, dass er sich vom Zeiger weg bewegt, sobald dieser zu nahe kommt. Die Botschaft ist klar: MINI kann gut Hindernissen ausweichen.

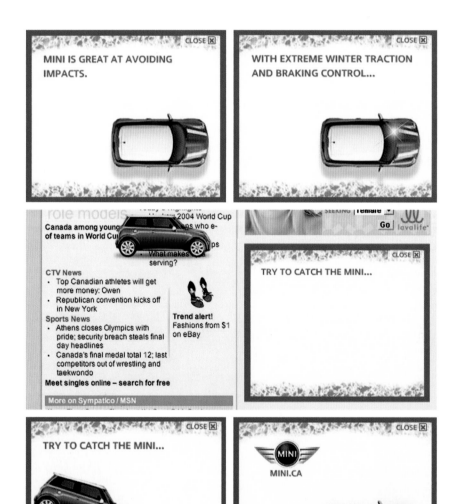

CONCEPT: These banner executions were part of a print and billboard campaign for MINI Canada designed to convey MINI's substantial safety and performance features. The distinctive white roof of the MINI was used as part of a "fill in the blanks" style execution where the audience was asked to complete the sentence. For example one of the billboard featured the phrase "_ _ _ _ like a Jackrabbit." Of course, two weeks later a repost of the billboard revealed the answer "goes like a Jackrabbit." These banners were developed as an interactive way to extend this concept online.

CONCEPT : Dans le cadre d'une campagne d'affichage public et d'encarts presse, la filiale canadienne de Mini a fait concevoir des bandeaux pour faire connaître les nouvelles options de sécurité des modèles. Le toit blanc de la voiture imitait une case de formulaire que le spectateur devait remplir afin de former une phrase complète. Par exemple, une affiche portait la phrase incomplète « _ _ _ _ comme un lapin ». Deux semaines plus tard, de nouvelles affiches révélaient « rapide comme un lapin ». Les bandeaux ont été déclinés de façon interactive pour la publicité en ligne.

KONZEPT: Diese Banneranwendungen waren Teil einer Print- und Werbetafel-Kampagne für MINI Canada und sollten MINIs umfangreiche Sicherheits- und Leistungsfeatures vermitteln. Das unverwechselbare weiße Dach des MINI wurde als Teil der „Füll die Lücken"-Anwendung verwendet, bei der das Publikum einen Satz vervollständigen musste: Beispielsweise enthielt eine der Reklamewände die Phrase „_ _ _ _ like a Jackrabbit." Zwei Wochen später enthüllte das Billboard die Antwort „goes like a Jackrabbit". Diese Banner wurden als interaktive Methode entwickelt, dieses Konzept online zu verbreiten.

FEATURED ON THE DVD **CAMPAIGN:** MINI JCW GP – Gone Fast <www.mini.com/gone_fast>. **PRODUCT:** MINI Cooper S with JCW GP Kit. **YEAR:** 2006. **AGENCY:** Interone Worldwide, Hamburg <www.interone.de>. **PRODUCTION TIME:** 3 months. **CREATIVE DIRECTOR:** Mike John Otto. **ART DIRECTOR:** Mike John Otto, Meike Ufer. **FLASH DEVELOPER:** Michael Ploj. **COPYWRITER:** Stephen James. **CONTENT DEVELOPMENT:** Anke Schliedermann. **PRODUCER:** Sven Heckmann. **TECHNICAL PROJECT MANAGER:** Eva Sürek. **PROGRAMMER:** Rico Marquardt, Sebastian Vogt. **PHOTOGRAPHER:** Uwe Düttmann. **POST-PRODUCTION:** Effekt-Etage. **SOUND:** V8 Studio. **TECH ASPECTS:** The new MINI Cooper S Gp with JCW Kit online-special breaks down the frontiers between the two media Internet and 3D/film and gives new life to the strained term "interactive".

TASK: Creation of an online special for the market launch of the on 2,000 cars limited MINI Cooper S with Gp Kit that transports the overall communication theme and claim of the car: "Gone Fast." **IDEA:** The Creation of an highly emotional Online Special that invites the User to experience the car in an interactive 3D Movie. We wanted to present the car like a "wild-cat" in a box. The car is presented in a dark hall in a very suspensive way. The 3D Clips are cutted in a way which allow the user to spend quite a time inside the spezial. **RESULTS:** Strong communication impulse for the brand in quantity and quality. The Module was rolled out into 6 markets.

MISSION : Création d'un site spécial pour le lancement en l'an 2000 de la série limitée Mini Cooper S avec kit de préparation moteur, véhiculant le thème général de la campagne « Vite partie ». **IDÉE :** Conception d'un site émotionnel qui convie l'usager à découvrir la voiture grâce à un film interactif en 3D. Nous voulions présenter la voiture comme une es-pèce de fauve en cage. Le modèle apparaît dans un couloir sombre, dans une atmosphère de suspense. Le montage des clips en 3D permet à l'internaute de naviguer assez long-temps à l'intérieur du site. **RÉSULTATS :** Gros impact pour la marque, en qualité comme en quantité. Le module a été décliné sur 6 marchés.

AUFGABE: Entwicklung eines Online-Specials für die Markteinführung des auf 2.000 Exemplare limitierten MINI Cooper S mit Gp Kit, das das allgemeine Kommunikationsthema und den Slogan des Autos transportiert: „Gone fast". **IDEE:** Die Entwicklung eines emotio-nalen Online-Specials, das den Benutzer einlädt, das Auto in einem interaktiven 3D-Film zu erleben. Wir wollten das Auto wie ein Raubtier im Käfig präsentieren. Es wird auf span-nende Weise in einer dunklen Halle gezeigt. Die 3D-Clips sind auf eine Weise geschnitten, die es dem Benutzer ermöglichen, sich eine ganze Weile in diesem Special aufzuhalten. **ERGEBNISSE:** Starker Kommunikationsimpuls für die Marke bezüglich Quantität und Qualität. Das Modul wurde in 6 Ländern eingesetzt

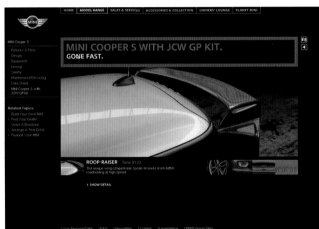

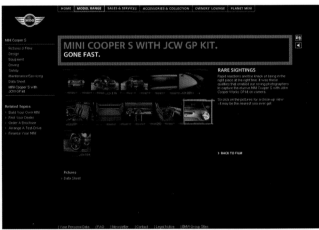

CAMPAIGN: MINI Cabrio Film Clips <www.mini.com/cabrio>. **PRODUCT:** MINI Cabrio. **YEAR:** 2004. **AGENCY:** Interone Worldwide, Hamburg <www.interone.de>. **PRODUCTION TIME:** 3 months. **CREATIVE DIRECTOR:** Martin Gassner. **ART DIRECTOR:** Margit Schröder. **FLASH DEVELOPER:** Michael Ploj. **COPYWRITER:** Stephen James. **CONTENT DEVELOPMENT:** Dirk Lanio. **PRODUCER:** Pina Pech. **TECHNICAL PROJECT MANAGER:** David Athey. **PROGRAMMER:** Sven Busse, Kevin Breynck. **FILM DIRECTOR:** Hans Horn. **POST-PRODUCTION:** Effekt-Etage. **TECH ASPECTS:** The new MINI Cabrio online-special breaks down the frontiers between the two media Internet and film and gives new life to the strained term "interactive". **AWARDS:** New York Festival, ADC Deutschland, The One Show Interactive, Cannes Cyber Lions, CLIO Award, International Automotive Advertising Award.

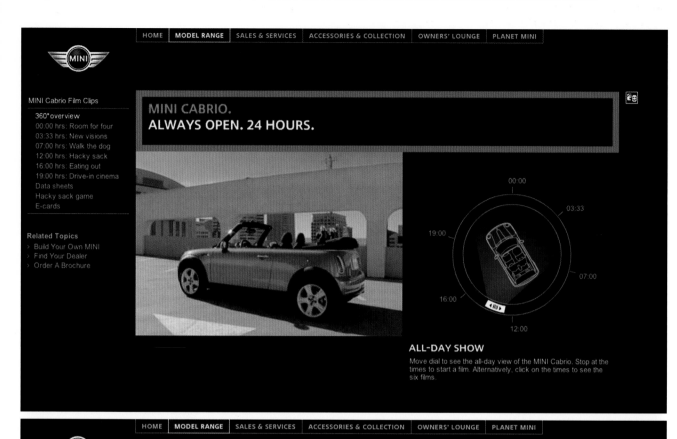

CONCEPT: Creation of an online special for the market launch of the new MINI Cabrio that transports the overall communication theme and claim of the car: "Always open." **IDEA:** twenty-four hours in the lives of two buddies, their dog and a MINI Cabrio. **DESCRIPTION:** six movie clips – filmed especially for the online module – are integrated into an interactive Flash MX module. With their mouse users can rotate the camera on a circular path around the MINI Cabrio to get an all-round impression of the car. During the rotation around the car a time span of 24 hours is also covered. At six points on the camera orbit, users can stop the rotation and seamlessly start the six film clips. Every film offers different possibilities of interaction with the actors and the product, always different, always surprising and, of course, always open. **RESULTS:** Strong communication impulse for the brand in quantity and quality. The Module was rolled out into 25 markets. The traffic on the websites has increased about 50%.

CONCEPT : Création d'un site spécial pour le lancement du nouveau cabriolet Mini, qui véhicule le thème général de la campagne avec le slogan « Toujours ouvert ». **IDÉE :** Vingt-quatre heures de la vie de deux amis, leur chien et leur Mini Cabrio. Six clips, tournés spécialement pour le support, sont intégrés dans un module en format Flash MX. Avec la souris, l'internaute peut faire pivoter la caméra autour de la voiture pour obtenir une vue d'ensemble. La rotation de la caméra est censée couvrir 24 heures. Sur six points de l'orbi-te, le visiteur peut stopper la rotation et visionner les six clips correspondants. Chaque clip offre des possibilités d'interaction avec les acteurs et la voiture, chaque fois différentes, chaque fois surprenantes, et bien sûr, « toujours ouvertes ». **RÉSULTATS :** Excellent retour pour la marque, en qualité comme en quantité. Le module a été décliné sur 25 marchés. Le trafic sur les sites a augmenté de 50%.

KONZEPT: Entwicklung eines Online-Specials für die Markteinführung des neuen MINI Cabrios, das das allgemeine Kommunikationsthema und den Slogan des Autos transportiert: „Always open". **IDEE:** 24 Stunden im Leben von zwei Freunden, ihrem Hund und einem MINI Cabrio. Beschreibung: Sechs Filmclips – speziell für das Online-Modul gedreht – werden in ein interaktives Flash-MX-Modul integriert. Benutzer können mit ihrer Maus die Kamera im Kreis um den MINI Cabrio herum drehen, um einen Eindruck des kompletten Autos zu bekommen. Während der Rotation wird auch der Zeitraum von 24 Stunden abgedeckt. An sechs Punkten der Kamerafahrt kann der Benutzer die Rotation stoppen und nahtlos die sechs Filmclips starten. Jeder Film bietet verschiedene Möglichkeiten der Interaktion mit den Schauspielern und dem Produkt, jedes Mal anders, immer überraschend und, natürlich, immer offen. **ERGEBNISSE:** Starker Kommunikationsimpuls für die Marke bezüglich Quantität und Qualität. Das Modul wurde in 25 Ländern eingesetzt; die Besucherrate auf den Webseiten stieg um ca. 50%.

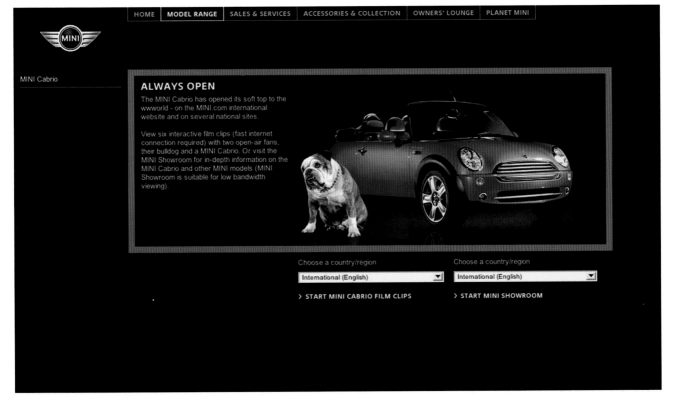

FEATURED ON THE DVD **CAMPAIGN:** MINI Counterfeit <www.counterfeitmini.org>. **PRODUCT:** MINI Counterfeit DVD. **YEAR:** 2005. **AGENCY:** Crispin Porter + Bogusky <www.cpbgroup.com>. **PRODUCTION TIME:** 2 months. **EXECUTIVE CREATIVE DIRECTOR:** Alex Bogusky. **CREATIVE DIRECTOR:** Andrew Keller. **INTERACTIVE CREATIVE DIRECTOR:** Jeff Benjamin. **ASSOCIATE CREATIVE DIRECTOR:** Steve O'Connell. **ART DIRECTOR:** Paul Stechschulte, Tiffany Kosel. **COPYWRITER:** Franklin Tipton, Rob Reilly. **DESIGNER:** Rahul Panchal, Michael Ferrare. **PHOTOGRAPHER:** Sebastian Gray. **DEVELOPMENT PARTNER:** Exopolis, iChameleon. **FLASH DESIGNER:** Luis Santi. **TECH ASPECTS:** Slap Some Sense game was built in Macromedia Flash. **MEDIA CIRCULATED:** Broadcast TV, outdoor, magazine inserts. **AWARDS:** Cannes Lions 2005 (Cyber Gold, Film Gold), Communication Arts 2005 (advertising & design), London International 2005 (Winner, Finalist), Young Guns 2005 (Gold, Silver).

CONCEPT: In a pro-active measure against iconic brand counterfeiting, we established the Counter Counterfeit Commission (CCC) who pervaded the public with a 10-minute DVD, a magazine insert, alerts in automotive classified publications and a grass roots effort at the NY Auto Show. Along with these efforts the CCC's website, counterfeitmini.org is a resource for consumers to learn more about the problem and post suspected fakes. Mini4Auction.com, auctions counterfeit MINIs, although the auctions are all conveniently closed. To further legitimize the CCC's claim, we created a pop-up on miniusa.com that warned surfers that counterfeit MINIs are on the loose. The pop-up provided a viral phone number and encouraged them to call and report any 'counterfeit' MINIs they may have seen. **RESULTS:** Traffic to the Counterfeitmini.org was host to millions of unique visitors. The 'hoax' was responsible for 6800+ calls whose over 800 voicemails reported "suspicious counterfeit activity" to the CCC. At the CCC site more concerned citizens posted nearly 400 images of their own suspected counterfeits. Over 550 informed consumers followed through on the warning and ordered the CCC's Counterfeit DVD. The CCC certainly gained a lot of attention. But more importantly, real MINIs were the stars of the hype, evidenced by a 23% YTD increase in sales vs. 2004.

CONCEPT : Dans le cadre d'une initiative pour lutter contre la contrefaçon, nous avons créé la Commission Anticontrefaçon, dont le message s'est répandu dans le public grâce à un DVD de 10 minutes, un insert magazine, des articles dans la presse automobile et une intervention au salon de l'auto de New York. Pour accompagner ces actions, le site de la Commission, counterfeitmini.org offre des informations sur le problème, et encourage à dénoncer toute voiture suspecte. Le site Mini4Auction.com vend aux enchères des Mini de contrefaçon, mais les enchères sont toutes closes. Pour légitimer le message de la Commission, nous avons conçu une fenêtre pop-up sur miniusa.com qui alertait les internautes sur une recrudescence de fausses Mini. La fenêtre affichait un numéro de téléphone à contacter pour dénoncer les éventuelles contrefaçons. **RÉSULTATS :** Le site Counterfeitmini.org a reçu des millions de visiteurs uniques. Le canular a déclenché 6800 appels et plus de 800 messages témoignaient de l'existence d'une activité de contrefaçon. Le site de la Commission a reçu 400 images de la part de propriétaires de Mini pensant avoir acheté une contrefaçon. Plus de 550 consommateurs ont suivi les recommandations en commandant le DVD. La Commission a attiré énormément l'attention, mais le plus important, c'est que les « vraies » Mini sont devenues des stars, et la société a enregistré une hausse des ventes de 23% en un an.

KONZEPT: Als aktive Maßnahme gegen Markenfälschung entwickelten wir den Counter Counterfeit Commission (CCC), der die Öffentlichkeit mit einer 10-Minuten-DVD, einer Magazinbeilage, Hinweisen in Autozeitschriften und einem Auftritt bei der NY Autoshow durchzog. Neben diesen Bemühungen stellt die Webseite von CCC, counterfeitmini.org, eine Informationsquelle für Kunden dar, die mehr über das Problem wissen möchten. Auf Mini4Auction.com gibt es Auktionen für gefälschte MINIs, die aber alle geschlossen sind. Um CCC weiter zu legitimieren, erstellten wir auf miniusa.com ein Pop Up, das Surfer warnte, dass gefälschte MINIs im Umlauf sind, und sie aufforderte, gefälschte MINIs zu melden, falls sie welche sehen. **ERGEBNISSE:** Millionen von Besuchern wurden auf counterfeitmini.org registriert. Der Hoax führte zu über 6800 Anrufern, von denen 800 Voicemails dem CCC „verdächtige Fälschungsaktivitäten" meldeten. Auf der CCC-Seite veröffentlichten besorgte Bürger fast 400 Bilder verdächtiger Autos. Über 550 informierte Kunden bestellten die DVD. CCC erhielt große Aufmerksamkeit. Was noch wichtiger war: Die echten MINIs waren die Stars des Hype, was der Anstieg der Verkaufszahlen um 23% gegenüber 2004 bewies.

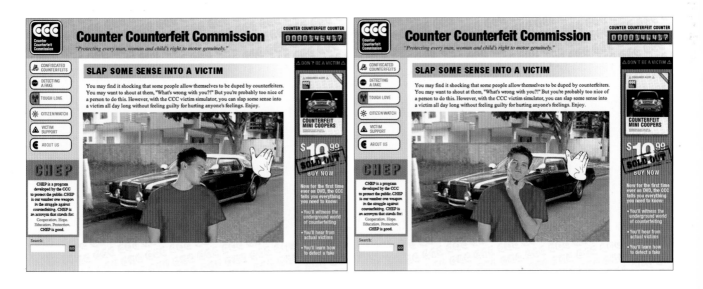

CAMPAIGN: MINI Robots r50r. **CLIENT:** MINI. **YEAR:** 2004. **AGENCY:** Crispin Porter + Bogusky <www.cpbgroup.com>. **EXECUTIVE CREATIVE DIRECTOR:** Alex Bogusky. **CREATIVE DIRECTOR:** Andrew Keller.
INTERACTIVE CREATIVE DIRECTOR: Jeff Benjamin. **COPYWRITERS:** Mike Lear, Bob Cianfrone, Roger Hoard. **ART DIRECTORS:** Dave Swartz, Paul Keister, Juan Morales. **PROGRAMMER:** Beam Interactive. **MEDIA CIRCULATED:**
Magazine print, several online sites, downloads on MINIUSA.com, OOH. **AWARDS:** London International 2004 (Interactive Winner, Finalist for Automotive Category), Young Guns 2004 (Silver), One show Pencils 2005 (Silver) Interactive,
Bronze Interactive), D&AD 2005 (Book entry), CLIO 2005 (Silver, Bronze).

CONCEPT: We created a new form of interactive fiction to help start an urban legend. It's based on a character named Colin Mayhew who, hoping to make roadways safer, starts building a huge humanoid robot from parts of MINI Coopers. **RESULTS:** Approximately 1 million unique visitors to the site. Over 150,000 robot configurator and large robot downloads on miniusa.com. The buzz for the site led many people to post on boards about whether or not the legend was true. Sometimes their posts were answered by Colin Mayhew himself.

CONCEPT : Concevoir une nouvelle forme de fiction interactive pour lancer une rumeur. Le personnage central, Colin Mayhew, désireux de rendre les routes plus sûres, se met à construire un énorme robot humanoïde avec des pièces détachées de Mini Cooper. **RÉSULTATS :** On a comptabilisé 1 million de visiteurs uniques sur le site. Plus de 150 000

téléchargements de « configurateur de robot » sur miniusa.com. Le buzz qui a entouré la campagne a engendré nombre de questions sur les forums concernant la véracité de l'histoire. Parfois, Colin Mayhew répondait personnellement au courrier.

KONZEPT: Wir entwickelten eine neue Form interaktiver Fiktion, um eine urbane Legende zu entwerfen. Sie basiert auf einer Figur namens Colin Mayhew, der die Straßen sicherer machen will und mit dem Bau eines großen menschlichen Roboters beginnt, den er aus Teilen eines MINI Cooper zusammensetzt. **ERGEBNISSE:** Ca. 1 Million Seitenbesucher. Über 150 000 Roboterkonfigurationen und Downloads auf miniusa.com. Die Aufregung um die Seite trieb viele Besucher dazu, in Foren zu diskutieren, ob die Legende wahr ist oder nicht. Manchmal wurden ihre Kommentare von Colin Mayhew persönlich beantwortet.

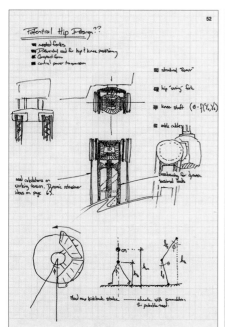

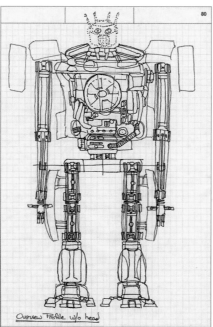

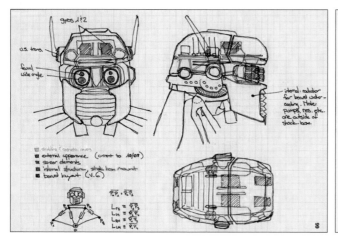

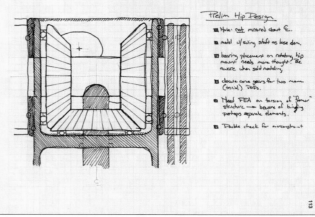

CONCEPT: MINI Canada wanted to extend the launch of the new Convertible, online. The print ads featured headlines suggesting situations or passengers and a checkbox over a MINI Convertible with an open or closed roof. For example, the headline "Three Bean Burrito," was mercifully paired with an open convertible. The Convertible-izer-ometer expanded on this concept by inviting visitors to use their own judgment as to whether the roof should be open or closed. Users were challenged with three different categories, including a speed round, and then evaluated based on their score.

CONCEPT : Etendre la campagne de lancement de la nouvelle décapotable sur Internet. Les annonces dans la presse contenaient des légendes suggérant des personnes ou des situations et une décapotable surmontée d'une case à cocher. Il fallait déterminer si la voiture devait être décapotée ou non. Par exemple, le titre « Burrito aux haricots » était associé à la voiture capote ouverte. Le « décapote-omètre » dérivait de ce concept et invitait l'usager à décider par lui-même si la capote devait être levée ou baissée. Un concours présentait trois séries d'épreuves, dont une de rapidité, et les internautes étaient classés selon leur score.

KONZEPT: MINI Canada wollte die Einführung des neuen Cabrios online unterstützen. Die Überschriften der gedruckten Anzeigen wiesen auf Situationen oder Mitfahrer und ein Ankreuzfeld bezüglich eines MINI Cabrios mit offenem oder geschlossenem Verdeck hin; z.B. wurde die Überschrift „Three Bean Burrito" mit einem offenen Cabrio kombiniert. Das „Convertible-izer-ometer" weitete dieses Konzept aus, indem es Besucher einlud, sich ein eigenes Urteil darüber zu bilden, ob das Verdeck offen oder geschlossen sein sollte. Es gab drei Kategorien, einschließlich eines Wettrennens, und die Benutzer wurden entsprechend ihrer Punktzahl bewertet.

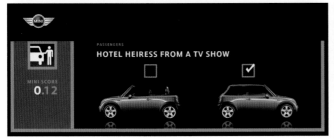

FEATURED ON THE DVD CAMPAIGN: Mini Rally Race <www.minirallyrace.com>. PRODUCT: Mini Cooper. YEAR: 2006. AGENCY: Crispin Porter + Bogusky <www.cpbgroup.com>. PRODUCER: Domani Studios <www. domanistudios.com>. PRODUCTION TIME: 2 weeks. CREATIVE TEAM: Crispin Porter + Bogusky. PROGRAMMER: Domani Studios. TECH ASPECTS: Macromedia Flash AS 2.0, audio, XML. MEDIA CIRCULATED: Banners.

CONCEPT: Create an engaging and branded gaming interactive experience within an expandable rich-media banner placement. The banners feature a multiplayer game that directly associates a childhood slot-car race with the power and excitement of the MINI Cooper. The game features realistic jumps, intelligent physics. multiple 3D renderings, spin outs, crashes, and slot car sounds to engage users. **RESULTS:** These banners are a great example of pushing an engaging user experience directly into a banner placement. While expandable banners are often times a less-than-rewarding experience, the game play in these banners was immediately gratifying. The game's "challenge a friend" feature led to a highly competitive leader board area where user's where continually beating peers with race times. The project has been very successful in driving traffic to MINI's dealer locator page, which was the ultimate goal of each MINI online placements.

CONCEPT : Créer une expérience de marque à travers un jeu interactif placé sur une bannière extensible en rich media. Il s'agit d'un jeu en réseau qui associe un circuit miniature et la puissance d'une Mini Cooper. Le jeu propose différentes figures en 3D, des cascades, des vrilles, et des accidents spectaculaires sur un fond sonore de circuit électrique. **RÉSULTATS :** L'opération a démontré la capacité des bannières à générer une expérience interactive de qualité. Alors que les bannières extensibles sont souvent une expérience inin-téressante, celle-ci est immédiatement gratifiante. La possibilité de se mesurer à un ami a incité les joueurs à rivaliser de vitesse pour figurer dans le tableau des meilleurs scores. Le projet a généré une hausse de trafic sur les sites des concessionnaires locaux, ce qui était l'objectif poursuivi par chaque module en ligne.

KONZEPT: Ein einnehmendes und interaktives Markenspielerlebnis mit der Platzierung eines erweiterbaren Rich-Media-Banners kreieren. Die Banner enthalten ein Spiel für mehrere Spieler, das ein Slotcar-Rennen aus der Kindheit mit der Power und der Aufregung des MINI Cooper assoziiert. Das Spiel umfasst realistische Sprünge, intelligente Bewegungen, ein 3D-Umfeld, Spin Outs, Unfälle und Slotcar-Geräusche, um den Benutzer einzunehmen. **ERGEBNISSE:** Diese Banner sind ein gutes Beispiel dafür, wie man eine Interaktion mit dem Benutzer direkt in die Bannerplatzierung einbinden kann. Während erweiterbare Banner oft kein lohnenswertes Erlebnis darstellen, ist das Spiel in diesen Bannern sofort befriedigend. Das Feature „challenge a friend" führte zu einem umkämpften Anführerbereich, wo sich Benutzer permanent gegenseitig mit ihren Zeiten übertrafen. Das Projekt war sehr erfolgreich, indem es zu einer erhöhten Besucherrate auf der Seite des MINI-Händlers führte das ultimative Ziel aller Online-Platzierungen von MINI.

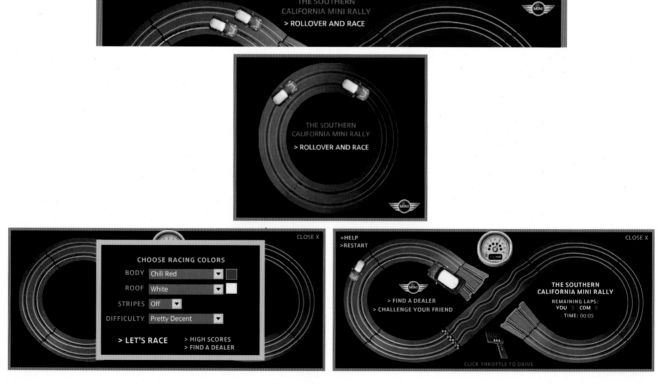

FEATURED ON THE DVD CAMPAIGN: Saab 9-3 – The Infinite Drive. CLIENT: Saab Automobile. YEAR: 2004. AGENCY: LOWE Tesch <www.lowetesch.com>. CREATIVE DIRECTOR: Johan Tesch. ART DIRECTOR: Johan Öhrn, Patrik Westerdahl. COPYWRITER: Tom Eriksen, Dan McDonald. ACCOUNT DIRECTOR: Nils Lindhe. AGENCY PRODUCER: Caroline Déas-Ehrnvall. WEB DEVELOPER: Niklas Fransson, Tobias Löfgren. FILM PRODUCTION: Flodell film. DIRECTOR: Joakim Sandström. CLIENT'S SUPERVISOR: Fredrik Gustafsson, Andreas Eskengren.

SYNOPSIS: This is for all of you that hasn't got the opportunity to drive the new Saab 9-3 Convertible through a sunny Californian landscape. Saab created an interactive car experience where you can push the story forward by clicking on the movie. The journey also brings intriguing thoughts to life, things that pops up during inspiring moments in your Saab.

SYNOPSIS : La pub est destinée à ceux d'entre vous qui n'ont pas la chance de conduire la nouvelle décapotable Saab 9-3 dans un paysage ensoleillé de Californie. Saab a créé une expérience interactive où l'on peut faire avancer l'histoire en cliquant sur la vidéo. Le trajet est également agrémenté de pensées insolites, de choses qui viennent à l'esprit au volant d'une Saab.

SYNOPSIS: Dies ist für alle, die keine Gelegenheit hatten, mit dem neuen Saab 9-3 Cabrio durch eine sonnige kalifornische Landschaft zu fahren. Saab entwickelte ein interaktives Autoerlebnis, bei dem man der Geschichte folgen kann, indem man den Film anklickt. Die Reise erweckt außerdem faszinierende Gedanken zum Leben – Dinge, die durch Pop Ups in inspirierenden Momenten im Saab erscheinen.

FEATURED ON THE DVD **CAMPAIGN:** Saab 9-3 – Heaven's above. **CLIENT:** Saab Automobile. **YEAR:** 2005. **AGENCY:** LOWE Tesch <www.lowetesch.com>. **CREATIVE DIRECTOR:** Johan Tesch. **ART DIRECTOR:** Johan Öhrn. **COPYWRITER:** Cissi Högkvist, Dan McDonald. **ACCOUNT DIRECTOR:** Nils Lindhe, Johanna Persson. **AGENCY PRODUCER:** Anna Kjellmark. **MOTION DESIGNER:** David Andersson, Tobias Löfgren. **3D ANIMATIONS:** Visual Art. **PHOTOGRAPHER:** Erik Grönlund. **CLIENTS SUPERVISOR:** Fredrik Gustafsson, Andreas Eskengren.

Interactive Driving

The cockpit-inspired interior in the Saab 9-3 allows intuitive interaction with the driver and it has many smart features to help you concentrate on driving. Advanced Voice Recognition (AVR) lets you to control the infotainment system using your voice, while ComSense delays incoming phone calls during heavy braking or steering, so you can stay focused on the road ahead

Illuminating information

The most frequently used instruments and controls are in the primary zone right in front of you. Saab's Night Panel function reduces distractions at night, by displaying only the most important dials and instruments, turning off the other readouts unless they are required. The soft green illumination of the instrument panel and displays is designed to be easier on the eyes

Practical versatility

Don't be fooled by the sporty looks. You'll find plenty of intelligent solutions inside, such as a bag holder net, under-floor storage and a twin cargo floor which divides the luggage compartment Put the 9-3 SportCombi to work for business, with the family or at leisure and the cargo possibilities are virtually limitless

SYNOPSIS: The all new 9-3 SportCombi – with genes from jets. **TARGET GROUP:** Young couples and families looking for a practical car to cater for leisure or family needs while not compromising on style and sportiness.

SYNOPSIS: La nouvelle voiture sportive de Saab, 9-3 SportCombi, possède des gènes d'avion à réaction. **GROUPE CIBLE :** Les jeunes couples et les familles qui recherchent une voiture pratique pour satisfaire les besoins de la famille et ses activités de loisirs, sans pour autant faire de compromis sur le style et l'allure sportive.

SYNOPSIS: Der neue 9-3 SportCombi – mit Genen von Jets. **ZIELGRUPPE:** Junge Paare und Familien, die nach einem praktischen Auto für Freizeit oder Familie suchen, ohne Kompromisse bezüglich Stil und Sportlichkeit machen zu wollen.

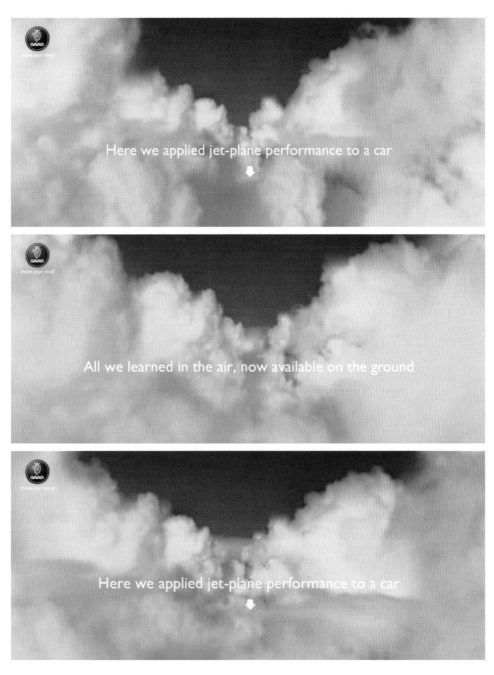

FEATURED ON THE DVD **CAMPAIGN:** Saab 9-5 – Animal Vision. **CLIENT:** Saab Automobile. **YEAR:** 2005. **AGENCY:** LOWE Tesch <www.lowetesch.com>. **CREATIVE DIRECTOR:** Johan Tesch. **ART DIRECTOR:** Tim Scheibel. **COPYWRITER:** Stephen Withlock. **ACCOUNT DIRECTOR:** Nils Lindhe. **AGENCY PRODUCER:** Caroline Déas-Ehrnvall, Anna Kjellmark. **ADVERTISER'S SUPERVISOR:** Fredrik Gustafsson, Andreas Eskengren. **MOTION DESIGNER:** Daniel Isaksson. **TECHNICAL ADVISOR:** Johan Öhrn. **FILM PRODUCTION:** Zermatt. **DIRECTOR:** Joakim Sandström. **ADVERTISING CONCEPT:** Lowe Brindfors. **CREATIVE DIRECTOR:** Magnus Wretblad.

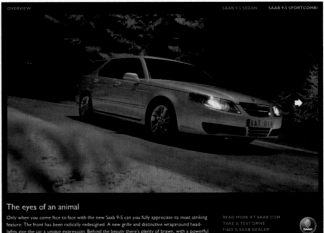

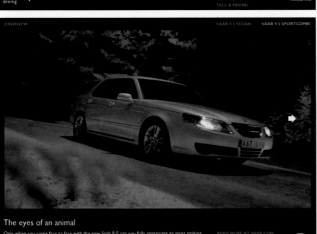

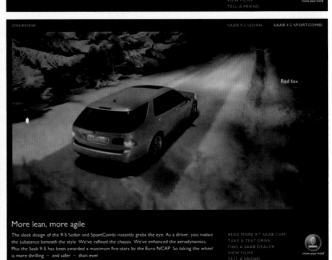

SYNOPSIS: It's winter. It's freezing. It's the middle of the night. You are alone in a dense forest somewhere in Sweden. Only you are not alone. Surrounding you are wild animals. Including one extremely exotic creature – the new Saab 9-5. By clicking on the eyes of the animals, you can switch between different perspectives. See the car from a low angle as a red fox would. Look from the height of a moose. Get a bird's eye view by gazing down like an eagle owl. See it like a lynx, or a wolf. Then you can move in for a closer look. Prowl around the car. How you approach it depends on the animal you have become.

SYNOPSIS : C'est l'hiver, il fait glacial. La nuit est tombée. Vous êtes seul dans une épaisse forêt quelque part en Suède. Mais en réalité vous n'êtes pas tout seul. Vous êtes entouré de bêtes sauvages. Dont une extrêmement étrange : la nouvelle Saab 9-5. En cliquant sur les yeux des animaux, la perspective change. On voit la voiture en contre-plongée comme le ferait un renard roux. On la voit d'en haut, comme un élan. On a une vue d'ensemble com-

me l'aurait un hibou. On la regarde à travers les yeux d'un lynx, ou d'un loup. On peut aussi s'approcher pour la regarder de plus près, rôder alentour. L'approche dépend de l'animal que vous êtes devenu.

SYNOPSIS: Es ist Winter. Es ist eiskalt. Es ist mitten in der Nacht. Sie sind allein in einem dichten Wald irgendwo in Schweden. Aber Sie sind nicht allein. Sie sind von wilden Tieren umgeben. Einschließlich einer sehr exotischen Kreatur – dem neuen Saab 9-5. Indem Sie auf die Augen der Tiere klicken, können Sie zwischen verschiedenen Perspektiven wechseln. Betrachten Sie das Auto von unten wie ein Fuchs. Schauen Sie von der Höhe eines Elches darauf herab. Sehen Sie es aus der Vogelperspektive wie eine Eule. Betrachten Sie es mit den Augen eines Luchses oder eines Wolfs. Sie können sich bewegen, um es aus der Nähe zu sehen. Umrunden Sie das Auto. Die Art, wie Sie sich ihm nähern, hängt von dem Tier ab, zu dem Sie geworden sind.

FEATURED ON THE DVD **CAMPAIGN:** Saab 9-3 – Caution. **CLIENT:** Saab Automobile. **YEAR:** 2006. **AGENCY:** LOWE Tesch <www.lowetesch.com>. **CREATIVE DIRECTOR:** Niklas Wallberg. **ART DIRECTOR:** Patrik Westerdahl. **COPYWRITER:** Cissi Högkvist. **ACCOUNT DIRECTOR:** Johanna Persson. **AGENCY PRODUCER:** Anna Axelsson. **ADVERTISERS SUPERVISOR:** Jessica Persson, Fredrik Gustafsson. **MOTION DESIGNER:** Tobias Löfgren, Peter Eneroth. **ANIMATIONS:** Per Kjellström, Morgan Kane. **SOUND/MUSIC:** Anders, Morgan Kane. **PHOTOGRAPHER:** Kjell Peterson, Agent Bauer.

SYNOPSIS: Saab Sport Combi/Sport Sedan is born from jets and therefore G forces may occur and have devastating effects on the surrounding content.

SYNOPSIS : Le combi sport et berline Saab 9-5 est né d'un avion à réaction, les forces gravitationnelles peuvent donc avoir des effets dévastateurs sur l'environnement immédiat.

SYNOPSIS: Der Saab Sport Combi/Sport Sedan ist aus Düsenflugzeugen entstanden; daher können Beschleunigungskräfte auftreten, die verheerende Auswirkungen auf den Inhalt haben.

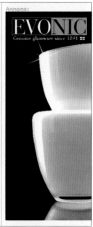

FEATURED ON THE DVD **CAMPAIGN:** SEAT Toledo – Website "Ya no hay límites" <www.seat.toledo.es>. **PRODUCT:** SEAT Toledo. **YEAR:** 2005. **AGENCY:** DoubleYou <www.doubleyou.com>. **PRODUCTION TIME:** 6 weeks. **CREATIVE TEAM:** Edu Pou, Frédéric Sanz, Blanca Piera, Joakim Borgström, Xavi Caparrós, Elisenda Losantos. **PROGRAMMER:** Xavi Caparrós, Joakim Borgström, Gonzalo Rodríguez.

CONCEPT: The original concept of this website reinforces the positioning of the new SEAT Toledo, a car which breaks the traditional sector boundaries. The campaign claim "Now there are no limits" is the linking thread, the basis for the entire site. Each of its letters (Ya no hay limites) serves as a milestone in an interactive discourse covering the main features of the Toledo. The scroll is the only means of surfing the site, which is built up as one moves horizontally from frame to frame. The apparent simplicity is speckled with small, yet spectacular interactive sections, which come out to meet the visitor, reinforcing, illustrating or supplementing information on the car. Finally, the sound effects caused by the user link in with the campaign's TV spot, providing harmony and unity.

CONCEPT : Le concept de ce site renforce le positionnement de la nouvelle Seat Toledo, une voiture qui sort du cadre traditionnel. Le slogan de la campagne « Maintenant il n'y a plus de limites », est le fil rouge, la base du site entier. Chacune des lettres sert de jalon pour un discours interactif présentant les caractéristiques principales de la voiture. La barre de défilement sert à naviguer sur le site, qui se développe en passant horizontalement

d'une image à l'autre. La simplicité apparente est parsemée de rubriques interactives spectaculaires qui viennent à la rencontre du visiteur, renforçant, illustrant ou complétant les informations sur la voiture. Enfin, les effets sonores rappellent le spot télévisé, contribuant à un effet d'unité et d'harmonie.

KONZEPT: Das ursprüngliche Konzept der Webseite bekräftigte die Positionierung des neuen SEAT Toledo; ein Auto, das die traditionellen Grenzen überschreitet. Der Kampagnenslogan „Jetzt gibt es keine Grenzen mehr" ist die Verbindung, die Basis für die gesamte Seite. Jeder Buchstabe (Ya no hay limites) dient als Meilenstein in einem interaktiven Diskurs, der die Hauptmerkmale des Toledo abdeckt. Nur durch Scrollen kann man auf der Seite surfen, die so aufgebaut ist, dass man sich horizontal von Frame zu Frame bewegt. Die offenbare Einfachheit ist mit kleinen, aber spektakulären interaktiven Bereichen gespickt, die dem Besucher Informationen über das Auto vermitteln. Schließlich sorgt der Soundeffekt, der durch den Link mit dem Fernsehspot der Kampagne entsteht, für Harmonie und Einheit.

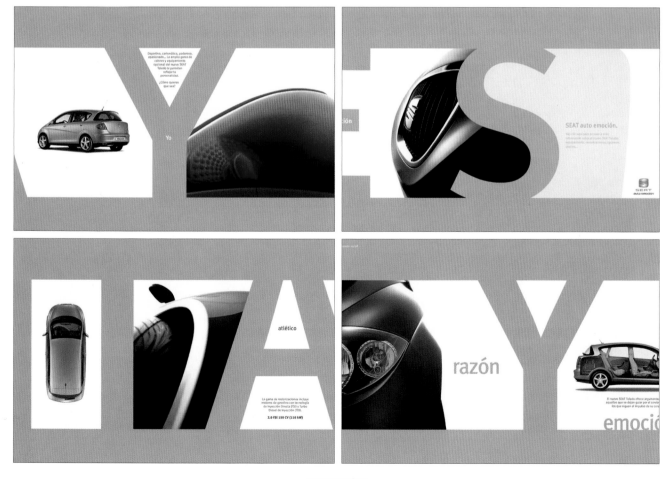

FEATURED ON THE DVD **CAMPAIGN:** SEAT Toledo – Campaign "Ya no hay límites". **PRODUCT:** SEAT Toledo. **YEAR:** 2005. **AGENCY:** DoubleYou <www.doubleyou.com>. **PRODUCTION TIME:** 1 week. **CREATIVE TEAM:** Joakim Borgström, Edu Pou, Frédéric Sanz, Blanca Piera, Xavi Caparrós, Elisenda Losantos. **PROGRAMMER:** Dani Fernández, Joakim Borgström, Xavi Caparrós. **TECH ASPECTS:** Macromedia Flash. **MEDIA CIRCULATED:** ABC, Expansión, Marca, MSN, Repsol YPF, TVCatalunya, Yahoo!.

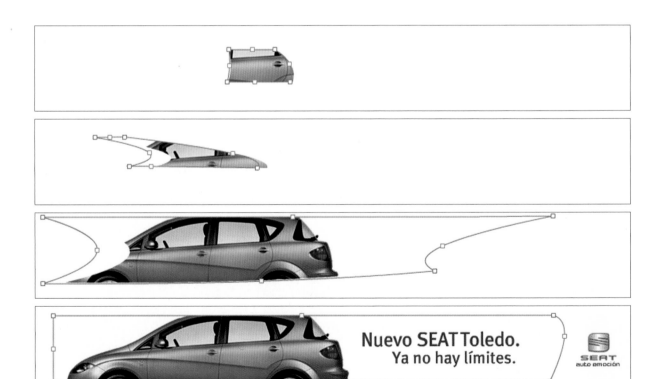

CONCEPT: If there are "no limits" for the new SEAT Toledo, then there shouldn't be any limits either for the online campaign to mark its launch. A dynamic figure, in constant, organic movement, not limited to the banner space but rather fluctuating within the screen. This served as a teaser and began to take on meaning when the user interacted by placing the cursor over it to reveal the hidden message. This set off the dialogue; if there is no interaction, there is no message. The learning that takes place has to be active if the resulting discovery is to reinforce the positioning of the Toledo in the user's mind. In conventional banners skyscrapers and killerpages... it's always the same game, it's the expanding banner that brings the medium to life. The piece is based on the portal site content, taking the "Now there are no limits" line quite literally.

CONCEPT : Si la Seat Toledo ne connaît aucune limite, alors la campagne en ligne qui accompagne son lancement ne doit en connaître aucune. Une forme dynamique, sans cesse en mouvement, comme organique, qui ne se limite pas à la bannière mais qui fluctue sur tout l'espace de l'écran. Cette accroche ne prend tout son sens qu'au moment ou l'internaute place le curseur dessus afin de révéler le message caché. Le dialogue s'enclenche alors. Sans interaction, il n'y a pas de message. Pour renforcer le positionnement de la Toledo dans l'esprit de l'internaute, il faut qu'il obtienne les informations de manière active. Dans les bandeaux classiques, gratte-ciels ou autre, c'est toujours la même chose, c'est la bannière extensible qui anime le médium. Le module s'inspire ici du contenu du site de la marque, prenant le slogan « Maintenant il n'y a plus de limites » au premier littéral.

KONZEPT: Wenn es für den neuen SEAT Toledo „keine Grenzen" gibt, sollte es für die Online-Kampagne, die seinen Launch begleitet, auch keine Grenzen geben: eine dynamische Figur in konstanter, organischer Bewegung, die nicht auf das Banner begrenzt ist, sondern sich auf dem gesamten Bildschirm bewegt. Dies diente als Teaser und bekam Sinn, wenn der Benutzer durch Anklicken die versteckte Botschaft offen legte. Dies eröffnete einen Dialog – ohne Interaktion keine Botschaft. Der stattfindende Lernprozess muss aktiv sein, wenn er dazu führen soll, dass der Benutzer die Marke Toledo im Gedächtnis behält. Bei konventionellen Bannern, Skyscrapern und Killerpages erweckt stets das sich erweiternde Banner das Medium zum Leben. Hier basiert das Banner auf dem Inhaltsseitenportal und nimmt den Slogan „Jetzt gibt es keine Grenzen mehr" ziemlich wörtlich.

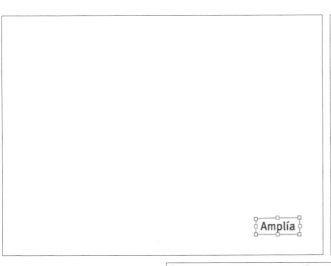

FEATURED ON THE DVD **CAMPAIGN:** Toyota Aygo <www.aygo.se>. **YEAR:** 2005. **AGENCY:** North Kingdom <www.northkingdom.com>. **PRODUCTION TIME:** 4 weeks. **COST IN HOURS OF WORK:** 600 h. **CREATIVE TEAM:** North Kingdom & SWE. **PROGRAMMER:** North Kingdom. **TECH ASPECTS:** Syndicate, Riviera. **MEDIA CIRCULATED:** First done for online, then adapted for 10" TV-spot. **AWARDS:** Favorite Website Awards (Site of the Day).

CONCEPT: Toyota wanted to reach a younger audience then their normal consumers when launching this car. The key message that we wanted to come across was to show that with this Toyota car, you can NOT actually buy it, you can only subscribe to it for about 200 euro/month. With the mailbox the connection to newspaper subscription communicated everything very effectively. Technically, the key challenge was how to make something extra of the animation. **RESULTS:** Fad 112,000 unique visitors in December of 2005, which is a record by far for any Toyota Sweden online campaigns.

CONCEPT : Avec le lancement de la Aygo, Toyota voulait toucher un public plus jeune que ses clients habituels. L'essentiel du message que nous devions communiquer était qu'on ne peut pas acheter cette voiture, on ne peut que s'y abonner pour 200 euros par mois, comme on le ferait pour un journal. Nous avons donc fait arriver la voiture par la fente d'une boîte aux lettres. Le défi technique était de dépasser l'animation traditionnelle. **RÉSULTATS :** Un engouement de 112 000 visiteurs uniques en décembre 2005, ce qui est de loin un record pour n'importe laquelle des campagnes de la filiale suédoise de Toyota.

KONZEPT: Toyota wollte beim Launch dieses Autos ein jüngeres Publikum als ihre normalen Kunden erreichen. Die Schlüsselbotschaft sollte zeigen, dass man diesen Toyota NICHT kaufen konnte, sondern ihn für ca. 200 Euro/Monat leasen musste. In Verbindung mit der Abonnierung einer Zeitung fand eine sehr effektive Kommunikation statt. Aus technischer Sicht bestand die größte Herausforderung darin, etwas Besonderes aus der Animation herauszuholen. **ERGEBNISSE:** Über 112 000 Besucher im Dezember 2005 – ein Rekord gegenüber allen Toyota-Online-Kampagnen in Schweden.

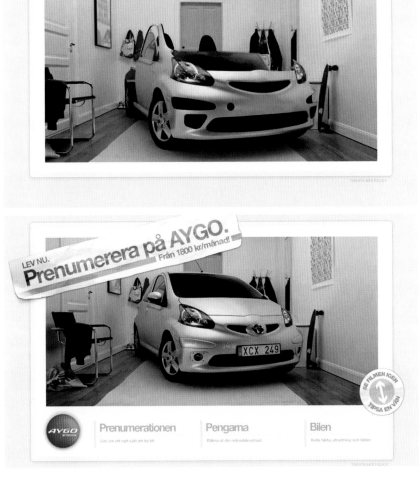

FEATURED ON THE DVD **CAMPAIGN:** Heart of Volvo. **CLIENT:** Volvo Car Corporation. **YEAR:** 2005. **AGENCY:** Forsman & Bodenfors <www.fb.se>. **PRODUCTION TIME:** 3 months. **ART DIRECTOR:** Martin Cedergren, Mikko Timonen, Anders Eklind, Mathias Appelblad, Andreas Malm. **COPYWRITER:** Filip Nilsson, Jacob Nelson. **DESIGN:** Jerry Wass, Lars Johansson. **PRODUCER:** Mathias Appelblad, Eva Råberg. **ACCOUNT MANAGER:** Maria Zachrisson, Gustav Aschan. **ACCOUNT EXECUTIVE:** Meta Ågren, Olle Victorin. **FILM PRODUCER:** Åsa Jansson, Magnus Kenhed. **3D:** Perssons Pixlar. **SOUND:** Delorean. **PHOTO:** Lennart Sjöberg. **PROGRAMMER:** Itiden, Kokokaka, Astronaut, Stink. **TECH ASPECTS:** Macromedia Flash. **MEDIA CIRCULATED:** Online ads, kiosk, virals. **AWARDS:** Cannes Lions 2005 (2x Finalist), CLIO Awards 2005 (4x Finalist), D&AD 2005 (Finalist), Epica 2005 (Bronze), Eurobest 2005 (Finalist), Favorite Website Award, Flash Forward 2005 (Finalist), London Internation Advertising Awards 2005 (2x Finalist), Adobe 2005 (Site of the Day), New York Festivals 2005 (Silver, Finalist), One Show 2005 (Finalist).

CONCEPT: For over 75 years, the design of every Volvo has been guided by the concern for the safety and well-being of people. Over time, this commitment grew into three core Volvo values: Safety, Quality and Environmental care. To answer the question "Why Volvo?", everybody is invited to Göteborg, Volvo's hometown for a true VIP experience. Welcome!

CONCEPT : Depuis plus de 75 ans, la conception de chaque Volvo a été guidée par la sécurité et le confort des usagers. Au fil du temps, cet engagement s'est développé suivant trois valeurs essentielles : sécurité, qualité et souci de l'environnement. Pour répondre à la question « Pourquoi choisir Volvo ? », les clients sont invités à Göteborg, le siège de Volvo, pour une visite officielle. Bienvenue !

KONZEPT: Seit über 75 Jahren wird das Design eines jeden Volvos von der Sorge um Sicherheit und Wohlbefinden der Menschen bestimmt. Mit der Zeit wuchs diese Verpflichtung zu drei Kernwerten: Sicherheit, Qualität und Umweltschutz. Um die Frage „Warum Volvo?" zu beantworten, ist jeder nach Göteborg, Volvos Heimatstadt, zu einem VIP-Erlebnis eingeladen. Willkommen!

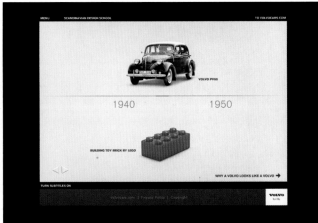

FEATURED ON THE DVD **CAMPAIGN:** The Cape Town Experience. **PRODUCT:** Volvo X-Sea Challenge. **CLIENT:** Volvo Car Corporation. **YEAR:** 2006. **AGENCY:** Forsman & Bodenfors <www.fb.se>. **PRODUCTION TIME:** 2 months. **WEB DIRECTOR:** Martin Cedergren. **ART DIRECTOR:** Martin Cedergren, Andreas Malm. **COPYWRITER:** Jacob Nelson, Filip Nilsson. **ACCOUNT EXECUTIVE:** Meta Ågren. **ACCOUNT MANAGER:** Cilla Glenberg. **DESIGN:** Mikko Timonen, Lars Jansson, Viktor Larsson, Jerry Wass. **PRODUCER:** Martin Sandberg. **PROGRAMMER:** B-ReeL, Itiden, Zooma. **TECH ASPECTS:** Macromedia Flash. **MEDIA CIRCULATED:** Online ads, dr, print.

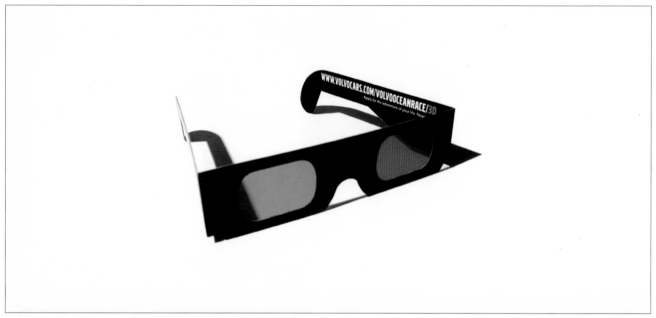

CONCEPT: This is a documentary part of the global testdrive event called Volvo X-Sea Challenge. The 3D glasses were sent out to Volvo prospects around the world with a special VIP link printed on them. Enter the website and experience the first stop of the Volvo X-Sea Challenge in Cape Town. And the Internet in 3D!

CONCEPT : Partie documentaire de la vaste opération d'essais sur route nommée Volvo X-Sea Challenge. Des lunettes en 3D ont été envoyées aux clients potentiels du monde entier, accompagnées d'un lien VIP. Entrez sur le site et faites un premier arrêt à Cape Town, au volant de la Volvo X-Sea. Et tout cela en 3D.

KONZEPT: Dies ist der dokumentarische Teil des weltweiten Testfahrt-Events Volvo X-Sea Challenge. 3D-Brillen wurden mit einem speziellen VIP-Link bedruckt und an Volvo-Kunden in aller Welt verschickt. Betreten Sie die Webseite und erleben Sie die erste Station des Volvo X-Sea Challenge in Kapstadt. Und das Internet in 3D!

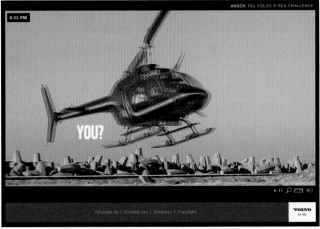

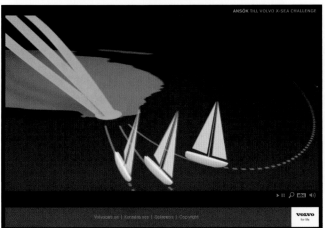

FEATURED ON THE DVD **CAMPAIGN:** Virgin Banners: Massage, Haircut, Dreams, Feather, Bounce, Golf, Flirt. **PRODUCT:** Virgin Atlantic Airways Upper Class. **YEAR:** 2004. **AGENCY:** Crispin Porter + Bogusky <www.cpbgroup. com>. **PRODUCTION TIME:** 2 months. **EXECUTIVE CREATIVE DIRECTOR:** Alex Bogusky. **CREATIVE DIRECTORS:** Bill Wright, Andrew Keller. **INTERACTIVE CREATIVE DIRECTOR:** Jeff Benjamin. **COPYWRITER:** Franklin Tipton, Dustin Ballard, David Gonzalez, Justin Kramm. **ART DIRECTOR:** Michael Ferrare, Juan-Carlos Morales. **DESIGNER:** Rahul Panchal. **PROGRAMMER:** Barbarian Group, Milky Elephant, Juan-Carlos Morales. **TECH ASPECTS:** Macromedia Flash, Iframe. **MEDIA CIRCULATED:** Print, OOH, broadcast, Pay-per-view. **AWARDS:** Cannes Lions 2004 (Gold), London International 2004 (Finalist – Interactive Banner and Online Campaign), Young Guns 2004 (Finalist – Cyberactive Online Advertising category), Viral Awards 2004 (Finalist – Best Interactive Viral category), Andy Awards 2005 (2x Bronze), One show 2005 (Gold/Silver – Pencil-Interactive category, Finalist – Interactive category), D&AD (Book entry), CA Interactive 2005 (Winner), CLIO 2005 (Bronze), Cannes Lions 2005 (Bronze), Communication Arts 2005 (Winner), London International 2005 (Finalist – Online Campaign).

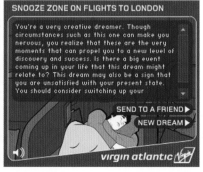

CONCEPT: This was a branding assignment for Virgin Atlantic Airways that was designed to extend the Go Jet Set Go! campaign. **MASSAGE:** People are asked to massage the banner and the banner responds with massage moans and rippling textures almost as if it was real – and lets users experience first hand relaxation on a Virgin flight. **HAIRCUT:** People are asked to upload a picture and give that person a haircut, just like they could get on a Virgin flight. Choose a hairstyle, cut and blow-dry your client a new style. Caution: blow-dryer gets hot! **DREAMS:** Type in what your last dream was about. Then have it analyzed by this dream interpreter. **FEATHER:** Tickle the Virgin Upper Class passenger as they lie in their suite. **BOUNCE:** People are asked to make a business man jump, bounce, flip, and belly flop off the largest fully flat bed in business class. **GOLF:** People are asked to play three rounds of miniature golf on board a Virgin flight. Touring the Upper Class Cabin and getting on board golf out of their system while passengers react. **FLIRT:** People are asked to flirt with a Virgin Atlantic passenger. Anything can be asked. Any pickup line can be used. All of it gets a reaction from either a male or female passenger. Letting users experience some of the fun in flying on Virgin Atlantic. **RESULTS:** After the Go Jet Set Go! campaign ran, Virgin's awareness was up 43%. Consideration was up 50% and trial had increased significantly. Articles were written about the online campaign in ADWEEK, Creativity, NYT and WSJ. It was named Ad Age Online Campaign of the Year. Virgin Atlantic enjoyed its most profitable year since 2000.

CONCEPT : Créer la publicité en ligne pour Virgin Atlantic Airways dans le cadre de la campagne Go Jet Set Go ! **MASSAGE :** L'internaute peut « masser » la bannière qui réagit par des grognements de plaisir. La texture de la bannière se met à onduler comme une peau et invite les utilisateurs à faire l'expérience de la relaxation à bord. **COIFFURE :** On télécharge l'image d'un visage et on lui fait une nouvelle coupe de cheveux, comme on peut en bénéficier sur les vols Virgin. On choisit un style, on coupe et on sèche. Attention, le séchoir peut brûler ! **RÊVES :** On écrit le dernier rêve que l'on a fait. Et on le fait interpréter par un « analyste. » **PLUME :** On chatouille les passagers de la classe affaires pendant leur sommeil. **REBONDS :** On fait sauter et rebondir sur le ventre un passager de la classe affaires sur un immense lit. **GOLF :** On peut jouer trois parties de minigolf sur un vol Virgin. On se promène dans la cabine de luxe et on propose aux passagers de relever le défi. **FLIRT :** On peut s'amuser à draguer un passager. On peut poser toutes les questions, utiliser toutes les astuces. Et on obtient la réaction du passager, homme ou femme. Une façon de goûter les distractions proposées par Virgin Atlantic. **RÉSULTATS :** A la fin de la campagne, la notoriété de la marque était en hausse de 43%. Les intentions d'achat ont augmenté de 50% et l'audience a explosé. La campagne a été commentée dans Adweek, Creativity, NYT et WSJ. Elle a été nommée Meilleure Campagne en ligne de l'Année par Ad Age. Virgin Atlantic a connu son année la plus rentable depuis l'an 2000.

KONZEPT: Dies war eine Kampagne für Virgin Atlantic Airways, die entworfen wurde, um die Go Jet Set Go!-Kampagne auszuweiten. **MASSAGE:** Man wird gebeten, das Banner zu massieren, und es antwortet mit gewellter Oberfläche und wohligem Stöhnen, als wäre es echt – und macht den Benutzern damit die Entspannung während eines Virgin-Fluges aus erster Hand erfahrbar. **HAARSCHNITT:** Man soll das Bild einer Person hochladen und dieser einen Haarschnitt verpassen, wie man ihn auf einem Virgin-Flug bekommen könnte. Wählen sie eine Frisur, schneiden und föhnen Sie Ihrem Kunden einen neuen Stil. Vorsicht: Der Föhn wird heiß! **TRÄUME:** Geben Sie in Ihren Computer ein, was Sie als letztes geträumt haben. Ein Traumdeuter wird diesen Traum interpretieren. **FEDER:** Kitzeln Sie den Virgin Upper-Class-Passagier, während er in seiner Suite liegt. **HÜPFEN:** Man soll einen Geschäftsmann dazu bringen, auf dem größten, komplett flachen Bett zu springen, zu hüpfen, sich zu drehen und auf den Bauch zu plumpsen. **GOLF:** Man soll drei Runden Miniaturgolf an Bord eines Virgin-Fluges spielen. Dabei tourt man Golf spielend durch die Upper-Class-Kabine, während Passagiere reagieren. **FLIRTEN:** Man soll mit einem Virgin-Atlantic-Passagier flirten. Man kann alles fragen. Jeder Anmachspruch kann verwendet werden. Auf alles erhält man eine Reaktion von einem männlichen oder weiblichen Passagier. **ERGEBNISSE:** Nachdem die Go Jet Set Go!-Kampagne startete, stieg der Bekanntheitsgrad um 43%, die Kaufabsicht um 50% an. In ADWEEK, Creativity, NYT und WSJ wurden Artikel über die Online-Kampagne veröffentlicht. Man nannte sie „Ad Age Online Campaign of the Year". Virgin Atlantic genoss das ertragreichste Jahr seit 2000.

Remain calm and click here>>

⚠ Attention Upper Class Passengers

CLICK & DRAG MOUSE TO CONTROL HANDS AND MASSAGE

OCCUR IN EVENT OF MASSAGE

go jet set, go! virgin atlantic

Remain calm and click here>>

⚠ Attention Upper Class Passengers

DEPRESSURIZATION MAY OCCUR IN EVENT OF MASSAGE

go jet set, go! virgin atlantic

Remain calm and click here>>

⚠ Attention Upper Class Passengers

DEPRESSURIZATION MAY OCCUR IN EVENT OF MASSAGE

go jet set, go! virgin atlantic

Remain calm and click here>>

⚠ ...tion Upper Class Passengers

DEPRESSURIZATION MAY OCCUR IN EVENT OF MASSAGE

go jet set, go! virgin atlantic

SHOULD YOU ENCOUNTER FLIRTING REMAIN CALM

go jet set, go!™ virgin atlantic

SHOULD YOU ENCOUNTER FLIRTING REMAIN CALM

Can I interest you in a drink?

▶Woman ▶Man

go jet set, go!™ virgin atlantic

SHOULD YOU ENCOUNTER FLIRTING REMAIN CALM

You have the most beautiful eyes

▶Woman ▶Man

go jet set, go!™ virgin atlantic

NO
BOUNCING
ON THE
LARGEST
FULLY FLAT
BED IN
BUSINESS
CLASS.

virgin atlantic

Now rolling out
across the fleet

go jet set, go!

virgin atlantic

Click here in an
orderly manner >>

go jet set, go!

virgin atlantic

Click here in an
orderly manner >>

go jet set, go!

virgin atlantic

Click here in an
orderly manner >>

go jet set, go!

virgin atlantic

virgin atlantic

IT MAY BE
DIFFICULT
TO WAKE UP
ANOTHER
PASSENGER.

virgin atlantic

IT MAY BE
DIFFICULT
TO WAKE UP
ANOTHER
PASSENGER.

virgin atlantic

Click here. Quietly. >>

virgin atlantic

Upper Class Suites on
flights To London

virgin atlantic

FEATURED ON THE DVD **CAMPAIGN:** Gypsy Cab Project <www.gypsycabproject.com>. **PRODUCT:** Volkswagen Rabbit. **CLIENT:** VW. **YEAR:** 2006. **AGENCY:** Crispin Porter + Bogusky <www.cpbgroup.com>

CHIEF CREATIVE OFFICER: Alex Bogusky. **EXECUTIVE CREATIVE DIRECTOR:** Andrew Keller. **INTERACTIVE CREATIVE DIRECTOR:** Jeff Benjamin. **CREATIVE DIRECTOR:** Rob Strasberg. **ART DIRECTOR:** Ka

Morris. **COPYWRITER:** Rob Thompson. **INTERACTIVE ART DIRECTOR:** Conor McCann. **TECHNICAL DIRECTOR:** Scott Prindle. **SENIOR LEAD PROGRAMMER:** Jordi Ortega, Larry Gordon. **QA ENGINEER:** Peter Mlodzik

INTERACTION DIRECTOR: Matt Walsh. **SENIOR SYSTEMS ARCHITECT:** Jordan Kilpatrick. **SYSTEMS ARCHITECT:** Adam Heathcott. **MEDIA CIRCULATED:** Online banners and small space print advertisements.

CONCEPT: For the launch of the new VW Rabbit, Volkswagen wanted to emphasize the excellent city-driving capabilities of the newly designed vehicle. So they dressed it up to look like an NYC cab, and hired Denver-based actor/filmmaker Steve Capstick to drive it around the Big Apple. Steve had never been to NYC before, so he had to rely on the kindness of strangers to get around town. In return, Steve would provide his passengers with a courtesy ride. For two weeks, Steve traveled around NYC, picking up locals and tourists, and learned the essential tools of city driving. The fares were broadcast on the Internet on gypsycabproject.com, where viewers could watch the live feed from the Gypsy Cab or view select edited fares. **TECH ASPECTS:** In order to make the Gypsy Cab Project a reality, we relied on a suite of technology products. The Rabbit was equipped with several pinhole cameras, which were wired to the trunk of the Rabbit. In there, four Apple Mac Minis captured the footage and dumped it onto four external firewire hard drives. CP+B also set up a wireless network in the back of the Rabbit, and with the help of a high-gain antenna mounted on the roof, broadcast the signal to a chase vehicle that followed the Rabbit. Inside the chase vehicle, a Mac Book Pro using Apple Remote Desktop 3 allowed for remote access to each camera. It also allowed the production team in the chase vehicle to view all the cameras and the content that was being acquired. The Rabbit was also equipped with a GPS tracking device from Webtech Wireless. The GPS transmitted the Rabbit's signal to a remote servers. Viewers on the site were then able to see the location of the Rabbit that corresponded to each fare Steve picked up. All the equipment in the car was powered from a 1000-Watt inverter connected directly to the Rabbit's battery. A group of editors worked around the clock for two weeks in a Manhattan apartment. They used seven Apple G5 editing suites to compress and upload the full length streams and to edit and archive select fares. **RESULTS:** At the end of the two weeks, Steve had a better grasp of the NYC landscape, a solid understanding of an ever-expanding city-driving dictionary, and a long list of fares and friendships that came from a somewhat-brief (depending on the traffic) interaction in a Volkswagen Rabbit.

CONCEPT : Pour le lancement de la nouvelle VW Rabbit, Volkswagen voulait souligner les excellentes qualités urbaines de cette voiture au design revisité. Ils l'ont donc déguisée en taxi new-yorkais et ont engagé Steve Capstick, un acteur/réalisateur de Denver, pour la conduire dans New York. C'était la première fois que Steve mettait les pieds à New York, alors il devait compter sur l'amabilité des inconnus pour trouver son chemin. En échange, la course était gratuite pour ses passagers. Pendant deux semaines, Steve a conduit dans New York, offrant ses courses aux New-Yorkais et aux touristes, et a appris les bases de la conduite en ville. Les courses étaient diffusées sur Internet sur gypsycabproject.com. Les visiteurs pouvaient voir les images du taxi en direct ou choisir parmi une sélection de courses. **ASPECTS TECHNIQUES :** Pour donner vie au projet Gypsy Cab, nous avons utilisé toute une palette de produits technologiques. La Rabbit était équipée de plusieurs petites caméras à sténopé connectées au coffre, où quatre Mac Mini Apple capturaient les séquences et les transféraient sur quatre disques durs externes FireWire. CP+B avait aussi monté un réseau sans fil à l'arrière de la Rabbit et, grâce à une antenne à gain élevé montée sur le toit, transmettait le signal à un véhicule qui suivait la Rabbit. Dans ce véhicule, un Mac Book Pro équipé du Remote Desktop 3 d'Apple permettait de contrôler chaque caméra à distance, et l'équipe de production pouvait aussi voir les images en cours d'acquisition sur toutes les caméras. La Rabbit était également équipée d'un système de positionnement GPS de Webtech Wireless. Le GPS transmettait le signal de la Rabbit à des serveurs distants. Les visiteurs du site pouvaient donc voir la position qui correspondait à chaque course de Steve. Tous les appareils de la voiture étaient alimentés par un convertisseur de 1 000 Watts connecté directement à la batterie de la Rabbit. Un groupe de monteurs a travaillé 24 heures sur 24 pendant deux semaines dans un appartement de Manhattan. Ils utilisaient sept plateformes de montage Apple G5 pour compresser et télécharger les séquences brutes et pour monter les courses sélectionnées. **RÉSULTAT :** À la fin des deux semaines, Steve s'était familiarisé avec le paysage new-yorkais, avait acquis une solide connaissance du dictionnaire de la conduite urbaine, en constante évolution, et avait collectionné une longue liste de courses et d'amitiés nées d'une interaction somme toute assez courte (en fonction de l'état de la circulation) dans une Rabbit Volkswagen.

KONZEPT: Für den Launch des neuen VW Rabbit wollte Volkswagen die großartige Eignung des neu designten Fahrzeugs für die City betonen, also gestalteten sie das Auto wie ein New Yorker Taxi und mieteten den Schauspieler und Filmemacher Steve Capstick, der es durch den Big Apple fuhr. Steve war noch nie in New York City gewesen und daher von der Freundlichkeit Fremder abhängig. Im Gegenzug für deren Hilfe lud Steve seine Passagiere zu einer Spritztour ein. Zwei Wochen lang fuhr Steve durch die Stadt, nahm New Yorker und Touristen mit und lernte die wesentlichen Tools des Fahrens in der Innenstadt kennen. Die Fahrten wurden im Internet auf gypsycabproject.com gezeigt, wo Besucher die Live-Übertragung des Taxis ansehen oder editierte Fahrten auswählen konnten. **TECHNIK:** Um das Gypsy-Cap-Projekt zu realisieren, bedurfte es mehrerer technischer Produkte. Der Rabbit war mit mehreren Lochkameras ausgestattet, die mit dem Kofferraum des Rabbits verkabelt waren. Dort nahmen vier Apple Mac Minis das Videomaterial auf und sendeten es auf vier externe Festplatten. CP+B errichteten im hinteren Teil des Rabbits außerdem ein kabelloses Netzwerk und sendeten mit einer auf dem Dach befestigten Antenne das Signal zu einem Fahrzeug, das den Rabbit verfolgte. In diesem Wagen sorgte ein Mac Book Pro mit Apple Remote Desktop 3 für den Fernzugriff auf jede Kamera. Außerdem konnte das Produktionsteam alle Kameras und aufgenommenen Inhalte sehen. Der Rabbit war außerdem mit einem GPS-Gerät von Webtech Wireless ausgestattet. Das GPS übertrug das Signal des Rabbits auf entfernte Server. Die Besucher der Seite konnten den Standort des Rabbits lokalisieren, an dem Steve einen Fahrgast einstiegen ließ. Die gesamte Ausstattung des Autos wurde von einem 1000-Watt-Inverter betrieben, der direkt an die Batterie des Rabbits angeschlossen war. Eine Gruppe von Editoren arbeitete zwei Wochen lang rund um die Uhr in einem Apartment in Manhattan. Sie verwendeten Editiertools von Apple G5, um die Streams in voller länger zu komprimieren, hochzuladen und ausgewählte Strecken zu archivieren. **ERGEBNISSE:** Nach zwei Wochen kannte sich Steve besser in New York City aus – er besaß ein fundiertes Wissen des stetig wachsenden Stadtverkehr-Vokabulars und eine lange Liste von Bekanntschaften, die durch ein relativ kurzes (je nach Verkehr) Gespräch in einem Volkswagen Rabbit entstanden waren.

GypsyCabProject

100 fares in 14 days to uncover what it takes to be the ultimate city driver.

hop on board | **favorite fares** | about the project | city driving dictionary | send to a friend

SOUND **ON** OFF

1 0 3 fares total

legal disclaimer | terms and conditions | privacy policy | vw.com

GypsyCabProject

100 fares in 14 days to uncover what it takes to be the ultimate city driver.

What happens if you take a guy who's never been to New York and make him a cab driver? The answer is something we call the Gypsy Cab Project 6/10-6/24. It's gonna be a fast, chaotic and unpredictable two weeks. It's also gonna be filmed and broadcast every day right here. **Everybody in.**

 watch the latest favorite fare ›

hop on board | favorite fares | about the project | city driving dictionary | send to a friend

SOUND **ON** OFF

1 0 3 fares total

GypsyCabProject

00 fares in 14 days to uncover what it takes to be the ultimate city driver.

Back to the map ›

013

I had 3 passengers in the Gypsy Cab that I won't ever be able to forget. With a little prompting, I'm sure I'll be able to remember pretty much every ride I've given. But this is different. This particular experience will always be floating around in my head and won't need any prompting to reach total recall. I am still somewhat speechless. Here it is in a nutshell:

Asian supermodel with friends, booze, and attitude.
(please note that I had no part in the "booze"...they were coming out of a restaurant).
I was way out of my comfort zone.
I survived and I had fun. Actually, I still feel a little funny (as in peculiar).

The End.

hop on board   **favorite fares**   about the project   city driving dictionary   send to a friend   SOUND **ON** OFF

103 fares total

GypsyCabProject

00 fares in 14 days to uncover what it takes to be the ultimate city driver.

Tell someone you know about the Project

Your friend's name

Your friend's email

Your name

Your email

SEND ▶

hop on board   favorite fares   about the project   city driving dictionary   **send to a friend**   SOUND **ON** OFF

103 fares total

FEATURED ON THE DVD **CAMPAIGN:** VW Golf – Porcupine. **PRODUCT:** Volkswagen Golf. **CLIENT:** Volkswagen Brazil. **AGENCY:** AlmapBBDO <www.almapbbdo.com.br>. **PRODUCTION TIME:** 30 days. **CREATIVE DIRECTOR:** Marcello Serpa, Sérgio Mugnaini. **ART DIRECTOR:** Isabelle De Vooght, Cesar Finamori, Julio Andery. **COPYWRITER:** Luciana Haguiara, Dulcidio Caldeira, Andre Faria. **DESIGNER:** Isabelle De Vooght. **TECHNICAL DIRECTOR:** Flavi Ramos. **PRODUCER:** Ana Maria Machado. **ACCOUNT EXECUTIVE:** Joanna Guinle, Vanessa Previero, Ana Beatriz Porto. **ADVERTISER'S SUPERVISORS:** Paulo Kakinoff, Sergio Szmoisz, Fabio Souza. **ILLUSTRATOR:** Adelmo SOUND TRACK: Lua Web. **PHOTOGRAPH:** Getty Image. **TECH ASPECTS:** Macromedia Flash, video, sound. **AWARDS:** El Ojo de Ibero America 2005 (Bronze), MMonline/MSN 2005 (Merit), London Festival 2005 (Shortlist).

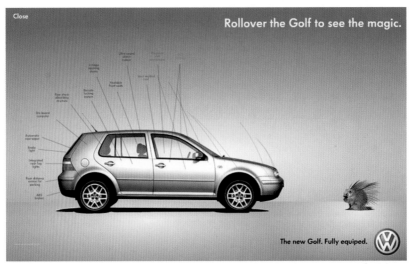

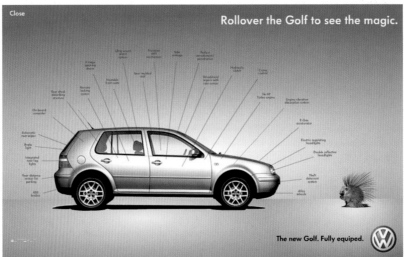

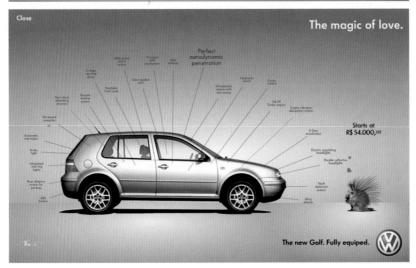

BACKGROUND PROFILE: The new VW Golf had as much new features that a campaign in offline and online was created to stand out its characteristics. **THE IDEA:** Show all features of the Golf in one and only ad, without being boring and to rational. **SOLUTION:** A superstitial. It starts with a soundtrack inspired by the music "Formidable", of Charles Aznavour. The Golf enters in scene, as well as a small pocupine. The text says: "Rollover the Golf to see the magic." With the interaction, the Golf's features appear in the same way that the porcupine leaves its spiny thorns. The porcupine shows signals of love. The text says: "The magic of love." **CLAIM:** "The new Golf. Fully equipped."

CONTEXTE : La nouvelle Golf VW avait tellement de nouvelles options qu'une campagne en ligne et hors ligne a due être spécialement réalisée pour décrire ses caractéristiques. **IDÉE :** Présenter toutes les options dans une pub globale sans être ennuyeux ni trop rationnel. **SOLUTION :** Une vidéo superstitielle. Elle démarre sur la musique de « Formidable", un titre de Charles Aznavour. La Golf entre en scène, ainsi qu'un petit porc-épic. Une légende indique : « Cliquez sur la Golf pour voir la magie ». De façon interactive, les équipements de la Golf apparaissent, tandis que le porc-épic laisse tomber ses piquants. Le porc-épic montre des signes d'amour. Légende : « La magie de l'amour ». Slogan : « La nouvelle Golf. Totalement équipée ».

HINTERGRUND: Der neue VW Golf hatte so viele neue Features, dass offline und online eine Kampagne erstellt wurde, um die Eigenschaften zu präsentieren. **DIE IDEE:** Alle Features des Golf in einer einzigen Anzeige darstellen, ohne langweilig und zu sachlich zu sein. **LÖSUNG:** Ein Superstitial. Es beginnt mit einem Soundtrack, der von dem Stück „Formidable" von Charles Aznavour inspiriert wurde. Der Golf erscheint, zusammen mit einem kleinen Stachelschwein. Der Text lautet: „Rollover the Golf to see the magic." Während der Interaktion erscheinen die Features des Golf auf dieselbe Weise, in der das Stachelschwein seine spitzen Stacheln verlässt. Es gibt Liebessignale. Text: „Die Magie der Liebe." Aussage: „Der neue Golf. Voll ausgestattet."

FEATURED ON THE DVD **CAMPAIGN:** Volkswagen GTI Configurator <www.vwfeatures.com>. **PRODUCT:** Volkswagen GTI Mk V. **YEAR:** 2006. **AGENCY:** Crispin Porter + Bogusky <www.cpbgroup.com>. **PRODUCTION TIME:** 1.5 month. **CHIEF CREATIVE OFFICER:** Alex Bogusky. **EXECUTIVE CREATIVE DIRECTOR:** Andrew Keller. **INTERACTIVE CREATIVE DIRECTOR:** Jeff Benjamin. **CREATIVE DIRECTOR:** Rob Strasberg, Tony Calcao. **ASSOCIATE CREATIVE DIRECTOR:** Scott Linnen. **ART DIRECTOR:** Tiffany Kosel, Geordie Stephens, Mike Ferrare, Rahul Panchal, Aramis Israel. **COPYWRITER:** Scott Linnen, Mike Howard, Franklin Tipton, Jeff Gillette. **DESIGNER:** Conor McCann. **PROGRAMMER:** IQ Interactive. **TECH ASPECTS:** Dynamic video player built in Macromedia Flash with external audio files. **MEDIA CIRCULATED:** Broadcast, web banners, print.

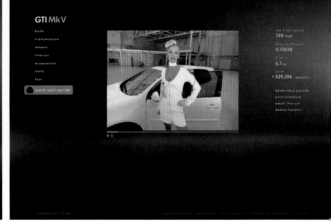

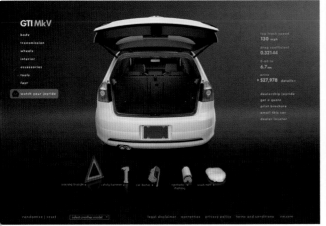

FEATURED ON THE DVD **CAMPAIGN:** VW Banners. **CLIENT:** Volkswagen. **YEAR:** 2006. **AGENCY:** Crispin Porter + Bogusky <www.cpbgroup.com>. **PRODUCER:** Domani Studios <www.domanistudios.com>. **PRODUCTION TIME:** 2 weeks. **CREATIVE TEAM:** Crispin Porter + Bogusky. **PROGRAMMER:** Domani Studios. **TECH ASPECTS:** Macromedia Flash AS 2.0, audio, XML. **MEDIA CIRCULATED:** Banner placements.

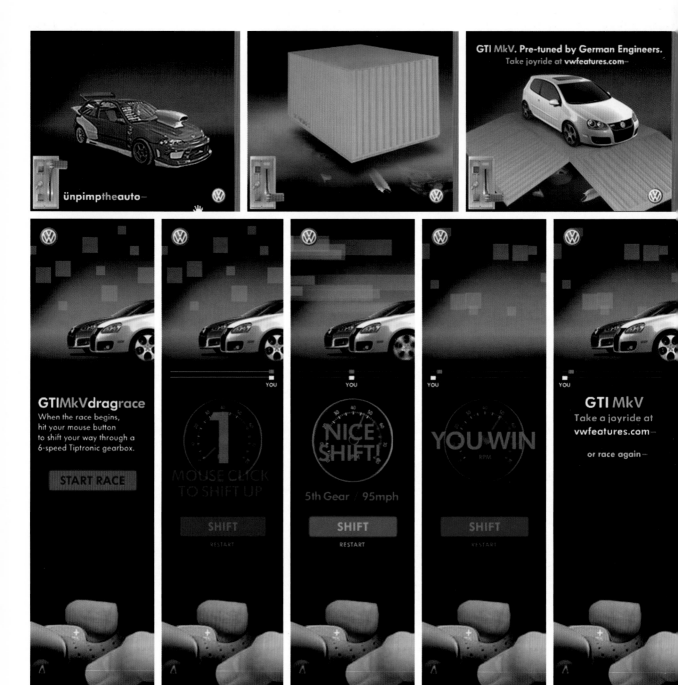

CONCEPT: Create engaging and branded interactive placements that could be experienced within an online banner. The banners feature a user-controlled shifting racing game, a dramatic animation of a car getting crushed by a new GTI, and a full-screen takeover of a GTI racing across multiple site web pages. **RESULTS:** Serving as an online reinforcement of the brand's broadcast placements, these interactive banners have been very successful in capturing the user's attention and ultimately driving traffic to VW.

CONCEPT : Créer des modules de marque interactifs et séduisants dans une bannière en ligne. Les bannières contiennent un jeu de course automobile à activer, une animation montrant un véhicule écrasé par une GTI, et une vidéo plein écran d'une GTI fonçant au travers de sites Internet. **RÉSULTATS :** Destinées à renforcer les annonces télévisées de la marque, ces bannières interactives ont réussi à capter l'attention du visiteur et ont généré une hausse de trafic sur le site de VW.

KONZEPT: Einnehmende und interaktive Markenplatzierungen entwickeln, die innerhalb eines Online-Banners erfahrbar wären. Die Banner enthalten ein benutzerkontrolliertes Rennspiel, eine dramatische Animation eines Autos, das von einem neuen GTI zerdrückt wird, und ein GTI-Rennen mit Überholmanövern in Volldarstellung über multiple Webseiten. **ERGEBNISSE:** Als Online-Verstärkung der gesendeten Markenplatzierungen waren diese interaktiven Banner sehr erfolgreich damit, die Aufmerksamkeit der Benutzer zu erregen und die Besucherrate zu erhöhen.

FEATURED ON THE DVD **CAMPAIGN:** Legend of Omaha. **PRODUCT:** VW Crossfox. **CLIENT:** Volkswagen Brazil. **YEAR:** 2004. **AGENCY:** AlmapBBDO <www.almapbbdo.com.br>. **PRODUCTION TIME:** 30 days.
CREATIVE DIRECTOR: Sérgio Mugnaini. **ART DIRECTOR:** Sérgio Mugnaini. **COPYWRITER:** Luciana Haguiara. **DESIGNER:** Sérgio Mugnaini. **TECHNICAL DIRECTOR:** Yves Apsy. **PRODUCER:** Egisto Betti, Verusca Faria.
DIRECTOR: Luis Ferré. **ACCOUNT EXECUTIVE:** Andre Furlanetto, Saulo Sanchez, Joanna Guinle. **ADVERTISER'S SUPERVISORS:** Marcelo Olival; Fabio Souza. **FILM PRODUCER:** Cine. **SOUND PRODUCER:** Lua Web.
TECH ASPECTS: Macromedia Flash, video, sound. **AWARDS:** El Ojo de IberoAmerica 2005 (Silver), MMonline/Msn Brazil 2005 (Silver), Cannes Lions 2005 (Shortlist), London Festival 2005 (Shortlist).

BACKGROUND PROFILE: The Volkswagen wanted to launch in the market the CrossFox: the first compact off-road vehicle in Brazil. For this, a campaign in two phases was developed: teaser and launching. **THE IDEA:** In the teaser phase, ads, outdoors and online campaign had been created with: DHTML, pop-up and box. But the main action in the Internet was viral, and started with the email marketing. The email, as well as the online campaign, took the users for a fictitious site especially developed for the viral action. In it, the user could see small indications of the new CrossFox, but nothing clearly reflects that it was a Volkswagen hotsite. **SOLUTION:** The site, named "The Legend of Omaha", was the page of a program about wild life. The presenter, Dr. Maxwell Adams, showed its profile, curiosities and the set of the documentary "Baboons of Tanzania". A movie, filmed and produced only and exclusively for the Internet, spoke on an unusual discovery: a new native species of off-road vehicle in Brazilian lands. The success was as much that the Dr. Maxwell Adams gained communities of fans in the Orkut and the 200 more than Beltrano and received e-mails. Many people had entered in contact to ask for information on the new CrossFox, looking for vacant of assistant and more episodes of the program. The site *The Legend of Omaha* received more than 80 thousand visitors in 15 days and more than 20 thousand people had attended the film.

CONTEXTE : Volkswagen voulait lancer sur le marché le modèle CrossFox, le premier véhicule tout terrain pour le Brésil. La campagne a été élaborée en deux phases : annonce, puis lancement. **IDÉE :** Dans la phase d'annonce, la campagne en ligne et hors ligne a utilisé le langage DHTML, les fenêtres pop-up et les bandeaux. Mais l'opération principale était de type viral, et s'est faite par mailing. Un message électronique invitait les internautes sur un site fictif spécialement élaboré pour l'opération. Sur ce site, on décelait quelques indications concernant le CrossFox, mais rien n'indiquait clairement qu'il s'agissait d'un site Volkswagen. **SOLUTION :** Le site, intitulé « La légende de Omaha », s'inspire des programmes animaliers. Le présentateur, Dr Maxwell Adams, introduit le sujet et le décor du documentaire « Babouins de Tanzanie ». Le film, tourné et produit en exclusivité pour Internet, parle d'une découverte inattendue, une nouvelle espèce endémique de véhicules tout terrain au Brésil. Le succès a été tel que le Dr Maxwell Adams a été l'objet d'un véritable engouement sur les sites de communautés virtuelles comme Orkut, et a été submergé de courrier. De nombreuses personnes l'ont contacté pour obtenir des infos sur le nouveau CrossFox, se proposer comme assistant, ou s'enquérir des prochains épisodes. Le site a reçu plus de 80 000 visiteurs en 15 jours et plus de 20 000 personnes ont visionné le film.

AUSGANGSSITUATION: Volkswagen wollte den CrossFox auf denMarkt einführen: der erste kompakte Geländewagen in Brasilien. Hierfür wurde eine Kampagne in zwei Phasen entwickelt: Teaser und Launch. **DIE IDEE:** In der Teaser-Phase wurden Online-Kampagnen entwickelt mit: DHTML, Pop Up und Box. Aber die Hauptaktion im Internet war viral und begann mit dem E-Mail-Marketing. E-Mail- und Online-Kampagne führten den Benutzer auf eine fiktive Seite, die speziell für die virale Aktion entwickelt worden war. Dort konnte man kleine Hinweise auf den neuen CrossFox sehen, aber nichts wies eindeutig darauf hin, dass es sich um eine Volkswagenseite handelte. **LÖSUNG:** Die „The Legend of Omaha" genannte Webseite war die Seite eines Programms über Tiere in freier Natur. Der Sprecher Dr. Maxwell Adams zeigte das Profil, Kuriositäten und das Set der Dokumentation „Baboons of Tanzania". Ein Film, der exklusiv für das Internet produziert worden war, berichtete von einer ungewöhnlichen Entdeckung: eine neue Spezies von Geländewagen in Brasilien. Der Erfolg war so groß, dass Dr.-Maxwell-Adams-Fangemeinden im Orkut entstanden und er zahlreiche E-Mails erhielt. Viele kontaktierten ihn, um Informationen zum neuen CrossFox zu erlangen und nach Episoden der Sendung zu suchen. Die Seite „The Legend of Omaha" wurde von über 80 000 Besuchern innerhalb von 15 Tagen angeklickt, und über 20 000 Leute sahen den Film.

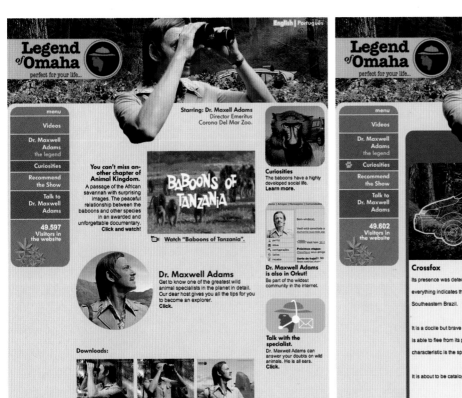

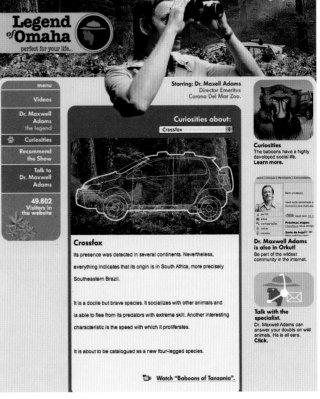

FEATURED ON THE DVD **CAMPAIGN:** VW Fox – Fractal. **PRODUCT:** Fox. **CLIENT:** Volkswagen Brasil. **AGENCY:** AlmapBBDO <www.almapbbdo.com.br>. **PRODUCTION TIME:** 30 days. **CREATIVE DIRECTOR:** Sérgio Mugnaini. **ART DIRECTOR:** Sérgio Mugnaini. **COPYWRITER:** Luciana Haguiara. **DESIGNER:** Carmelo Di Lorenzo. **TECHNICAL DIRECTOR:** Yves Apsy. **PRODUCER:** Ana Maria Machado. **ACCOUNT EXECUTIVE:** Andre Furlanetto, Saulo Sanchez, Joanna Guinle. **ADVERTISER'S SUPERVISORS:** Marcelo Olival, Fabio Souza. **TECH ASPECTS:** Macromedia Flash, video, sound. **AWARDS:** Mmonline/Msn 2005 (Merit), London Festival 2005 (Shortlist).

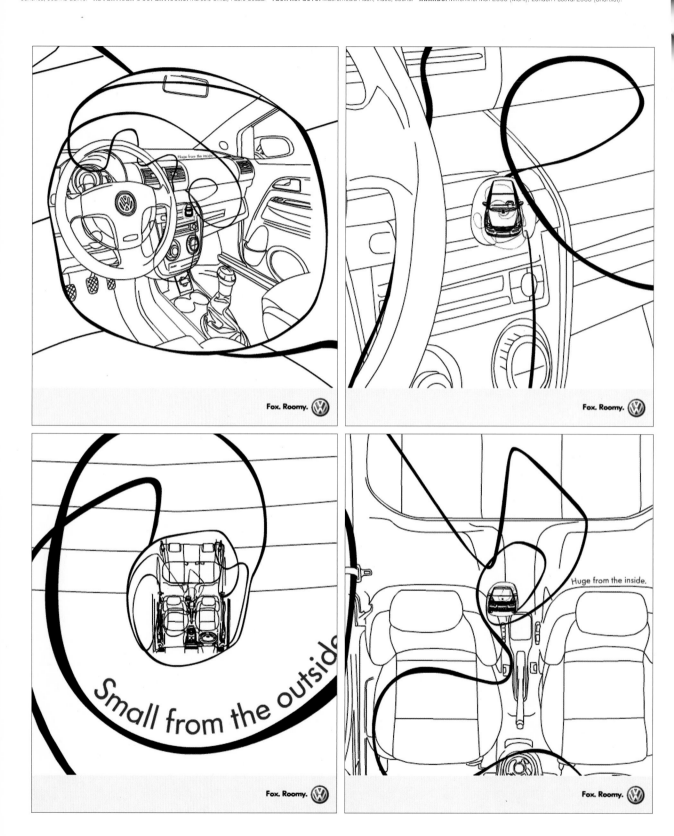

BACKGROUND PROFILE: The VW Fox is a revolutionary car, designed following the standard "Designed Around the Passengers." Its interior was projected before the exterior, to locate comfortably five passengers, and to foreseeing all the spaces and elements of versatility that the families and demanding drivers wants. **THE IDEA:** Fox. Compact for those who see it. Giant for those who drive it. **SOLUTION:** A superstitial. The image of the exterior and the interior of the car are integrated and moving in an infinite loop. Almost like a ballet. The message that we read in its interior and exterior is, respectively: "Smal from the outside. Huge from the inside." **CLAIM:** "Fox. Roomy."

CONTEXTE : La VW Fox est une voiture révolutionnaire, respectant la notion de « conception autour des passagers ». L'habitacle a été imaginé avant l'extérieur, pour que 5 personnes y soient à l'aise, et tout a été étudié pour assurer la polyvalence des espaces et des accessoires voulus par les familles et les conducteurs exigeants. **IDÉE :** La Fox. Compacte pour ceux qui la regardent. Géante pour ceux qui la conduisent. **SOLUTION :** Un superstitiel vidéo. L'image de l'extérieur et de l'intérieur de la voiture s'enchaînent dans une boucle infinie. Comme un spectacle de ballet. Les messages inscrits à l'extérieur et à l'intérieur indiquent respectivement : « Petite dehors » et « Enorme dedans ». **SLOGAN :** La Fox. Spacieuse.

HINTERGRUND: Der VW Fox ist ein revolutionäres Auto, das gemäß dem Standard „Designed Around the Passengers" entworfen wurde. Die Innenausstattung wurde vor dem Äußeren herausgestellt: Sie sollte bequem Platz für fünf Insassen bieten wie auch den Raum und die Flexibilität, die Familien und anspruchsvolle Fahrer brauchen. **DIE IDEE:** Fox. Kompakt für jene, die ihn sehen. Gigantisch für jene, die ihn fahren. **LÖSUNG:** Ein Superstitial. Die Bilder der äußeren und inneren Ausstattung werden kombiniert und bewegen sich in einer unendlichen Schleife, fast wie ein Ballett. Darin lesen wir jeweils die Botschaft: „Klein von außen. Riesig von innen." (*Small from the outside. Huge from the inside.*) **AUSSAGE:** „Fox. Geräumig."

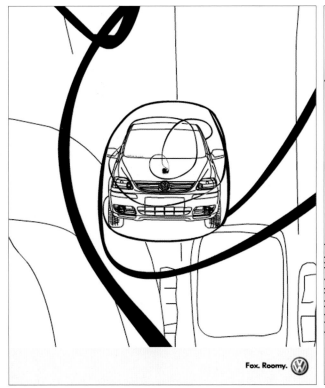

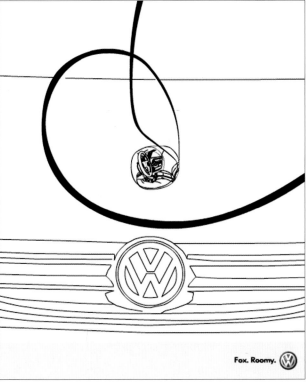

FEATURED ON THE DVD   **CAMPAIGN:** Love Hurts <www.lovehurts.ws>.   **PRODUCT:** VW Fox.   **YEAR:** 2006.   **AGENCY:** AlmapBBDO <www.almapbbdo.com.br>.   **CREATIVE DIRECTOR:** Sérgio Mugnaini.   **TECH ASPECTS:** Macromedia Flash, film, sound.

IDEA: CrossFox was already a sales success and Volkswagen decided to give continuity to this success. Behaviour changing idea: a viral movie was spread on the web and its link would take users to a tailor made hotsite. The story revolved around a Panda that had a romance ruined by a CrossFox. The action is composed of a viral movie, a hotsite and a campaign.

IDÉE : Le CrossFox était déjà une réussite commerciale et Volkswagen a décidé d'exploiter ce succès. La nouvelle idée : Un film viral lancé sur le Net, accompagné d'un lien renvoyant l'usager à un site dédié conçu sur mesure. Le scénario met en scène une Panda dont l'histoire d'amour est gâchée par une CrossFox. L'opération est composée d'un film viral, d'un site et d'une campagne..

IDEE: CrossFox war bereits ein Verkaufserfolg; diesem Erfolg wollte Volkswagen Dauer verleihen. Im Netz wurde ein viraler Film verbreitet, dessen Link zu einer maßgeschneiderten Hotsite führte. Im Film ging es um einen Panda, dem ein CrossFox eine Romanze vermasselt. Die Werbeaktion besteht aus einem viralen Film, einer Hotsite und einer Kampagne.

FEATURED ON THE DVD **CAMPAIGN:** ShortButFun.com <www.shortbutfun.com>. **PRODUCT:** Volkswagen Fox. **YEAR:** 2005. **AGENCY:** Tribal DDB, Hamburg <www.tribalddb.de>. **PRODUCTION TIME:** 1 month.
COST IN HOURS OF WORK: 170 h. **CREATIVE TEAM:** Hartmut Kozok, Jörg Meyer. **PROGRAMMER:** Moritz Neelmeier, Daniel Knobloch, Per Hiller. **TECH ASPECTS:** Backend: Microsoft ASP.NET, C# (CSharp), Microsoft IIS, Microsoft
SQL Server 2000-Database. Frontend: JavaScript, Macromedia Flash, HTML, CSS. **MEDIA CIRCULATED:** TV-Spots, Edgar Cards.

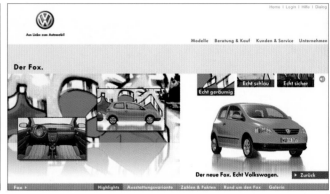

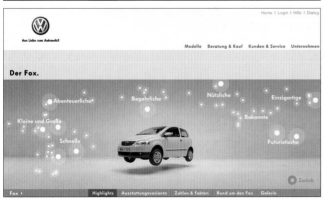

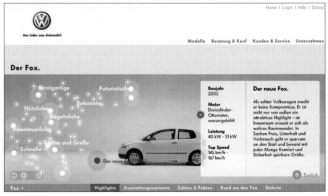

CONCEPT: Due to the small Media Budget, the Shortbutfun.com Website played a key part in the overall campaign. It was designed to multiply the message communicated in TV-Spots on MTV and VIVA and at the same time measure the traffic that resulted from the Links. The TV-Spots carries the Internet-Address and links Users to the website shortbutfun.com. On the site users can find the whole range of spots, ready to view, rate and send to a friend. Although the sender was Volkswagen, the website was designed to appear as a "self-made" fun portal, in order to be more authentically. The only hint was a Volkswagen Fox banner ad placed on top of the website and linking to the Fox Showroom on volkswagen.com. **RESULTS:** After the TV-Spots went on air the site got enormous traffic, not only linked from the TV-Spots but also placed as a topic in several communities and discussion forums. In the space of time from November 12th until November 15th 2005 (while the TV-Spots were on Air) the homepage was viewed approximately 32,000 times. The TV-Spots were viewed over 100,000 times overall. The traffic on Volkswagen.de/Fox Showroom increased by 25% compared to usual numbers.

CONCEPT : Compte tenu de la modestie du budget média, le site Shortbutfun.com devait jouer un rôle capital dans la campagne globale. Il devait renforcer le message communiqué par les spots télé de MTV et VIVA, tout en mesurant le trafic généré par les liens. Le spot télé donne l'adresse Internet et envoie les usagers sur shortbutfun.com. Les internautes retrouvent sur le site la série des différentes annonces, qu'ils peuvent visionner, évaluer et envoyer à un ami. Bien que l'annonceur ait été Volkswagen, le site était conçu pour ressembler à un site personnel amusant, afin de paraître plus authentique. La seule allusion à la marque était une bannière Volkswagen Fox en haut de la page, qui renvoyait au site du constructeur. **RÉSULTATS :** Après la diffusion des spots télé, le site a connu une énorme fréquentation, également due à l'exploitation du contenu sur les forums et communautés virtuelles. Entre le 12 et le 15 novembre 2005, (durée d'exploitation des spots télé), la page d'accueil a été vue environ 32 000 fois. Les spots télé ont été visionnés plus de 100 000 fois en tout. Le trafic sur le site de Volkswagen a connu une hausse de 25% comparé au trafic ordinaire.

KONZEPT: Wegen des kleinen Media Budgets spielte die Webseite Shortbutfun.com eine Schlüsselrolle innerhalb der Gesamtkampagne. Sie sollte die Botschaft multiplizieren, die in Fernsehspots auf MTV und VIVA kommuniziert wurde und gleichzeitig die durch die Links erzeugte Besucherrate messen. Die Fernsehspots zeigen die Internetadresse und verweisen Zuschauer auf die Webseite shortbutfun.com. Hier findet man die ganze Reihe der Spots, die man ansehen, bewerten und an Freunde senden kann. Obwohl der Auftraggeber Volkswagen war, sollte die Seite als „self-made" Funportal erscheinen, um authentischer zu wirken. Der einzige Hinweis war ein Volkswagen Fox Banner, das oben auf der Seite platziert war und zum Fox Showroom auf volkswagen.com führte. **ERGEBNISSE:** Nach der Ausstrahlung der Fernsehspots erhielt die Seite zahlreiche Treffer – nicht nur durch den Link der Fernsehspots, sondern auch als Thema in zahlreichen Internetgemeinden und Diskussionsforen. Zwischen dem 12. und 15. November 2005 (während die Spots gesendet wurden) wurde die Homepage ca. 32 000-mal angesehen. Die Fernsehspots wurden insgesamt 100 000-mal angeschaut. Die Besucherrate auf Volkswagen.de / Fox Showroom stieg um 25%.

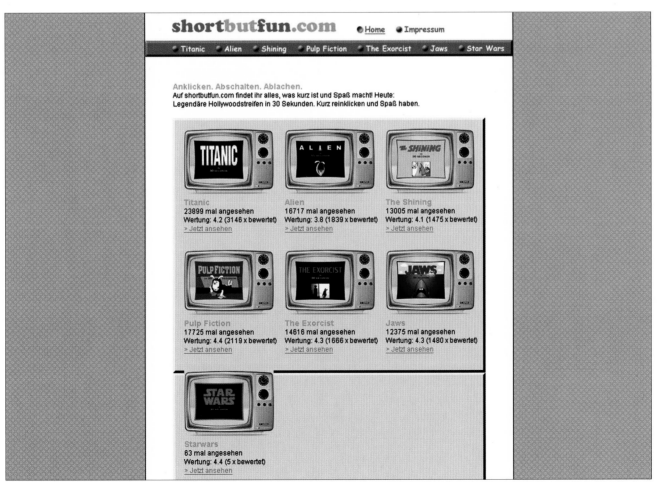

FEATURED ON THE DVD CAMPAIGN: VW Passat Features Minisite. YEAR: 2005. AGENCY: Arnold Worldwide <www.arnoldworldwide.com>. CHIEF CREATIVE OFFICER: Ron Lawner. EXECUTIVE CREATIVE DIRECTOR: Alan Pafenbach. CREATIVE DIRECTOR: Chris Bradley, Chris Carl, Dave Weist, Colin Jeffery. ART DIRECTOR: Paulo Lopez, Paul Lee, Phillip Squier, Colin Jeffery. COPYWRITER: Chris Carl, Dave Weist. PRODUCER: Tom Lerra, Amy Favat. PROGRAMMER: Roy Wetherbee (Tech Manager). FLASH PROGRAMMER: The Barbarian Group. MECHANICAL SUPERVISOR: Judy Wong. INFORMATION ARCHITECT: Dale Cumberbatch. ACCOUNT SERVICE: Mike Zagorsek, Alison Starr, Nicole Harvey.

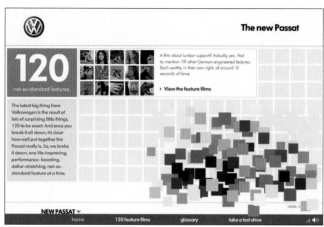

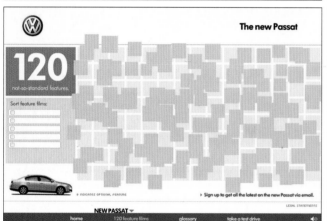

FEATURED ON THE DVD CAMPAIGN: VW "Pinball" banner. **PRODUCT:** Volkswagen GTI MkV. **YEAR:** 2006. **AGENCY:** Crispin Porter + Bogusky <www.cpbgroup.com>. **PRODUCER:** Domani Studios <www.domanistudios.com>. **PRODUCTION TIME:** 2 weeks. **CREATIVE TEAM:** Crispin Porter + Bogusky. **PROGRAMMER:** Domani Studios. **TECH ASPECTS:** Macromedia Flash AS 2.0, audio, XML. **MEDIA CIRCULATED:** Banner placements.

CONCEPT: Pushing further the treatment of Volkswagen's sporty cars as delightful toys, the pinball banner entices the user to launch the car into action and rewards him/her with full motion and sound simulating a tear-ass race across "neighboring" web pages. Reinforcing the brand's broadcast placements, these interactive banners arrest the user's attention and drive traffic to VW.

CONCEPT : Poussant plus loin le concept des sportives de Volkswagen vues comme des jouets extraordinaires, la bannière en forme de flipper invite l'internaute à démarrer la voiture et le récompense en l'entraînant dans une course effrénée à travers les pages des sites voisins, dans un vrombissement de moteurs. Accompagnant la publicité télévisée, ces bannières interactives ont attiré l'attention et généré du trafic sur le site de VW.

KONZEPT: Um die Konnotation der Sportwagen von Volkswagen als wunderbare Spielzeuge auf die Spitze zu treiben, fordert das Banner die Benutzer dazu auf, das Auto anzuklicken und belohnt sie mit Full Motion und Soundeffekten, die ein Rennen über „benachbarte" Webseiten simulieren. Die gesendete Markenwerbung bekräftigend, erregen die interaktiven Banner die Aufmerksamkeit der Benutzer und erhöhen die Besucherrate zu VW.

FEATURED ON THE DVD **CAMPAIGN:** VW "Popup" banner. **PRODUCT:** Volkswagen Jetta. **YEAR:** 2006. **AGENCY:** Crispin Porter + Bogusky <www.cpbgroup.com>. **PRODUCER:** Domani Studios <www.domanistudios.com>.
PRODUCTION TIME: 2 weeks. **CREATIVE TEAM:** Crispin Porter + Bogusky. **PROGRAMMER:** Domani Studios. **TECH ASPECTS:** Macromedia Flash AS 2.0, audio, XML. **MEDIA CIRCULATED:** Banner placements.

CONCEPT: This rich media banner auto detects the user's system to feed a window-graphics accurate 'fake' pop-up ad, into which a Jetta 'crashes' – with random particle effects for a different crash every playback. The concept humorously plays off of the aggrevation of pop-up ads, while offering a legitimate sub-ad placement in the clickable 'fake' popup. Dynamic audio heightens the experience if users choose to play the ad again. The ad feeds the vw.com site and highlights the front-end crash safety record of the Jetta.

CONCEPT : Cette bannière en rich media détecte automatiquement le système d'exploitation de l'internaute pour afficher une imitation de fenêtre pop-up, dans laquelle vient s'encastrer une Jetta, avec un effet de particule différent à chaque ouverture de page. Le concept joue sur la contrariété qu'engendrent les fenêtres pop-up, tout en offrant un mes-

sage légitime dans la « fausse » fenêtre à cliquer. Les effets sonores dynamiques renforcent l'expérience si l'internaute décide de repasser la publicité. Celle-ci dirige vers le site de VW et souligne les performances de sécurité de la Jetta en cas de choc frontal.

KONZEPT: Dieses Rich-Media-Banner erkennt automatisch das Benutzersystem, um ein der Windowgrafik entsprechendes Fake-Pop-Up zu laden, in dem ein Jetta einen Unfall hat – mit jeweils anderen zufälligen Partikeleffekten bei jedem neuen Crash. Das Konzept spielt humorvoll mit dem Ärger über Pop-Up-Werbung und bietet gleichzeitig eine legitime sub-ad-Platzierung im anklickbaren Fake-Pop-Up. Dynamisches Audio intensiviert das Erlebnis, wenn der Benutzer die Werbung wiederholt abspielt. Die Anzeige wirbt für die vw.com-Seite und betont die Unfall-Sicherheitsprotokolle des Jetta.

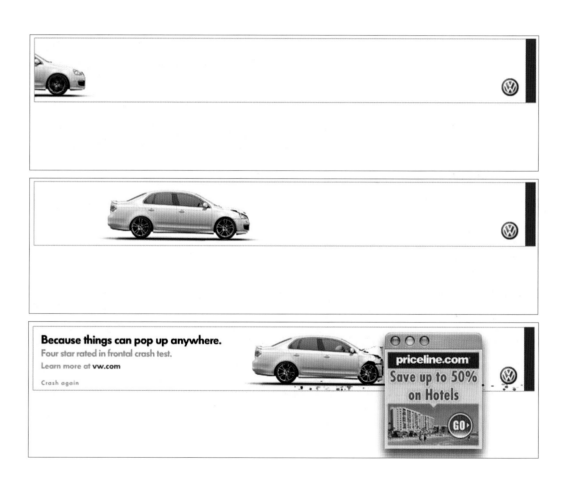

CAMPAIGN: VW "Scroll" banner. **PRODUCT:** Volkswagen Jetta. **YEAR:** 2006. **AGENCY:** Crispin Porter + Bogusky <www.cpbgroup.com>. **PRODUCER:** Domani Studios <www.domanistudios.com>. **PRODUCTION TIME:** 3 weeks. **CREATIVE TEAM:** Crispin Porter + Bogusky. **PROGRAMMER:** Domani Studios. **TECH ASPECTS:** Macromedia Flash AS 2.0, audio, XML. **MEDIA CIRCULATED:** Banner placements.

CONCEPT: This technically challenging banner grabs attention by following the user's scroll behavior. As a user scrolls down the page, a Jetta 'crashes' into the top of the browser window and continues to scrape and crunch its way down the page as the user scrolls. The programming includes actual physics to relate speed of the user's scroll onto the impact of the car while also calculating random debris with the same considerations. The ad feeds the vw.com site and highlights the front-end crash safety record of the Jetta.

CONCEPT : Ce bandeau techniquement élaboré attire l'attention en suivant le comportement de la bande de défilement de l'internaute. Quand on défile vers le bas de la page, la Jetta s'écrase en haut de la fenêtre de navigation et continue sa chute le long de la page au fur et à mesure du défilement. La programmation a intégré des éléments de physique afin d'associer la vitesse de défilement avec la violence de l'impact et ses conséquences. La publicité nourrit le site de VW et souligne les performances de sécurité de la voiture en cas de choc frontal.

KONZEPT: Dieses technisch herausfordernde Banner erregt die Aufmerksamkeit des Benutzers, indem es seinem Scroll-Verhalten folgt. Scrollt man die Seite, stürzt ein Jetta von oben in das Browserfenster und schabt und knirscht weiter seinen Weg nach unten, wenn der Benutzer scrollt. Die Programmierung beinhaltet wirkliche Physik, damit die Geschwindigkeit des Scrollens sich direkt auf das Auto sowie zufällige Schuttteile auswirkt. Die Anzeige wirbt für die vw.com-Seite und betont die Unfall-Sicherheitsprotokolle des Jetta.

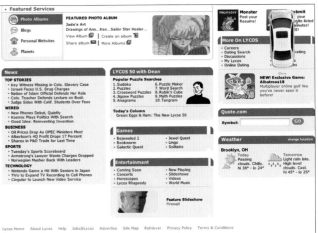

INDEX

AGENCIES

20:20 LONDON
www.2020london.co.uk
UNITED KINGDOM
56 [Commando VIP/Channel Five], 58 [CSI-NY/
Channel Five], 60 [The Farm/Channel Five], 78
[Trauma/Warner Brothers], 198 [BP Ultimate], 320
[FIFA Street/Electronic Arts], 326 [24: The Game/
PlayStation], 354 [Audi A3 Sportback], 360 [Audi A4],
380 [Lotus Elise].

2ADVANCED STUDIOS
www.2advanced.com
USA
332 [Metroid Prime 2 Echoes].

AGÊNCIA CLICK
www.agenciaclick.com.br
BRAZIL
18 [Coca-Cola Light], 22 [Coca-Cola], 23 [Coca-
Cola], 24 [Learn to drink Tequila/Abaetuba Group], 65
[MSN Woman/PMS Magazine], 105 [Furry Island/
WWF], 171 [Banco de Olhos], 175 [Ecco], 178
[Proanima], 195 [Bradesco Bank], 235 [C&A], 291
[INDT], 311 [Gear Up/Brasil Telecom], 372 [Brazil
Grand Prix], 373 [Fiat Stilo Connect], 374 [Fiat Idea].

AGENCY.COM
www.agency.com
112 [John Lewis Direct], 144 [NSPCC], 206 [Dulux],
226 [BT Broadband/British Telecom], 362 [British
Airways/e-Services], 364 [British Airways Club World].

AKQA
www.akqa.com
32 [Peperami Noodles], 98 [Axe Pulse], 100 [Axe
Clickmore], 188 [3M], 214 [PG Tips], 322 [Xbox
Forza], 324 [Xbox Origen].

ALMAPBBDO
www.almapbbdo.com.br
BRAZIL
36 [Pepsi Pro Contest], 43 [Bauducco], 72 [Super
Interessante Magazine], 420 [Volkswagen Golf], 426
[Volkswagen CrossFox], 428 [Volkswagen Fox], 430
[Volkswagen Fox].

ARNOLD WORLDWIDE
www.arnoldworldwide.com
218 [Freedom of the Seas/Royal Caribbean's], 434
[Volkswagen Passat Features].

BIG SPACESHIP
www.bigspaceship.com
USA
74 [Alfie], 75 [Underworld: Evolution], 76 [Sin City],
80 [War of the Worlds], 82 [Wolf Creek], 126 [MoMA:
Contemporary Voices].

BLUESPONGE
www.bluesponge.com
CANADA
122 [MadeinMTL].

CRISPIN PORTER + BOGUSKY
www.cpbgroup.com
14 [Burguer King/Subservient Chicken], 20 [Coca-
Cola], 124 [Method Come Clean], 148 [Pink Panty
Poker/Victoria's Secret], 164 [GAP], 196 [Borders
Giftmixer 3000/Borders Bookstore], 392 [Mini/
Counterfeit DVD], 394 [Mini], 396 [Mini], 412 [Virgin
Atlantic Airways Upper Class], 416 [Gypsy Cab
Project/Volkswagen Rabbit], 422 [Volkswagen GTI Mk
V], 424 [Volkswagen], 435 [Volkswagen], 436
[Volkswagen Jetta], 437 [Volkswagen Jetta].

DEL CAMPO NAZCA SAATCHI & SAATCHI
ARGENTINA
101 [Ariel], 104 [Buenos Aires Zoo], 224 [Answer
Seguro On-Line], 225 [Answer Seguro On-Line].

DENTSU INC.
www.dentsu.com
JAPAN
73 [Slam Dunk/Takehiko Inoue], 94 [One Show 2005
Call for Entries/The One Club for Art & Copy], 108
[Interactive Salaryman/Self-promo], 130 [World
Terakoya Movement/National Federation of UNESCO
Associations in JAPAN], 174 [Japan Advertising
Council], 234 [Sankyo Co.], 312 [TOSHIBA Presents
FM Festival '04], 378 [Honda Icon Museum].

DIGIT
www.digitlondon.com
UNITED KINGDOM
20 [Coca-Cola Zero/World Chill], 62 [Howard's
Studio], 150 [Five Poker Room/Channel Five], 292
[Motoglyph/Motorola].

DM9DDB BRASIL
www.dm9ddb.com.br
BRAZIL
156 [Super Bonder], 173 [Cia. Athletica], 228
[Speedy/Telefônica Broadband], 237 [TAM Express
Courier].

DOMANI STUDIOS
www.domanistudios.com
USA
118 [Kid Cupid V-Day Game/Self-promotion], 220
[Starwood Meetings/Starwood Hotels and Resorts],
424 [Volkswagen], 435 [Volkswagen], 436
[Volkswagen Jetta], 437 [Volkswagen Jetta].

DOUBLE YOU
www.doubleyou.com
SPAIN
16 [Cacique Rum], 19 [Coca-Cola Blak], 194
[Atrápalo], 254 [NIKE/The San Silvestre Vallecana],
260 [NIKE Sprint Sister], 265 [NIKE/The San Silvestre
Vallecana], 267 [nikeplay.com], 318 [1st Worldwide
Search Championship YAHOO!], 352 [Attitudes], 356
[Audi A3 Sportback], 358 [25th Anniversary of Audi
Quattro], 359 [Audi A4], 403 [SEAT Toledo website],
404 [SEAT Toledo campaign].

EURO RSCG 4D
www.eurorscg4d.com.br
BRAZIL
44 [Bavaria Premium Beer], 166 [Nugget Leather
Cleaner], 167 [Nugget Shoe Wax], 168 [Poliflor], 169
[Rodasol], 170 [Rodasol], 230 [TIM International
Roaming], 232 [Brokeback Moutain/2001 Video
Store], 288 [Intel Centrino], 289 [Intel Centrino], 308
[Nokia N-Gage], 309 [Nokia Trends Festival].

CLIENTS

DVD CONTENTS

CHAPTERS
Campaigns featured on the DVD

ACKNOWLEDGMENTS

I would like to start thanking the E-mail. This book has taken more than a 1000 E-mails to this point, and without this simple tool I believe many of the things we do today wouldn't be possible. At least regarding the speed that E-mails allow us to reach people everywhere. Thus the speed to solve problems. On a Blackberry myself, I am not at all stressed with the fact that I am 24/7 reachable. Quite the opposite, it is a relief to me to be able to coordinate things no matter where I am. That allows me to have a much more flexible working flow. That's what technology should be about: make life better. But this book is also about making brand experience better, using for it the king of interaction that a company didn't have before. So we collected outstanding examples of "interactive" works that show how brands and people can develop a relationship in the digital world.

This is the second book of the series Advertising Now!, featuring this time just campaigns and websites focused on interactive. I have to thank first of all Daniel Siciliano Brêtas, that worked until the last moments to improve the publication. My right hand.

Also Christoph Krahl from Cologne for making the DVD work and feel as if you were going to an interactive festival. Which is actually the idea of having it. We hope many of you can now sit on the sofa and enjoy all these brilliant ideas produced for the internet, mobile and hand-pads. Christoph has cre-ated a superb viewing experience out of his multi-faceted talent.

As usual, Stefan Klatte has been our right hand in the production front, always making things for us easier and finding solutions to make the book more beautiful.

Moreover Andy Disl has been always our support enhancing always the design he created for the series. His way of seeing the publication has many times surprised us and elevated the level of the publication.

Before it is too late, I want to thank all Creative Directors that have written the texts for the book, Bob Greenberg, Matt Freeman, Johan Tesch, Lars Hemming Jorgensen, Daniel Solana, John Otto, Jan Leth, PJ Pereira and Ricardo Figueira. These early-adopters and fathers of the revolution have made this book a base for anyone working or willing to work with interactive.

At last, but not at least, I must thank all Creative Directors, agency PR teams, assistants, Art Directors, and agency managers not only for the great stuff they have been doing, but for the amazing collaboration in this publication. These guys are also the creators of this revolution named by many "digital," that is changing the face of communication.

JULIUS WIEDEMANN

IMPRINT

To stay informed about upcoming TASCHEN titles, please request our magazine at www.taschen.com/magazine or write to TASCHEN, Hohenzollernring 53, D-50672 Cologne, Germany, contact@taschen.com, Fax: +49-221-254919. We will be happy to send you a free copy of our magazine which is filled with information about all of our books.

Design: Sense/Net, Andy Disl and Birgit Reber, Cologne & Daniel Siciliano Brêtas
Layout: Daniel Siciliano Brêtas & Julius Wiedemann
DVD Production, Editing, Sound: Christoph Krahl, Cologne
Production: Stefan Klatte

Front cover: from the Sabrina Setlur's website <www.sabrina-setlur.de> by Neue Digitale. Artwork by Bejadin Selimi <www.bejadin.info>. Photography by Bernd Bodtländer.
Back cover: illustration by eBoy <www.eboy.com>, MAG_peecolposter_final.tif.
Endpapers: Del Campo Nazca Saatchi & Saatchi for Ariel (Procter & Gamble), Argentina, 2005.

Editor: Julius Wiedemann
Assistant Editor: Daniel Siciliano Brêtas
French Translation: Claire Allesse
German Translation: Claudia Dziallas
Spanish Translation: Mar Portillo
Italian Translation: Marco Barberi
Portuguese Translation: Alcides Murtinheira

Printed in China
ISBN-13: 978-3-8228-4956-9
ISBN-10: 3-8228-4956-1

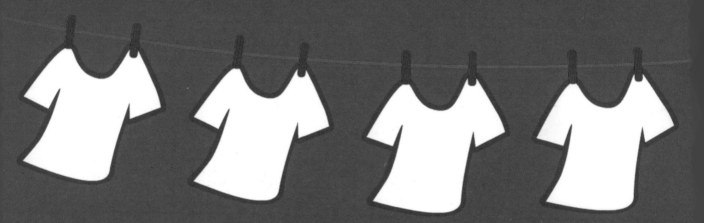

COMPLETED